Books by Louis Sheaffer

O'Neill: Son and Playwright

O'Neill: Son and Artist

O'NEILL
SON AND ARTIST

The "Sea-Mother's Son" draped with ropes of seaweed

O'NEILL
SON AND ARTIST

by LOUIS SHEAFFER

with photographs

PARAGON HOUSE
New York

First Paragon House edition, 1990

Published in the United States by

Paragon House Publishers
90 Fifth Avenue
New York, NY 10011

The author is grateful to Yale University as legatee under the will of
Carlotta Monterey O'Neill, and to the Collection of American
Literature, Beinecke Rare Book and Manuscript Library, Yale
University, for permission to quote from selected letters, poems,
articles and other writings by Eugene O'Neill.

All hitherto unpublished quotations from Eugene O'Neill copyright
© 1973 by Yale University as legatee under the will of the late
Carlotta Monterey O'Neill.

Acknowledgements for permissions to quote copyrighted material
appear in "Acknowledgements" on pages 721-728.

Library of Congress Cataloging-in-Publication Data

Sheaffer, Louis.
    O'Neill, son and artist / by Louis Sheaffer. — 1st Paragon
House ed.
        p.   cm.
    Reprint. Originally published: Bost : Little, Brown, 1973.
    Bibliography: P.
    Includes index.
    ISBN 1-55778-184-2 (pbk.)
    1. O'Neill, Eugene, 1888-1953—Biography. 2. Dramatists,
American—20th century—Biography. I. Title.
    [PS3529.N5Z797   1990]
812'.52—dc19
[B]   88-21476
                                                               CIP

Manufactured in the United States of America

In memory of my father,
Abraham Slung

How shall a man escape from his ancestors, or draw off from his veins the black drop which he drew from his father's or his mother's life?

Ralph Waldo Emerson, "Fate," *The Conduct of Life*

Preface

To Eugene O'Neill playwriting, as Brooks Atkinson puts it, was "not so much his profession as his obsession." In the first book of my two-volume biography I was particularly concerned with probing the evident sources of his obsessional drive, above all the familial source, for O'Neill was an emotional hemophiliac whose family-inflicted wounds never healed. In his relations with his parents and one sibling, an elder brother, are to be found the fountainhead of his passion and power, as well as much of his subject matter. In this respect he was unlike any other major playwright except Strindberg, his self-acknowledged model, who also, turning repeatedly to his own life for his material, transmuted private history and secret anguish into art.

Among the shyest of men, O'Neill was torn between two opposed impulses: one, a desire to sequester himself from the world, a passion for privacy; the other, a need to explain and justify himself to the world. At once concealing and revealing himself in his writings (but ultimately baring all in *Long Day's Journey Into Night*, which he wanted withheld from the public till decades after his death), he constantly "went for broke." Even some of his poorest plays, after his apprenticeship, possess exceptional power and a sense of urgency. He always wrote from his guts.

Heredity and circumstance worked together, at the expense of his peace of soul, to make him a dramatist. His father, James O'Neill, was among the most promising actors of his day until he had the "good bad luck" to appear in an adaptation of *The Count of Monte Cristo*, an enormous success that finally became his cloak of Nessus. Long unable to shake it off, for the public flocked to see him in large numbers only when he impersonated the Dumas hero, he grew to hate the play, especially its most famous line: "The world is mine!" Yet haunted all his life by a fear of poverty, the result of a mean, hungry childhood, he played his one really popular role on and off for thirty years. In the process his talent decayed, his career lost distinction. "That's what caused me to make up my mind that they would never get me," Eugene once said. "I determined then that I would never sell out."

His mother's initial misfortune was that she fell in love with and married an actor. Timid, fastidious, devoutly Catholic, a product of gentle rearing and convent schools, Ella O'Neill was fatally unfit to be an actor's wife; she felt lost, a perpetual alien, in the semibohemian world of the theater. The birth of Eugene, her third and final child (the second died in infancy), proved disastrous to her and the rest of the family. Since Ella had a difficult delivery and was slow to recover, her doctor gave her morphine — at the time widely and freely used as medicine — to allay her pain and relieve her anxious frame of mind. Before she knew the name and nature of her marvelous panacea, she had become a morphine addict. Eventually Ella broke free of her addiction but during more than a quarter of a century she knew the tortures of the damned.

"When you're in agony and half insane," the mother cries out in *Long Day's Journey*, "[the doctor] holds your hand and delivers sermons on will power! He understands nothing! And yet it was exactly the same type of cheap quack who first gave you the medicine. I hate doctors! They'll do anything . . . to keep you coming to them. They'll sell their souls! What's worse, they'll sell yours, and you never know it till one day you find yourself in hell!" .

Nearly fifteen when he first learned of her addiction, Eugene felt shattered, particularly since her "curse," as the family alluded to it, had begun with his birth. Formerly quiet and well behaved, now burdened with a crushing sense of guilt, he began turning into a rebel, openly defiant. His faith in the divine scheme of things destroyed (if God were benevolent, how could He allow his pious mother to fall?), the youth rejected Catholicism and all other orthodoxies. Yet essentially a person of religious temperament who felt lost without a governing creed, he became a disciple of Nietzsche and attempted to establish a position "beyond good and evil." Under the tutelage of his brother Jamie, a cynical, dissolute alcoholic, he took to drink and at a relatively early age became familiar with whorehouses. "Gene learned sin more easily than other people," Jamie used to say. "I made it easy for him."

The anger and darkness in O'Neill demanded an outlet, a target. Unable to move against the source of his bad conscience, a drug addict who collapsed at the first critical word or, still worse, resorted to a defense that intensified his guilt feelings, he joined forces with his brother in a running feud against their father. They questioned his religion, derided his chauvinism about the Irish and, echoing Ella's charge that he had engaged a "cheap quack" to attend her at Eugene's birth, blamed her "curse" on his strain of penuriousness. But unlike his bachelor brother, who adored his mother and was hostile to the father, Eugene derived little satisfaction or ease from his sorties against the aging actor.

A dropout from Princeton after one year, he prospected for gold in Spanish Honduras, went to sea, knocked around the water fronts of Buenos Aires, Southampton and New York with derelicts, drifters, other lost souls, and was once in such despair that he attempted suicide. During his years of drifting about New York he married and shortly deserted one Kathleen Jenkins, who bore his first child; the marriage, he laconically said later, was "a mistake."

Starting in childhood, O'Neill had a need to verbalize his thoughts, feelings and fantasies on paper, but his literary ambition long centered on becoming a poet, one worthy of his idols Byron, Swinburne and Baudelaire. It was only after his health broke down and he spent six months in a tubercular sanatorium in 1912–1913, when he was twenty-four, that he decided to become a playwright. Disdainful of his father's contrived, artificial theater, he was determined "to use whatever I can make my own, to write about anything under the sun. . . . And I shall never be influenced by any consideration but one: Is it the truth as I know it — or, better still, feel it? If so, shoot, and let the splinters fly where they may."

Plays, both short and long, poured out of him once he began. He studied playwriting for a year under Professor Baker at Harvard, but he gained more valuable instruction from seeing his works performed, initially by a band of amateurs on Cape Cod headed by George Cram ("Jig") Cook, a visionary from Iowa. Before long O'Neill was recognized as the leading writer of the play-makers, who moved to Greenwich Village and, taking the name of their birthplace, called themselves the Provincetown Players.

In the winter of 1917–1918, in the backroom of a Village saloon popularly called the Hell Hole, O'Neill met a charming magazine writer named Agnes Boulton, whom he married some months later. The following year in Provincetown, where they had settled, Agnes bore their first child, a boy named Shane.

O'Neill, Son and Playwright, my first volume, ended early in 1920 with

O'Neill's successful launching on Broadway with *Beyond the Horizon*. At the première James O'Neill, who for years had despaired over Eugene, watched the unfolding of *Horizon* through tears of happiness; it appeared that his onetime prodigal son was going to bring new distinction to the ancient name of O'Neill.

This book, like my previous one, is based almost entirely on original research and primary sources. Besides drawing on all the standard sources, I interviewed scores of persons whose memories of O'Neill had hitherto been untapped by the subject's chroniclers, and I had the use of hundreds of letters written by O'Neill and his last two wives, in addition to other documents new to his biography. The reader will find here a portrait of the playwright somewhat different from his generally accepted image, as well as an account of episodes in his life that until now had remained private.

L. S.

Brooklyn Heights, N.Y.
December 1972

Contents

[xiii]

Contents

Illustrations

[xv]

Illustrations

O'NEILL
SON AND ARTIST

1

The Old Actor's Finale

Taken as a whole, the correspondence between O'Neill and Agnes in the first months of 1920, when he was in New York for *Beyond the Horizon* and she was confined to Provincetown with their infant Shane, reflects all the major elements in their relationship: affection, sexual passion, a great need for one another, a constant hunger for reassurance, an undercurrent of mistrust, resentment, hostility. The letters provide in fact an emotional profile of their marriage and, from hindsight, afford occasional glimpses of the atmosphere of accusation and bitterness — chiefly on his side — in which the marriage was to end.

He had scarcely left for New York, early in January, when Agnes wrote: "Oh, Gene, I am missing you so! *I didn't appreciate* you [her underscoring]. The first hours after you left were simply torture — I felt like running down the street after you. . . ." And a month or so later: "I just can't *believe* that God has been so good to me, to give me the wonderful, blessed gift of your love . . . I want no other religion, no other belief — it is all there — in *you* — in us." Nearly all her letters of the period contain such impassioned declarations.

In like vein he said at different times: "I'll be back the first second I possibly can." . . . "After this experience we must never again be separated for so long." . . . "God, how I need you and want you! The whole thing is without meaning without you!"

But Agnes was unhappy in being tied down on Cape Cod with a baby when her husband's first Broadway production was opening ("Oh Beloved, I have been with you when you were suffering, when despair and loneliness were upon you, and I needed to be with you triumphant!") They had promised to write one another daily, and whenever a day or two passed without her hearing from him she felt neglected, diminished, relegated to a minor role in his life; understandably, a note of grievance occasionally crept into her letters.

Easily hurt, quick to take offense, Eugene once shot back in reply: "If you and I, who love each other so much, cannot keep petty hate from creeping into our souls like the condemned couple in a Strindberg play; if our letters are to become an added torture to our hearts already tortured by separation . . . if we cannot stand back to back to face failure or the equally fatal possibilities contained in success; if the morale at home cannot reinforce the morale at the front when that falters — then we are lost; and my only remaining hope is that the 'Flu,' or some other natural cause, will speedily save me the decision which would inevitably have to come at my own instance. If you and I are but another dream that passes, then I desire nothing further from the Great Sickness but release."

In the main, however, their correspondence is that of a loving couple, greatly dependent upon one another and deeply attached. Worried by his frequent mention of working long hours and not feeling too well, Agnes constantly urged him to take better care of himself, especially now that influenza was raging, while he kept writing back that he would have had her and the baby join him if New York were not a "plague spot." Once, though, lamenting their separation, he said that "it would all be so simple if Shane were not in our midst."

Barometerlike, his letters provide a series of readings of his changing moods, with apprehension the predominant one. Right after *Beyond the Horizon* opened, he was jubilant: "You'll see what a knockout *Beyond* was when you get the [reviews]. Whatever it may or may not do in a financial way, it has done all I ever expected of it already — and more. . . . My Own, I have made them take my work — and like it! . . . *Beyond* is now the big talk [of Broadway]."

From feeling on the crest of a wave, with his successful launching on Broadway, he soon fell into the depths. Even had everything continued favorably, it is doubtful, given his temperament, that his euphoric state would have lasted much longer anyway, but circumstances were against him. On February 4, a day after his play had opened, he saw Helen Hayes in *Clarence* at George C. Tyler's insistence. Tyler, planning to cast her in *The Straw,* wanted O'Neill to look her over, and this was to be her last night in *Clarence.* Eugene went reluctantly, as he was exhausted from the ordeal of the *Horizon* rehearsals and première; in addition, the weather was vile — cold and damp, with snow piled up in the streets. No taxi was to be found when he and his mother left the theater, with the result that Ella, inadequately dressed, was chilled and wet by the time they returned to the Prince George Hotel. The following day she was coughing, but, hostile as ever to doctors, refused to see one till medical care became imperative; she had, it turned out, a "trace of pneumonia in one lung." Within hours of her illness Eugene himself came down with the flu, contracted, he assumed, from his mother.

The doctor expected him to recover in several days, but it was nearly three weeks before he felt well enough to venture from the hotel. Thrown into panic by his illness, Agnes reminded him of his friend Hutch Collins, who had succumbed quickly to flu and pneumonia, and added, "NOW YOU MUST NOT DO ANYTHING TO GET COLD AFTER YOU ARE BETTER. I beg and plead with you not to take any chances . . . if anything happens to you I will not live in this world without you." The only thing that made him feel "alive at all" was a drink, but whiskey, now that Prohibition was in effect, was hard to find. Even his father, who had good contacts, was reduced to drinking rum, which he had never liked, and then port, till even his source of wine dried up.

For about a year now father and son had been drawing closer together. James O'Neill took pride in his boy's success ("I tried to drag you into the theater through the back door [as an actor] and you walked in through the front [as a playwright]"), while Eugene, long so critical of the aged actor, had grown to view him with sympathy. Once Eugene began to feel better, he spent almost all his time in his parents' suite, he and James playing cards as they talked themselves out — one looking ahead with dreams of glory, the other looking back and lamenting the years he had wasted on *Monte Cristo*. In the son's words afterward, James O'Neill realized too late that the Dumas adaptation had been his "curse," that he had "fallen for the lure of easy popularity and easy money." The playwright son would remember these confessional nights when he wrote of Edmund and Tyrone baring their souls while playing cards in *Long Day's Journey Into Night;* although *Long Day's Journey* is set in 1912, its moments of rapport between Tyrone and his younger son were inspired by the harmony between Eugene and his father in 1919 and 1920.

Their improved relationship left his brother Jamie not only jealous but feeling isolated, particularly when Ella, echoing her husband, criticized him for wasting his life and praised Eugene as an example for him to follow. Apparently Jamie spent as little time as possible around his parents and brother, for there is only one passing mention of him, referring to something in the past, in all Eugene's letters to Agnes during this period. At one point she asked whether Jamie was in New York, but he never answered. Another indication of the strained feeling between the brothers is available from Charles Webster, who had been in O'Neill senior's vaudeville tour in *Monte Cristo*. During a chance meeting with Jamie in Times Square, several weeks after *Horizon* had opened, Webster was surprised to learn that only now was he going to see his brother's play.

One night, after Eugene thought he had practically recovered from the flu, he awoke with a pain above his heart so severe that he feared death was imminent; but the doctor diagnosed it as a case of localized neuralgia. "Life with me now," he wrote to Agnes in mid-February, "consists of wondering: 'What new ill is going to hit me tomorrow?' Stripped, I look like a medical student's chart, every muscle outlined and every bone and bit of sinew. I weigh about 125. . . . Just think! I haven't been out of this hotel since the Friday after *Beyond* opened! And all 'the honor and the glory' passes by in the street below."

With his new prominence came invitations to be a speaker or guest of honor at various affairs ("If that's fame they can leave me out"); requests for interviews ("Success has meant to me the meaningless futility I always knew it would be — only more so"); a query about the place and date of his birth, the "exact hour and minute," for a book of horoscopes of "notable Americans." Unable to fend off all the interview requests, he submitted to several, including one by a woman from *Theater* magazine. He felt "punk and pessimistic," he told Agnes on February 21, and the woman "insisted on my divulging my philosophy of life. I gave it to her as bitter and poisonous as I could. You'll laugh when you see it. I probably said two million things I'll be sorry for. . . . She took leave of me by saying she was so afraid she would find me a disappointment to look at after reading my plays. 'But I'm not! They're all there — in your eyes,' she remarked enthusiastically. So be prepared to read of my 'great, sad eyes.' Toward the end they must have been great pools of grief — I was wondering when in hell she was going away and leave me to cough in peace!"

As he began to convalesce, he was further cheered by *Beyond the Horizon*, which was playing to near-capacity houses in spite of the flu epidemic and snowstorms, and by certain of the tributes lavished upon him, including a letter from Anglo-Irish St. John Ervine. "I am proud to think," wrote Ervine, "that so beautiful a thing was made by a man with Irish blood." (When the British playwright's career declined a few years later, he turned on O'Neill and, in his role as a drama critic, exploited every possible opportunity to attack him.)

[6]

Producer John D. Williams, meanwhile, was trying to book a theater so that *Horizon* could expand from its schedule of "special matinees" to a regular nightly run. At the same time, George C. Tyler's production of *Chris* (the title had been shortened from *Chris Christopherson*) was shaping up with Emmett Corrigan as the old bargeman and Lynn Fontanne, a rising young English actress, as his daughter. The sea play was to try out in Atlantic City and Philadelphia before opening on Broadway. O'Neill still had not seen a rehearsal of *Chris* because of his illness, but he had confidence in director Frederick Stanhope as a man with "four years' experience before the mast."

Late in February he felt well enough to write Agnes a long letter full of news. He was upset after a phone call from Stanhope that William ("Scotty") Stewart, one of Eugene's drinking cronies at the Hell Hole and a member of the Provincetown Players, was being dropped from the cast; though Scotty had seemed gifted in the Greenwich Village productions, he looked amateurish alongside of professionals. Now the *Chris* company, Eugene suspected, was annoyed with him for foisting Stewart on them, and Stewart must be nursing a grievance that O'Neill had failed to back him up. "Well," the playwright vowed, "never again! No more of that friendship game in business!" Helen Hayes, his letter continues, had scored a hit in Boston with *Bab*, her new vehicle, and rehearsals of *The Straw* were to begin shortly for a special matinee up there to determine whether she was right for the part of Eileen Carmody. The *Horizon* matinees, he added, were still thriving, but publication of the play was being delayed by "trouble with the printers. [Horace] Liveright is tearing his hair out but hopes to have it out in a week." His cough was better and he told Agnes to cheer up as "pretty soon I'll have had everything and then I'll have to get well."

Already tense and fidgety from his confinement, he became desperate that evening when Agnes and Lillian Brennan, his garrulous cousins from New London, Connecticut, called on his parents. After enduring them for a time he fled to the Hell Hole, where some Hudson Dusters and other "rough-necks" welcomed him as a "brother," they had a whiskey ("of a kind!"), and he was soon "as full as a tick." He spent the night in a room upstairs and awoke the next day feeling, he informed Agnes, "100% better — except for my nerves which are somewhat tattered. . . . But what would any doctor say was the cause of my being cured of my cough and the pain in my chest, I wonder, after all the medicines had failed. Alcoholic Christian Science is my only hope!"

Unable to bear their separation much longer, he intended to catch a

Jamie
in his early
thirties

James O'Neill
in his late
sixties

rehearsal or two of *Chris* and slip away to Provincetown for a few days, but he had reckoned without Tyler; Tyler insisted on his presence at the final practice sessions in New York and the dress rehearsal in Atlantic City, where *Chris* was to open on March 8. Before Eugene had much time to feel sorry for himself, his father, unwell for months, suffered a stroke; for forty-eight hours Eugene went without sleep as the old actor hovered between life and death. In the midst of the crisis the doctor, intensifying the gloom, disclosed that Mr. O'Neill had cancer of the intestines and should be operated on at once, but his heart was too weak for surgery. "And Mama and I," Eugene lamented to Agnes on March 1, "have to go around nursing him, watching his every movement, and pretending to kid him and cheer him up! . . . To have this happen just at the time when the Old Man and I were getting to be such good pals! I'm not going to write any more. I'm all broken up and begin to cry every time the meaning of it all dawns on me."

Adding to his anxiety, Agnes wrote that she was not well and had summoned the doctor; though a day or so later she was all right again, her brief indisposition gave him an idea. When his father rallied slightly, Eugene told Tyler that his wife was seriously ill, without anyone to take care of her, and rushed back to Provincetown. The final rehearsals and the out-of-town opening of *Chris* took place without him, but his presence would have been of little help; in performance the play proved weak and far too long.

Rejecting a summons from the producer, O'Neill replied on March 10 that Agnes was "still very ill" and suggested certain script revisions. Tyler by now was critical of Atlantic City audiences as "principally composed of tango lovers and chewing-gum sweethearts," while O'Neill, on further studying his script, decided that the last scene was "all wrong and must be radically rewritten before the play has a New York showing." He belatedly realized that he had so concentrated on the old bargeman that he had scanted the young couple and failed to individualize them.

After its first several performances *Chris* was cut drastically, yet it remained sluggish and undramatic. Led by Tyler's reports to expect a fiasco, Eugene professed to find the reviews in Philadelphia, where the play opened on March 15, a "pleasant surprise. At least all [the critics] got the idea that I was trying to do something new and outside of the carpentered flip-flap that constitutes the usual American play. To me this is the highest tribute and flattery that I desire." He was, however, rooting for crumbs of comfort among the notices and pretending to be satisfied;

in reality, feeling that no amount of tinkering would materially improve *Chris*, O'Neill had already decided to scrap it and start afresh. "In the back of my mind," he informed Tyler, "there are already inklings as to how this could be done. . . . Suffice it to say that of the present play I would keep without change only the character of Chris — I'd give you a real daughter and lover, flesh-and-blood people — and the big underlying idea of the sea.

"When I could do this, I don't know, as it would all depend on the back of my head which works independently of urgings and won't be forced to turn out ideas." As for Tyler's suggestion that he see the play before it folded in Philadelphia, he said: "Up here I see the real faults inherent in the play itself — my faults. But the only thing I ever get out of seeing a presentation is the actors' faults, which never fail to set me in a rage. I'd rather keep a pleasant memory of the *Chris* cast than to have to hate at least fifty percent of them for the rest of my life."

A few days later, calling *Chris* a "technical experiment," he said that he had tried to "compress the theme for a novel into play form without losing the flavor of the novel. [He had once thought of making such an experiment with *Beyond the Horizon*.] The attempt failed. Perhaps such a bastard form deserved to fail. Perhaps I was attempting the impossible." But, undiscouraged, he was to continue "attempting the impossible" on a scale far more ambitious than *Chris*, for one of his strongest drives as a playwright was to create something with the depth and scope, the large qualities of a novel. Eventually, ignoring standard dramaturgy and what everyone thought theatergoers would accept, he would write *Strange Interlude*, *Mourning Becomes Electra* and *The Iceman Cometh*, multiact mammoths that run over four hours.

The failure of *Chris*, on top of his father's ill health, spurred O'Neill's tendency to look on the dark side of things. In March *Horizon* settled at the Little Theater on Forty-fourth Street for an indefinite run, yet its success could not prevent him from developing a sense of grievance about the critics. Where he had once rejoiced over the reviews, he now felt that they had been unfair to certain aspects of the play, particularly its structure. Expressing a common view, Alexander Woollcott of the *Times* had found in the play a "looseness and a certain high-and-mighty impracticality. . . . Certainly it was a quite impractical playwright who split each of his three acts into two scenes, one outside and one inside the Mayo farmhouse."

O'Neill, who had purposely devised this pattern to get "rhythm" into the story, complained to Barrett H. Clark: "You remember when you read *Beyond*, you remarked about its being an 'interesting technical experiment.' Why is it, I wonder, that not one other critic has given me credit for a deliberate departure in form in search of a greater flexibility? [Apparently he had forgotten that Kenneth Macgowan in the *Globe* had praised the indoor-outdoor pattern as an example of the "new imaginative freedom" in playwriting.] They have all accused me of bungling through ignorance — whereas, if I had wanted to, I could have laid the whole play in the farm interior, and made it tight as a drum à la Pinero. . . . I've been longing to protest about this to someone ever since I read the criticisms by really good critics who blamed my youthful inexperience — even for poor scenery and the interminable waits between the scenes!"

Originally he had favored Tyler's plan to test *The Straw* with a matinee in Boston, but now, declaring that he had been opposed all along, he welcomed a rumor that the performance was likely to be canceled. "I am firmly convinced," he wrote to the producer on March 26, "that Helen Hayes is not old enough either in stage or life experience for the part. The role of 'Eileen' is so tremendous in its requirements that only one of our very best and proved dramatic actresses should be allowed to attempt it." John Westley, who had a dual assignment to portray Stephen Murray and to stage the play, also came under attack. O'Neill dismissed him as a "farce actor," expressed doubts about his ability as a director, and said that *The Straw* should be produced with the greatest care as "the best play" he had yet written, "better even than" *Horizon.*

Contrary to rumor, the projected matinee in Boston had not been canceled. Tyler was confident that Miss Hayes would be ideal as Eileen and called Westley "a good deal of a genius." O'Neill withdrew his objections to the two actors but was doubtful of Westley as a director; he yielded after Tyler said that Westley was "very intelligent" and "so crazy" about the play. O'Neill remained skeptical, however, about the project, as he felt that "to produce a play so drastic in its subject matter as *The Straw* in a town as conventional and hide-bound as Boston is to reduce the play's chances to a minimum." (A year later, though, he urged Tyler to try out one of his plays there, because "the Bostonians have been strong for me from the start when my first one-acters appeared.") He also said that he would regard the matinee as a test not of the play but of the principals' qualifications for their roles. As it turned out, *The Straw* was never given in Boston, for Miss Hayes finally decided it would be too hard on her to appear in *Bab* and rehearse for the other work.

Besides corresponding with Tyler, Eugene kept in touch with the Provincetown Players. In March the group presented a bill that included

"Exorcism," the one-acter based on O'Neill's suicide attempt at Jimmy the Priest's, with Jasper Deeter, a newcomer at the MacDougal Street theater, as the would-be suicide. The reviews were mixed. Alexander Woollcott, praising the work as "uncommonly good," said that O'Neill has a "surplus creative energy which enables him . . . to people [the play] with original and distinctive characters." Heywood Broun of the *Tribune* thought the playlet had "moments of intense poignancy" and was "powerfully successful in painting the atmosphere" of the water front flophouse but as a whole was below the author's standard. The man on *Variety*, taking a moralistic stance, assailed it as a "most depressing affair, devoid of all uplift. . . . The weakling's observations on life and things are of the most morbid kind, showing a depraved, degenerate mind which nothing can alter."

Of all O'Neill's early works, "Exorcism" is the clearest indication that a biographical impulse, a need to bare and justify himself, was a major element in his creative makeup. But once he had written "Exorcism," he began to have doubts: it was too nakedly autobiographical, too revealing about the bleakest period in his life. By the time it opened in the Village, he regretted its existence and, in the only course open to him, directed "Fitzi" — M. Eleanor Fitzgerald, secretary of the Players — to return all the scripts, every single one of them. " 'Exorcism' has been destroyed," he said in 1922, "and the sooner all memory of it dies the better pleased I'll be."

Shortly after his return to Provincetown he resumed working on *Gold*, a full-length version of his one-acter, *Where the Cross Is Made*. Here again, contending with madness, is Captain Bartlett, haunted by the ghosts of seamen murdered at his order and, against all evidence, convinced that his ship is not sunk but will return. Although O'Neill indulged in private symbolism in both the one-acter and the long play, his emphasis in the two works is different. In *Where the Cross* he had in mind the central tragedy in his family: his mother's years of drug addiction, while the O'Neill men desperately hoped for her cure and return from the depths. In *Gold*, however, the symbolism primarily concerns James O'Neill and *Monte Cristo:* just as James had frittered away his talent on the Dumas dramatization, Bartlett, "one of the smartest whaling skippers," betrays his better self by treasure-hunting; just as the fortune James made from *Monte Cristo* (in which buried treasure also figures importantly) failed to bring him a sense of security, since he lost most of the money in bad investments, so the cache in *Gold* proves worthless — the supposed precious gems are actually cheap trinkets. Finally, again like

James O'Neill, who had sought wealth not merely for his own sake but for that of his family, Bartlett, trying to justify his greed and crimes, says he wants to give his wife and children, especially his wife, the best of everything.

Since *Monte Cristo* loomed in O'Neill's thoughts as he worked on *Gold*, it was perhaps inevitable that the artificial Dumas piece should influence the tone and quality of his writing. An old-fashioned sort of work, the new play was contrived, melodramatic, given to overly theatrical confrontations between the principals. The characters, with the lone exception of Captain Bartlett, a figure of some stature and force, are colorless; the dialogue tends to be florid and stilted: "Hands off, ye dog! I'm takin' care o' this chest." . . . "It wasn't me you ran away from, Isaiah. You ran away from your own self — the conscience God put in you." . . . "What man that's a real man wouldn't be against you, sir?"

Although O'Neill usually thought his latest play his best, he "hated" *Gold* when he finished it, considering it "the punkest thing ever written." He felt differently a few months later, however, when John D. Williams placed it under option and so exacting a critic as George Jean Nathan praised it as better than *Beyond the Horizon*. In thanking Nathan, Eugene disclosed that for about a year an idea had been growing "in the back of [his] head" for a work "so large in outline" and so original that it would "take some years of intensive and difficult labor to fill in." What he had in mind is unknown, but his words give some notion of the size and reach of his ambition. In another letter to the critic, after the *Smart Set* ran a Nathan article on O'Neill's career to date, he said: "I am familiar enough with the best modern drama of all countries to realize that, viewed from a true standard, my work is as yet a mere groping. I rate myself as a beginner — with prospects. I acknowledge that when you write: 'He sees life too often as drama. The great dramatist is the dramatist who sees drama as life,' you are smiting the nail on the head. But I venture to promise that this will be less true with each succeeding play. . . . God stiffen it, I am young yet and I mean to grow!"

Late in April, while he remained in Provincetown a few more days to outline some ideas for future work, Agnes visited New York, where she at last caught a performance of *Horizon* and gave the elder O'Neills their first sight of Shane. It was an emotional visit at the Prince George Hotel; while Ella wept softly, James, partly recovered from his stroke, walked up and down several times with Shane in his arms, but he tired quickly and handed the infant back to Agnes. He recalled that when he first learned of her pregnancy, he had hoped for a grandson and thought of all he could do for him; Ella, however, said that she had hoped for a girl, intending to get her a pink layette at Best's, where she had purchased all of Eugene's baby clothes.

O'Neill in Provincetown missed his son, missed him more, he said, than he had expected, but it is doubtful that he felt as bereft as Mrs. Fifine Clark, the O'Neills' housekeeper, who began to center her life on Shane from the first days he was entrusted to her care. "Fifine," Eugene wrote to Agnes, "is lost without him. She keeps repeating what a hole his absence has left in her existence. She is really all broken up about it." Mrs. Clark, who never had children of her own, considered Shane a remarkable youngster. When he was several years old she told Agnes that he had a natural talent for the movies, as she had never known anyone "like him to show his feelings by the expressions on his face. I do not think there could be any child smarter or more adorable. I often look at him in wonder and say to myself, 'Shane, you are certainly going to make your mark in this world.' "

Contrary to her prediction, Shane Rudraighe O'Neill, named after a legendary warrior hero of ancient Ireland, was to grow up a dreamer without a sense of direction, without drive, without the protective skin almost everyone develops after the naked vulnerability of childhood. Essentially, in fact, he was to remain a child most of his life, a lost, quietly despairing child. But he had little if any chance to turn out otherwise. During his early, formative years he was reared, because of the family's special mode of living, in near-isolation. He became a center of conflict and competition between Mrs. Clark, in effect his second mother, and Agnes, with the two women vying for his primary love and devotion. His father, whom he worshiped, felt at a loss with the young, particularly his own. If Shane, originally a demonstrative, affectionate youngster, grew up shy and remote, it was partly, no doubt, because he had unconsciously patterned himself on a withdrawn father whose plays, not his flesh-and-blood offspring, were his "children."

Agnes and the baby were visiting with her parents in West Point Pleasant, New Jersey, by the time Eugene arrived in New York at the beginning of May. After fortifying himself with some drinks, he saw *Beyond the Horizon* again, for Agnes had written to him critically of the performance. Like her, he found that several of the principals were overacting; according to E. J. ("Teddy") Ballantine, who accompanied him, he kept muttering complaints about Richard Bennett. Shortly before the final curtain, he tore up the aisle and when an usher asked if he were ill, snapped: "No, I'm the author!" Ballantine managed to dissuade him from "giving Bennett hell," but the conversation in the actor's dressing room was less than amicable.

At the Provincetown Playhouse a lackluster season was ending. There had been two one-acters by O'Neill, *The Dreamy Kid* and "Exorcism," neither of them among his best; nothing from Susan Glaspell, one of the group's best writers; and worthwhile scripts were so scarce that the Players for the first time in their history put on a foreign work, Schnitzler's *Last Masks* — a move Edna Kenton promptly denounced. "We could understand now why the Washington Square Players and the Theater Guild had sought foreign dramas," she later wrote. "And yet our claim to fame, and the only justification for our simple resources was just precisely that of maintaining an experimental stage for American playwrights."

Miss Kenton, who later wrote the first history of the group, was not the only one dissatisfied; the season was marked by criticism both within and without the ranks. Burns Mantle declared that "these earnest amateurs" are "not living up to their promise of a few seasons ago." Some members complained that Djuna Barnes became "arrogant" after a play of hers was singled out for praise. Following disputes between Jimmy Light and Ida Rauh, codirectors during George Cram ("Jig") Cook's sabbatical, Ida withdrew. Yet the Provincetown Players continued to function. New faces replaced those who dropped out; William and Marguerite Zorach returned briefly as scenic artists; Helen Westley took time from acting with the Theater Guild to direct several plays; and a few Players proved themselves nothing if not versatile. Both Jimmy Light and Charlie Ellis designed sets, acted, and directed, while Edna St. Vincent Millay gave some radiant performances in comedy, directed, and in *Aria da Capo* wrote the group's outstanding play of the season.

But the one most vital to the theater's day-to-day existence was, as always, Fitzi, tall and serenely commanding, who had a stabilizing influence on everyone. "What are the geniuses and near-geniuses up to now?" she used to say in a humorously indulgent tone. Since she had no illusions of being artistically talented herself, she could wholeheartedly devote her energy to the essential chores behind the staging and acting of plays. The title of executive secretary gave but scant indication of Miss Fitzgerald's activities, for she handled the paper work, presided at the box office, served as the group's most effective fund-raiser (she made people feel that it was both their duty and their privilege to support the Provincetown), and was mother-confessor to them all. "Fitzi," said Edmund Wilson, "was touched by an essential nobility that seemed proof against bitterness and disappointment," and e. e. cummings thought her the "incarnation of a mystery."

The 1919–1920 season, as became evident later, ended the first phase in the life of the Provincetown Players; in the fall, chiefly because of O'Neill, they would start concentrating their efforts on full-length scripts. For some time O'Neill, no longer interested in one-acters, had urged his associates to graduate to more substantive fare, and now, heartened by his Broadway success with *Horizon*, a growing number of the group shared his view. A spirit of fresh enthusiasm, in spite of a mediocre year and a sizable deficit, animated the Players. Jig Cook was writing a long play entitled *The Spring*, for which he had high hopes; his wife, Susan Glaspell, had a long one in mind; and all were counting on O'Neill to contribute importantly to their new season.

Not long after Eugene's return to Provincetown in May, he had fresh cause for concern over *The Straw*. From his literary agent, Richard J. Madden, he heard that Tyler planned to try it out that summer in Atlantic City; from his brother Jamie, that Tyler, while visiting the elder O'Neills, had said that it was a "*Romeo and Juliet* play" and that "all the coughing and spitting would have to be cut out." Eugene thought it incredible, he told the producer on June 3, that after the experience with *Chris* he would consider presenting his other play in Atlantic City. *The Straw* bore no resemblance to the Shakespearean work, he said, but was "a play of the significance of human hope and the TB background of the action is as important as the action itself in bringing out my meaning." He offered, if Tyler doubted that *The Straw* could succeed in its present form, to take back his play and return the thousand dollars he had had in advances.

In a heated reply the following day, Tyler disputed Jamie's account, made a slighting reference to *Chris*, contended that an August audience in Atlantic City was a "pretty wise crowd, mainly from New York," and complained that Eugene had formed "the rather youthful impression that I am an idiot manager who knows nothing whatever about the artistic side of the theater and have only an ambition to succeed financially!" The new flurry of correspondence ended inconclusively, with O'Neill neither taking back *The Straw* nor Tyler testing it in the New Jersey resort. Months later O'Neill apologized to the producer for his "over-strained letters . . . written during a period of great worry and nervous tension when I was scarcely responsible. That I should seriously quarrel with so old and dear a friend of my father's is absurdly wrong."

As *Beyond the Horizon* began its final weeks at the Little Theater — it closed after its one hundred and forty-fourth performance on June 26 — O'Neill received word that it had won the Pulitzer Prize as the season's best American play. His first reaction, since he had never heard of the award, was: "Oh, a damned medal! And one of those presentation ceremonies! I won't accept it." After learning that it meant a windfall of one thousand dollars and no ceremony, he "practically went delirious! I was broke or nearly," he said. "It was the most astoundingly pleasant surprise of my life."

His ignorance of the prize is not as surprising as it seems today; in 1920 the Pulitzer awards in drama, literature and journalism, established several years earlier by newspaper publisher Joseph Pulitzer, were so little known that to the public at large they carried almost no prestige. Actually, as was announced, the drama jury would have chosen *Abraham Lincoln* by England's John Drinkwater had it been eligible; but the prize could be awarded only to an American work, one which "best represents the educational value and power of the stage in raising the standards of good morals, good tastes, and good manners." A few years later, after the national outlook had become more sophisticated, after "good morals, good tastes, and good manners" had changed drastically under the impact of Prohibition and the Jazz Age, the drama award citation would eliminate the Sunday School verbiage.

In all, with the Pulitzer thousand, O'Neill made six thousand two hundred and sixty-four dollars from the New York engagement of *Horizon*, which grossed just over one hundred and seventeen thousand dollars. Though far from one of the season's big money-makers (where *Horizon* averaged around sixty-five hundred dollars a week, *East Is West*, a piece of exotic trash, took in twelve thousand dollars in its sixty-eighth week), the O'Neill play did prove, to the future health of the Broadway theater, the existence of a sizable audience for serious contemporary American drama. The success of the play, both commercially and critically, was especially gratifying to Eugene because it all happened while his actor father was still living. "Yes," he told a friend, "it was the greatest satisfaction [my father] knew that I had made good in a way dear to his heart. And I thank 'whatever Gods may be' that *Beyond* came into its own when it did and not too late for him."

James O'Neill's condition, which varied in the first months after his stroke, occasionally aroused hope in his family that he still had considerable time to live. At one point the old actor felt so much better that he intended to visit New London to attend to some business matters, chiefly with the view of improving his financial situation for Ella's sake; he also

Eugene's response to word that his Pulitzer Prize for Beyond
the Horizon *included a thousand-dollar cash award*

O'Neill and Agnes

O'Neill and Shane

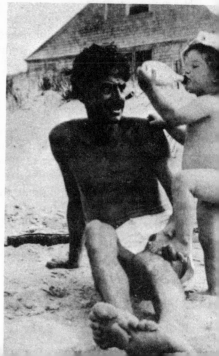

Before the station

The station being claimed by the sea, 1931

transferred to her most of his real estate, in the possibility that she would have little if any taxes to pay on his estate. But on May 14, vomiting and in agony, he was rushed by ambulance from the Prince George to St. Vincent's Hospital.

"Friday night and Saturday," Jamie wrote to his brother several days later, "nurses and Drs. at St. Vincent's gave the Governor up — yesterday he sat up and took his broth — & orange juice. [Dr. John] Aspell says, 'Isn't it wonderful?' — & when Mama asked how he accounted for it today, he said, 'Maybe the noise and rattle of dishes at the hotel were responsible for the former pain and vomiting.' . . . Yesterday he told her tho Papa was better apparently — he'd surely have another attack — & could not possibly live anyhow. . . . All I know is Papa says he has no pain. . . . I believe he's going to die — and soon — but that he'll linger some time yet. Everyone — nurses, etc. — seem puzzled at the pain disappearing in a cancer case. It's costing $130 a week for room & two nurses — not to speak of that dear Dr. Aspell — He won't have to linger a hell of a while to leave Mama on the rocks for cash. You missed great characters & Material for your work by not being around that hospital — Talk about your tragedy Comedy – Comedy Tragedy! If it had been someone else's father I would have died laughing. . . .

"I wept and felt horribly grief-stricken myself when I really believed the end was at hand — but my after-thoughts of all that happened down there — except those few solemn moments are comic memories that will stay with me for life. That's all the news — Mama was on the verge of a breakdown & staying up purely on her nerve. She's rested a bit since his rally — but it's fierce to think she'll have it all to go thru' again — & to boot — the horrible Elks — K. of C. — Thames Club — Engine Co.'s — Father Fitzsimon Ceremonies in New London."

On June 10, after nearly a month in the New York hospital, Mr. O'Neill was transferred by ambulance and train to the Lawrence and Memorial Associated Hospitals in New London. He had always looked forward, after weary months of touring, to his summers in the quiet, elm-lined town, where he would trim the hedge and putter around the grounds of his cottage on Pequot Avenue, spend gossipy hours at Nat Keeney's fish market on nearby Scott's dock, drink away leisurely afternoons with his cronies at the Crocker House bar, and look after his extensive real estate holdings. Now he had come home to die.

As he faded, Ella, although Jamie had feared her "on the verge of a breakdown," grew stronger, more resolute; now that she no longer could lean on her husband, she drew on her own inner resources. She was at the hospital every day from morning to night, though James had nurses around the clock, and kept a vigilant watch over the care given to him; little conversation passed between them but it was obvious to the hospital people that he derived comfort from her mere presence. Among themselves the staff members referred to her as "the charming widow," for she already dressed in black, wearing part of the smart mourning wardrobe she had acquired, while still in the city, at Bendel's, Lord & Taylor's, and other Fifth Avenue shops. Ella had formerly thought the jewelry James had given her was too ostentatious, but now, probably to please him, she always wore one of the pieces. The nurses found her polite but distant — "You could get so close to her," one recalls, "and no further."

In Provincetown Eugene expected a summons any day to his father's bedside, yet Mr. O'Neill, against all expectations, retained a grip on life. June passed and July was nearly over when Eugene, torn between a desire to see his father before the end and a reluctance to participate in the deathwatch, received the word that sent him hurrying to New London. At the hospital on the twenty-ninth, he told Agnes he was writing her while "Papa is lying in bed watching me, his strange eyes staring at me with a queer, uncanny wonder as if, in that veiled borderland between Life and Death in which his soul drifts suspended, a real living being of his own flesh and blood were an incongruous and puzzling spectacle. I feel as if my health, the suntan on my face contrasted with the unhealthy pallor of his, were a spiritual intrusion, an impudence. And yet how his eyes lighted up with grateful affection when he first saw me! It made me feel so glad, so happy I had come!

"The situation is frightful! Papa is alive when he ought to be dead. The disease has eaten through his bowels. Internal decomposition has set in — while he is still living! There is a horrible, nauseating smell in the room. . . . His face, his whole body is that of a corpse. . . . Only his eyes are alive — and the light that glimmers through their glaze is remote and alien. He suffers incredible tortures, in spite of all their dope. Just a few moments ago he groaned in anguish and cried pitifully: 'Oh, God, why don't You take me! Why don't You take me.'" And Mama and I silently echoed his prayer. . . .

"One very pitiful, cruelly ironic thing: He cannot talk plainly any more. Except when he cries out in pain it is impossible to understand him. And all through his life his greatest pride has been in his splendid voice and clear articulation! His lips flutter, he tries hard to say something, only a mumble comes forth. . . .

"Death seems to be rubbing it in — to demand that he drink the chalice of gall and vinegar to the last bitter drop before peace is finally his. And, dear God, why? Surely he is a fine man as men go, and can look back to a long life in which he has kept an honorable faith and labored hard to get from nothing to the best attainment he knew. Surely the finest test of that attainment is the great affection and respect that all bear him who knew him. . . . And he has certainly been a husband to marvel at, and a good father, according to his lights . . . looking at it dispassionately, he seems to me a good man — in the best sense of the word — and about the only one I have ever known. . . .

"I'm afraid you'll find this letter a false note of drama. It isn't. It's sincere as hell! Perhaps I'm too keyed up to write convincingly. . . .

"Later — He was asleep when I was writing the above. Then he woke up and called me over. He made a dreadful effort to speak clearly and I understood a part of what he said. 'Glad to go, boy — a better sort of life — another sort — somewhere' — and then he mumbled. He appeared to be trying to tell me what sort — and although I tried my damndest I couldn't understand! . . . Then he became clear again: 'This sort of life —froth! — rotten — all of it — no good!' There was a bitter expression on his poor, sunken face. And there you have it — the verdict of a *good* man looking back over seventy-six years: 'Froth! Rotten!' "

These were the last intelligible words Eugene would ever hear from his father.

Shortly before he left Provincetown, he and Agnes had had a quarrel during which he had referred to their marriage as "an unhappy one," arousing in her "the greatest antagonism," but they had patched up their differences. Now, sitting beside his dying father, he wrote: "Oh, My Own, we just mustn't fight and hurt each [other] any more! *We mustn't!* It's the unforgivable sin — a crime against the spirit of our love! I can see that the great thing my father brings to his heart as something vital, not froth or rotten, is my mother's love for him and his for her. He has thrown everything else overboard but that remains — the real thing of the seventy-six years . . . the justification of his life because he knows that, at least, is fine and that it will go with him wherever he is going. . . .

"They expect Father to go any moment now. . . . His pulse is almost out."

Yet he lingered, "hanging on," Eugene said on the thirtieth, "by the merest thread. The head [doctor] says that it is only Papa's *marvelously strong heart* that is keeping him alive! And that fool in New York was afraid to operate on him months ago because he claimed his heart was too weak!"

For days James O'Neill lay in a coma and on August 10, sometime after midnight, his wife and sons were summoned back to the hospital; Agnes, who by now had joined her husband, was with them. To a friend who drove them to the hospital, Jamie, who had been drinking, grumbled, "Helluva time for the Old Man to die." The end came at four-fifteen in the morning, with Ella and a nurse in his room at the time; Ella, who was standing beside his bed as the death rattle signaled his end, broke into hysterical weeping and clung to the nurse.

In death, as during a great part of his life, James O'Neill was bound to *Monte Cristo*. Newspapers throughout the country, paying memorial tribute, dwelled on his long association with the Dumas work and a number regretted that he had wasted years on Edmond Dantès that should have been devoted to Shakespeare. The ultimate word on him would not be said, however, until years later when it was written by his son and pronounced by James Tyrone in *Long Day's Journey Into Night*: "That God-damned play I bought for a song and made such a great success in, it ruined me with its promise of an easy fortune . . . and by the time I woke up to the fact I'd become a slave to the damned thing and did try other plays, it was too late. I'd lost the great talent I once had through years of easy repetition."

Ella had been staying with the Sheridans, her cousins, at 55 Channing Street, and here her husband's body was laid out, dressed in the full uniform, complete with baldric and sword, of the Knights of Columbus, fourth degree, in which he would be buried. When he was first brought from the funeral parlor, Ella, like a solicitous mother who wanted her child to look his best, fussed over his clothes. Eugene, also a guest of the Sheridans, together with Agnes, tried to be as inconspicuous as possible during the two days his father was on display in the front parlor. Ella made repeated attempts to have him join the crowd in front, but he generally remained in a rear room; one relative recalls him staring morosely into an artificial fireplace. Jamie, however, stayed close to his mother, excepting the time when he and Eugene disappeared for hours. They went off and, according to Tom Dorsey, Mr. O'Neill's old drinking crony, "mourned their father in the true Irish fashion — by drowning their sorrow."

One side of Eugene would have preferred a quiet, simple exit for his father, but another side was gratified by the display of attention and respect: throngs of people at the Sheridan house, a deluge of letters and telegrams, a mass of floral tributes. Eugene's lone grievance, which he harbored for years, was that The Players, the club founded in New York by Edwin Booth, "absolutely ignored [the] death — sent no flowers, no word, nothing. My mother was deeply hurt," he said, "and my brother and I were furious, as well we might be! For my father had been a friend of Booth's, and played with him, and was one of the club's oldest members!" (He later learned that his father's death had been overlooked during a change of management at The Players, and eventually relented enough to accept honorary membership in the club.)

In one of New London's most impressive funerals in years, St. Joseph's Roman Catholic Church was packed with notables of the community, theater people from New York, and delegations from the many fraternal and Irish organizations to which James O'Neill had belonged. George Tyler was in Europe but William P. Connor, Tyler's associate and James's advance man for years, attended, and his floral piece, a large wreath of white roses, lay on the casket. In mid-service a dumpy woman, all in black and carrying a suitcase, clumped down the aisle, stared around with an irate expression, and joined the family group; it was Mrs. Margaret Platz of Cincinnati, one of James's two surviving sisters, and she wanted the coffin opened for a last view of her illustrious brother. Though James had never been close to any of his sisters, he occasionally used to send a check to Mrs. Platz, who was of limited means. Mrs. Platz finally was mollified when the coffin was opened briefly at St. Mary's Cemetery. She later called on Ella, who had retreated to a room at the Mohican Hotel, to inquire about her brother's will; on learning that he had left everything to his widow, Mrs. Platz immediately departed for home.

As Eugene and Agnes returned to Provincetown, he found that his father's final words were "written indelibly — seared on [his] brain," along with the bitter regrets James had voiced earlier about *Monte Cristo* and his unfulfilled career. The son regarded it all as a "warning from the Beyond to remain true to the best that is in me though the heavens fall."

2

※

The Provincetown's Costly Success

A SEMIAMPHIBIOUS man with a strain of atavism in his makeup,
O'Neill felt in his element at Peaked Hill Bars, where he had "the
Atlantic for a front lawn, miles of sand dunes for a backyard." Only a
few steps from his summertime home, a former United States Coast
Guard station, and he was at ease in the water, cradled by the waves.
Hazel Hawthorne, who likewise preferred the primeval beauty of "the
Outside" to the orderly charm of Provincetown proper, recalls that
Eugene "would be idling by in the sea when I passed on shore, and would
raise an arm in greeting with a flash of smile that I never saw when he
was ashore." While swimming rather far out once, he raised his head and
was startled to see, only a few feet away, a dark sleek head with whiskers
and large dark eyes regarding him with grave curiosity; for a fleeting
second he had the eerie feeling that he was looking at an image of himself. It was a seal, presumably seeking a playmate, but Eugene, reacting
instinctively, turned and raced furiously for the beach.

In August Boston newspaperman Olin Downes trekked over the dunes
one day, hoping for an interview, and was fortunate enough to find the
playwright, normally so taciturn, in a reminiscent mood. Between long
reflective silences, he talked of his childhood and various schools, his gold-
prospecting in Honduras, his time at sea, his being "on the beach" in
Buenos Aires and on the New York water front. At one point he asked
Downes (later a noted music critic) whether he had ever heard "chanties
sung on the sea. You never did? It's not surprising. There are even fewer
sailing vessels now than there were ten short years ago when I pulled out
for the open. They don't have to sing as they haul the ropes. They don't
humor a privileged devil who has a fine voice and hell inside of him, as he
chants that wonderful stuff and they pull to the rhythm of the song and

[25]

the waves." Like everyone else who visited Peaked Hill, Downes fell under the spell of the old station: "The wind hummed in the timbers, and I should not have been the least surprised if I had seen, sailing through the foggy sky, the body and spars of the *Flying Dutchman.*" Equally impressed by O'Neill himself, he came away feeling that he had never met anyone "whose life, personality and work seemed more of a piece."

Besides *Gold*, finished in the spring, O'Neill was to compose three more plays in 1920. His father's death, rather than so upsetting him that he was unable to write, seems to have had, if anything, an opposite effect on him: reminded, presumably, of his own mortality, he could not create fast enough. Facing him on the desk where he worked was a photograph of his father at a late age, a side view that recalls the son's description of him: "His face has begun to break down but he is still remarkably good-looking – a big, finely shaped head, a handsome profile."

To letters of condolence Eugene replied that his father's death had left "a big hole" in his life. "My one reconciling thought," he told Nina Moise on August 29, "is that he suffered such incredible tortures the last three months of his life that death was for him a true release – and peace." Informing her that he had a ten-month-old son, he added that the child "howls with his deceased grandfather's far-famed voice."

Shortly after his return from the funeral O'Neill resumed working on a new version of *Chris*, which he had begun earlier in the summer; it was finished on September 18. He retained the character of old Chris virtually unchanged, just as he had predicted to Tyler, and completely transformed the two young lovers. Instead of portraying Anna Christie as a stenographer who had been properly reared in England, he made her a prostitute who, as a child, had been exploited by brutish relatives on a Minnesota farm. Rather than pairing her with a colorless young American, he drew on his memories of Driscoll, his swaggering stoker friend, to draw the hero, now called Mat Burke, as a crude but romanticizing Irishman with great self-confidence.

The new version, first called "The Ole Davil," then "Tides," finally *Anna Christie*, greatly improved on the old one. With the sea as a menacing background, Chris's efforts to dissuade Anna from marrying a sailor, her self-torment over whether she has a right to accept Mat, and Mat's outrage on learning of her past all serve to keep the story rolling and pitching on a course almost continuously absorbing. The author's spokesman in the play, Anna not only shares his mystical feeling for the sea but voices one of his summary views of life. "There ain't nothing to forgive, anyway," she says, when Chris blames himself for his daughter's misfortunes. "It ain't your fault, and it ain't mine, and it ain't [Mat's] neither. We're all poor nuts, and things happen, and we yust get mixed in wrong, that's all." Twenty years later O'Neill would express a similar thought through the mother in *Long Day's Journey Into Night:* "None of us can help the things life has done to us. They're done before you realize it, and once they're done they make you do other things until at last everything comes between you and what you'd like to be, and you've lost your true self forever."

A work of mixed quality, *Anna Christie* embodies both clichés, such as regeneration through love, and fresh material derived from the author's familiarity with the sea and water-front life. Similarly, Anna herself rings true in her grievance against society, especially her hostility to men, and her ambivalence toward her father; yet she also recalls one of the stalest of literary stereotypes – the prostitute with a heart of gold, the fallen woman who has remained basically pure. As for Mat Burke, he too is drawn with vitality and personal color, but his Irishness is painted on so thick that he sometimes verges on being a stage Irishman. Whatever its flaws, *Anna Christie* was to prove one of the author's most popular works, and it is possible that certain of its excesses and stock features contributed to its success.

All the while he was working on *Anna Christie*, O'Neill was conceiving yet another play, which he began writing in mid-September. "When I get an idea I put it down," he once said, "or I may work on it until I can't see how it will turn out. Then I put it aside and work on something else. Later on I may get an idea that picks me up where I left off, and I take up the thing until I finish it."

Several years previously a friend of his, a circus man who had toured the West Indies with a tent show, had told him that Vilbrun Guillaume Sam, onetime president of Haiti, used to boast that "his enemies would never get him – that if he were overthrown he would kill himself, but not with an ordinary lead bullet; only a silver one was worthy of that honor." Fascinated by the image of the black potentate and the silver bullet, O'Neill made a note of the anecdote. Months later he conceived the idea of having a deposed ruler in flight through the jungle, "but I couldn't see how it could be done on a stage, and I passed it up again. A year elapsed. One day I was reading of the religious feasts in the Congo and the uses to which the drum is put there; how it starts at a normal pulse-beat and is slowly intensified until the heart-beat of every one present corresponds to the frenzied beat of the drum. There was an idea and an experiment. How would this sort of thing work on an audience in a theater?"

His physical surroundings helped to activate the play forming in his mind. As Old Snail Road led from the highway toward the dunes and Peaked Hill, it passed through a clump of woods in which the overarching trees were so thick that they shut out the sky; even in daytime the area, over a hundred paces long, seemed broodingly quiet and secretive, but at night "the dark place," as Provincetowners called it, was altogether spooky. Whenever O'Neill traversed "the dark place" it reminded him, he said, of his gold-prospecting in Spanish Honduras – particularly the bottomless black nights in the Honduran forests.

Augmenting his own experience, the playwright, who had read practically all of Conrad, was influenced, apparently, by *Heart of Darkness*. Like the play O'Neill wrote in fall 1920, the Conrad novelette dwells on the oppressive nature of the jungle ("The woods were unmoved, like a mask – heavy, like the closed doors of a prison") and conjures up the unsettling sound of tom-toms ("The monotonous beating of a drum filled the air with muffled shocks and a lingering vibration . . . the beat of the drum, regular and muffled like the beating of a heart – the heart of a conquering darkness"). Even more to the point, both the novelist and the playwright tell essentially the same story: the nightmarish disintegration of a man, an outsider, in an aboriginal land of omnipresent terror.

In writing "The Silver Bullet," later retitled *The Emperor Jones*, O'Neill was evidently swayed by yet another book, Gordon Craig's *The Theater Advancing*, which he had read earlier this year. A compilation of Craig's radical views, it champions a freer, more imaginative stagecraft: "Dancing, Pantomime and the Marionette, three essentials of the old Dramatic Art, have been allowed to go to seed, and people wonder why the Dramatic Art of today is so indifferent in quality." All three features, as well as masks, Craig maintained, were indispensable if the contemporary theater hoped to regain some of its onetime stature and magic. Inspired, presumably, by Craig's vision, O'Neill used masks, pantomime and dance, especially pantomime, in *The Emperor Jones;* and while he never actually resorted to marionettes, he had them in mind as he described the figures in the dumb-show interludes of his play: "Their movements are those of automatons – rigid, slow, and mechanical. . . . There is something stiff, rigid, unreal, marionettish about their movements."

Finally, as Professor Travis Bogard has pointed out, the new O'Neill work was indebted also, "in its dramatic form and in many aspects of its theme," to Ibsen's *Peer Gynt*. Among other parallels, both plays send their eponymous heroes fleeing for their lives, both reduce these so-called emperors to "the condition of groveling animals," both confront them with accusatory scenes from their pasts.

The entire scheme for *The Emperor Jones* was so clear in O'Neill's mind that its composition took only about two weeks; he finished the play on October 2. For its Negro protagonist he drew on various sources: his acquaintance, chiefly through gambler Joe Smith, with the "black belt" of Greenwich Village (an aspect of Manhattan that dwindled as more and more blacks flocked to Harlem); his readings about Toussaint L'Ouverture and Henri Christophe; the Jamaican blacks, strapping men with natural dignity, who had been crew members of the sailing vessel *Charles Racine;* and Adam Scott of New London, a Baptist Church elder who worked as a bartender. "I'm a religious man on Sunday," Scott was fond of saying, "but the rest of the week I puts my Jesus on the shelf." Similarly, the author has Brutus Jones say: "It don't git me nothin' to do missionary work for de Baptist Church. I'se after de coin, an' I lays my Jesus on de shelf for de time bein'."

Placed on a West Indian island "as yet not self-determined by White Marines," the story dramatizes the downfall of Brutus Jones, an ex–Pull-man porter from Harlem who has set himself over the natives through luck and guile; they believe he possesses supernatural powers. As the play opens he swaggers about, resplendent in a red-and-blue uniform with gold chevrons and patent-leather boots; his pearl-handled revolver contains five lead bullets and a silver one — only a silver bullet, he boasts, can kill him. The palace, he soon discovers, is ominously empty, for the people have at last revolted, and he begins his flight as a drumming, low yet insistent, is heard from the distant hills; the rebels are working up courage to hunt him down.

Still self-confident as he enters the jungle, Jones intends to follow an escape route he had once marked out in anticipation of his day of reckon-ing. His is a journey not only in time and space, however, but into the darkest recesses of his soul. As he loses his way, he is hounded less by his enemies — except for their tom-toms which steadily grow faster and louder — than by frightful images conjured up by his mind. In brief cinemalike scenes the play projects his hallucinations. Episodes from his criminal past return to haunt him, then scenes epitomizing the tragic history of the Negro in America, and at last Jones, stripped of his veneer of civilization, reverts to the primitive condition of his Congo forebears. Each ghostly encounter ends with his firing in panic, till all his bullets, including the silver one, are spent. Throughout the night, as the drumming accelerates, he has been running in a great circle and he finally returns to his starting point, where his enemies greet him with a gun loaded with silver bullets.

Exciting, imaginative, richly theatrical, with an undercurrent of dark lyricism, *The Emperor Jones* was a splendid achievement, easily the author's finest work to date. Various sides of O'Neill — the poet, the experimentalist, the born dramatist, the dreamer in love with strange exotic places — all found expression in *Jones*. Nothing else he had yet written signaled so clearly that he was his own man, blazing his own trail in the theater. Against all the rules and conventions, the play had a black man as the protagonist, there was no love interest, and even its form and length were unorthodox — no intermission, lasting only about an hour. The play is, moreover, almost a monologue; except in the first and final scenes, Jones is isolated among phantoms born of his memories and atavistic fears.

If the play has a fault, it is predictability: once Jones has fired at the Little Formless Fears, vague creatures writhing up from the ground, the pattern is set, the course of the story evident. Any shortcomings, however, are far overbalanced by the virtues. To some extent Jones's portrait conforms to the old stereotype of the American Negro — superstitious, only half civilized, given to violence; but at the same time he is endowed with a quick intelligence, a strong will and, despite his rather comic airs as monarch of the island, innate dignity, a commanding personality. All in all, an impressive figure. Essentially, O'Neill was not trying to demonstrate that the American black is only a short step from his African ancestors; he was suggesting something more universal — that an apprehensive primitive being lurks just below the surface of us all.

After word from O'Neill that he had written an unusual new play, Susan Glaspell and Jig Cook, their curiosity aroused, labored across the dunes on a day so stormy that it was a "thrilling struggle" just to get to the old station. The turbulent weather was a suitable overture, they later thought, to the play they heard the author read that night before a blazing fire. "This marks the success of the Provincetown Players," Cook said to his wife the following morning as they recrossed the dunes. "Gene knew there was a place where such a play would be produced. He wrote it to *compel* us to the untried, to do the 'impossible.' " To Susan it did seem "impossible to give this play on our few feet of stage," but Cook was determined. "We will work out new ways of doing things. Our very limitations will create," and, as he became more and more excited, "I'll get the afternoon train."

[30]

"One thing," he said to Susan as she walked with him to the train, "we've got to put in a dome. Money or no money — the Emperor has got to play against that dome."

Jig had long dreamed of a dome, a plaster cyclorama such as advanced European theaters were using, a device that would give an illusion of spaciousness to the tiny stage at 133 MacDougal Street; but the Players had never been able to afford it. At present, with some of last season's debts still unpaid, they had only five hundred and thirty dollars — subscriptions were coming in slowly — with which to launch their 1920–1921 season. In New York, Cook was immediately embroiled in controversy with other executive-committee members. Praising *Jones* as O'Neill's best play, he said that it would launch their season with excitement, that its story and form demanded a dome, while the others maintained that it was unthinkable at this time and suggested deferring *Jones* to later in the season, when they might be able to mount it properly.

Finally, after heated sessions with the others, none of whom had yet read the play, Cook took matters into his own hands. One day Edna Kenton, dropping by the Provincetown in hopes that O'Neill had sent down some copies of the script, got a disturbing response from Fitzi when she asked for Jig ("What Jig hasn't done! I thought he hadn't called you up") and went to see for herself. She found him alone on the stage "in a clutter of steel netting, iron bars, and bags of cement. He looked up as I came down the aisle, then turned his back on me and finished throwing in his batch of mixed plaster.

"'There's to be no argument about this,' he said suddenly. 'I've had enough from everybody. The Emperor has *got* to have a dome. You see, Edna, it begins . . . thick forest at first . . . steadily thinned out . . . scene after scene . . . to pure space.' And as he went on, it began to happen — one of his hours of creative talk of the rarest and finest. Many, many times I was to see that play that made Gene O'Neill famous, played against the dome downtown, against wrinkled cycloramas uptown, in theaters large and small. . . . But I was never to see it so clearly as it played itself that morning in the dim little theater, with no voice but one, with no audience but one. From the Little Formless Fears to the Crocodile God the figures emerged and moved in relation to all their scenic values . . . against the rough unfinished dome."

With Jig and a few helpers doing all the labor, the dome cost five hundred dollars in materials alone. Not without disadvantages, it occupied eight precious feet of the small stage and in addition made the actors' entrances and exits more difficult; but, vindicating Cook's dream, it gave the stage an "actual sense of infinity" and "like the heavens it was itself a source of light." The Players were never to exhaust the scenic effects and the lighting possibilities of their dome, the first ever in the American theater.

While the device was under construction another argument broke out, this time over the casting of Brutus Jones; some Players, led by Ida Rauh, insisted that he should be played by a Negro, and others maintained that the public would prefer a white man in blackface for such an important part. Charles Ellis, one of the group's better actors, was eager for the role, but at last the pro-Negro advocates prevailed. Jasper Deeter, who was to play the Cockney trader Smithers, suggested an actor named Charles S. Gilpin who had had a small part as a slave in Drinkwater's *Abraham Lincoln,* and, after some queries in Harlem, he was tracked down to Macy's, where he was running an elevator.

"Are you Charles Gilpin?" a deputized Provincetowner inquired as he got on the elevator. "Yes. Corsets, ladies' underthings — second floor." "Are you an experienced actor?" "Yes. Glassware, silverware, household furnishings." "We have a good part for you in a play by Eugene O'Neill." "How good? Draperies, upholsteries, linens." "The leading part. Would you like to act again?" "Yes, what's the pay? Furniture, bedclothing, bathroom supplies — fifth floor." "The best we can pay is fifty dollars." "It's a deal. Going down. Where do I go?"

He had read but a few lines at the Provincetown when all present felt that he was the man for the role; in fact the selection of Gilpin as Brutus Jones — the first Negro ever cast by a white American company for a major role — was to prove one of the ideal combinations of actor and part in American theater history.

From Richmond, Virginia, endowed with a good mind and natural ability, Charles S. Gilpin had managed, in spite of the great odds against him, to accumulate considerable stage experience by the simple expedient of not being "fussy." He appeared in vaudeville, musical comedy, Negro stock companies, fly-by-night minstrel shows ("Away we'd start with a show, get paid for the first night or so, and then we'd live on 'art' for a while"), and for a time produced recent Broadway hits at the Lafayette in Harlem. But he never had a chance to build a career; from the footlights he kept returning to jobs as a printer, a barber, a Pullman porter, anything to earn a living. Now in his mid-forties exact age unknown ("A colored man doesn't have dates — he is just born"), he was ready, after years of frustration and waste, to bring Brutus Jones alive on the stage.

Charles Gilpin and Jasper Deeter had the only roles of consequence, with Christine Ell appearing briefly as an old native woman and Charles Ellis as a tribal chief. Appearing "deeply excited and gaudily indifferent all at once," O'Neill came down from Provincetown for the first readings, was impressed by Gilpin, and returned for the final rehearsals. Shortly before the opening, Cook, who was directing *Jones*, and his aides decided that the scenery, a succession of heavy standing screens, required too much time for the constant changes of scene. In the emergency Deeter enlisted a young artist friend of his, Cleon Throckmorton, to devise a new production scheme. At first "Throck" felt discouraged about the playhouse and its facilities. "In the cellar," he recalls, "there was three inches of water, with planks laid across for the actors to reach the dressing rooms. It all looked hopelessly amateurish to me — I couldn't see how they got anything done." But, working day and night, he came through with some lightweight hanging silhouettes that enabled the scenes to be changed swiftly. "The last five days, after Throck came on and the work of three weeks was torn to pieces," according to Miss Kenton, "were nothing short of cyclonic."

Adding to the preopening confusion, Charlie Chaplin, who had become friendly with some of the Players, particularly Christine Ell (he enjoyed her earthy humor and thought her a born mimic), volunteered to appear under the name of "Harry Spencer" in the pantomime scenes at the première. Although a number of Provincetowners welcomed his offer, it was declined, before O'Neill ever heard about it, when others protested that if news leaked out that the famous comedian was to take part, the play would be overshadowed.

Since three Broadway productions, in addition to *The Emperor Jones*, opened on November 1, 1920, a Monday, the reviewers did not see the Village production till later in the week. But from the excited response of the first-nighters, it was obvious that *Jones* would be a hit; even after the actors had taken many curtain calls — the place rang with cheers for Gilpin — the audience refused to leave, so the curtain was rung up, the stage cleared of its "thick forest," and the dome shown off with a series of lighting changes. Word spread fast and the following morning saw the first line at the box office in the theater's history, a line that grew longer as the reviews began to appear.

Heywood Broun in the *Tribune* on November 4: " . . . the most interesting play which has yet come from the most promising playwright in America. . . . Gilpin is great. It is a performance of heroic stature." Kenneth Macgowan in the *Globe* the same day: "An odd and extraordinary play, written with imaginative genius. . . . Gilpin's is a sustained

[33]

and splendid piece of acting. The moment when he raises his naked body against the moonlit sky and prays is such a dark lyric of the flesh, such a cry of the primitive being, as I have never seen in the theater." Alexander Woollcott in the *Times* on November 7: " . . . an extraordinarily striking and dramatic study of panic fear . . . for strength and originality [O'Neill] has no rivals among the American writers for the stage." And summing up the general view, the Brooklyn *Eagle* on November 9: "The Provincetown Players have justified their season if they do nothing else this winter."

Tribute was paid to the dome ("episodes of glorious beauty") and particularly to the use of the tom-toms, but their effect was best described by a critic who saw a later production in London: "A persistent drum beat punctuates *The Emperor Jones*, beginning slowly, quickening as scene follows scene, culminating in a headlong prestissimo, but never ceasing for a moment, not even in the intervals between scenes. Of course your nerves are affected. You throb responsive to the drum. You have a feeling of tense expectation. Finally you are exasperated and yearn only for relief from the persistent agonizing sound. It is a nightmare."

The Provincetowners had begun the season "deep in the hole," but with *Jones* the entire picture changed: the number of subscriptions jumped to fifteen hundred; the actors were getting paid for the first time (Gilpin's fifty dollars a week was the only sizable salary), a policy that spurred competition for roles; Fitzi had difficulty coping with box office matters and the paper work, even though she now had two assistants, Susan Jenkins, Jimmy Light's wife, and Pauline Turkel; hard-eyed Broadway managers, who previously would have scorned *Jones* as uncommercial, besieged the Villagers with offers to move the work to Times Square. It appeared, in short, that the band of semiamateurs had at last established themselves; but actually, behind the scene, their situation was becoming precarious.

The group had managed to endure through six years of scant funds and hit-and-miss experimentation, animated and sustained by their freewheeling amateur spirit; success, with the problems that arose in its wake, was to prove fatal for them. The previous season they had doubled their schedule for each bill to two weeks, an ill-advised move, since they had usually played to half-empty houses in the second week; now the theater was too small to accommodate all who wanted to see the exciting new hit. The more idealistic Players urged that after *Jones* had completed the standard two-week engagement, it should be released for royalties to a Broadway producer, with the group remaining intact to continue as a laboratory for experiment; but most, hungering for Broadway acclaim, felt that the production should be moved uptown. After its Village engagement had been extended a few times, the play was taken to Broadway with the original company — leaving the downtown ranks depleted — under the auspices of producer Adolph Klauber for a series of special matinees and finally was installed in its own theater for an indefinite nightly run. But, as Edna Kenton said, "We were not getting rich. We were paying 'uptown' actors 'uptown' salaries. Jealousies arose. And expenses leaped bewilderingly." The Players were to survive only one more season.

Jig Cook had contributed substantially to the success of *Jones* not only by building the dome against all opposition (thereby becoming a hero to his associates) and sleeping in the theater to save rent money toward its cost but by driving everyone, himself most of all, to give of their best. Later he was to complain that the play had infected the group with a fever for Broadway, yet he himself was among the infected. Moreover, he benefited from the play's commercial success; in the Village *Jones* had been coupled with *Matinata*, a curtain raiser by Lawrence Langner, but on Broadway it was given with *Tickless Time*, by Jig and his wife Susan Glaspell. Envious of O'Neill, Cook left for Provincetown shortly after the première of *Jones* to complete *The Spring*, hoping it would at last bring him recognition as a playwright.

If *Jones* became a costly success to the Players, it eventually proved a personal disaster for Charles Gilpin. Defensively proud of being black, resentful of all he had had to endure because of his color, he was vulnerable, understandably, to the pressure and intoxication of overnight fame. It was of little consequence to the Players that he reportedly "was acting the Emperor all over Harlem." It was another matter when he tampered with his role; balking at the word "nigger," as frequently required by the script, he changed it to "Negro" or "colored man" and began taking other liberties with the dialogue. Furious about it, O'Neill threatened to have him fired but finally vented his feelings by telling him, "If you change the lines again, I'll beat the hell out of you!" For relief from all that was weighing on him, Gilpin resorted to liquor, not only during his leisure but, at times, before and even during a performance. Although he generally managed to give a good account of himself onstage, there were nights, as he waited in the wings for a set to be changed, that he would whisper to the stage manager, "What's the scene, what's the scene?"

But even those who had lost all patience with him were outraged the following year when the New York Drama League sought to discriminate against him. The trouble began when the league, polling its members to choose the ten persons who had contributed most to the 1920–1921 season, found that Gilpin was a leading candidate. After some racist objections within the organization, the directors announced that if Gilpin were one of the ten, he would not be invited to the league's annual dinner. A storm of protest arose from the people of the theater, especially from the other winners in the poll — among them O'Neill, David Belasco, Jacob Ben-Ami, an actor from the Yiddish stage who had scored on Broadway in *Samson and Delilah,* and Gilda Varesi, star and coauthor of *Enter Madame,* who said that she would be "proud" to sit next to Gilpin at the dinner. O'Neill, besides being among the first to protest the league's decision, joined critic Kenneth Macgowan in rallying support from others.

Greatly outnumbered, the bigots had to retreat. After the league had reversed its stand — Gilpin would be welcome — reservations for the dinner poured in. Where normally about two hundred and fifty attended, more than twice that many turned out, and Gilpin won the biggest hand of the night. He had intended, he said afterward, to drop by for "about four minutes," pay his respects, and then "retire gracefully. I stayed four hours and had the time of my life. No, it didn't take much nerve to go and face the crowd. I could count on the artists treating me fairly, and I didn't care a hang about the others. They could sit there and stare at me as though I were some kind of a prize monkey and it wouldn't disturb me at all. . . .

"I like to keep the footlights between me and the public. I don't go in much for sociability and hobnobbing. If I can give anyone pleasure with my acting I am very happy to do so. But that's all. A close-up of Charles Gilpin does not look very inviting. I have my own little circle of friends and I love them. I live quietly up in Harlem where I belong. When I leave the theater, I like to leave it.

"I am really a race man — a Negro and proud of being one, proud of the progress the Negroes have made in the time and with the opportunity they have had. And I don't want the public to think anything different."

Gilpin continued in *The Emperor Jones* throughout its first New York run — in all it gave two hundred and four performances — and two seasons on the road, after which his life again became a struggle. In 1923 O'Neill told a friend: "Yes, Gilpin is all 'ham' and a yard wide! Honestly, I've stood for more from him than from all the white actors I've ever known — simply because he was colored! He played Emperor with author, play and everyone concerned. There is humor in the situation but I confess mine has worn out. I'm 'off' him and the result is he will get no chance to do it in London. He was drunk all of last season and, outside of the multitude of other reasons, I'd be afraid to risk him in London. So I've corralled another Negro to do it over there . . . a young fellow with considerable experience, wonderful presence and voice, full of ambition and a damn fine man personally with real brains . . .

"No, I don't think Gilpin's color had much — or anything — to do with the 'warping' you speak of. He's just a regular actor-brain, that's all. Most white actors, under the same circumstances, would have gone the same route. The point is, none of them would have *dared* go so far. Gilpin lived under the assumption that no one could be got to play his part, and took advantage accordingly."

The unnamed actor mentioned in the letter was Paul Robeson, who first appeared as Jones when the play was revived on MacDougal Street in 1924. In the audience the first night was Gilpin, anxious to see the young actor who was being touted as his equal (overtouted, actually, for Robeson, in spite of superb natural attributes, could not match the sensitivity, force and total conviction of Gilpin's portrayal). As Gilpin was leaving the theater he met James J. ("Slim") Martin, one of the Provincetowners, who invited him to have a drink. "No, Slim, I feel kind of low. I created the role of the Emperor. That role belongs to me. That Irishman, he just wrote the play."

Where Robeson went on to score as Brutus Jones in London and to other triumphs as actor and singer, Gilpin was reduced to appearing in occasional revivals of the O'Neill work. Moss Hart, who supported him in a pinchpenny production of *Jones* in 1926, recalled "a timeless resignation and disenchantment about everything he did or said." But when he extended himself on the stage, Hart writes, the "effect was shattering. He had an inner violence and a maniacal power that engulfed the spectator. . . . Had he not been a Negro . . . he would have been one of the great actors of his time." Gilpin died in 1930 on his small chicken farm in New Jersey, where he had lived out his final years in near-poverty.

On several occasions in later years O'Neill told interviewers that of all the actors who had appeared in his plays, only three — Gilpin among them — had completely satisfied him. But in 1946 he said: "As I look back now on all my work, I can honestly say there was only one actor who carried out every notion of a character I had in mind. That actor was Charles Gilpin. . . ."

[37]

O'Neill's surge of creativity in 1920, during the final months of his father's life and a short period afterward, produced not only *Gold, Anna Christie* and *The Emperor Jones* but another drama. He had scarcely written the last word of *Jones* early in October when he went to work on *Diff'rent*, finishing it on October 19, three days after his thirty-second birthday. Its basic idea came from French-born Mrs. Clark, who, as an outsider, took a sharp-eyed interest in Provincetown life. "Fifine," Eugene wrote to Agnes earlier this year when she was in New York, "has handed me a lot of old village tales — one of which don't forget to remind me to tell you. It would make a bear of a story or short play." The tale in question concerned an aging spinster of the community who, after being scrupulously respectable most of her life, turned into a pathetic coquette.

As O'Neill developed the story, no one could be more proper than Emma Crosby at the start of *Diff'rent* or more foolish and pitiable years later. Her fatal weakness is that she considers herself "diff'rent" from the people around her — not better, she protests, but "diff'rent" — and she feels similarly about her fiancé, Caleb Williams, an upright young whaling captain. Their marriage, she is certain, will be "diff'rent." Severe and inflexible in her romanticism, she reacts violently on learning that Caleb had slept with a native girl during his recent sailing in the South Seas. Though Caleb had stoutly resisted all temptation until, in one instance, circumstance overwhelmed him, Emma no longer feels that he is "diff'rent," and to everyone's amazement, cancels their wedding. Caleb vows that he will wait, no matter how long it takes, for her to accept him.

Thirty years later, in the second and final act, Emma is a caricature of youth — dyed hair, much powder and rouge, frilly clothes — desperately trying to make up for lost time. Where she had rejected Caleb in 1890 for a single misdeed, she now makes a fool of herself over his weak and despicable nephew, Benny Rogers. Benny finds her a ridiculous "old hen" but kids her along for the money he can wheedle from her. When Caleb learns of her infatuation and at last sees her clearly, he hangs himself; and she in turn, after Benny shows how he actually views her, joins Caleb in death.

Diff'rent, though of some merit, is on the whole unsatisfactory. Like *The Emperor Jones* it is less than standard length, but where *Jones* appears fully developed, the new play seems an early draft of what should be a longer work. In the first act things happen too quickly, too much exposition is crammed in — the author, one feels, was in a hurry to get to

Emma's transformation – and the double suicide at the end appears more contrived than inevitable. Potentially, the most interesting part of *Diff'rent* is the part O'Neill never wrote: the transitional period in which Emma, reacting to the cold touch of passing time, takes the first giggling steps on a course that will change her into a grotesque flirt. And yet, though her story is unconvincing, the breath of life is in Emma herself; if she were only a puppet, we would not be so irritated by her prissy romanticism at the start or feel so uncomfortable later when, moistening her lips with her tongue, she tries to question Benny about his sexual experiences.

Emma prefigures to some extent Lavinia Mannon of *Mourning Becomes Electra*, for both are inhibited, sex-starved, rigid in their convictions, embodying the puritanic strain in the New England soul. Both also serve to set up a contrast between their stiff-necked backgrounds and the warm, sensuous life of the South Pacific islands. Emma's strongest resemblance, however, is not to Lavinia but to a pair of other O'Neill women, Mrs. Keeney of *Ile* and Mary Tyrone (actually Ella O'Neill) of *Long Day's Journey Into Night*. Like Emma, these two have a romantic view of life and, to their eventual sorrow, overly idealize their men. Where Mrs. Keeney initially regarded her husband as one of the "old Vikings in the storybooks," Mary Tyrone thought hers "different from all ordinary men." Thus, the first-act portrait of Emma Crosby incorporates, in part, some of the playwright's ideas about his mother as a young woman.

At Thanksgiving Eugene and Agnes, who had moved from Peaked Hill to winter quarters in Provincetown proper, played host for a few days to his mother and Jamie – the first and last time Ella ever visited the old fishing village where her younger son made his home. Agnes's chief memory of the visit is that when they all went to the movies one evening, Ella questioned the propriety of including Mrs. Clark.

In the few months since her husband's death, Mrs. O'Neill, though she would always shy away from people, had grown more self-assured. When Eugene first went to New London to be with his dying father, he had written to Agnes that the "Old Man's business affairs are in a hellish tangle and my Mother is worried sick. I'm afraid when the end comes and the tension she is now under relaxes, she'll collapse." Instead, however, Ella had proceeded to administer the estate with an efficiency that surprised her sons. The estate, most of which Mr. O'Neill had placed in Ella's name in the final period of his life, consisted chiefly of New London realty and was worth over one hundred and fifty thousand dollars.

"[My father's] leaving her to untangle his chaotic affairs," Eugene wrote to George Tyler, "has proved to be the most merciful in the world. She has not had time to think or brood. And, although it may sound strange to you, she is developing into a keenly interested business-woman who seems to accept this unfamiliar responsibility with a great sense of relief. Under her hand, I honestly have a hunch that some dividends may finally accrue from the junk buried on the island of [Monte Cristo]." Delighted to hear about her "taking a real interest in things," Tyler replied: "You see, she never had a chance before — your dear father loved her so much that he couldn't bear to see her be anything else than an ornament."

Ella was not the only one who had changed; the change in Jamie was even more radical. Now that his lifelong enemy was dead and he had his "Cynara," his mother, to himself, he had given up drinking at her request, as well as his other dissipations. Virtually inseparable, dividing their time between New London and New York, mother and elder son made a handsome pair — Ella always dressed smartly in black, with a black velvet ribbon around her neck, Jamie immaculate in a stiff collar, derby and chesterfield, pink-faced, generally looking as though he had just left the barber shop. Although he had drunk, whored, and hung around Broadway since youth, he seemed perfectly content with his present decorous mode of living. The lone trace of his former life was a love of playing the horses, a passion curbed only by his limited funds; he spent much of his time studying the "dope" sheets. Occasionally Ella would arouse his deepest resentment, setting off bitter words between them, by saying that he should emulate Eugene and try to make something of himself (the portrait of Jamie in *Long Day's Journey* is based not only on his personality in 1912, the time of the play, but on his jealous attitude later as Eugene became successful). Most of the time, though, all was harmony between mother and bachelor son.

One of the Sheridan family who saw a good deal of Jamie felt that he was "a wasted talent, . . . he had a lot of ability and never did anything with it. He talked well, he had poise, a great sense of humor — he was very likable. Sarcastic? Yes, he was sarcastic, he was a belittler, but he did it in a kidding way. I remember one story he used to tell, because he told it so often. After Eugene became famous and people thought he'd learned about the theater from acting with his father, Jim said he was little more than a walk-on once. In this scene, according to Jim, two men appeared and one said, 'It's a bad night on the sea tonight, mate,' and the other one said, 'Aye.' Well, Jim would finish, the one who said 'Aye' was Gene."

[40]

To O'Neill's surprise, George Tyler suggested this fall that he write a new version of *Monte Cristo*. "Being your father's son," the producer wrote, "I should imagine it might appeal to you." Eugene's initial feeling was negative; he had a "direct grudge" against the play for preventing his father from becoming "one of our greatest actors," yet some part of him was teased by the challenge. He replied on December 9, 1920, that he could imagine "only one way in which the project would call forth any genuine creative interest on my part. If I could say to myself: Throw everything overboard — all precedent, all existing dogmas of what is practicable and what is not in the theater today. . . . Create your own [play] just as you did in *The Emperor Jones*. And, above all, make the Count and the others *human beings*, which they never are in either book or old play. . . .

"Of course the revenge motif would remain the same. It is only the treatment I refer to." The new *Monte Cristo* never materialized, however, for he had too many ideas of his own that interested him more.

Since he wanted Tyler to concentrate his efforts on *The Straw*, O'Neill waited months before informing him that he had written a new version of *Chris*, entitled "The Ole Davil." Tyler, who held the option from renewing his contract for *Chris*, liked the revised play "very much indeed," sent it to Lionel Barrymore, hoping to sign him for the part of Mat Burke, and informed Eugene he wanted to produce either "Davil" or *The Straw* this winter — "both of them if possible, but we should have perfect casts for both." Barrymore, however, was committed elsewhere, news that left the playwright feeling increasingly frustrated. "The Ole Davil" was going to be difficult, it seemed, to cast properly; *The Straw* was no closer to production than it had been for a year, as Helen Hayes had scored on Broadway in *Bab*, forcing Tyler to seek another Eileen Carmody; and John D. Williams, who had hoped to present *Gold* this winter, had likewise run into casting difficulties. "Either I get a production soon," Eugene told Tyler on December 15, "or I will have to give up writing for the time and go in for plumbing or some other more lucrative trade. I have even had to ask the Provincetown Players for a mite of royalty per week on *Jones* — something I have never done before — in order to keep going. [The play had not yet moved to Broadway.] Of course if *Jones* catches on when it goes up to the Selwyn, that will relieve matters somewhat. . . .

"I beg of you to believe that this letter is no veiled plea for financial assistance. I want nothing from anyone, nor would I accept it, except what my plays can bring if given a chance."

[41]

A month later, asking whether Tyler had any definite plans for *The Straw*, O'Neill said that apart from "the very deplorable financial aspects of the case, these delays affect the playwright's whole career. . . . I have a lot of work planned out that I ought to be busy on but it is impossible for me to concentrate properly on anything new as long as I live in constant expectation of being called down for rehearsals of the old. . . . Although I note by the press that I am the White Hope of playwriting, I might just as well be the scurviest typewriter-puncher of the lot — in fact, far better be, for they have theaters planned out for their plays in advance and have no difficulty in getting a hearing while my plans wait upon every fortuitous wind that blows."

He had hoped for income from *Beyond the Horizon*, which was on "the road" this fall, but the expenses of touring kept it from being profitable and shortly ended its existence. In Chicago the Shuberts, the leading theater owners in the country and among the most active producers, had closed *Horizon* just as its ticket sale was starting to grow, because they wanted the theater for one of their own presentations, a routine piece of commercialism. Such experiences left O'Neill with an abiding contempt for "the real estate theater sharks" and others in control of "the show-shop."

Late in December he came to New York for rehearsals of *Diff'rent*, scheduled to open on the twenty-seventh as the Provincetown Players' second offering of the season. O'Neill, who regarded it as "one of the best things I have ever done," expected that "any of our home talent will look mighty sick with the memory of Gilpin's work so fresh in everybody's mind." For the role of Emma Crosby, the Players chose Mary Blair, a newcomer to MacDougal Street but an old friend of Jimmy Light and his wife Susan Jenkins who had been in one or two things on Broadway. A thin-faced girl with an intense quality about her, Miss Blair compelled attention more through her personality than her technical ability; an uneven performer, her acting could vary widely from one evening to the next; it all depended on her emotional state and frame of mind at the time.

The other chief parts were filled by Jimmy Light as Caleb and Charles Ellis as the heartless nephew, with Charles O'Brien Kennedy, an aide of Broadway producer Arthur Hopkins, directing in his first association with the Players. A man of few words, a loyal Irishman, a devout Catholic without insisting on it or trying to save the backsliders, Kennedy got along well with O'Neill from the start. Recalling his first impression of the playwright, Kennedy says: "His speech was slow and hesitant, and he laughed with his eyes, the most luminous eyes I ever saw in a human. Here was a man, I thought, who could experience all the emotions without making any noise. But beneath this quietude one could discern deep-seated rebellion."

Inevitably, the press compared *Diff'rent*, to its disadvantage, with *The Emperor Jones:* the new work was more conventional, it had none of the poetic quality and stunning theatricality of the other play, and, in the view of most critics, it told an "unpleasant" story. The reviewers were particularly embarrassed by the scene in which Emma flirts with the nephew and dances skittishly around the subject of sex. Alexander Woollcott declared that the episode was "so brutal and ugly that most minds would be revolted by it," while Lawrence Reamer was even more critical: "To see dramatic use made of the dangerous years of life is too clinical for artistic respect. . . . Even the easy horrors of the Grand Guignol pause at this point."

(In contrast to the press's indignant clucking over *Diff'rent*, O'Neill had a letter from the librarian at Sing Sing prison praising his realism: "A chap walked into my office here the other day and said, 'For the love of Mike, lend me something to read.' It developed that he was sick of reading the ordinary line and wanted something 'different,' so I lent him my copy of *The Moon of the Caribbees* [the collection of sea plays]. He wasn't at all enthusiastic when he took it but two days later he came back [and] said, 'Gee, it's great. There ain't a character in it that don't walk around like he had a pair of nuts and a pecker like a regular man.' ")

Nearly all the reviewers found things to praise in *Diff'rent* ("The characters are boldly drawn and closely scrutinized." . . . "The man who writes the strongest, truest, finest and most inherently honest dramatic dialogue in America is Eugene O'Neill"), but their predominant tone was one of impatience. Going beyond their strictures about this particular play, they charged the author with being overly pessimistic, with focusing almost exclusively on somber and neurotic aspects of life. "Life," said Heywood Broun, "is too complex to be reduced to any formula or pattern as simple and as pat as that of O'Neill. . . . The great artist belongs to no army. He is with the men who fall and also with those who triumph. He is the defeat and the victory."

The performance, as O'Neill had predicted, was found wanting – Charles Ellis's nephew was the only portrayal roundly praised – but he had not expected the attacks on his subject matter. Though the play went on to give a total of one hundred performances, in the Village and on Broadway, the criticism rankled so that the playwright stated publicly:

"*Diff'rent*, as I see it, is merely the tale of the eternal, romantic idealist who is in all of us — the eternally defeated one. In our innermost hearts we all wish ourselves and others to be 'Diff'rent.' We are all more or less 'Emmas.' . . . There are objections to the play as pathological, but . . . that is putting the accent where none was intended . . . and someone has said to me that all the people in the play were either degenerates or roughs — at which I was properly stunned, because I consider all of the characters, with the exception of Benny, to be perfectly regular human beings even as you and I. Dividing folks into moral castes has never been one of my favorite occupations."

In another view of his attitude, Carlotta Monterey, who became his third wife, once summed up: "Gene was never shocked at *what* people did. He was only interested in *why* they did it."

Throughout the fall O'Neill had worked too steadily to do any real drinking — liquor almost never tempted him when he was writing — but in the city, where he felt nervous and out of his element, he as usual fell off the wagon. Under Prohibition the drinking scene in Greenwich Village, like everywhere else, had changed drastically, but while most of the saloons and taprooms were now out of business, a few places struggled on. Tom Wallace, who had "pull" with Tammany Hall and, consequently, with the police, boarded up the windows of the Hell Hole, after putting on display a few medicine bottles and other pharmaceutical items in a feeble pretense of running a drugstore. At Luke O'Connor's Working Girls' Home the front door was permanently locked, but the side entrance on Christopher Street led to a room where O'Connor served the best whiskeys and beers he could buy from wildcat breweries; and in certain restaurants, including Barney Gallant's place and Sam Schwartz's Black Knight, the regular patrons were provided with liquor in teacups.

O'Neill patronized all these oases but his favorite, partly because it afforded the most privacy, was a dingy cold-water flat on West Third Street, around the corner from the Provincetown Players — a combination of winery, speakeasy, and the bachelor quarters of Willie Fernandez, known to his customers as "Spanish Willie," who periodically returned home to his family in Brooklyn. He made his own brand of muscatel (it tasted, according to Eugene, as though "extracted from an elephant with a giant syringe") and sometimes managed to come up with a bottle of bonded liquor. Eugene was fond of Willie, an easygoing chap with a mouthful of gold who was too unbusinesslike, as well as too fond of drinking, to be a successful bootlegger; Eugene felt that he was a "real" person, as contrasted with the bohemians and other aesthetic souls of the

Village. On his side Willie worshiped O'Neill, not for his growing fame but as a natural aristocrat who treated Willie as his equal.

Malcolm Cowley, who lived across the street, was in the speakeasy one evening and (according to an account he later wrote) Willie said, "Did you hear that Gene was in town?" "Gene who?" "Why, Gene O'Neill, of course. You know Gene, don't you? He's a regular prince. The boys tell me he's coming around tonight." O'Neill shortly appeared and, after brushing away some cockroaches, sat down at a table with the two men. "I'm glad," he said, "to hear that you're feeling better, Will."

"Aw, Gene, that cough wasn't so much. I oughta knowed better than to sleep in the gutter all night. [Several years later Fernandez died of tuberculosis.] Say, I just got some fine Scotch off the boat. Won't you have a drink on me?" Cowley meanwhile, as the other two fell to talking, was "observing O'Neill as he twisted his long nervous hands above the table. There was no trace of patronage in his manner. No slang, no artificial breeziness, no effort to talk down to his host. He was just as grammatical, just as considerate as if he were holding a conversation with Shakespeare or the Prince of Wales. Perhaps this was why all the West Side gorillas worshiped him, and even attended his plays.

"This evening in Spanish Willie's, he was talking about the old scenes which both of them had known. I wish I could report their conversation. Every time I try, the words seem to lose their magic. They were speaking of ships and docks and crimes and politics; of gangsters, sailors, stevedores, ward politicians and square-shooting black gamblers — all the figures of that life which seethed between wharves and crimping houses, between dance halls and saloons; all the glamour of a Manhattan which is almost totally unknown. I sat in silence, listening. The Elevated went rumbling past, while empty glasses shivered on the tables. Finally it was time for him to go.

" 'Well, you saw him again. Ain't he a regular prince?' asked Spanish Willie."

Another evening Eugene, Agnes and some friends, including the Jimmy Lights and Charles O'Brien Kennedy, dined at a Second Avenue restaurant patronized by Jewish intellectuals of the lower East Side. Once the playwright was recognized, people began to crowd around his table, a situation that became still less pleasant when Kennedy misunderstood a remark about the Irish and started throwing punches. In the midst of the melee two girls began to force a path toward O'Neill as one of them called out, "I want to talk to you about Dostoevski."

Nursing a hangover, Eugene was glad to return to Provincetown and his work. "Art may not be for Art's sake," Gordon Craig said in *The Theater Advancing*, "but the artist is certainly for the artist's sake. That is to say, he is selfish to the core. . . . He works for happiness. Experiencing nothing but sorrow in his life, he is incessantly searching for happiness in his work — and he finds it. Day after day it comes to him." Paraphrasing Craig, perhaps unknowingly, O'Neill once said: "A work of art is always happy; all else is unhappy."

3

Uneven Playwright

O F all the major playwrights, O'Neill is, with little doubt, the most
uneven. During the larger part of his career — until in fact the final
few years, when he at last found his truest voice — he kept producing, almost
alternately, good plays and bad. His checkered record was partly due,
clearly enough, to faulty judgment and taste, but the chief cause seems
to have been the subjective nature of his talent. He struggled not only
with literary and theatrical problems that could be solved but with in-
soluble personal matters, with contradictions within his character and
conflicts in his life. Basically, this Catholic apostate used the drama as a
confessional; his chief objective was certainly not popular success, not
even critical acclaim or literary immortality, but his own salvation. He
sought through his writings to ease the pressures and storms within him,
to justify himself to himself, if not to the world.

Early in 1921, not long after creating so imaginative and original a play
as *The Emperor Jones,* he wrote *The First Man,* a prosaic, unconvincing
story about an anthropologist who bears a distinct resemblance to O'Neill,
particularly in his attitude as a husband and his total commitment to his
work. One noteworthy aspect of the play is that it marked the first time
the author had lifted his story idea from ancient literature — the legend
of Jason and his quest of the Golden Fleece. Paralleling the early fable,
Curtis Jayson is about to embark on an important expedition to a remote
land; and just as the old hero used and finally sacrificed Medea to his
advancement, the scientist has exploited his wife in his career. But where
the early fabulists told the story without taking sides, O'Neill, though he
tried to be fair to Martha Jayson, was essentially concerned with vindicating her egocentric husband.

The First Man would have us believe that its couple was so grief-stricken when their two children died suddenly, years before the time of the story, that they vowed never to have any more. Now Jayson is stunned, he feels betrayed, on learning that Martha can no longer accompany him on his travels to primitive regions because she has become pregnant. His reproaches ("Haven't we been sufficient, you and I together? Isn't that a more difficult, beautiful happiness to achieve than — children? Doesn't it mean anything to you that I need you so terribly — for myself, for my work — for everything that is best and worthiest in me?") are strikingly similar to things Eugene once said to Agnes; "I wanted you alone . . . in an aloneness broken by nothing. Not even by children of our own. I don't understand children, they make me uneasy." Or, as Agnes summarized his attitude: "To be alone with me — that was what he wanted; we had everything — work, love and companionship. Never, *never* let anything interfere with work or love!"

In view of Curtis Jayson's self-centered nature and his vehement opposition to Martha's pregnancy, it is difficult to believe that this man had ever cared for children, that he had been devastated when their first ones died. If he had really loved his young, he most likely would have been eager for others to replace those he and his wife had lost. The play is based, in other words, on a premise one cannot accept.

At times, as Jayson argues that he and Martha should be as one, of one mind, one will, one dream ("You are me and I am you!"), while she struggles against his attempt to dominate her, the two prefigure the Strindbergian pair O'Neill was to depict in *Welded*. To Martha's distress, Jayson suggests an abortion, but she has her child after a long, particularly painful delivery — her offstage screams punctuate the proceedings onstage — during a harrowing scene that ends with her death. Too bitter at first to look at his infant son, whom he assails as a "murderer," Jayson finally relents and is swept up in a surge of parental love. Consigning the child's care to a great-aunt who dotes on the infant — Jayson, with good cause, dislikes his other relatives — he vows to return in a few years and assume the role of a loving father. A heavy-handed play, a forced, indeed an inept conclusion. The playwright's view of life was such that he always seems weakest and least credible when, as at the end of his new drama, he tried to speak affirmatively.

O'Neill conceived the idea for *The First Man* not long after Agnes had borne Shane, yet his own birth, not his son's, seems to have inspired the new work. "I am one of the happiest old ladies in New York tonight to know I have such a wonderful grandson," Ella O'Neill had written to Eugene in November 1919 on first learning about Shane, "but no more wonderful than you were when you were born and weighed *eleven pounds* [her underscoring] . . ." Apparently his mother's letter aroused memories in Eugene that helped to shape and color his next play, for the Jayson child also weighed eleven pounds ("that's what made [the delivery] so difficult," says the nurse in *The First Man*). In both cases, moreover, that of the fictional and the real-life child, their births proved calamitous to their mothers: Martha Jayson died, while Ella O'Neill, condemned to a living death, was plunged into the private hell of drug addiction.

The play contains other story elements of an autobiographical nature. Set in a small Connecticut city and dealing with some of its prominent citizens — Jayson's relatives are bankers, lawyers, clubwomen, in general a smug, malicious lot — *The First Man* gave its author a chance to vent his feelings about the New London gentry, such as the Chappells, who used to look down on James O'Neill and his family. "We considered the O'Neills shanty Irish," says a Chappell girl, who married a man named Sheffield, "and we associated the Irish with the servant class." In revenge the playwright son, who took great pride in his Irish ancestry and never forgot a slight, named a pompous couple in the play Sheffield. Primarily, though, *The First Man* is concerned not with New England snobbery but with the relationship of Jayson and Martha, with Jayson's attitude as a family man.

Whenever O'Neill and Agnes were apart he practically always wrote that he missed their son and asked her to kiss the baby for him; he sounds, in short, like the usual devoted father. But other, more substantial evidence indicates that he was deficient in parental feeling. In summer 1920, about the time he presumably was conceiving *The First Man*, he told Agnes that he wanted to make an extended trip with her the following year on the Amazon River (such a trip would have taken months) and proposed leaving Shane with her parents. When they moved into a cottage in Provincetown in fall 1921, he suggested that a nursery, with sleeping quarters for Mrs. Clark, be arranged in the basement. Though the basement was clean and dry, Agnes objected, for it seemed to her that there was something wrong with the idea; perhaps she felt, unconsciously, that establishing Shane's quarters in the lowest part of the house would be a kind of symbolic burial.

The primary image of Eugene O'Neill that emerges from his writings is that of an eternal son, a man constantly examining and dramatizing his ambivalent feelings toward his mother and father, forever bound to them emotionally, a man never able to mature fully, never free to be a real parent himself. In a basic sense, he was free only to be a writer, a man trying to make peace with himself.

". . . everyone who does not *need* to be a writer, who thinks he can do something else," says Georges Simenon, "ought to do something else. Writing is not a profession but a vocation of unhappiness. I don't think an artist can ever be happy . . . if a man has an urge to be an artist, it is because he needs to find himself. Every writer tries to find himself through his characters, through all his writings."

Despite George Tyler's assurance that he would produce *The Straw* or the new *Chris* play before long, prospects of either being done in the 1920–1921 season faded. Tyler tried to sign Alice Brady, a gifted young actress, for *The Straw*, but her father, producer William A. Brady, who guided her career, prevented the deal; he would approve the O'Neill play only if it included a role for another of his clients, boxer Jack Dempsey. It had been a discouraging season for Tyler; after several of his productions failed, he approached the Theater Guild to coproduce the *Chris* play with him or take it over completely, offering terms that Eugene thought "most generous," but the Guild found them excessive. In a letter to Eugene on February 12, 1921, Tyler said, "Of course the Provincetown Players and the Theater Guild can cast most any amateur in any of the parts and have them accepted by the press as heaven-sent geniuses. We 'commercial' managers cannot get away with that sort of thing." But the playwright, nursing his own grievances, had little sympathy to spare for the producer: "I wonder if you can realize what it means to have three long plays under contract, and not a damn one of them produced — while the papers keep wondering why you haven't a long play this year to follow *Beyond the Horizon*."

In mid-February he and Agnes visited New York for ten days, where he attempted to see John D. Williams regarding *Gold*, but Williams proved, as usual, elusive. O'Neill was photographed by Nicholas Muray, a young Hungarian who had opened a studio next door to the Provincetown Players (the newspapers and magazines were after Eugene for portraits of himself); spent some time with Kenneth Macgowan and Robert Edmond Jones, with whom he had become friends; and to his regret, as he told Macgowan, saw Lionel Barrymore in *Macbeth:* "My principal reaction to the production was a rage at Barrymore. He got between the production and me. That is my main trouble in theatergoing, by the way, and the real reason why I avoid the show-shops. I can't help seeing with the relentless eye of heredity, upbringing, and personal experience every little trick they pull as actors. Thus in the most tense moment of a play I am struck — with amusement or disgust as the case may be — by the sly, insidious intent — plain to me — of a gesture, a fillip, a change in tempo, a body wriggle. The actor stands revealed, triumphant in his egotistic childishness."

One play that he arrived in town too late to see was Jig Cook's *The Spring*, a curious mélange of frontier history, mysticism, and psychic phenomena which won a more favorable press than it deserved. The reviewers extended themselves to be generous, one suspects, in appreciation of Jig's leadership of the Provincetowners and all the years he had devoted to the group. "*The Spring*," said Heywood Broun, "has true dramatic interest despite its discursiveness," and Macgowan called it "a remarkable and arresting drama."

Fired by the reception of his play, which gave the Provincetown Players their third success in a row, after *Jones* and *Diff'rent*, Jig, a man of great dreams and, in the throes of an idea, boundless drive, turned almost incandescent with enthusiasm to build a new playhouse, an ideal home for his group. Throughout the winter and spring he made detailed sketches, drawn carefully to scale, of theaters incorporating the most advanced technical features. In a newspaper article he said that the projected theater "will have a new structural invention which makes it possible to raise the curtain and give your play in pure space. Nothing there but infinity and the stage. . . . It will now be possible for an artist to let his human figures and chosen objects receive mystically deep significance from their background of infinity."

Besides making numerous sketches of his dream theater and composing dithyrambs about it, Cook, sounding quite businesslike, labored over a prospectus to attract investors. "All through our seventh season," he said in one draft, "appreciative subscribers and friends have been coming to us with proffers of free financial support amounting to many thousands of dollars. We have worked out a sound method of raising the necessary capital. . . . The Provincetown Playhouse Trust Company, to own the land and building, is being incorporated for $150,000. Shares of stock will be issued in proportion to the amount of each subscription . . ."

O'Neill, a trustee of the company, together with Jig, Susan, Fitzi, and attorney Harry Weinberger, who handled the theater's legal affairs, listened to Cook's ambitious plans without having much faith or interest in them. His hopes were centered on Broadway, especially on the possibility that Arthur Hopkins might take over the new *Chris* play when

Tyler's option expired. Tyler, who rated *The Straw* over the other work ("It's too great a play to fail, if properly produced"), decided that he had finally found the right Eileen in Margalo Gillmore, a comparative newcomer who had won some acclaim on Broadway this season. O'Neill felt that she was "too inexperienced for such a difficult emotional role," but the producer, with characteristic hyperbole, maintained that she "possesses absolute genius and has the possibility of a great position in the near future." Weary of the long delay in mounting the script, O'Neill yielded, and Miss Gillmore was signed. *The Straw*, after being on the verge of production for over a year, was now scheduled for fall 1921, with John Westley still set to double as Stephen Murray and the director.

In March, after completing the first draft of *The First Man* and setting it aside "to smolder for a while in the subconscious and perhaps gather itself a little more flame," O'Neill began a new play — his sixth in little more than a year. He had long thought of attempting a poetic work in an effort to acquire more grace in his writing but was undecided between two story ideas. One concerned an African chieftain, brought to America in the early nineteenth century and sold into slavery, who struggles with forces that would break his spirit. The other idea, like the one for *The First Man*, came from literature, but this time O'Neill's imagination was stirred by "the recurrence in folklore of the beautiful legend of a healing spring of eternal youth." Perhaps the memory of his father's final days, as the once-vigorous actor wasted away, had aroused his interest in characters struggling against time and old age. In *Diff'rent* he had written of a woman's pathetic attempt to reverse the calendar, and now he decided to tell his own version of Juan Ponce de León's search for the Fountain of Youth.

The writing of *The Fountain* went slowly, not only because the author was striving for a literary style but because his story demanded extensive research and background reading. Though more concerned with "the truth" behind Ponce de León's career than with historical accuracy, he still had to familiarize himself with life in old Spain and the conquistadores' era in America. "Could you," he asked Macgowan, "suggest any books that might be of help in the way of atmosphere, mood, method or myth?" . . . "If you should happen to go to the library, will you see if there is anything about Moorish minstrels and minstrelsy during their occupation of Spain?" But in the midst of his reading he wondered whether he was wasting his time. ". . . the more I ponder over this play," he wrote his friend on April 6, "the more I feel that the less I know of the real Juan Ponce, the better. I want him to be my Spanish noble, none other — not even his historical self. . . . I am afraid too many facts might obstruct the vision I have and narrow me into a historical play of spotless integrity but no spiritual significance. Facts are facts, but the truth is beyond and outside them."

His pursuit of "the truth" in *The Fountain* proved exceptionally difficult; more than a year later, after a second draft and extensive rewriting, he had "worked harder" on it, he said, than on any previous play. And this was not all, for in the following several years, he was to revise it still further, yet the end product fell far short of distinction; formal poetic writing, language with the sort of measured grace and silken texture required here, was beyond him. Also, the story failed to activate his deeper creative powers; the characters, instead of living in their own right, are merely so many mouthpieces for the author's views.

A multiscene work spanning over twenty years, the play depicts Ponce de León as a blend of adventurer, dreamer and independent thinker, a man dedicated to Spain but hostile to the Church. Accompanying Columbus on his second voyage, he hopes for military glory in the ancient civilizations of the East but ends, instead, as the governor of primitive Porto Rico, aged, disenchanted, hungry for romance and love. Seeking a Fountain of Youth promised by local legend, he runs into an ambush set by the Indians; shortly before his death he attains serenity through a mystical vision: "I begin to know eternal youth! . . . O Fountain of Eternity, take back this drop, my soul!"

For all the talk about the fountain, O'Neill, though he apparently never realized it, became less interested in the old legend than in the white man's harsh and greedy invasion of the New World as the origin of a dark strain in the American character. Virtually all the better passages in the play touch on this theme. Indeed, *The Fountain* is, in some respects, a prologue to "A Tale of Possessors Self-Dispossessed," a multiplay cycle O'Neill later worked on in which he aimed to show where, in his view, this country went wrong, how and why it betrayed its original ideals; he intended the Cycle as his masterwork and ultimate statement, but ill health prevented him from realizing the project.

"Look at the men of this fleet," Juan says to Columbus in a passage that foreshadows the Cycle. "Adventurers lusting for loot to be had by a murder or two; nobles of Spain dreaming greedy visions of wealth to be theirs by birthright; monks itching for the rack to torture useful subjects of the Crown into slaves of the Church! . . . Looters of the land, one and all! There is not one who will see it as an end to build upon! God pity this land until all looters perish from the earth!"

Shortly after O'Neill began *The Fountain* in 1921, a prosaic concern interrupted his preoccupation with Moors, Spanish grandees and high-born señoritas. His teeth were in "frightfully dilapidated shape" from years of neglect, and he decided to have them fixed by his good friend Saxe Commins, who longed for a literary career of his own but who had had to settle for dentistry. "I warn you," Eugene wrote to Saxe, now practicing in his hometown of Rochester, "to polish up all your racks and thumbscrews, for I'll probably need them all." On receiving the letter Commins, a softhearted man, felt as apprehensive as his prospective patient.

En route to Rochester O'Neill made a side trip to New York in mid-April to attend final rehearsals of *The Moon of the Caribbees*, in revival for the Players' last program of the season. The production impressed Eugene as markedly superior to the original one and cemented his regard for Charles O'Brien Kennedy, who had staged it; but otherwise the scene on MacDougal Street depressed him. Ever since the success of *The Emperor Jones*, the life of the playhouse had deteriorated into cliques and "tiresome bickering," with one main faction headed by Jig Cook, Ida Rauh and Edna Kenton, the other by Jimmy Light and Charlie Ellis, while Fitzi tried to mediate between them. Much of the present conflict arose from everyone vying for roles in a double bill of *Jones* and the one-acter *Suppressed Desires* that was scheduled for London this summer. Charles Gilpin later fell ill, forcing cancellation of the overseas presentation, but the dissension left scars and lasting cleavages among the Players. Financially, their most successful season was proving the costliest; although they had taken in nearly as much money this season as their total receipts of the previous four seasons, most of it vanished. "Our finances had got out of the hands of economists among us," said Edna Kenton. "We were spending money like drunkards."

In Rochester O'Neill stayed with Commins's parents, Jewish immigrants from Latvia who never had much money and yet had managed to send all their six children to college. Saxe, a bookish, idealistic soul, was a true son of his parents, although he was retiring where his tiny mother, a sister of Emma Goldman, the anarchist, was assertive and forceful. She read Goethe, Schiller and Heine in the original German and constantly quoted them to illustrate homey things in her daily life. Mr. Comminsky, a quiet man, had a deep feeling for justice, even in minor matters; when one of his grandchildren wept that a playmate had struck him, he quizzed the child and gently led him to realize that he had provoked the assault. "Saxe's people are fine folks," Eugene wrote Agnes. "They are all as kind as they can be" — but, he continues, they could not compensate for his separation from her. "I have a poignant pain of emptiness inside of me as if I'd lost the vital spiritual organ without which the rest of the machine is a mere whirring of wheels . . . it won't be long until we're Us — One & Indivisible — again. I love you so!"

While undergoing the tortures of dentistry, he was further dispirited by news from Stella Ballantine, one of Saxe's sisters, that John D. Williams was going to stage *Gold* with Willard Mack as the old sea captain. Eugene was already angry at Williams for trying to sell his rights to the play for "a large cash sum" to the Theater Guild without telling the author anything about it; he had also "hawked *Gold* around to every film company in the country," in an effort to finance the stage production, "as if it were a dime novel." O'Neill considered the casting of Mack, a melodramatist who generally starred in his own plays, "outrageously inept" and resolved to "fight the production tooth and nail," but at the same time conceded that Mack was rated an "excellent actor according to current standards." Several days later, after hearing from Williams about his arrangements for *Gold*, he felt that it "doesn't sound so bad . . . his cast sounds very good — especially Teddy [Ballantine, Stella's husband] who will be able to keep me posted from the inside."

Encouraged by a movie scriptwriter visiting in Provincetown, Agnes, who had begun a novel, thought of trying to earn some easy money from Hollywood, but Eugene was indignant when he heard about it. "For Christ's sake, don't think of the movie writing. My God, you have a soul to express which will create beauty in your novel, etc., if you will only work hard. . . . The film would ruin all that chance — and what for? A mess of garbage! You may think you can trifle with the film and still do your real work, but you can't. The experience of everyone else is against it. [Apparently he never informed Agnes that he himself, as a fledgling playwright, had tried repeatedly to be a movie scenarist.] . . . If the above sounds rather excited, pardon me! I just have [had] a tooth pulled and then your letter comes hinting you'd like to be a movie writer! These are gray days."

Agnes was enduring her own gray days in moving the family from winter quarters in Provincetown to Peaked Hill Bars. The weather was sharp and rainy; the stove at the old Coast Guard station had to be repaired after Terry Carlin, who could get things out of order by merely looking at them, had used it; the oil heater misfunctioned on one of the coldest days; and, as Agnes complained to her husband, she had lost all patience with Mrs. Clark's "loud, strident voice talking, talking — if not to me, then to Shane. No peace — no quiet. . . . I feel now as if the exhausting struggles of running this place spoiled the pleasures of it — that it is all right for two people alone when they can live simply as you & I did that first summer — but when it comes to a family — !"

Weary from two weeks of dentistry, Eugene recuperated for a few days at Peaked Hill before going to New York early in May, accompanied by Agnes, for rehearsals of *Gold*. The advance word from Teddy Ballantine had been encouraging ("Williams is on the job sober every second"), but the playwright found the production a shambles. Williams, nowhere in sight, was drinking again; Willard Mack, who had failed to learn his lines, was improvising; and director Augustus Saint-Gaudens was having difficulty with the company, especially with Mack, who was accustomed to being a little dictator in his own productions. After attending several rehearsals, O'Neill "got good and pickled to chase the memory of it away" — his first drinking in months — and fled back to Provincetown, leaving Agnes behind as his surrogate. She made several attempts to see Williams at his office and finally, on learning his home address, called at his hotel apartment, where she found him drunk, sprawled over a sofa and clutching a telephone. Pulling himself together in a show of stiff dignity, he declared that he "would take the production in hand," a promise that never materialized.

After a hurried trip to Provincetown to solace her husband, Agnes returned to New York for the opening of *Gold*, which had been postponed from May 23 to June 1. On reaching town she was cheered to hear that Willard Mack had withdrawn and been replaced by George Marion, his understudy, who was reported to be much better. But the news proved false; after being absent a few days, Mack turned up at the dress rehearsal and insisted on opening in the play. Agnes immediately notified Richard Madden, who regretted that time was insufficient to obtain an injunction against Mack's appearance. Madden was in an indignant mood when he phoned Williams to demand an explanation, but he turned meek when the producer stated, in an icy voice, that Marion had simply rehearsed as the understudy and that of course Mack would play the role.

Most of the reviewers lauded Mack — though Heywood Broun called his performance "an amazing mixture of good and bad" — and criticized the O'Neill script, with a number again complaining of what one said was "his propensity to look only upon the dark side of human nature. He must learn, before it is too late, to study all sides of life. Otherwise he will become a dramatist for a cult which will bring him no lasting importance in the world of the theater." Maida Castellun of *The Call* adopted a facetious tone: "Admirers of Eugene O'Neill will soon have to pray 'From madness, murder, and sudden death, O'Neill, deliver us.' . . . Beginning blithely with two murders in the first act, continuing with a death in the last, O'Neill in *Gold* does not quite equal the record of Shakespeare in *Hamlet;* but for the twentieth century 't is enough, 't will serve." The play lasted thirteen performances.

Fortunately for O'Neill's morale, Arthur Hopkins, whom he admired, acquired the sea play when Tyler's option expired and planned to present it in the fall with Pauline Lord, a gifted young actress, as Anna Christie, and Robert Edmond Jones designing the production. "So the future," O'Neill exulted to Saxe Commins on June 19, "holds promise of a fine and lasting association with the best people in our theater. Not to speak of my hope that Hopkins will take my Fountain of Youth play when it is finished, have [Jacob] Ben-Ami act in it, and Jones again for the scenes. . . . There is only Tyler's *The Straw* to face with fortitude as a possibly very unpleasant experience."

Despite the quick failure of *Gold*, the playwright was in fairly good financial shape from the Broadway engagements of *The Emperor Jones* and *Diff'rent*, Horace Liveright's publication of his plays, the options on *Anna Christie* and *The Straw*, and the growing number of little theaters that were staging his plays. "Every hat in Indianapolis," wrote the director of one group, "is off to you, Mr. O'Neill." In all, the playwright later estimated, he made about fifteen thousand dollars in 1921.

Now that they could afford it, the O'Neills hired a local girl to look after Shane at Peaked Hill, while Mrs. Clark did the cooking and general housework. The first time the girl, Agnes Carr, saw the playwright, she "wanted to cry — I felt so sorry for him. I once asked Mrs. Clark why he looked so unhappy, and she said that his birth was the cause of his mother's becoming sick [Ella's morphine addiction], and he hated himself for it. The thing I'll always remember are his eyes, black and piercing they were, the most piercing I've ever seen. They looked right through you, and beyond. You felt that underneath he was restless, forever reaching out for something."

Actually, regardless of the impression he gave, he was relatively happy, cheered not only by his forthcoming association with Hopkins and Jones but by his progress for a time with *The Fountain*. "It's great joy doing," he informed Macgowan, "and seems to be behaving as I would wish." If anyone in the family was restless and dissatisfied, it was Agnes, who had more time for herself than she knew how to fill. Though she continued to write (two of her *Smart Set* stories won honorable mention in the 1920 and 1921 editions of Edward O'Brien's *Best Short Stories*), she did not have O'Neill's all-consuming need for self-expression. What she primarily needed for contentment was a more satisfying relationship with her husband, but generally he was so preoccupied with his work that she often felt slighted, taken for granted. According to her, he was far more fervent in expressing his love when they were apart — in his letters — than when they were together. Yet the passion in his letters sounds genuine enough: "God, how I wish you were here! I love you so! It truly is a love that passeth beyond all bounds, beyond which there is nothing." . . . "I feel quite intolerably lonely and I miss you in every atom of me. I simply can't live — really live — without you any more." Apparently he expected Agnes, in their daily life, to sense how he felt about her, but she longed to be told. She was once so unhappy about their sexual relationship, feeling he had allowed it to dwindle to a matter of routine, that she dashed into the ocean with a threat of drowning herself.

Another source of her discontent was Fifine Clark, who always sided with O'Neill in the family disputes and who, possibly without realizing it, tried to monopolize Shane's affection. As it was, if the two women were in a room with the child and he wanted something, he always went to "Gaga," as he called her, rather than to his mother. Inevitably, there was friction between the two, yet they had to get along as best they could and even put on a mask of liking one another, since both O'Neill and the child were attached to the housekeeper-cook. The temperature at any given time of Agnes's feelings toward the other woman was evident in how she addressed her: if hostile, she called her "Mrs. Clark"; if fairly well disposed, "Clarkie"; and in moments of warmth, "Gaga." On her side, Mrs. Clark (O'Neill was always "Gene" to her) addressed her mistress as "Mrs. O'Neill," but behind her back used to refer to her as "she" or "that one." The housekeeper often complained to intimates that once O'Neill started to be successful, Agnes, turning less friendly, began treating her as a servant.

Much as Clarkie loved Shane, she was not above using him. Sometimes when he disobeyed her, or after a dispute between her and Agnes, she threatened to quit — he would never see her again — whereupon the child would start wailing until reassured that Gaga was remaining. She was like a musical virtuoso, with Shane as her instrument. A sturdy beautiful child with ringlets of golden hair from the sun, he was of a variable disposition, now racing about in high spirits, now sitting quietly on the beach, a small replica of his father, and staring out to sea for a long time. He might be in the midst of a meal in the kitchen — he always ate with Clarkie and the nursemaid, never with his parents, who spent little time with him — when he would fall to dreaming and forget his food. "Is he sick? He looks so far off," the Carr girl once said to the housekeeper, only to get the reply, "If you grew up living this kind of life, you'd be far away, too."

Like his father, he loved the water and was never so happy as when playing around in the shallows. As a group was sitting on the beach one day, Mrs. Clark suddenly asked about Shane, and looking around they spied him drifting out on his rubber float, some distance from shore. Eugene raced out in his kayak, afraid as he approached that the child might reach toward him and fall overboard, but Shane waited contentedly, looking perfectly at home as he rocked on the waves. When the two returned to shore, O'Neill said, "He was headed for Ireland, I guess."

Whether primarily concerned with giving his son a playmate, in his isolation from other children, or with pleasing himself, for he was fond of dogs, O'Neill bought an Irish terrier and promptly dubbed him "Mat Burke," after the seaman in *Anna Christie*. The dog proved fine in one respect — he and Shane became inseparable friends — but it was a constant problem to keep him from tangling with the other family pet, a cat from a coal barge that had been beached close to the station during a storm. The barge still hulked above the shore, providing a booming sounding board for the waves and a favorite playground for Shane and Mat. O'Neill took enough interest in the cat to name it "Anna Christie," since Anna in the play is associated with a coal barge, but like his son, he preferred the terrier, while Agnes was partial to the cat.

One of the O'Neills' first guests this summer, Jamie, still on the wagon and content in his reformation, detached himself from his mother long enough to spend a week at the oceanside retreat. Although the two brothers constantly bantered each other, one could sense a serious undertone in their relationship, a deep bond between them, as though they shared secrets they could never divulge to anyone else. Between Agnes and Jamie there was little warmth, but for Eugene's sake they kept up appearances. With the prime exception of his mother — and possibly one or two other women he had known — Jamie took a low view of the sex, regarding them less as persons in their own right than as objects for venereal pleasure. When Eugene first became interested in Agnes Boulton, Jamie had seemed fond of her, but in time, turning critical, he used to disparage her to his friends. One Christmas Agnes, who had almost forgotten him in her gift-buying, sent him a wallet at the last minute; as she later heard, Jamie considered the wallet a gibe at his chronic shortage of funds, his dependence on his mother for pocket money.

Always neatly dressed, usually in a double-breasted navy blue suit, even when he went walking on the beach, he looked out of place in the informal life of Peaked Hill. He spent much of his time around Clarkie and Agnes Carr, charming them with theatrical anecdotes and his humorously cynical line of talk, but he appeared serious when he once praised the nursemaid as pretty enough to go on the stage. Eugene, however, warned her against it: "There are already enough actresses, and you don't have the training. You ought to marry and raise a family." But another day he said to her, "Whatever you want in life, reach out for it, work for it."

The O'Neills played host, after Jamie's visit, to Robert Edmond Jones, whom Eugene admired as an artist and liked as a person. A striking-looking individual whose long pale face and large gray eyes were set off by a beard, mustache and unruly shock of reddish-brown hair, he recalled a medieval image of Christ. An improbable mixture of artist, mystic, and shrewd Yankee, with a veneer of preciousness, he was totally dedicated to the theater and, like O'Neill, took refuge in his work. Where O'Neill felt that he did not "need vacations. Writing is my vacation from living," Jones said of himself: "Too weak to live life, but strong enough to make it." Inspired originally by the pioneering ideas of Gordon Craig and the productions of Max Reinhardt, he went on to achieve by his own inner light. He might dream high but when he translated his dreams to paper, they were drawn precisely to scale and were at once imaginative, beautiful and eminently practical. "He is essentially a poet," said Gilbert Seldes, "the creator of the imagined lands in which a pillar rising to the sky in *The Jest* is the image of the late Renaissance, or a guttering candle in a dark room becomes the Russia of *Redemption*."

From his appearance and manner, one would never guess that Jones had grown up in poverty on a farm, but his background, as in O'Neill's case, always haunted him; he would shudder as he recalled the stony existence of his early years in New Hampshire. "It is dreadful here," he wrote to his friend Mabel Dodge, while visiting at home. "All the people are sad and tired and anxious and afraid — and everywhere there is misery. Meaningless and unnecessary. Sterility." And from another letter to Mabel: "It is horrible here. There has been rain for three weeks and the seeds have rotted in the ground. We are planting again. My mother has had some kind of an apoplectic attack since I was here and spends half her time in a snoring stupor. There are New England rumors that she is losing her mind. The whole world is sodden: lean, strained figures slump and gibber through it. I realize that I have always been an old tired man, and that my profoundest feelings have been those of age, and weariness, and horror." Jones's gothic images of his family background would help shape O'Neill's thinking when he wrote about New England in *Desire Under the Elms* and, in particular, *Mourning Becomes Electra*.

In July Kenneth Macgowan and his wife spent a week at the station but they saw little of their host, who was wholly absorbed in *The Fountain* ("I never felt so tremendously keyed up and eager to work"). He hoped, however, that the couple looked on his neglect of them as a compliment – he was treating them like old friends. Though O'Neill generally kept his distance from drama critics, he respected Macgowan's writings and took a liking to the man himself, a lanky Bostonian with a boyish face, attentive ears and thinning hair. He regarded Kenneth not "as a critic but as a fellow-worker for the best that we can fight for in the theater."

Macgowan had begun reviewing while a Harvard undergraduate. At a Boston theater one night he descended on H. T. Parker of the *Transcript* to complain of his failure to review a production by the Harvard Dramatic Club – Kenneth had been the stage manager. Impressed by the young man's spirit, the noted critic apologized, invited him to supper, and soon afterward began giving him assignments as a second-stringer. Before he and O'Neill met, Kenneth had successively been many things – Parker's full-time assistant at twenty-five dollars a week, amusement editor of a Philadelphia paper, press agent for Broadway shows, publicity man for film-maker Sam Goldwyn, feature writer for the New York *Tribune* – and now, as the *Globe's* drama critic, he was helping to raise the level of Broadway commentary. With Stark Young of the *New Republic* and Alexander Woollcott of the *Times* he represented the new breed of critics, thoughtful, well informed, receptive to the new, as contrasted with J. Ranken Towse of the *Post*, a crotchety septuagenarian who had been reviewing since the 1880s, and Alan Dale of the *American*, another old-timer, a dapper little man with a large vein of malice which he fondly considered wit. As for George Jean Nathan, he was an original, an impish yet serious scholar of the theater, a superior intellect who delighted in playing the jester and firing off his idiosyncratic views like so many roman candles.

At Peaked Hill, where the playwright worked all summer on *The Fountain*, the old station no longer seemed so isolated from the outside world. Louis Kalonyme, a free-lance newspaperman and a celebrity-collector who had made himself useful to O'Neill, running and fetching for him, was quartered in a nearby shack; Saxe Commins paid a visit, followed by Nicholas Muray, who photographed both Eugene and Agnes; and Terry Carlin drifted in and out. Neither age — he was now in his late sixties — nor Prohibition could slow down Carlin, ragged, perpetually broke, yet serene. As Larry Slade, "the old Foolosopher" in *The Iceman Cometh*, he prefers to sit on the sidelines and observe the antics of others; in life he was not merely a spectator but a constant source of interest and amusement to his friends. In an unfortunate experiment, he built a huge wooden wheel, equipped with a free-swinging bosun's chair, to traverse the dunes, but on one of his first rides he fell off and cracked several ribs. Instead of Prohibition discouraging his thirst, it sharpened his ingenuity. He made wine from berries of the area, burying the bottles in the sand to ferment; experimented with mushrooms and other produce ("Skunk cabbage," he said, "is the only plant no good for either eating or drinking"); and when all else failed him, would strain "canned heat" (Sterno) through a not overly clean bandanna. One day he said dreamily, as though thinking aloud, "I'll have to stop drinking wood alcohol. It's beginning to affect my eyesight."

Through Bobby Jones the O'Neills became friendly with Eben Given, a painter, and his sister Thelma, a concert pianist, whose parents had filled their house in Provincetown with antiques and mementos of their European travels. There was a close relationship among Eben, Thelma and their Dresden figurine of a mother — the father was rarely around — that somehow suggested an old sorrow in the family background. Eben, a frequent visitor at Peaked Hill, recalls that O'Neill generally appeared detached, lost in himself, no matter how many persons were present. "Gene used to move about the place," he says, "like a ghost. He didn't seem to have any contact with the mechanics of daily living — the plumber, the carpenter, any of that. Agnes was a buffer between him and the rest of the world."

In contrast to his disheveled earlier years, O'Neill now had a passion for order, neatness, regularity, and as far as possible made a schedule of his life. Immediately after breakfast he would retire to his upstairs study, where paper and pencils were tidily arranged on his desk. Sometimes he was so absorbed in his work that he wrote all day, passing up lunch, but generally his afternoons were spent in swimming, paddling out in his kayak, pounding away at a punching bag, and taking long walks on the beach, with the same amount of time usually allotted to each activity. Although in fine physical condition, he was somewhat hypochondriacal and would worry over a cold; once, on spitting blood, he became frightened about a recurrence of tuberculosis and lamented to Eben Given that he "always knew it would be like this. Just as I'm starting to be a success, my health fails." But Eben's father, who had studied medicine, assured him after an examination that the trouble was simply a ruptured blood vessel in his throat.

As he was completing *The Fountain* late in August, Agnes visited New York to rent an apartment for their stay in the city this fall while *Anna Christie* and *The Straw* were in rehearsal. Agnes also spent a few days in New Jersey with her parents and the child of her first marriage, Barbara Burton, who was being reared by the Boultons. During Agnes's absence fire destroyed the coal barge beached at Peaked Hill, and, as Eugene wrote her, he feared that the sparks would set the station aflame: "The ordeal of the conflagration had me quite as much of a wreck as the charred remains of the barge. . . . I've been terribly lonely and lost for the past few days. It seemed as if the fire was a disruption of mood that knocked me off the creative heights where I had been clawing for a foothold for the past two months and let me down physically and mentally into a melancholy backwash where the world looks gray indeed. Probably my regular August attack of melancholy was about due to hit me, anyway. [His "August melancholy" probably originated in childhood, when late summer meant the end of comfortable months in New London and the start of the family's gypsylike existence on the road with their actor father.]

"If I really believed that *The Fountain* were as rotten as it seems to me now I'd hang the script out on the hook in the toilet. Either it is a dead thing or I am. . . . Come home and bring my life back! These days crawl sufferingly like futile purgatories."

Already in an apprehensive state, he was frightened that night by an electrical storm that flashed and rumbled for hours, the worst he had ever experienced at Peaked Hill. O'Neill, who shared primitive man's awe of the elements, including a great fear of lightning, took refuge in a closet when the storm was at its height. Years later he would project something of his atavistic feeling onto the Reverend Light and his son Reuben in *Dynamo*, a strange, cloudy drama with a mystical attitude toward electricity.

In September O'Neill received a telegram that so elated him that, in Agnes Carr's words, "he jumped around like a kid and yelled." The wire probably told about Arthur Hopkins placing *The Fountain* under option, a development that occurred around this time. To celebrate, the play-

[63]

wright decided to give a dinner party and told Mrs. Clark to order squab and other special foodstuff from Boston for "the best spread we've ever had." All summer long, since the *Gold* fiasco, he had scarcely touched liquor, but the night of the party both he and Agnes had their share of drinks. After the guests had left, as Clarkie and the Carr girl were cleaning up, the Irish terrier Mat Burke charged at the cat Anna Christie and the two tore around, barking and yowling. Agnes, seizing a poker to separate them, struck the dog. His eyes blazing, Eugene warned her, "Don't hit him again or I'll kill you!" whereupon she hit her husband with the poker. He grabbed her neck, then swung her around back of him, holding onto her by her long hair, and started dragging her toward the beach, as Agnes cried out, "Gene! Gene!" When the nursemaid tried to intervene, Clarkie brushed her away ("This has happened before"), so the girl ran to the shack where Terry Carlin and Louis Kalonyme were staying, and they finally succeeded in pacifying O'Neill. The next morning he was all remorse and, as Mrs. Clark said, "hated himself."

While he cared little for the cat, he had a superstitious notion that the fate of *Anna Christie* was linked with that of its namesake. Worried when the animal's tail became infected, he rushed the cat to Dr. Daniel Hiebert in Provincetown for surgery, then took her back several more times when the gangrene continued to develop. "You must keep her alive," he urged Hiebert, before leaving for New York, "at least until the play opens."

Broadway was having a poor season. A record number of productions had folded quickly, and O'Neill, always expecting the worst, did not "anticipate making a nickel" from either *Anna Christie* or *The Straw*. After attending a few rehearsals of *Anna Christie*, however, he told friends that if it failed, he could blame only his script. In Arthur Hopkins he at last had a producer-director of his own kind, a man of integrity and vision. The function of the theater, Hopkins held, "is to release the inner potentials of all people concerned – dramatists, actors, and particularly audiences." Practically unique among the Broadway producers, his primary reason for choosing a script was not that he believed it would succeed but that he felt it "should be done. From then on," he said, "you become the willing servant of the play." His modesty and his attitude as a director were equally exceptional: "We have heard of actors who were made by directors. This is a miracle I have never witnessed. . . . A performance that is hung on an actor by a director is false fruit wired to a tree that has not flowered. . . . The greatest gift that the director can bring to the actor is faith, faith in the actor's own rich potentials." True to his word, he functioned so tactfully and unobtrusively that many of his actors felt that they had not been directed at all. Instead of telling them what to do, he encouraged them to eliminate all stock gestures, all the old tricks, and project the essence of their roles. He established a reassuring atmosphere which set actors at ease and heartened them to give their best — a method that worked fine with players of talent and experience, but not so happily with those who required firm guidance.

At one of the final rehearsals of *Anna Christie* Pauline Lord, an actress plagued with self-doubt, threw her arms around Hopkins and wept, "That's all I can do with it." "I should hope so," he replied. "Nobody could stand much more."

Even his appearance was reassuring: a short chubby man with pink cheeks, "Hoppy" suggested a middle-aged Kewpie doll in a derby. He and O'Neill were similar not only in their dedication to the theater but in their dislike of small talk. The producer in fact was, if anything, even more taciturn than the playwright. Sometimes when Eugene called on him, the two would sit for ten or fifteen minutes in complete silence, but, according to Oliver Sayler, Hopkins's press agent, they were "in conference."

Hopkins had served his apprenticeship by writing, producing and booking vaudeville acts. As a legitimate producer, he had been among the first on Broadway to discard the ultrarealism of David Belasco and favor the imaginative new stagecraft dreamed into being by Adolphe Appia and Gordon Craig. Few other producers could approach, still less equal, his record. In Tolstoi's *Redemption*, in the Bard's *Richard III*, in Benelli's *The Jest* — with John Barrymore starring in all three and his brother Lionel costarring in *The Jest* — Hopkins mounted productions that were at once commercial hits and artistic triumphs. Their genuine brilliance was due not only to their stellar portrayals but to the scenery, costumes and lighting of Robert Edmond Jones, a true artist in his field.

After waiting so long for *The Straw* to materialize, O'Neill had lost interest in the TB sanatorium play, yet, unable to ignore it, he underwent a "hectic, nerve-wracking" period shuttling between rehearsals of Tyler's and Hopkins's productions. In the midst of his professional concerns he took time for a personal matter — making the acquaintance of his first-born son, now aged eleven. Months before, he had received a letter from a lawyer to the effect that since he had become a success, his former wife, the onetime Kathleen Jenkins, hoped that he would pay for their son's education. Presently married to George Pitt-Smith, an office employee, and living on Long Island in modest circumstances, Kathleen wanted her son, her only child, to have advantages beyond her means; otherwise, she would never have approached her ex-husband. O'Neill immediately agreed to help, and the two of them, feeling that personal contact would be too awkward, continued to communicate through her attorney. Finally O'Neill, after some hesitation, said he would like to meet his son. Actually, he shrank from the prospect, for fear that the youngster might be hopelessly ordinary; but other, deeper feelings were also at work in him — a sense of guilt, an apprehension that the boy might resent or even hate him, the absentee father who suddenly appears after so many years.

Eugene O'Neill, Jr., had been five when his mother remarried, at which time he was given the name of Richard Pitt-Smith and told that Mr. Pitt-Smith was his father. Although Kathleen used to maintain that the two got along well together, she once admitted that her husband, who also had been married before and had a son, would have preferred her childless; and there seems to have been conflict between Mrs. Katie Jenkins, Kathleen's mother, who adored her grandson, and Pitt-Smith, who thought that she "spoiled" him. Pitt-Smith would like to have seen Kathleen more attached to his own son, a boy about young Eugene's age, who lived with his mother and spent weekends with his father and stepmother. The crosscurrents here were probably no stronger than in many households, yet Pitt-Smith's entry into the family apparently had an unsettling effect on young Eugene, accustomed as he had been to the indulgence and undivided love of both his mother and his grandmother. Formerly well behaved, he became so rebellious that he was sent off, just as his real father had been, to boarding school — in his case, a military academy, traditionally a place for difficult youngsters. Like his father, too, he was unhappy at school and felt that his mother was rejecting him; several times he ran back home, only to be returned to school again.

He was wearing his khaki uniform the day his grandmother brought him to 36 West Thirty-fifth Street, Manhattan, where the O'Neills were sharing an apartment with Bobby Jones. While Mrs. Jenkins waited in the lobby, the boy went up to meet the famous playwright whom he had recently learned was his father. Nervous about the occasion, O'Neill had Macgowan present for moral support and to help maintain conversation, but the precaution proved unnecessary. At first father and son were shy — O'Neill's hands were shaking — but they soon fell to talking easily, chiefly about baseball and school, and O'Neill grinned as he recalled that he had been a bad boy at prep school and college. The visit went off more pleasantly than either had anticipated; O'Neill was gratified to find his son alert and handsome, apparently without animus toward him, while it was obvious to the boy that he had favorably impressed this distinguished-looking man, his father. He was invited to visit Peaked Hill the following summer. On returning home he told his mother he was luckier than most boys, since he had two fathers, whereas others had only one. Though relieved that the occasion had gone satisfactorily, Kathleen admitted to a friend that she felt "peculiar" about it — "They hit it off so well that I feel I'm losing my son."

Months earlier O'Neill had sent a script of *Anna Christie* to George Jean Nathan and was worried when the critic found the ending unduly optimistic. Sounding rather defensive, he wrote back: "Anna forced herself on me, middle of third act, at her most theatric. In real life I felt she would unconsciously be compelled, through sheer inarticulateness, to the usual 'big scene,' and wait hopefully for her happy ending. And as she is the only one who knows exactly what she wants, she would get it.

"And the sea outside — life — waits. The happy ending is merely the comma at the end of a gaudy introductory clause, with the body of the sentence still unwritten. (In fact, I once thought of calling the play *Comma.*) . . . My ending seems to have a false definiteness about it that is misleading — a happy-ever-after which I did not intend."

His apprehension was well founded. The play, which opened on November 2, 1921, at the Vanderbilt, was favorably received but a number of critics assailed the ending and, indeed, more than a few accused the author of catering to the box office. Burns Mantle, for one, called it the first work in which "the morbid young genius compromised with the happy ending all true artists of the higher drama so generously despise"; and Stephen Rathbun, not alone in his suspicion, wondered whether the author "is gradually degenerating into a Broadway playwright."

Although he could have taken heart from the tenor of the reviews ("Towers above most of the plays in town." . . . "For sheer realism, stripped to its ugly vitals, *Anna Christie* is the finest piece of writing O'Neill has done." . . . "O'Neill has never so fully achieved his dramatic purpose"), the praise was nullified in his view by the charge that he had sold out to Broadway. Angry and hurt, impelled to make "not a defense but an explanation," he stated publicly: "In the last few minutes of *Anna Christie* I tried to show that dramatic gathering of new forces out of the old. I wanted to have the audience leave with a deep feeling of life flowing on . . . of a problem solved for the moment but by the very nature of its solution involving new problems.

"Since the last act seems to have been generally misunderstood, I must have failed in this attempt. . . . A kiss in the last act, a word about marriage, and the audience grows blind and deaf to what follows. . . . It would have been so obvious and easy — in the case of this play, even conventional — to have made my last act a tragic one. But looking deep into the hearts of my people, I saw it couldn't be done. It would not have been true. They were not that kind. They would act in just the silly, immature, compromising way that I have made them act. . . .

"Lastly, to those who think I deliberately distorted my last act because a 'happy ending' would be calculated to make the play more of a popular success, I have only this to say: The sad truth is that you have precedents enough and to spare in the history of our drama for such a suspicion. But, on the other hand, you have every reason not to believe it of me."

While O'Neill was justified in resenting charges that he was turning venal, he seems in error about his denouement. His mistake was that he wanted the audience to share Chris's apprehensions at the end; he tried, as Professor Travis Bogard puts it, "to force Chris's view of the sea as a malevolent force . . . onto the play as a whole." But Anna is the playwright's chief spokesman here, especially in her mystical response to the sea; and, moreover, she is the most sympathetic character, so that we are led to identify with her, to hope with her that things will turn out well, despite Chris's ominous muttering about "dat ole davil," the Sea.

Still smarting under the press's criticism of the final act, O'Neill told Oliver Sayler, Hopkins's aide, that he considered *Anna Christie* "the very worst failure I have experienced, and the most ironical joke ever played on me — for probably its success depends on the audience believing just what I did not want them to. If it were not for the others concerned in its production, I assure you I would pray for its closing next Saturday." At first he resented the way the play was generally interpreted, then began to resent the play itself, and eventually came to underrate it. Some years later when Joseph Wood Krutch asked permission to edit a volume of his plays, O'Neill replied: "Sure, use your own judgment, with one proviso: *Anna Christie* must not be among them."

Whatever their reservations about the script, the critics had only praise for the performance headed by Pauline Lord, George Marion as Chris, and Frank Shannon as Mat Burke. Miss Lord, after years of transforming roles of dross into something finer, at last had a part and a play worthy of her; with a wounded mouth, a plaintive voice that always seemed about to choke with suppressed emotion, brave gestures that subsided into helpless fluttering, she gave an irresistible portrayal. The Vanderbilt rang with cheers as she ended the impassioned outburst in which Anna tells the two men the facts of life, the sordid facts of her life: "I was in a house, that's what — yes, that kind of a house — the kind sailors like you and Mat goes to in port — and your nice inland men, too — all men, God damn 'em! I hate 'em! Hate 'em!"

That night, after the première, the O'Neills and Bobby Jones threw a party at their apartment, a wild mixture of Broadway figures, Province-town Players, and some of Eugene's barroom friends from the Village, including Spanish Willie. Ella O'Neill and Jamie were not present, since Agnes, in charge of the arrangements, thought that her mother-in-law would be offended by the drinking and goings-on; but she miscalculated. Ella, in spite of a show of affection for Agnes, had never approved of her son's marriage, partly because Agnes had been married before and had a child but chiefly because she was not Catholic. Both Ella and Jamie, ready to find fault with her, took it as an affront that they had not been invited and complained to Eugene, who in turn charged his wife with poor judgment, if not discourtesy toward his mother and his brother.

All this would come out later, though; the night of the party Jones, surveying the throng, said, "The goats are lining up on one side, the sheep on the other." To O'Neill the celebration was an ordeal made bearable only by drink; after a woman from Dublin tried to converse with him in Gaelic, he retreated with a bottle to the bathroom, pulling Charles O'Brien Kennedy along in his wake. Sitting on the edge of the bathtub, he outlined the story of a play he had long thought of writing. Based on his stoker friend Driscoll, whose suicide in 1915 had seemed so out of character for the swaggering seaman, the play, like the short story O'Neill had once written about him, was to be called *The Hairy Ape*. O'Neill not only had the play well developed in mind by this time but felt that the right man for the central role was Louis Wolheim, a friend of Kennedy's, who had a hulking build and a face like a battering ram. Both Wolheim and Kennedy worked for Arthur Hopkins in various capacities, now as actors, now as production assistants. At the play-wright's request, Kennedy called his friend the following day and bluntly asked, "Would you play the homeliest man in the world if Eugene O'Neill wrote the play?" Replied Wolheim, "If O'Neill writes it, I'll play it."

Two nights after the première of *Anna Christie*, George Tyler pre-sented a single performance of *The Straw* in New London, figuring that here, if anywhere, the author would get a sympathetic hearing; but O'Neill himself did not attend, for the *Anna Christie* party had launched him on one of his marathon binges and he now was holed up at Spanish

[69]

Willie's. Drawn by reports that *The Straw* was set in a tuberculosis sanatorium, almost every doctor in New London was at the Lyceum Theater, as were Ed Keefe, Art McGinley and other of Eugene's friends. Also present was Ella O'Neill, accompanied by a young local acquaintance named Alice Sheridan. Mrs. O'Neill was so little known to the townspeople, even though she had summered on Pequot Avenue for over thirty years, that only a few recognized her and came to her box to congratulate her on Eugene's growing fame. She said little before the performance and not much more afterward, telling Miss Sheridan only that she found the play "interesting."

But her cousins the Brennans had a great deal to say, all of it in an indignant vein, for they considered it a slap at themselves that Eugene had given their name to one of the play's most distasteful characters. "The Brennans are infuriated at me," he informed Ed Keefe. "They take the old harridan stepmother as an insult directly aimed at their mother, whom they insist is a lady and not the creature of the play at all — all because of the name, 'Brennan'! Can you beat it! I've tried to explain that every city directory is pretty full of Brennans but it's no use."

He must have written tongue-in-cheek to Keefe, for he had never liked the Brennans, particularly the old-maid Lillian, a pious busybody, and her mother, a matriarch of emphatic opinions. Back in 1914, after reading *Thirst*, O'Neill's first published collection of plays, Mrs. Brennan had thrown it into the furnace and declared: "Someone ought to tell Eugene to get out of the gutter!" It is relevant to note also that one of the Brennan girls became a Rogers through marriage — relevant because the young scoundrel in *Diff'rent* is named Rogers. A hoarder of grievances, Eugene O'Neill had a long memory.

In the New London tryout of *The Straw* John Westley proved inadequate as the young newspaperman and was replaced by Otto Kruger for the opening at the Greenwich Village Theater on November 10. The majority of the reviewers found the play of uneven quality and its subject matter depressing. Alan Dale, in his customary witty fashion, thought that the author will "probably write a musical comedy around cancer later on." Louis V. De Foe, in a discussion of both *The Straw* and *Anna Christie*, said: "Only that which is sordid or gloomy or doleful in life appears to arrest his attention." Unless he overcame this "unfortunate predilection," De Foe predicted, it would, despite his "great ability," vastly restrict his usefulness and influence in the theater." But at the same time (to give some idea of how O'Neill's writings left the reviewers confused) the critic felt that both *The Straw* and *Anna Christie* "have a poignancy and power that make all the other plays now on the boards seem pallid and inept."

In poor shape from his binge, O'Neill fled back to Provincetown without seeing *The Straw*, which closed after two and a half weeks of sparse attendance. Its failure, Tyler wrote the playwright, could not be blamed on the location of the downtown theater, since other presentations had thrived there. "People seemed to have the idea," he said on November 29, "they would catch tuberculosis by going in the building."

"Better luck next time!" Eugene replied on December 2. "As you say, the fault must be in the subject matter. Having been so close to its background once, I was never able to feel any shudder about it but I guess most people did. So the fault for the failure, if there is a fault in it, is all mine." Forgetting, or glossing over, that both he and Tyler had once been highly optimistic about the play's prospects, he continued: "And I want to express my gratitude to you for staking everything on a play that any other manager would have turned down as a 'hopeless hope.' I know you must have always appreciated how little chance for financial success the play had; and yet you went ahead because you believed it a good play that deserved a hearing. . . . Perhaps I'll be able to bring you a success sometime that will make up for *Chris* and *The Straw*." This marked the end, however, of his professional association with his father's good friend and longtime producer.

4

❀

The Mother's End

JUXTAPOSING two letters from O'Neill to Oliver Sayler in December 1921, it appears that a man's conscious mind may drift in the shallows at the same time that his creative unconscious is functioning most actively, and, in fact, is about ready to assert itself. On the fifth the playwright said that in his present mood he found it "exceedingly difficult to think anything about the theater, or feel anything, or give a damn one way or another. I am in one of my periods of uncreative doldrums — read only the papers and the *Sat. Eve. Post*, think not at all, walk much, and for emotional reaction have only a great and self-blighting loathing for the world in general. . . . But these moods of the Great Loathing never last very long with me when the dunes are within walking distance, and I hope to report to you in my next [letter] that I am fully resurrected."

Only two days later he began writing *The Hairy Ape* with a "mad rush," as he informed Sayler on the tenth: "Think I have got the swing of what I want to catch. . . . It is one of those plays where the word 'inspiration' has some point — that is, either you have the rhythm or you haven't and if you have you can ride it, and if not, you're dead."

To Charles O'Brien Kennedy, three days afterward, he reported that the play "is coming along in great shape. I've got the swing of it now, I think. Believe me, it is going to be strong stuff with a kick in each mitt — and stuff done in a new way, along the lines of *Emperor Jones* in construction but even more so. You can tell Wolheim for me that the lead will be a bigger part than Brutus Jones. If I could go ahead without interruption, I think I would have the whole thing completed — in longhand — by the first of the year. But darn it, the chances are I'll have to go to New York for a few days to see my mother and Jim who are leaving for California soon to be gone a year. But whatever interruptions, I've got a stranglehold on the play now and the rest is only a question of how soon."

He had the "swing" of it so well that he wrote the play in only two and a half weeks, finishing it on December 23; but it had been developing in his mind for years. "The search for an explanation of why Driscoll . . . should kill himself," he has said, "provided the germ of the idea of *The Hairy Ape.*" Where Mat Burke of *Anna Christie* is a romanticized surface image of the husky stoker Eugene used to drink with at Jimmy the Priest's, Yank of the new play embodies the author's view of the essential Driscoll, the man fated for an untimely end.

Originally O'Neill had intended to make Yank an Irishman but instead he drew him as "a New York tough of the toughs, a product of the water front turned stoker." Yank, dominating the hold by his exceptional strength and truculent personality, glories in feeling that he "belongs." When Paddy, a nostalgic old-timer, laments the passing of the sailing ships, Yank bursts out: "I belong and he don't. He's dead but I'm livin'. . . . Hell in de stokehole? Sure! It takes a man to work in hell. . . . I'm at de bottom, get me! Dere ain't nothin' foither. I'm de end! I'm de start! I start somep'n and de woild moves! . . . I'm de ting in coal dat makes it boin; I'm steam and oil for de engines; I'm de ting in noise dat makes yuh hear it; I'm smoke and express trains and steamers. . . . And I'm what makes iron into steel! Steel, dat stands for de whole ting! And I'm steel, steel, steel!"

Yank's paean to steel resembles certain passages in the title poem of *Smoke and Steel,* a collection of Carl Sandburg's verse that O'Neill had read earlier this year. Listen to Sandburg:

> *Steel barbwire around The Works.*
> *Steel guns in the holsters of the guards at the gates of The Works.*
> *Steel ore-boats bring the loads clawed from the earth*
> *by steel, lifted and lugged by arms of steel. . . .*
> *The runners now, the handlers now, are steel; they dig*
> *and clutch and haul . . . they are steel making steel . . .*
> *Liners on the sea, skyscrapers on the land; diving steel*
> *in the sea, climbing steel in the sky.*

It appears, then, that the poem acted on O'Neill as a catalyst, speeding the crystallization of a play that had been evolving in his mind for years. As the first scene ends, Yank snaps to nostalgic old Paddy: "Aw yuh make me sick! Yuh don't belong!" Thereafter the drama proceeds to show his brutal awakening to the realization that he himself does not "belong" and never has. Precipitating his downfall, a neurotic heiress, the daughter of a steel tycoon, visits the infernolike hold in search of thrills and is horrified when confronted by the huge, sweating half-naked Yank. "Take me away!" she cries. "Oh, the filthy beast!" and then faints. As one stoker says, she acted as though "she'd seen a great hairy ape escaped from the zoo."

Brooding over the insult, Yank whips himself into a fury and swears to avenge himself on her and her kind; but all his attempts end in frustration and defeat. The "bulls" hustle him away from the dock before he can "spit in her pale mug." The wealthy churchgoers on Fifth Avenue, whom he tries to taunt into a fight, ignore him as though he does not exist; and when someone finally notices him, he lands in jail. Once free, Yank visits a local of the Industrial Workers of the World and volunteers to dynamite "all de factories, steamers, buildings, jails — de Steel Trust and all dat makes it go." Suspecting him of being a police agent, the Wobblies throw him out.

In the author's initial conception Yank returned to the stokehold, to what he now saw as a prisonlike existence, but as the play was taking shape, Yank became stubborn, as it were, and refused to go back. He continues on to the zoo, from a confused notion that he might learn something there, and, standing outside the gorilla's cage, feels that the animal is more fortunate than himself. "I ain't on oith," he says, "and I ain't in heaven. . . . I'm in de middle tryin' to separate 'em, taking all de woist punches from bot' of 'em." He opens the cage and tries to make friends with the gorilla, but the beast wraps him around in a bone-crushing hug, tosses the limp body into the cage, and shuffles off as Yank cries out, "Christ, where do I get off at? Where do I fit in?" Then he dies. "And, perhaps," in the author's concluding words, "the Hairy Ape at last belongs."

To the playwright, Yank was both an individual and "a symbol of man who has lost his old harmony with nature, the harmony which he used to have as an animal and has not yet acquired in a spiritual way. . . . Yank can't go forward, and so he tries to go back. . . . But he can't go back to 'belonging' either. The gorilla kills him. The subject here is the same ancient one that always was and always will be the one subject for drama, and that is man and his struggle with his own fate. The struggle used to be with the gods, but is now with himself, his own past, his attempt 'to belong.'"

Basically, Yank is modeled not on Driscoll the stoker but on Eugene

O'Neill, a man haunted throughout his life by a feeling he did not "belong." As a husband he tried to counter his sense of isolation by becoming "One & Indivisible" with Agnes, and when the darkness was on him he felt aggrieved and bitter toward her that they fell short of total union, total rapport. (This side of him, his straining to attain an impossible relationship with Agnes, which he had already dramatized to a limited extent in *The First Man*, would be plumbed in his 1923 play, *Welded*.) As a renegade Catholic, a man of spiritual temperament who felt lost without a faith, he tried to make a religion of the theater. Hence his contempt for "the Broadway show-shop" and, conversely, the envy in his voice when he used to talk with Jig Cook and Jimmy Light about the old Greek theater, where, like religious services, the performances partook of ritual, mystery, and traffic with the gods. During his career O'Neill was to experiment in many styles and with various devices; he would exploit virtually the full vocabulary of the theater — not only dialogue and action but masks, pantomime, song, dance movement, sound effects, speaking choruses and responsive chanting. The one constant behind his restless experimentation was his effort to elevate the theater to a temple, to help create a place where he could "belong."

While writing *The Hairy Ape* he took time to submit to an interview by correspondence with Malcolm Mollan, his onetime city editor on the New London *Telegraph* and presently a free-lance newspaperman. (Though Mollan had been rather hard on cub reporter O'Neill, the playwright felt sorry for him, a man with a drinking problem who had fallen on lean times.) To Mollan's question about whether he would ever produce a play that ended happily, he replied that he would "write about happiness if I ever happen to meet up with that luxury, and find it sufficiently dramatic and in harmony with any deep rhythm of life. But happiness is a word. What does it mean? Exaltation; an intensified feeling of the significant worth of man's being and becoming? Well, if it means that — and not a mere smirking contentment with one's lot — I know there is more of it in one real tragedy than in all the happy-ending plays ever written.

"It's a sheer present-day judgment to think of tragedy as unhappy! The Greeks and the Elizabethans knew better. They felt a tremendous lift to it. It roused them spiritually to a deeper understanding of life. Through it they found release from the petty considerations of everyday existence. They saw their lives ennobled by it."

O'Neill read *The Hairy Ape* one evening in Provincetown to Jig, Susan, and several other friends, all of whom were greatly impressed.

Shortly afterward Agnes's father, Edward Boulton, visited Provincetown and wrote his daughter Margery that the play "is a wonder. If you read it, you can't sleep."

Imaginative, powerful, nightmarish, *Hairy Ape* interweaves realism and the stylized mode known as Expressionism, that "drama of disorder," as one writer put it, which tries "to represent concretely on the stage what happens inside a character's mind." Born chiefly of Strindberg's *The Dream Play* and *The Spook Sonata*, Expressionism became a movement, at the same time acquiring its name, as Wedekind, Toller, Kaiser and other continental playwrights followed Strindberg's lead. O'Neill had first dabbled in Expressionism with *The Emperor Jones*, but this time he made greater use of its characteristic features: masks or masklike faces; distorted settings that suggest a claustrophobic world in which everything is askew; depersonalized characters confined to their own orbits and unable to make contact with anyone else. In the Fifth Avenue scene of *Ape*, for instance, the churchgoers are presented as "a procession of gaudy marionettes, yet with something of the relentless horror of Frankenstein in their detached, mechanical unawareness."

Of two minds about Expressionism, O'Neill conceded that *Ape* belonged in part to the genre but denied that he had been influenced by Toller and the others. Calling *Ape* a "direct descendant" of *Jones*, he said that the earlier play was "written long before I had ever heard of Expressionism." Nevertheless, despite a manifest relationship between his two plays, O'Neill, prior to composing *The Hairy Ape*, had seen and greatly admired an Expressionist film, the now-classic *Cabinet of Dr. Caligari*, and had read *From Morn to Midnight*, a prototypal Expressionist drama. The new O'Neill play, in fact, basically resembles the Georg Kaiser work: in both the lowly protagonist is jolted out of his rut by encountering a "Lady" and at last finds peace, after a series of bewildering experiences, in death.

"I personally do not believe," O'Neill has said of Expressionism, "that an idea can be readily put over to an audience except through characters. When it sees 'A Man' and 'A Woman' — just abstractions, it loses the human contact by which it identifies itself with the protagonist . . . the character of Yank remains a man and everyone recognizes him as such."

Here is the crux of the matter, the chief reason why he sought to draw a distinction between his play and one such as *From Morn to Midnight*, in which the central figure, a bank employee, is called simply "A Cashier." Yank meant so much to O'Neill personally — he realized later that the play was "unconscious autobiography" — that he resented Yank's being grouped with the dehumanized, rather faceless principals common to Expressionism.

The Hairy Ape was slated for the Provincetown Players, since O'Neill took for granted that so unconventional a play would have to prove itself downtown before it could find an uptown sponsor. Looking ahead, he wrote to Arthur Hopkins about his new drama and expressed the hope that the producer would eventually take it over; Hopkins replied that he not only was interested but volunteered to help in staging *Ape* on Mac-Dougal Street.

From O'Neill's extant correspondence between late December 1921 and early 1922, it appears doubtful that he visited New York, as he had intended, to see his mother and Jamie before they left for California. For months Ella had suffered periodically from severe headaches, brought on, she thought, by the strain of trying to straighten out her late husband's tangled business affairs. Adding to her burden, she had had to contend with a lawsuit brought by Tom Dorsey, the part-time realtor and full-time toper who had sold Mr. O'Neill most of his New London property. (The playwright son would make unflattering references to Dorsey, under the name of "McGuire," in *Long Day's Journey Into Night*.) In a flimsy, trumped-up case, Dorsey, who apparently had considered Ella too timid to fight back, sued the estate for thirty-five hundred dollars allegedly due him in unpaid commissions. His suit was dismissed finally but it dragged on for over a year, adding to Ella's expenses and worries. Now she was going to California both for her health and to check on some land in Glendale which James O'Neill had bought early in their marriage; once rated almost worthless, the property had grown in value as Los Angeles expanded close to the area.

On January 10, 1922, a week after her departure with Jamie, Eugene wrote Harold DePolo that his brother had been on the wagon for a year and a half and that his "sobriety has had a wonderful effect on his judgment of the ponies. He follows a system of his own with religious rigidity, has accumulated quite a small bankroll in reserve, and spends hours a day in intensive doping. He has been beating them for the past year almost." His mother and Jamie planned, he said, to remain on the Coast till spring.

By unfortunate chance, production of his plays went in spurts. First there had been *Beyond the Horizon* and *Chris* in rehearsal concurrently, then *Anna Christie* and *The Straw*, and now he again faced the "ghastly joy of attending two sets of rehearsals at the same time" — *The Hairy*

Ape and *The First Man,* the latter presented by and starring Augustin Duncan at the Neighborhood Playhouse. But when the time came, O'Neill avoided the ordeal by the simple expedient of ignoring the Duncan production. For a while it had appeared that the Theater Guild, prodded by Lawrence Langner, one of its managing directors, might present *The First Man.* In response to an enthusiastic letter from Langner about *Anna Christie* and *The Straw,* both of which the Guild had rejected, O'Neill sent him *The First Man,* but this, too, was turned down. Shortly afterward, Langner suggested to stockbroker Maurice Wertheim, another Guild director, that he should finance O'Neill for a year or two, during which he would be free of money cares to concentrate all his thoughts on writing plays; when Wertheim responded favorably, Langner relayed word to the playwright.

Nonplussed by the offer, O'Neill replied that the Guild was contradicting itself, since it had consistently rejected his plays but now was ready to subsidize his future work. If all the other producers and theatrical groups had taken the Guild's tack, he said, he would not have a past or present on which to base his future. The Guild could prove its faith in him, he added, only by producing his plays, but it seemed to him that he and the organization were fated to go separate ways forever.

Things went badly at first when the O'Neills returned to New York late in January for *The Hairy Ape.* Agnes was stricken almost immediately with influenza, and shortly afterward Bobby Jones, who was codesigning the sets with Cleon Throckmorton, collapsed from overwork. Originally, Charles O'Brien Kennedy was supposed to direct the play, but Jig Cook was so eager for the assignment that O'Neill, against his better judgment, yielded. Jig had been in low spirits for months, ever since the failure of *The Spring* at an uptown theater, produced with funds he himself had raised, for the Provincetowners had voted against backing it. On the third night of the engagement four tickets were sold; the following night the play closed. Equally disheartening to Jig, the Players were having a poor season, their poorest in fact: *The Verge,* one of Susan Glaspell's lesser efforts; *The Hand of the Potter,* a dreary work by Theodore Dreiser; a bill of mediocre one-acters. The Players were so demoralized that, unable to come up with a fourth program in time, they sublet the theater to another group for a few weeks till *The Hairy Ape* would be ready.

The rehearsals of *Ape* began with O'Neill in a supervisory capacity and Jig as director, but it shortly developed that Jig, though he had done well enough with *The Emperor Jones,* was unequal to the new play, a far

[78]

more exacting script. As O'Neill increasingly took command of the production, Cook felt diminished, slighted, relegated to a corner. One night Pauline Turkel, an assistant to Fitzi, found him at the corner of Grove and MacDougal — he was drunk — trying to pry a brick loose from a building. "Things need loosening up," he said, clawing at the cement. "I'm trying to loosen 'em up." Another evening Floyd Dell, once a close friend of Jig's, was dining with Arthur Davison Ficke in the downstair grill of the Brevoort when Jig, who was again intoxicated, joined them and urged that they should all go back to Davenport, Iowa, and turn it into "the Athens of America." Growing more and more excited, he marched around the room, striking a plate with a knife in what he called a "pyrrhic dance."

Jig had convinced himself by this time that he had not failed but that others, particularly O'Neill, had failed him. He felt that O'Neill had exploited him and the Provincetown Players, and now, tossing him aside, was using the MacDougal Street playhouse merely as a tryout place for Broadway. That the Players had capitalized on O'Neill's talent, that their record would have been far less impressive without his plays, that possibly his writings had saved the group from an early demise — all this Cook preferred to overlook. After reviewing his situation and what had happened to the Players since the disruptive success of *Jones*, he came to a decision. "It is time," he told Susan Glaspell, "to go to Greece." This had been his supreme dream all his life, to walk where Aeschylus, Sophocles and Euripides had walked, but now he was going not simply on pilgrimage to the past but to find refuge from the present.

On February 23 Jig and Susan, Edna Kenton, Fitzi, Cleon Throckmorton and Harry Weinberger, the attorney for the Players, met with O'Neill at his apartment on Thirty-fifth Street to decide the future course of the playhouse. They agreed to follow *Ape* with *Chains of Dew*, a new work by Susan, as the season's final bill; to incorporate, in order to preserve the name of the Provincetown Players, with the seven of them as the directors of the corporation (Jimmy Light, who had frequently been in conflict with Jig, was squeezed out at the insistence of the Cooks and their ally, Edna Kenton); and to recess for a year, during which time the theater would be sublet to another group. At a farewell party a few nights later, when Jig became eloquent with drink, he spoke of his dreams while growing up in Iowa, of his great hopes for the Players, and finally got into an acrimonious exchange with O'Neill. Intending to be away about a year, the Cooks sailed on the S.S. *Themistocles* on March 1; they did not want to be around to witness the acclaim they expected for *The Hairy Ape.*

After Cook's death in 1924, O'Neill said that he was "the big man, the dominating and inspiring genius of the Players. Always enthusiastic, vital, impatient with everything that smacked of falsity or compromise, he represented the spirit of revolt against the old worn-out traditions. . . ." But in 1922 O'Neill's predominant feeling toward him was one of exasperation. While appreciating all that Cook had contributed to the Players, he also felt that Jig had discouraged fresh talent, had been high-handed, had too often shown poor judgment.

At a less demanding time, Eugene would have been more affected by the rift between him and Jig, by his and Susan's departure, but the situation came to a head when he could think of little except *The Hairy Ape.* Usually the last one to leave the playhouse, he had never before worked so hard on a production, not alone because it meant so much to him — it would always be among his favorite works — but because of the difficulty of staging the eight-scene drama on the tiny stage at 133 Mac-Dougal. Since the theater had no "flies" and there was no backstage to speak of, where the sets might be stacked, they would have to be dropped through a hole to the basement.

The playwright had chosen Louis Wolheim for Yank on the basis of his battered face and rugged build — he weighed around two hundred pounds — but at the same time was worried that the actor, whose experience had been limited to minor roles, might prove inadequate for a character who is nine-tenths of the play. Despite his plug-ugly appearance, Wolheim was a man of superior intelligence, a college graduate with degrees from two institutions, a linguist versed in French, German and Spanish. His forbidding looks were chiefly the result of his nose being smashed while he was on the Cornell football team ("That guy," he used to say, "smeared my nose from ear to ear"), and he also had a cauliflower ear from college boxing. Though basically good-natured, he was touchy about his appearance and easily provoked, more than once taking on several opponents at a time. While he was teaching at Cornell Preparatory School, Lionel Barrymore, in Ithaca with a film-making troupe, induced him to appear in the movie. Subsequently, Wolheim, a restless soul, interspersed teaching jobs with bit parts in the movies and the theater, and spent some time in Mexico as a mining engineer, where he became involved in revolutionary activity; more recently he had concentrated on the theater, chiefly in Arthur Hopkins's employ. As rehearsals of *The Hairy Ape* progressed and Wolheim dug into his part, O'Neill felt increasingly confident that he had chosen well, a feeling that the critics and the public were to verify. At the age of forty, Wolheim, somewhat like Charles S. Gilpin, who also had had to wait so long to prove his mettle, was ready to give a definitive, thrilling performance in the sort of role actors dream about.

After some discouraging months a spirit of excitement animated the MacDougal Street playhouse (the decision to suspend for a year, at the end of the season, was known only to the directorate) as *The Hairy Ape* began to take form. Unlike so many productions at the theater, which were put together with prayers, day-to-day improvising, and casts plagued by absenteeism, the new work was being staged with meticulous care. Wolheim, a perfectionist, had a stimulating, if sometimes abrasive effect on the rest of the cast. Overcoming limited physical resources with imagination and ingenuity, Bobby Jones, who had regained his health, and Throckmorton wrought wonders with the sets. ("That preposterous little theater has one of the most cramped stages New York has ever known," a critic was to say, "and yet on it the artists have created the illusion of vast spaces and endless perspectives.") Blanche Hays, an experienced hand, designed the costumes, while O'Neill was in overall command, with Jimmy Light assisting him and Arthur Hopkins standing by to make suggestions. The role of Mildred Douglas, the steel heiress who precipitates Yank's ruin, was being played by Mary Blair, who had first appeared with the group as the desperate spinster in *Diff'rent*.

Initially in *The Emperor Jones*, for the witch doctor, and now in *The Hairy Ape*, for the robotlike churchgoers on Fifth Avenue, O'Neill resorted to the mask. Years later, regretting that he had not utilized the device more extensively, he said that "all the figures in Jones's flight through the forest should be masked. Masks would dramatically stress their phantasmal quality, as contrasted with the unmasked Jones, intensify the supernatural menace of the tom-tom. . . . In *The Hairy Ape* a much more extensive use of masks would be of the greatest value in emphasizing the theme of the play. From the opening of the fourth scene, where Yank begins to think, he enters into a masked world; even the familiar faces of his mates in the forecastle have become strange and alien. They should be masked, and the faces of everyone he encounters thereafter, including the symbolic gorilla's."

Early in February, while engrossed with *The Hairy Ape*, Eugene was alarmed to hear from his brother that "Mama" had suffered a stroke. Several days later in another telegram Jamie reported that her condition was less serious than it had seemed, and that they would return East as soon as she was better; but this was followed a week or so afterward by word that she was dying. Jamie urged his brother to hurry to the Coast, but Eugene wired back that he was unwell, a matter of "nerves." To another, more insistent message, he replied: "No question of temperament. Be fair. Specialist says means complete nervous collapse if undertake trip present condition. Would not help Mother or you. Also, you wire she is unconscious, will not know me. Want to help in any possible way. Everything I have at your command. Wire me what and how. Just consulted Jelliffe, famous specialist here, on Mama's case. He says hopeless but last resort call best man on Coast, Samuel D. Ingham, Los Angeles. Mention Jelliffe. My plans depend on health. Would leave immediately if able. You must accept truth. I am in terrible shape."

The Jelliffe of his wire was Dr. Smith Ely Jelliffe, a psychoanalyst whose patients included a number of theatrical and literary people, among them Arthur Hopkins, who had a liquor problem, and Robert Edmond Jones, who suffered from periods of great depression. On Jones's advice, O'Neill had seen Jelliffe a few times about his drinking and the strain of hostility in his relations with Agnes.

Actually, despite what he told Jamie, Eugene was in fairly good health at the time. Most likely he would have refused to go to California even had he not been involved with *The Hairy Ape* or some other production. Unable to cope with ordinary problems and difficulties of quotidian life — he used to shunt onto Agnes responsibilities that should have been his as head of the family — he was completely at a loss in a crisis. "The thought of death," Agnes says, "unnerved him. He hated anything that had to do with death." Whether a defect in his character or an aspect of his hypersensitive nature, he ran from situations that other persons would have felt duty-bound to face. When his good friend Louis Holladay died suddenly from an overdose of heroin at a Greenwich Village spot, he had burrowed into himself, instead of lending a hand in the ensuing emergency. Much as he had wanted to see his father before his death, it was with considerable reluctance that he had gone to New London when the old actor's life was ebbing. Now that his mother was dying far away, it was easier for him to escape the deathwatch; but even though he never went to the Coast, he was not to be spared a close-up view of her wretched end.

In Los Angeles Mrs. O'Neill and Jamie, after taking a furnished apartment at 118 South Oxford Avenue, had gotten in touch with several persons from the East, including a hairdresser named Libbie Drummer whom Ella had known for years ("a fine type of woman," according to

Eugene, "although comparatively uneducated"), and Marion Reed, a friend of Jamie's who had been in a few Broadway shows and now was a movie bit player. When Ella had her initial attack she forbade Jamie to call a doctor, an injunction he obeyed in deference to her old hostility to doctors; but medical attention shortly became imperative, as she suffered a second stroke on February 16. Jamie also summoned Mrs. Drummer and several other acquaintances on that date as witnesses to his mother's will, which gave him the Glendale property, divided the remainder of the estate between him and Eugene, and named Marion Reed as executrix. Mrs. Drummer was badly shaken by the evening, in part because Jamie was drinking and seemed to her too intimate with Mrs. Reed but chiefly because Ella was semiparalyzed and scarcely able to talk. When Fred A. Luth, an attorney and a friend of Mrs. Reed's, asked if she understood that this was her last will and testament, she managed to say "yes" but was unable to sign her name; with Luth guiding her hand, she made an "X."

By this time Jamie was in communication not only with his brother but with Frank W. Dart of New London, the administrator of the O'Neill estate. On February 28, after word to Eugene, he wired Dart: "My dear friend, my mother died this morning. I know your devotion to yours so you can appreciate the awful desolation that has come into my life."

No matter how darkly Eugene may have visualized his mother's final days — he suspected that his brother had resumed drinking — his imaginings must have fallen short of reality. But eventually he had the full unhappy picture from a letter Mrs. Drummer wrote to a Mrs. Phillips, an old friend of the O'Neill family who in turn forwarded it to Eugene. Mrs. Drummer's letter in part: "I am so glad you told me about the funeral. I was so worried. I did not know if Jamie would ever reach New York alive. He was in a dreadful condition . . . when he left. Well, dear, the whole thing is *very sad*, and it will take me a long time to get over it, if ever. I am going to tell you just what happened and you can place yourself in my position. It was dreadful . . . I received a card from Mrs. O'Neill that she was in town and would love to see me. Well, I went out to call on her. When she opened the door, I felt very bad. She dragged one foot . . . and her mouth was a little crooked. She spoke of a Mrs. Reed and said that this Mrs. Reed's husband was a friend of Mr. [James] O'Neill's. Before I left Jamie came in. He was not drinking at that time and I invited them both to dinner the following Sunday. . . .

"Well, I did not see her again until they came to dinner. I will never forget [that] Mrs. O'Neill was dressed lovely and her whole face was all to one side. I felt more like crying every time I looked at her. She wanted to stay with me the worst way but I did not have room for them. If she had been alone I would have kept her right with us. She never mentioned her condition and you know me I would not speak of it, only I told them to see a doctor.

"I did not see them again until the following Thursday. Jamie came to the store and said that his Mother had another stroke and would I come out there. I went out and oh what a sight. All of her right side was dead from head to toe. And Mrs. Reed and some gentleman friend of her's was there, also a trained nurse. . . . This Reed woman was running everything. She is married and has two little sons. She did not like it one bit that I was there and let me see it, but I stayed for a few hours as Mrs. O'Neill wished me to. I think that was the day that Jamie started drinking. He is very weak. This Mrs. Reed had him over to her home day and night. I did not like her and could see through her from the first moment I met her. . . .

"Then Jamie came to the store and asked me to come out that night [February 16] as his mother was going to make her will and he wanted me for his witness. So Min [Mrs. Drummer's sister] and I went and when we got near the house we met Jamie and he said a new complication had set in. His mother's jewelry, her deed to the Glendale property, and the return tickets were missing. While we were talking this Mrs. Reed came along and asked Jamie where he was going and he said to have something to eat, and she went with him. . . .

"Along about eight o'clock they came back and the lawyer came. He was a friend of Mrs. Reed's and from what I understand they — Jamie and this Reed woman — were at the lawyer's all afternoon. The lawyer went in to Mrs. O'Neill and roused her, told her that he had come to draw her will, and she seemed to understand. . . . She gave equal division to Jamie and Eugene to everything but the Glendale property. Her mind was made up and seemed very clear. Jamie wanted the New York property but she wanted Eugene to have half. The Glendale property is worth twenty thousand. The nurse said that she intended giving Jamie the New York property but changed her mind that morning and nothing could change her. It was the saddest thing that I have ever witnessed. She seemed to be quieter after that and I went to her and held her hand and asked her if she was satisfied with what she had done. She said yes, and I said now you will rest better and she said yes.

"Well, she seemed to get worse every day and Jamie kept drinking harder all the time and the worst part of it [is] I think she knew he was drinking before she died and realized everything and was helpless.

"Then she passed away the following Tuesday morning. . . . The next day [the nurse] phoned me and wanted me to come out to the house to see if I could do anything with Jamie. . . . Min and I went and oh, my dear, it was pitiful. The two nurses were there with him and his condition was dreadful between dope and drink and his mother at the undertaker's, and he wanted to ship her home to Eugene as this Mrs. Reed wanted him to remain here. He was a little afraid of me and when he mentioned it I said by no means, you are going back with your mother or I wire Eugene. Then the next day I went to the undertaker's and had a talk with them. He had left the whole thing to them, even to buying his ticket. I told them not to let the body go back without him. . . . The nurse came the next day and said that she and this Mrs. Reed and her gentleman friend had seen him off and that he had ten bottles of whiskey with him and that he had a compartment. The nurse said that he had found the tickets and the deed but no jewelry. They were in the trunk and only three people had been in it — Mrs. Reed, Jamie, and Mrs. Reed's friend — so it must be one or the other that took it. [The jewelry was later found.]

"Jamie gave each of the nurses a dress and a pair of Mrs. O'Neill's shoes. Mrs. Reed got her silk stockings and he gave her a check for 150 dollars and no doubt she took other things. What she wanted was the fur coat. They had a quarrel over it, the nurse said, before Mrs. O'Neill died, and he wouldn't give it to her. He didn't give me a thing and I sure didn't want anything. I would have liked a little picture of her. I don't know when I felt so bad for anyone as I did about Mrs. O'Neill. It was the saddest closing chapter of any story I have ever read."

For several days after Ella's death Eugene was worried at not hearing from Jamie, but on March 4 he received a wire that Jamie was leaving that day. With thoughts of his mother and brother weighing on him, O'Neill paid scant attention to *The First Man*, which opened on the fourth to a tepid response from the critics and the public. The train bearing Jamie, as well as Ella's coffin, arrived in New York on the ninth, the same night *The Hairy Ape* was roaring through its first performance in the Village. While Agnes attended the première with Saxe Commins, Eugene was supposed to meet the train at Grand Central, accompanied by William P. Connor, one of his parents' oldest friends. As the time approached, however, he became increasingly agitated; his nerve failed him. He telephoned Connor that he was unable to join him and turned stubborn when the other, a man of stern character, tried to insist that he fulfill his duty.

Connor, who took along his nephew, Frank W. Wilder, had no difficulty locating Ella's coffin. When the passengers had debarked, the two men, standing on the long empty platform, saw the coffin removed to a luggage wagon — but no Jamie in sight. After looking in vain through the cars and checking with the stationmaster about Jamie's compartment, they found him in a drunken stupor, with empty bottles all around; beyond knowing them, all he could do was mumble incoherently. With the aid of two redcaps half carrying him, they got him into a taxi, then deposited him in a hotel off Times Square, after which Connor telephoned Eugene and in a voice of cold disgust gave him a report.

At the Provincetown Playhouse *The Hairy Ape* excited the first-nighters to calls of "Author! Author!" but Agnes and Saxe, thinking of Eugene's mission this evening, left the theater heavyhearted. At the Netherland Hotel, where the O'Neills were staying, they found him uninterested in the première, and reticent about his meeting with Jamie; feeling guilty over his defection, he relayed a few things Connor had told him, giving the impression that he had been to Grand Central. Suddenly he said to Saxe that he had to get out, he wanted to walk, and the two set off for Central Park, where they kept circling the reservoir most of the night.

At first Commins, trying to inspirit his silent friend, talked of the enthusiastic response to *The Hairy Ape*, till Eugene said, "It doesn't really mean anything." Then the floodgates opened and out poured a tide of reminiscence full of old grief and bitterness about his family, matter that one day would be reworked and distilled into *Long Day's Journey Into Night*. He recalled his mother's piety and sheltered upbringing, her falling in love with James O'Neill — a mistake, for she should never have married an actor — and her drug addiction, which had been a blight on all their lives. Thinking of his father, he recalled his despair at being chained so many years to *Monte Cristo*, his fear of poverty, and the fortune he had lost through investing in gold mines that had no gold, in oil wells without oil. And there was Jamie, who had thrown his life away, Jamie, whom Eugene considered more talented than himself; he was smart, he was witty, he had a genuine feeling for literature, and yet it had all come to nothing, a life wasted on sex, drinking and other pleasures. Probably Jamie, his brother felt, was the most unfortunate of them all, for he had had scarcely anything to sustain him, nothing except his love for his mother.

[86]

The funeral services were held on the morning of the tenth at St. Leo's on East Twenty-eighth Street, near the Prince George Hotel, which Ella used to attend, but Jamie was absent. When Mrs. Wilder, Connor's sister, and her son Frank stopped by his hotel, they found him in the midst of sending a bellhop for liquor, still drunk but able to recognize them. In reply to Mrs. Wilder's question whether he would attend, he gestured helplessly and said he was too broken up. The priest who officiated at St. Leo's, a Father Fogarty, turned out to have been a classmate of Eugene's at his first school, St. Aloysius Academy on the grounds of Mount St. Vincent. Among the mourners was another, far more important figure from his past: Sarah Sandy, who had once been to him more like a second mother than a nursemaid. For some reason he avoided her at the church, unwilling to talk with her, and became evasive when Agnes tried to question him about it; possibly in his mind Miss Sandy was associated with too many painful memories of the family. This was, in any case, the last time he ever saw her.

After the services the coffin was transferred to a train for New London, with Eugene and Agnes making the trip, and Ella was buried that same day in the family plot in St. Mary's Cemetery, next to her husband, mother, and infant son Edmund (whose name Eugene would borrow for himself in *Long Day's Journey*). To the distress of the Sheridans and the Brennans, there was no church service in New London – only prayers said at the grave – for Eugene wanted the rites held to a minimum. All was not over, however, between him and his mother; her image, like an unquiet ghost, was to haunt a number of his dramas, among them *A Moon for the Misbegotten*.

If, as O'Neill said, he wrote *Long Day's Journey* with "deep pity and understanding and forgiveness" for all his family, including himself, he wrote *A Moon for the Misbegotten* as absolution for his brother, called James Tyrone, Jr., in both plays. He had to write it, had to absolve him, since Jamie was never able in life to forgive himself, especially for his outrageous behavior on the train from California. It seems, as he confessed to Eugene, that he was driven by a compulsion to wallow in the mud, to profane his thoughts of his mother, and, as related in *The Misbegotten*, he picked up "a blonde pig who looked more like a whore than twenty-five whores, with a face like an overgrown doll's . . . one of the smuttiest-talking pigs I've ever listened to. . . . So every night – for fifty bucks –"

Although O'Neill wrote the play some twenty years later, his brother's agony and self-loathing are conveyed as sharply as though he had suffered through it all only yesterday. Set in 1923 the play finds Jim Tyrone vainly trying to drown the recent past in liquor. The one thing uppermost in his torturing thoughts, the subject he constantly returns to, like a wound he is exacerbating, is his conduct on the train: "It was like some plot I had to carry out. The blonde – she didn't matter. She was only something that belonged in the plot. It was as if I wanted revenge – because I'd been left alone – because I knew I was lost, without any hope left. . . . No, I didn't forget, even in that pig's arms! I remembered. The last two lines of a lousy tear-jerker song I'd heard when I was a kid kept singing over and over in my brain: And baby's cries can't waken her / In the baggage coach ahead."

In 1931, to a query from an old schoolmate, O'Neill replied: "No, my brother is not alive. He died in 1923. Booze got him in the end. . . . He and I were terribly close to each other, but after my mother's death in 1922 he gave up all hold on life and simply wanted to die as soon as possible. He had never found his place. He had never belonged. I hope like my 'Hairy Ape' he does now."

The Hairy Ape drew a bewildering assortment of reviews, ranging from "the most powerful thing he has done" (Robert Benchley, *Life*), "a bitter, brutal, wildly fantastic play" (Alexander Woollcott, the *Times*), and "the best play by an American we have ever seen" (Arthur Pollock, the Brooklyn *Eagle*) to "an exceedingly juvenile performance" (J. Ranken Towse, the *Post*), and "A little of it is fine. Much of it is dull" (Heywood Broun, the *World*). A number likened it to *The Emperor Jones*, with some finding it superior to its forerunner, others, not as good; and one or two, viewing it as radical propaganda, scolded the author on patriotic grounds.

By now O'Neill was accustomed to being "misunderstood" by the press, but he would never become resigned to it. In 1933 he told a friend that the more he read "of the professional critics' comment, either pro or con, past & present, the wearier feeling I get that all they say is something between them and their trade but, so far as the reality of my play goes, totally irrelevant, except as boxoffice help or hindrance. Not that I am not properly grateful for the sympathetic breaks they give – but . . . I do not write for critics. They are too steeped in the theater and they react from that standpoint and not from the insight of one living in life. They see the play first and life second – whereas I write first about life and then try to cram it into a play form." To another friend he expressed himself succinctly: "I like to read what the reviewers find in my plays — things I never knew I had put there."

Despite the carping voices, the general reception of *The Hairy Ape* indicated that O'Neill had at last consolidated his position: at the age of thirty-three he no longer was seen as "our most promising playwright" or "the leading young American playwright" but as the best this country had yet produced. "It seems rather absurd," Woollcott said, "to fret over much about the undisciplined imagination of the young playwright towering so conspicuously above the milling, mumbling crowd of playwrights who have no imagination at all. . . . We have a turbulent and tremendous play, so full of blemishes that the merest fledgling among the critics could point out a dozen, yet so vital and interesting and teeming with life that those playgoers who let it escape them will be missing one of the real events of the year." Stark Young, even more laudatory, said: "O'Neill has done what happens only once in a dramatic generation and almost never then, he has invented a fable. He has created a story that begins and moves and ends in a line so right, so just, so simple and inevitable that it might easily be taken for granted."

In 1947 Arthur Hopkins, reviewing the playwright's career, said: "In my opinion *The Hairy Ape* remains O'Neill's most important work. This is true O'Neill, the inspired dramatic poet. Here are perception, compassion and prophecy. The world today is full of desperate Yanks, frantically determined to destroy an inhuman scheme that provides no place for them.

"The shocking headlines of today were set up by O'Neill thirty years ago."

Like Gilpin in *The Emperor Jones*, Wolheim won immediate fame, but where the Negro actor had nowhere else to go, Wolheim was to move on to *What Price Glory?*, one of the decade's outstanding plays, and finally to stardom in Hollywood. "No actor we know," Burns Mantle said of his Yank, "could roar more effectively, swear with more freedom and give less offense, or suggest the pathetic groping of a primitive human better than he did." O'Neill himself was enthusiastic; he used to say that of all the actors in his plays, only three had completely realized what he had had in mind, two of whom were Wolheim and Gilpin.

After Ella's funeral Eugene tried to get his brother to sober up, then he himself went on a binge; it was several weeks before he could pull himself together and return to Provincetown. At first, realizing the despair and self-flagellation behind Jamie's wallowing with "the blonde pig" on the train, he was sympathetic, but he turned critical as he learned of his brother's behavior on the Coast. Early in April he received "a horrible document" (Mrs. Drummer's account of his mother's death), and shortly afterward a letter from Marion Reed to Jamie (forwarded by Frank Dart) that shows her in a particularly unflattering light. Mrs. Reed directed Jamie to write her "in full of your return trip — how Gene is — if anyone met you — how you have been *every minute* since leaving here. Very sincerely do I want to hear from you about all personal matters. You cannot slip away from me like that. Just how much you recall before leaving I don't know. Upon reaching N.Y. you were going to send back to me some or all dresses you packed and shoes if they were 5-½ size. You were going to send me some perfume. Instead I should like some more bath powders such as your mother used. . . . Anything at all, James, you do not give Agnes I shall be very glad to have. . . . I fear you have been miserably sick since arriving East and hope that your failure to write is not because you do not care to. . . . You thought you knew a lot. You terribly accused me and unjustly too. . . .

"Are you ever coming back? The wonderful thing wasn't much, was it? . . . I wish you were to be here to celebrate my birthday with me next month (April 25th). Had hoped for a good time. Fear like many other such plans all will go up in smoke. Every last one seems to fail me and my only pleasure is in doing something for the other fellow."

Ella O'Neill left a net estate of about one hundred and fifty thousand dollars, the largest part in New London realty, the rest being chiefly a building at 53 Columbus Avenue, in New York City, with an equity of twenty-six thousand dollars, and the Glendale tract, worth twenty thousand dollars. Frank Dart and the New London law firm of Hull, McGuire and Hull had special problems before they could file the will for probate, since Jamie for a time was either too drunk or too sick to sign the necessary papers; also, the attorneys had difficulty persuading Mrs. Reed to withdraw as executrix. Suspecting a plot to deprive her of a substantial fee, she made veiled threats in her letters. "While James O'Neill was here, before and after the death of his dear Mother," she wrote to the probate court judge, "he told me many things (and I wonder if he recalls them and would care to have them repeated to parties of whom he talked)" — she was referring, no doubt, to Eugene and Agnes. "I have information in my possession," she warned the lawyers, "that would make not only your firm sit up and take notice, but a number of others as well." And from a letter to Eugene: "I realize you are no doubt very deep in thot [*sic*] on your future plays and present successes but, may I beg of you to drop me a line. . . . I am very slow to anger but I am much longer to recover when once I consider I have been crossed. . . . " In the end Mrs. Reed yielded, after a personal plea from Jamie, and after learning that she would have to come East at her own expense to administer the estate.

Arthur Hopkins, as had been expected, decided to sponsor *The Hairy Ape* on Broadway, but at his insistence Mary Blair was being replaced as the steel heiress. Hopkins's choice was Carlotta Monterey, one of Broadway's foremost beauties, who usually played adventuresses, "the other woman," the type vanquished by the good wife shortly before the final curtain. Miss Monterey, who had a proud air and an emphatic voice, was dramatic-looking – glossy jet hair, a pale complexion, a fine profile, eyes of glowing darkness ("They looked," someone said, "like wet grapes"). The rest of her was less striking, for she had short legs, strong stubby hands, a figure inclined to plumpness. One friend of hers thought she appeared "Javanese or Russian, or something mysteriously exotic," while others, because of her stage name, took her to be Latin. Her real name was Hazel Neilson Tharsing, and she had been born in Oakland, California, to a Danish father and a mother of mixed origin, chiefly French Swiss, New York Dutch, and German. Several months younger than O'Neill, she eventually was to become his third and final wife.

"Carlotta," says Nicholas Joy, "was about the most nervous actress I've ever played with. She tore her handkerchief to pieces, was just as nervous after seven weeks, on the final night, as she was at the opening. She looked stunning and had a wonderful voice, but she was so nervous that it was a smart thing when she retired from the stage." Giving a woman's view, Ilka Chase, who once acted with her, writes that she "always dressed rather dowdily, but everything was expensive and of the finest material, and her shoes were made to order of special leathers, at great cost. She was the most immaculate creature I've ever known . . . even at a time when she was sweeping New York as the town's most sultry glamour queen, her apartment shone like a fresh-minted coin. Her bills were paid on the dot, she wore no jewels, and she dressed like a Dutch burgher's wife from the provinces. She was kind and funny, remarkably ribald, and she hated the theater."

Miss Monterey, according to her own account, was reluctant to be in *The Hairy Ape*: "I had already been in two things that season, and I was tired, I wanted to go out to California and see my mother and child. Another reason I didn't want to be in it was that I felt the company would hate me, since I was replacing one of their members. But Hoppy had been good to me and it was hard to refuse. He told me it was not a large part but an important one. She wasn't a real girl, in *The Hairy Ape*, but a symbol of a spoiled, neurotic one."

Her first meeting with O'Neill was inauspicious. He slipped into the Plymouth Theater one day as she was having trouble with a scene and "blowing" her lines. As the rehearsal ended she made some disparaging remarks about the play and its author, then joined Hopkins and a stranger seated next to him in the auditorium. Hopkins, in her account, said: " 'I want you to meet Mr. O'Neill,' and I said, 'How do you do?' to which he replied 'Hello' or something like that, but nothing more, no thank-you for going into his play, not even a go-to-hell. I whispered to Hoppy, 'Is this Eugene O'Neill?' I was so surprised. From all I'd heard, I expected someone in old pants, a sweater and needing a shave, but he was neat in a dark suit and white shirt, without a hair out of place. 'Don't listen to all the gossip,' Hoppy whispered back, 'just believe what you see yourself.' " On his side, O'Neill later told Jimmy Light that while he agreed with Hopkins that she looked the part better than Mary Blair, he was unimpressed by her acting.

At the première of *Anna Christie* he had lurked backstage — Pauline Lord noticed him hiding behind a large trunk — but for the uptown opening of *The Hairy Ape* on April 17 he bought his first dinner jacket, invited some racketeers and bootleggers he knew from the Village (he was curious about their response to a play dealing with the sort of characters they knew), and was in the front of the Plymouth to welcome them. "Gee, kid," one said, as the playwright grinned, "you sure look great in your soup-and-fish." The racketeers, who were sharply turned out in loud, checked jackets and flashy neckties, proved enthusiastic spectators. Sitting in the balcony they startled the house by clapping and cheering in the third scene when Yank, in response to the engineer's whistle from above, shouts: "Toin off dat whistle! Come down outa dere, yuh yellow, brass-buttoned, Belfast bum, yuh! Come down and I'll knock yer brains out! Yuh lousy, stinkin', yellow mut of a Catholic-moiderin' bastard!"

During the Village engagement no one had objected to the rough language of the play; after the play opened at the Plymouth, however, the police department, trying to close it, filed a complaint with the magistrate's court that it was "indecent, obscene and impure." Days later, the chief magistrate, after reading the script, dismissed the complaint without comment, but O'Neill said of the censorship attempt: "This stupidity was to be expected. Morons will be morons."

While a decision was pending on the complaint, the playwright received word from Columbia University, which administers the awards, that *Anna Christie* had won him a second Pulitzer Prize. "I seem," he jested to Oliver Sayler, "to be becoming the Prize Pup of Playwriting — the Hot Dog of Drama. When the Police Dept. isn't pinning the Obscenity Medal on my Hairy Ape chest, why then it's Columbia adorning the brazen bosom of Anna with the Cross of Purity. I begin to feel that there is either something all wrong with me or all right. Both the *Tribune* [a conservative newspaper] and *Solidarity* — the I.W.W. organ — praise me editorially — both for something I didn't mean. 'It's a mad world, my masters!' "

5

※

Echoing Strindberg

U NLIKE most writers, O'Neill never feared he would run dry; his
problem was not dreaming up something, not finding something
to write about, but deciding which of his story ideas had developed
sufficiently in mind to be realized on paper. In him the creative unconscious seems to have been exceptionally active, forever transmuting
his thoughts, feelings and fantasies – his responses to reality and experience – into material for his writings. Among the main sources of his
creativity, as with Joyce and Proust, the archetypal fictionists of our
century, was a biographical impulse, a penchant for looking back; while
his body was confined to the shapeless, ever-changing present, his mind
tended to voyage in the past, seeking significance and some kind of
pattern in his history, in various lives that had touched his own. His
fertility was such that he sometimes worked on two plays concurrently
and when he became stalled with one, would turn to the other. He had
enough story ideas, he often said, to keep him writing for the next ten
years.

In slightly over two years since his Broadway debut with *Beyond the
Horizon* he had been represented in the theater by eight long plays, such
worthy achievements as *Beyond the Horizon, The Emperor Jones, Anna
Christie* and *The Hairy Ape*, two creditable efforts, *Diff'rent* and *The
Straw*, and two jejune works, *Gold* and *The First Man*. During most of
1920 and 1921 he had been especially prolific, but the spring and summer of
1922 found him relatively unproductive, for his mother's death had left
him restless and uneasy. While he and his father had finally made their
peace, attaining some degree of rapport and mutual understanding, a
shadow had always lain between him and his mother: neither could ever
forget that his birth, by triggering her drug addiction, had caused her to

live a large part of her life in hell. Now that she was dead, their unresolved relationship was sealed forever. Eugene felt within him an aching void, a kind of suspension of his own life; without naming the cause, he told Eben Given that he felt as though he had died, that an essential part of himself was dead.

His brother, in a more extreme reaction to their common loss, was clearly bent on drinking himself to death. Holed up at the apartment on Thirty-fifth Street, Jamie, on May 20, 1922, lamented to Frank Dart: "You would not know me — I weigh less than 150 pounds and resemble the Governor as he lay in bed during his last illness. For five days and nights I threw up and threw up. . . . I never was so miserable or suffered so in my life. . . . I never was so near the 'Great Adventure.' "

Besides worrying over his brother, Eugene was depressed about the Provincetown Players. He had had a letter from Jimmy Light, he informed Fitzi on May 28, "relative to next year and the future in general and asking my cooperation. I had replied sort of hinting that his plan is impossible — legally. [Light wanted to organize a group to take over the theater.] The whole situation puts me in a hell of a position where no matter which way I jump or don't jump I tread upon a friend's corns. It makes me sick — this mess. Primarily, as you undoubtedly will agree, it is all Jig's fault. As I look back on it now, I can see where he drove all our best talent, that we had developed, away from the theater for daring to disagree with him. . . .

"I think the only thing to do is absolutely to reorganize from top to bottom as soon as Jig and Susan return. Otherwise, ignoble death by slow — or sudden — starvation. A meeting should be held in which all those who had ever been important PPs since the founding should be present. Everything in the past and everything for the future should be threshed out openly. Let the chips and insults fall where they may. And then a secondary meeting where everyone should be invited who is interested in our future — everyone with talents, ambitions, ideas, like Bobby Jones, Kenneth [Macgowan], [Norman] Bel Geddes, etc., for a fine experimental theater. . . . New blood — lots of it — or death. That's the alternative as I see it.

"Jig will probably oppose this. He will see it as a deliberate attempt to further ruin him by taking *his* theater out of *his* hands. But unless something of this kind is done a year from now, I am going to resign instanter, there is no good sitting up with a corpse. And I will be making the plea not on my own behalf — for through Hopkins I now have an outlet . . . but because I think it best for all concerned."

Except for revising *The Fountain,* which he expected Hopkins to produce in the fall, and cutting *The First Man* for publication, O'Neill accomplished little at Peaked Hill in 1922; he spent most of his time reading, loafing, swimming, and he also drank heavily, influenced to some extent by Jamie, who stayed at the station over two months and was scarcely ever sober. Provincetown had long been dry under local ordinance, but it was easy to bring in a supply from elsewhere; and now that Prohibition had invested liquor with the glamour and excitement of the forbidden, almost everyone was drinking. There were various ways of evading the ban: bootleggers, bathtub gin, home brew, a prescription for bonded stuff from a sympathetic doctor, or, when all else failed, a local concoction known as "Tiger Piss" which burned as it went down – it was best to gulp it quickly – and had a terrific wallop.

Indulging a desire ever since Prohibition to spend a hundred dollars on quality liquor, O'Neill splurged with the cooperation of a local bootlegger, and started drinking with a few cronies at Frank Shay's home. When Shay tried to kiss his daughter good-night, the child, repelled by his smell of whiskey, turned away; immediately furious, he began throwing dishes against the wall, a pastime in which Eugene joined him, and after the two had exhausted the supply of chinaware they completed making a shambles of the place by overturning all the furniture. Another night, in the presence of Bobby Jones and Terry Carlin at Peaked Hill, O'Neill urinated into a half-empty bottle of whiskey and then drank from it, an act that clearly tells of self-hatred, an impulse toward self-abasement. Jones shuddered with disgust when he told Macgowan about the incident.

For years Jones had been trying to persuade Eugene and Agnes to visit his friend Mabel Dodge in Taos, New Mexico, where she had married a Navajo, immersed herself in the life and culture of the Indians, and tried to get close to the simple life. But she still, as during the period when her Greenwich Village salon had helped foster a revolution in American culture and morals, liked to have celebrities and creative personages around her. Bobby, who thought that O'Neill would find spiritual solace in the Southwest, especially in the desert with its atmosphere of eternity, reported to Mabel from time to time on the progress of his campaign: "I'm doing very subtle and continuous work on the O'Neills to get us all out there for a long time. They are always full of all sorts of fears and dreads but I feel as though it might happen." . . . "Gene and Agnes and I plan to come to Taos just as the aspens begin to turn and stay all the fall and see all the Christmas and New Year's dances". . . . "I hear you are planning to have the O'Neills and D. H. Lawrence and me all together. I warn you that won't work". . . . "I shall slip away, probably for six weeks to Taos, but probably without the O'Neills who loathe the idea of Lawrence and are rendered will-less by liquor anyhow, so they can't decide anything. I worship the O'Neills, they are the noblest spirits there are here, and they know nothing about anything except suffering and hell generally."

Like someone out of Strindberg, Eugene's feelings toward Agnes were hopelessly ambivalent; he felt incomplete, lost, a shell of himself when they were apart ("He really loved her," says Thelma Given, "make no mistake about that"), but when he drank his undercurrent of hostility was likely to surface. At the Artists' Association ball, a costume affair, he attacked Agnes for wearing a black lace mantilla that had belonged to his mother; tearing it off her head, he declared: "Go back to the gutter you came from!" Equally melodramatic was his appearance: a dark mahogany from the sun, he wore a leopard-skin loincloth, an orange-red fright wig, such as circus clowns wear, and nothing else; he suggested someone ready for savage rites in the jungle. Aware of his mood that evening, most of his friends gave him a wide berth, but a Boston newspaperwoman approached him with a piece of paper and began rubbing it on one of his arms; mistaking his tan for makeup, she wanted a souvenir of the eminent playwright. He glanced at her sideways, as though at an insect, and then swung an arm so forcibly that she went reeling across the floor, her mouth puckered up in fright.

After the ball some were going to a party at the Wilbur Daniel Steeles', and the O'Neills were supposed to be among them, but he was nowhere to be found. As a group started to pile into Eben Given's car, an open touring model, they were startled to see Eugene, his eyes blazing insanely, rise suddenly in the rear. "Let's go!" he commanded Agnes, grabbing her by the hair. "We're going home!" and over her cries of protest began pulling her toward the dunes and Peaked Hill. In later years, as their friends discussed the pair, such outbursts of hostility and acts of violence loomed large in their reminiscences, yet the moments of discord were the exception, not the rule. There was little to recall or tell of the long periods when the two lived together more or less harmoniously.

The O'Neills entertained a great deal this summer, usually throwing their parties in a barn equipped with a phonograph and a bar, where the guests danced to the latest jazz numbers. Eugene liked dancing, but as one prone to arm-pumping he was more vigorous than graceful. One night a séance was held at the instance of Eben, Thelma and Mrs. Given, all of whom believed in psychic phenomena (the early 1920s witnessed a surge of interest in the occult), and O'Neill appeared to take the event seriously. As the group sat around the table, a rapping was heard, and Eben asked, "Who are you, how did you die?" Decoding the taps, Eben said that the body of a seaman who had drowned off Peaked Hill Bars had been recovered and laid out on the same table where the séance was being held. Years later there were conflicting accounts about the end of the evening but, according to one participant, Eugene asked the spirit what had finally happened to him, and he replied that his body had been thrown back into the sea.

The girl in charge of Shane this summer, Louise Enos, was surprised at the family's style of living at the isolated station. "You couldn't say that they roughed it out there," she recalls, "not when I worked for them. They had the best of everything, the finest linenware and silver [most of it had been Ella's], and they bought their food from Burch's, the best grocery in town. I had to wear a white starched uniform when I waited on them at dinner; afterward, they used to have their coffee in the big room before the fireplace." Her chief job, however, was attending to Shane, as neither O'Neill, who said it made him nervous to have the child around, nor Agnes spent much time with him.

There were guests practically all summer, principally Jamie, Terry Carlin (the two were, Jamie said, "boozin' buddies," though he kept trying to hide his liquor from the old Irishman), free-lance journalist Louis Kalonyme, whom all except O'Neill found rather sycophantic, and Agnes's sister Margery, an attractive, good-hearted girl who typed for O'Neill. (Touched by her sympathetic personality, Jamie professed, half seriously, to be in love with Margery and advised her to marry him; she would not have to wait very long, he said, to be his widow and heir.) Kalonyme was quartered in a shack so located that he had the first view of persons coming over the dunes. At sight of anyone, he used to hurry to warn O'Neill, whereupon the playwright would hide in his upstairs study until he knew who they were and whether he cared to see them; he had no patience with the autograph fans and celebrity hounds who sought him out, even at his oceanside retreat. In August the guests included Eugene Jr. and Barbara Burton, Agnes's daughter, a shy, affectionate child of seven who adored Shane ("He had a golden heart," she says, "as well as a golden head of hair") and found Eugene Jr., "fun and full of zest."

Young Eugene, who immediately fell in love with Peaked Hill, envied his half brother's living in such wild, beautiful surroundings, but most of all he hungered for his father's approval and affection. By now he not only had read every one of O'Neill's published plays but had written one himself, and after some hesitation, passed around his script; set in Russia, the play had, someone recalls, "violence and death in every act." Where formerly the boy had been lax in his studies and difficult — prior, that is, to meeting his father — he now was eager to excel and please. At Horace Mann preparatory school in the Bronx, which he entered in fall 1922, he proved a fine student, and later at Yale developed into a brilliant classicist with promise of an outstanding career. At bottom, though, he was discontent, in conflict with himself, troubled chiefly, it appears, by a feeling that he had been deprived of his rightful heritage as Eugene O'Neill's son. At the age of forty, after becoming a heavy drinker, he killed himself. In the long run he probably would have been better off had he remained ignorant of his real father, had they never met.

O'Neill's "regular attack of August melancholy" was particularly severe in 1922 since he already was in a disturbed state. Early in September Agnes went to New York to attend to several matters, chiefly to find a boarding school for her daughter Barbara. After word from Agnes that she missed him, Eugene replied: "I can't tell you how it bucked me up when your wire came — a little thing but big in meaning to my loneliness. There was some warmth in the sun after that. I spent the day — or most of it — on the beach and in the water. Tried to swim myself out of this accursed lethargy . . . and it was a good cure as far as my body was concerned. Tonight it feels healthily tired and has lost its abnormal tension. Now if my mind will only return from those dim regions in which it seems to wander, a haunted thing, I may be able to greet you on your return my old self again, able to help and not hinder you in deciding on our future whereabouts, etc. . . . I love you with every bit of worth in me!"

Though his low spirits and his drinking were largely responsible for his relatively unproductive summer, the succession of guests seems to have been a contributing factor. "Long-forgotten progeny and other relatives, each with their own problems," he wrote Macgowan on September 23, "made a congregation out here which rather scrambled the mental eggs — at any rate, deferred any hatching." Voicing a similar complaint to Saxe Commins, he added, "I've done a lot of rewriting on *The Fountain* . . . [and] think I have improved it immensely.

"Just what I'll start to work on now I don't know yet. I feel in a sort of scrambled mood and will have to wait until the right moment comes for resuming the drama. There are a lot of things I want to do but I don't seem to be able to make a decision which to tackle first."

Only days later he began working on *Welded,* which he thought "demands evolving into some new form of its own if I am to say what I want to. My conception of it as Strindberg *Dance of Death* formula seems hard to fit on," he informed Macgowan. "But I have no inkling yet of the 'belonging method.'" His reference to the Swedish author is significant — not on technical grounds, as his words suggest, but in regard to content, for *The Dance of Death* concerns a husband and wife who are mortal enemies and try to destroy one another. *Welded,* one of O'Neill's most concentrated works, was an attempt, in a kind of exorcism, to come to terms with the conflict between him and Agnes, the ugly passions that sometimes flared up in their marriage. It expresses some of his deepest feelings and — despite what he apparently considered an affirmative ending — darkest forebodings about their union.

Written in the fall and winter of 1922–1923, *Welded* tells of a playwright, Michael Cape, and his actress wife Eleanor, trapped in a love-hate relationship — a pair closely based on Eugene and Agnes. The author's description of the thirty-five-year-old Cape (O'Neill was now thirty-four) is a striking self-likeness: "His unusual face is a harrowed battlefield of supersensitiveness, the features at war with one another — the forehead of a thinker, the eyes of a dreamer, the nose and mouth of a sensualist. One feels a powerful imagination tinged with somber sadness — a driving force which can be sympathetic and cruel at the same time." As for Eleanor ("blue-gray eyes . . . high, prominent cheekbones . . . the first impression of her whole personality is one of charm"), she is similarly true to her model. One is practically eavesdropping on the O'Neills in the following exchange, as Cape says: "You can't imagine how wonderful it's been up in the country. There's just enough winter in the air to make one energetic. No summer fools about. Solitude and work. I was happy — that is, as happy as I ever can be without you." Eleanor, sarcastically: "Thanks for that afterthought — but do you expect me to believe it? When you're working I might die and you'd never know it."

At another point, Cape: "I've grown inward into our life. But you keep trying to escape as if it were a prison. You feel the need of what is outside. I'm not enough for you." Eleanor: "You insist that I have no life outside you. You hate my need of easy, casual associations. . . . You're jealous of everything and everybody. You're too severe."

As *Welded* opens, Cape has just returned to town and their reunion is rapturous, for a few moments, then discord arises and shortly escalates to open hostility. Though O'Neill wanted, apparently, to display the two as equally at fault, the play itself indicates that the husband (as seems true with the O'Neills) was chiefly to blame in this war of the sexes. Cunningly, deftly, though seemingly unconscious of what he is about, Cape forces his wife onto the defensive, arousing in her guilt and self-hatred, till she feels impelled to fight back. "It's so beautiful," she says of their love, "and then — suddenly I'm being crushed. I feel a cruel presence in you paralyzing me, creeping over my body, possessing it . . . then grasping at some last inmost thing which makes me — my soul — demanding to have that, too! I have to rebel with all my strength. . . . And yet I love you! It's because I love you! If I'm destroyed, what is left to love you, what is left for you to love?"

After she falsely confesses to a love affair, Cape, rushing out, declares that he will "stamp [his love] into the vilest depths! . . . I'll murder it — and be free!" In a semihysterical state he picks up a streetwalker who is bewildered by his talk, a torrent of venom and passion, of self-hatred and disgust with the world. Realizing finally that he and Eleanor are inextricably bound together, that they are "welded," he returns home. Paralleling his night with the prostitute, Eleanor tries to give herself to a theatrical producer who has long loved her (he is based to some extent on Kenneth Macgowan at a projected later age) but, like her husband, she cannot be unfaithful. The play ends on a note of febrile ecstasy as they accept their sadomasochistic relationship and whatever the future may bring. " . . . we'll torture and tear," Cape says, "and clutch for each other's souls! — fight — fail and hate again — (*He raises his voice in aggressive triumph*) but! fail with pride — with joy!" Eleanor: "Yes."

In a study of Edgar Allan Poe (with whom O'Neill felt a kinship), D. H. Lawrence says some illuminating things about the dark underside of love, particularly the danger of loving to excess, as he traces a connection between Poe's writings and what Lawrence held to be Poe's basically destructive feelings toward his wife. Certain of Lawrence's commentary seems to apply equally to O'Neill:

"Love is the mysterious vital attraction which draws things closer together, closer, closer together. For this reason sex is the actual crisis of love. For in sex the two blood-systems, in the male and female, concentrate and come into contact, the merest film intervening. Yet if the intervening film breaks down, it is death." (In *Welded* Cape says to his wife: "You and I — year after year — together — forms of body merging into one form. . . . I've become you! You've become me! One heart! One blood! Ours!" Similarly, before Eugene and Agnes were married, he told her: "I wanted you alone . . . in an aloneness broken by nothing. Not even by children of our own. . . . I want it to be not you and me, but *us, one* being, not two.")

"So there you are," Lawrence continues. "There is a limit to everything. There is a limit to love.

"The central law of all organic life is that each organism is intrinsically isolate and single in itself.

"The moment its isolation breaks down, and there comes an actual mixing and confusion, death sets in. [Eleanor, referring to the start of their romance, says: "Oh, it was beautiful madness! I lost myself. I began living in you. I wanted to die and become you!" Cape: "And I, you!"].

"But the secondary law of all organic life is that each organism only lives through contact with other matter, assimilation, and contact with other life, which means assimilation of new vibrations, nonmaterial. Each individual organism is vivified by intimate contact with fellow organisms: up to a certain point.

"So man. He breathes the air into him, he swallows food and water. But more than this. He takes into him the life of his fellow men, with whom he comes into contact, and he gives life back to them. This contact draws nearer and nearer, as the intimacy increases. When it is a whole contact, we call it love. Men live by food, but die if they eat too much. Men live by love, but die, or cause death, if they love too much. . . ."

An important biographical document, *Welded* reveals more about its author than he probably intended or ever realized. Agnes herself has called it "a carbon copy" of their relationship. At the same time, unfortunately, it is a repetitious, wearisome drama. The whole thing is pitched so high that it seems to have been written more with exclamation marks than with words, as though the author, finding language inadequate, sought to convey his meaning through sheer intensity. At one point Cape, half sobbing, exclaims: "I want to say so much what I feel but I can only stutter like an idiot!"

In concentrating on the pair's tortured relations and excluding everything not absolutely essential to his communiqué from the marital battlefront, O'Neill went too far. He sought to give the heart of the matter, to create a drama overpowering in its single-minded focus, but instead produced a bloodless duel of words. Despite all the talk about love and anguish and loneliness, none of it seems real, none of it touches us, since the protagonists are unreal; they are abstractions, incarnations of O'Neill's feelings about Agnes and how he imagined hers about him. He was so preoccupied with probing and analyzing that he failed to create characters with the breath of life, characters who could arouse our concern.

Beyond its biographical content, *Welded* is of interest for its foreshadowing of certain of his other plays, for dealing briefly with material that he would exploit more fully later on — a recurrent tendency in O'Neill that establishes a greater continuity among his works than may be apparent on the surface. The streetwalker, for example, whom Cape picks up is first shown realistically as typical of her kind, then, in a touch of romanticism, as defensively proud, and finally as having an instinctive sort of wisdom; she is a preliminary sketch for the idealized prostitute in *The Great God Brown*. Similarly, *Strange Interlude*, which has the characters disclosing their unvoiced thoughts, is prefigured by the scene in which Cape and his wife "speak, ostensibly to the other, but showing by their tone it is a thinking aloud to oneself, and neither appears to hear what the other has said." There is, finally, a parallel between something Eleanor says to Cape (". . . you're such a relentless idealist. That was exactly what drew me to you in those first days. I'd lost faith in everything. Your love saved me") and the way Elsa in *Days Without End* feels about her husband, a "romantic idealist": "I have my share of scars. But the wounds are all healed . . . John's love has done that for me."

As the time approached to leave Peaked Hill station in fall 1922, O'Neill, who had tired of Provincetown proper, was undecided about his next move. "Our plans for the winter remain chaotic," he informed Macgowan on September 23. "We will probably, in a fit of desperation, wind up in China. I'd like that, too, while Europe somehow means nothing to me. Either the South Seas or China, say I. I'm willing to omit the sophisticated stage. . . . But until *The Fountain* is definite, all plans are useless."

His hopes for the 1922–1923 season were to be disappointed, for Arthur Hopkins was unable to find a suitable Ponce de León. Both John Barrymore, whom the author had particularly wanted, and his brother Lionel rejected the script; John was to play Hamlet in a Hopkins presentation (his Dane would be hailed as the greatest of the American stage in decades), while Lionel, disenchanted with the theater, was starting to concentrate on film-acting. Jacob Ben-Ami, who had won praise on Broadway after an apprenticeship in the Yiddish theater of Second Avenue, was eager to play Ponce de León but his accent made him unsuitable. "Who can you think of," the author asked Macgowan "for that part?" Two years later, discussing the still-unproduced drama with Stark Young, he said of his father's generation: "Here's the difference:

the actors those days would not have understood my play but they could act it; now they understand it but can't act it."

Despite his talk of China and the South Seas, O'Neill yearned to put down roots, to "belong" somewhere. Earlier this year he had bought his first automobile, a red custom-made touring car, and now he drove around in Connecticut seeking a place within easy commuting distance of New York. Although he had not yet received anything from his mother's estate, he was in better financial shape than ever before, earning in all about forty-four thousand dollars in 1922. The largest part of the income came from *Anna Christie;* in addition to royalties from the Broadway run of one hundred and seventy-seven performances and a road tour still continuing, *Anna* had been sold to the movies for twenty-five thousand dollars, with the sum split equally between the playwright and his producer. (Released in 1923, with Blanche Sweet as Anna, the film impressed O'Neill as a "delightful surprise . . . remarkably well acted and directed, and in spirit an absolutely faithful transcript." Remade years later for Greta Garbo's talking debut, the script brought the author an additional seventy-five hundred dollars. While he considered "the lady was damn good in her work," he never saw the sound version, figuring it would be "all to the Garbo and very little of the O'Neill left in it.") His other chief sources of income this year were *The Hairy Ape*, the publication of his plays, and the little-theater presentations of his works.

For a time the playwright thought of buying Stormfield, the Italian-style villa Mark Twain had built in Redding, Connecticut; in youth Eugene had read a good deal of Twain and he fancied the prospect of living in the celebrated author's former home. He was talked out of it, however, by Eben Given and Wilbur Daniel Steele, who argued that the place needed extensive repairs that would be costly. After further search the playwright bought for thirty-two thousand five hundred dollars Brook Farm in Ridgefield, an estate of thirty acres dominated by a handsome white clapboard house of Colonial style with fifteen rooms. The property, half in woodland, included an apple orchard, a pond, brooks, and a flower garden with a fountain — all in all, the sort of place Ella and Jamie, who had looked down on the modest Monte Cristo cottage, had desired in New London.

In keeping with their new style of living, the O'Neills hired a Japanese butler named Kawa, a man for the outdoor work, Vincent Bedini, and Bedini's wife for part-time help in the house. As befit a country squire, Eugene, who took great pride in being an O'Neill, a descendant of the early kings of Ireland, acquired an Irish wolfhound that he named Finn

Mac Cool after the legendary warrior-ruler in ancient Ireland. A huge gray formidable-looking creature, Finn was gentle with people, especially children, allowing Shane and Agnes's daughter Barbara to try riding him like a pony, but he was an instinctive killer of livestock. Margery Boulton was walking him one day when he broke away at the sight of some chickens and within minutes had killed over a score; he next charged at a herd of cattle but was thwarted when the animals, backed against a wall, lowered their heads to form a semicircle of horns.

Bringing the past with him into his new home, O'Neill fell prey to memories as he unloaded barrels of his father's books and theatrical effects. The possessions had been in storage ever since an auction in New London was cut short because of inadequate bidding; one woman, for instance, paid fifty cents for a trunk full of clothes and costume jewelry from James O'Neill's production of *Monte Cristo*. Following the abortive sale, held not long after her husband's death, Ella had given some costumes to friends, who cut them up for party clothes for their children; but most of the effects ended up in Ridgefield, where they became playthings for Shane and his young friend, Silvio Bedini. The movie of *Monte Cristo* was among the contents of the barrels, but it is uncertain whether Eugene ever screened it: Jimmy Light says that he did, but, according to Macgowan, he refrained for fear the movie, including his father's performance, would strike him as ludicrous.

In November, as the family was establishing itself at Brook Farm, Eugene heard from C. Hadlai Hull, an attorney for the estate, that his brother had been drunk in New London for weeks and was involved with a pair of notorious gamblers. Hull feared that the two might defraud Jamie of four thousand dollars he was about to receive as down payment for the Glendale property, which had been sold for eighteen thousand dollars. Eugene, who did not reply till December 13, a full month later, said apologetically: "My only excuse is that I have been so busy winding up arrangements for the production of my plays in London next spring [*Anna Christie* was the only one definitely scheduled], and getting settled in my new place up here, that I have not wanted to think about this trouble about my brother.

"I don't know what to say. . . . It seems there is nothing I can do about it. The last I heard of him he was still in pretty bad shape. In New York he phoned to me, but I have not seen him. I had too much else on my mind at the time. And I have learned by experience that the more I should urge him toward one course of action, the more obstinate and determined he will be to do the opposite. So what can I do?"

O'Neill never considered having his brother live with him, since a perpetually drunken Jamie would interfere with his work. Also, Jamie had grown venomous toward Agnes; he suspected that she resented his inheriting the Glendale property and was poisoning Eugene's mind against him. The problem of Jamie was settled for a time through Harold DePolo, the pulp writer, who was an old friend of both brothers; after talking things over with Eugene, DePolo, who had just rented a house in Darien, Connecticut, took in Jamie for an indefinite stay. Harold, himself a hard drinker, and his wife Helen enjoyed Jamie's company so long as he behaved himself but other times found him impossible. "He had the wittiest, most ruthless tongue I ever knew," says DePolo. "He'd find out your weaknesses and play on them all night. The next morning he couldn't remember what he'd done and would ask, 'Was I terrible?' 'Yes, you were.' 'Christ! It's the old spirit of the perverse in me again.' "

He drank constantly and used to stand before a mirror for long periods, gazing at himself with loathing, while he called himself every foul name he could think of. Deprecatory about virtually everyone — the lone exception was Ella, whom he always referred to as "my sainted mother" — he perpetually ran down Eugene, jealously claiming that he had given him the ideas for many of his plays. But Christmas Day, sober and in a reminiscent mood, he played marbles on the floor with the DePolos' two children and, with tears in his eyes, recalled that this was the first Christmas he had ever spent in a home; all the other ones, he said, had been a dreary round of hotel rooms, trains and backstage as he toured with his father.

William F. Batterham, another guest at Darien, thought that Jamie possessed more native ability than Eugene, that he could have gone far in the theater, either as actor or writer, had he applied himself. "He had one of the most fertile minds I've ever come across, the fastest repartee," Batterham says. "He could make up stories, scenes, whole acts at the drop of a hat, and sometimes he entertained us by playing three or four parts from one of his father's old plays — and doing them brilliantly. But usually he was hard to take. He monopolized the conversation, he wanted to be the center of attention all the time."

Formerly a natty dresser, always freshly groomed, Jamie now slopped around in pajamas, overcoat, a derby and, since his ankles were swollen from drink, bedroom slippers. If he wasn't announcing to the world that he was "stinko profundo," he was likely to say, "Where's Helen? I want to fill her with pups!" He had been in Darien only a short time when the DePolos regretted that they had ever invited him (according to Agnes, he was paying the household expenses), but they were reluctant to ask him to leave. Smoking in bed one evening, he set the mattress on fire, and Helen, who was alone with him in the house, rushed it outside.

The situation came to a head on the night of February 16, 1923, when Jamie and the DePolos attended a performance in Stamford of the touring *Anna Christie*. After making a nuisance of himself by repeatedly coughing on a woman in front of him, Jamie suddenly stood up in mid-performance and declared: "Why shouldn't my brother, the author, know all about whores?" – then went on to make a scurrilous reference to Agnes and Helen. As the actors paused momentarily, confused by the voice from the auditorium, and people craned their necks, DePolo rushed him out of the theater, tongue-lashing him all the while. The following morning DePolo and Batterham dumped him onto a train for New London, after which Harold telephoned an account to Eugene. Eugene immediately wired C. Hadlai Hull that his brother had made a "most disgraceful scene" at the Stamford theater and would be arrested if he returned to the area. "Any measures however drastic you see fit to take to restrain him in New London will have my full approval."

Although ordinarily he was at peace with himself while writing, even relatively happy, *Welded* had the opposite effect on him. This time he was not dramatizing and fictionalizing material from the past but dealing with a painful aspect of the present – the discord in his relations with Agnes. The play, in other words, had him reliving the unhappy moments that inspired it; for a time he was in a "vale of despair." Ordinarily, too, he never drank while engaged on a play, but he weakened a few times during the writing of *Welded*. While Agnes was in New York one day, he worked himself into such a rage as he drank that he cut up every photograph of her he could find and scattered the pieces on the floor. He also kicked a hole in a Thomas Eakins portrait of her father, a quiet, retiring painter who had been a protégé of Eakins; not that Eugene had anything against Mr. Boulton – he actually was fond of him – but he knew that Agnes cherished the painting. When she returned home, he confronted her at the door, demanding to know "what man" she had seen in the city.

Once *Welded* was finished, O'Neill became easier to live with, but its subject matter, the reality behind it, bulked too large in his life for him to view the play with any degree of objectivity. While conceding that the first draft might have "preliminary imperfections," he thought it "ought to be the very finest, deepest, and the most vital thing" he had written. Both George Jean Nathan and H. L. Mencken, however, found the drama below the author's usual standard. Stubbornly maintaining that *Welded* was his "best yet," the playwright replied to Nathan on May 7: "I'm glad to get Mencken's letter but I must confess the greater part of his comment seems irrelevant as criticism of my play. To point out its weakness as realism (in the usual sense of the word) is to confuse what is obviously part of my deliberate intention.

"Damn that word 'realism'! When I first spoke to you of the play as a last word in 'realism,' I meant something 'really real' in the sense of being spiritually true, not meticulously life-like. . . . Mencken says: 'The man haranguing the streetwalker is surely not a man who ever actually lived.' Well, he surely is to me and, what is more to my point, he is also much more than that. [Here O'Neill falls into the sort of mystical pretentiousness he was prone to in discussing the deeper meanings of his plays.] He is Man dimly aware of recurring experience, groping for the truth behind the realistic appearance of himself, and of love and life. For the moment his agony gives him vision of the true behind the real.

"I can't agree that the speeches in this scene are 'banal.' . . . In fact, I'm positive it's the deepest and truest, as well as the best-written scene I've ever done. Perhaps it isn't 'plausible' — but the play is about love as a life-force, not as an intellectual conception, and the plausibility of reasons don't apply. Reason has no business in the theater anyway, any more than it has in a church. They are either below — or above it."

Viewing *Welded* more soberly several months later, he called it "an attempt at the last word in intensity in the truth about love and marriage. Not that I pretend to have succeeded but I think the result is interesting." Ten years later he lumped it together with *The Fountain, The First Man* and *Gold* as "too painfully bungled" to merit reviving.

In spring 1923, as the Hopkins production of *Anna Christie* was about to open in London, O'Neill appeared on the verge of winning a reputation abroad commensurate with his name at home. Ever since *Beyond the Horizon*, but especially after *The Emperor Jones*, Europe had been hearing of a new American playwright of originality and talent as foreign critics and theater people returned to their countries with enthusiastic reports. Also, Macgowan and Jones, touring the Continent in 1922 to gather material for a book, had helped to spread the word in their meetings with Reinhardt and other impresarios. By this time O'Neill was known to English theater fans, for his plays were now being published in London (he took the surname of his protagonist in *Welded* from Jonathan Cape, his British publisher) and several of his lesser works had been given in a small theater club. But *Anna Christie,* with the original cast nearly intact and headed for a regular West End theater, was to be his first major overseas presentation and the forerunner of others scheduled on the Continent.

The London first-nighters, though notoriously reserved, were "wildly demonstrative" over *Anna Christie*, and the following day the critics hailed both the cast, above all Pauline Lord, and the playwright. "What Walt Whitman is to poetry," one said, "Eugene O'Neill is to drama." Nevertheless, the London presentation, like a portent of O'Neill's record in Europe for the next several years, had a disappointing run. In Berlin, at a version that had Anna shooting herself at the end, audiences were openly bored, chiefly because of an inept translation by a Hungarian. "Apart from his admiration of the play," said German journalist Rudolf Kommer, "his qualifications as a literary go-between were limited to a Berlitz acquaintance with English and German. What he may have guessed in English, he was utterly unable to express in German." For the engagement, which lasted only three performances, the playwright received from inflation-wracked Germany a royalty of 7,840,000,000 marks – or, in American currency, $1.39.

A Berlin production of *The Emperor Jones*, even though it boasted a good translation and cast, also failed. The trouble was, according to Kommer, that the play-makers "thought they could only cope with the primeval forest by entrusting its execution to a neo-Expressionist of the most radical brand. The result was so perplexing that even an Elizabethan signboard, if added to the scenery, could not have convinced the audience that it was sitting in front of a forest. Furthermore, concentrating upon the spiritual side of the play, the producers overlooked the fact that Jones's revolver was supposed to go off from time to time – and so it didn't. Strange are the ways of producers."

In Moscow *Anna Christie* did achieve a long run but without adding a kopeck to the author's income, since the Russians did not believe in paying royalties to the authors of capitalistic, exploitive nations. O'Neill's sole dividend was some amusement when his friend Michael Gold, who divided his time between writing and radical politics, wrote him from Russia about the production: "The first act opens in a saloon with a crowd of Russian roughneck men in leather coats and blouses, women in shawls and red gypsy kerchiefs, drinking and singing 'Chinatown, My Chinatown' . . . from which they switch to a queer version of 'Yankee Doodle Dandy' done gypsy style and accompanied by a guitar and concertina. A lot of rough humor, horseplay and laughter – and then opens the real play. Johnny the Priest in long black ulster and immense derby with a high crown. The old captain with white side whiskers, a pea jacket and red muffler . . . Anna a blond, loud, breezy female in loud summer clothes. . . . The whole was played at about six times the New York tempo — very melodramatic and filled with Russian gestures and moods."

Moving back to Peaked Hill each summer entailed a great amount of work — shoveling away the sand, piled up by the winter storms, that almost buried the station to its roof; lugging supplies, equipment and personal possessions across the dunes; replacing broken pipes; inducing a temperamental water pump to function properly. Usually O'Neill was out of humor at such times, but he was in high spirits as the family returned in June 1923; he had been so troubled while writing *Welded* that his present mood was perhaps a natural, pendulumlike reaction. "It's wonderful," he wrote to Fitzi, "same old sea & all. Haven't started working yet. Too full of the joy of just being alive. Haven't known it except in spare moments in years. Seem to be ten years younger — all pep! . . . a regular rebirth from the vale of despair which about reached its worst when you were out at Ridgefield in December."

Shortly after resettling by the ocean he had a letter from Maxwell Bodenheim, whom he had not seen in years, congratulating him on his success. O'Neill replied on July 5 that they had not met in such a long time because he visited the city as little as possible and "avoided the Village more and more. Why? Well, the saddest part of the 'acclaim' you mention is not that I take it seriously but that other people do. . . . Some hate me for it, or envy me, or like me, or use me, or flatter me — all for it — while they seem absolutely unable to see the me they knew ever again. Yet I'm sure I'm still that 'me,' and that I'm lonely, and that it is these stupid folk who change me by their suspicions into a suspicious one. Not that I don't realize all this is inevitable — but it's distressing and I've learned for my sensitive skin's sake to duck and dodge. . . .

"So much for the 'well-lit corridors' you assume for me. You know deeper than that. All relative, no? God's gas flickers alike for all in the same dimness. I suspect we're all acrobats and I know we enjoy being tired. At all events, it doesn't matter much, does it? We work. The rest is nonsense, as Hamlet might have said.

"Writing to you makes me feel a bit hilariously nutty, Max. Much gratitude to you. Everything is so sane these days. Not that I complain. On the contrary I have sedulously willed it so — for work's sake."

Not long after he had finished *Welded* another project began to take shape in his thoughts. "I can't write plays fast enough," he said, "to keep up with the production-imagination section of my 'bean'!" He had always been fascinated by the Orient but had never thought of setting a play there until, researching for *The Fountain*, he ran across references to Marco Polo that aroused his interest (in *The Fountain* Ponce de León expects to fight in "lands beyond strange seas — Cipango and Cathay — the cities of gold that Marco Polo saw"). As O'Neill's image of Polo came into focus, it owed less to the telescope of history than to the satiric eyes of Sinclair Lewis, the Lewis who immortalized the prototypal go-getting American businessman as "Babbitt." Under the playwright's scheme for *Marco Millions*, his eponymous hero was to be a twentieth-century Babbitt peddling his wares between thirteenth-century Venice and Cathay.

Where the author had suffered in the writing of *Welded*, the new play was a "grand pleasure." He read everything available on Marco Polo, took "millions of notes," and bought recordings of Chinese music, which he listened to for hours at a time. Late in the summer, after writing a lengthy scenario and the opening scene, he set the project aside to concentrate on plans for reactivating the MacDougal Street playhouse.

When Jig and Susan left early in 1922, they intended to return in about a year and authorized Edna Kenton to cast their votes, during their absence, as executive-committee members of the Provincetown Players. Once in Greece, though, they began to put down roots, and Jig, being Jig, went to excess. He grew a luxurious beard and mustache, wore the traditional garb that the nationals brought out only for holidays, and spent much time at the outdoor cafés drinking the strong resin-flavored wine and making friends with his enthusiasm for everything Grecian. He went through manic phases — up one day, the next one down — that are reflected in his correspondence. "The real Greeks of today," he wrote to Eugene and Agnes, "are shepherds & sailors — as always. They are bed-rock-better than Hell-Hole's best. And God what a language! Two or three times as good as classic Greek. On Parnassus the women spin and delve. The men devote themselves to the more important matter of singing — when just drunk enough. They can stay just drunk enough for 12 hours. Come."

But another day, in another mood, he unburdened himself to Edna Kenton: "*My* Provincetown Players never swerved ½ inch right or left for money in that New York hog trough. . . I have had an automatic pistol revolver for two years — I have lived with that implement . . . now that youth is gone, I'm keen for a good cause to die in."

Once it became evident that the Cooks would remain abroad indefinitely, O'Neill took the initiative about resuming activities on MacDougal

Macgowan, O'Neill and Jones

Jones, Macgowan and O'Neill

Jig Cook in Greece

Street. As he told attorney Harry Weinberger, he thought the new regime should emphasize "*experiment in production,* utilizing any play ancient or modern, foreign or native, to that end." By "production," he meant "experiment in acting, directing, scenery — everything. It is to be a directors' theater, as it had been a playwrights'." He was in constant touch with Kenneth Macgowan, whom he wanted to head the group, and with Bobby Jones, who intended to take part. Tired of "the old bickering democracy," he told Macgowan: "To hell with democracy! — Director with a capital D! — you'll need to use all you can extract of theater blood from our eager frames but never let anyone think his blood is what keeps the theater going — one of the old PP got to think that [a reference, presumably, to Jig Cook]. When each became sure of it the theater up and died of anemia which insulted each so each blamed everyone else!"

One point of difference between them was that Macgowan wanted to retain the name of the Provincetown Players, figuring it would stimulate subscription sales, and O'Neill was opposed. The issue was complicated and sharpened by the obstructionist tactics of Edna Kenton, who considered Macgowan "sweet" but a lightweight, disdained Fitzi for trying to get along with everyone, and thinking O'Neill overrated, resented his success. She was determined that the new theater group should not be endowed in name with a distinction she felt had been achieved by the Provincetown Players largely through the work of Jig and Susan. In a voluminous correspondence she kept the Cooks informed of everything going on or planned, giving a critical, biased account, and they in turn wrote back objections.

"Frankly, things are happening a bit as I had dreaded," Eugene complained to Macgowan in fall 1923, "and I already see a wild-eyed Jig Cook returning hot-foot from Greece to denounce the kidnapping of his child. . . . I by no means share in the belief about the commercial value of 'PP.' They were absolutely dead financially when the *Ape* came — and no one knew that better than the subscribers. I believe the name will be a hindrance rather than an asset. Personally, the mere idea of being *actively* associated where any of the old bickering has a legal right to operate kills all my interest instanter. I won't be mixed up in any organization which has to straddle the old and the new. . . . After all, when it comes down to it, I feel this new thing has no right to the PP name. The new group stands for an entirely opposed policy to the old — or so I have understood it."

Critical also of a manifesto Kenneth had drafted for the press and potential subscribers, his letter continues: "Just give them a promise that something mysterious, new, daring, beautiful and amusing is going to be done by actors, authors, designers — that the purpose of this theater is to give imagination and talent a new chance for such development — ask them to subscribe because you promise them things which they *can't* see anywhere else — and then keep your promise to them! . . . I think you ought to inject a lot of the Kamerny [the adventurous Moscow theater] spirit into your statement with the emphasis on imaginative new interpretations, experimentation in production. That's what the theater ought to mean in New York today, Kenneth! That's what N.Y. lacks right now! That's the gap we ought to fill. . . . But where is it in your manifesto? Nowhere! And do you know why? Because that old man of the sea, PP is on your neck. You're trying to collect subscriptions in the name of a dead issue, in the spirit of a straddling compromise.

"Don't mind if this letter is a bit carping in spots. I'd like to see this a real Big Thing, Kenneth, for you as much as for myself, for the Theater more than for either of us."

6

❖

Legacy from Jamie

O'NEILL, who had last seen his brother at the DePolos' in Darien, kept in touch with him mainly through the attorneys of their estate. In New London Jamie, becoming the town scandal, figured in drunken scrapes, threw around his money, and hung out with unsavory characters — bootleggers, gamblers and, though by now he had lost all sexual desire, prostitutes — until his health collapsed. Nearly blind from "bad booze" and temporarily irrational, he was removed in June 1923 to an asylum at Brewster's Neck, Norwich, as word spread around town that he had been taken there raving and in a straitjacket. About a month later, after his condition had improved, he was transferred to the Riverlawn Sanitarium in Paterson, New Jersey, which accommodated alcoholics and mild mental cases.

Darien, it turned out, was the last time Eugene ever saw his brother alive; after Jamie's death Eugene, trying to ease his sense of guilt, criticized Agnes for not persuading him to visit his brother at the sanatorium, but at the time he was loath to go. He knew Jamie had set out to destroy himself, he was convinced there was nothing he could do about it (but he sent a specialist to Paterson several times to try and help), and he preferred to avoid a reunion that could only be painful on both sides. Angry from frustration and helplessness, he complained to Saxe Commins on August 7: "What the hell can be done about him is more than I can figure. He'll only get drunk again, after he gets out and then he'll be all blind."

Even at Riverlawn Jamie managed to obtain liquor; during a visit from his cousin Philip Sheridan and Alex Campbell, another New Londoner, he brought out a bottle hidden under his bed and they all had a drink. He had aged years in a period of months and looked like a burned-out old man — thin, pale, his whole body atremble — though Sheridan, who saw him in September, thought he was "on the road to recovery." In mid-October, paralleling his mother's terminal period, he suffered a stroke and grew progressively weaker. He had been out of his mind for days when the end came on November 8, from arteriosclerosis and cerebral apoplexy, two months after his forty-fifth birthday.

Shortly before Jamie's death Eugene had gone on a binge that began in Ridgefield and ended with Agnes tracking him down in Greenwich Village. Still in bad shape when informed about Jamie, he retreated into himself, heartsick at the thought of his brother's wasted life, and left the final arrangements to Agnes. Accompanied by her sister Margery, she was dismayed to find at the funeral parlor in New York that Jamie, who had had a large wardrobe, was dressed only in underwear; all his other clothes had been stolen somewhere along the line. The undertaker, prepared for such emergencies, had a stock of "half-suits," only the front half, and dickeys — a sartorial convenience that struck Agnes as an obscene kind of economy, particularly for someone who had been a snappy dresser. When the undertaker asked her about the coffin, all she could think of was an old-time song in which the phrase "a plain pine coffin" recurs. "A plain pine coffin!" the undertaker exclaimed. "Why, you can't do that. This is James O'Neill's son!"

Finally, after Jamie, in a half-suit, was stowed in a proper coffin, services were held an hour late at St. Stephen's Church on East Twenty-eighth Street before a handful of impatient mourners. Using his hangover as an excuse to escape the worst of a painful day, Eugene neither attended the rites nor accompanied Agnes and Margery to New London, where Jamie was buried in the family plot in St. Mary's Cemetery, close to his lifelong enemy, his father, and his "sainted mother."

"I have lost my Father, Mother and only brother within the past four years," Eugene lamented to a friend. "Now I'm the only O'Neill of our branch left. But I've two sons to 'carry on.' However, neither of them will be pure Irish, so I must consider myself the real last one. It makes me feel old and a bit weary sometimes."

As sole heir to an estate with a net valuation of about one hundred and forty thousand dollars, he seemed more prosperous than he actually was, for much of the New London property was in such poor condition that it was hard to rent or sell; he was to have heavy legal, administrative and other expenses before all the property was sold, over a period of years, and in the end would receive substantially less than he had once anticipated.

Probably his most important legacy from Jamie was not the other half of the estate but a sense of freedom, with Jamie's death, to exploit the family history any way he chose. Indeed, he had already embarked on such a course in the final months of his brother's life, knowing that only Jamie, who would never be able to read the play, could detect the biography behind the fiction of *All God's Chillun Got Wings*, the story of a white girl, neurotic, unstable, full of fears, married to a black man who is trying to climb in the world. The girl is named Ella, the man Jim, names that were not chosen lightly, for the couple embody some of the playwright son's ideas of his parents and their relationship.

When O'Neill suspended work on *Marco Millions* at Peaked Hill, he had intended to resume shortly in Ridgefield; but George Jean Nathan asked him for a one-acter to be published in *American Mercury*, a magazine he and Mencken were founding as a successor to *Smart Set*. The result of Nathan's request was *All God's Chillun Got Wings*, something that had been evolving in O'Neill's mind for years.

A number of parallels can be drawn between the real-life models and their fictional counterparts in the new play. Where James O'Neill, overcoming early poverty and the anti-Irish bigotry of his day, rose to be a famous actor, Jim Harris of *All God's Chillun*, hoping to become "a Member of the Bar," struggles against racial prejudice and self-doubt. Where Ella O'Neill had felt lost in the theatrical world and, because of her drug addiction, became a semirecluse, the girl in *All God's Chillun* feels drowned in a sea of black faces and she too, viewing herself as a social leper, hides from people. In the play, as was true in life, Ella is utterly dependent upon her husband, and in both cases the husbands, feeling they had married above themselves, place their wives on a pedestal. O'Neill's idea of depicting his parents in a black-white confrontation originated, possibly, in his father's fondness for quoting Othello's defense of his marriage to Desdemona ("Most potent, grave, and reverent signiors . . ."), a passage that suggests an analogy between his parents and the Shakespearean couple: just as gentle Desdemona is attracted to the Moor by the romance of his strange and dangerous past, so Ella Quinlan had looked on James O'Neill as the glamour of the theater incarnate. Perhaps the actor had favored the Othello passage because he himself, unconsciously, felt a kinship with the blackamoor.

While viewing the pair in *All God's Chillun* as based on the author's parents sets the play in a revealing perspective, this is scarcely the full picture. There are other elements here — some fictional, some borrowed from other realities — that, taken all together, make the drama more than a camouflaged story about Ella and James O'Neill.

Affording a glimpse of the way O'Neill's creative mind worked, as well as an idea of how long he might harbor material for a play, *All God's Chillun* was partly inspired by an actual tragedy of an earlier decade. While he was a reporter in New London in 1912 and closely attending the day's news, a front-page story in the nation's press told of the suicide of Mrs. Jack Johnson, wife of the heavyweight champion. Her first name was Etta. "I am a white woman," she said a few weeks before she shot herself, "and am tired of being a social outcast. I deserve all of my misery for marrying a black man. Even the Negroes don't respect me; they hate me. I intend to end it all." Minutes before carrying out her threat, Mrs. Johnson summoned her two black maids, asked them to join her in prayer, and with an arm about each knelt at her bedside. As she arose, Etta, pressing her hands to her face, said: "God pity a poor woman who is lonely!"

Unlike Etta Johnson, who took refuge in suicide, Ella Harris finds escape through insanity, a development that recalls O'Neill's childhood fear that his mother was mentally unstable when she used to "drift around the house like a ghost" — a fear that haunted the boy for years till he learned of her drug addiction. In *All God's Chillun* Ella, bitterly opposed to her husband's ambition to be a lawyer, since it would authenticate his superiority to her, prowls about the apartment with a knife, interfering with his studies and his sleep. Yet even after she calls him a "dirty nigger," his love for her persists. In a lucid moment she asks, "Will God forgive me, Jim?" to which he replies: "Maybe He can forgive what you've done to me; and maybe He can forgive what I've done to you; but I don't see how He's going to forgive — Himself."

All God's Chillun Got Wings was decades ahead of its time in its sympathetic treatment of the racial question. "You with your fool talk," Harris says to his sister, "of the black race and the white race! Where does the human race come in?" Though inferior to *The Hairy Ape* and *The Emperor Jones*, the new work was decidedly better than *Welded;* this time the two protagonists, as well as Jim's mother and sister, are credible human beings. If the writing is often rather flat, it does attain moments of singing passion, as in Jim's response when Ella asks about his latest attempt to qualify for the bar:

JIM (*looking at her wildly*) Pass? Pass? (*He begins to chuckle and laugh between sentences and phrases, rich, Negro laughter but heart-*

breaking in its mocking grief) God Lord, child, how come you can ever imagine such a crazy idea? Pass? Me? Jim Crow Harris? Nigger Jim Harris — become a full-fledged Member of the Bar! Why the mere notion of it is enough to kill you with laughter! It'd be against all natural laws, all human right and justice. It'd be miraculous, there'd be earthquakes and catastrophes, the seven Plagues'd come again and locusts'd devour all the money in the banks, the second Flood'd come roaring and Noah'd fall overboard, the sun'd drop out of the sky like a ripe fig, and the Devil'd perform miracles, and God'd be tipped head first right out of the Judgment seat!

Despite George Jean Nathan's request for a one-acter, O'Neill had so much he wanted to say that he wrote *All God's Chillun* in two acts of seven scenes. Though somewhat shorter than standard length, it spans some seventeen years and covers a varied range of story material, not only a husband-wife relationship and the larger issue of whites vis-à-vis blacks but the changing scene and personality of New York City. O'Neill's dislike of the city — he found it alien to the human spirit, oppressive, overwhelming — is reflected in a number of his plays, including *All God's Chillun*, which takes place in a racially mixed neighborhood of lower Manhattan.

In the first scene there are "street noises — the clattering roar of the Elevated, the puff of its locomotives, the ruminative lazy sound of a horse-car, the hooves of its team clacking on the cobbles. From the street of the whites a high-pitched nasal tenor sings the chorus of 'Only a Bird in a Gilded Cage.' On the street of the blacks a Negro strikes up the chorus of: 'I Guess I'll Have to Telegraph My Baby.' As this singing ends, there is laughter . . . from both streets." The description is nostalgic, affectionate, but in time the scene becomes menacing: "The street noises are now more rhythmically mechanical, electricity having taken the place of horse and steam. . . . There is no laughter from the two streets. . . . The buildings have a stern, forbidding look. All the shades are down, giving an effect of staring brutal eyes." Eventually the playwright's aversion to the city would become almost tangible in *Hughie*, a two-character work in which the sounds of New York, especially intrusive and disturbing at night, constitute virtually a third character.

At the start of November, while O'Neill was working on *All God's Chillun*, he had as weekend guests Malcolm Cowley and his wife Peggy — the former Peggy Baird, one of Eugene's early intimates in Greenwich Village — and their friend Hart Crane. The playwright had first met the poet at a party a week before, and favorably taken with both the man and his verse, invited him and the Cowleys to Ridgefield. The visitors were impressed by the O'Neills' estate and style of living, but where Cowley felt somewhat constrained, Hart afterward described the weekend as a "roisterous time! Cider, belly dances and cake walks . . . no end of fun and celebration." Their opposite responses tell something about the two men: Cowley, an intellectual, an analytical mind, considered that he and his host had failed to communicate, while Crane, a manic depressive, reacted exuberantly on feeling that the famous dramatist and his "charming" wife liked him.

Extending himself to be hospitable, O'Neill, according to a written account of the weekend by Cowley, was "extraordinarily kind to a shabby young man without a reputation [Cowley]." At one point O'Neill, showing Malcolm a book by Wilhelm Stekel on sexual aberrations, said that it contained enough case histories "to furnish plots to all the playwrights who ever lived." O'Neill seemed particularly interested in an account of an only son who went insane after his mother had seduced him.

In a tour of the house Cowley found his host's study, a large upstair room, "so meagerly furnished that it looks like an abbot's cell" — no pictures on the walls or other decorations but chiefly a bed, where O'Neill did his writing on a lapboard, and a mahogany secretary. He brought out several medium-sized ledgers, in which he wrote his plays, and opened one to *The Emperor Jones*, the entire text consisting of less than six pages in a handwriting so small that it was illegible without a magnifying glass. Malcolm thought of "the Lord's Prayer engraved on the head of a pin." That night Eugene took him and Crane to the basement, ostensibly to show off a large steam-heat furnace with "pipes radiating in all directions like the arms of an octopus," but he also called their attention to three barrels in the shadows, filled with hard cider made from his own apples. Crane, disappointed that the visit thus far had been dry, suggested that they broach a cask. At first O'Neill demurred, saying that he didn't know how, then consented when Malcolm volunteered that he did. "I can see the beaded bubbles winking at the brim," Hart intoned after his host had returned with a pitcher and three glasses.

"Gene takes a sip of cider," in Cowley's account, "holds it in his mouth apprehensively, gives his glass a gloomy look, then empties the glass in two deep nervous swallows. After a while we fill the pitchers again. When I go upstairs to bed, long after midnight, Gene is on his knees drawing another pitcher of cider, and Hart stands over him gesturing with a dead cigar as he declaims some lines composed that afternoon."

Since he himself had once striven to become a poet (and, secretly, still wrote an occasional verse), Eugene empathized with Hart Crane's struggle in his art. But for a time, at a later period, he cooled toward Crane in the belief that he and Agnes were becoming too friendly — Agnes, to arouse her husband's jealousy and passion, was sometimes a bit flirtatious. As soon as Hart learned of O'Neill's suspicions, he took him aside and divulged, as many of his friends knew, that he was homosexual, a disclosure that set his friendship with the O'Neills on a more comfortable basis. Agnes has described him as "a wonderful guy in his crazy, tragic, boisterous way," while O'Neill said years later: "I consider him one of the few modern American poets possessed of real genius. I only met him during 1923 and 1924, and most of the times I did see him we were both cockeyed." In saying that Crane was "possessed" of genius he used the right word, for Crane *was* possessed, a man even more driven and self-tormented than O'Neill, a son even more drastically affected by his relations with his parents, a poet whose works were painfully wrung out of a disordered and, at times, violent life. In 1932, after prematurely exhausting his talent and spirit through drink, reckless sex adventures and other excesses, Hart Crane, aged nearly thirty-three, jumped overboard in mid-ocean; his body never was recovered.

As Crane and the Cowleys left Brook Farm after the weekend, Malcolm's predominant impression was that "the O'Neills rattle around in this big country house like the last dried peas in a box — or better, like castaway sailors who have blundered into a deserted palace on the shore. But the sailors would laugh if they found wine in the cellar, where Gene hardly even smiles."

O'Neill had no occasion to smile, since he was working at the time on *All God's Chillun*, a drama that evoked in him somber memories of his parents; also, in the midst of playing host that weekend, he knew that his brother was dying. He continued drinking after his guests had left and, while Agnes was out, took a taxi to the nearest railroad station, where his trail vanished. Agnes spent several frantic days in New York telephoning his friends and visiting his old Village haunts until, on her last call at the Hell Hole, the proprietor disclosed that Eugene had drunk himself into a coma in the back room. "To avoid trouble with the police," Cowley writes, "he had been stashed away in the mysterious upstairs that none of us had seen, where Gene said that a crazy old woman wandered through the hallways, opening and closing doors." A day or two after his return home he had word of Jamie's death.

It took him over two months, including the time lost on his binge and other interruptions, to write *All God's Chillun*. Late in September he was "madly riding" it, working eight and ten hours a day in an effort to complete the first draft before the family moved from Peaked Hill to Ridgefield. As soon as he had the play revised and polished in December, he told Nathan that it was in two acts and suggested its publication in two successive issues of *American Mercury*. "I think I've done the right thing by an intensely moving theme and that the result has a real beauty." Nathan, who liked it, favored running the drama in one installment, while Mencken was against publishing it at all. In the end Nathan prevailed — *All God's Chillun* appeared in the second (February 1924) issue of *Mercury* — but at a cost, for the dispute brought to the surface differences between the two old friends over editorial policy. Where Nathan wanted the new magazine to foster literary talent, as in the old *Smart Set,* Mencken was increasingly eager to do battle with the politicians, the hard-shell Baptists, "the booboisie," and everyone else who did not share his views on social, economic and other public matters. The conflict between the two men was to intensify until Nathan left the *Mercury* a few years later.

The new regime in MacDougal Street — headed by Kenneth Macgowan with "full and final power both in production and business management" and O'Neill and Bobby Jones as associate directors — had originally planned to open with *All God's Chillun*. However, since it was not ready in time for the first issue of *American Mercury*, the playhouse, under O'Neill's agreement with Nathan, had to postpone it. Strindberg's *The Spook Sonata* was scheduled instead, at O'Neill's suggestion (to Macgowan he confided that "the Mummy" in the play, a grotesque creature who lives in a cupboard, reminded him of his mother's reclusive existence during most of her married life).

The rehearsals did not progress smoothly. Jones, codirecting *The Spook Sonata* with Jimmy Light and codesigning the scenery with Cleon Throckmorton, had respectfully approached the play as a modern classic, but he came to feel that he was working on a "gravestone for a pile of stinking dead." In the absence of O'Neill, who was too absorbed in his own work to pay much attention to the production, Jones did all he could to soften the play's macabre character. When Kyra Markham, who designed the costumes, saw one of the last rehearsals, she felt that Jones had "wrecked the play, that Gene's ideas were totally lost" and blurted out: "Why, every true Strindbergian line has been cut!" Macgowan rushed over and tried to soothe her, while Bobby Jones, turning white, dashed out of the theater, pursued by Jimmy Light and others. Jones finally returned, arms outstretched, and said, "It's all right, Kyra, I love you just the same."

With a cast that included Clare Eames, Mary Blair, Mary Morris and Walter Abel, *The Spook Sonata* opened on January 3, 1924, to a press that, generally speaking, was bored, baffled or derisive. One reviewer called it "much ado about nothing," another said that "it is negligible," and George Jean Nathan, in the unkindest cut of all, described the play as one "which Strindberg wrote when he was on his way to the nutatorium and which has been produced by the Provincetown Players headed momentarily for the same destination." O'Neill could not have been more upset had one of his own works been ridiculed. In an article for the playbill he had declared that in "establishing a modern theater which we hope will liberate . . . a fresh elation and joy in experimental productions, it is the most apt symbol of our good intentions that we start with a play by August Strindberg. . . . Strindberg still remains among the most modern of moderns, the greatest interpreter in the theater of the characteristic spiritual conflicts which constitute the drama — the blood — of our lives today. He carried Naturalism to a logical attainment of such poignant intensity that, if the work of any other playwright is to be called 'naturalism,' we must classify a play like *The Dance of Death* as 'super-naturalism,' and place it in a class by itself. . . .

"The old 'naturalism' no longer applies. It represents our Fathers' daring aspirations toward self-recognition by holding the family Kodak up to ill-nature. But we have taken too many snapshots of each other in every graceless position; we have endured too much from the banality of surfaces . . . we have been sick with appearances and are convalescing; we 'wipe out and pass on' to some as yet unrealized region where our souls, maddened by loneliness and the ignoble inarticulateness of flesh, are slowly evolving their new language of kinship.

"Strindberg knew and suffered with our struggle years before many of us were born. He expressed it by intensifying the method of his time and by foreshadowing both in content and form the methods to come. All that is enduring in what we loosely call 'Expressionism' — all that is artistically valid and sound theater — can be clearly traced back through Wedekind to Strindberg's *The Dream Play*, *There Are Crimes and Crimes*, *The Spook Sonata*, etc. Hence, *The Spook Sonata* at our Playhouse. One of the most difficult of Strindberg's 'behind-life' (if I may coin the term) plays to interpret with insight and distinction — but the difficult is properly our special task, or we have no good reason for existing. Truth, in the theater as in life, is eternally difficult, just as the easy is the everlasting lie."

Perhaps O'Neill's only convert with his sermon on Strindberg and "the banality of surfaces" was his thirteen-year-old son, Eugene, who was so eager to please him. Taking a hand in the boy's development, the father dispatched him to the play with a note: "Be sure and go. I've written them to expect you. You'll see an unusual play unusually produced. . . . The experience will be of use to you in your writing."

In mid-January the Provincetowners, already dispirited by the response to *The Spook Sonata*, were saddened by word from Greece that Jig Cook had died. His was a shabby death in view of his dramatic talk of killing himself, of finding "a good cause to die in"; he succumbed to glanders, a disfiguring and painful death, contracted from his pet dog. In spite of his mean illness, however, his final hours and burial were touched with honest glory, for during his brief years in Greece he had become a local legend through his generous, passionate love of the country. As Susan Glaspell tells it: "When the word went up Parnassos that he was sick, shepherds left their flocks with boys and came down the mountain. And when in Delphi they were told he would not be with them again, they did not go back to their flocks, but stayed on in the house of this man they loved — through the day, the night, another day, and until midnight, they were there. Villagers and shepherds carried him, uncovered, through the street of Delphi, round the bend of the mountain to the graveyard" near the Temple of Apollo. From miles around peasants and other plain people, including many who knew of George Cram Cook only by report, came through the snow bearing homemade wreaths for the funeral. Climaxing the tributes, the Greek government, at the urging of many, paid him signal honor by allowing a sacred stone to be removed from the Temple of Apollo, where it had lain for twenty-five centuries, and placed on the grave of Kyrios Kouk as his headstone.

None of the other Provincetowners was more distressed than O'Neill. He felt that he had lost "one of the best friends I had ever had or ever would have — unselfish, rare and truly noble! And then [from a letter to Susan] when I thought of all the things I hadn't done, the letters I hadn't written, the things I hadn't said, the others I had said and wished unsaid, I felt like a swine, Susan. Whenever I think of him it is with the most self-condemning remorse."

For their second bill "the Triumvirate," as Macgowan, Jones and

O'Neill were called, presented on February 3 *Fashion*, the nineteenth-century comedy by Anna Cora Mowatt in a new acting version with songs of the period. Though O'Neill would have preferred something more substantial and adventurous, he deferred to Jones, who loved to evoke earlier, more romantic eras. Both press and public were enchanted by *Fashion*, which, in the words of Deutsch and Hanau's *The Province-town*, "steered just the right course between authentic reproduction and travesty." Theatergoers nightly cheered the hero, hissed the villain, and happily stamped their feet as the curtain rolled down with a thud after each act to reveal a painting of "a languorous lady surrounded by cupids and flowers." After playing to capacity for eight weeks, the period comedy was transferred to the Greenwich Village Theater, a larger house at Sheridan Square, where it ran another fifteen weeks, and finally was moved to Broadway for an indefinite engagement. Heartened by its success and a large number of new subscribers, the Triumvirate decided to operate both the Greenwich Village Theater and the Provincetown the following season.

One day early in 1924 O'Neill, in an excited voice, told Macgowan that for the first time in his life he had dreamed a play, one that he felt had great possibilities. As he outlined the projected work, Kenneth (though he never mentioned this to O'Neill) thought it a case of "unconscious plagiarism," for its story of an aged farmer, his young wife and her lover, by whom she has a child, resembled a new play he had lent Eugene a short time before, *They Knew What They Wanted* by Sidney Howard. Howard had become friendly with the Triumvirate through his wife, Clare Eames, now appearing in the Village productions. While undoubtedly the Howard play helped to inspire *Desire Under the Elms*, which O'Neill wrote in the winter and spring of 1924, the two, except for their basic situation, are totally different in all respects; O'Neill adapted and transformed the Howard story to his own purpose.

They Knew What They Wanted, set in the California vineyards, concerns a warmhearted Italian farmer; his mail-order bride, a brave little sparrow from the city; and the foreman of the place, whom the farmer regards as almost a son. All three in their separate ways are decent and likable, as benevolent as the California sun. By contrast, a critic said of the principals in O'Neill's drama, set in mid-nineteenth-century New England: "These people — unlike the people in everyday life! — are cruel and greedy; they talk freely of shameful things fit only to be printed in the Bible." There is seventy-five-year-old Ephraim Cabot, harsh as the stony earth he tills, who has "slaved" two wives into early graves and has just taken a third; constantly quoting Scriptures to justify himself and viewing God in his own image as a super-Ephraim, he maintains that "God's hard, not easy!" There is the embittered son of his second marriage, Eben Cabot, who contends that his mother was cheated out of the farm by Ephraim and covets it for his own. Completing the unholy triangle, Abbie Putnam, sensual, calculating, has married Ephraim for the sake of a home, though she detests him and at the first sight of Eben hungers for his strong ripe body. Eben too is attracted but, regarding her as an interloper bent on depriving him of the homestead, tries to suppress his rising desire for his young stepmother.

In the Howard play the girl becomes pregnant through a single misstep, but her husband Tony, after a brief explosion, forgives her and accepts the child as his own. Wilder, more elemental emotions are loosed in the Cabot household. Abbie and Eben glory in their passion till Eben, led to believe she has cold-bloodedly used him to gain an heir, turns against her. To win him back, to prove she loves him above everything, even their infant son, she suffocates the baby, as Ephraim finally learns that he has been duped and cuckolded. The two lovers are under arrest as the play ends, while Ephraim, after weakening momentarily and thinking of joining his elder two sons in the California gold mines, says: "Mebbe they's easy gold in the West, but it hain't God's gold. It hain't fur me. I kin hear His voice warnin' me agen t' be hard an' stay on my farm."

Both *Desire Under the Elms* and *They Knew What They Wanted* are considered outstanding plays of the 1920s, yet what a distance between them! — the distance between genius and talent, between O'Neill and the other leading American playwrights of his day. Howard's play, for all its onetime glow onstage, appears today a faded valentine of goodwill; the O'Neill drama remains a combustible mixture of granite and fire. O'Neill was not only more gifted than his contemporaries but more ambitious, more daring. In his struggle to develop as an artist he was ready to tackle any theme, challenge all conventions. If the old Greeks could dramatize such dire matters as incest and infanticide, he was ready to dare as much. "I intend to use whatever I can make my own," he has said, "to write about anything under the sun in any manner that fits."

The Howard play and the Greek classics (*Hippolytus* in particular) are not the only literary sources of *Desire*. When the Abbey Players appeared in New York in 1911 one drama that made a deep impression on O'Neill was *Birthright*, T. C. Murray's story of a hard, unloving Irishman who has developed "a cold, poor place" into a thriving farm, his drudge of a wife, and their two sons, totally unlike one another, who are rivals for the farm. O'Neill, who had used some of this material in *Beyond the Horizon*, borrowed again as he told of ill will between Eben and his two half-brothers, hostility between father and sons, and the struggle for the farm. Although Murray's farmer served as a model for Ephraim Cabot, the Irish precursor is only a sketch – a mean thin mouth and pinched nose – compared to Ephraim, among O'Neill's richest portraits. It is one measure of his complexity, of his abundance of human nature in all its contradictions, that he has reminded Professor John Henry Raleigh of such disparate figures as old Karamazov (O'Neill had read *The Brothers Karamazov* several years previously), a Grant Wood portrait, and legendary Paul Bunyan. With his pious talk yet lust for the flesh, his scorn for his sons yet strange tenderness toward his herd of cows, his hickory toughness, his at once miserly and religious feeling for the land, his bursts of wild extravagant humor, Ephraim takes on epic dimensions.

Yet another literary source, Stekel's book on sexual aberrations, specifically his account of the mother who seduces her son, can be detected in the scene where Abbie, overpowering Eben's defenses, makes him her lover. The two are in the tomblike parlor, where his mother's body had been laid out years before, and he senses her presence in the room, her unquiet spirit. As he remembers that she used to sing for him, he breaks down weeping.

> ABBIE (*both her arms around him – with wild passion*) I'll sing fur ye! I'll die fur ye! (*In spite of her overwhelming desire for him, there is a sincere maternal love in her manner and voice – a horribly frank mixture of lust and mother love*) Don't cry, Eben! I'll take yer Maw's place! I'll be everythin' she was t' ye! Let me kiss ye, Eben! . . . Don't be afeered! I'll kiss ye pure, Eben – same's if I was a Maw t' ye – an' ye kin kiss me back's if yew was my son – my boy – sayin' good night t'me! . . . (*They kiss in restrained fashion. Then suddenly wild passion overcomes her. She kisses him lustfully again and again and he flings his arms about her and returns her kisses.*)

As one might surmise from Eben's grieving over a mother who has been dead for years, memories of the author's own family, sharpened by the recent death of Jamie, who had been so deeply – and disastrously – attached to his mother, were at work in O'Neill as he wrote *Desire Under the Elms*. He even invested the Cabot homestead itself with a maternal aspect: "Two enormous elms are on each side of the house. They bend their trailing branches down over the roof. They appear to protect and at the same time subdue. There is a sinister maternity in their aspect, a crushing, jealous absorption."

The immediate real-life model for the Cabot setting was a homestead located only a short distance from Brook Farm, visible from the highway, which O'Neill must have seen hundreds of times. In the front yard of the old Smith farm, as it was known, were two tremendous elm trees that overhung, shaded and framed the house. The Smith place in turn seems to have reminded O'Neill of the Monte Cristo cottage in New London, where trees, including elms, hugged the house and, as Ella used to complain, made it gloomy. From the description in *Desire* it appears that trees and Ella's lachrymose spells while under the influence of morphine were strangely interwoven in the playwright son's imagination: "[The two elms] brood oppressively over the house. They are like exhausted women resting their sagging breasts and hands and hair on its roof, and when it rains their tears trickle down monotonously and rot on the shingles."

Also linking the author's past with the present, the Monte Cristo place had a "dry" wall in the rear yard, while Brook Farm had one, among many of the region, running before its front lawn. By now the walls, made of local stones and laboriously put together by earlier generations, symbolized to O'Neill the rude, flinty existence of old-time New England, as he indicates in a key image of *Desire*. "Stones," says old Ephraim. "I picked 'em up an' piled 'em into walls. Ye kin read the years o' my life in them walls, every day a hefted stone, climbin' over the hills up and down, fencin' in the fields that was mine."

O'Neill had grown to dislike Brook Farm by the time he wrote *Desire Under the Elms*. The house seemed to him too formal and large, the winters were harsher than in Provincetown, and he felt hemmed in by the nearby hills. Prey to strange fancies, he at times had the sensation that someone was peering over his shoulder as he wrote, and one night he thought he heard footsteps outside, going round and round the house. Traces of his nervous state are evident in *Desire* as Ephraim complains to Abbie: "It's cold in this house. It's oneasy. They's thin's pokin' about in the dark — in the corners." Fretting another time about "somethin' " in the house, he says, "Ye kin feel it droppin' off the elums, climbin' up the roof, sneakin' down the chimney, pokin' in the corners! They's no peace in houses, they's no rest livin' with folks. Somethin's always livin' with ye."

In certain respects Cabot resembles James O'Neill, since both had a peasant's hunger for the land, as well as a peasantlike penuriousness, and both were in conflict with their sons. Essentially, however, old Cabot — even though Eben embodies an aspect or two of the author — is another of the playwright's self-portraits. Ephraim scorns whatever is easy, whatever can be won without a struggle; similarly, "easy" was one of the most damning words in O'Neill's lexicon. Ephraim, like O'Neill, is a difficult, demanding husband and an inadequate father. Finally, nothing was more true of O'Neill than that he suffered from an abiding sense of isolation, of being misunderstood by those closest to him, another central characteristic shared by old Cabot. In the scene where Ephraim, seeking to make contact with his new wife, tries to explain and justify himself, the refrain "I was allus lonesome" runs through the account of his life. "Will ye ever know me — 'r will any man 'r any woman?" he says scornfully to Abbie. "No. I calc'late 't wa'n't t' be." (In 1928 O'Neill said, "I always have loved Ephraim so much! He's so autobiographical!")

A lean, sinewy drama, *Desire Under the Elms* manages to encompass a good deal of story material. It is at once a portrait of the New England Puritan, harder on himself than on anyone else, who founded the work-and-thrift ethic in America, and a celebration of human needs, represented by Abbie and Eben, at war with that puritanism. Thus, without pausing in its headlong storytelling to belabor the point, *Desire* dramatizes an aspect of the American past that helps to explain the continuing American character. The play is also revealing on a psychological level. Though O'Neill used to deny that he had borrowed from Freud, Eben's hostility to Ephraim is in accord with Freudian theory about the Oedipus complex; it seems particularly significant that the father's farm, which the son had long desired so ardently, becomes relatively unimportant to him once he has plowed, and left his seed in, his father's wife.

But *Desire,* greater than the sum of its Freudian, Stekelian, etc., parts, is an organic work of art, not a medley of echoes of what other men had said. Mastering his materials this time, O'Neill raised an uncompromising drama — one, it should be added, that occasionally verges on melodrama — to the exhilarating level of tragedy. At the end, possibly facing the gallows, Abbie and Eben exult in their love, instead of feeling guilty or blasting one another with recriminations; their fulfillment in one another is worth the ultimate cost. As to Ephraim, he accepts a heavier burden on his ancient shoulders, regarding it as just and proper, and thereby grows taller in defeat.

To settle all the playwright's major debts, his austere view of New England owed something to the stories Robert Edmond Jones used to tell of his grim New Hampshire background. Just as Eugene was haunted by the Monte Cristo cottage, where his mother had drifted in the depths of morphine, Jones, according to one of his biographers, could never forget a "house full of the forms and figures of Old New England, which seems to have some relation to antique tragedy. . . . The memory of this house, with its secret interior drama — the drama of strong, devoted, violent, cross-grained characters — is to Jones more powerfully living than anything he has seen in the wider world." Jones himself, looking back, summarized his impression of New England in words applicable to the O'Neill play itself: "violent, passionate, sensual, sadistic, lifted, heated, frozen, transcendental, Poesque."

While writing *Desire Under the Elms*, between January and mid-June 1924, O'Neill had to suspend the work from time to time for rehearsals of other of his plays. During part of February and March he was busy with *Welded*, which the Triumvirate was producing in association with the Selwyns. The direction of the play had been entrusted to Stark Young at the request of Mrs. Willard Straight, a friend of Young's who had contributed generously to the Triumvirate's season on MacDougal Street and was now among the chief backers of *Welded*.

Costarring in the play were Jacob Ben-Ami, an alumnus of the Yiddish theater who had a kind of rabbinical fervor, and Doris Keane, who was best suited to costume roles — her Madame Calvacanti in Edward Sheldon's *Romance* was among the celebrated portrayals of the previous decade — but she hoped for réclame in contemporary stories. Though eager to be in something by O'Neill (several years earlier she asked him to write a play for her), shortly after *Welded* entered rehearsal she felt miscast and wanted to withdraw. Stark Young, who had suggested her for the wife's role, persuaded her to remain by appealing to her as a trouper. But the situation only grew worse; besides disliking her part and the play, Miss Keane came to view Ben-Ami, a lesser "name," as distinctly below her caliber and made no attempt to disguise her feeling. "The temperature between them dropped," says Curtis Cooksey, one of the cast, "to a freezing point."

According to a published account by Stark Young years later, O'Neill appeared quite satisfied with the rehearsals. "I know," Young says, "that Gene's personal life in the period that *Welded* came out of had not been all smoothness, not between two such vivid temperaments as he and Agnes, for all the love between them, and I felt that this play was in the nature of a confession and a benediction. I can see them now at some of the rehearsals sitting side by side there in the third row and listening to every speech, good or bad, and taking it all as *bona fide* and their own."

Another time, speaking privately, he put it more bluntly: "Those God-awful speeches! Yet Gene and Agnes drank it all in as though it were poetry."

Despite Young's account, O'Neill was dissatisfied with the way the production was developing. Not only was he critical of both leading players but halfway through rehearsals, when it was too late to change the settings, he decided that they should have been symbolic rather than realistic, that they helped to throw his script off-key. Usually he was against pre-Broadway engagements, for he felt that he could evaluate and improve his scripts through rehearsals alone, without the aid of audience response; but he and his colleagues were so dubious about *Welded* that they tested it for a week in Baltimore, where the playwright attended several performances and made last-minute revisions.

When *Welded* opened on March 17 at the Thirty-ninth Street Theater — the first O'Neill production since *The Hairy Ape* two years before — certain critics tried, from regard for the author, to find things to praise, but with only an exception or two the reviews were severe. Alexander Woollcott in the *Herald* the following day: "a somewhat dolorous function . . . prodigiously dull." The *Sun*'s Gilbert W. Gabriel: "doleful reiteration, a constant, wearing, unrelieved intensity." *Welded* became known as the "I love you, I hate you" play, and one night Doris Keane overheard a man sitting down front say: "If that fellow [Ben-Ami] says it again, I'll throw a chair at him."

Edna Kenton, who seized every possible opportunity to score off O'Neill, gloated on April 4 to Carl Van Vechten: "I am told the audiences at *Welded* titter and laugh outright nightly at the dialogue. The author's friends are consumed with pity for him, and unbearable pain at seeing on the stage scenes witnessed in the playwright's own home. 'He has torn out his heart and put it on his sleeve for stupid peckers to peck at,' said one. 'I suppose it was something he MUST do.' "

When the play closed after twenty-four performances, O'Neill blamed the performance rather than the script. "The actors," he said, "did about as well as they could, but the whole point of the play was lost in the production. The most significant thing in the last act was the silences between the speeches. What was actually spoken should have served to a great extent just to punctuate the meaningful pauses. The actors didn't get that." There were quite a few things in the script the actors did not "get." At one point, for instance, the couple, according to a stage direction, convey with a look that it "becomes impossible that they should ever deny life, through each other, again."

All O'Neill had wanted from the actors, in other words, was for them to create with their acting the play he had seen in his mind but had failed to produce on paper. In time he came to regret *Welded* and wished that he had never written it, yet he could not in honesty disown its content; it expressed, however clumsily, his basic feelings and thoughts about his relationship with Agnes. When the play was published he inscribed a copy to her with some of Cape's words to his wife, a passage that ends: "I love you! Forgive me all I've ever done, all I'll ever do."

7

⊠

Besieged Playhouse

As the season developed on MacDougal Street, after the productions of *The Spook Sonata* and *Fashion*, the playhouse came under attack from within and without. O'Neill tried to remain clear of the intramural struggle, waged chiefly between Edna Kenton and Kenneth Macgowan, but he was repeatedly pulled into it by Miss Kenton, who was determined to discredit him to Susan Glaspell, now back from Greece. Her partisanship intensified by Cook's death, Edna, maintaining that the Provincetown was largely Jig's creation, argued that the Triumvirate should change the name of both the theater and the group, because their policy was different. The dissension would have been rather absurd — such undue importance was given to the issue of the name — had it not become so acrimonious. In her campaign against them, Miss Kenton led Susan to believe that O'Neill and his associates had already forgotten Jig, since they had done nothing to memorialize him (in reality they were trying to decide how to honor him properly). After the smoke of battle had cleared, the Provincetown Playhouse had retained its name, the group was now called Experimental Theater, Inc. — though practically everyone continued referring to it as the Provincetown Players — and both Susan and Edna had resigned.

Later, after some correspondence between her and O'Neill, Susan wrote a tribute to her husband which appeared in one of the theater's playbills, and she chose the wording, from Jig's writings, for a bronze wall plaque in his memory. But in the other attack, from without the walls, there was to be no truce or reconciliation, no quarter given.

The Village producers had expected *All God's Chillun Got Wings* to arouse some controversy, but they were caught off-balance by the sniping and finally all-out assault that developed months before the O'Neill drama was staged. At first all was deceptively calm when the New York *Herald* announced on January 31, 1924, just after *American Mercury* had published the text, that the Provincetown Playhouse would produce *All God's Chillun* with a Negro actor and a white actress as husband and wife. (Despite the acclaim for Gilpin in *The Emperor Jones*, the practice of casting whites in blackface for important Negro roles remained widespread. *White Cargo*, a hit of the 1923–1924 season, had a white actress as a sexy half-caste married to a proper Britisher, while in another play of the season, *Roseanne*, a story of Negro life in the South, all the characters were enacted by blackened whites.)

In February several newspapers reported that an actress as yet unidentified had consented to appear opposite Paul Robeson, "a full-blooded Negro," after the part had been rejected by other white actresses, among them Helen MacKellar, who had played Ruth in *Beyond the Horizon*. "The play requires," said the *American*, "that the white girl kiss the negro's hand on the stage." The Brooklyn *Eagle*, the first to identify the actress as Mary Blair, quoted her on February 22 as saying, "I deem it an honor to take the part of Ella. There is nothing in the part that should give offense to any woman desiring to portray life." The Players, denying that Miss MacKellar had ever been approached, told the press that Mary Blair was the first and only person offered the role.

Giving national publicity to what had been a local story, a news syndicate sent out a photograph of Mary headed: WHITE ACTRESS KISSES NEGRO'S HAND. Thereafter, although this is but a minor incident in the play, the countless news stories of the controversy almost always mentioned it. (Many years later when Miss Blair was dying, she wryly joked that the obituaries would probably identify her as the actress "who kissed a Negro's hand" – a prediction that came true.) The photograph and caption, lighting the fuse, inflamed some persons to fire off indignant letters to the city authorities, the newspapers, and the Village playhouse. At the theater Fitzi told a *World* reporter, as printed on March 3: "We are producing the play because it is beautiful. . . . Some people may storm our doors, but if they wait and see the play they will go away humble." In the same account O'Neill, professing bewilderment over the objections, said, "The racial factor is incidental. The play is a character study of two human beings."

While most newspapers confined themselves to reporting the developments objectively, several, particularly the *Morning Telegraph*, a sheet dedicated chiefly to the edification of horse players, and Hearst's *American* were openly biased; they used all their journalistic wiles to keep the controversy aflame. Resorting to such phrases as "rumor has it" or "it is said," the two ran stories full of innuendoes and distortions of fact, and solicited the comments of public figures hostile to anything liberal, advanced or experimental. The Village group was particularly vulnerable at the time, since it was conducting a campaign to raise funds for operating both the Provincetown Playhouse and the Greenwich Village Theater the following season.

"It is reported," the *American* said on March 2, that Otto H. Kahn, the Wall Street broker and patron of the arts, "has intimated a desire to withdraw his support should the play go on," and his position was "said" to be supported by Mrs. Willard Straight, another of the Provincetown's leading "angels." Adding its own embellishments the *Telegraph* said: "Yesterday a persistent rumor floated around Broadway that both [Kahn and Mrs. Straight] had withdrawn their subscriptions and would have nothing to do with the Provincetown Players henceforth. . . . In Harlem there is as much interest as in other parts of the city, and it is understood that scores of negroes have become subscribers. The opportunity of witnessing a white woman kissing a black man's hand and engaging in love scenes with him [there is no lovemaking in the play] will be one that the average negro would not care to miss. It is now certain that the Provincetown Theater will not be large enough to accommodate the negroes who will flock there."

No sooner had the Provincetowners denied one rumor than another was rushed into print. There were stories that the hand-kissing episode was being dropped, that Miss Blair, fearful for her career, had resigned and been replaced by an "octaroon," that O'Neill, now worried about *his* career, had withdrawn the play. All the rumors proved to be false, including the one about Otto Kahn and Mrs. Straight; instead of ending their support, they increased their gifts to the fund drive.

The adverse pressure continued to mount as women's organizations and church groups passed condemnatory resolutions; and day after day the *American* summoned to the witness stand the gray voices of reaction and repression. On March 12 John S. Sumner of the Society for the Prevention of Vice declared the play "might easily lead to racial riots or disorder, and if there is any such possibility, police powers can be exercised." On the thirteenth, a clergyman: "There is no good or uplifting thought in the play. It should be condemned by every clean-thinking man and woman in the city." On the seventeenth, S. Edward Young of the Society for the Prevention of Crime: "Although I have not read the play, from the representations made to me, I infer that it is a damnable thing to put on the stage . . . guarantees an appeal to the lewder qualities of the audience."

In its inflammatory campaign the Hearst sheet went to ridiculous lengths. As though the Provincetown group normally rehearsed in the middle of Washington Square, the *American* ran a story headed: SECRET DRILLS IN RACIAL PLAY / REHEARSALS OF 'ALL GOD'S CHILLUN' GO ON BEHIND CLOSED DOORS. The headline was based on the mere fact that a reporter who invaded the theater while rehearsals were in progress was shown the door, but the account conveyed the impression that the play-makers were engaged in something furtive and shameful.

From the start of the controversy the press had reported that the city authorities were, at least for the time, powerless to act. License Commissioner August W. Glatzmayer, noting that the Provincetown was an unlicensed club with admission limited to its subscribers, said it was outside his jurisdiction. District Attorney Joab H. Banton, a Southerner eager to bar the O'Neill drama, stated that his office could move against "obscene and indecent" plays only after they had been produced. Chief Magistrate William McAdoo said, according to the *World* on March 3: "I should think that in a country where racial prejudice is so deep-seated, any play of such character as described might prove very dangerous," but he added that the police could not act until the peace had been disturbed.

Yet the opposition kept calling for official action. Whether they had volunteered the opinion or were prompted (a reporter can often elicit a desired reply by the way he frames his question), many quoted in the *American* stories feared that the O'Neill drama would inspire public violence. Gradually it became apparent that the journal was trying to force Mayor John F. Hylan's hand; after stating on March 14 that the mayor had no legal right to close a theater "arbitrarily," the *American* expressed belief that he could prevent the play from opening "if it were shown the presentation might incite race riots. The danger of race riots," it added ominously, "has been pointed out in many protests." The following day, above a story of little substance, the paper ran a seven-column streamer: RACE STRIFE SEEN IF 'GOD'S CHILLUN' IS STAGED.

The Provincetowners had intended to present *All God's Chillun* as their third program, after *Fashion*, in early March. But it had to be postponed, initially because *Fashion* was kept running on MacDougal Street till another Village theater could receive the hit, then because Mary Blair fell ill and was incapacitated for a month. Revising its schedule, the playhouse presented in April a double bill of Coleridge's *The Ancient Mariner*, in "a dramatic arrangement" by O'Neill, and Molière's

George Dandin. O'Neil had simply cut the ballad, with some of its verse and his own interpolations serving as stage directions, but it gave the Villagers a chance to experiment with masks, lighting, and pantomime. Most reviewers found the venture ill-advised. Heywood Broun called it "base metal from a cracked test tube in the Provincetown laboratory," while Woollcott felt that Coleridge, in his "collaboration" with O'Neill, "got somewhat the worst of it."

In his single-minded approach to his art and his determination to tell "the truth" as he saw it — "let the splinters fly where they may" — O'Neill never took into account how Negroes might feel about *All God's Chillun*. By and large they were against it. A notable exception was W. E. B. Du Bois, the writer, an eloquent and dauntless champion of his people, who said: "Any mention of Negro blood or Negro life in America for a century has been occasion for an ugly picture, a dirty allusion, a nasty comment or a pessimistic forecast. The result is that the Negro today fears any attempt of the artist to paint Negroes. He is not satisfied unless everything is perfect and proper and beautiful and joyful and hopeful. He is afraid to be painted as he is, lest his human foibles and shortcomings be seized by his enemies for the purposes of the ancient and hateful propaganda.

"Happy is the artist that breaks through any of these shells, for his is the kingdom of eternal beauty. He will come through scarred, and per-haps a little embittered — certainly astonished at the almost universal misinterpretation of his motives and aims. Eugene O'Neill is bursting through. He has my sympathy, for his soul must be lame with the blows rained upon him. But it is work that must be done."

For every Du Bois there were ten Powells and Browns. Calling the play "intensely harmful," the Reverend A. Clayton Powell, pastor of the Abyssinian Baptist Church (and father of the late congressman), said it was "harmful because it intimates that we are desirous of marrying white women." The Reverend J. W. Brown of Mother African M. E. Zion Church felt that the O'Neill drama could do his people "only harm," while the Chicago *Defender*, a leading Negro paper, assailed the play for having "an educated, high-minded Negro, whose sister is a school teacher, take into his home a wife who has come from the streets."

Nettled by the barrage of criticism, especially from the white racists, O'Neill, counterattacking in a statement to the press, said that virtually all the protests "very obviously come from people who have not read a line of the play. Prejudice born of an entire ignorance of the subject is the last word in injustice and absurdity. . . .

"As for the much discussed casting of Mr. Robeson . . . I believe he can portray the character better than any other actor could. That's all there is to it. . . . The question of race prejudice cannot enter here. And it is ridiculous in the extreme that objections should be made to Mr. Robeson. Right in this city two years ago in a public theater he played opposite a distinguished white actress, Margaret Wycherly, in a play called *Voodoo*. In one of the scenes he was cast as the King and she the Queen. A King and Queen are, I believe, usually married.

"Miss Blair is cast for 'Ella' because I have always had her in mind. Her performance in the very difficult role of my *Diff'rent* three seasons ago convinced me that she is one of the most talented actresses on our stage. [O'Neill was eager to praise her publicly as he felt guilty, even though he was not responsible, about her being replaced by Carlotta Monterey when *The Hairy Ape* was moved to Broadway. Also, there is reason to believe that Mary Blair accepted the role after Helen MacKellar and others had rejected it.] She is playing 'Ella' in *God's Chillun* because she likes the play and the part. As a true artist, she does not recognize any considerations but these as having any bearing.

"The play itself, as anyone who has read it with intelligence knows, is never a 'race-problem' play. Its intention is confined to portraying the special lives of individual human beings. It is primarily a study of the two principal characters, and their tragic struggle for happiness. To deduce any general application from *God's Chillun*, except in a deep spiritual sense, is arbitrarily to read a meaning into my play which is not there. . . . . Nothing could be further from my wish than to stir up racial feeling. I hate it. It is because I am certain *God's Chillun* does not do this but, on the contrary, will help toward a more sympathetic understanding between the races . . . that I will stand by it to the end. I know that all the irresponsible gabble of the sensation-mongers and notoriety hounds is wrong. They are the ones who are trying to rouse ill feeling."

Parts of his statement were widely printed in the press on March 19. While the *Times* noncommittally headed its account, 'ALL GOD'S CHILLUN' DEFENDED BY O'NEILL, the *American*, true to form, ran the headline: O'NEILL DEFIES PUBLIC OUTCRY / GABBLE OF SENSATION MONGERS WRONG, ASSERTS AUTHOR.

Applauding the playwright's stand, Arthur Pollock said in the Brooklyn *Eagle:* "Othello through his black makup has been kissing Desdemona these many years with no resultant outcry. . . . We see no reason why a white actress should not, so long as she is willing, be allowed to kiss a hand that is dark by nature, not by grease paint."

O'Neill had been restrained in his public statement, but writing to a friend months later he expressed how he really felt about his assailants: "It seemed for a time there as if all the feeble-minded both in and out of the K.K.K. were hurling newspaper bricks in my direction – not to speak of the anonymous letters which ranged from those of infuriated Irish Catholics who threatened to pull my ears off as a disgrace to their race and religion, to those of equally infuriated Nordic Kluxers who knew that I had Negro blood, or else was a Jewish pervert masquerading under a Christian name in order to do subversive propaganda for the Pope! This sounds like burlesque, but the letters were even more so."

Although he could be facetious afterward, the hate campaign at the time was anything except humorous. The Provincetowners kept assuring one another that nothing would happen, but the atmosphere at the playhouse was thick with apprehension. The mail included poison-pen letters not only for O'Neill but for Mary Blair and Paul Robeson. "A great many," Jimmy Light recalls, "were obscene or threatening or both, but Mary and Paul didn't see the largest part because we began holding them back. I remember one in particular to Mary, really filthy, pathological. And Gene had a letter from the K.K.K. in Georgia, on their official stationery, signed by the Grand Kleagle, which began reasonably enough and then got increasingly worse. 'You have a son,' it said. 'If your play goes on, don't expect to see him again.' You know what a tiny handwriting Gene had – well, he returned the letter after writing at the bottom in a large hand: 'Go fuck yourself!' Another letter from the Ku Kluxers, this time a bunch on Long Island, was unsigned. It said: 'If you open this play, the theater will be bombed, and you will be responsible for all the people killed.' "

When the Coleridge-Molière program proved too weak to run its allotted four weeks, the Provincetown, as a stopgap till *All God's Chillun* was ready, revived *The Emperor Jones* on May 5 with Paul Robeson starred. It was the smartest move the theater could have made: the revival, turning the spotlight away from *Chillun*, focused attention on Robeson as an actor rather than as a center of controversy. The first-nighters, many of whom had seen Gilpin's thrilling performance, were at first cool to Paul, then, after a scene or two, warmer, and by the end enthusiastic – as were the reviews the following day. Paul Robeson, aged twenty-six, had begun his climb to theatrical renown. An honor graduate of Rutgers University and a member of Walter Camp's 1918 All-American football team, he was generously gifted by nature with a superb physique, a fine mind, and a splendid voice (from the reviews: "a voice that is unmatched in the American theater" . . . "not merely a large and powerful voice but one rich in shadings and emotion." . . . "One wonders if he has ever tried to sing"). Unlike Jim Harris of *All God's Chillun*, who repeatedly flunks the bar examination, Robeson was a graduate of Columbia University's law school, but he had practiced only a short time when he was forced to conclude that his color would be less of a hindrance to him in the theater than in law.

After the opening performance of *Jones* a party was held in Cleon Throckmorton's apartment above the theater, but O'Neill was more interested in the tom-tom used in the play than in the celebration. He played it for hours, starting on the stage, where Jimmy Light found him in semidarkness, and continuing without a pause as he climbed the stairway to join the party. Apparently he was working off an accumulation of tension through the instrument. He often said that he tried to get "rhythm" into his writing; he held that people were more sensitive and responsive to rhythm than they realized. Now the rhythmic drumming seemed to have a strangely soothing effect on him. During the party Light, Robeson and Throckmorton took off their shirts to compare their physiques, and Agnes, proud of Eugene's, urged him to display his; he acceded amiably, with hardly a word, then returned bare-chested to his drumming. It was a warm night, the windows were open, and finally a policeman materialized to relay complaints about the noise; but he turned friendly on learning that an O'Neill was the culprit. Eugene and a few others adjourned across the street to Barney Gallant's downstairs restaurant, where he drummed away most of the night, communing, it seemed, with himself.

All God's Chillun was scheduled to open on May 15 — "in the face," said the Brooklyn *Eagle*, "of opposition from all sides." Even some Broadway figures were against it, for fear its controversial nature might lend ammunition to bluenoses trying to impose censorship on the theater. Interviewed a few days before the première, O'Neill denied that there was "a genuine prejudice against my play. Judging by the criticism it is easy to see that the attacks are almost entirely based on ignorance of *God's Chillun*. I admit that there is prejudice against the intermarriage of whites and blacks, but what has that to do with my play? I don't advocate intermarriage in it. I am never the advocate of anything in any play — except Humanity toward Humanity.

"The persons who have attacked my play have given the impression that I make Jim Harris a symbolical representative of his race and Ella of the white race — that by uniting them I urge intermarriage. Now Jim and Ella are special cases and represent no one but themselves.

"Of course, the struggle between them is primarily the result of the difference in their racial heritage. It is their characters, the gap between them and their struggle to bridge it which interests me as a dramatist, nothing else. I didn't create the gap, this cleavage — it exists. And members of both races do struggle to bridge it with love. Whether they should or not isn't in my play. . . . What is the theater for if not to show man's struggle, whether he is black, green, orange or white, to conquer life; his effort to give it meaning?"

To another interviewer he said the basic tragedy of the play "is that the woman could not see their 'togetherness' — the Oneness of Mankind. She was hemmed in by inhibitions. Ella of the play loved her husband, but could not love him as a woman would a man, though she wanted to, because of her background and her inherited racial prejudice. . . . We are divided by prejudices. Prejudices racial, social, religious — Life is hard and bitter enough without, in addition, burdening ourselves with prejudices."

Only hours before the curtain was due to rise on *All God's Chillun,* New York City officially moved to block the presentation. A local ordinance required all theaters, even unlicensed ones such as the Provincetown, to obtain permission to employ child actors, but such permission was a routine matter and practically always granted. On May 13, two days before the première, the playhouse applied to the mayor's office for children's work permits, as the opening scene of *All God's Chillun* has black and white youngsters at play together. It was not until late afternoon of the fifteenth that Mayor Hylan's chief clerk telephoned the theater that the application had been rejected. No explanation was given, no pleas or protests could change the decision. (Several days later, after adverse newspaper publicity, a spokesman for the mayor, denying that racism was involved, said the rejection was based on "the tender age" of the children. Those in question ranged in age from eleven to seventeen; that same week a play opened on Broadway with a child of seven.)

Already keyed up and nervous, the Provincetowners were stunned by the new development. In the initial shock and bewilderment someone suggested deferring the première till the youngsters could be replaced by midgets, but finally a simpler solution was found. As the first-nighters began to assemble, tension was evident both backstage and in the auditorium. Hart Crane had written to friends: "There will be some kind of mobbing or terrors . . . and I expect to be there with my cane for

[142]

cudgeling the unruly!" Police were on duty inside the theater and out, ready, presumably, to stop the performance should the child actors appear or to quell any disorder that might occur. Suspicious by now of the authorities, the Provincetowners, rather than rely solely on police protection, had taken their own precautions. With the help of James J. Martin, a steelworker and Village hanger-on who occasionally acted at the playhouse, the group hired a few of his huskier coworkers, stationing them at Robeson's and Miss Blair's dressing rooms and at both ends of the theater's short block on MacDougal Street.

When all was ready, Jimmy Light, who had directed the play, appeared before the curtain to announce that the first scene could not be performed and, after explaining why, proceeded to read the scene — a procedure that would be followed throughout the engagement. A feeling of constraint was evident as the performance began — Miss Blair in particular was nervous — but the players gradually warmed to their roles before an attentive, respectful audience, and the evening went off without incident. It was, in O'Neill's words, "a dreadful anti-climax for all concerned, particularly the critics who seemed to feel cheated that there hadn't been at least one murder."

A majority of the reviewers found the play itself anticlimactic. Nearly all had read *All God's Chillun* beforehand but apparently some had hoped it would appear more impressive onstage than in print. Heywood Broun called it "very tiresome," Burns Mantle cautiously termed it "an interesting exhibit," and Percy Hammond, no O'Neill fan, said, "A bit overdone and breathless, it is a vehement exposition of a marriage between a stupid negro and a stupid white woman. If it is possible for you to get an emotion out of that situation, here is your opportunity." In a hatchet job, as might be expected, the man on the *American* declared: "It seems the most useless thing in the theater, does this groaning, creaking, dismal caricature of hearts that quiver beneath an assortment of skin-hues."

Robert Benchley, on the other hand, was less interested in appraising the play than in ridiculing its enemies: "The production, long dreaded by the champions of Nordic supremacy and the guardians of the honor of white womanhood, has taken place, and at a late hour last night, white women were still as safe on the streets of New York as they ever were and the banner of purity still floated from the ramparts of our Caucasian stronghold."

Alexander Woollcott called the play "a strained, wanton and largely unbelievable tragedy . . . it did not come to life truly and vividly on the stage. . . . It seemed one of those tragedies in which the author can be heard panting so hard in his exertions to thrust two puppets into a cruel trap that when he steps back and bursts into compassionate tears over their dreadful predicament, a certain want of sympathy has been engendered on the other side of the footlights."

O'Neill was almost as upset by the reviews as by the attacks of the "sensation-mongers and notoriety hounds." Though he used to pretend indifference to the critics, his mask was transparent. In 1929, when another of his plays was roundly criticized, he wrote to a friend: "Ah, well, it is not the first time and, I hope, not the last — for when [the critics] begin accepting you without protest it's a sure sign that you're good and dead. And compared with what I had to take on *All God's Chillun*, the present panning is gentle and sweet." The very next day, though, warming to the subject, he said he had "heard dramatic critics called sons of bitches — and, speaking in general, believed it — ever since I was old enough to recognize the Count of Monte Cristo's voice!"

When speaking for the record, however, he was more discreet. Reviewers, he stated, could be "divided into three classes: Play Reporters, Professional Funny Men and the men with the proper background or real knowledge of the theater of all time to entitle them to be critics. The play reporters just happen to be people who have the job of reporting what happens during the evening, the story of the play and who played the parts. I have always found that these people reported the stories of my plays fairly accurately. The Professional Funny Men are beneath contempt. What they say is only of importance to their own strutting vanities. From the real critics I have always had the feeling that they saw what I was trying to do and whether they praised or blamed, they caught the point."

Thanks to its enemies and the notoriety, *All God's Chillun*, despite the reviews, had a profitable engagement. For a while it alternated in repertory with *The Emperor Jones*, then played continuously a month, and after a summer hiatus ran two more months to nonsubscription audiences at the Greenwich Village Theater. In all the play gave one hundred performances, but since it was presented in small houses the author's royalties totaled only thirteen hundred dollars.

On balance the Triumvirate's first season could be considered a moderate success. There had been two productions that practically no one had liked (*The Spook Sonata* and the Coleridge-Molière bill), a solid hit that brought in new subscribers and fresh financial support (*Fashion*), and the two O'Neill plays, one of which, as Macgowan said, "received more publicity before production than any play in the history of the American theater, possibly the world." O'Neill always believed that the uproar over its racial aspects set the play in the wrong perspective; he maintained for years that it was among his most "misunderstood" works and once, seeking to emphasize its personal man-and-woman relationship, proposed reviving it with a white Jim Harris.

Once *All God's Chillun* had opened, O'Neill resumed writing *Desire Under the Elms* and on completing the first draft in June, said, "It's my very completest best so far." Usually Agnes's sister Margery typed his scripts, but she being ill early this summer, he enlisted the services of Bernard Simon, a young employee of the Provincetown. Though Simon was delighted at the opportunity to know the playwright better, the week he spent at Brook Farm was uncomfortable at times, beginning with a drive to Ridgefield in virtual silence as O'Neill discouraged his attempts at conversation.

"At first I thought he was contemptuous of me," Simon recalls, "but he simply wasn't geared for small talk. He was also short with Agnes at lunch the first day. Trying to make conversation, mostly for my sake, I guess, she mentioned something about the Democratic convention coming up — this was an election year — and said she hoped the Republicans would win. Why, O'Neill wanted to know. Well, he jumped on her when she said the Republicans had more money and were better theatergoers. 'We can't look at it that way,' he said. 'The Democrats are more progressive and liberal, they're more concerned with the people, while the Republicans cater to big business.' "

Several times O'Neill had Simon accompany him on the long walks he took almost daily for exercise; during one he called the young man's attention to the old stone walls along the way and expatiated on their symbolizing, in his view, the hard life of the early New England farmers. Another day, though Simon was practically a stranger to him, he complained about Agnes: "She's using me to get in with the social crowd. She invites them up here for a weekend to meet her husband or throws parties, and I hate it. I don't care for those people. I like plain ones like Terry Carlin and Slim Martin, but she doesn't make them feel very welcome. Agnes wants the goddamned *Social Register* crowd. I don't learn anything about human beings from them. They're living corpses.

"There's an old Swede who cuts the grass, a helluva good egg who lives down the road a mile or so. Sometimes when Agnes throws these parties, I frustrate her. I get the old fellow and go down to the barn, where we get drunk."

Shortly before Bernard Simon's stay, O'Neill had a visitor he had not seen in years, Felton ("Pinky") Elkins, his millionaire classmate at Harvard, who used to predict: "Gene is going to be the greatest dramatist in America!" Elkins, whose marriages, divorces and polo-playing were duly chronicled in the society news columns, was still trying to win recognition as a playwright. He turned up in Ridgefield with his latest wife and, in hopes the Provincetown might be interested, his latest script. Although Eugene liked Pinky and enjoyed the visit — the two sat up late drinking and reminiscing about the other students and Professor Baker — he did not care to become intimate with the Elkinses, while Agnes, he thought, was eager for them all to become close friends.

Sculptor Edmond T. Quinn and his wife were other guests this spring, but Quinn, a member of the National Institute of Arts and Letters, had a mission to perform. A year before, the institute, after awarding O'Neill its annual gold medal for drama, had found him elusive about accepting the medal, so finally Quinn was delegated to dispose of the matter. The playwright informed the institute on June 2: "Mr. Quinn made a glorious presentation on our front lawn. Nothing could have been more impressive. I made a humble speech of two words: 'Thank you,' and the whole affair was voted by all a stunning success.

"The principal reason I never came around to get [the medal] was my complete ignorance of what procedure I should properly take. This was my first medal and I naturally felt a bit bashful about it — added to which was the horror that I might be expected to say something."

O'Neill, who had earlier met Quinn through Agnes — he was a friend of her father's — liked both him and his sculpture. After seeing a bust of Edgar Allan Poe by Quinn, he had heads made of himself and Agnes which he proudly displayed at the Ridgefield house. He felt an affinity with the sculptor, a large quiet man who took great pride in his Irish heritage, lived for his art, and tried to stave off his wife's efforts to involve him in social activities. While Eugene thought well enough of Mrs. Quinn, a handsome woman from a good family, he felt that she too, like Agnes, was overly fond of social life. However, his complaint to Bernard Simon that Agnes filled the house with socialites seems exaggerated; he was imagining, apparently, what she would do if he were not so opposed.

"Regardless of what he ever told anybody," Agnes says, "I wouldn't have dared give a party without Gene's approval — you know what he could be like when he drank — and the guests were practically always friends of ours, both his and mine, or people he wanted to see for business reasons." Their most frequent guests were Fitzi, Bobby Jones, Arthur

Hopkins, Jimmy Light and Susan Jenkins — the two had separated by this time but remained friends — Hart Crane, Mary Blair and her writer husband Edmund Wilson, actress Helen MacKellar (who, to Agnes's annoyance, had a crush on O'Neill), Eben Given and his sister Thelma, the Wilbur Daniel Steeles, and the Macgowans, who lived in nearby Brewster ("I never," says Kenneth, "saw any society people at Brook Farm").

Through the Quinns the O'Neills met Padraic and Mary Colum, a young literary couple from Ireland who knew all the big guns at home — Yeats, Joyce, Lady Gregory, Synge, Lennox Robinson — and played host to them one weekend. O'Neill was particularly interested in Joyce and asked so many questions about his play *Exiles*, which he had not heard of before, that Colum afterward sent him a copy. Charmed by the Irish pair, Eugene for a time thought of accompanying them, with Agnes, on a trip to Ireland this year; but summer 1924 found him again at Peaked Hill, functioning in a fresh surge of creative energy. Besides resuming work on *Marco Millions*, which he had not touched in nearly a year, he wrote a detailed scenario for a new play, *The Great God Brown*, and made some notes for another one, *Dynamo*, which loomed in his thoughts "queer and intriguing."

Eager to make some money of her own — finances were a chief matter of contention between the O'Neills — Agnes, with her husband's encouragement, turned playwright this summer. Under the pen name of Eleanor Rand (the wife in *Welded* was named Eleanor), she wrote a full-length drama entitled *The Guilty One* from a long scenario Eugene had written years earlier for a projected play called "The Reckoning." His synopsis of eighteen pages dealt with a man's forced marriage to a girl he has made pregnant, his rise in the world to industrialist and United States senator, and conflict between him and his wife, whom he has grown to hate, over their son. It all ends happily, though, in a vein of the baldest hokum. As the son marches off to World War I, the father, who has finally learned to appreciate his wife, says: "He'll come back to us, Mother — when it's all over. I know on my soul he will. The good God owes us that."

Written in Provincetown about 1918, "The Reckoning" was one of O'Neill's abortive attempts during his lean early years at something commercial. Although unpromising as fiction, the scenario is not without interest as biography, for some of it recalls the author's own history. Specifically, it reminds one of Eugene's being sent away to boarding school at an early age, of his marriage to Kathleen Jenkins because of her pregnancy, of his mother's shy and fearful course through life, of his father's climb to theatrical eminence from early poverty (there is, needless to say, a distinct resemblance between politicians, including senators, and actors). "The Reckoning" offers, if nothing else, further evidence that the biographer in the playwright was never far from the surface.

With some help from her husband, Agnes finished the play late in the summer and sent it to Richard Madden, who felt that it had commercial possibilities. Before long Madden relayed the good news that William A. Brady had placed *The Guilty One* under option, but he wanted some revisions.

O'Neill meanwhile, in the midst of working on *Marco Millions*, paused occasionally to fire off advice and criticisms to Macgowan about their approaching season at the two Village theaters. Strindberg's *There Are Crimes and Crimes* ("No one else dares to do him") was one of his suggestions, and he also favored Wedekind's *Lulu*, a combination of his *Erdgeist* and *Pandora's Box* ("It's the best thing of its kind ever written"). As for his own plays, *Desire Under the Elms* was scheduled for the Greenwich Village Theater, and another of his works was to be chosen for the Provincetown; one possibility was *The Book of Revelations*, which he, along the lines of his Coleridge adaptation, had arranged for the stage.

Dissatisfied on the whole with the way the programs for the two theaters were shaping up, he wanted them to be "much more adventurous. Some of our choices" he told Kenneth, "don't seem to me very imaginative or original . . . there isn't a play on either of our lists to represent any of the 'Big Men' we recognize as the masters of Modern Drama. Two plays by Stark [Young] and two by [Edmund] Wilson and two by me and none by Strindberg, none by Wedekind, none by Hauptmann, none by Ibsen, none by Andreyev, etc., doesn't seem right to me." (Operating the two theaters was to prove more difficult and complicated than they had anticipated; in the end, since it was easier to restage familiar scripts than to produce ones new to the group, there would be not two but four O'Neill productions — *Desire Under the Elms* and three revivals.)

"Am working hard as hell on *Marco*," Eugene reported to his colleague, and added that it is "coming along in great shape. . . . It's going to be as humorous as the devil if the way it makes me guffaw as I write is any criterion — and not bitter humor, either, although it's all satirical. I actually grow to love my American pillars of society, Polo Brothers & Son. It's going to be very long in first draft, I imagine, but I'm letting the sky be the limit and putting every fancy in. I imagine it's pretty nearly half-done now."

Worry over his financial situation offset his pleasure over *Marco Millions*. In 1922 he had earned about forty-four thousand dollars, in 1923 nearly thirty-five thousand dollars, but this year had been a lean one, with no prospects for immediate improvement (in all he was to make around ten thousand dollars in 1924). At the same time, largely because of the Ridgefield estate, his living expenses had grown heavier. Seeking an advance on *Desire Under the Elms*, he told Macgowan on August 19: "Next month is a bad one — with the income tax installment, my son Eugene's quota for schooling as per contract with my former frau, and the summer's bills . . . this firm is rapidly drifting toward insolvency. There has been nothing coming in of any account now in over a year and my back is beginning to crack under the strain. *Welded*, the biggest asset, didn't bring enough to pay the income tax on last year's prosperity. . . . The O'Neill estate continues quiescently in probate. An endeavor to auction off a choice lot of New London real estate failed lamentably. A large crowd gathered, but they evidently thought it was a philanthropic outing, for the highest bid was thousands below real value and the estate bid it in."

After Kenneth had sought advice and help from Otto Kahn — Kahn offered a loan of several thousand — Eugene replied, "Either he's there for the big help or he isn't. A couple of thou. would only put me that much more in debt without getting me anywhere nearer a solution. . . . The case is simple enough. The estate has no debts but lawyers' and administrator fees. All else is clear. But it has no cash wherewith to pay said fees and so must remain in probate no-man's land accumulating more administrator fees to pay. A simple ruinous circle!" He estimated that the estate had a net value of about one hundred and twenty-five thousand dollars and that it would cost approximately fifteen thousand dollars to get it out of probate. "Unless I get help," he said, "I see no end to the mess except a gradual taking over of the whole thing by the lawyers, etc. In five years they'll automatically own it all!"

In Provincetown Frank Shay, who usually confined himself to writing books and running a bookstore, organized a theater and as his major offering revived four of O'Neill's sea plays — *Bound East for Cardiff*, *In the Zone*, *Moon of the Caribbees* and *Long Voyage Home* — under the collective title *S.S. Glencairn*. Eugene went reluctantly, expecting an amateurish performance, and was gratified to find not only that it was quite good but that the one-acters "go together in great shape." At the same time the production aroused in him memories that crystallized into a feeling of loss and regret. "Seeing the *Glencairn* cycle," he said, "makes me homesick for homelessness and irresponsibility and I believe — philosophically at any rate — that I was a sucker ever to go in for playwriting, mating and begetting sons, houses and lots, and all similar snares of the 'property game.'" His sense of being trapped in domesticity was intensified several months later when Agnes became pregnant, but as the word got around he told friends he hoped the next child would be a girl.

Except for a short binge when a ten-gallon tin of pure alcohol was "cast up on our doorstep by the sea" (it probably had been jettisoned by a rumrunner), O'Neill worked hard at Peaked Hill. Late in August, feeling stale, he vacationed for a week with Agnes at the Wilbur Daniel Steeles' place in Nantucket and, though liquor was plentiful, he remained on the wagon. Among those he met at the Steeles' were critic Ernest Boyd and his wife Madeleine, a literary agent; Thomas Beer the writer; and Dudley Digges, one of the Theater Guild's finest actors. Madeleine Boyd, who remembered seeing Eugene and Agnes throwing things at one another in the Hell Hole, was impressed by his present sobriety, especially since everyone else was drinking.

During the visit he told his hosts that he regretted buying Brook Farm; aside from the place proving too costly for him, he had always hated cold weather and found the Ridgefield winters interminable. "I've spent too many winters in New England," he once said, "where there's nothing to do but chop down trees and drink hard cider and try to forget." The Steeles, who had spent considerable time in Bermuda, spoke so enthusiastically about its climate and year-round swimming that O'Neill decided to try the island this winter.

Refreshed by the Nantucket visit, he resumed work at Peaked Hill on *Marco Millions* and finished the first draft early in October. It was long, about twice as long as the standard play, and would be costly to produce. A fanciful excursion into the thirteenth century, the episodic work displays Venetians and knight crusaders, Tartar merchants and Indian snake charmers, Buddhist, Taoist and Confucian priests, not to mention a splendid assemblage of wives, warriors and courtiers at the palace of Kublai, the great Kaan. Unfortunately, despite its Mardi Gras of characters, its constant change of scene, each more exotic than the other, its continual philosophizing and poetizing, the play is more surface show than satisfying theater. It satirizes the materialism of Western civilization by placing a Babbitt-like Marco Polo in the legendary East and contrasting his values with those of a society superior to him in every respect —

intellectually, culturally, spiritually — though he of course looks down on the Orientals as benighted infidels. While the play's central idea has possibilities, O'Neill was not the man to develop them. In the hands, say, of Shaw, the story could have been thoughtful, witty comedy along the lines of *Caesar and Cleopatra;* but O'Neill, though he had a sardonic sense of humor and an Irishman's flair for comic exaggeration, was too slow on his feet for the kind of verbal Ping-Pong his story required.

Another weakness is Marco himself; concerned solely with making money and getting ahead, he is too consistent, too predictable to be interesting. Spanning some twenty years, the play takes him from Venice to Cathay, where Kublai, a wise ruler with a whimsical turn of mind, is fascinated by the callow traveler from the West. "This Marco touches me," he says, "as a child might, but at the same time there is something warped, deformed — Tell me, what shall I do with him?" Replies Chu-Yin, his venerable adviser: "Let him develop according to his own inclinations. . . . And let us observe him. At least, if he cannot learn, we shall."

Appointed ruler of a large city, Marco becomes the Kaan's most effective fund-raiser by simply reversing "the old system. For one thing," he explains, "I found they had a high tax on excess profits. Imagine a profit being excess! Why, it's humanly impossible! I repealed it. And I repealed the tax on luxuries. I found out a great majority . . . couldn't afford luxuries." As a "democratic" measure he imposes "a law that taxes every necessity in life, a law that hits every man's pocket equally, be he beggar or banker!" While the author's attempts at satire are ponderous, he is somewhat more successful with the bittersweet romance between Princess Kukachin, the Kaan's granddaughter, and Marco, who is too obtuse to realize she loves him. While Kublai finally wearies of him ("A jester inspires mirth only so long as his deformity does not revolt one") the princess regards him as a "strange, mysterious dream-knight from the exotic West." At the end he returns to Venice laden with riches to marry the giggling middle-aged virgin who has been awaiting him all these years, as flowerlike Kukachin, having lost the will to live, fades away into death.

By design *Marco Millions* has a dual personality, for the playwright wrote in two different styles to contrast the Venetian's sterile, money-grubbing nature with the exquisite sensibilities of classical China. Marco's language is always flat, banal, cliché-ridden ("There's no place like home . . . I've had my fun and I suppose it's about time I settled down"), while the Orientals express themselves in quasi-lyrical fashion. "You have

[151]

been a golden bird singing beside a black river," the Kaan tells his grand-daughter. "You took your mother's place in my heart when she died. I was younger then. The river was not so black — the river of man's life so deep and silent flowing with an insane obsession — whither? — and why?"

Here again, as in *The Fountain*, O'Neill sought to prove himself as much poet as playwright, but verbal felicity was not his forte; when he strove for lyricism, his writing tended to become soft, diffuse, "poetic" in the pejorative use of the word. At the same time, O'Neill *was* a poet of the theater in his conceptions, in the total effect of his better scenes, in his fresh, imaginative use of stagecraft — masks, settings, pantomime, back-ground sounds — and behind all was his tragic view of life, another sign of the poet.

8

※

A Drama of Masks

On paper Macgowan, Jones and O'Neill had their 1924–1925 season well organized. The Provincetown Playhouse, continuing its original policy, was to feature "experiment," the Greenwich Village Theater "repertory," five productions were to be given at each house, and "a beginning will be attempted toward a true repertory company. A single group of players will appear at both theaters. All will work toward a creative ensemble." As the season actually turned out, the Provincetown staged eight productions, the other theater only three; all distinction faded between the "experiment" of the one and the "repertory" of the other; and, as Helen Deutsch and Stella Hanau recount in *The Province-town*, "Life was a bewildering maze of openings and closings, of meetings and dovetailed rehearsals, of voyages back and forth between the two theaters, which were only four blocks apart. [The staff members] were endlessly in transit, carrying properties, costumes, programs, scribbled messages."

The Greenwich Village was to open with *The Saint*, a story of the Southwest by Stark Young, the Provincetown with *The Crime in the Whistler Room*, a mixture of realism and fantasy by Edmund Wilson. O'Neill had hoped that *Desire Under the Elms* would launch the season at the Greenwich Village, but difficulty in finding an actor for old Cabot had forced its postponement; the other two leading roles had been filled early, with Mary Morris, who had been in *The Spook Sonata* and *Fashion*, cast as Abbie, and Charles Ellis as Eben.

With Bermuda in mind Eugene wrote to Macgowan on September 21, 1924, that he wanted to know the "definite date *Desire* is to open. In fact, I must know approximately. I've been counting on its going on four weeks after *Saint* [due on October 11] and making plans accordingly

[153]

. . . I won't be in Ridgefield where I can get to town any time — not after the middle of November." Since he had previously made his financial situation seem critical, he had not yet informed Kenneth that he was going to incur further expense by wintering in Bermuda, but he said: "I'm very anxious to see you and talk over my winter's plans. I've made a discovery about myself in analyzing the work done, etc., in the past six winters which has led me to a decision about what I must do in the future."

The "discovery" was that the caliber of his work generally declined with the seasonal drop in temperature. Reviewing the past he found that his weakest plays had been written entirely or in large part during the cold months: *Chris*, winter 1918–1919; *Gold*, winter 1919–1920; *The First Man*, winter 1920–1921; and *Welded*, fall and winter 1923–1924. Conversely, he had generally been more productive and written better in the milder seasons: final draft of *The Straw* (he still felt in 1924 that it contained "some of the best writing I've ever done"), spring 1919; *Anna Christie*, summer 1920; *The Emperor Jones* and *Diff'rent*, fall 1920; first draft of *The Fountain*, spring and summer 1921; *The Hairy Ape*, fall 1921; final draft of *The Fountain*, summer 1922; *Marco Millions*, the summers of 1923 and 1924; *All God's Chillun Got Wings*, summer and fall 1923; and *Desire Under the Elms* (an exception in part), winter and spring 1924. After finding such a pattern in his work, he decided that not only would he winter in Bermuda but that henceforth he would so arrange his life as to have warm weather the year around.

Considering his particular nature, it does seem possible that the cold could adversely affect his writing, for he generally was in a better frame of mind when he had the sun, the beach and swimming. A man with a deep love of and mystical feeling toward the sea, one who felt more at ease in the water than on land, he found swimming almost as essential as writing to his mental and emotional well-being. (In the late 1920s he thought of writing an "autobiographical" play, "the grand opus of my life," which, significantly enough, he intended to call "Sea-Mother's Son"; the project never materialized, however. Years still later, in *Long Day's Journey Into Night*, which contains, presumably, some elements of the "autobiographical" play he originally had in mind, he wrote: "It was a great mistake, my being born a man, I would have been much more successful as a sea gull or a fish. . . .")

O'Neill spent his final days at Peaked Hill reading proof for a two-volume edition of his "complete works" to be published by Horace Liveright. "It's a hell of a job," he said, "but it does serve to acquaint me with stuff that is so forgotten, it's new." This time he simply checked his plays for printers' errors, but for a four-volume edition of his works the following year he made revisions that, among other changes, shortened *Beyond the Horizon, Gold, The Straw* and *Welded*. He took great care with the publication of his plays; no matter how many drafts he might have written or how much revising he had done during rehearsals, he always went over his plays again before allowing them to appear in print. He wanted his published works to be as good as possible, for he looked to future generations of readers, rather than to the public of his day, for the important verdict on his writings.

On returning to the city in fall 1924 he was involved immediately with rehearsals of both *Desire* and *S.S. Glencairn;* prompted by the success of Frank Shay's production, the Village group was packaging the sea tales at the Provincetown. "The individual plays are complete in themselves," O'Neill had said previously, "yet the identity of the crew goes through the series and welds the four one-acts into a long play." The reviewers by and large were delighted with *S.S. Glencairn*, which opened on November 3, lavishing on it such praise as "vividly pulsating drama" and "a richly memorable evening." The author himself considered the production "on the whole excellent," but he joked to Frank Shay that *Bound East for Cardiff* was not "as good as the original PP wharf production (because I didn't play the mate, what?)."

He was chiefly interested, however, in *Desire Under the Elms*, rehearsing with a cast headed by Mary Morris, Charles Ellis and, in the role of Ephraim Cabot, a newcomer in the New York theater — Walter Huston. Rangy in build, with a pleasantly plain, typically American face (he was from Toronto, of Irish-Scotch parentage), Huston had been in show business for years but his experience had been confined almost entirely to vaudeville, as a song-and-dance man, and to stock companies in the "sticks." Now aged forty, Huston had finally emerged from obscurity early this year when he appeared on Broadway in the title role of *Mr. Pitt*, a sentimental tale of small-town America. Huston was so convincing as Pitt — a meek, pathetic figure — and as a similar character in *The Easy Mark*, a subsequent Broadway piece, that almost everyone considered him typecast in the two plays. His image both times was directly opposite to the one he was now required to project as the harsh, tough old farmer in *Desire Under the Elms*.

Robert Edmond Jones, serving as both designer and director for *Desire*, had suggested Huston for the part. At first O'Neill was skeptical, thinking that Bobby might have been influenced by his friendship with

Charles Gilpin in The Emperor Jones

Walter Huston in Desire Under the Elm

Louis Wolheim in The Hairy Ape

Huston's sister (years later he married her), but Jones's recommendation of Walter Huston proved to be one of his major contributions to the production. "There have been only three actors in my plays who managed to realize the characters . . . as I originally saw them," O'Neill said toward the end of his career, and he proceeded to name Gilpin in *The Emperor Jones*, Wolheim in *The Hairy Ape*, and Huston in *Desire Under the Elms*. "There have been other good actors and actresses in my plays," he continued, "but only those three lived up to the conceptions I had as I wrote. There are too many actors and actresses who just go out there and play themselves. It's not a good thing, either for acting or for playwriting. The playwright comes to depend on the physical presence of the actors to fill out their characters for him. . . . I've always tried to *write* my characters out."

As one thoroughly versed in the theater, starting "from the back wall," he also used to write out "every detail of the setting and action, even the lighting," and make sketches to guide his designers. *Desire* posed a special scenic problem, since the action constantly shifts from one room of the farmhouse to another or to the outside, and at times occurs simultaneously in separate places. As a solution, O'Neill conceived a full end of the two-story farmhouse, specifying that the outer wall of the house should be detachable in sections so that any part or parts of the interior could be bared as the action required; the general effect was to be of the entire farmhouse placed on the stage.

Working from four sketches by O'Neill, Jones devised a set faithful to the author's conception: stark, whitewashed exterior, mean little windows, pinched rooms, sinister overhanging elms. For some episodes the structure worked fine; in the scene where old Cabot tells his life story to his wife, as she stares hungrily toward Eben's bedroom, the multiple setting also shows Eben in his room, restless and uneasy. As the text says: "Their hot glances seem to meet through the wall. Unconsciously he stretches out his arms for her and she half rises." On the whole, though, the setting was a mixed blessing. If the rooms and other playing areas, all of them small, suggested the constricted life of the Cabots, they also cramped the action; perhaps it would have been better had Jones, disregarding the O'Neill sketches, provided a freer, more impressionistic set. In fact O'Neill himself was dissatisfied, for he later complained that the play had not been produced as he wrote it: "There has never been the elm trees of my play, characters almost, and my acts were chopped up into four distinct scenes through lack of time to get the changes perfected in blackouts; the flow of life from room to room of the house, the house as character, the acts as smooth developing wholes have never existed."

As *Desire* was having its première at the Greenwich Village on November 11, the playwright took refuge in the basement workshop of the theater and, occupying himself like a rustic, whittled one piece of wood after another. A few days earlier he had told an interviewer that *Desire* contained "a surprise" (he presumably had in mind Abbie's slaying of her own child), and now he awaited the response to his Greek tragedy set in old New England.

The following day the press notices, with only a few exceptions, failed to do justice to what remains one of the author's outstanding works; the critics passed more accurate judgment on themselves, so to speak, than on *Desire Under the Elms*. Alan Dale denounced the new play as "cantankerous, cancerous proceedings" full of "hideous characters" — as could be expected, since he was on the *American*, the Hearst sheet that had tried to repress *All God's Chillun*. Yet Dale was not alone in finding *Desire* repellent. The man on the *Post* dismissed it as "a tale of almost unrelieved sordidness," while *Time* magazine pontificated that it was "the kind of thing the spectator will object to on the score that existence cannot possibly be so brutal." In a more balanced verdict Burns Mantle said that it should be seen by everyone seriously interested in the theater, then added: "But none should see it unadvisedly — without knowing that it is a story in which lust and murder, incest between son and stepmother, and infanticide, ugliness, sin and appalling freedom of speech are frankly illustrated."

Heywood Broun, blowing hot and cold, thought that *Desire* could have been the author's finest work if not for excess and some strokes of old-fashioned theatricality. "In many external things," he said, "O'Neill is a pioneer among the playwrights. He has spread before us new forms. But he is still the true son of the man who played *The Count of Monte Cristo* more than a thousand times. . . . Heredity has left in O'Neill the actor's greediness for every last potential twist and turn in any given situation." In Alexander Woollcott's case it appears that he was so distracted by the set ("pesky contraption") that he could scarcely see the play, and what he did see failed to impress him. On the other hand Stark Young, who was now on the *Times*, called the setting "profoundly dramatic" and thought that the party scene contained "such poetry and terrible beauty as we rarely see in the theater."

The most enthusiastic as well as perceptive review came a fortnight later from Joseph Wood Krutch, the newly appointed critic of the

Nation. Discussing not only *Desire* but the author's work in general, he said on November 26 that in "this age of intellectualized art there is an inevitable but unfortunate tendency to assume of Eugene O'Neill, as of every other arresting artist, that his greatness must lie somehow in the greatness or in the clarity of his thought; to seek in *All God's Chillun* some solution of the problem of race or in *The Hairy Ape* some attitude toward society; and then, not finding them, to fail in the fullest appreciation of the greatness which is his. It was not thought which drove him, as a young man, to seek adventure among the roughest men he could find, and it was not thought which he brought back from this and other experiments in life. Something tempestuous in his nature made him a brother of tempests, and he has sought wherever he could find them the fiercest passions, less anxious to clarify their causes for the benefit of those who love peace than eager to share them, and happy if he could only be exultantly a part of their destructive fury. It is a strange taste, this, to wish to be perpetually racked and tortured, to proceed from violence to violence, and to make of human torture not so much the occasion of other things as the raison d'être of drama; but such is his temperament. The meaning and unity of his work lies not in any controlling intellectual idea and certainly not in any 'message,' but merely in the fact that each play is an experience of extraordinary intensity."

Still aggrieved over the general reception of his play, O'Neill protested months later to George Jean Nathan (among those who underestimated *Desire*): "What I think everyone missed in *Desire* is the quality in it I set most store by — the attempt to give an epic tinge to New England's inhibited life — but, to make its inexpressiveness practically expressive, to release it. It's just that — the poetical (in the broadest and deepest sense) vision illuminating even the most sordid and mean blind alleys of life — which I'm convinced is . . . my concern and justification as a dramatist.

"There's a lot of poetical beauty in *Marco Millions* . . . but there the poetic is more or less obviously called forth by the theme and background. It's where the poetic is buried deep beneath the dull and crude that one's deep-seeing vision is tested."

Shortly after *Desire* opened, Sidney Howard's *They Knew What They Wanted* arrived in town to unanimous acclaim, and several critics, noting that the two plays had similar stories, drew comparisons between them to O'Neill's discredit. Robert Benchley, for instance, felt that Howard "has done the better job, for his comedy has moments of great pathos, a necessary thing for comedy, but O'Neill's tragedy has moments of unconscious comedy, a terrible thing for tragedy." Howard himself, though, admired *Desire* and felt so strongly that it was being underrated that he wrote a letter to the *Times* in which he said that the play has "the power, starkness and nobility which only real tragedy can assume. If it strikes snags, they are heroic snags . . . I only ask to be shown anything produced by the English-speaking theater of recent generations which is half so fine or true or brave as *Desire Under the Elms*." (Months later, on learning that his play had won the Pulitzer Prize, he said that the award should have gone to O'Neill.)

Unlike Howard's comedy-drama, which immediately became a major Broadway hit, it appeared that the O'Neill tragedy would have only a limited run in the Village. Despite O'Neill's reputation and past successes, none of the Broadway producers rushed to move his new play uptown; they apparently considered it too grim to be commercial. Fortunately, Cleon Throckmorton, who had done some favors for Jones and Green, a firm normally occupied with the *Greenwich Village Follies* and similar frivolous fare, persuaded them to see the play. Favorably impressed, the pair joined forces with the Triumvirate in moving *Desire* to the Earl Carroll Theater and later to the smaller George M. Cohan, where it ran until fall 1925. Produced at a cost of four thousand dollars, it wound up grossing three hundred and ninety-five thousand dollars and earning twenty-four thousand dollars for its author. What saved the play, though, and fueled its lengthy run, was that a few weeks after the move to Broadway the city authorities, urged on by persons and organizations dedicated to purity and decency, tried to close it as "immoral and obscene." In the ensuing notoriety its audiences grew larger.

As O'Neill prepared to leave for Bermuda he had two scripts still awaiting production, *The Fountain*, which the Theater Guild had placed under option when Arthur Hopkins relinquished his rights, and *Marco Millions*. At first O'Neill had sought to place *Marco* with Max Reinhardt and Morris Gest, hoping they might stage it on a scale comparable to their spectacle *The Miracle*, which cost half a million dollars, but when this dream never materialized he turned to David Belasco, another impresario with a flair for showy productions. Only a few years earlier Eugene had scorned Belasco's offerings as typical of the "Broadway show-shop," just as Belasco had once assailed the Village presentations as "vicious, vulgar and degrading," but the times and the theater had changed.

Acknowledging a congratulatory note from Belasco, the playwright replied on November 22, 1924: "I now have a play to submit to you. . . . It has these defects from a production standpoint: It is costly to put on, involving a forestage, music, many scenes, large crowds, etc. – and also *it seems to last two nights* — to be *two* plays, in fact!" As to its merits, he said that it was *"comedy satire . . .* of our life and ideals," despite its historic background; expressed confidence that its love story and Eastern background possessed *"real* poetic beauty," and concluded that he would regard it as "a great favor" if Belasco read the script.

From resentment, apparently, over the *Desire* reviews, O'Neill had begun drinking the day after the première, but his forthcoming departure for Bermuda forced him to exercise restraint so that he could get his affairs in order. Shortly before sailing on November 29, he took the precaution to discourage headhunters in Bermuda who might want to lionize him or draw him and Agnes into the social whirl; he sent word ahead, as appeared in the *Royal Gazette and Colonist Daily*, the island's newspaper, that he intended doing "much work whilst here and is therefore looking forward to peace and quiet rather than the gaieties of our season."

But his desire to arrive unobtrusively was thwarted by his Irish wolfhound, Finn Mac Cool, who was frantic at being cooped up aboard ship. As soon as the liner was berthed, Finn, the *Royal Gazette* reported on December 6, "brought a steward ashore at a speed never before attained on Front Street. The captain of the *Fort St. George* had serious intention of manning the front tackle and running the dog ashore in a breeches buoy, but a reckless steward volunteered to risk his life, and a rapid landing was accomplished to the great admiration of the crowd. Bermuda opinion as to his breed has run riot. The oldest inhabitant does not remember the island ever being invaded by anything like it; and the youngest generation looks on in wonder."

After a fortnight at a hotel in Hamilton, the island's capital, the O'Neills moved to a pair of isolated wooden cottages called "Campsea" and "Crow's Nest" — the first as living quarters for them all, the other as a place for Eugene to work — on the south shore in Paget Parish (today the site of the posh Coral Beach Club). The cottages, while small and plain, were magnificently located on a high, thickly wooded area that led down to cliffs overlooking the sea, and the property of some thirty acres included a long span of unspoiled beach. Here, as at Peaked Hill Bars, O'Neill could "feel a true kinship and harmony with life. . . . Sand and sun and sea and wind — you merge into them, and become as meaningless and as full of meaning as they are."

During his early weeks on the island, however, as he drank 1924 out and 1925 in, he was in no condition to enjoy his new refuge by the sea. More than once in the past, but particularly since his brother's slow suicide by alcohol, he had attempted to quit drinking forever as the only solution to his weakness, for he generally could not stop till he was sick and vomiting. Doctors had warned that the prolonged binges would shorten his life, but the deep sense of guilt in his makeup and concomitant, though unconscious, need to punish himself, continued to rule him. At the same time, countering his self-destructive impulse, he had a passion for physical fitness and took pride in his lean athletic build. It is symptomatic of the contradictions in the man that during his drinking he sought to keep in shape, whenever he could muster the energy, by swimming and taking hikes along the beach.

When he finally tapered off in January he also began a new effort to quit smoking, as he was something of a hypochondriac and suspected that he was "sensitive" to nicotine; most of the time he smoked only moderately, but when he wrote it was one cigarette after another. He used to record in his diary the days that passed without his having a drink or a smoke, and one day jubilantly noted that he had exceeded his "non-smoke record of 42 consecutive days of last year." He also, after some weeks of healthful living, recorded his measurements: "chest, 40; expand, 41; biceps, 13-½, 13; forearm, 11; waist, 31, etc."

Shortly after his binge a local physician lent him an issue of *The Practitioner*, an English medical journal, that was entirely devoted to the subject of alcoholism. O'Neill found the issue "very interesting and applicable to me" — a comment that most likely was inspired by an article by Sir James Purves-Steward on what was known at the time as "paroxysmal dipsomania." "This is a recurrent psychosis," Sir James said, "consisting of attacks during which the patient has an irresistible impulse to take alcohol in excess. The dipsomaniac individual sometimes drinks himself into a state of acute alcoholic poisoning. . . .

"Careful inquiry into the history of such patients shows that many of them have a marked neuropathic heredity, and that practically all of them, before they happen to acquire the habit of paroxysmal excessive drinking, have had previous neuropathic symptoms, such as phobiae, obsessions, emotional depression, visceral discomfort, etc. . . . the patient discovers that he can mask his deficient will-power and 'drown his sorrow' by a dose of alcohol, which comforts him for the time. . . . He drinks heavily for a few days until his bout is brought to an end by alcoholic gastritis. . . . His attack then subsides, and he is free from alcoholic craving, and full of good resolutions, perhaps for weeks or months, until his next attack. Sometimes during this interval he even has a positive distaste for alcohol. But his psychosis inevitably recurs."

In January, after being informed by Richard Madden that Belasco would take an option on *Marco Millions* if it were cut to "one long evening," O'Neill, working some days as long as ten and eleven hours, finished the new draft in slightly over a week. A fortnight later he received an effusive cablegram from the producer that he "loved" the play, and shortly afterward word that Belasco wanted Robert Edmond Jones to design the production; he intended to spend between seventy-five thousand and one hundred thousand dollars, a large sum for the day, the sort of money usually expended on a musical comedy.

The playwright's affairs were now flourishing: *Desire* was playing at the Earl Carroll to over nine thousand dollars weekly, more than any of his other plays had ever grossed; *S.S. Glencairn*, after six weeks in the Village, had been moved uptown, first to the Punch and Judy, then to the Princess; and a new revival of *The Emperor Jones* at the Provincetown was about to transfer to the Punch and Judy. In addition, a London producer was interested in *Jones* and *The Hairy Ape*, and there was talk of making a film of *Ape* with Louis Wolheim in his original role (but only the London *Jones* was to materialize).

Among the first persons the O'Neills met in Bermuda were Mrs. Charlotte ("Tottie") Barbour, an Englishwoman who worked for a New York book publisher and knew some of the Provincetown Players, and her sister Alice Cuthbert, a beautiful blond, well tanned, who loved outdoor sports. The two women, guests at the Elbow Beach Club, a hotel within walking distance of Campsea, often joined the O'Neills for picnic lunches and in the evening. While Agnes liked them both, she was starting to lose her shape from pregnancy and could not help being jealous of Alice, as Eugene, obviously enjoying the girl's company, spent time with her almost daily. Mrs. Clark, who missed little and ventured occasionally to needle her mistress, inquired one day with an innocent face: "Weren't they swimming holding hands?" When Agnes upbraided him, Eugene maintained that they were merely "swimming tandem." The socializing with "Tottie" and Alice continued, despite some arguments between the O'Neills; but eventually Agnes, concluding that Alice had no designs on her husband and that he was not falling in love with her, admired her as having "a rare & beautiful quality."

Apparently Eugene's feeling toward the girl was idealistic rather than romantic or sexual; there was something innocent about her, something inviolate that he admired and envied. He wrote a poem about her (which Agnes considered "very near the truth") that includes the lines, "We are wise/But you are whole," and ends:

You, the sun, & sea
Trinity!
Sweet spirit, pass on
Keep the dream
Beauty
Into infinity.

From all available evidence, it appears that in the ten years O'Neill and Agnes were together he never, except toward the end, was unfaithful to her. Not because he was so content in his marriage but, apparently, because sex in itself did not tempt him sufficiently for him to complicate his life with an affair or even a brief fling; he wanted regularity and peace for his work. While his letters to Agnes suggest a passionate lover, he was not, according to her, particularly sensual. The ironic thing about their relationship was that although he yearned for total union with her, he basically was unsuited for it, unable to give wholeheartedly of himself not only to Agnes but to any woman. A man of contradictory impulses and needs, with a strain of misogynism, he would always keep a crucial part of himself remote, secret, untouchable.

Late in January, after revising *Marco* for Belasco, O'Neill went to work on *The Great God Brown,* for which he had prepared a scenario months earlier. About half the time in his work he began with a scenario, "which means," he said, "that some ideas develop fully and clearly before a word is written, others won't. But here's the queer part, having written a detailed scenario, I rarely ever look at it when writing the play or follow it at all except in the bare outline – and rarely in that!" When he prepared the scenario for *Brown,* however, he felt that he had the play entirely "doped out," but as he began writing he found it "coming out all different" from the way he had planned. "This," he said, "is a strange one!"

As he struggled with *Brown,* trouble was brewing in New York for *Desire Under the Elms.* On February 20, 1925, he had a letter from Richard Madden that the police were "after" *Desire* – news that he took lightly until a "wild cable" the following day from the literary agent that his play was "about to be indicted." The threat against the O'Neill drama was part of a general campaign, the latest in a number of crusades, to clean up the New York stage. Earlier in the 1924–1925 season a voice or two had spluttered briefly and ineffectually against *What Price Glory?,* Laurence Stalling and Maxwell Anderson's ribald comedy of men at war, but the new drive, launched in mid-February by the police authorities, was the broadest, most determined effort at censorship to date. At the same time, complicating the situation, certain producers whose shows were failing tried to boost business by filing anonymous complaints against their own attractions as "indecent."

The greatest confusion was generated by William A. Brady, whose production *A Good Bad Woman* was the first to attract the censors' fire; from one day to the next he changed position, now siding with the censors, now complaining about being made a scapegoat, now assailing other producers' offerings. Brady had made himself vulnerable through a publicity hoax in which his leading woman had protested to the press that certain dialogue in her vehicle was offensive. It appears in fact that his hoax touched off the agitation for censorship, and throughout the ensuing controversy, which eventually engulfed a dozen or so plays, Brady played a half-serious clown. At one point he declared that he had produced *A Good Bad Woman* "to shock the theatergoing public into such reforming zeal as would purify the New York stage"; another time he suggested "a theatrical suicide compact under which all the bad plays would immolate themselves by agreement among the producers." Apparently he could not decide whether to pose as a public benefactor by supporting the authorities or to try to promote *Bad Woman*, which had drawn adverse reviews, into a profitable run. In any case, his presentation was denounced as "irreclaimably vicious" and ordered closed by District Attorney Joab H. Banton. Brady, after twisting and turning, complied finally, as Banton aimed his sights on bigger game.

Another play, Banton declared, was even "worse," but at first he refused to identify it for fear this would "advertise it, and thus send greater crowds to its box office." The one he had in mind, it soon became clear, was *Desire Under the Elms;* seeking revenge for his failure to muzzle *All God's Chillun* the previous year, the southern-born prosecutor had seized on the current crusade as a chance to suppress the latest O'Neill work. Calling it "too thoroughly bad to be purified by a blue pencil," he threatened to seek an indictment from the grand jury unless it were closed immediately.

While the district attorney viewed with alarm, conciliatory voices in the theater suggested activation of the "citizens' play-jury," an arrangement under which plays allegedly objectionable would be tried by special juries functioning outside the regular judicial system. Conceived by leading Broadway figures, with the backing of Actors' Equity, as a means of averting official harassment, the plan called for a panel of several hundred persons in the arts and the professions — a panel selected by the head of Equity — from which the juries would be formed. Although the authorities had accepted the plan when proposed several years earlier, at the height of another censorship drive, it had never been tried.

Kenneth Macgowan now endorsed the idea, in response to Banton's ultimatum, and said that he and his colleagues were willing to abide by a play-jury's verdict. Banton tried to dismiss the offer on the grounds that the system was nonexistent and would take too long to implement, but under criticism from the press, which in general championed O'Neill, he began to soften his pronouncements. He conceded that perhaps Macgowan's proposal was practical after all; finally, confronted with tributes to the O'Neill drama from leading clergymen, educators and other notables, he washed his hands of the entire matter, relegating *Desire* and the other allegedly immoral works to the play-juries.

The notoriety, just as he had feared, boosted business at *Desire*, with the weekly gross jumping immediately from about twelve thousand dollars to over thirteen thousand dollars and shortly to nearly sixteen thousand dollars. "God bless Gene!" Macgowan said, taking a practical view. O'Neill himself had mixed feelings; while he welcomed the high grosses and relished the thought of Banton's discomfiture, he was distressed to hear that the "wrong audience" now flocked to his play. It was attracting, he complained, "the low-minded, looking for smut, and they are highly disappointed or else laugh whenever they imagine double-meanings."

The first plays submitted to the special juries — a different jury tried each one — were Edwin Justus Mayer's *The Firebrand*, a sophisticated comedy about Benvenuto Cellini; *They Knew What They Wanted*; and *Desire*. On March 13, exactly a month after the cleanup effort had begun, the O'Neill and Howard plays were unanimously acquitted of any indecencies, but the *Firebrand* jury suggested that a balcony scene, "culminating in a prolonged osculation, be shortened." At once seeking new publicity, William Brady called the verdicts "comical," said that any jury finding *Desire* "guiltless" would have "hung a medal" on *A Good Bad Woman*, and announced his intention to revive it. A few months later O'Neill, recalling Brady's equivocal role in the censorship drive and his slur at *Desire*, intervened when the producer wanted to renew his option on Agnes's *The Guilty One*; at Eugene's urging (he also was motivated by the feeling that the play, on which he had done some work, was not good), Agnes withdrew her script.

Though his latest brush with the authorities gave him some uneasy moments, O'Neill was so engrossed with *The Great God Brown* that *Desire* had seemed outside his "range of worry." What he was trying to achieve in his new play, which he had begun on January 28, was "so damn complicated and subtle" that at times his progress was slow; but working steadily he completed *Brown* on March 25. Toward the end he became so emotional that he finished the play "in tears! Couldn't control myself!" The following day, expressing the belief that it "marks my 'ceiling' so far," he described it in a letter to George Jean Nathan as "a devastating, crucifying new one."

As his words to Nathan, not to mention his private tears, suggest, the play is among his most subjective works. Indeed, when you search for Eugene O'Neill in his writings a chief place to look is *The Great God Brown*, particularly at the character of Dion Anthony. "You're not weak," someone comforts Dion. "You were born with ghosts in your eyes and you were brave enough to go looking into your own dark — and you got afraid." At another point Dion apostrophizes the night: "Why must I live in a cage like a criminal, defying and hating, I who love peace and friendship? (*Clasping his hands above in supplication*) Why was I born without a skin, O God, that I must wear armor in order to touch or to be touched? Or rather, Old Graybeard, why the devil was I ever born at all?"

A strange and uneven drama, *The Great God Brown* is mystical, poetic, at times profound and beautifully written, other times hopelessly pretentious, and eventually so tortuous in its course and so difficult to follow that it becomes exasperating. In several earlier plays, particularly *The Hairy Ape*, the author had flirted with masks; in the new one his characters are constantly masking and unmasking in their efforts to protect themselves from or to make contact with others. The playwright, almost exhausting the vocabulary of masks, also used them to indicate split personalities, to differentiate between the characters' private and social selves, and as a device to transfer one man's personality to another. His use of the masks owed more to Freud than to Aeschylus. "For what, at bottom," he has inquired rhetorically, "is the new psychological insight into human cause and effect but a study in masks, an exercise in unmasking?"

So many reviewers voiced bewilderment when *Brown* opened in 1926 that the playwright wrote what was supposed to be an explanatory article, but while it clarified some aspects of the play, in general it deepened the fog. He disclosed that the names of his principals were symbolic. Thus, Dion Anthony was named after both Dionysius ("the creative pagan acceptance of life") and St. Anthony ("the masochistic, life-denying spirit of Christianity") — two opposing forces that, when embodied in one person, could result only in "mutual exhaustion," in both sides of the man being tortured. Dion's wife Margaret was envisioned as a descendant of Faust's Marguerite, "the eternal girl-woman . . . properly oblivious of everything" but perpetuating the race. The other woman in Dion's life, though a prostitute, is essentially a dauntless Earth Mother, serene, compassionate, instinctively wise; she is called Cybel, after the nature goddess Cybele who was worshiped by the Greeks and Romans as "the Great Mother of the Gods." And William A. Brown, the fourth principal, was named in an ironic sense after the martyred abolitionist ("John Brown's body lies a-moulderin' in the grave," etc.); he represents the acquisitive, materialistic spirit in American life that "goes marching on."

After explaining his characters' names, O'Neill continues: "Dion's mask of Pan . . . is not only a defense against the world for the supersensitive painter-poet underneath it, but also an integral part of his character as an artist. . . . Dion's inner self retrogresses along the line of Christian resignation until it partakes of the nature of the Saint while at the same time the outer Pan is slowly transformed by his struggle with reality into Mephistopheles."

Aware that his explanation was becoming as involved and confusing as the play itself, O'Neill sums up: *The Great God Brown* "is Mystery — the Mystery any one man or woman can feel but not understand as the meaning of any event — or accident — in any life on earth." To Barrett H. Clark he made the same point more simply: "In one sense *Brown* is a mystery play, only instead of dealing with crooks and police it's about the mystery of personality and life."

A play the biographical dramatist *had* to write, *The Great God Brown* was, basically, the second time he had written it. Stripped of its complicated use of masks, its flights of mysticism, its poetic language, *Brown* tells the same story as the author's very first full-length work, "Bread and Butter," for both are concerned with a failed artist, crucified by life and imprisoned in marriage, who takes refuge in self-induced death. Just as *Brown* is richer, more imaginative than the early drama, so Dion Anthony is more complex and interesting than his precursor; both, however, like certain other O'Neill protagonists, bear a marked resemblance to their author. In *The Straw* he had given a fairly accurate, though sketchy image of himself as an egocentric young writer; in *Welded*, probing more deeply, he had shown himself as husband and lover; now in *Brown*, despite the fiction and ambiguities in Dion Anthony's portrait, he reveals more of himself than ever before. This is, however, neither the complete picture nor a flattering self-likeness, for the situation of Artist versus Society activated the adolescent strain in O'Neill's emotional makeup; he conceived Dion chiefly in terms of romantic self-pity and narcissistic self-dramatization. (No wonder, then, considering the author's identification with his ill-fated hero, that he wept as he finished the play.)

For most of its length *Brown* is perfectly intelligible. Dion Anthony loses all zest for living once he realizes that his is only a minor talent ("I want to be an artist or nothing," fledgling playwright Eugene O'Neill said in 1914); but at the urging of his wife – they have three children – he goes to work for his old friend Billy Brown, a mediocre yet successful architect. Theirs has always been an uneasy friendship, for Brown envies the other's charm and ability, and moreover he believes himself in love with Dion's wife. "No!" Dion tells him. "That is merely the appearance, not the truth! Brown loves me! . . . because I have always possessed the power he needed for love, because I am love!"

Allowing for certain modifications required by the story, the relationship between Dion and Brown resembles the one between the O'Neill brothers; yet such is the complexity of the play that Dion, though largely an image of Eugene, also contains elements of Jamie's personality and in fact occasionally represents Jamie. At such times Brown, generally a Jamie-figure, becomes momentarily a Eugene-figure. To illustrate: after an outburst by Dion Anthony against his rival, Cybel says, "But you like him, too! You're brothers, I guess, somehow. Well, remember, he's paying, he'll pay – in some way or other." To which Dion replies: "I know. Poor Billy! God forgive me the evil I've done him!" (In life Jamie did "evil" to Eugene, not conversely – a subject the playwright was to explore in the harrowing fourth act of *Long Day's Journey* as the older brother strips down to his tortured soul.)

Dion, who is drinking himself to death (like Jamie), finds his sole consolation in Cybel, whom he playfully refers to as "Old Sacred Cow," "Old Filth" and "sentimental old pig." She is the one person who accepts his real self, the martyred soul beneath the Mephistophelian exterior ("Haven't I told you," she once admonishes him, "to take off your mask in the house?"); and she in turn, removing the mask of "the hardened prostitute," discloses only to him her true face – the indomitable, all-compassionate Earth Mother. Their mutual understanding is so profound that no one can disturb it, not even Brown; covetous of everything Dion has, Brown buys Cybel as his mistress but he can never really possess her. Up to this point *The Great God Brown* is clear enough, but once Dion

[169]

Anthony dies and Brown, using the other's mask, assumes his place with Margaret, the play becomes too metaphysical and obscure.

Despite its cryptic finale and other arcane moments, *Brown* is revealing biography, and nowhere more so than in Dion's dependence upon Cybel, particularly when this is contrasted with his attitude as husband and father. Although he professes great love for his wife, his feeling for her is tepid compared to his relationship with Cybel — an aspect of Dion Anthony that expresses a crucial side of O'Neill himself, namely, his need of a "mother." It all goes back to O'Neill's apprehensive childhood when, feeling shut out by his addicted mother, he used to take refuge under the firm wing of Sarah Sandy, his nursemaid and in effect his second mother. Later, as an adult, Eugene yearned for another Sarah Sandy to shelter him from the world. When he was courting eighteen-year-old Beatrice Ashe in New London in 1914 — he was then twenty-six — he often referred to her as "Mother" and in one letter said: "I feel the impulse of the tired child who runs to his mother's arms and lays his head upon her breast, and sobs for no reason at all. Be my mother! Let me place my head on My Place and weep out my woes, Soul Mother of Mine." Haunted by the image of a strong mother-figure, the playwright created such a character not only in Cybel but years later in the massive farm girl in *A Moon for the Misbegotten*. Moreover, in *Strange Interlude* he has Nina Leeds say: "The mistake began when God was created in a male image. Of course, women would see Him that way, but men should have been gentlemen enough, remembering their mothers, to make God a woman!"

As a story *Brown* was partly inspired by the history of O'Neill's New London friend Edward Keefe, who, abandoning his struggle as an art student in New York, returned home to practice architecture. (The Dion Anthony character in the original draft of the play was named "Stanley Keith.") At first, Keefe worked for an architect whose sole qualification was that he had the right political connections to get commissions to design official buildings — a situation paralleled in the professional relationship of Dion and Brown.

Another source of the play appears to have been a letter Agnes wrote to her husband a few years earlier. "I had," she said, "a frightful dream last night. You, it seemed, had broken your promise to me [about drinking] — and you came home — oh, quite a ghastly wreck — and, worst of all, a person whom it seemed I no longer knew, who no longer meant anything to me. I looked at you — with a sickening pain in my heart — and thought — 'But this *isn't* Gene. Where is he?' And suddenly I seemed to realize that I'd *never* have you in my life again — or that you weren't *you* — funny! It — oh, I can't tell you the horror of it!" In the play Margaret never recognizes her husband when he unmasks ("Who are you? Why are you calling me?") and she grows terrified once when he persists in showing her his true face: "Dion! Don't! I can't bear it! You're like a ghost! You're dead! Oh, my God! Help!"

Keefe's history, Agnes's dream (Eugene told her she was the model for Margaret), the playwright's obsessional interest in masks, certain of his reading, particularly Nietzsche (the eternal recurrence), Freud, and Wilde's *The Picture of Dorian Gray*, which made an "indelible impression" on O'Neill in youth — they all contributed to *Brown*. Primarily, though, the play is rooted in the author's view of himself and his history. In the most moving passage of the play Dion Anthony recalls his father: "What aliens we were to each other! When he lay dead, his face looked so familiar that I wondered where I had met that man before. Only at the second of my conception. After that, we grew hostile with concealed shame. And my mother? I remember a sweet, strange girl, with affectionate, bewildered eyes as if God had locked her in a dark closet without any explanation. I was the sole doll our ogre, her husband, allowed her and she played mother and child with me for many years in that house until at last through two tears I watched her die with the shy pride of one who has lengthened her dress and put up her hair."

If *The Great God Brown* rises at times to honest grace, as in Dion's elegiac remembrance of his parents, it also descends to such tasteless phraseology as "bad boy Pan," one of Dion's self-descriptions. Considering the various things wrong with the play — an uneven command of the language, pretentious symbolism, an overintellectualized scheme, ultimate confusion — one would expect it, on the whole, to fail; yet, somehow, most of the play is engrossing. Part of the credit belongs to O'Neill's vivid sense of theater, but the heart of the answer is probably to be found in what Stark Young said of his writings in general: "What moved us was the cost to the dramatist of what he handled."

To the end of O'Neill's life, *Brown* remained one of his prime favorites. For the 1942 anthology *This Is My Best*, with various writers choosing from their own works, O'Neill selected a portion of *Brown* — Act 1, scene 3, the first meeting between Dion and Cybel. "I still consider this play," he said, "one of the most interesting and moving I have written. It has its faults, of course, but for me, at least, it does succeed in conveying a sense of the tragic mystery drama of *Life*. . . . And this, I think, is the real test of whether any play, however excellent its structure, characterizations, dialogue, plot, social significance or what not — is true drama or just another play."

A few years later he said: "Of all the plays I have written, I like *The Great God Brown* best. I love that play!" His remark — taken in conjunction with a study of the play — tells as much, possibly, about the essential O'Neill as anything else he ever said on record.

9

Dion Anthony's Course

"THE climate is grand," O'Neill said. "There's absolutely nothing interesting to do, and the German bottled beer and English bottled ale are both excellent. And the swimming is wonderful. If you like such, which I do above everything. It has proved a profitable winter resort for me. I've gotten more work done than in the corresponding season up north in many years. The frost and hard cider of too many successive New England winters are slowly being rendered out of my system."

His letter to George Jean Nathan on March 26, 1925, is similar to others he wrote during this period in its suggestion that he was doing little except work, swim, and relax in near-isolation. Even while writing *The Great God Brown*, however, he led a fairly active social life of beach picnics, guests in for lunch or tea, dining out with friends, sailing parties, and several times, at the gentle urging of Mrs. Barbour and her sister Alice, he allowed himself to be roped in for a hotel dance. He would always be more or less ill at ease around strangers, he would never develop a facility for small talk, but warmed by the leisurely outdoor life of Bermuda he ventured partially and tentatively out of his shell.

A new acquaintance who aroused his interest — he found her "very intriguing-looking" — was Mrs. Olga Collinson from New York. Though she was a good friend of Susan Jenkins, Fitzi and others at the Provincetown Playhouse, the O'Neills had never met her till she got in touch with them in Bermuda. Chiefly because of her eyes, which were uncommonly prominent (from a thyroid condition) and had an intense expression, she impressed the playwright as being of a passionate nature; in writing *Strange Interlude* he would borrow Olga's predominant feature for Nina Leeds (her eyes are "beautiful and bewildering, extraordinarily large"), but Alice Cuthbert was to be the chief model for Nina's general appearance: "tall with broad square shoulders, slim strong hips and long beautifully developed legs – a fine athletic girl of the swimmer, tennis player, golfer type. Her straw-blond hair, framing her sun-burned face, is bobbed."

An omnivorous reader, O'Neill happened to be reading Freud (he thought *Group Psychology and the Analysis of the Ego* "very interesting," *Beyond the Pleasure Principle* "interesting but dully written or translated") around the time he heard from several persons who wondered whether he was indebted to Freud for certain aspects of *Desire Under the Elms*. O'Neill resented the question, replying to one correspondent: "Playwrights are either intuitively keen analytical psychologists or they aren't good playwrights. I'm trying to be one. To me, Freud only means uncertain conjectures and explanations about truths of the emotional past of mankind that every dramatist has clearly sensed ever since real drama began. Which, I think, covers your question. I respect Freud's work tremendously – but I'm not an addict! Whatever of Freudianism is in *Desire* must have walked in 'through my unconscious.'"

To a friend he expressed himself more bluntly: "The Freudian brethren and sisteren seem quite set up about [*Desire*] and, after reading quite astonishing complexes between the lines of my simplicities, claim it for their own. Well, so some of them did with *Emperor Jones*. They are hard to shake!"

In contrast to his professed reservations about Freud – which seem a case of his protesting too much – he still admired Nietzsche, whom he had first read while going to Princeton; at Campsea he browsed again in the philosopher's *Joyful Wisdom* ("wonderful stuff") and *The Birth of Tragedy* ("most stimulating book on drama ever written!"). He read with total concentration; a frequent visitor at the O'Neills' remarked that when he was "immersed in a book it requires some moments before he can be brought back to the present."

In April the family had two houseguests, first, for a week, O'Neill's elder son, who was on Easter vacation from school, and afterward Jimmy Light. Young Eugene's visits with his father, initially at Peaked Hill and now in Bermuda, were high points in his life, events that he looked forward to for months. The playwright escorted his son, who was nearly fifteen and growing tall, into Hamilton and bought him some British tweeds. Another day he hired a sailboat and took a small party – Agnes, Eugene Jr., Mrs. Barbour, Alice and Jack Pierce, a recent Princeton graduate who was courting Alice and later married her – for a picnic on an island beyond Somerset.

O'Neill had not touched anything alcoholic since early January, but at the picnic he had some ale in what proved to be the unobtrusive start of another marathon binge; during the rest of 1925 he would, in fact, be more or less under the influence of drink or suffering its aftereffects a large part of the period. While one can only theorize, it seems likely that young Eugene's presence and Agnes's pregnancy were the chief factors that set him off this time, for his immature, Dion Anthony side resented both.

Despite O'Neill's measure of fondness for his namesake, his disposition toward the youth was, basically, that of a man of conscience, with guilt feelings, fulfilling an obligation rather than that of a real father. There are indications that he chafed at the obligation. In, for instance, *The Hairy Ape*, written shortly after Kathleen Jenkins approached her ex-husband about the support of their son, the playwright has a stoker say: "Jenkins — the First [Mate] — he's a rotten swine!" If the mate's name is coincidence, it is the sort of coincidence that led to the harridan in *The Straw* bearing the surname of the playwright's bigoted New London cousins.

As for Agnes's unwitting role here, it seems significant that Eugene also went on a long binge when she bore Shane. As he had said after *S.S. Glencairn* in Provincetown, the sea plays made him "homesick for homelessness and irresponsibility" and left him with regret that he had ever gone "in for playwriting, mating and begetting sons. . . ."

O'Neill was still confining himself chiefly to beer and ale when Jimmy Light arrived in mid-April seeking his support for the Provincetown Playhouse. Artistically, the theater had had an unimpressive season, and its financial record was even more discouraging — thirty-five thousand dollars in debt, as compared to a deficit of three thousand dollars at the Greenwich Village Theater. The Provincetown had incurred the larger deficit not only because of its smaller seating capacity, which limited its profit from a success, but because it had staged eight productions, the Greenwich Village only three. It was Light's fear that the Triumvirate might abandon the Provincetown.

In a season that had scarcely been as "experimental" as was promised, the Provincetown had fallen back three times on O'Neill revivals (*S.S. Glencairn*, *The Emperor Jones* and *Diff'rent*), and when it had sought to be adventurous — Edmund Wilson's *Crime in the Whistler Room*, Hasenclever's *Beyond* — the results were less than stimulating. So far as pleasing its audience was concerned, the theater had fared better with a tabloid edition of Gilbert and Sullivan's *Patience* — "tabloid" because

[175]

nine "lovesick maidens" instead of the standard twenty were all the tiny stage could accommodate.

"I wish," O'Neill wrote to Macgowan, "we had more definite proof that there *are* interesting experiments all written for the doing at the PP. . . . If there ain't none, what's the good of hanging on to the PP?" Another day, boasting that *The Great God Brown* was "grand stuff, much deeper and poetical in a way than anything I've done before," he said, "but wait till you read it!" Thinking ahead to next season, when *Brown* was to be given at the Greenwich Village, he mentioned several actresses as possibilities for the roles of Cybel and Margaret, then added, "But the man? The man?"

He later concluded that only John Barrymore, whose Hamlet in the 1923–1924 season had won him recognition as America's most brilliant young actor, could realize the full potentiality of the Dion Anthony part. "Your Hamlet," O'Neill had written to him at the time, "was the very finest thing I have known in the theater — an inspiring experience for me! Discouragement with our stage becomes a rotten pose when one faces such an achievement. I was immensely elated. When one is trying to create oneself, in however humble a way, there is nothing so wonderfully stimulating as seeing Art really live and breathe. It leaves no alibi to a playwright. Everything becomes possible — if he is."

Chances that Barrymore would accept the *Brown* part were remote, since he had become a major name in films, but O'Neill, who always believed in "shooting for a star," wired him in Hollywood: "Am taking liberty send you my latest play *The Great God Brown* thinking may interest you as a vehicle. Dion in first half and Brown in rest of play should be played by same actor but you alone could do this. Would not bother you except I honestly believe play unusual and strong enough to merit your consideration." Barrymore replied that he looked forward to reading the script, but subsequently turned it down. (He would not return to the stage till some twenty years later, when, a shell of his former self from drink and other dissipation, he clowned, never more than half sober, through a cheap farce that exploited his private life.)

For Agnes's sake, Eugene moved the family in April to Southcote, a substantial old house about a half-mile inland from Campsea and Crow's Nest; though the two cottages were adequate most of the time, they were uncomfortable on cool days and had leaky roofs. Agnes had intended originally to enter the hospital for her confinement but now she decided to have her baby at Southcote. Once, when she asked Eugene to kiss her good-morning, he complied, and, sounding rather like Dion Anthony, said something about their being an "old, married child-bearing couple."

"Our twin daughters," he informed Macgowan on May 1, "are expected any moment now — but then ladies always make you wait, don't they? — but it's getting on my nerves while Agnes is as calm as calm." He was concerned also about *The Fountain*, because the Theater Guild, like Arthur Hopkins previously, had dropped its option. Starting to regard it as "a play with a jinx attached," he told Kenneth that he would not "do anything about 'F' until you and Bobby arrive and I have read it over in the meanwhile. Maybe I'll decide to produce and publish it myself — in a good hot stove!"

The letter to Macgowan was one of the few he wrote in a period of several months, for he was drinking too heavily by now to bother with correspondence. One day, as Agnes recorded in her diary, he had "three drinks of whiskey before breakfast, which combined with 'hangover' got him into a delightfully so-soish state. He is at present composing a poem — a thing he hasn't done for years — with a red hibiscus flower behind his ear." But the euphoric moments were rare; generally he was in a somber mood or miserable from being hung over. Turning on Agnes, he once, as she wrote, "raved bitterly against me because after seven years I didn't know how to help him!" The poems he wrote during this period offer revealing glimpses of the desolate landscape where his mind wandered. The following extract is typical:

> *A ghost that was Domitian* [*said*] . . .
> "*If you'll remember*
> *A silly soothsayer once told me*
> *I'd be stabbed in the back*
> *So I put mirrors on every wall*
> *And nobody came behind me*
> *That I couldn't see.*
> *Yet,*" — (*and his rheumy eyes grew startled*)
> "*Someone did*
> *And stabbed me in the back —*
> *It's hell to live in a world of mirrors,*" *he said*
> "*The murderer was —*
> *The assassin was —*
> *Well — hmm — never mind*
> *You'll have to prove me guilty*"
> *And he dove into a lake of flame*
> *To escape from Hell!*

Evidently *Lazarus Laughed*, the next play he would write, was starting to dominate his thoughts, for one of the poems deals with Caligula, a leading figure in the Biblical drama, while the following verse concerns Lazarus himself:

> *How many we are!*
> *We scarce can drag one thought after another*
> *Up the long tiresome hill to Calvary*
> *To keep our Tryst*
> *With Thou and the two thieves;*
> *Where now they crucify us all*
> *On Question marks.*
> *And that man there,*
> *And this man here,*
> *Who beats his brains against a rock,*
> *And I myself*
> *We are all Lazarus*
> *And we accuse Thee!*

In yet another poem there is a passage that seems biographically significant:

> *And Nero said to me:*
> *"Oh, yes, my mother was a good woman*
> *And I only killed her because —*
> *(How vague time makes one!) — well,*
> *Because she had a wart on her chin*
> *And because I was God!*
> *Don't you think it's a bit degrading of God*
> *To have a mother? . . ."*

The passage seems significant because Agnes had a wart on her chin.

Fortunately for the O'Neills, one of their new friends was Mrs. Louis E. Bisch, a former registered nurse whose husband was a New York psychiatrist. Capable and kind-hearted, Maude Bisch remained close at hand during the final days of Agnes's pregnancy, performing many little services for her, and she also helped O'Neill, who was not sleeping well, by supplying him with paraldehyde. On May 13 Agnes, who had suffered relatively little discomfort so far, felt well enough to walk with Eugene all the way from Southcote to the beach, where he took a swim to clear his head. Early the next morning, following a short period of labor pains and only twenty minutes after the doctor's arrival, she gave birth to a girl, a beautiful child with dark hair and large dark eyes that, slanting upward, gave her a charming, faintly oriental look. From a list of Irish names supplied earlier by Edmond T. Quinn with the help of writer James Stephens, the baby was named Oona because her parents "liked the sound of it with O'Neill."

Usually Eugene found infants unattractive but even he was impressed, and, according to Agnes, said that Oona was "the only very little baby [whose appearance] he ever liked." As for Agnes, she doted on the child, and thinking of Mrs. Clark's possessive attitude toward Shane and the close — too close, she felt — relationship between them, vowed to herself: *This one* is going to be mine!

"It's a goil," O'Neill cabled Macgowan. "Allah be merciful. According to indications will be the first lady announcer at Polo Grounds. Predict great future grand opera. Agnes and baby all serene." All was not "serene" with him, however, for after sending off a flock of cables, he resumed drinking. It was as though writing *The Great God Brown* had placed him under some compulsion, in a case of life imitating fiction, to follow the self-destructive course of hard-drinking Dion Anthony.

Agnes, wavering between sympathy for him and resentment that his alcoholism had clouded her joy over Oona, was reduced to tears one evening when, with drunken repetition, he took up an old argument between them about Finn Mac Cool. Insisting that the wolfhound be allowed in the house, he declared that "dog fleas don't hurt anybody." All Agnes could think of was that he would make a determined effort to go on the wagon when "something 'important' turns up," such as the appearance of Macgowan and Jones, who were due shortly, but that he was not making such an effort for her and their baby.

Late in May, after nearly two months of drinking, O'Neill tapered off so that he would be sober by the time Dr. Louis Bisch arrived for a visit with his wife; O'Neill wanted advice and help from the psychiatrist. The two men hit it off well, with Bisch, partly through shrewd flattery, favorably impressing the playwright. Energetic and ambitious, not content with success in his profession, Bisch was the author of *The Complex*, a psychological drama that had a brief run on Broadway shortly before his visit to Bermuda; in subsequent years he wrote another play, countless articles, and, among other books, a nonfiction best seller whose popular approach may be surmised from its title, *Be Glad You're Neurotic*.

Trying to excuse his drinking, O'Neill told the psychiatrist that he generally went into a depression after finishing a play, as it never turned out as well as he had envisioned it. While this was true enough – about his depressed mood afterward – Agnes's pregnancy seems to have been more responsible for his latest binge. Eugene was sorry to see Bisch leave after a brief visit, and said he would consult him further in New York.

When Macgowan and Jones arrived on June 6 they found their colleague in fairly good spirits, looking fit and eager for them to read *The Great God Brown;* both were "much impressed" with the play. By this time, since no Broadway manager was interested in *The Fountain,* O'Neill had decided to have the Greenwich Village Theater present it also. For a week the three men talked shop, reviewing their newly ended season, planning the next one, and in their most important decision agreed to concentrate their activities at the Greenwich Village. Under the new setup, the Provincetown Playhouse was to be headed by Jimmy Light as artistic director and Fitzi as business manager, though the Triumvirate retained final authority.

After his two friends had left, O'Neill's mood sagged again. He felt bored and nervous, but he resisted a desire to drink and hoped that a projected change of scene would raise his spirits. Figuring that Peaked Hill would be "too primitive" because of Oona, he and Agnes had decided to summer in Nantucket. The family arrived in New York on July 1, and after they had checked into the LaFayette Hotel, O'Neill called the same day at Dr. Bisch's office to start treatment for his nerves. A week later Agnes, Mrs. Clark and the children left for Nantucket, with Eugene remaining behind to see Dr. Bisch and attend to his theatrical affairs.

His treatment by Bisch was medical rather than psychiatric – it chiefly entailed sedatives – but, curious about psychoanalysis, he questioned the psychiatrist about the possible efficacy of analysis in his case. Two of O'Neill's friends who met Bisch (Bisch later could not recall their names) told him privately that they feared psychoanalysis could harm or even ruin O'Neill as a playwright. Bisch, disagreeing, thought that "it might make him even freer. But I warned them that O'Neill would be a difficult man to analyze because he had such a strong ego. Most people who are very shy, I told them, have strong egos; they are certain of their own powers but afraid others won't recognize those powers. I felt analysis of this would help him; I said it would probably enhance, rather than repress, his genius." (Months later O'Neill consulted a psychiatrist who, unlike Bisch, thought that long analysis might have an adverse effect on his creativity.)

During an afternoon with David Belasco the playwright found "the Old Master very long-winded when he starts reminiscing over his past but sharp and direct enough when it comes to practical present details." Though O'Neill failed to pin him down as to when *Marco Millions* would be produced, he was heartened by Belasco's enthusiasm for the script. Another day, after lunching with Walter Huston, whom he found refreshingly natural for an actor, O'Neill agreed with Bobby Jones that Huston should be tested for Ponce de León in *The Fountain*. Lionel Atwell, who had scored opposite Helen Hayes in a Theater Guild production of Shaw's *Caesar and Cleopatra*, had been the leading candidate for the part, but he was now "demanding all sorts of impossible money, comparing himself to Irving & Mansfield & Barrymore — in short, playing the jackass."

After writing Agnes his theatrical news, Eugene ended: "I'm damn lonely! Every second I spend alone in the [hotel] room I miss you like the devil — and I miss Oona over on the couch. I really love her! Never thought I could a baby! And I love you . . . more than I have power to say!"

Though generally averse to interviews, O'Neill, to help publicize the forthcoming season at the two Village theaters, submitted amiably to extensive quizzing by a woman from the *World*. Rather than striking her as "the morose, silent, distant person some have painted him," Flora Merrill reported on July 19 that he could be "an animated, easy and entertaining conversationist. "Oona," she added in a burst of enthusiasm, "will find in him an ideal play-fellow."

It was hot and stifling in the small upstairs office of the Greenwich Village Theater that day; trucks rumbled up and down Seventh Avenue, often drowning out O'Neill's low voice; Macgowan and others kept popping in and out; but nothing seemed to disturb his composure. Miss Merrill, recalling his father's renown in *Monte Cristo* and other "good, old roaring melodrama," wondered why he had written plays so different. "I suppose," he replied slowly (he practically always spoke slowly, weighing each word as though words were traps through which he had to pick his way carefully), "if one accepts the song and dance complete of the psychoanalysts, it is perfectly natural that having been brought up around the old conventional theater, and having identified it with my father, I should rebel and go in a new direction." Grinning suddenly, he added: "I think it would be quite amusing, however, to revive *Monte Cristo* sometime, because, as I look back upon all the old romantic melodramas, that was the best."

As usual, he was questioned about his personal philosophy. Voicing one of his basic views, he said, "The tragedy of life is what makes it worthwhile. I think that any life which merits living lies in the effort to realize some dream, and the higher that dream is, the harder it is to realize. Most decidedly we must all have our dreams. If one hasn't them, one might as well be dead – one is dead. The only success is in failure. Any man who has a big enough dream must be a failure and must accept that as one of the conditions of being alive. If he ever thinks for a moment that he is a success, then he is finished. He stops."

Impressed by his looks, the reporter "marveled" that O'Neill had "escaped being lionized." Now thirty-six, he was dramatically handsome with his rangy build, his lean face a dark mahogany from the Bermuda sun; but most of all there were the eyes – large, dark, extraordinarily piercing – and now that his black hair was whitening at the temples, the eyes, by contrast, seemed more prominent than ever. Most writers resemble everyone else; from their appearance they could be bankers, plumbers, something prosaic, but in O'Neill's case he looked what he was: a smoldering individualist, dedicated, intense.

The difficulty of casting *The Fountain* and *Brown* was on his mind, for when asked about developments in the theater, he replied that the stage "has progressed furthest in production but also tremendously in playwriting, and in acting not at all, if you leave out one man who is the exception to all rules, because he has real genius, and that is John Barrymore [a calculated compliment, for Barrymore had not yet rejected *Brown*]. I feel very strongly about the matter of acting in this country, and in my opinion it is impossible to carry on much further until the actors catch up."

After hearing about the night life flourishing in Harlem at such spots as Small's Paradise, Connie's Inn and the Cotton Club, Eugene went uptown with Paul Robeson to look around and during the evening fell off the wagon. But this time he could scarcely help himself, for as word spread that the author of *The Emperor Jones* and *All God's Chillun* was present, everyone pressed drinks on him. His next few days were a blur of drinking at his hotel, at his cousin Phil Sheridan's apartment, at a speakeasy in Times Square, where he ran into his old friend Bill Clark, the onetime circus daredevil "Volo the Volitant," who now was working as a barker for sightseeing buses. Trying to sober up, he spent several days at the Macgowans' in Brewster, New York ("I must have been a pretty sorry sight to have about the house," he afterward wrote to them, "and by no means a welcome addition to any family retaining their sanity"); but he was still tapering off when he returned to the city. On July 27 he saw

Walter Huston audition as Ponce de León — "not inspiring," he thought — and left that evening by boat for Nantucket.

Besides having "the shakes" when he arrived, Eugene, in Agnes's words, appeared "peculiar, he acted all doped up." He had been taking Veronal, prescribed by Dr. Bisch to help him sleep, but he apparently fought off its effect (probably because he had used Veronal in his suicide attempt at Jimmy the Priest's), and consequently was groggy from both the medication and insufficient sleep. The family's accommodations in Nantucket were no help to his spirits, for the house at 5 Mill Street was small and, being near the center of town, afforded little privacy. The day after his arrival he went to Royal Beach, intending to swim, but, accustomed to the solitude and beauty of Bermuda's beaches, he immediately left. "Not for mine," he said. "Cheap Narragansett stuff."

He revised *The Fountain*, though he could not "get interested in the old thing — probably because I'm really anxious to get going on something new and yet my conscience makes me go over this." He assured Macgowan that he was "very much on the old cart again and feel as well now as I ever did, what with swimming, boating and the rest of it." Shortly afterward, though, feeling restless and nervous, he resumed drinking and was more or less under the weather during a large part of August.

Edward Keefe of New London dropped by to see him, only to learn from Agnes that he was "off on a tear and she didn't know where he was." Keefe, who had arrived in Nantucket on the schooner of friends, managed to track him down and took him out to the vessel, which was anchored some distance from shore. "After a while," Keefe recalls, "my friends turned in, but Gene and I kept drinking. At one point — I don't know what was eating him — he threw his watch against the mast, breaking it into a thousand pieces. [Timepieces seem to have had an unfavorable connotation for O'Neill: in a New London bar he once smashed his watch against a wall; another time, while drinking in Ridgefield, he threw his watch out into the snow, where it remained lost till the snow had melted.] Finally the two of us went to bed, but some time later a seaman with us woke me to say that my friend was overboard."

Fully clothed and threshing about in the water, O'Neill was pulled aboard, dried, and put to bed. Toward morning the seaman again woke Keefe to report, "There's a lady alongside in a rowboat" — Agnes had finally located her husband. The last Keefe saw of them, Eugene was slumped over in the stern and Agnes, looking spent, was rowing.

In September O'Neill, besides polishing *The Fountain*, wrote scenarios for his next two projects, *Lazarus Laughed* and *Strange Interlude*, which had him "enormously excited," and fired off letters to Macgowan about *The Great God Brown* and *The Fountain*, both of them still uncast. Charging that his own theater was neglecting his plays to concentrate on lesser works, he told Kenneth that if *Brown* could not be cast adequately by the first of the year he would "much prefer to do it with Jimmy [Light] at the PP. . . . If we must have poor acting, let's have it where the audience is somewhat willing to make allowances in that respect."

Critical of Maxwell Anderson's *Outside Looking In,* which had launched the Greenwich Village's new season on September 7, he maintained to Macgowan that it was "totally without significance as far as you or Bobby or I imagined we wanted in the theater. Then why? Nothing better we had the capacity or ability to produce? Then let's be honest and either give up the ghost or give up pretending to mean anything new or deep or significant . . . our first season at the PP was ten years in advance of what we are now! It seems to me we're just nothing but another New York theater. Candidly, Kenneth, I'm not interested in such an idea. . . . I somehow feel we're going bad and have become a young organization with a brilliant past."

His sense of grievance welled up again when Fitzi asked him for an article to be used in the playbill of the Provincetown's opening production. Declaring himself unable to write something constructive, he replied that his "faith in theaters, Provincetown or otherwise, has bogged down a bit. I'm miscast among the conception of miracles . . . I don't belong, get me? because I don't believe." Fulminating at length about the present state of acting and the stage in general, he held that there was "no possibility of real progress in the creative interpretation of fine new plays . . . until we develop a new quality . . . in actors and actresses. . . . Great acting has frequently made bad plays seem good, but a good play cannot penetrate bad acting without emerging distorted — an uneven, bumpy ugly duckling of an offspring at whom the playwright father must gaze with a shuddering 'And Mama theater says you are mine! I think she must have spent some dark moments in the alley with an actor!' " . . .

"Are the actors to blame for the present conditions in all theaters which restrict them to the easy goals of type-casting at the cost of painstaking self-training in the acquiring of an art? Certainly not! And if actors are to blame then we others of the theater are equally to blame. Do we give them parts other than the apparent one God cast them in as persons? Do we take a chance on them? We do not. We cannot afford to in an era of the theater as primarily a realtor's speculation. One mistake and then comes the landlord with a notice of eviction. . . . He could see Shakespeare boiled alive in Socony gasoline and have qualms only as to our diminishing national Standard Oil reserves. The answer? Repertoire, my children. We all know it — it is like truth — so why don't we live & work accordingly.

"I'll wind up with a sharp report and a puff of smoke. What is the Provincetown going to do about acting? Is it going this time to attempt to correct its great weak spot, the source of its failure in times past? The present future of the theater is in the actor. Until he goes on we others — I speak as a playwright — can't, except by the inadequate written word. My motto just now is 'Write 'em & leave 'em!' and my morose intuition is that it is better not to do things at all — especially the most beautiful things — than to run the slightest risks of doing them badly. Beauty is in poor enough repute already!"

He ended: "Yours for the Revolution!"

It was scarcely the sort of response the Provincetowners wanted, yet they were so eager to exploit his name that his jeremiad, after careful editing, was used. Certain language was softened, passages that struck too painfully close to home were eliminated, and the letter appeared in the program under the heading "Are the Actors to Blame?"

On quitting Nantucket early in October, O'Neill, while the rest of the family went directly to New York, spent two days in New London attending to business affairs. Earlier this year, thanks to the success of *Desire Under the Elms,* he had finally paid the fees and commissions necessary to get his estate out of probate. In New London he conferred with his attorneys and went around inspecting his various properties, the residue of his father's lifelong quest for security. Although the Monte Cristo cottage was no longer part of the estate, he stopped by 325 Pequot Avenue and stood for a long time before the gray old house. Vacant for years, in need of paint and repairs, it had a desolate appearance that, to the playwright son, was intensified by the faded signboard, MONTE CRISTO, still over the doorway. Summing up his impression, he wrote in his diary: "Decay & ruin — sad."

At a party that night at Dr. Joseph Ganey's, where everyone got "blotto," Eugene drank his full share and was so hung over the next day that he needed more liquor before he could proceed to New York. He later joked to Art McGinley about the evening as a "debauch with your brother Tom, Eddie Keefe, Scott Linsley, Doc Ganey and the rest of that corrupt herd," but the aftermath of the party was less than humorous. Edgy and tired as he rejoined his family, he flared up when Agnes, worried about his drinking, reproached him for indulging again. The ensuing argument, which continued fitfully in Ridgefield, became so bitter as both revived old grievances that for a while he considered divorce as the only solution. Too upset to work, he took long hikes and, possibly as both exercise and an outlet for hostile feelings, spent many hours chopping down trees.

In calmer spirits finally, he began writing *Lazarus Laughed* in the latter part of October. It poured out of him at such a rate that he completed half of the first draft in three weeks, even though he took time to attend rehearsals of *The Fountain* and further revise the script. Since no one better seemed available, he had given his reluctant consent to Walter Huston as Ponce de León. Eager to qualify, Huston had spent weeks working on the part with his sister, Mrs. Margaret Carrington, an inspiring voice teacher who had coached Barrymore for his memorable Hamlet; but unfortunately, as O'Neill had feared, Huston's efforts were wasted. For all his excellence in certain parts, Huston lacked the grace and panache for a grandee; he was honest cotton and kersey where lace and silk were required.

One day the playwright took time from a *Fountain* rehearsal to audition several players, among them Leona Hogarth, for *The Great God Brown*. To Miss Hogarth, who won the part of Margaret, her first meeting with the playwright was an experience that remained vivid as she wrote about it more than thirty years later. "I'd been playing in a John Golden production that didn't come into town," she says, "when I received a call to come to the Greenwich Village Theater and see Eugene O'Neill. He interviewed me in a tiny cubbyhole up some stairs. We sat on two straight chairs with our knees almost touching. I wanted terribly to play in an O'Neill play and so I was nervous. And Mr. O'Neill seemed at a loss for words. We just looked at each other.

"Finally he said, 'You don't look like a John Golden actress [Golden specialized in comedies and other lightweight fare]. What are you doing there?' And I said, 'I have to eat, don't I?' He immediately smiled — only the slightest movement of his face but his whole expression lit up like a lamp. And — this I can't describe adequately — but his eyes seemed to look through and through me as though he were searching for something. Well, I had nothing to hide from him — I loved the theater and I knew my business and that I was capable of as much in the performance as he would ask from me — and so I absorbed that stare and in my mind I said to him: 'YES, YES.' Now that might not make sense, but that's what happened and I've never forgotten the experience. There was nothing of attraction or repulsion — there was only a searching and an acceptance of the search. He was an exceptional human being and it was my privilege to have had that moment of contact with him."

Pleased with his progress on *Lazarus*, O'Neill was in good spirits when he saw Miss Hogarth, but the following day, after attending another *Fountain* rehearsal, he was so "disgusted" that he went on a "bust" with Edmund Wilson and his wife Mary Blair and sat up all night drinking, talking, and denouncing the theater. He tapered off after nearly a fortnight, but then, feeling bored ("Ridgefield is no home for me! Dull as hell"), he shortly returned to the bottle and continued indulging practically to the end of December. Not that he was continuously drunk but simply that there was scarcely a day when he was completely sober.

"I liked him," Agnes's sister Cecil says, "but Gene was a different person – he could be a fiend – when he drank." Cecil was probably thinking of the night she and her husband, Edward Fiske, were drinking with O'Neill in his study when he took a revolver out of his desk and sighted along the barrel. "See that little thing on the wall there? I'm a good shot, I could put a bullet right through it." Suddenly the unsteady gun was pointed at Cecil, seated a few feet away, as he said, "I could shoot you right in the middle of your forehead." She and her husband sat paralyzed for long seconds, till he finally put the gun away.

When *The Fountain*, in a production designed and directed by Robert Edmond Jones, opened December 10 at the Greenwich Village, the author was in Ridgefield drinking heavily; the next day, figuring he knew "how bad they must be," he refused to look at the notices. They were about as he had expected: while one or two reviewers had a kind word for him, the majority found his play verbose, undramatic, more pretentious than poetic. It was a costly failure for the Triumvirate; although Jones had worked a miracle of economy with the sets and costumes, the multiscene work cost eighteen thousand dollars to produce, as compared with four thousand dollars for *Desire Under the Elms*.

In the last days of 1925 O'Neill intensified his effort to quit drinking, for he was eager to assist in staging *The Great God Brown*, now in production with actors new to the Village group – Robert Keith as Dion Anthony, William Harrigan as Brown, Anne Shoemaker as Cybel, and Miss Hogarth as Margaret. Although a "bit corned up," he attended an early rehearsal and was momentarily cheered that all the principals looked "fine" to him. At a Christmas Eve party, he again hit the bottle and felt so miserable the next day that he tried to numb himself with more liquor. Right afterward, though, telling himself that he "must get in shape" for *Brown*, he began to cut down; on the final day of the year he went on the wagon.

10

❈

O'Neill's Reformation

"K ENNETH has made date with Hamilton for me," O'Neill noted in his diary shortly before he stopped drinking. "A ray of hope amid general sick despair."

Hamilton was Dr. Gilbert V. Hamilton, a psychiatrist with a commission from a scientific organization to research the sex life and problems of married people. For more than a year now he had been developing his program through the systematic questioning of an eventual total of one hundred husbands and one hundred wives — not a hundred couples, since only the wife or the husband was involved in some instances. Although sexual matters were his central concern, Hamilton's quizzing covered virtually every important aspect, past and present, of his subjects' lives, for his investigation was "in a measure a study of the child in the adult." He believed that "almost from the day of birth, the state, society and most persons (including our parents) whose lives intimately touch our own, unwittingly conspire to make us bad and stupid when we grow up."

The Macgowans were part of the survey, and Kenneth thought that Dr. Hamilton might be able to help the O'Neills with their drinking problem and the conflict between them. All the participants were entitled, after their questioning was complete, to a reasonable number of free consultations with Hamilton concerning their marital and other personal problems.

To his surprise, Dr. Hamilton had little difficulty from the start in enlisting persons for his project, and he was further pleased that nearly all spoke quite frankly of intimate matters; but they were scarcely representative of the public at large, for most came from the arts and the professions. According to Stella Bloch Hanau, the press agent of the two

Village theaters, the participants were "interrelated, nearly everyone knew everybody else. The first ones who were recruited brought in their friends, and the latter recommended others, and so forth."

O'Neill took an immediate liking to Dr. Hamilton, paternal-looking, prematurely white-haired, who bore some resemblance to philosopher John Dewey. Hamilton had, besides a reassuring personality, a comfortable, unobtrusive way of conducting his interviews. In a modification of the Freudian couch he had his subjects sit in a chair fastened in position, facing away from him, and silently handed them one at a time file cards containing questions of a searching personal nature. The subject could answer as briefly or fully as he chose, free of all interruption. One participant, for example, raced through all the questions — there were over three hundred — in about two hours, the usual running time of each session, while another took more than thirty hours in all; but most subjects required about eight hours. Hamilton never commented on the replies or indicated any reaction but simply wrote down everything that was said. He also noted any agitated behavior during the interviews, and concluded that questions about "erotic self-love and homosexuality appeared to be much more upsetting to the men than to the women"; the women, on the other hand, were more likely to show evidence of "emotional upset while . . . answering the questions concerning incestuous imaginations, impulsions, etc."

In 1929 the psychiatrist published *A Research in Marriage*, in which he listed the questions, gave a detailed breakdown through charts of all the replies, and summarized his findings. (Acknowledging him as a forerunner, the Kinsey Report called his book one of the few "studies [of sex] which are scientific, based on more or less complete case histories.") Since the book never names the people in the survey, it is impossible to tell from the charts who gave a particular reply — impossible, that is, in all cases but one. In this instance fifteen men, answering questions about friction between their parents, said that their mother was chiefly at fault; some blamed her "scolding" and "nagging," others, her "nervous instability," while one — undoubtedly O'Neill — replied that his mother's "drug habit" had been the primary cause of discord within the family.

A man with great respect for artistic talent, Hamilton was both eager to help the playwright and apprehensive that he might do him more harm than good. In his view the talented are so complex, the roots of their creativity so often entwined with the sources of their neuroses, that psychoanalysis could possibly benefit them as persons at the same time that it injured them as artists. Consequently, he treated O'Neill with special care; but O'Neill, instead of being discouraged by his cautious attitude, found it easy to talk to the solicitous, fatherly doctor.

In all, for both the sex-research interviews and the consultations afterward, Eugene saw the psychiatrist over a period of only six weeks; yet in this time he arrived, almost miraculously, at a major turning point in his life: he resolved never to drink again. Except for several isolated falls from grace, he was to remain abstinent the rest of his days. Unquestionably, Hamilton played some part in his reformation, but it is difficult to estimate both the nature and the extent of Hamilton's contribution. Authorities on alcoholism agree generally that the afflicted are rarely cured by psychoanalysis, even by years of treatment, yet here was O'Neill taking the pledge while in therapy just a few weeks.

Dr. Hamilton, who told him that he had an Oedipus complex (according to both Macgowan and Jimmy Light), apparently believed that O'Neill was able to reform once he accepted that oedipal impulses, with consequent guilt feelings, were at the root of his self-destructive drinking. Hamilton seems to have been alone, however, in his view. "Gene kidded about it," Jimmy Light recalls, "when he told me that after much probing and questioning, Hamilton found he had this complex. 'Why, all he had to do,' Gene said, 'was read my plays.' "

As Agnes remembers, O'Neill thought well of Dr. Hamilton personally but was disappointed in his findings and felt somehow, on his own, he had finally mustered the strength to renounce liquor. Siding more or less with her view, Macgowan thinks that "Gene quit when it came down to a choice between his writing and his drinking. He knew he couldn't go on indefinitely as he had — all that drinking in the previous year — and his writing meant everything to him. That's what turned the trick, I think, more than anything Hamilton told him."

His participation in the research project and his consultations afterward with Hamilton (which he incorrectly used to call his "analysis") launched O'Neill on a journey into the past that led to his drawing up two papers in which he summarized his early years and the familial forces that had shaped him. The two documents are in a script so minuscle that they almost defy reading even with a magnifier; he evidently tried to make them illegible, except to himself, in case they ever fell into another's hands.

One paper, a diagram, outlines his relations from birth into adolescence with his parents and his nursemaid, Sarah Sandy. (The diagram is reproduced in *O'Neill, Son and Playwright*, p. 506.) Here is its single reference to drinking: "At early childhood father would give child whisky & water to soothe child's nightmares caused by terror of dark. This whisky is connected with protection of mother – drink of hero father." The paper goes on to mention his "resentment & hatred of father as cause of school (break with mother)," and says of his first Catholic boarding school: "Reality found & fled from in fear – life of fantasy & religion in school – inability to belong to reality."

The language of the diagram is, on the whole, explicit, except for the words "discovery of mother's inadequacy," which guardedly refer to the traumatic night in New London when his mother tried to drown herself and he at last was informed that she was a morphine addict, that her addiction had begun with his birth. In *Long Day's Journey Into Night* he says through Edmund, his counterpart: "It was right after that Papa and Jamie decided they couldn't hide it from me any more. Jamie told me. . . . God, it made everything in life seem rotten!"

The other document, also on one side of a single page, summarizes a great deal of the background history that would be divulged in his family portrait. Taken as a unit, the two papers can be considered his first step toward writing, some fifteen years later, *Long Day's Journey Into Night*.

Wherever he turned during the early weeks of 1926 O'Neill found himself confronted by his past – in his sessions with Dr. Hamilton, at rehearsals of *The Great God Brown*, one of his most subjective works, and now Barrett H. Clark wanted his cooperation for a biographical and critical monograph. But O'Neill, as Clark wrote of their meeting, "feels he has hardly got into his stride. A book! Already! He wonders if it's necessary to be so darned personal about it? His life belongs to himself, doesn't it? Surely I'll have enough material if I stick to the plays, and leave the man out of the picture?

"No, I can't do that. The man is a part of the whole thing. A long pause – a wry smile.

"Personal accounts of the young playwright have already crept into print, several lies and exaggerations; a lot of legendary anecdotes are going the rounds, and there will surely be more.

"Once again the wry smile. He must face the situation. If I don't do the job, someone else will, so we'd better get the facts straight right now. Very well, but let's not either of us take the thing too seriously. If some kind of book must be written, the ground has got to be cleared. He tries to help; he gives me a sober account of some apocryphal legend, but thinks it best for me to go to other people for an outline of his life. When the MS. is ready he will look it over. He'll tell me what I haven't been able to learn from anyone else. . . . Another pause. So that's that, and for the rest of the afternoon we talk about *Desire Under the Elms* and *The Fountain*, the Provincetown Players, plans for new plays to be written next year, and the year after that, but mostly about *The Great God Brown*. I have had the MS. with me for the past week and as he takes it he asks how I like it. . . . He listens intently."

After reading Clark's manuscript months later, Eugene wrote back: "When all is said and done — and this is, naturally, no conceivable fault of yours — the result of this first part is legend. It isn't really true. It isn't I. And the truth would make such a much more interesting — and incredible! — legend. That is what makes me melancholy. But I see no hope for this except someday to shame the devil myself, if I ever can muster the requisite interest — and nerve — simultaneously! The trouble with anyone else writing even a sketch is that I don't believe there is anyone alive today who knew me intimately in more than one phase of a life that has passed through many entirely distinct periods, with complete changes of environment, associates, etc. And I myself might not be so good at writing it; for when my memory brings back this picture or episode or that one, I simply cannot recognize that person in myself nor understand him nor his acts as mine (though objectively I can), although my reason tells me he was undeniably I."

Produced at a cost of four thousand dollars, *The Great God Brown* was taking shape at the Greenwich Village under the direction of Bobby Jones, who also was designing the sets and costumes. Though O'Neill regularly attended rehearsals, where he hovered around like an anxious parent, he never discussed the play or their parts with the actors but conferred quietly with Jones. The players would have welcomed his comments, since they found Jones of little help to them in coping with an elusive play. Anne Shoemaker recalls with a sniff that he advised her to read one speech "like a ship coming into harbor" (the image, being of the sea, probably originated with O'Neill). Leona Hogarth, likewise critical of their director, says that "there was so much talk of overtones and subtle meanings that the cast was tied up tight as knots. The last act was always obscure and the more Jones tried to explain it the more clouded it grew. I don't believe Mr. O'Neill was satisfied with [the final part] because we spent so much time on it."

January 23, 1926, had been chosen for the première because it was a Saturday; thus, the reviewers would have plenty of time to grope among their reactions and write something coherent, for Monday's papers, about a play that was certain to bewilder them in some degree. At a late hour on opening day O'Neill and his colleagues decided that the critics would need more than time to deal with the play – they would need the text of the play itself. A rush job of typing up additional scripts began; a copy was hurried to O'Neill at the Hotel Lafayette so that he could incorporate in it changes he had made during the final rehearsals, and as the first performance took place he was too busy transcribing revisions to worry about how *Brown* was faring.

Some reviewers were confused yet impressed, others just plain confused, but virtually all found that the play becomes hopelessly obscure when Dion Anthony dies and Brown, using the other's mask, assumes the dead man's identity. Frank Vreeland of the *Telegram*, voicing a common view, thought the play showed the author "at his most metaphysical, at his most cryptic, at his best and at his worst." After declaring that *Brown* "at least half of the time is as eloquent and stirring and richly imaginative as anything" O'Neill had written, Richard Watts, Jr., added in the *Herald Tribune* that it "remains in the end a fascinating, half-mad enigma."

In a generally favorable notice that pleased the playwright by its constant reference to him as "a poet," Gilbert W. Gabriel of the *Sun* said: "If Mr. O'Neill writes for anything beyond the satisfaction of his own urge, it is for posterity, not for popularity. Here he experiments bravely and strangely. The poet and technician in him come to grips and fight it out along their own lines through more than a dozen unequal but always interesting scenes."

At the *Times* there had been a succession of reviewers in a few years: Woollcott the prima donna, who had transferred his pouter-pigeon stance to the *World*, John Corbin, who had rarely ventured off the fence, and Stark Young, whose astute analyses were now a feature of the *New Republic*. Starting what would be a long, distinguished career, the new *Times* critic was Brooks Atkinson, a learned New Englander, a bird-watching disciple of Thoreau, and above all a high-minded lover of the theater. In a sympathetic review, he said: "What Mr. O'Neill has succeeded in doing . . . is obviously more important than what he has not succeeded in doing. He has not made himself clear. But he has placed within the reach of the stage finer shades of beauty, more delicate nuances of truth and more passionate qualities of emotion that we can discover in any other single modern play. . . . From passages of winged poetry he shifts quickly to mordant irony; from the abstract he passes to the concrete without missing a beat. And the implications of [the play] carry us far afield among the cruelest uncertainties of a pleading, skeptical mind. Obscure or clear, *The Great God Brown* is packed with memorable substance."

The masks were of course discussed extensively, and here the reviewers were sharply divided. For every Woollcott who detested them ("cramp the actors' style to the ragged edge of strangulation"), there was a Stark Young speaking in their defense: "Coming on and off the faces as they do when these human beings confront one another, they say quickly and clearly certain things that need to be said. They are made immensely economical . . . They say what nothing else in the play says or could quite say."

O'Neill himself was dissatisfied with the masks and complained afterward that they "only get across personal resemblance of a blurry meaninglessness. Whose fault? No one's. Not enough time to see them. Perhaps the result the script calls for is impossible to attain by the method of combination masks the script describes." Still unhappy about them a year later he told a friend that "we had neither the time nor the money to experiment and get them right before we opened — the old story that prevents anything really fine from ever being done in the American theater! When you read what I wanted those masks to get across — the abstract drama of the forces behind the people — as it is suggested in the script you will remember more clearly how wrong they were. They suggested only the bromidic, hypocritical & defensive double personality of people in their personal relationships — a thing I never would have needed masks to convey."

Despite all the talk in the press about its obscurity, *Brown* flourished at the Greenwich Village; there must have been some who disliked it, many who found it difficult to follow, yet night after night the audiences were silently attentive. At one performance, as Dion and Cybel were playing solitaire, a leg fell off the sofa, but the only audience reaction was a gasp, no laughter. After five weeks at the small downtown house the production was moved to the five-hundred-seat Garrick, on Thirty-fifth Street, and about a month later to the Klaw, eight hundred seats, in Times Square. In all it gave two hundred and seventy-eight performances, for a gross of one hundred and ninety-three thousand dollars, with the author netting ten thousand dollars.

O'Neill regarded its success not only as a vindication of his determination to write as he pleased (it heartened him in writing the almost impossible *Lazarus Laughed* and the marathon *Strange Interlude*) but as a tribute to the public. "There was," he said in 1932, "some misunderstanding, of course. But so is there always misunderstanding in the thing beyond what is contained in a human-interest newspaper story. In the main, however, *The Great God Brown* was accepted and appreciated by both critics and public – a fairly extensive public, as its run gives evidence.

"I emphasize this play's success because the fact that a mask drama, the main values of which are psychological, mystical, and abstract, could be played in New York for eight months, has always seemed to me a more significant proof of the deeply responsive possibilities in our public than anything that has happened in our modern theater before or since."

On returning to Bermuda late in February 1926, the O'Neills settled at Bellevue, an imposing estate in Paget Parish dominated by a fine old main house with carved woodwork, sweeping stairways, and wide verandahs that offered vistas of the sea through a long lane of great cedars. The twenty-five acres contained several other handsome houses, groves of palms and pines, and an immaculate private beach bordered by bay grape trees – all this for only one hundred and fifty dollars a month. "You simply must come down!" Eugene exulted to Macgowan. "Must! . . . lots of room . . . really the nicest house I've ever seen here."

He had left New York feeling poorly from a siege of dentistry, but warmed by the sun, cradled by the waves, he shortly was in good shape and spirits. His mood at the time is evident in motion pictures taken by Nicholas Muray, the theatrical and fashion photographer, who visited Bermuda early in March. The man shown here could hardly be more different from the common image of him as a gloomy soul: relaxed, grinning, he teases a parrot with a punching bag, trots along the beach with the jaunty stride of a young athlete, but seems most at ease as he heads into the water, swimming out with long, powerful strokes. Another time, presenting himself before the camera as an amphibious creature, he had ropes of seaweed draped all over his shoulders (an image that flashed into Agnes's mind nearly thirty years later when she first heard of his death).

Scarcely had the family unpacked at Bellevue when O'Neill was hard at work on *Lazarus Laughed*. From time to time he sent word to Macgowan about his progress: "*Lazarus* is going strong. I'm going over what I've already written in the light of many new and richer notions, chiefly connected with a working out of my mask scheme. It gains significance and depth in every way daily. I'm sitting on the top these days." . . . "*Lazarus* coming bigger & bigger! . . . Have almost entirely reconstructed & rewritten 1st 2 scenes. Ten times better!"

Some idea of the amount of reading he did in his work, especially for his historical plays, can be gained from a letter he wrote on March 1 to Manuel Komroff, an editor at Liveright's. With *Lazarus* and other

O'Neill, Agnes and Oona in Bermuda in 1926

Mrs. Clark and Oona

projects in mind, he requested Bergson's *Laughter* and "anything else you know printed about the spirit of laughter among the Greeks or Ancients of any sort"; Frazer's one-volume *The Golden Bough*, as well as the separate volumes from the complete set that pertain to "the worship of water whether in oceans, rivers, pools or what not"; Müller's *Chips from a German Workshop* and "any good volume readily accessible about the philosophy of the very early Greeks up to and including Pythagoras"; Jonson's *The Alchemist* and George Moore's *The Brook Kerith*. "Is there," he asks, "a decent history of Imperial Rome? If so, I need it. I have Ferrero [*The Greatness and Decline of Rome*] and Suetonius' *Lives* and Saltus's *Imperial Purple*. I want especially a more complete history of Rome from the time of Tiberius on."

He asked Komroff another day for translations of the Talmud and the Koran, saying, "I'm going in very heavily these days for the study of religion along certain definite lines I have mapped out as a sort of large background for certain work in the future. Am also starting to study ancient Greek which I never 'took' at college or prep. If in three or four years I'm able to read Greek Tragedy in the original and enjoy it – the mind as well as the meaning – I'll have made a grand refuge for my soul to dive deeply and coolly into at moments when modern life – and drama – become too damn humid and shallow to be borne."

Although *The Great God Brown* was proving more popular than anyone, including its author, had expected, its success was not enough to offset the Triumvirate's failures at the Greenwich Village, chiefly *The Fountain*, twenty-eight performances, and a Rostand translation, only sixteen. *Brown* was in fact to be the trio's final presentation and the end of their operations at the Village playhouse, but to the last they kept hoping for a windfall that might enable them to continue.

After *Brown* was transferred uptown, O'Neill suggested to his colleagues a revival in the Village of *The Hairy Ape* with Louis Wolheim, who had become a major star in *What Price Glory?* He also urged Macgowan to promote a London production of *Brown* by enlisting the support of Noel Coward, a clever young Englishman who had scored on Broadway this season as both an actor and a playwright. But neither of his hopes materialized, and in a further disappointment, Belasco dropped *Marco Millions* as too costly, too great a gamble. One newspaper said it seemed that "no stage except that of the Metropolitan Opera House will ever be able to afford *Marco Millions* – and there is no music."

Adding to O'Neill's financial worries, his royalties, as he kept complaining, were overdue. Spelling out his grievances, with his ire centered on

Alexander McKaig, the Greenwich Village's business manager, he told Macgowan on April 28: "No royalty from [the touring *Desire Under the Elms*] since week ending March 6th! No royalty from PP for *Jones* except one week. . . . Nothing from *Brown* — which has been making money — since week of Feb. 27 at GV two months ago! Now where in the hell do I get off at under such an arrangement? I am not Otto Kahn. I have a larger family to support, for one thing. Do you want me to begin selling the investments I made before I left N.Y. [with funds from the sale of New London property] in order to pay my bills down here? It is damn close to that now. . . .

"I don't want to seem hard on you, Kenneth. I know the financial worry on your shoulders, but I must still insist on my opinion that paying me weekly would not have added to that worry a damn bit, while the reverse has certainly added to my worry. I can least afford to play philanthropist just now when I'm making my first determined effort to get my own affairs stabilized so that I can work steadily ahead for the next few years in peace. The amount of my income tax I have to pay in installments for last year would paralyze you — nearly 3000 bucks! — and yet where most of the income leaked away to is one of those enigmas."

To an extent his financial situation was his own fault. While he had a penurious streak — expressed chiefly in his relations with Agnes — he also had lordly tastes and was inclined to spend beyond his means. The year before, for example, feeling prosperous from *Desire Under the Elms*, he turned in his first automobile for a new, more costly DuPont, even though he made little use of cars. The result of such ill-advised expenditures was inevitable: since his income fluctuated from one year to the next, while his expenses mounted, he often found himself short of cash. In all, he was to earn around eighteen thousand dollars in 1926, including ten thousand dollars in royalties from *Brown*, a drop of some six thousand dollars from the previous year.

"Tell McKaig," his letter continues, "to put me on the salary list as an actor. Then paying me will be done as a matter-of-fact, without heartache. . . .

"My advice is: Steal my royalties from the GV, abscond on the first boat & come here! I will stake you to the fare as your collector's commission, and in spite of my professional ire will bed and feed you as if you were an honest man and not a manager."

When he spoke of his "family" being larger than Otto Kahn's he probably had in mind — besides his immediate dependents and Eugene

Jr. — his in-laws and Agnes's daughter Barbara. After the O'Neills had separated and were wrangling over alimony terms, he claimed that he not only had been generous with Agnes but had "staked all the members of her family . . . repaired their houses, paid their doctor bills, [and] supported her child." From other sources, though, it appears that he greatly exaggerated. He did come to the Boultons' aid once or twice at a time of crisis, but otherwise did little if anything to alleviate their chronic financial struggle. All the Boulton girls had gone to work at a relatively young age, and the mother took a job from time to time.

Agnes's sister Margery, who had stayed with the O'Neills at Peaked Hill and in Ridgefield for extended periods, was now with them in Bermuda, not as a leisured guest but, at a modest salary, as a working member of the household. Besides giving Mrs. Clark a hand with Shane, she helped Eugene answer his correspondence and typed his scripts. Margery recalls that he was greatly impressed by Joyce's *Ulysses*, which, though banned in the States, was openly available in the Bermuda bookstores, a large paperback for five dollars. O'Neill read the seminal book at a strategic time, for not long afterward, in writing *Strange Interlude*, he would borrow Joyce's stream-of-consciousness technique.

Saxe Commins, who spent a fortnight at Bellevue in April, was among the first to know of the playwright's next project. During a discussion of Dreiser's *An American Tragedy*, the literary sensation of the day, O'Neill remarked, according to Saxe, that "Dreiser had written the novel of the unexceptional man, whereas he was [planning] a novel in dramatic form of an exceptional woman." It would be, he said, of a "revolutionary length."

In high spirits after completing *Lazarus*, he apologized on May 14 to Macgowan for his complaints ("Not getting paid any royalty *by anyone* had gotten me as crotchety as any other philanthropist") and reported that he was going to work almost immediately on *Strange Interlude* ("my creative urge is all for going on").

The man's fertility and drive were remarkable. He had just finished an unusual, difficult drama; he was about to start another one far more demanding; and beyond that, as he informed Kenneth, he had "many new ideas — for a play similar in technique & length to *Emperor Jones* with Mob as the hero — or villain rather! Done with masks entirely — showing the formation of a lynching mob from more or less harmless, human units — (a white man is victim of the lynching) the gradual development as Mob & disintegration as Man until the end is a crowd of men with the

[199]

masks of brutes dancing about the captive. . . . I have a fine ironic title for it, 'The Guilty Are Guilty.'

"And many more new ideas. They will wait."

As for *Lazarus,* he said: "Certainly it contains the highest writing I have done. Certainly it *composes* in the theater more than anything else I have done. Certainly it is more Elizabethan than anything before & yet entirely [non-Elizabethan]. Certainly it uses masks as they have never been used before and with an intensely dramatic meaning that really should establish them as a sound and true medium in the modern theater. Certainly, I know of no play like *Lazarus* at all, and I know of no one who can play Lazarus at all — the lead, I mean. Who can we get to laugh as one who had completely lost, even from the depths of the unconscious, all traces of the Fear of Death? But never mind. I felt that about *Brown.* In short, *Lazarus* is damned far from any category."

But, unfortunately, his enthusiasm was misplaced, for *Lazarus Laughed* is at once among his most ambitious and least satisfying works; O'Neill the playwright had been led astray this time by O'Neill the mystic. In his new play, an overblown mixture of metaphysics and unconvincing drama, he presents a Lazarus who has returned from the grave free of all fear, all weaknesses of the flesh. "Laugh!" he tells his family and friends in Bethany. "Laugh with me! Death is dead! Fear is no more! There is only life! There is only laughter!"

Although many reject his message, practically no one — not even those who fear and hate him as a threat to their particular faith or to the established order — can resist his heroic laughter. He sways great crowds into laughter with him; he wins converts to his joyous gospel wherever he goes, even at the dissolute and bloody imperial court of Rome, but only transiently, for once he moves on, his momentary followers sink into their old fears.

It may seem strange that O'Neill, who during his lifetime was almost never known to laugh aloud, should celebrate a character who defines himself in laughter; that O'Neill, a man who distrusted life and who was always "a little in love with death," should now, affirming life, deny the finality of death. Yet it is precisely a man of this sort who would conceive such a play, such a protagonist: Lazarus is a figure of wish fulfillment, representing a spiritual state the author longed to attain; he is the shadow of a giant cast by a cripple who dreams of being whole. Essentially, the play is a debate not between Lazarus and Caligula, who hates the world, particularly himself, or between Lazarus and Tiberius Caesar, who despises everyone, including himself, but a debate within O'Neill, the homeless renegade Catholic who was trying to exorcise his own darkness and fears. *Lazarus* is also the ultimate statement of a recurrent thought in his plays. "To learn to love life — to accept it and be exalted," says Cape in *Welded*, "that's the one faith left to us!" In *The Great God Brown* the same theme is sounded by Cybel: "Always spring comes again bearing life again! . . ." The new drama was chiefly foreshadowed, though, in *The Fountain*, as the dying Ponce de León has a vision: "Age — Youth — They are the same rhythm of eternal life! . . . Death is no more [This phrase, or slight variations thereof, is repeated what seems a thousand times in Lazarus]. . . . I see! Fountain everlasting, time without end! Soaring flame of the spirit transfiguring Death! . . . All things dissolve, flow on eternally!" At the heart of the metaphysical concept is Nietzsche's doctrine of eternal recurrence, just as there is something of Zarathustra at the core of Lazarus.

Summing up the play, O'Neill wrote to theater historian Arthur Hobson Quinn that the fear of death "is the root of all evil, the cause of all man's blundering unhappiness. Lazarus knows there is no death, there is only change. He is reborn without that fear. Therefore he is the first and only man who is able to laugh affirmatively.

"His laughter is a triumphant Yes to life in its entirety and its eternity. His laughter affirms God, it is too noble to desire personal immortality, it wills its own extinction, it gives its life for the sake of Eternal Life. . . . His laughter is the direct expression of joy in the Dionysian sense, the joy of a celebrant who is at the same time a sacrifice in the eternal process of change and growth and transmutation which is life. . . . And life itself is the self-affirmative joyous laughter of God."

One is tempted to say that if O'Neill's execution had matched his conception, *Lazarus Laughed* would have been — as, in some respects, he always thought it was — among his peak achievements. Yet actually the conception was precisely of a kind most likely to produce his worst writing. While he could create images of beauty, a sense of universality, from narrow lives on a harsh New England farm or from "hairy apes" in grimy stokeholds, he generally, as in *The Fountain* and at times in *The Great God Brown*, overwrote when dealing with poetic or lofty subject matter. Paradoxically, he could soar only if he kept his feet on the ground. Inevitably, then, O'Neill, trying to attain the transcendant heights with *Lazarus*, constantly fell into pretension and grandiloquence.

Influenced by both the Greek classics and Catholic ritual, he freely exploited the opportunities in his biblical fable for masks and music, dance movements, speaking choruses and responsive chanting. In an effective bit of symbolism, he has all the characters masked except Lazarus, the only unified and harmonious being among them, the only one without fear. But in spite of the pageantry and surface color, this is a ponderous drama, tireless and tiresome in hammering away at its mystical message. The basic trouble is that O'Neill tried through *Lazarus Laughed* to provide an experience no longer available, he felt, from the church.

Explaining what he meant by his subtitle for *Lazarus* — "A Play for an Imaginative Theater" — he said: "I mean the one true theater, the age-old theater, the theater of the Greeks and Elizabethans, a theater that could dare to boast — without committing a farcical sacrilege — that it is a legitimate descendant of the first theater that sprang, by virtue of man's imaginative interpretation of life, out of his worship of Dionysius. I mean a theater returned to its highest and sole significant function as a Temple where the religion of a poetical interpretation and symbolical celebration of life is communicated to human beings, starved in spirit by their soul-stifling daily struggle to exist as masks among the masks of living!"

Normally too much of a theater man to write "closet drama," he was more or less guilty of it here, since the part of Lazarus is virtually impossible to enact. In despair over the problem, O'Neill suggested to Macgowan that the role be translated into Russian for Feodor Chaliapin, not only a great singer but a fine actor, with the rest of the cast speaking English. "It would be a wonderful strange effect," he said, "and as far as most of an average audience understanding what Lazarus means, why it would probably be a lot clearer to them in Russian! Does this sound like pessimism? Well, it is and I am. No director in the world can make anything of my play but a horrible, humiliating fizzle — for me! — until a right Lazarus is found."

After Chaliapin had, understandably, proven cool to the idea, O'Neill proposed to Paul Robeson that he play the role in whiteface. "He's the only actor," Eugene told Agnes, "who can do the laughter, that's the important point. It would be good showmanship, too, no end to the publicity it would attract. Now all we have to do is raise the money!"

As a published work *Lazarus* was admired by Lewis Mumford ("a great, an exhilarating achievement"), but Conrad Aiken's response was more typical. He thought it as a whole "too romantic, too purple, too humorlessly serious; there is a kind of grandiosity about it which if not intellectually hollow is very close to it. . . . The whole thing is pitched just a little too high." But it might, he added, make "a first-rate libretto" for an opera.

Never produced on Broadway, the work has been staged twice in this country. Given full scale in 1928 as a community project at Gilmore Brown's Pasadena Playhouse (the production used four hundred costumes, three hundred masks and as many wigs), with Irving Pichel as Lazarus, Gilmore Brown as Tiberius and Victor Jory as Caligula, the play was well received. "It is as a pageant, perhaps, more than as a play," said one reviewer, "that *Lazarus Laughed* succeeded tonight." At its next presentation, however, twenty years later by the Fordham University Theater, Brooks Atkinson found it "practically unbearable theater," while Richard Watts, Jr., called it "verbose and strangely tedious."

Not long after the family settled at Bellevue, O'Neill was on the verge of extending his lease for several years, at one thousand dollars a year, when he fell in love with and bought a two-hundred-year-old house on Little Turtle Bay, called "Spithead," for seventeen thousand five hundred dollars. While this may seem extravagance in view of his professed money troubles, he actually, thanks to rentals and piecemeal sale of his New London realty, was in better financial shape in 1926 than his complaints suggested; reminiscent of his father, he was inclined to talk "poor-mouth."

Like Peaked Hill station, Spithead was located by the water and commanded a panoramic view. Unpretentious compared to Bellevue, it was a two-story residence of native stone and had the simple architecture typical of early eighteenth-century Bermuda homes. Its interior was in poor shape and the flooring dangerous, since no one had lived there for many years; but while "just a shell," as O'Neill said, it was "a very fine shell" and he looked forward to making it livable again. The restoration would take many thousands, money he intended to raise by selling Brook Farm.

At the same time that he had a desire for roots, as evidenced by his purchase of Spithead, he was prey to a great restlessness, a hunger for change, that had long been growing in him, a feeling that not even the move to Bermuda had stilled. When he left Provincetown in 1924 he had no idea that he would never again see the old Coast Guard station; but the place had been inconvenient the following year because of Oona, and since then he had undergone a change of heart about returning. "I feel sick of all past connotations," he told Macgowan on April 4, "and think it behooves me to shake them — even Peaked Hill — for the next few years anyway. . . . Bermuda is really a start on a new tack — was last year, for that matter. The thought of going back to P'town, much as I love Peaked Hill, rather wearies me and makes me sad. The old truth is no longer true. Too many 'somethins' hide in the corners [a reference to old Cabot's

Shane with his parents

Finn Mac Cool with his Irish-American m

Spithead before alterations and restoration

feeling about the farmhouse in *Desire*]. What I need for my new voyage is fresh fair winds and new ports of call."

What he meant by "somethins in the corner" can only be surmised, but apparently Terry Carlin, Frank Shay and other of his hard-drinking friends were part of the reason why he now chose to avoid Province-town — he was avoiding temptation. "Not that I'm afraid any more," he assured Macgowan, "but it's no use making it harder for one's self." He finally decided to spend the summer with his family at a lake in Maine that had been recommended to him by Elizabeth Marbury, a partner of his agent Richard Madden; she herself had a vacation place nearby. It was a fateful choice for O'Neill: in Maine, in one of Miss Marbury's house-guests, he was to meet a temptation of greater consequence in his life than any he might have encountered at Provincetown.

11

Actress in Maine

As O'Neill returned to the States in mid-June 1926, one thing on his mind was the recent merger of the Greenwich Village Theater with the Actors' Theater, a group unofficially sponsored by Actors' Equity that had staged Ibsen, Shaw and Wilde on Broadway. O'Neill had been opposed at first, even though Macgowan had initiated the merger and was slated to head the combined forces, for he feared that Kenneth would be hampered by the old guard in the other group. Kenneth was confident, however, that he would have a free hand in running the new organization. "Daring!" Eugene wrote to his colleague on June 3, after the deal had gone through. "Remember that, old Top, with this new venture! It seems to me most emphatically a case of shooting at a star or being a dud!"

His idea of "daring" was, not surprisingly, a production of *Marco Millions*. He suggested that Macgowan try to enlist the support of banker Otto H. Kahn, the leading contributor to the two Village playhouses and also an "angel" of the Actors' Theater. Kenneth was doubtful about *Marco*, considering it too costly for his group, but after reading *Lazarus Laughed* and being exposed to the author's enthusiasm for it, he decided to concentrate his fund-raising efforts on a presentation of *Lazarus*.

During the week O'Neill was in New York he called on Horace Liveright, something he rarely did, for he did not care to become socially involved with his publisher, a gregarious, flamboyant individual whose establishment in an old brownstone on West Forty-eighth Street (a site now occupied by Rockefeller Center) was most unconventional: barflies, pretty girls and late-hour parties were as much part of the scene as manuscripts and editorial conferences. "Why doesn't Gene ever come to see me?" Horace used to say. But while O'Neill had reservations about him personally, he respected him as an adventurous force in the literary world. Besides sponsoring such new voices as Sherwood Anderson and e.e. cummings, Eliot, Pound and Hemingway, not to mention O'Neill himself, Liveright, more than any other book publisher, was in the van of battles against the censors.

O'Neill visited the publisher in fulfillment of an old promise to Hart Crane that he would try to persuade Liveright to bring out *White Buildings*, Crane's first collection of poems. Crane, whose writings had appeared only in the little magazines, was desperate by now for the cachet of book publication, a possibility that had seemed more than once on the verge of materializing. Originally Liveright had rejected *White Buildings*, then had reversed himself when he heard that O'Neill would write a foreword, but he again cooled when the playwright's contribution did not materialize.

For more than a year O'Neill, who found nondramatic writing difficult, had procrastinated about the introductory piece; an article of any length cost him nearly as much thought and effort, he has said, as a play. Shortly before leaving Bermuda, though, he wrote a foreword of some eight hundred words, but he was so dissatisfied that he never sent it to Crane or even told him about it. Following is an extract from his hitherto unpublished introduction:

"Hart Crane's poetry is not 'easy.' It bears no relation to that readable American commodity, magazine verse. The poems are not topical, nor appealing, nor wistful. They stir no easy familiar sympathies. They are a fresh vision of the world, intensely personalized in a new creative idiom. . . . Crane wields a sonorous rhetoric. His blank verse, the best medium he controls, is Elizabethan — measured and richly textured. But his spiritual allegiances are outside the English tradition. Melville and Whitman are his avowed masters. In Crane's sea-poems, 'Voyages,' in allusions to the sea throughout his work, there is something of Melville's intense brooding on the mystery of 'the high interiors of the sea.' "

Concerned that Crane might be aggrieved, O'Neill later wrote to him that he had felt all along that he "wasn't qualified [to write the foreword] . . . considering the difficult nature of the poems for the layman-reader, you needed a poet or a critic of poetry who could not only understand your purpose sympathetically (I could do that) but also make a clear, well-devised statement of your use of means to your end. . . . I felt my introduction might prove a damn poor piece of work — and a poor piece of writing, no matter how glowing its praise, is never justifiable on any occasion because it always defeats its purpose."

Eventually Liveright published *White Buildings* with a foreword by Allen Tate (who generously offered to sign O'Neill's name to it) and a blurb on the dust jacket by the playwright: "Hart Crane's poems are profound and deep-seeking. In them he reveals, with a unique power, the mystic undertones of beauty, which move words to express vision."

Aside from a general desire to be in O'Neill's good graces, Liveright, in agreeing to publish Crane, had a special reason for pleasing the playwright: he was eager to produce *Marco Millions*. A restless, dynamic soul who expended only a fraction of his energy on publishing books and battling the censors, a man who rather suggested an actor — piercing dark eyes, sensuous lips, a bold nose, a lordly air — Liveright had found the excitement and glamour his nature craved by becoming involved with Broadway. His record included Edwin Justus Mayer's *The Firebrand*, an adaptation of Dreiser's *An American Tragedy*, and a modern-dress *Hamlet* that aroused considerable talk. O'Neill was perfectly willing for his publisher to double as his producer but he doubted that Horace could raise the sort of money *Marco* required. Though Liveright's publishing house was flourishing — his books at the time included Dreiser's *Tragedy* and Anita Loos's *Gentlemen Prefer Blondes* — he chronically was pressed for funds from high living and playing the stock market.

Before driving his family to Maine, O'Neill, much as he shrank from public display, attended the Yale commencement as one of the notables of the day. At the urging of Professor George Pierce Baker, who had left Harvard to head a newly established drama department at Yale, he had agreed to accept an honorary degree of Doctor of Literature. Professor Baker felt, as he wrote Eugene, that the degree would not only honor him but would establish the precedent that universities "should recognize [a playwright of] genuinely significant achievement. . . . It is another milepost." In his reply on May 21 O'Neill said: "Coming from Yale, I appreciate that this [degree] is a *true* honor . . . and hope that this recognition of my work really should have a genuine significance for all those who are trying, as I am, to do original, imaginative work for the theater." But his main reason for accepting the tribute, he later informed a friend, was that "it meant so much to Professor Baker and I know how hard he had worked to get it for me. I was his best-known pupil, and Yale was really honoring him through me. In short, I was on the spot, liking him as much as I did."

There was, in his view, an ironic aspect to Yale's new theater center, which had been financed by a gift of one million dollars from Standard Oil heir Edward S. Harkness. In earlier years Eugene, as a fire-breathing

Socialist in New London, used to shake his fist in the direction of Harkness's Waterford estate and inveigh against "the power of Mammon." At a later date, combining Harkness (actually a shy individual) with his neighbor Edward Crowninshield Hammond (a brusque snob) for a composite character, the playwright would ridicule them as Harker, an offstage figure in *Long Day's Journey Into Night,* and as T. Stedman Harder, a bewildered tweedy squire in *A Moon for the Misbegotten.* Despite the similarity, though, of Harder's and Harker's names to Harkness's, they are primarily based on Hammond, not on the Standard Oil man.

Of the sixteen who received honorary degrees at Yale on June 23, 1926, the most prominent were Andrew W. Mellon, the secretary of the United States Treasury, and O'Neill. O'Neill, who was so seated that he could observe Mellon, thought him "the epitome of the cold banker. You couldn't read anything there. What a cold face, what cold piercing eyes! The skin of his face was tightly drawn, the color of old, silvery parchment." Introducing O'Neill, who received "a tremendous ovation," Professor William Lyon Phelps declared: "He is the only American dramatist who has produced a deep impression on European drama and European thought . . . he has redeemed the American theater from commonplaceness and triviality." Yale President James Rowland Angell in bestowing the degree described him as "a creative contributor of new and moving forms to one of the oldest of the arts."

The commencement was less trying, O'Neill said afterward, than he had feared: "To my surprise, in spite of a large dose of stage fright — and the horrible feeling of a virgin circus horse when 'pee-rading' under the elms between lines of blasé New Havenites — I had a fine time. . . . One reason for my taking on the whole business was to test myself out along a new line. The whole experience did me a lot of good inside, I feel."

The feeling shortly evaporated, however; he would continue to avoid public appearances as much as possible. On being informed years later that Princeton, his alma mater, wanted to honor him, he criticized honorary degrees in general and added: "[The ceremony is] a torture, not a pleasure. I made up my mind after the Yale ordeal in '26, never again."

En route to Maine the O'Neills stopped in New London, two days after the Yale event, to enjoy the spectacle of a high-spirited throng flaunting Harvard crimson or Yale blue in neckties, blazers, pennants and parasols. It was Boat Day again. The small city by the Thames overflowed with tens of thousands — students and alumni with their families, gamblers and bootleggers, pickpockets, souvenir hawkers and just plain sports fans — who had gathered to watch, or profit from, the annual contest between the racing shells of the two schools. The crowd had poured in not only by automobile and train but by boat, hundreds of them, all sizes, all shapes, ranging from craft that were scarcely more than a sail and a plank to oceangoing yachts that now, a wildly democratic armada, rode on the broad reaches of the Thames. It was, said one news story, "as colorful a scene as any sports event in the world has to offer."

To O'Neill the college regatta was an old story and among his few unclouded memories of New London, but time and change had taken their toll of the event's former glamour and atmosphere of munificence. In earlier years the yachts, a flotilla of them, and the deluxe railroad cars used to arrive days before the race, for a week of parties and champagne; by now the celebrating, more tumultuous than glamorous, was confined to a day or so.

The 1926 Boat Day was, however, among the most festive in years — and would be one of the last with a sprinkling of the old-time glitter. Climaxing the day, a new record was set for the four-mile run upstream in a thrilling race. After Yale had taken an early lead, the contest became, as one newspaper recounts, "a long, heartbreaking stern chase, with the white-hatted Crimson oarsmen never losing hope and coming through with a spurt as they came to the last half-mile that had the crowded observation trains bellowing with excitement. . . . The Crimson crawled up an agonizing boat's length, but one and a half length's distance was as close as it came to the sliding Blue ghost tonight." (With the spectacle and cheering fresh in his mind, O'Neill would use the duel on the river as background for a climactic scene in *Strange Interlude*.)

After the race Eugene, who left his family behind at a hotel, made a brief excursion into the past by driving "very slowly and reminiscently" along Pequot Avenue. Here was Maibelle Scott's onetime home, which he had visited only once because her parents were opposed to his courting her (a page of his history he would treat with humorous nostalgia in *Ah, Wilderness!*); now he was passing the Monte Cristo cottage at 325, still vacant, shabbier than ever; and further along, at 416, the home of the Rippins — Jessica, Emily and Doll, but above all Mrs. Rippin, sympathetic and tactful, who had mothered him when he was convalescing from tuberculosis. Eugene had thought of calling on the Rippins but the house was dark, and he continued to Ocean Beach, where he and Beatrice Ashe used to picnic in an isolated corner near Alewife Cove and shut out the world. He was jarred from the past, though, by the sight of "atrocities committed at the beach" — Coney Island–like improvements — and rushed back to the hotel. The next morning, without further sightseeing, he resumed the drive to Maine.

The O'Neills' place at Belgrade Lakes, a two-story log cabin surrounded by pines, was called Loon Lodge. "The above name of our camp," he wrote to Frank B. Elser, a friend, on July 10, "is no horrible jest but a fact! After a winter spent in a 'Bellevue,' I'll say it looks as if God had taken to symbolism, what? However, I remain not only sane but also sober."

The family was joined shortly by Eugene Jr., who at sixteen was nearly as tall as his father, and Agnes's daughter Barbara, five years younger, who found him "so dashing and handsome and full of exuberance" that she fell "madly in love" with him. Her infatuation lasted all summer. "I think he enjoyed it," she says, "for he constantly played jokes on me which served to both inflate and deflate my ego." A sensitive, affectionate girl who was eager to be of service, Barbara recalls that during her stays with her mother and stepfather, she usually was assigned a household task. "At Belgrade," she says, "it was to get breakfast, and I did it right down to making muffins. I felt pretty important getting a complete breakfast for the entire family every day. I have no specific recollections of Eugene Sr. that summer, but I always remember him as a gentle, shy man with a soft light flickering in his eyes.

"We had some kind of competition among ourselves — Shane, Gene Jr., and myself — as to who could catch the most fish over the summer. It turned out that the smallest, Shane, who was only six, caught the most. He was always a wonderful fisherman and seemed to have some affinity for the silent sitting and waiting involved in fishing."

For young Eugene the summer marked the start of a lifelong friendship with Frank Meyer, whose parents had a place by the lake not far from the O'Neills. Both youths were bright, both loved to read, and in comparing notes learned that they both had been impressed by Hector C. Bywater's *The Great Pacific War*, a novel set in the future that dealt with a war between this country and Japan. At the O'Neills' camp, where young Meyer became a frequent visitor, they played a game inspired by the book, a kind of water polo in which each participant — Shane, Barbara, the two youths — represented a different country. At times O'Neill joined in. "I found him," Meyer says, "very kind and gentle. What I especially liked was that he talked to you as an equal, none of that talking down because you were a kid. The three of us, including young Gene, discussed Bywater's prophecy of war between the United States and

Japan in the 1930s, and we agreed that it was very likely to come true. Another time we talked about Freud. I remember in particular our discussing puns and slips of the tongue in connection with the unconscious."

O'Neill, who had begun *Strange Interlude* in Bermuda and was eager to continue, found it difficult to write at Loon Lodge, for the walls were so thin that he could hear any sound in the place. "He needed complete quiet when he worked," Agnes says. "That's why he couldn't have the children around most of the time." Noting that he was becoming restless, his face "longer and longer," Agnes discussed the problem with Elizabeth Marbury and at her suggestion had a small one-room shack built out of earshot of the lodge. The playwright worked here all morning, seven days a week. Afterward, looking tense when he first appeared at the lake, he silently, without a word or even a nod to anyone, would swim across and back, about two miles in all, and then, looking relaxed, would join the others. On the whole he relished the change to fresh water, he enjoyed the rowing and canoeing, yet, as he said, the lakes "aren't the sea."

In July he spent a long afternoon dredging up the past for the benefit of David Karsner, an old admirer of his work who had been on the *Call*, a Socialist newspaper now defunct. Clearly awed by his subject, Karsner said in his account, which appeared in the *Herald Tribune* on August 8, 1926, that in "twenty years of meeting the great, the near-great and ordinary mortals in all stages and degrees of elation and reverses . . . I cannot recall a single person whose burning eyes [and] intense, almost nervous exterior had upon me the same effect as Eugene O'Neill . . . as a playwright [he] did not disturb me at all, but the man disturbed me much. It was what gave those eyes of his their burning luster and what contributed to his intense, almost jerky exterior that mattered."

He brightened, however, when Karsner mentioned that he had recently seen a copy of *Thirst*, O'Neill's first collection of plays, priced at eight dollars; O'Neill "clapped his hands and his laughter could be heard across the lake." So few copies were sold originally, in 1914, that the publisher had offered him virtually the entire edition at twenty-five cents apiece. (Today a copy in mint condition, with a dust jacket, brings about one hundred and fifty dollars.)

Where Eugene had granted an interview to Karsner as a favor to an old fan of his, he welcomed Elizabeth Shepley Sergeant because he admired her writings, particularly a "portrait study" of Robert Edmond Jones, and wondered how she would depict him. Her biographical sketches, which appeared in the *New Republic*, were personal, searching, interpretative, rather than the usual objective account. Miss Sergeant, who spent two days at Loon Lodge, wrote an article that impressed O'Neill as "the best thing ever done about me. The others," he told her, "have been pretty dull and lame. Yours is the only one!" One result of the article, subtitled "Man with a Mask," was that the playwright admitted Miss Sergeant to his circle of friends. O'Neill, her article begins, "has ever walked alone, and seemed a stranger to those about him. While still unaware who and what he was, he suffered from the isolation and tried to destroy it by putting on a disguise of romantic adventure. In his photographs you will see a mask of arrogant disdain. The tortured dreamer's eyes, the tossed black head, with its streaks of white, the scowling thunderous face, glimpsed at some formal dress rehearsal, escaping from praise, seem also to confirm the legend. But if you corner the playwright you will find him sorry and uneasy in his aloofness. And it may be that some flash of understanding will bring out, from behind the barrier, with a smile of doubting trust, the sensitive 13-year-old boy whom you recognize as O'Neill the poet.

"Always thus hiding, always thus revealing himself, the Irish-American mystic, with his strange duality of being, has made his plays a projection of his struggles with the unmanageable universe."

Having written nearly two acts before he left Bermuda, O'Neill thought he was "well into" *Strange Interlude;* but after a fresh look at the script, he wrote another second act and then, still dissatisfied, a third version. Discouraged by his slow progress, he felt that his present entourage was partly responsible. "I could do with less progeny about," he complained to Macgowan, on August 7, "for I was never cut out, seemingly, for a *pater familias* and children in squads, even when indubitably my own, tend to 'get my goat.'" Trying to soften the remark, he adds, "However, they have their recompensing sides, too" — but there is little evidence he really thought so. "Gene seems to think," Agnes informed her mother on August 10, "it would be much better for his work if there were *no* kids here but Shane and Oona, as he hasn't got a thing started so far this summer, and as we have *no* prospective plays going on in the fall, *Laz* and *M. Millions* both seeming to have a hard time getting any backers." Eugene Jr. and Barbara, who were supposed to remain to the end of August, were dispatched several weeks earlier.

(In a romantic image that both suggests and glosses over O'Neill's inadequacy as a parent, Elizabeth Sergeant ended her article: "When O'Neill steps lightly along some pagan shore with Shane, he walks a little behind, a tall figure, in a bathing-suit, with limbs burnt to a pagan blackness; and on his face the look, not of a 'father,' but of some trusting elder child who has grown up into a strange world.")

Worried about *Lazarus* and *Marco*, the playwright needed, and of course found, a scapegoat. In a letter to Macgowan he criticized "this Actors' combine. Combine? As far as I can see, the GV has simply been swallowed up by a vastly inferior, quite brainless organization! You made one grand mistake when you let them keep the name of Actors' Theater and all the paraphernalia of their ridiculous letter-head staff! [The board of directors read like a *Who's Who* of the American stage — Ethel Barrymore, John Barrymore, Laurette Taylor, John Drew, Jane Cowl, etc. — while the group's backers included John D. Rockefeller, Jr., Coleman Du Pont, Otto Kahn and Marshall Field.] What have we gained, for Christ's sake? We have no money to do any real work with, we haven't even got a theater to plan ahead with — and we've lost our absolute control [though Macgowan was in charge, O'Neill believed that his "dictatorship" would collapse once he sought to implement his ideas]. . . .

"I tell you candidly, Kenneth, if it weren't for our friendship, I'd be out of this combine — script of 'L' and all — as fast as I could get to the telegraph office! . . . I'm not denying the GV was finished financially and that something had to be done, but I think we have been cheated into giving our good names for nothing. . . . I think if you started to raise a howl — in my name, which will let you out of the responsibility — it may have some salutary effect. Tell whoever should be told that . . . if the Actors' Theater cannot raise the money to insure time and material for a proper production of either *Marco* or *Lazarus*, then I wish to be publicly announced as out of it."

Broadening his attack to cover the theater in general, he said that "a deep sense of insult and injury has been growing & brewing in my mind ever since I've realized how little we've got in exchange for the GV labors. I'm sick of your having to beg money . . . for my plays. I'm sick of your submitting them to [people] whose opinion is worthless. It's humiliating for you and for me. . . . This putting my stuff up for auction in the slave market spoils the game for me . . . like Yank in [*The Hairy Ape*] I question the moon above Broadway dolefully, 'Where do I get off at? Where do I fit in?' "

Macgowan, who had his own grievances after "three hellish seasons of worry and struggle" in the Village, was angered and hurt by the letter, which goes on for pages, since it questioned his association with the Actors' Theater. But in his reply several days later he patiently took up, one by one, the points his indignant colleague had raised. After citing data to prove that the merger was a better setup than the Greenwich Village had ever been, he said on August 12 that since *Lazarus* would cost at least fifty thousand dollars to stage, additional "outside" money would have to be found. "If you want to put your plays out in large form, then the risks for you as well as for any theater — and the delays — are going to be considerable. There's *Marco* to prove it. If the plays were hokum and still had your rep behind them that would be different. But in any case a huge production with 120 people doesn't slip onto the American stage very quickly or easily."

While conceding that perhaps he had been too severe on the Actors' Theater, O'Neill in a follow-up letter renewed his general complaint: "What's the use of my trying to get ahead with new stuff until some theater can give that stuff the care and opportunity it must have in order to register its new significance outside of the written page. . . . I'm sick and tired of old theaters under old conditions, of 'art' theaters with fuzzy ideals and no money or efficiency — in fact, of *the* American theater as it exists."

He had earlier suggested to Kenneth, as an alternative to merging with the actors' group, that they try to establish a theater that featured his writings. Returning to the subject, he said: "There must be a Maecenas somewhere in the U.S. if we could but find him who would have the faith and generosity to gamble artistically for a few years on my new plays & revivals of old ones as a basis, and give us the chance to start clean, clear of old people & old conditions. . . . I may be a fool but I believe in this. I believe if we knew how to go after this opportunity, we'd find it. (Baker found Harkness.) In fact I don't believe much in anything in the theater but this dream. It is this theater I'm writing for."

O'Neill was discontented not only with his career but, as he confessed to Macgowan, with his personal life. He felt that he and Agnes "could do with more real friends to talk with. Especially I feel that I could for, my days of rum being, I am quite confident, over forever in this world, I rather feel the void left by those companionable or (even when most horrible) intensely dramatic phantoms and obsessions, which, with caressing claws in my heart and brain, used to lead me for weeks at a time, otherwise lonely, down the ever-changing vistas of that No-Man's-Land lying between the D.T.s and Reality as we suppose it. But I reckon that, having now been 'on the wagon' for a longer time . . . than ever before since I started drinking at fifteen, I have a vague feeling of maladjustment to this 'cleaner, greener land' somewhere inside me. It is not that I feel any desire to drink whatever. Quite the contrary, I rather wonder that I ever had sought such a high-priced release, and the idea of it is (what must be fatal to any temptation!) dull and stupid to my mind now. But it is just like getting over leprosy, I opine. One feels so normal with so little to be normal about. One misses playing solitaire with one's scales."

His malaise seems inevitable when one views him as a man with a deep sense of guilt whose binges had been a form of self-punishment, a way, unconsciously, of doing penance. (Miss Sergeant's article again: "One might trace his life like one of those dry, southwestern roads where the Penitente Brothers have laid down the dead man they are carrying. O'Neill's plays, up to now, are crosses that mark the laying down of some outworn shell of existence. Follow the road he travels and you will often hear the sound of flagellation. Look and you will see that the cruel whip is brought down by a tormented soul on his own back.")

Having abjured drinking, O'Neill needed a substitute, something else with which to torture himself. This need would be a factor — though not, by any means, the sole or predominant one — in the relationship that shortly developed between him and Carlotta Monterey ("the famous beauty" he called her on August 18, in writing to the Rippin family), who was Elizabeth Marbury's houseguest for the summer.

The playwright and the actress, who had not met since her appearance in *The Hairy Ape* in 1922, approached one another warily the first time he and Agnes came to tea. Recalling the occasion, Miss Monterey says, "I nodded coolly when we were introduced and didn't say much. My hostess — she was crippled, a large woman with tiny feet that didn't support her — and Agnes, they did most of the talking. Finally Miss Marbury asked me to take Mr. O'Neill down to the bathhouse, so he could have a swim. On the way there he said, 'You don't like me, do you?' I gave it to him plain. 'You're the rudest man,' I said, 'I've ever met. When I went into that play of yours, I didn't want to. I had just finished one thing and wanted to go out to California and see my mother and daughter. But Hoppy [Arthur Hopkins] kept after me, so I did, with hardly a rehearsal, and you never had the decency to thank me.'

"Well, he went into the bathhouse and the only suit he could find was a woman's. Oh, my, it was the most ridiculous thing; it was much too large for him, but that didn't seem to bother him — he wanted his swim. I thought to myself, He can't be so stuck on himself if he'd do something like that."

Agnes was unconcerned in Maine about her husband and Miss Monterey, since, as far as she could see, "nothing was happening between them. I didn't worry about her because she didn't seem smart enough for him. I remember her telling us that she had read all of de Maupassant and how much she loved his stories — and Gene and I just looked at one another. It seemed to me he was more amused by her than anything else. But I suddenly remember something he said — I guess this was after he began to have some feeling about her: he said that she had eyes like his mother's."

In the four years since *The Hairy Ape* Carlotta had appeared decoratively, if with little other distinction, in a few plays and had gone through another marriage — a third one for both her and caricaturist Ralph Barton. A slight, dapper chap with patent-leather hair, boyish good looks and a zest for pleasure, Barton liked nothing better than throwing parties and surrounding himself with celebrities. Carlotta, however, for all her smart facade and confident manner, was less sure of herself than she appeared; she felt "out of things" among Barton's clever, quick-witted friends and professed to find most of them "shallow." In Charlie Chaplin's opinion — he and Barton were good friends — Miss Monterey wanted "to be all sufficient to a man of genius, to cut him off from everybody and minister to his genius, while she herself shone in reflected glory." Voicing a similar view, Ilka Chase, who saw a good deal of the Bartons, says, "Carlotta wanted to possess her men and be everything to them. She felt Barton was wasting his talent with his playboy socializing. She had a sense of mission and wanted to help him achieve himself."

Miss Chase, who became friends with Miss Monterey when they appeared in "an incredible stew" called *The Red Falcon* in 1924, writes that the Bartons' "life together was stormy and passionate, and she would arrive at the theater in a seething emotional turmoil and pour her misfortunes into my willing ears. As she was very beautiful, Ralph Barton was not the first man who had made her unhappy." The couple had a studio apartment in the Hotel des Artistes, 1 West Sixty-seventh Street, and Ilka "used to love to go there, because they had wonderful books and pictures and delicious little dinners; but they dined at half-past six even when Carlotta wasn't playing, and I never could understand why. It had something to do with their temperaments, I imagine; their temperaments were prominent, and everybody relaxed when they got a divorce." The marriage collapsed early in 1926 when Carlotta, who had been in a play out of town, returned home unexpectedly one night and found Barton in bed with another woman.

Like O'Neill, who was to become her fourth and final husband, Carlotta Monterey had a bent for self-dramatization, a distrust of the world, and, though one might never suspect it from her proud way of carrying herself, a deep strain of insecurity in her makeup; as compensation, she had great drive, a highly developed sense of self-preservation. As in O'Neill's case, she had been painfully shy in childhood and had thought herself unwanted, unloved. Moreover, she too felt shadowed by her family background, but where O'Neill examined his past with a relentless eye, trying to understand it, she romanticized, giving others a glossier account than her history warranted.

The actress was the sole offspring of a marriage that broke up early. Christian Neilson Tharsing, her father, left home in Denmark when he was sixteen and knocked around the world as a seaman before he settled down in California to fruit farming. Physically well favored, he was both handsome and powerfully built, a man weighing over two hundred pounds, but his disposition was as hard as his massive arms. If a horse disobeyed him, Tharsing would pinch its nostrils and with a quick twist of the nose flip the animal to the ground. He was a childless widower of forty when eighteen-year-old Nellie Gotchett of Oakland, at the urging of her strong-willed mother, married him for security; security was all she found, for little if any affection developed on either side. Nellie was, however, as fertile as the California earth, and Chris had to do little more than look at her before she became pregnant. Feeling trapped, she induced a series of miscarriages by horseback riding (in a scandal of the neighborhood, she wore men's jeans for riding), but one pregnancy resisted her efforts. During Christmas week of 1888, several months after Mrs. James O'Neill on the opposite side of the continent had with difficulty borne her third son, Nellie gave birth after great pain — she was in labor for forty-eight hours — to a girl who was christened Hazel Neilson Tharsing.

When Hazel was about four, her mother walked out on Tharsing, deposited the child with one of her sisters, Mrs. John Shay of Oakland, and proceeded to make her own way in the lusty, flourishing San Francisco of the 1890s. Capable, hardworking, with a passion for cleanliness that must have been a legacy from her ancestry — German, New York Dutch, French Swiss — Nellie would take over a run-down lodging house, get it into spotless condition, and shortly have it filled with acquaintances from sporting and theatrical circles. Once it was thriving, she would sell the place at a good price and repeat the process with another shabby rooming house. Nellie profited also from her love affairs. Although unexceptional-looking, she made the most of herself by dressing with smart simplicity and attracted men with her vitality, her zest for

Eugene, age about ten

Nellie Tharsing and her daughter Hazel

Hazel, age about six

living. She enjoyed food, played a shrewd hand of poker, and had an uncorseted sense of humor. Her lovers — only in succession, never concurrently, for Nellie was too practical to be promiscuous — were usually men of some means; one of her longest affairs was with the leading undertaker of Sacramento.

The Shays, who had two sons slightly older than Hazel, treated her like a daughter, and her mother came to see her fairly often, but, according to one Shay boy, she was "terribly shy for a long time." Mr. Shay, whose library included Shakespeare, Scott, and Washington Irving, liked to read to his family in the evening, a pastime that gave Hazel an early love of books. Mrs. Shay, a rather strict but conscientious mother, as well as a devout Baptist, did her full duty by Hazel. To help the child overcome her shyness, she enrolled her in an elocution school, a place the child long disliked; but after a year or so she began to enjoy being a center of attention as she recited, and announced that she was going on the stage when she grew up.

After living with the Shays till she was thirteen, Hazel spent three years, except for the summers, at St. Gertrude's, a Catholic academy in Rio Vista, California. The other girls found that she not only liked to star in the school plays but was inclined to dramatize in daily life. She used to unnerve her classmates by describing in detail an eye operation she had undergone before entering the school. The doctor, according to her account, removed an eyeball, placed it on her cheek before doing some scraping and cutting in the socket, and then returned the eye to its place. (After several years of wearing glasses, she rebelled, but later in life, plagued by recurrent eye trouble, she wore them in private. While she long disregarded the doctor about glasses, she heeded him in another respect; on his advice that it benefited her eye condition, she held her head back, her chin up, a position that gave her a rather arrogant air and that possibly, as a result of the impression she made on people, figured to some extent in the formation of her personality.)

Recalling that "Hazel always made a mystery of things," a schoolmate adds: "She used to sign other girls' memory books with the name of 'Jane C.,' and if you asked why, she would say it was going to be her stage name, but she never told us what the 'C' stood for. [Her mother's protector at the time was George Clark, the Sacramento undertaker.] When the rest of us got a package of food or candy, we'd tell who it was from — our parents or a friend or some relative. But not Hazel. If you asked, she just looked mysterious about it. She was selective about the girls she became friendly with — they usually were from the better families — but I would say she had no real friends, no close ones. She was a loner more or less. When we went walking on Sundays, she'd be up at the head of the line, talking to the nuns and playing up to them. We all felt she was going to amount to something."

For a time Miss Tharsing (like O'Neill's mother at convent school) thought of taking the veil. "I was attracted," she says, "by the color of it — the music, the rituals, the nuns' dress — it was like theater to me. But the mother superior was wise. She told me, when I was about to graduate, to spend a year at home, and if I still felt the same, to come back to them." Several years after St. Gertrude's, Hazel wrote to one of the nuns: "You know I always wanted a skull; I have one at last. I keep it in my bedroom, often look at it, and think of what I shall one day be." (This was no passing fancy or bit of youthful weltschmerz, for she again had a skull in her bedroom toward the end of her life and used to fondle it.)

To prepare for the stage and, according to a relative of hers, acquire some polish that would enhance her matrimonial prospects, the Oakland girl spent five years abroad, 1906 to 1911, taking French, ballet and fencing lessons in Paris, singing and acting courses in London. To her private displeasure, since she had more substantial ambitions, she was named "Miss California" in a beauty contest in 1907 after her mother had submitted her photograph. Hazel returned briefly to this country for the national finals — she came in second — then went back to Europe, this time accompanied by her mother. Nellie later complained to the Shays that even when they lacked the funds to eat properly, Hazel insisted on their having "a good address." After studying at Sir Herbert Beerbohm Tree's Academy of Dramatic Arts (which later became the Royal Academy), where her classmates included Cedric Hardwicke and Roland Young, she made her first and final appearance on the London stage in a revival of *The Geisha*.

Her first husband, whom she met abroad and married in New York in 1911, was John Moffat, a Scottish lawyer of distinguished appearance, good family background and variable means. Nine years her senior, he was deeply in love with her. Before they met he had run through a fortune by speculating in mining stocks, but he hoped to make another with the help of his family connections — he belonged to the Coates thread clan. The Moffats' several years of marriage were spent first in Europe, then in California, where they finally became dependent on Nellie Tharsing after Moffat was cut off, by World War I, from his funds in England. When Hazel sued him for divorce, she alleged that he once threatened to shoot her, another time to kill himself by jumping from their hotel room. (The two, nevertheless, remained fond of one another, and toward the end of their lives carried on an affectionate correspondence.)

After choosing a stage name suitable to her Latin appearance, Carlotta Monterey (the surname came from the town in California) made her Broadway debut in March 1915 opposite Lou Tellegen in *Taking Chances*, a sex farce. The reviewer for the *Sun* noted appreciatively on March 18 that she appeared in "an almost negligible negligee in the last act and made a seductive picture."

In her first interview as an actress, an article headlined "A Girl of Extremes" in the New York *Tribune* on April 18, Miss Monterey agreed with a friend's description of her as "a girl of strong emotions" and said, after listing her scrambled parentage: "I have often wondered if the mixed blood of those different nationalities had much to do with it. It seems that I am always vacillating between extremes, and never choose a compromising and restful middle course. There are times when I feel within me a calling for the primitive, the wild and the elemental in nature and in art. . . . Then at times I crave the very reverse, the exquisite and the ultra-refined. . . . It is not pleasant to be like a living pendulum swinging between two natures. Please, do not think me morbid or abnormal, for I take too wholesome an interest in life to become that, thanks to the healthy outdoor life of my girlhood. I enjoy too thoroughly to fight for my place in the world."

The following season she toured the country as the ill-fated Luana in *The Bird of Paradise*, a bravura role made famous by Laurette Taylor and Lenore Ulric; but unlike her predecessors the California actress failed to arouse any excitement except in the California press, which hailed her as a native daughter. Adding to her discontent, she "loathed" touring. (A person of "extremes," she never liked or disliked things; it was always a matter of her either "loving" or "loathing" something.) "I would rather not work at all," she said after her stint in *Paradise*, "than go on the road. To me [it] represents all that is distasteful — the middle-of-the-night 'jump'; the stuffy, dirty hotel rooms; the stomach-racking meals; the loneliness."

In October 1916 Miss Monterey married Melvin C. Chapman, Jr., of Oakland, a law student seven years her junior — she was now twenty-seven. The new union created a rather involved family setup, for Nellie Tharsing had long been the mistress and housekeeper of young Chapman's widowed father. A leading attorney of the Bay Area, Chapman Sr. had wanted to marry Nellie but his son, who found her "bossy" when she first appeared on the scene, gave Senior the choice of marriage to his mistress or his son's affection; he had no objection, however, to his father's liaison. The father in turn (a rather ineffectual man outside his profession) raised no objections when the youth began courting Carlotta. "Nellie persuaded me to do it," young Chapman recalls, "but I was already infatuated and thought I loved her." And Carlotta married him because, she later told him, she wanted a child; Lou Tellegen had advised her that she would never be a good actress until she became a mother.

Ten months after her marriage to Chapman she gave birth to a girl, who was named Cynthia Jane, and less than a year later, leaving the child to be reared by Nellie, she returned to the stage. In 1923 Chapman sued for divorce at her request — so that she could marry Ralph Barton — while Nellie Tharsing said, as the San Francisco *Call* reported on April 23 of that year, "[My daughter's] love for art destroyed her love for home and family."

For about a half-dozen years, in a relationship that started before and outlasted her marriage to Barton, Miss Monterey was the mistress of James Speyer, an elderly Wall Street banker whose "philanthropies were many and varied." Widowed and childless, he gave away in his lifetime a sizable part of his fortune. Although they never lived together, he made Carlotta one of his private philanthropies by establishing a trust fund which provided her, to the end of her life, with an annual income that averaged close to fourteen thousand dollars. For all his generosity, he was displeased when Carlotta, who had a passion for shoes, spent fifteen hundred dollars for a pair of sandals inlaid with semiprecious stones. She generally contented herself, Ilka Chase says, with slippers "made to order of special leathers, at great cost" — but a cost substantially less than fifteen hundred dollars. (An architect who designed a home for O'Neill and Carlotta in the 1930s said that "he had eight thousand books, she had three hundred pairs of shoes.")

While Carlotta gained financially from knowing Speyer, her friendship with Elizabeth Marbury was of social and professional benefit to her. An outstanding play agent for decades (her clients ranged in time from Sardou and Wilde to Shaw, Barrie and Maugham), Miss Marbury knew practically everyone of consequence in the arts on both sides of the Atlantic, and in addition she moved in high society; her friends included Mrs. Jack Gardner of Boston, Anne Morgan, the financier's sister, and Mrs. William K. Vanderbilt. Generous and outgoing, a woman at peace with herself and well adjusted to the world, she was widely liked. At an earlier time Carlotta Monterey might have hesitated at a close friendship

*Carlotta and her daughter Cynthia
in the early twenties*

*A photo that helped Hazel Tharsing
win the title of "Miss California"
in the 1907 beauty contest*

Carlotta, seated on the floor, with Jane Haven in The Bird of Paradise

James Speyer

Caricature of Carlotta by Ralph Barton

Carlotta and Barton

Ralph Barton's between-the-acts curtain for the Chauve-Souris, *a hit 1920s revue*

This reproduction of Barton's curtain highlights O'Neill and those of the audience who figure in his history. They are:

FIRST ROW, *left to right: David Belasco and John Barrymore*

THIRD: *Kenneth Macgowan and Alan Dale*

FOURTH: *Alexander Woollcott, Heywood Broun, Doris Keane and Percy Hammond*

FIFTH: *Lillian Gish and Elizabeth Marbury*

SIXTH: *Otto H. Kahn*

SEVENTH: *Lynn Fontanne, George M. Cohan, Jacob Ben-Ami and Robert Benchley*

NINTH: *O'Neill*

TENTH: *Charlie Chaplin and Ralph Barton*

LAST: *Oliver Sayler and Robert Edmond Jones*

The entire audience is listed on page 700.

Playwright and actress

Carlotta in a fetching pose

*Eugene Jr.'s pleasure at being with his fat
is evident in his face*

with her, for Miss Marbury, though she had always been discreet, was known in her circles as one who loved her own sex; for decades she and Elsie de Wolfe the decorator were inseparable. By now she was an enormously stout woman of seventy who had difficulty walking, but apparently neither age nor infirmity impaired her affectionate nature; according to one of Carlotta's relatives, Miss Marbury wrote to Nellie Tharsing that she wanted to adopt her daughter and would designate Carlotta as her heiress. However, Carlotta, as one or two persons in Maine began to suspect, had other plans.

The summer colony at Belgrade Lakes included actress Florence Reed and her husband Malcolm Williams, whose place was not far from the O'Neills' lodge. Seeking "friends to talk with," the playwright fell into the habit of calling on the couple, but he impressed Miss Reed as "absolutely the most withdrawn person I've ever known. People would drop by while he was sitting on the porch, and he'd remain in the corner, wet bathing suit, teacup shaking — you couldn't make him one of us. He didn't even appear at ease with Bess Marbury, his own agent. [Actually, Richard Madden, Miss Marbury's partner, was his agent.] My husband and he got on famously — I guess that's why he kept dropping in — but while we were friendly, I never felt really close to him.

"As soon as Gene was in the water, though, he loosened up, he was a different person. He used to go for a swim every time he came over, and I remember his telling me the story of *Lazarus* one day while swimming sidestroke. I was paddling alongside, in a canoe."

While he was visiting the couple one day, Carlotta and Miss Marbury came by with several other persons. After all their guests had left, Williams asked his wife whether she had noticed the actress trying to draw out the reticent playwright; he also pointed out that Carlotta had left a scarf behind. When Miss Reed said she would return it by their maid, her husband replied, "Don't bother, she won't thank you for it. She'll be back for it herself tomorrow, when Gene's here."

Like her mother, Carlotta had a passion and a gift for domestic order. Rather than acting the lady of leisure as Miss Marbury's guest, she, in Florence Reed's words, "took over, and Bess was happy to have her do it. Carlotta ran the servants, ordered the food, supervised the cooking — she took care of everything and did it superbly. She had, I'm not exaggerating, a genius for it." As others would later think also, Miss Reed felt that Carlotta's talent as a homemaker was one of the factors that eventually won over O'Neill. "He was especially impressed," says Miss Reed, "because Agnes was quite the reverse. One day I called at their place and right in the living room – they didn't know who might drop by – there were baby things hanging up that hadn't been washed properly. They smelled a little."

It is true that Agnes had nothing like Carlotta's flair for domestic management, yet a comparison of the two households is somewhat unfair. One was a large renovated house full of fine antiques, where the owner had summered for years; the other, an unpretentious lodge overrun by youngsters – Eugene Jr. and Barbara were still around at the time. As domestic help, the O'Neills had Mrs. Clark (who was better at cooking than cleaning house) and, for the summer, a Canadian girl to take care of Oona and keep an eye on Shane.

Carlotta, who had little if any subtlety in her makeup, sought out O'Neill on every possible occasion, but her open, direct approach served to forestall rather than to excite suspicion. Both Agnes and Miss Marbury assumed that Carlotta's interest in him was chiefly that of an actress trying to ingratiate herself with a noted playwright. In a snapshot of the two in Maine, she is holding his arm with a pleased, rather proprietary air. Ever since a traumatic experience in early childhood, when her father had tried to force her to learn to swim, she had been deathly afraid of the water; but she used to appear at the O'Neills' camp in a daring one-piece garment ("a boyish white wool knit bathing suit," says Barbara Burton, "with no overskirt such as suits usually had") and would venture out onto the lake in a canoe with O'Neill.

By early September the playwright, after some discouraging weeks, was making good progress on *Strange Interlude*, but his satisfaction with his work was shadowed, as he told George Jean Nathan on September 3, by concern over his unproduced scripts: "The Actors' Theater crowd are still trying to raise money to do *Lazarus Laughed* from among the ranks of their million-talking, jitney-giving Lorenzos. It will cost around $40,000 [in Macgowan's estimate, over fifty thousand dollars] . . . I am afraid I shall soon have to go on a search for an insane – and therefore a truly generous – millionaire and start my own theater.

"Seriously, I honestly am getting awfully fed up with the eternal show-shop from which nothing ever seems to emerge except more show-shop. It's a most humiliating game for an artist. Novelists have all the best of it."

The image of playwright vis-à-vis novelist was in his thoughts at the time because *Strange Interlude*, shaping up as a multiact mammoth, was essentially a novel in play form. He already was thinking ahead, no doubt, and worrying about finding a producer for *that* one. As he worked on

Strange Interlude, Frank B. Elser sent him a play he had adapted from one of his own novels. O'Neill liked it ("a damn fine sound job"), although he was discouraging in another respect: "If you want to be a playwright, you have sure done it, you are! But why want to be one? I speak with exceeding acrimony — for *Marco* still lacks a lover with money enough to support it in the style it needs, and *Lazarus Laughed* is weeping fruitlessly (so far) for actors with emotional — and spiritual — guts enough to approach its roles. . . . So it seems to me if I were a novelist, instead of a Ham-strung & manager-strung idiot, I should get down on my knees and say a prayer to Something."

12

❖

Strange Interlude

FOR months O'Neill's hopes regarding *Lazarus Laughed* kept rising and falling. At one point Max Reinhardt was supposed to be eager to stage it in Berlin, and possibly afterward on Broadway; there was word that Nemirovich-Danchenko, cofounder with Stanislavski of the Moscow Art Theater, was considering a Russian-language presentation; a new group at the Goodman Theater in Chicago was on the verge of accepting the play. But none of these projects ever materialized. Interest in *Marco Millions* was quickened, however, when George Jean Nathan wrote enthusiastically about it in the August 1926 issue of *American Mercury*. The Theater Guild was willing to place the work under option but could not stage it for at least a year, while Gilbert Miller talked of producing it this fall if he could find a proper actor for Marco.

On returning from Maine in mid-October the playwright called on Miller as soon as possible, only to learn that the producer's initial choice for the part, Glenn Hunter, had proven unsuitable. Hunter "gushed about [the] play," Eugene reported to Agnes on the fifteenth, "but showed Miller he didn't know what it was about — the satire — he wanted his Marco to be [a] romantic, handsome hero! Dear actors, what!"

With Macgowan as his guest, O'Neill celebrated his thirty-eighth birthday on October 16, 1926, by attending a Yale-Dartmouth football game in New Haven, where they sat in President Angell's seats on the fifty-yard line. "Old Doc. O'Neill, the Yale grad," he boasted to Kenneth, "has his rights!" After the game the two spent some time with Professor Baker, who had earlier said that he wanted to produce *Marco* for the opening of the Harkness Theater in December; but eventually Baker, deciding that the O'Neill work would be too difficult for a school production, chose a play by one of his students.

Since Brook Farm, which had been rented for the summer, was still occupied when the O'Neills left Maine, Eugene stayed for a while at the Harvard Club in New York, Agnes and the children with her parents in New Jersey; but even when the family returned to Ridgefield for a short stay, Eugene spent most of his time in the city. After all his hopes and efforts for a production of *Marco* or *Lazarus*, if not both, he had to settle for a revival of *Beyond the Horizon*, now in rehearsal as Macgowan's first and final offering at the Actors' Theater. Macgowan, just as O'Neill had predicted, ran into "trouble" and "rows" once he tried to assert his leadership of the group. *Horizon* being O'Neill's "only chance of an income for the winter," he did his utmost to strengthen its chances of success by cutting the script, which now struck him as verbose, and working closely with Jimmy Light, who was the director. O'Neill felt "mighty uncertain" about the play, for it seemed to him "such a past thing. I couldn't reestablish any contact. It left me cold and dissatisfied."

In the midst of busy days largely devoted to *Horizon* rehearsals and fresh efforts to arouse managerial interest in *Marco* and *Lazarus*, the playwright found time to consult Dr. Gilbert Hamilton in regard to the psychological aspects of *Strange Interlude*, which was now about half written. He also resumed seeing Carlotta Monterey, who had an immaculate, tastefully furnished apartment at 20 East Sixty-seventh Street. According to a rather garbled account she gave many years later, O'Neill telephoned to ask whether he might call and, starting with his first visit, poured out his heart to her. Her account, pieced together from several interviews, follows:

"He came up on three afternoons. . . . I hardly knew the man . . . and he paid no more attention to me than if I were that chair, and he began to talk about his early life — that he had had no real home, that he had no mother in the real sense, no father in the real sense, no one to treat him as a child should be treated . . . those three afternoons I sat and listened to this man — at first I was a little worried, and then I was deeply unhappy. I thought of all people to be so stricken, a man who has talent, and he has worked hard and all, and his face would become sadder and sadder and he would talk and talk, and then finally he would say, 'Do you know what time it is . . .?' And I would say, 'There is a clock there.' And he would say, 'I have to go, I have to go,' and he would rush out, come back the next day and go on. . . . He never said to me, 'I love you, I think you are wonderful, I think you are grand.' He kept saying, 'I need you, I need you, I need you,' and sometimes it was a bit frightening. I had been brought up in England and nobody had ever gritted their teeth and said they needed me. And he did need me, I discovered . . . he was never in good health. He always had a cold. He wasn't properly fed or anything. . . . Well, that's what got me in all my trouble with O'Neill — my maternal instinct came out.

"After he'd been to tea several times, he invited me to have lunch with him, a nice restaurant, he said, in his hotel — he was at the Wentworth. . . . I had a broken fingernail that day and asked him for a nail file. He didn't think he had any but we went up to his room and I looked in his suitcase for a toilet kit. All he had in that beaten-up suitcase was one shirt, a pair of pajamas that needed buttons, two pairs of union suits and two pairs of cheap socks. Afterward I went right to Abercrombie and Fitch and got him a half-dozen union suits, half-dozen pair of socks, half-dozen shirts, a fitted case of toilet articles, and had them sent to his hotel. When he phoned me, he sounded so grateful. 'You must have spent,' he said, 'an awful lot of money!' "

Certain things in Miss Monterey's account do not square with the picture given by other sources; the bulk of available evidence tends, for one thing, to cast her, not O'Neill, in the role of pursuer. It also seems that her reminiscences telescope the past, that some things O'Neill said to her about a year later — such as, "I need you, I need you" — have been moved up to his visits this year. Carlotta, at any rate, was not the first woman to try to interest him during his marriage to Agnes, but she was more attractive, more resourceful and, above all, more determined than any of the others. She informed him of her fourteen thousand dollar annuity but said that it came from a childless aunt of hers, in California, who was now deceased. (After learning about the annuity, O'Neill joked to Agnes, "Now I know Carlotta has everything.")

At first O'Neill was merely flattered by Carlotta's attentions; he did not intend or, at least consciously, want to become involved in a grand amour that might overturn his life. But his defenses began to crumble after she made an impassioned declaration of love; and she also aroused his sympathy with a revised history of her family background and marriages. Earlier this fall he and Agnes — with the children left behind in Mrs. Clark's care in Ridgefield — had enjoyed ten "wonderful days" together in the city, a kind of second honeymoon after their congested domesticity in Maine. Yet now he felt drawn to Carlotta, not only by her beauty and professed love for him but by her strength, her solicitude; the gift of clothes from Abercrombie and Fitch, reflecting a maternal attitude, was an inspired tactic. The more he saw of her, the more desirable she appeared on all counts. She was sympathetic, she was understanding, she was intensely interested in his work (Agnes used to say that she was "bored" by so much talk of the theater), and when he complained of his professional troubles, Carlotta's strictures against Broadway matched his own contempt for the "show-shop." But most of all, her strength attracted him: "Agnes was uncertain of herself," says Elizabeth Shepley Sergeant, "so she couldn't help Gene any, while Carlotta always appeared perfectly at ease. She was reassuring to him."

O'Neill wanted to buy a kayak at Macy's but, loath to be engulfed by streams of people in the mammoth department store, he kept postponing the shopping trip till Carlotta heard about it and offered to accompany him. With Carlotta steering him with a firm, confident hand, he felt safe and protected at her side. Almost before he realized what was happening to him, he was swept out of the shallows of gratified ego into tumultuous depths.

His final days in New York found him in an agony of indecision and conflicting desires, but he was not ready to disentangle himself from Agnes and the life they had built together. Agnes and the children left for Bermuda on November 20, while he remained behind to supervise rehearsals of *Beyond the Horizon*, which was to open at the Mansfield on the thirtieth. Following an emotional parting from Carlotta ("Everything will come out," she said, "as we wish it"), he sailed on the *Fort St. George* on the twenty-seventh. The liner had scarcely left New York Harbor when, seeking relief from his feelings by verbalizing them, he began writing a letter to Carlotta. The ship, he said, was "rolling now off [Sandy] Hook. I can remember in my sailor days what a thrill of release it gave me to feel the great ocean ground swell start to heave the ship under me. It meant freedom then. . . . Now that old thrill is gone. The ground swell is just salt water. The rhythm is lost. The self that it excited to dreams was long since buried at sea some night when I was sleeping. Sometimes when I loll on deck as a passenger I can feel it running under the keel of the ship, the haunting soul of a drowned one, wailing lamentable sagas of the past or mocking me in the blasphemous irony of the forecastle. 'What did they give yer, Gene the Yank, in place of the sea.' 'Oh,' I reply airily, 'there's fame, you know.' . . . 'It won't go down with me, that tale,' he says. 'And it won't go down with the sea 'ceptin' to drown and dissolve in it.' 'Well,' I reply shamelessly, 'there's money and a house [at this point O'Neill wrote, and afterward deleted: "and wife and kids"] – and security and ease.' 'And flowers in the front yard?' he sneers. 'Aw, hell, what does that git yuh?' . . . And so on. Quite like the Hairy Ape, that old long-drowned self of mine, who comes back to haunt the bitterest, loneliest hours.

"As now. My soul is a black cell of loneliness and longing, longing for you, my love. . . . God has turned his back and slammed the door and gone away and all the prison is darkness. . . .

"But what a sad letter to be writing to you, Dear One! And especially when, of all things, I don't want to bring you sorrow, of which you've had more than your fill already, God knows! Forgive me! It's rank ingratitude for the great, deep joy your love has given me . . . only just now you seem so far away, so lost to me and I find myself temporarily in such a helpless fog. But I know 'the sun will come — soon!' "

The letter is such a mixture of genuine feeling, self-pity, and romantic posturing that one can hardly tell which predominates. Despite his lamentation, some part of him was gratified by his situation. Carlotta not only brought him "great, deep joy," she served him as a means of self-torment.

The flagellant in him, the man who needed to "play solitaire" with his "scales," is more visible in his next letter to her, written shortly after his return to Bermuda: "The two days on the boat were 'bad uns.' I never left my cabin from dock to dock — but I took many journeys into diverse exquisite torture chambers of the soul. Well, what of it? Life is not a free picnic — what a bore if it were! — and there is no reason why I, in my old age, should feel as plagued and put upon as if I'd just made the discovery. For one's moments of vision of the rare and beautiful, one has to pay — and one should do so, in the pride that no price can be too cruel that one would not give it gladly again and again."

O'Neill lost no time in telling Agnes about Carlotta. In his words, "There are some things I couldn't lie about — even by silence," but he insisted that his feeling for Agnes was greater and that he had no intention of breaking up their marriage. According to his account, he never slept with Carlotta (whether or not true, Agnes believed him); he maintained that neither of them was to blame that Carlotta had fallen in love with him and that he should be attracted to her. Agnes was badly shaken, but after recovering her balance, she wrote to her rival in a generous vein, and received the following reply: "I think of you & Gene & Shane often &, in a way, envy you your life of ease & sunshine & blue water — But altho' we are not all so fortunate we fill our lives with other things. I hear all the music I can and read my eyes out!

[236]

"This Holiday Season gives me the 'blue devils' beyond belief — Why — God knows — for I have no happy Christmas's to remember!

"I hope to be as *splendid* as you are — and that's saying a lot!"

It was a particularly difficult period for Agnes, for she learned of her husband's infatuation only a short time after her father, who had long been unwell, was found to be tubercular. He was now in New Haven Hospital waiting to be admitted to a sanatorium. O'Neill, who was fond of Mr. Boulton, wrote to him on December 20: "I know, from my own experience, what you must be going through now. The first weeks at a San. or a hospital are the devil's own for getting one at the bottom of depression. But never mind! After that it gets better and better until you begin to find a new and interesting life going on around you. . . . I honestly didn't mind my six months in a San. — after the first one was over."

But while he felt sorry for his father-in-law, his own situation dominated his thoughts. To Macgowan, the only one of his friends in whom he had confided, he disclosed his inner state: "I'm not what you could call perfectly at peace with God. The two days' voyage was a beautiful little inner hell. The high cost of living seemed horribly exorbitant. One was tempted to refuse to pay the bill. I envy those simple souls to whom life is always either this *or* that. It's the this *and* that . . . that slow-poisons the soul with complicated contradictions. . . . [Agnes] is fine. So are the heirs. And it is good to be home again. And luckily I left when I did — for I love her and them and my home — nothing could ever take their place — but oh Christ, there are other things — 'on the other side of the hills.' "

He sent Macgowan a check of twenty-five dollars to get Carlotta some roses for Christmas ("My God!" she recalls. "Macgowan came with a box of flowers as big as a coffin!"), and on December 16 he cautioned Kenneth, "Don't 'understand' in your letters. They are read not only by me!" In his first days in Bermuda he felt as though he had been "shot into the sky" and was being "blown about like a cloud, with only my shadow moving down on the earth, where there are houses and people who live in them." A month later he still felt adrift, but to those around him he gave little if any indication of his inner state; like his masked Dion Anthony, he cultivated a sardonic manner. Hubertine Zahorska, an American girl who ran a linen shop in Hamilton and did part-time typing for O'Neill, felt that he was "playing Carlotta against Agnes and deriving some kind of satisfaction from the situation."

His one source of unalloyed pleasure was Spithead, which he was sure would be "a wonder when it is finally fixed up — absolutely ideal for me and will surely pay me big dividends in the work I shall do here. I love it." By the time he was through renovating and improving the property — besides restoring the house he built a concrete dock and a tennis court — he would spend about twenty thousand dollars beyond his purchase price of seventeen thousand five hundred dollars. Located at the water's edge and commanding a sweeping view of Great Sound with its sailboats, sea gulls and many islets, Spithead possessed genuine charm. Sturdily built of native stone, the sand-colored eighteenth-century house had plain honest lines, thick walls and, after the alterations, a double stairway with "welcoming arms" that led up to the second story from the outside. Built by Captain Hezekiah Frith, a privateer who grew rich from capturing Spanish and French merchant ships, Spithead originally served as both living quarters and a storehouse for booty. According to a local legend that delighted O'Neill's romantic soul, Spithead was haunted twice over; earlier tenants were said to have seen the ghosts of both Captain Frith and his son, Hezekiah Jr., who was killed by lightning while on Granaway Deep.

In addition to the main house, the property included a sizable cottage, an ancient buttery with massive stone walls, and in the middle of the dock, a well-like fishpond, fed by the sound, in which the tide rose and fell. Here Shane, a quiet boy who moved rather slowly and tentatively, as though unsure of the ground beneath him, was to spend many hours daydreaming between nibbles at his line.

The renovation of Spithead proceeded so slowly that for several months the family had to endure "a hell of an overcrowded time" in the cottage, where O'Neill wrote in "a bedroom with children, carpenters, plumbers, masons . . . doing all sorts of telling chorus work in the near vicinity." Normally he would have found it impossible to write under such circumstances ("How Gene works," Agnes said, "is beyond me"), but to keep from brooding over personal matters, he pushed ahead. Hoping to spur a production of *Marco Millions*, he had decided to let Liveright publish it and spent part of December revising and cutting it sharply. He also worked hard for a fortnight on *Lazarus*, and after making extensive changes felt that he had a much better play. On the last day of the year, wondering what 1927 would bring, he again took up *Strange Interlude*, which he estimated was about half written. "With all that's inside me now," he had told Macgowan on December 7, "I ought to be able to explode in that play in a regular blood-letting."

He shortly was "deep" in *Interlude*, "groaning in spirit and sweating blood at the immense amount of labor" still before him, but sustained by the belief that it would be "a great thing — if it comes off." Despite his adverse working conditions, he made good progress, writing five acts in two months, and finished the play at the end of February. "It's the biggest ever," he exulted to Macgowan on the twenty-eighth. "I'm tremendous[ly] pleased with the deep scope of it. Nothing like it has been done before."

After nursing a dream for years of "wedding the theme for a novel to the play form in a way that would still leave the play master of the house," he finally had achieved his ambition, chiefly by making the work as long as he deemed necessary. In two parts, consisting of nine acts and covering twenty-five years, *Strange Interlude* explores the history of Nina Leeds and the three men in her life: Sam Evans, a bumbling innocent who is grateful that she married him; Dr. Edmund Darrell, who prides himself on his cool, scientific detachment till Nina destroys his independence by pulling him into orbit around herself; and Charles Marsden, family friend, genteel novelist, and "one of those poor devils who spend their lives trying not to discover which sex they belong to!"

In striving for novelistic qualities O'Neill broke with convention not only in the extraordinary length of his new drama but in its "thought asides," as he called them, an extension of the old technique in which the characters spoke directly to the audience, supposedly out of earshot of the others onstage. This time, however, the asides and soliloquies are used more boldly and freely than ever — they constitute over a third of what the audience hears — to give voice to the characters' secret thoughts. Although the innovation was briefly foreshadowed by a scene in *Welded* in which the husband and wife think aloud without hearing one another, Joyce's *Ulysses*, which O'Neill read about the time he began writing *Strange Interlude*, probably inspired him to make such prominent use of a stream-of-consciousness pattern. In his hands it led to mixed results. Time and again the asides heighten the emotion or significance of a scene, provide ironic contrast, or add to a characterization; equally often, though, they seem either repetitious, telling us what we already know, or merely an easy way for the author to get across exposition he should have woven unobtrusively into the dialogue.

Like nearly all his plays, *Strange Interlude* ("our lives are merely strange dark interludes in the electrical display of God the Father!") had a long gestation. He first made notes for it in Provincetown in 1923 when he "heard from an aviator, formerly of the Lafayette Escadrille, the story of a girl whose aviator fiancé had been shot down just before the Armistice. The girl went to pieces from the shock. She later married, not because she loved the man but because she wanted a child. She hoped through motherhood to win back a measure of contentment from life."

Starting with this glimpse of a woman's history, O'Neill developed a through-the-years saga of guilt feelings, promiscuity, latent homosexuality, insanity, adultery, illegitimacy, neurotic motherhood with an undercurrent of incestuous desire, and (not surprisingly) emotional exhaustion, all this to illustrate the instability of human relations, the erosive workings of time. Like a kaleidoscope, the play is never still, its picture keeps changing; and at the center of this shifting complex of love, hostility and frustration is Nina Leeds, at once one of the author's most fascinating and least credible women. It appears that he consciously sought to create a heroine who would personify a cross-section of all womanhood; what he actually created was an embodiment of his ambivalent feelings toward the sex, a femme fatale who is both victim and victimizer.

Strange Interlude was based not only on the story O'Neill heard in Provincetown but, apparently, on Shaw's *Man and Superman*, with its portrait of Ann Whitefield as "Everywoman." Thinking of Ann, Shaw said that "if women were as fastidious as men, morally or physically, there would be an end of the race." In the play itself there are exchanges that would fit perfectly into the O'Neill work:

TANNER: . . . that's the devilish side of a woman's fascination: she makes you will your own destruction.

OCTAVIUS: But it's not destruction: it's fulfillment.

TANNER: Yes, of her purpose; and that purpose is neither her happiness nor yours, but Nature's. Vitality in a woman is a blind fury of creation. She sacrifices herself to it: do you think she will hesitate to sacrifice you?

What Shaw rather primly called the "Life Force" is clearly at work in Ann Whitefield and Nina Leeds; yet, though *Man and Superman* and *Strange Interlude* share a basic theme and a somewhat similar view of Woman, they are poles apart in treatment: one is all wit, intellect and verbal grace, the other, much soul-searching and passion and suffering. While the Shaw comedy concedes the facts of life by including a pregnancy, it is asexual in tone (it is difficult to imagine its couples coupling); the O'Neill drama on the other hand is constantly preoccupied with the bedeviling flesh.

O'Neill once thought of calling his play *The Haunted*, since all the principals are haunted in one way or another, chiefly by the ghost of Gordon Shaw, a demigod at college and Nina's fiancé, who died in World War I. Bitterly regretful that they never consummated their love, Nina, feeling that she "owes" it to Gordon, becomes a nurse and gives herself to crippled soldiers; but her form of penance only deepens her sense of guilt. Seeking salvation through motherhood, she marries Sam Evans, who not only adores her but joins her in worshiping at the shrine of Gordon Shaw (Gordon's surname is doubly appropriate, since everyone looked on him as a "superman" and the Shaw play helped to inspire O'Neill's).

All seems well till Nina discovers that, unknown to her husband, his family is tainted with insanity. After an abortion, she persuades Dr. Edmund Darrell, who had encouraged her marriage to Evans, to sleep with her; they will be, she says, "guinea pigs" in an experiment to produce a healthy child. The two fall in love, of course, and are torn with indecision about whether to declare themselves to the unsuspecting Evans. As things work out, she continues as Sam's wife and Darrell's mistress and in addition forms a daughter-father kind of relationship with Marsden — "dear old Charlie," who has always loved her in his timid fashion. "My three men!" Nina says in the quintessential scene. "I feel their desires converge in me! . . . to form one complete beautiful male desire which I absorb . . . and am whole . . . they dissolve in me, their life is my life . . . I am pregnant with the three! . . . husband! . . . lover! . . . father!" Then, thinking of her infant son, she adds: ". . . and the fourth man! . . . little Gordon! . . . he is mine too! . . . that makes it perfect!"

Step by step *Strange Interlude* carefully rationalizes her development from idealistic virgin to self-sacrificing wanton to dutiful wife to a devouring kind of Earth Mother, and so forth. Yet she becomes increasingly less plausible, for no amount of elucidation can disguise that she is acting out a succession of roles designed to exhibit the major aspects of Woman. By the end, after contending with so many problems and woes, she seems like nothing so much as a prototype of the beleaguered heroines of soap opera.

Unlike many of O'Neill's other works, *Strange Interlude* contains no one character who serves as his persona, but fragments of the author can be found in Nina, Darrell, and especially Marsden, who, to some extent, resembles an impotent O'Neill. Through Marsden the playwright expressed his strain of hostility to women, his fear of life (like Dion Anthony, Marsden was "born afraid"), and his disdain for the dollar-hustling aspects of the American scene. O'Neill also, recalling his traumatic whorehouse initiation into sex while going to prep school, included a similar experience in Marsden's history. In yet another biographical touch the playwright son, who could never forget his dead, mourned his father in Marsden's opening words: ". . . how dim his face has grown! . . . he wanted to speak to me just before he died . . . the hospital . . . smell of idoform in the cool halls . . . hot summer . . . I bent down . . . his voice had withdrawn so far away . . . I couldn't understand him . . . what son can ever understand? . . . always too near, too soon, too distant or too late!"

Primarily, though, the character was based on Charles Demuth, the painter, whom O'Neill had known in Provincetown and Greenwich Village; and the playwright also had in mind another noted artist, Marsden Hartley (hence the name "Charles Marsden"), who was a good friend of Demuth's. The two artists were homosexual – as is the play's Marsden, though he flees from himself – and Demuth, like his fictional counterpart, had a strong, protective and jealous mother. "I like 'Marsden' . . . very much myself – next to 'Nina,' " O'Neill once said. "I've known many Marsdens on many different levels of life and it has always seemed to me that they've never been done in literature with any sympathy or real insight."

In drawing such a character he was again indebted to Shaw, for *Man and Superman* has a Marsden in Octavius Robinson ("Men like that," says Ann Whitefield, "always live in comfortable bachelor quarters with broken hearts, and are adored by their landladies"). Finally, O'Neill used Shaw's John Tanner as one of his models for Darrell; just as Tanner regards himself as too knowing about the nature and wiles of Woman to succumb, the *Strange Interlude* physician considers himself "immune to love through his scientific understanding of its real sexual nature." Both men, needless to say, are overpowered in time by the "Life Force."

Darrell, who was named after an islet within view of Spithead, bears some resemblance to the author: he is dark, wiry and handsome, "doesn't care for children," and has "a quality about him, provoking and disturbing to women, of intense passion." The two men otherwise have little in common, for it is impossible to imagine O'Neill wrecking his life for love, as Darrell does, or going along for years sharing a woman with her husband; he was far too possessive and jealous to endure a three-sided romance indefinitely. Yet Darrell's long relationship with Nina, the wife of his best friend, was probably inspired by a page from O'Neill's own history: his comparatively short affair in the World War I period with Louise Bryant, both before and after her marriage to John Reed, a man

Charles Demuth, the chief model for Charles Marsden in
Strange Interlude, *and the playwright in Provincetown
in the early twenties*

Agnes, from movies of the family taken by Nicholas Muray

O'Neill genuinely liked. "When that girl [Louise] touches me," Eugene told Terry Carlin at the time, "it's like a flame!" In the play Darrell thinks of Nina: "Christ! . . . touch of her skin! . . . her nakedness . . . those afternoons in her arms! Happiness! . . . what do I care for anything else? . . . to hell with Sam!"

While Nina in appearance was modeled on Alice Cuthbert and Olga Collinson, both of whom the playwright had met in Bermuda at about the same time, her personality was chiefly based on Louise Bryant, who had a voracious appetite for life, liked to be surrounded by men, and had few scruples in satisfying her desires. At the same time Nina is more than a fictionalized image of Louise, for she also, containing aspects of her author, serves as one of his spokesmen. Echoing a pet thought of his, she says, "How we poor monkeys hide from ourselves behind the sounds called words!"

Where Nina, Darrell and Marsden were drawn from a variety of sources, including the author's imagination, the unseen yet omnipresent Gordon Shaw was taken whole from life. Although he seems impossibly idealized, Shaw is virtually a replica of Hobart Amory Hare Baker, Princeton's incomparable "Hobey" Baker (1892–1918), who was "the most golden and godlike" collegian of his day and, according to one authority, "indisputably the best athlete in the history of Ivy League sports." Gordon Shaw's history parallels that of the Princeton man, for Baker, a member of the Lafayette Escadrille, fell from the sky in France. He was a hero who captured the imagination of his generation, including schoolmate F. Scott Fitzgerald, who felt that Baker was "an ideal worthy of everything in my enthusiastic admiration."

No listing of the sources of *Strange Interlude* would be complete without mention of Freud, even though O'Neill used to deny his influence. Joseph Wood Krutch, among the first to read the play, noted that some of it followed a Freudian line. Objecting only mildly, since Krutch admired the play, Eugene replied: "I feel that, although [*Strange Interlude*] is undoubtedly full of psychoanalytic ideas . . . any artist who was a good psychologist . . . could have written 'S.I.' without ever having heard of Freud, Jung, Adler & Co." But several years later, to a professor preparing a thesis on the psychological aspects of his work, the playwright was somewhat more vehement in his denial. He declared that there was "no conscious use of psychoanalytical material in any of my plays. . . . I most certainly did not get my idea of Nina's compulsion from a dream mentioned by Freud in *A General Introduction to Psychoanalysis*. I have only read two books of Freud's, *Totem and Taboo* and

Beyond the Pleasure Principle. [Actually, he had also read *Group Psychology and the Analysis of the Ego,* and possibly others.] The book that interested me the most of all those of the Freudian school is Jung's *Psychology of the Unconscious.* . . . If I have been influenced unconsciously, it must have been by this book more than any other. . . . But the 'unconscious' influence stuff strikes me as always extremely suspicious! It is so darned easy to prove! I would say that what has influenced my plays the most is my knowledge of the drama of all time — particularly Greek tragedy — and not any books on psychology."

Even if one agrees that the playwright was, as he liked to think, an "intuitively keen analytical psychologist," *Strange Interlude* contains phrases and thoughts that could have been written only by someone familiar with Freudian theory. O'Neill speaks from his own experience — particularly the period when he headed for the depths in Buenos Aires and at Jimmy the Priest's — when he has Darrell voice the fear that Nina may "dive for the gutter just to get the security that comes from knowing she's touched bottom, and there's no farther to go!" But the playwright merely echoes Freud when he has Darrell say that Nina "needs normal love objects for the emotional life Gordon's death blocked up in her."

An incredible heroine, a facile application of Freudian thought, a narrative that at times foreshadows today's soap operas, language that rarely rises above the commonplace — it is, in short, easy to fault *Strange Interlude.* Yet, rather paradoxically, its defects testify to the author's achievement, for the play, in spite of being so flawed, generates considerable force and emotion and holds one's interest almost continuously through its nine acts. Part of the answer is that the playwright, a true son of the Count of Monte Cristo, plunges his characters into one crisis after another. But the main thrust and power of the drama develops from a deeper source, something more genuine, as critic Robert Littell was to note; in a perceptive analysis that applies not only to *Strange Interlude* but to the author's work in general, Littell called O'Neill "an exception among writers in that his strength and his weaknesses are inseparable and that several of his faults, while they remain faults, serve also as allies of his strength. What distinguishes all of his plays here and there, and *Strange Interlude* most of the way through, is a groping, smoldering, passionate sincerity many times more intense, relentless and mysterious than that of any other American playwright — and nearly all foreign ones also. O'Neill seems to be burrowing in the depths of human nature, not so much because he finds interesting dramatic material in these psychological catacombs, but because the search profoundly concerns him personally. The endless burrowing is a mole's progress toward salvation – his own salvation far more than that of his characters.

"If O'Neill could cease to identify his own search with that of his characters, if he could stand further away from them, they would be clearer, realer, but they would lose much of the mystery and integrity which their author's fumblings, quite as much as his passion, help to give them. And if O'Neill had three grains more of the humor which causes a writer to laugh mistrustfully at his own solemnities, he could not indulge himself so freely in just those inarticulate cries of cosmic pain which make his characters, a great deal of the time, singularly strange and moving creations."

Early in March 1927 the family moved into the main house at Spithead, though the interior was incomplete, and almost immediately began playing host to a succession of visitors. Elizabeth Shepley Sergeant, among the first, spent six weeks with the O'Neills recuperating from an auto accident. As soon as Eugene heard about the mishap, he had invited her to stay with them after she left the hospital. By the time of her visit his feeling for Carlotta seems to have subsided, but his relations with Agnes were not entirely harmonious. Like so many reformed drinkers, he now was hypercritical about drinking, particularly in regard to Agnes, and wanted her, too, to abjure alcohol. Moreover, he was increasingly reluctant to socialize, another point of contention between them, for Agnes occasionally went to parties without him.

"Gene felt that Agnes was sorry he had turned teetotaler," Miss Sergeant says, "because Agnes, according to him, had been in command of the situation before, and didn't like it much now when he was in command. Whether this was true, I can't say, but that's what he believed. And Agnes herself once told me she thought she had married a bohemian, then found out that he was very set in his ways. I think she had come to feel sort of suppressed by him. I don't imagine that he was easy to live with, but it seemed to me that Agnes was too sure of herself. He was very dependent on her, she said. Whenever they had to be separated for a little while he would write, according to her, that he was lost without her."

Eugene Jr., who spent a week in Bermuda during his Easter vacation from school, told Miss Sergeant that he had been overjoyed when he learned a few years previously that he was the son of the celebrated playwright, especially since he did not care for his stepfather. The youth, who had switched by now from playwriting to poetry, liked to stand on the dock declaiming his own efforts. "It was as if," someone has said, "he was making love to his father with poetry." The following is characteristic of his verse:

> *They did not recognize me,*
> *Me, son of God!*
> *Born of a Virgin*
> *I told them who I was.*
> *They gave me a brain examination.*
> *They did not phase me,*
> *No! Not me!*

> *Jesus Christ come again to Earth.*
> *I preached my simple teaching.*
> *The world would not listen.*
> *They sent me to the electric chair,*
> *Crucified me again!*
> *But on the chair I laughed at them.*
> *They made me a Cynic! So I laughed.*

> *Did you have a funny dream, Eugene,*
> *That you laughed so in your sleep?*
> *Why are you still laughing?*
> *Did I not see something down there?*
> *In that Infinite Hole?*
> *Was it God?*
> *Or nothing?*
> *Maybe God is The Nothing.*

The seventeen-year-old youth, who was to enter Yale in the fall (O'Neill's honorary degree and his fondness for Professor Baker had led him to choose Yale for his son), appeared to Miss Sergeant to have a good relationship with both his father and stepmother. "Agnes was nice to the boy and seemed to like him. The one I felt sorry for was little Shane, a touching child, wandering around at the edge of the sea when children should be taken in by their parents. I remember one afternoon when I found him sitting listlessly on the dock. He was so delighted when I asked if he'd like to come inside and have me read to him. Neither Gene nor Agnes, as far as I could see, paid much attention to him. Gene once told me he didn't know how to talk to children and felt he couldn't have any connection with him until he grew up."

Though Hubertine Zahorska had a place of her own in Bermuda, she was another houseguest. Like Miss Sergeant, Hubie had been in an accident – she suffered a brain concussion from a bicycle fall – and was recuperating at the O'Neills; but her stay was not entirely restful. "I'd been there only a few days," she recalls, "when Agnes asked me how soon I could start typing *Strange Interlude*, as Gene needed it as soon as possible. I wasn't in good shape yet, but after some quiet pressure from Agnes, I started, and it pained me so that tears used to run down as I typed. Gene happened to pass the window once as I was typing and weeping, and he told Agnes I was the most appreciative audience he'd ever had. I never bothered to disillusion him but I did complain to Agnes about the difficulty of copying from bound notebooks. I wondered why he didn't write on loose sheets – it would be much easier for him too. Agnes gave me a long look and smiled, 'Gene knows their value!' I'm not sure whether she was referring to posterity or autograph dealers."

While *Strange Interlude* was being transcribed, one of the visitors at Spithead was Lawrence Langner of the Theater Guild, who had come to Bermuda for the dual purpose of recovering from an illness and improving his relations with O'Neill. O'Neill, he knew, was aggrieved that the Guild had never produced any of his plays (it rejected *The Straw, The First Man, Welded, The Fountain*, and, to its regret, *Anna Christie*); but it now appeared that America's first playwright and its foremost producing firm might finally work together, for the Guild, after long blowing hot and cold about *Marco Millions*, was again regarding it favorably. Though Langner came to discuss *Marco*, he was immediately interested on hearing that O'Neill had just completed an unconventional play that would take two evenings to perform; its length did not dismay him, he said, since the Guild had staged Shaw's mammoth *Back to Methusaleh*. Several days later, after another call at Spithead. Langner returned to his hotel with the first six acts of *Strange Interlude*. He intended to glance at it before going to bed shortly, but instead stayed up most of the night, reading with crescent excitement, and ended feeling that the play was among the greatest ever.

For all his enthusiasm, though, he thought that its length and downbeat character would prevent it from being popular; at the same time he was eager for his organization to produce it as a matter of prestige. Langner returned to New York all set to do battle for both *Strange Interlude* and *Marco Millions* with the Guild's five other managing directors.

Wary of placing too much hope in the Theater Guild and worried about finances ("The family *en masse*," he told Macgowan, "is praying for the sale of Ridgefield"), O'Neill felt desperate for a production. "I wish," he lamented to Kenneth on March 24, "our old Triumvirate were still alive. This being without any sympathetic outlet for my *Strange Interlude* — unless the Guild or Arthur [Hopkins] gets interested — isn't so good. There aren't many managers I'd want that submitted to." To George Jean Nathan he wrote on April 7 that the "old outlet for my stuff, via the PP and the Greenwich Village, was certainly not ideal but it had a lot on the present blind alleys."

His first report from Langner about *Marco* — the Guild had no *Strange Interlude* script as yet — was sobering. Most of the directorate liked the play but all felt that it required too expensive a production; designer Lee Simonson, on the executive board, estimated that the sets, costumes, props, and so on, would cost a minimum of thirty thousand dollars. O'Neill was asked not merely to trim the play but to drop whole scenes and scale it down drastically. The Guild heads were opposed to its lavish features not solely because of the projected cost, according to Langner, but because they felt that the story's human and humorous qualities would be submerged in an ornate production. His colleagues had begged him, he added, to exercise the utmost tact in corresponding with O'Neill.

"You have either to do it up to the last gasp of cost and magnificence," the playwright replied on April 5, "or else very simply. Any half-way measures would be ultra-fatal — and, candidly, I think Simonson's 30,000 cost would be a half and half way." He suggested a number of script changes, including the omission of full scenes, that would "cut down cast, costumes enormously" and hoped that his response "shows how far I am willing to go — and how desirous I am to work with the Guild." Subsequently informing Langner that a copy of *Strange Interlude* was on its way, he urged the Guild directors "to keep the theme and treatment of the play under their hats. Whatever their decision on it may be, I think you'll agree that the less that gets around about it before definite production is scheduled, the better."

After his colleagues had read *Strange Interlude*, Langner was distressed that not all shared his enthusiasm for the play. Campaigning for the two O'Neill works, especially the new one, he wrote a fervent letter to the other board members in which he hailed the nine-act drama as "probably the bravest and most far-reaching dramatic experiment" since Ibsen's revolutionary works and declared that it contained "more deep knowledge of the dark corners of the human mind than anything ever written before." Exhorting the others to do their duty by the American theater, he urged them not to be influenced by the possibility that they might lose money on *Strange Interlude*.

In April Agnes, whose father was dying, sailed for the States to visit him at the Laurel Heights Sanatorium (originally the Fairfield County State Tuberculosis Sanatorium) in Shelton, Connecticut. Modern and well equipped, Laurel Heights was the ultimate in hospital care compared to the pitifully inadequate farmhouses on the same site where O'Neill himself had briefly been a patient in 1912. (One whose wounds still bled decades later, the playwright son would memorialize the original Shelton place as the "state farm" in bitter arguments between Edmund and his father in *Long Day's Journey Into Night*.)

Agnes's departure plunged her husband into the depths. Although he generally felt at a loss when they were apart any length of time, he was affected so severely this time that some unconscious conflict and turmoil – involving, apparently, Carlotta – must have been at the bottom of his agitated state. Only hours after she sailed on April 15, he wrote to her: "God, how I miss you! . . . I actually broke down on the bed in our room in a fit of hysterical crying when I first went up there. I know this is a bit absurd when you are only going to be gone a week, but my whole control seems gone. . . . *I need you, need you, need you!* – intensely more now than ever before in our married life. I feel . . . as if this were a crucial period in my life, an ordeal, a test on which everything I have built depended – God knows what! – and our lives were in the balance."

In a calmer mood the following day, he told her that he loved Spithead, "and not with my old jealous, bitter possessiveness – my old man Cabotism! [a reference to *Desire Under the Elms*] – but as ours. . . . The thought of the place is indissolubly intermingled with my love for you, with our nine years of marriage that, after much struggle, have finally won to this haven. . . . 'And perhaps, the Hairy Ape at last belongs.' I have, as you know, never felt this deep peace or permanence about any place where we have lived before. Perhaps, a lot of this feeling is due to the change in us. In the old – and how really distant and improbable those days seem to me now! – alcoholic times there could be no confidence in the security of anything. Perhaps we should rechristen Spithead Water Wagon Manor! It is certainly connected in my mind with sobriety and sane living.

"But what I started out to say was that it is a very lonely home right now . . . as if the familiar spirit of our home whose presence alone gives it meaning and makes it *my* home, were gone. . . . I love you! For over nine years I have loved you and you alone."

Urging her not to doubt his devotion because of the Carlotta episode, he declared that he never loved Carlotta but had simply dramatized a boost to his vanity. He maintained that Agnes overestimated the actress's talent for intrigue if she were concerned that he might be tempted again by Carlotta; insisted that he had told her the complete truth about the episode; and warned her to be on guard in New York against "friends" carrying tales. He castigated himself for having placed Agnes in a position to be hurt and said that he would have forgotten Carlotta by now if only Agnes, who kept him feeling guilty, had stopped bringing up her name.

Besides visiting her father, Agnes performed some errands in New York for her husband that included checking with Arthur Hopkins about *Lazarus Laughed* (he was "impressed — but didn't 'get' it") and with Langner about the other two plays (he thought O'Neill should return for a conference with the Guild). Agnes also, at Eugene's request, called on Evangeline Adams, the astrologist, whom Bobby Jones had recommended as remarkably prescient. Miss Adams, predicting a "bad financial slump for next year for the U.S.," advised the playwright "to liquidate & get all overhead expenses cut down," but she also forecast that his economic situation would "pick up about October." Her final word was that he should "close" with the Theater Guild as soon as possible.

The Guild brass had practically decided by late April to produce *Marco* but they wanted the author to submit a "cut script" before they committed themselves to *Strange Interlude*. "Surely now that you have all read it and know the dramatic guts of it and its new method," he argued on May 1, "you ought to be able to make a definite decision. All it needs is an intensive cutting . . . from first act to last, such as I always do on all my plays — but certainly no drastic reconstruction is called for. . . . I have offered you the essential play and I don't want to do more work on it until I have the incentive of knowing it's going to be produced."

Since the Guild was not dealing with a tyro, he said, it should have enough faith in him to be able to anticipate what the play would be like in its final form. Macgowan, Jones, Hopkins, everyone with whom he had been associated, he continued, could verify his statement that he was constantly on the alert, up to the last days of rehearsal, for cuts that would improve his scripts.

As proof of his "eagerness" to work with the Guild, he was ready to accept what he considered a "pretty small advance," for the two plays, even though "I direly need all the cash I can grab." One thing particularly worrying him, though he had sworn to secrecy everyone who read the new play, was that word of his stream-of-consciousness method might leak out and be copied by another playwright before *Interlude* was staged. "So you see," his letter continues, "I need a prompt decision so that I can try for quick action elsewhere if you should not see your way to [do] it. Even a production at the PP might be preferable . . . to having the play in the air too dangerously long."

At the Guild's urging he visited New York in mid-May and, despite his demurring previously, brought along a revised script of *Strange Interlude* which was, he said, "only a first cutting [that] will be thoroughly gone over again later." The Guild placed both plays under option but was more hopeful about *Marco*, which was promptly added to its fall schedule, than about *Strange Interlude*, which was listed only as a possibility. To protect himself, since the organization was notorious for wavering a long time and then dropping a script, O'Neill reserved the right to repossess his nine-act drama if the Guild failed to produce it in the forthcoming season.

Although he had long resented the firm for turning down his plays, it appears fortunate for both parties that they did not join forces until he was universally recognized as the country's foremost playwright. Had the association begun earlier, it might have proven short-lived. The Guild was regarded by many around Broadway, in the words of one theater historian, as "arrogantly critical of playwrights" and "unnecessarily cruel in their treatment of actors." Theresa Helburn herself, one of the six managing directors, once admitted that a playwright's introduction to the Guild's committee system came as "a difficult ordeal." The trouble was, John Mason Brown sums up gently, that the directors "fought family quarrels, failing to remember that the playwrights they included in them were not members of the family." (In the 1930s some of our leading playwrights — Maxwell Anderson, S. N. Behrman, Sidney Howard, Elmer Rice and Robert E. Sherwood — became so aggrieved at the Guild that they formed the Playwrights' Company to stage their own works.)

In their dealings with Bernard Shaw, the Guild heads had always been on their best behavior; now they turned benign faces toward O'Neill. He felt, as he told Miss Helburn, that they would "work together with zest and enthusiasm."

The evening he dined with her and her husband happened to be a few hours after Charles Lindbergh had excited the world by his daring solo flight across the Atlantic. In "Terry" Helburn's mind thereafter, the aviator and the playwright would always be linked, for she thought of O'Neill as "a lone eagle in his chosen field." She found not only that he was very shy but that when alone with him he made "you realize your own shyness . . . you cannot keep on the surface very long . . . you must either dig deep or be silent."

Another evening he attended a fund-raising celebration for the Provincetown Playhouse. After struggling along for years and appearing more than once on the verge of collapse, the theater had gained fresh distinction this spring when Paul Green's *In Abraham's Bosom,* one of its productions, won the Pulitzer Prize. At the affair in the Village, where some notables urged support for the playhouse, O'Neill was asked to say a few words. Looking startled, he slowly rose to his feet and, after swallowing nervously, said: "The Provincetown did its best work when it didn't have a dime," then he added under his breath to himself, "Sit down, you son of a bitch, sit down!" Cutting short an awkward silence, Fitzi jumped up and said, "For the sake of Jig Cook's memory, let's not drop tears — let's drop dollars!"

A houseguest of the Langners during his week in the city, O'Neill reluctantly consented to their giving a small party for him. He used to drink, he said, to fortify himself when meeting people, and now that he was on the wagon, socializing was more difficult for him than ever. One reason he swore off liquor, he explained, was that he had been alarmed by a doctor's description of alcohol's effect on the brain: "It's just like turning the albumen in your brain into the white of a poached egg!"

Langner, who had cultivated a friendship with Shaw in the years that the Guild had been staging his works, wondered whether O'Neill had been influenced by him. More as a person, O'Neill said, than as a playwright, and recalled that while going to prep school he had been "wildly excited" over Shaw's *The Quintessence of Ibsenism.* At a later time, while in England, Langner discussed O'Neill with Shaw, who already was on record as calling him "a fantee Shakespeare who peoples his isle with Calibans." Apparently Shaw regarded the author of *The Emperor Jones* and *The Hairy Ape* as a kind of wild man whose talent was fueled by alcohol, for after learning from Langner that O'Neill had stopped drinking, the Irish playwright said: "He'll probably never write a good play again."

At the Langners' O'Neill first met Joseph Wood Krutch, a critic he highly respected. Krutch found it difficult "to see in him the tumultuous adventurer" of his earlier years but could sense "behind the mask of his brooding face and dark smoldering eyes the sleeping volcano of his temperament." Apparently Eugene, who took a quick liking to the critic, wanted to counter the popular view of him as a gloomy, forbidding figure; with the air of a "somewhat naughty boy" he told Krutch that sometimes when he was drunk in Bermuda he used to strip off all his clothes and, with a hibiscus tucked behind an ear, run along the beach in the moonlight reciting his own verse.

On May 30, shortly after his return home, he wrote to Macgowan that "it's grand down here and Aggie and the kids are good to be with again — and the sea. It's a bit lonely, though, and I feel isolated at times now that everyone we knew who was the slightest bit intelligent or amusing has blown for the season." Unlike the previous two years, when they had summered elsewhere, the O'Neills were remaining in Bermuda, both to preserve their funds and spur the renovation of Spithead, which was taking longer and costing more than they had estimated. "If the bankroll holds out," Eugene wrote Saxe Commins on June 18, "we will have a fine place." But Spithead, which he considered ideal for his work and his amphibious way of life, would still be unfinished when his marriage to Agnes broke up late this year.

13

O'Neill's "Vultures"

CONFINED to bed nearly a fortnight in July 1927 with a severe case of the flu, O'Neill was slow to regain his energy in Bermuda's worst heat wave in years ("You get so," he said, "you pray for a good old gray New England murky for 24 hours"); yet such was his drive that he accomplished a good deal this summer. He once again revised *Lazarus Laughed,* which was to be published in the fall; finished a detailed scenario for *Dynamo,* his next play; and, fertile as ever, conceived ideas for four new plays. His chief task, however, was cutting *Strange Interlude,* which he wanted in such shape that the Theater Guild would be unable to resist it. He was fairly confident of an early production, either by the Guild or another firm, for both Krutch and Nathan, two of the critics he most respected, had called the play his finest after reading the original, uncut draft.

"What you say about the slightness of even the best modern plays," he wrote to Krutch on July 15, "is exactly the way I feel . . . they are all too totally lacking in all true power and imagination." With unconscious irony the author of the nine-act *Strange Interlude,* among the longest plays ever written, continues: "But on the other hand, even the best of modern novels strike me as dire failures in another direction. They are all so wordy . . . the authors appear to me as timid recorders of life, dodging the responsibility of that ruthless selection and deletion and concentration on the essential which is the test of an author. . . . No, I think the novelists are worse than the playwrights — they waste more of one's time!"

In the first published comment on *Strange Interlude,* in the August 1927 *American Mercury,* Nathan hailed it as "the finest, profoundest drama" of O'Neill's entire career, one that made all his previous work

[255]

"seem trivial." Theresa Helburn objected to the article, since it divulged the play's method of asides and gave a detailed synopsis of the story, but O'Neill, replying on August 22, called it "grand stuff" that would arouse "a vast amount of advance interest." He had feared, he told Miss Helburn, that his method would "leak out and be copied before it has gone on record, but I think Nathan's article does just this. . . . In a way now it's copyrighted." He had another, more private reason for welcoming the magazine piece; in thanking Nathan he said that it "should certainly be of great assistance in helping the cautious Guild bunch to come to a favorable decision — or, for that matter, Hopkins or any other to whom it might be submitted."

Nathan's article, for all its high praise, seems almost lukewarm compared to one by Benjamin De Casseres that appeared the same month in *Theater* magazine. Reviewing the career of America's "one dramatic genius," with special emphasis on his newly published *Marco Millions*, the critic called it "one of the finest fantastic and philosophical plays of any time . . . not only a landmark in the American stage, but . . . probably the turning point in [O'Neill's] mental evolution." O'Neill and De Casseres had met briefly a few years before (his first sight of the playwright, De Casseres has said, "almost awed me . . . a grim, unsmiling face taut with suffering, he seemed to say to me: 'Excuse me for not being nice, but I've just returned from hell' "); they had exchanged a letter or two; but this summer they began a correspondence that shortly led to their becoming friends. One bond between them was their common admiration for Nietzsche.

"Your long letter," Eugene wrote, "was a treat. Here in Bermuda one rarely gets the chance, especially now in the slack season, to say a word to a human being above the intellectual and spiritual level of a land crab and this solitude gets damned oppressive at times. But it's a fine place to get work done . . . and that's why I'm here." He had had a script of *Lazarus* sent to De Casseres, feeling that he would "get the affirmative cry of it as perhaps no one else could," and now was greatly pleased that the other "found something of *Zarathustra* in it." *Thus Spake Zarathustra*, he said, "has influenced me more than any book I've ever read."

The *Theater* article gives some idea, apparently, of the way O'Neill saw himself, for he told the critic on August 11: "I immediately got the feeling that the person you were writing about was I and none other in body and spirit. This is an extremely rare and gratifying experience. . . . More idiotic bunk has been written about me than I like to remember." He took exception, though, to one point. The article, after noting that his sense of irony was "no longer bitter" in *Marco*, concluded that he had "stormed and conquered life, a Laocoon who has strangled his serpents, a Prometheus who has shooed away his vultures."

"My vultures," O'Neill said in rebuttal, "are flapping around, thank God, hungry and undismayed; and I am very proud of them, for they are my test and my self-gratification. I would feel a success and a total loss if they should ever desert me to gorge themselves fat and comforted on what the newspaper boys naïvely call fame. But luckily they are birds that fly from the great dark behind and inside and not from the bright lights without. Each visit they wax stronger and more pitiless — which is, naturally, a matter of boast between them and me! — and I look forward to some last visit when their wings will blot out the sky and they'll wrench the last of my liver out; and then I predict they'll turn out to be angels of some God or other who have given me in exchange the germ of a soul."

Aside from expressing his flagellant side and tortured yearning for salvation, the letter, together with other evidence, suggests that the idea of developing a "soul" was a constant in his thoughts. When he spoke a few years later of writing an autobiographical play called "Sea-Mother's Son," he said it would be subtitled "The Story of the Birth of a Soul."

De Casseres's magazine piece concentrates on O'Neill the playwright. In a newspaper article Montiville M. Hansford, an American working in Bermuda who saw him often, presents a close-up view of O'Neill the man. Describing him as "a slow mover," Hansford said he gives one "the feeling that [he] is continually undergoing a sort of physical helplessness, as if his mind did not know what to do with his body. . . . Coming slowly down the back stairs to join a group at Bellevue, I have watched him stand for two minutes trying, evidently, to decide upon which chair to sit, and wondering (certainly by his expression) what sort of human beings were these gathered together. Often there comes to his face an expression of astonishment, even on seeing his own family, as if undecided just where this or that child fitted into the general scheme of things. . . .

"Quite noticeable is O'Neill's helplessness in a rapid conversational bout — those quick-firing and snappy moments when smart stuff is being juggled back and forth . . . he will look around [with] bewilderment, as if wondering what it is all about. . . .

"I always feel that everything on earth is eternally new to O'Neill. . . . O'Neill would grace the head of the table clad in an undershirt, canvas trousers and barefooted. Calm, silent and contemplative — all with that childish wonder showing in his face, as if this were really the very first dinner he ever attended and the lamb stew and fish the first that had ever been cooked. . . . I believe that this man never feels quite at home with anybody . . . the one outstanding impression is that he does not belong anywhere."

Jimmy Light and his second wife Patti, who spent July at Spithead as a belated wedding gift from their hosts, sensed an undercurrent of strain between them at times. As Patti, an attractive brunette with dark eyes, was sunning one day on the dock, she overheard Agnes say to Mrs. Clark, "Don't you think she looks a lot like Carlotta?"

One point of contention between the O'Neills was whether the family should accompany him to New York, where he was to confer with the Guild. In the end he yielded to Agnes's view that, since their funds were low, it would be more sensible for him to go alone. The night before his departure on August 27, as they talked themselves out and made love on the front patio, they felt that they had never been closer. "Everything seems so right in our relationship now after all the nervous bickerings and misunderstandings of the summer," he wrote her from the ship the next day. "I feel deeply at peace now about you and me, as if we had achieved . . . a fresh faith to carry us on together through the rest of our lives with a love that will grow tenderer and be freed from all bitterness as the years pass. . . . It won't be long before I'll come down or you will come up. . . . In the meantime, don't worry about anything. . . . I'm hardly liable to be caught in any emotional storms again!"

But after a single day in New York, O'Neill, who had looked forward to a change of scene, felt utterly depressed, since he had arrived too early and had little to do. He had been eager to show his revised script to Theresa Helburn, who was still doubtful about *Strange Interlude*, but she was ill. Hopkins, Macgowan, Jones, Light, nearly everyone he knew was busy rehearsing something, and "I'm not," he lamented to Agnes on the twenty-ninth. "I had premonitions," he continues, "against this trip as is. I have them worse now. Of course, I'm due for sessions with the Guild bunch, collectively and individually, as soon as Helburn is well and Lawrence Langner returns [from Europe] but what am I going to do with the other 21 or 22 hours besides sleeping? . . . And I tell you again you have made a mistake! It is not good to force me to be lonely and homeless under the most unfortunate conditions when I'm sick in the bargain [besides feeling enervated from the Bermuda summer, he had an infection]. . . . You have thought of yourself and the inconvenience

O'Neill at the time he became associated with the Theater Guild

The managing directors of the Guild. Left to right, first row: Philip Moeller and Helen Westley; back row, Theresa Helburn, Maurice Wertheim, Lee Simonson and Lawrence Langner

moving the kids would cause you but you have not considered me or my work — or even my health. . . .

"All my love! I miss you like the devil or I wouldn't mind this so much. You must *realize* this!

"Not that my love or loneliness can mean much to you, judging by the way you've arranged this all-important fall season for me! By the time rehearsals start I ought to be a fine morbid wreck."

For days he was undecided whether to rush back to Bermuda, as Agnes urged, or have her join him immediately in New York or summon the whole family and reopen Brook Farm. At Mary Blair's invitation he spent part of the Labor Day weekend at the home of friends of hers in Connecticut, chiefly because it was close to his Ridgefield place, which he wanted to look over. The visit to Brook Farm left him "very sad." Despite all he used to say against it, he told Agnes that it "is so beautiful right now . . . I couldn't help feeling more keenly than ever that that's where our family ought to be." He maintained that reopening "our home" would cost less than their combined living expenses at present; Agnes countered with facts and figures that indicated the move would be more costly than he realized.

His first word from the Guild was discouraging: *Marco* would not begin rehearsing before mid-December, and nothing was to be done before then, either, about *Strange Interlude* — that is, if the Guild decided to produce it. As a result, since neither would open till the latter half of January, he could not expect any income from them for months. For a time he had hoped for early money from *Strange Interlude,* since Horace Liveright, confident that it would sell well, was eager to issue it as soon as possible, but the Guild was against its being published before production.

O'Neill remained in New York, instead of taking an early ship home, for medical as well as theatrical reasons. Over the years he had seen a number of doctors for various ailments, some of which seem to have been of a psychosomatic nature; his chronic problem was his "nerves." Feeling so on edge during his first days in town that he had an impulse to scream, he sought help from Dr. Alvan L. Barach, an expert diagnostician, and Dr. Harold H. Gile, a urologist. As he began undergoing examination, he weighed only one hundred and thirty-seven pounds in his clothes. At first neither physician found anything physiologically wrong with him, although they immediately saw, in his words, that his "nerves were all shot. It looks," he told Agnes on September 8, "as if I would have to put up with them philosophically as the inevitable paying the piper for my past, and that everything else that is wrong with me is all mental and up to Hamilton & Co."

After further tests, Dr. Barach diagnosed a thyroid deficiency and placed him on medication (the physician privately thought that O'Neill's feeling of "great fatigue" came chiefly from "inner tension and stress"). Barach also, O'Neill reported, "has given it out cold and clammy that I must stop smoking right away. . . . He says he never saw anyone so nervously sensitive to the effects of cigarettes before." (He exaggerates here; Barach actually found, he later said, that the playwright was among "the one in a hundred" who are so sensitive on this score that they "get an increase in pulse rate and blood pressure from the first cigarettes of the day, but this subsides after a while.") And Dr. Gile finally determined that O'Neill had a prostate condition and started him on treatments.

Enjoying himself more than he had expected, O'Neill had tea at the Ritz with George Jean Nathan and Lillian Gish, who were having a great romance, and found her "the exact opposite of all you imagine when you say 'movie queen.' She's quiet and has real brains . . . and fine eyes." (Miss Gish, who thought him "beautiful," says that his was "a face you never forgot. Most people today don't really have faces, but he stood out. He had a high forehead, a sculptured nose, and the eyes were like mid-August — burning. He smoldered. He was thin but well proportioned, like something on an Egyptian frieze.") Nathan suggested Miss Gish, who was considering a return to the stage, for the part of the Chinese princess in *Marco*, and O'Neill promised to pursue the matter (but the Guild brass rejected the suggestion because they feared "it would wreck their company with jealousy and dissension" to cast her in *Marco*).

On September 8 Eugene reported to Agnes that he was feeling better and also was heartened by the prospect of a buyer for Brook Farm. "I do love you so much," he said. "Remember that always and don't worry about anything!"

The following day, though, he was again ailing, the Ridgefield sale looked doubtful (it fell through), and he felt "rotten about everything! It seems," he lamented to Agnes, "as if we manage things in the exact way to make everything turn out all wrong — and this fall's mess certainly draws the prize! You must have framed it up with the idea of becoming a widow!" Then a postscript: "Forgive this! But I do feel sick and despondent."

On her side Agnes too was undergoing desolate days. "The place is as silent & still as death," she had written to him shortly after his departure, "and I have the feeling of being completely isolated from life . . . it's damned lonely for me here, I can tell you that." For a time she was unwell, and another day she was concerned about Oona's health, but generally her letters were more or less cheerful. After hearing of his social activities — he went to Belmont track one afternoon with Robert Rockmore, a lawyer friend of Jimmy Light's, and dropped ten dollars — she wrote: "Please do anything you want to do — anything that will make you happy or give you pleasure . . . it is necessary for you to try & get some sort of enjoyment . . . that will compensate for drinking." But, she added, "This does *not* mean that I am trying to force you into a love affair!"

Although O'Neill seems to have been little aware of his younger son's feeling for him — he voices doubt in one letter to Agnes that the boy misses him — Shane quietly worshiped his father. After single-handedly catching a ten-pound porgy off the dock, he immediately had his mother photograph him with the fish so that he could send a picture to "Daddy." Answering a letter from Shane about his various exploits, O'Neill called him the family's "prize fisherman" and asked him to look after the womenfolk "because they really are nice to have around . . . and you realize that when you're far away from them and all alone in a big city and exposed to temptation like I am now! But maybe you'd better not read Mother this part of my letter. She might get mad and raise hell with me when I get back."

Changeable, moody, prey to opposed desires and impulses that he could not acknowledge, O'Neill was feeling "vile, physically and mentally," as he wrote to Agnes on September 11. After reporting various developments in his theatrical affairs, he said that he had lunched the previous day with Carlotta, who had just returned from a rest cure in Baden-Baden. "She remarked on how thin and badly I looked compared to when she saw me last. She's quite right."

At which point he abruptly dropped the subject, knowing that he would be on delicate ground if he spoke further about Carlotta, for she had been so concerned over his health, so sympathetic about his theatrical frustrations and fruitless efforts to sell Brook Farm, so understanding in general that she made Agnes seem, by comparison, almost indifferent to his welfare. Trying to dwell on safe matters, he told about attending a tiresome party with Jimmy and Patti Light, about his problems with a realtor, but his sense of grievance against Agnes, sharpened probably by his reunion with Carlotta, again surfaced: "Every time I sit alone in this stuffy room [he had a four-dollar room in the Hotel Wentworth on West Forty-sixth Street] looking out over the dirty, smelly roofs and streets, feeling low and sick and depressed and lonely, I'm overcome by bitterness and a feeling that something is all wrong when you deliberately sacrifice me for your own designs and convenience. It isn't your work [Agnes had resumed writing]. You could have worked at Ridgefield. It isn't the sale of the place. Even if it were sold while we were there we could have put a limit before a purchaser could take possession. It isn't economy" — and he went on to rehash his argument for reopening Brook Farm.

He wondered whether her reluctance to return with him to the States was due to her having a lover in Bermuda; if this is so, his letter continues, he urges her to be honest with him and let their marriage end. In an obvious reference to Carlotta, he said that Agnes seemed unconcerned about the "temptation" in his present circumstances, declared that his coming to New York alone was fraught with potential disaster, and added that he felt like the Hairy Ape: "It's all dark, get me? It's all wrong!"

"I'm not well," he ends. "I'm lonely. I love you. That's the whole case in a nutshell."

While the letter seems, on the whole, a product of genuine emotion, it sounds an occasional spurious note, as though he were flogging himself to express his grievance with the utmost vehemence; and at times it turns "literary," suggesting that he derived some gratification from dramatizing his unhappy lot. Primarily, though, the letter reflects his ambivalent attitude toward Agnes as he in one breath accuses her of having a lover and suggests that they part and in the next avows his love. Consciously and unconsciously he was starting to justify to himself the dual change developing in his feelings toward her and Carlotta. In *Strange Interlude* he has Charles Marsden say: ". . . we must all be crooks where happiness is concerned! . . . steal or starve!" In life the playwright could not be so honest with himself.

The same ship that bore the bitter letter carried another of apology written two days later. He became so depressed at times, according to the second letter, that it seemed he would go out of his mind unless he unburdened himself to Agnes. After hoping that she would be sympathetic, he concluded: "Love and a million kisses, sweetheart. I hope it won't be so damned long now before I can come down and be with you again."

But Agnes was too hurt by his suspicions and charges to be comforted by his words of affection. She replied that "anyone with any practical or common sense" would realize that her remaining in Bermuda "is the thing that should have been done — however, it merely gives you an excuse to say that I must have a *lover* . . . if you know how damned bored & lonely I was here — never mind, I think I'll pack up & arrive in N.Y. next boat, kids & all — then we'll see how that will work. . . . Remember your conversation with me, in which you told me you wanted to divorce me — remember the days & days of silent dislike & hatred on your part. . . . Do you think I can forget all that — You love me & need me now, yes, because you're bored and lonely — but that love speedily deteriorates into an intense irritation as soon as we've been together two weeks. . . . I've got my little pistol locked up in a drawer. I lost the key — otherwise I think I'd take out the pistol & finish it right now, tonight. Bermuda is so empty & lonely, and then, on top of that, one hears again the old mistrust. . . .

"I'm glad Carlotta's nerves are gone. [He had written that Carlotta was in a nervous state before the cure at Baden-Baden.] Do you think she would be interested in taking charge of Spithead? If so, tell her I've given up the job. She is certainly much more beautiful than I am."

Turning conciliatory, Agnes wrote several days later that she had decided to close Spithead, since he thought that she had acted from "selfish" motives, and return with the children to reopen Brook Farm. She regretted that he was not enjoying himself and ended: "Good-bye, darling."

By mid-September Eugene was feeling energetic — something he credited to his thyroid tablets — and thought that the rest of his stay could be both stimulating and productive. Perhaps the hours he was now spending with Carlotta were more inspiriting to him than Dr. Barach's medication, but in any case he is in a cheery frame of mind as he informs Agnes on the fifteenth that his health has improved and that he is confident the Guild will sponsor *Strange Interlude*.

Still in good spirits as he wrote to her on the nineteenth — he had not yet received her recriminatory letter — he now realized that her decision to remain at Spithead was "undoubtedly a good deal wiser than my overwrought, morbid notions of feeling abused have been!" The Guild, he said, was going to produce *Strange Interlude* but would not meet till the end of September to decide "the where, when, how, and the possible casting, etc., and I simply must be in on it." His thyroid and prostate treatments were other reasons, he added, why he must remain in New York into October.

He was having "a pleasant time now, nothing hilarious but pleasant." He spent some evenings with Benjamin De Casseres ("A damned interesting man!"), went to the races again with Robert Rockmore ("You certainly must come with me to the track sometime!"), had lunch with Manuel Komroff, who had left Liveright's to write his own books ("A damned nice fellow!"), was to dine with Miss Gish ("That will be interesting"), and: "I've seen Carlotta a couple of times . . . she's been damned nice to me and I've enjoyed being with her — but that's all of it, from both sides."

After informing her about some theatrical and financial matters, he said: "Darling, I do wish you were here! But don't come! It would break us entirely just now with the bankroll so low."

That evening, before the letter was mailed, he received Agnes's heated rebuttal to his charges and immediately felt "terribly depressed." He acknowledged in a postscript that she had "a right to feel peeved" at him, but not to such a vehement degree. "After all, you might have taken into consideration that I have been palpably not myself mentally for the past few months and, as everyone up here noticed as soon as they saw me . . . physically sick. And why remember the bitter things I said and did? You said and did things just as wounding — more so! — and I assure you that I love you enough to have completely forgiven them. . . .

"I thought you wanted to come up to help me but evidently you're merely doing it out of anger and if you do come, I have only to expect a wife who will hate me! . . . why can't we understand each other, why couldn't you see that it was at bottom my loneliness and my love for you that made me write as foolishly as I did?"

He cabled her the following morning to postpone her decision about returning till she had received his latest letter, then added to it a second postscript in which he said: "All love, sweetheart. Forgive that crazy letter and forget it, please do! Remember we both desire so much to start a new life together." Mollified, she replied that it seemed he had been away "years, rather than a month," and hoped he would return before his thirty-ninth birthday in mid-October.

Since it would have looked suspicious had Carlotta's name disappeared from his letters, he referred to her briefly several times and once made a deprecating remark indicating, apparently, that she had lost all attraction for him. "I felt that the Carlotta thing," Agnes replied, "would turn out as you said."

O'Neill by now knew nearly all the major critics — Krutch, Woollcott, Broun, Stark Young and of course Nathan — the chief exception being Brooks Atkinson of the *Times*, a quiet pipe-smoking New Englander whose reserve cloaked a generous nature. The two had met fleetingly before, but they finally had a chance to become acquainted on

September 22 when Manuel Komroff brought them together for lunch. Afterward Atkinson, who had "long admired him from afar as one of the heroes, living in the far-off realm of poetry but firmly rooted in human existence," wrote in his diary that O'Neill "is graying around the edges and his face is marked with experience. It is not tired. It is vivid; there is something immediately magnetic about his personality. He has the physical strength of one who understands the strength of nature. Although he is generally unconscionably shy, even awkward, he was at ease today and talked on many themes. About his own work he is neither modest nor presumptuous. He talks of Art – of *Lazarus Laughed* and *Strange Interlude* . . . frankly, and smiles agreeably over his practical difficulties. With the arrogance of the true artist he is contemptuous of directors and actors who are not capable of producing him; he is charmingly frank in despising rich men who do not put huge sums of their private fortunes at his disposal for producing his work in proper style. I like him immensely for his ability to see all these minor forces in true perspective. Although he is gentle and sympathetic, I am sure he would trample down anything in his path. He is not to be denied. . . .

"We talked of human character, Maugham, Galsworthy, the current stage, the Dempsey-Tunney fight last night. . . . O'Neill is naturally a recluse. I was delighted to get on so swiftly with him. But he is the kind of man whose seclusion one instinctively respects, and, on his side, he never takes the initiative. He left me with a glow all afternoon. I felt that I had been in contact with the genuine article."

Hungry, it seems, for personal contact and stimulation after his isolation in Bermuda, O'Neill socialized in New York more than ever before. In addition to attorney Robert Rockmore, who wanted to become a theatrical producer, O'Neill's new acquaintances included Norman Winston, a shoe manufacturer and a friend of Rockmore's who had contributed money to the Provincetown Playhouse. "When I took Gene to the track," Rockmore recalls, "he said he'd always wanted to go but hesitated to get started, since horses, liquor and women had been his brother's downfall. The brother was the only one of the family he ever mentioned – always with great pity and affection. The first time we went I wanted to do the handicapping for him, but he took out a long sheet and said he'd rather play his own selections. He'd been up late the night before going over the entries. When I asked how he'd picked them out, he said he'd done it by numerology."

In return for his day at the track, O'Neill took Rockmore to the six-day bicycle races at Madison Square Garden, but the lawyer was not entertained. "What Gene saw in it," he says, "is beyond me. He had tickets for the whole series. I went once and left after several hours, bored as hell, but there he was, waiting for a 'jam.' He stayed, he later told me, till four in the morning."

Despite O'Neill's usual taciturnity, he talked on one occasion, according to Rockmore, for hours. "We were spending the day at City Island — I used to charter a boat on weekends — and Gene got started about his experiences as a seaman, the only time I ever saw him in a talkative mood. I'd been in the marines in the First World War and was not unfamiliar with rough language, but this was about the foulest I ever heard. What made it so surprising was that Gene's language was generally clean. [Agnes says that in their early years together he constantly used the four-letter words, but that gradually he changed.] He reminisced about the sailor bars, dirty movies and whorehouses in Buenos Aires, he recalled situations on ships because of seamen with homosexual proclivities. He was going to write it all out someday, he said, and have a few copies privately printed for his friends."

While spending a night at Norman Winston's home in Stamford, Connecticut, beside Long Island Sound, O'Neill and his host strolled down to the water. After gazing awhile at the moon's reflection, Eugene, repeating something he had told Beatrice Ashe, Maibelle Scott and other girls in New London years earlier, said that if he ever committed suicide, he would swim out on a moonlit night until he drowned.

His socializing in New York included theatergoing. Although he rarely went to plays — he preferred to read them, since he could "do a better production in my own mind" — he was fond of musical comedy. He had "a grand time" at Ziegfeld's Follies ("I laughed my head off at Eddie Cantor and enjoyed the semi-nude beauties"), saw *Good News* twice ("a fine show") and went backstage to meet Zelma O'Neill ("A real character!"), but was bored at *Sidewalks of New York* ("the lousiest musical show ever written . . . I sat behind Governor Smith, with [Mayor] Walker three seats away. . . . Illustrious company. All Tammany was there!")

Though *Marco Millions* and *Strange Interlude* remained in abeyance — the Guild was busy with its first productions of the 1927–1928 season — O'Neill found enough work to keep him occupied between "social excitements." To prepare for writing *Dynamo*, he visited a hydroelectric plant not far from Danbury, Connecticut; approached by a dirt road and located in an isolated spot beside the Housatonic River, the plant, with its intricate, mysterious-looking equipment, appeared in dramatic contrast to its verdant setting. The playwright was "taken all over and shown everything from roof to cellar. Quite an experience!"

Part of his time was spent on the proofs of *Lazarus Laughed*, due to be published in November, and he again made many changes. He felt that *Lazarus*, "with the possible exception" of *Strange Interlude*, was his best, and hoped, since none of the producers shared his opinion, that the biblical fable would create a great stir among its readers.

His published plays provided an increasing part of his income. Liveright issued them in regular trade editions, in sets, and certain ones in signed, limited printings, with the author getting a flat royalty of fifteen percent (his percentage, already above the standard rate, would be increased in 1929 to seventeen and one-half). His works were also regularly printed in England, and the major ones translated into the leading European languages, but the bulk of his book earnings came from this country. While he had reason to be concerned in 1927 about finances, the year would end with his making about twelve thousand dollars through Liveright alone, the bulk of the sum coming from *Marco*, published in April, and *Lazarus*. Following in approximate figures are his earnings from domestic publication for the years preceding 1927: 1920, three hundred and ninety dollars; 1921, eight hundred and sixty dollars; 1922, two thousand four hundred and fifty dollars; 1923, one thousand eight hundred and fifty dollars; 1924, two thousand eight hundred dollars; 1925, three thousand one hundred dollars, and 1926, six thousand nine hundred and thirty dollars, for a grand total from 1920 through 1927 of slightly over thirty thousand dollars.

Aside from the monetary return, O'Neill was gratified by the book sales because he believed that his permanent reputation depended on both readers and a theater of the future that could do justice to his scripts. Always dissatisfied to some extent with the staging of his works, he had written Krutch earlier this year that "there can be no such thing as a really good production in the American theater, and I gave up all hope of ever getting one years and years ago! I am tickled to death if a play of mine is done adequately. I expect bad productions. In a theater run as a commercial gamble . . . where more than four weeks' rehearsal is a dangerous financial risk, where directors, actors and actresses have no chance for any real training and no background or tradition of artistic feeling for their own calling, where — but why go on? You know the facts as well as I do — it is simply a proof of congenital imbecility in a dramatist to expect a good production . . . you can't build temples out of rotten wood. When we can afford time in the American theater, then and only then will things begin to pick up."

Softening a little, he hoped that the Guild would "do as well" by him as the Provincetown Playhouse and the Greenwich Village had with their productions of *The Emperor Jones, The Hairy Ape, Desire Under the Elms,* and *The Great God Brown.*

He had long had his heart set on Katharine Cornell, one of the country's finest young actresses, long-limbed, dark-haired, with an air of well-bred tragedy, playing the central role in *Strange Interlude.* He had sent her the script from Bermuda, feeling that "there is absolutely no one else who could touch what you could do with 'Nina.' " While he knew that she was scheduled to appear early this fall in Somerset Maugham's *The Letter,* he hoped that she would soon tire of the thriller and assume the role of his neurotic heroine. He was confident, he said, that *Strange Interlude,* "if done reasonably well," would "prove the biggest all around success of any of my plays." But Miss Cornell, while professing to like his play, rejected it. After *The Letter* opened in September, Eugene reported to Agnes, "No one thought anything of the play except as cheap melodrama but it will probably make money." Thinking presumably of his father's deterioration in ramshackle vehicles, he added, "She'll ruin herself."

Now that they had patched up their differences, his letters to Agnes were invariably reassuring. He said on September 23: "I'll be glad to get back home and rest. . . . The whirl [of my activities] keeps me from thinking too much about it but I'm very lonely inside." On the twenty-sixth: "It sure will be wonderful to have you in my arms again." On the twenty-ninth: "I only hope you are half as anxious to have me back as I am . . . !"

But the husband who wrote so affectionately was in conflict with himself and battling his conscience, for by this time he and Carlotta had begun their liaison. Dr. Gilbert Hamilton once said that O'Neill was "a one-woman man, not the sort to indulge in affairs," and O'Neill himself, in a letter to Agnes, declared that sex alone did not interest him, that only love mattered. He gave Carlotta a book of his plays — *Desire Under the Elms, The Hairy Ape* and *Welded* — which he inscribed with the following from *Ape:* "Sure! *You* get me. It beats it when yuh try to t'ink it or talk it — it's way down — deep — behind — you 'n' me we feel it! Sure! Bot' members of dis club!" Yet, in spite of her strong attraction for him and his sense of an affinity between them, it appears that he still felt "welded" in marriage. During September he repeatedly told Agnes he

[269]

would return early in October but when the month arrived he became busy (or so he said) with the Guild.

On October 11, after a cable from her telling him to remain as long as he deemed necessary, he replied: "I'm fed up with N.Y. and worn a bit ragged by my numerous goings here and there. But these goings are really doing me a lot of good — getting rid of my self-consciousness . . . and you'll find . . . that I'll be a much better husband in future and take you around everywhere when we're here together."

He returned to Bermuda on the twenty-first to rest and build up his strength for the ordeal that lay ahead with the two Guild productions. His relations with Agnes during his several weeks at Spithead seem to have been more or less as usual; there is no apparent evidence that he came to any crucial decision at the time. On the twenty-seventh he sent Macgowan a note to buy some flowers for Carlotta. On November 7 he informed De Casseres that he would see him shortly, for he intended to leave for New York in about a week.

"What would be ideal," he added, "would be if Bio [the critic's wife] and you would begin making plans now . . . to come back with me for a visit with us here when I return after the *Marco* opening. . . . And really stay with us a while."

But when he sailed on November 15, he would never again see Bermuda.

14

End of a Marriage

B Y the time O'Neill returned to New York the Theater Guild had
cast, subject to his approval, all the principals of his two plays except
the most important one — Nina Leeds. Looking outside its regular acting
company, the Guild had tried to sign Alice Brady, but she finally said no
(later calling this her greatest mistake), whereupon the firm turned to
Lynn Fontanne, its foremost actress and one of the best in the country,
especially for comedy. Without O'Neill's knowledge, she disliked *Strange
Interlude* and so, for that matter, did her husband Alfred Lunt, yet Lunt
urged her to accept the part. He thought that the play, because of its
exceptional length and novel technique, not to mention its author's
renown, would be "the event of the season. Everyone will be writing
about it and talking about it," he said. "Even if it is a flop, it will be
important and you will gain something by having played in it." On his
advice, she consented.

Usually teamed with her husband, another of Broadway's finest
players, Miss Fontanne had developed greatly since she enacted a colorless, properly reared Anna Christie in *Chris* before "tango lovers and
chewing-gum sweethearts" in Atlantic City; but O'Neill was unfamiliar
with her mature work except by reputation. To evaluate both her and
Lunt — the latter was to play the title role of *Marco Millions* — he
attended the Guild's revival of *The Doctor's Dilemma*, in which the two
played the Shavian artist and his wife. Normally astute in sizing up actors,
O'Neill this time misjudged somewhat. While he expected Lunt to be a
"remarkable" Marco, he thought Miss Fontanne "will give a very adequate performance but she will be far from . . . my 'Nina.' However,
who would be?" (In actuality she would contribute a brilliant portrayal.)
On the other hand he thought the leading male players of *Strange Inter-*

[271]

lude would be "splendid" — namely Tom Powers (Marsden), Glenn Anders (Darrell), and Earle Larimore (Sam Evans). "So," he wrote Agnes late in November 1927, "the cloud has its bits of silver lining. . . . The Guild is our best and they are doing their best by me."

The playwright's first days in town were largely spent at auditions for the many bit parts in *Marco* ("a long boring business"). The players supporting Lunt included Margalo Gillmore (the Eileen Carmody of *The Straw*) as the princess, Dudley Digges as Chu-Yin, Morris Carnovsky in two roles, and, at O'Neill's instance, Mary Blair. Though he practically never was swayed by personal considerations in casting his plays, he remained so grateful to Mary for appearing in *All God's Chillun*, particularly after she had been replaced by Carlotta Monterey for the Broadway engagement of *The Hairy Ape*, that he privately urged the Guild to engage her. While scarcely ideal for the part, Mary was cast as the eternal prostitute who repeatedly turns up in the Polos' travels, the only feminine role of any consequence after the princess.

O'Neill was also occupied in script conferences with Philip Moeller, one of the Guild executives, who was to direct *Strange Interlude*, and Rouben Mamoulian, who filled the same berth for *Marco Millions*. *Marco* was scheduled to open early in January, the other play late that month. O'Neill had been acquainted with Moeller ever since the days of the Washington Square Players, the forerunner of the Theater Guild, but Mamoulian, a young Armenian who had begun his career in Moscow, was a newcomer to Broadway. Rather surprisingly, in view of his foreign background, the Guild had entrusted him several months before with an indigenous work by the Du Bose Heywards, the all-Negro, now-historic *Porgy*, and he had staged one of the most exciting performances in years. O'Neill, who always tried to get "rhythm" into his plays, had been impressed by the ebb and flow, the rhythmic pacing of *Porgy*, and was pleased to have Mamoulian directing *Marco* as his second Guild assignment.

Rehearsals began at the Guild Theater for *Marco Millions* on December 5, for *Strange Interlude* a week later, and O'Neill used to slip quietly in and out of the darkened auditorium without anyone knowing he had been there. He once interrupted *Marco*, however, when Henry Travers, playing Marco Polo's father, resorted to a broad piece of business for an easy laugh. The playwright was immediately on the stage asking him to desist. "Oh, I wouldn't do that when we open, Mr. O'Neill — " but the other cut him short. "Don't tell me you wouldn't. *I know actors.* My father was one."

A legend would develop in time that whenever O'Neill gave the Guild a script, he said in effect: this is it, I won't make any changes or cuts, take it or leave it — and no argument could sway him. But the legend is greatly exaggerated (he would not turn stubborn until *The Iceman Cometh* in 1946). First on his own initiative, then at the Guild's urging, he had already substantially revised *Strange Interlude* to shorten its running time and *Marco Millions* to reduce its production cost; and now, as the two works were in rehearsal, he again made cuts. After one session of *Marco* he told Robert Rockmore that he had consented to drop a scene that had been "written in my blood." The Guild, among Broadway's most frugal managements, thought that *Marco*, if staged with sufficient economy, could be profitable, but it expected kudos rather than cash from the nine-act drama. It was so doubtful, in fact, about *Strange Interlude*'s commercial prospects that for a time it considered presenting the play as a "special" attraction only for its subscribers. O'Neill, somewhat more optimistic, believed that the play would be welcomed by intellectual theatergoers for a run of about three months.

Originally he and his producers had thought *Strange Interlude* would have to be performed on two nights, but after his first extensive revisions they agreed that it could, and should, be given "Bayreuth fashion" — that is, in one day, with a long dinner intermission. In rehearsal its running time proved much longer than he had expected and, under Moeller's patient pressure, O'Neill worked "like hell" to shorten it further. Otherwise, he informed Agnes, it "couldn't be done in an afternoon-evening, and that would be fatal." He and the director did not have too much trouble agreeing on most of the cuts, yet the revising finally became a kind of tug-of-war between them, chiefly because Moeller delighted in the script's comic moments and favored as many as possible, while O'Neill excised them whenever, in his view, they impeded the creation of emotion and drama in a scene.

To Moeller, who was to direct five O'Neill plays in all, the playwright appeared "one of the most far-away persons I ever knew, a deeply unhappy man searching for something, but I imagine that was part of his drive as a writer." While they never became close friends, O'Neill, who had formerly underestimated the director, recognized his ability and dedication once they teamed up for the nine-act marathon.

A shy, high-strung bachelor of aesthetic tastes and something of a dandy — he favored opera capes and used a long cigarette holder — Moeller suggested a dilettante; he actually was among the few creative directors around Broadway, one with an individual approach. Where most directors prepare in advance as thoroughly as possible, familiarizing themselves with the script, thinking out the stage "business" and blocking all the scenes, he would come to the first rehearsal, in Theresa Helburn's words, "strangely and deliberately unprepared." He kept himself "fresh for the first impact of the play" when read by the cast, and as the rehearsals progressed he relied on the inspiration of the moment. He was more like an imaginative participant with the actors than the instructor over them.

"We used to say rather wistfully," Miss Helburn recalls, "that it would be nice if Phil would read a play before he produced it." But this time, since *Strange Interlude* was so formidable an assignment — it was allotted seven weeks of rehearsal instead of the usual four — Moeller not only read the script in advance but immersed himself in it.

His overriding problem from the start was how to differentiate in performance between the "asides" and the dialogue proper. One of his ideas was to have a "special zone" of the stage to which the characters would repair when they expressed their supposedly silent thoughts; another would have required the actors to use a distinct change of voice; in a third method a complicated system of lighting would have isolated the person audibly communing with himself. In all the director dreamed up and discarded a half-dozen or so methods in his effort to arrive at "something simple and spontaneous" that would not call too much attention to itself.

While returning early this fall from Baltimore, he was wrestling with the problem when the train suddenly stopped. "Unconsciously," he says, "this may have been the hint," for after the train had resumed, a new thought occurred to him: "Why not, for a moment, stop the physical action of the play and allow the mental commentary to tell us its hidden secret simply, directly and without any obviously elaborate and intricate preparations?" And that was the way the drama was rehearsed and performed, with the other characters immediately freezing whenever one of them gave vent to a private aside. The length of *Strange Interlude*, Moeller adds, also posed a special problem: "What I had to do throughout this extraordinary play was to maintain the sensitive balance between what the actors could project and what the audience could receive. Here were nine acts for a company to learn and for the public to take almost at a stretch. I do not think the average audience realizes that much more of a play is acted by them — yes, I mean actually unconsciously acted by them! — than they know. Sometimes they do this for three and now and

[274]

then for four acts. But would they suddenly get on to themselves if urged to do this for nine? Would they "assist" us for as long as this?"

Because of its length and ultimate defeatist tone, the Guild expected *Strange Interlude* to last about six weeks, just long enough to accommodate its subscription audience. Although Moeller told O'Neill that the cast was "enthusiastic," Lynn Fontanne, grappling with one of the longest parts ever for an actress, had come to hate the play. She did not consider Nina worthy of such intensive scrutiny. "I thought," Miss Fontanne says, "she gave herself to those soldiers because she wanted to. She liked a lot of sex. She didn't feel sorry for them. I didn't ever feel O'Neill made her a tragic figure. I don't think he knew the first thing about women.

"I respect authors, I really do, but I have a great sense of what will 'go,' and I didn't care much for the writing in *Strange Interlude*. There was a woodenness at times, and so much of it was repetitious. I asked O'Neill to cut certain of my lines and he wouldn't do it, so, without telling anyone — Moeller, Helburn, Langner, anyone — I cut, cut, cut, and nobody ever realized it. I relied on the fact that the play was so long that not even O'Neill would remember what he'd written. Some of his scenes are ridiculous. I remember a passionate love scene with Ned [Darrell] and we were sporting about quite vigorously and then I was supposed to be thinking a lot of thoughts at the same time and the action was supposed to stop and we had to freeze while I was speaking my unconscious thoughts. Well, the audience would have just laughed out loud at me if I had done it. You can't stop in the middle of a nice sexual romp and have a brain wave."

With two plays in rehearsal concurrently and private matters weighing on him, O'Neill was in a highly nervous state (he reminded Miss Fontanne of "a horse in a fire"). Consciously he was torn with uncertainty about Agnes and Carlotta, but it seems likely that unconsciously he had already made his choice and now, reluctant to recognize the fact, was struggling to rationalize his decision. One evening he called on Benjamin De Casseres and his wife Bio, expecting nothing more than talk of writers and the theater. Though by now the two men had become friends, De Casseres knew little about the other's personal life and Bio even less, as this was her first meeting with the playwright. The couple had no idea, in short, that he was considering abandoning his wife for another woman.

While the playwright, stretched out on a chaise longue, talked with De Casseres, his wife sat quietly to one side studying him. During a lull in the conversation, Bio, who was part American Indian and dabbled in the occult, impulsively said she would like to read his hand, adding that she was supposed to have a gift for palmistry. Without expression, appearing totally indifferent, O'Neill extended his right hand. Bio was overwhelmed, she recalls, when she first looked at it, for she found "so much" in his palm. "You are not going back to Bermuda," she began excitedly, "never again . . . but your wife doesn't know this yet. . . . There is another woman you love — you first met her about five years ago. . . . There will be difficulties before you are free to marry her. . . . You are going to do a great deal of traveling. . . . You will live for a while in France and later in San Francisco. . . . There will be much notoriety in your life and — "

She stopped abruptly, embarrassed by her emotional state, since O'Neill had remained impassive. Bio felt that she had "unveiled a sacred, secret part of myself to one who did not understand. I should not have been so passionate, so full of authority, when reason and logic mock what I had done." Shortly after she broke off, O'Neill, still appearing indifferent to her sibylline pronouncements, said good-night and left.

Upset and depressed for having, as she felt, made a fool of herself, Bio spent a sleepless night, while her husband did his best to reassure her. The next morning the telephone rang and O'Neill, in a distant voice, asked for Ben; he wanted Ben to lunch with him. De Casseres returned home all excited, for O'Neill, far from being untouched by Bio's predictions, had been "bowled over." It was true, he told Ben, that he was in love with another woman and now was "in anguish as to how he should tell Agnes he was leaving her." Eager to question Bio, he wanted to see her again that very night. Though reluctant at first — she had "suffered too much the previous evening" — she finally consented at her husband's urging.

When O'Neill reappeared, he was, according to Bio, "smiling and human," and he apologized for not giving some indication that he was affected by her reading. In answer to his flood of queries, she told him, among other things, that his two Guild productions would be successes, that considerable time would elapse before he could wed Carlotta, that he would live another twenty-five years (in reality it would be twenty-six).

Shortly after his return to New York he had informed Agnes that Bobby Jones and Elizabeth Sergeant, both of whom had visited Mabel Dodge in Taos several times and found their stays among the Navajos a mystical experience, were insisting that he "*must* go. I was a great deal impressed this time. . . . Perhaps I might be able to go down for a few weeks after the plays get on. . . . I certainly won't feel in any mood to start writing a new one for some weeks after this ordeal is over, my nerves and vitality will undoubtedly be all shot, and some weeks in the desert might prove a wonderful reviver." He ended, "Much love, dearest," but his considering a trip alone to New Mexico indicates a major change in him; during their past separations he had always written that he was impatient for their reunion.

His next letter to Agnes, early in December, was chiefly about realty and financial matters. The Ridgefield place had been sold for thirty thousand dollars — which meant "a loss of at least $10,000" — and his share, because of the mortgage and agent's commission, would be only fourteen thousand dollars. By now he had over thirty-five thousand dollars sunk in Spithead, he still owed about eight thousand dollars of the purchase price and, he said, "that's aplenty for an artist who is trying to stick to being an artist. So please . . . don't go making plans for Spithead beyond what we've already agreed on, just because Ridgefield is sold. Later on, it may be a lot different but for the present the only sensible thing is to stand pat and have a good reserve for me to work on in peace in case the plays flop. . . ."

"Now here is something that is *very very important* and that I wish you would attend to *without fail* as soon as possible." He goes on to report that A. S. W. Rosenbach, the famous dealer in autographs and rare books, was "very much interested" in his manuscripts and wanted to see them. "It is no question of an immediate sale," Eugene says, "but, given the time, he thinks he can work them up to a big price." Rosenbach was leaving shortly on a long trip and O'Neill wanted to show him the material before his departure. He urged Agnes to send the scripts the safest way possible, to make certain she did not overlook any, and added: "Remember, this may be a big 'ace in the hole' for us and the kids. I really ought to have them in a safe deposit box, fire-proof — up here anyway, so they'd be absolutely safe."

His leaving the manuscripts behind is the clearest available indication that when he sailed in November he intended to return to Bermuda. Increasingly anxious as the days passed, he wrote in mid-December: "*Don't forget to send those scripts!* Important I get them soon." Farther in the letter he says, "Why don't you go out and enjoy yourself? Please don't think that I would have any objections. You are the boss of your own life, to live it in whatever freedom you desire, as I am with mine, and this must be the basis of our new understanding. You have been tied up too long and you deserve any happiness you can get. I feel that very deeply now that I have been able to get a real objective perspective on things." Yet in closing, he said, "Much love."

How Agnes felt about his declaration of independence under the guise of being fair to her is unknown, for her half of the correspondence between them in this period is lost; but his next letter must have quashed any lingering doubt she may have had regarding his new attitude. Still addressing her as "Dearest Aggie," he begins temperately enough with theater talk ("Rehearsals of 'S.I.' are coming along fine. Real enthusiasm among the company. 'Marco' is also blooming," etc.). Suddenly, with mock apology, he asks her to forgive him for "speaking so much about my plays. . . . It's quite evident to me that you're not interested since you never mention them. [He told the De Cassereses that she once fell asleep when he was reading to her one of his plays, as contrasted with Carlotta, who was passionately interested in his work.] . . .

"You never say a word about your plans. Are you coming up . . . ? I don't mean for the openings. . . . Leave them as entirely out of your considerations as, if you are frank, you must acknowledge they are out of your mind . . . please feel free to do as you wish without any compunction about hurting my feelings. I honestly don't care. You can't hurt me any more, thank God! You've tortured your last torture as far as I'm concerned. Something in me is so damn utterly dead that I don't care about anything any more – except doing my work. . . .

"A gloomy letter for Christmas? Well, it really shouldn't be for you. You are still young and beautiful and, with any sort of an even break from fate, you should have every chance for a real happiness before you – a happiness that it has become indubitably evident I never did and never can give you. And I certainly wish you to be happy, Agnes . . . what happened is neither your fault nor mine. It is simply the curse of the soul's solitude, the grinding, disintegrating pressure of time, that has destroyed us. . . . We both tried – and tried hard!

"So my Christmas present to you is really to give you back your absolute liberty in any way . . . you may desire. . . . I will always be your friend – your very best friend, I hope! . . .

"Look into your own heart and face the truth: You don't love me any more. You haven't for a long time. . . . Kiss the children for me. I hope they like their presents. I love them more than you give me credit for. But what do you understand of me, or I of you? And for their future happiness I am sure it's better for me to be more a friend and less a father than the reverse.

"God bless you and give you happiness!"

Trying to avert a permanent rupture, Agnes cabled that she "understood," thus indicating that she would allow him a fling with Carlotta; but he was not to be dissuaded from the course on which he was now embarked.

In an immediate reply he said that he "loved someone else most deeply" and that his affection was fully reciprocated. He reminded Agnes that they had often promised one another that if either of them ever fell in love with someone else, the other would step aside, knowing that "love is something which cannot be denied. . . . I am sure that I could accept the inevitable in that spirit if our roles were reversed." Declaring that he had always been faithful and had never sought another woman, he said that if his love for her had not died, another love would not have "come" to him. What had bound them together in recent years, he continues, had basically been "a fine affection and friendship. . . . There have been moments when our old love flared into life again but you must acknowledge that these have grown steadily rarer. On the other side of the ledger moments of a very horrible hate have been more and more apparent, a poisonous bitterness and resentment, a cruel desire to wound, rage and frustration and revenge. This has killed our chance for happiness together."

Considering the situation "objectively," he felt certain that "the freedom" to do as she pleased would mean a lot to Agnes. She would have the use of Spithead as a permanent home for life and could be "reasonably sure, unless catastrophe beans me, that you will always have enough income from me to live in dignity and comfort. . . . And, above all, you will have your chance of marrying someone else who will love you and bring you happiness. . . ."

He said that when she came to New York to discuss the situation "we must try to meet as friends who want to help each other, . . . we must avoid scenes and gossip and cheap publicity . . . we must act like decent human beings, realizing that we are both hot-tempered and sensitive to take offense at each other's words or looks or whatever. . . . I know how I would act if I were in your place – how I would force myself to act even if I loved you and your decision crushed me."

Asking her to postpone her trip till after the two openings, he said, "It isn't going to be easy for us . . . and for me it would make it terrifically difficult even to think of my plays just when they need my thought most. But if you feel you must come now, why come along. I don't want to be selfish about it."

Agnes took the first ship for New York and, against his express wishes, checked into the Wentworth. What chiefly worried him was Carlotta's reaction should she learn of Agnes's presence in the hotel. Only months before he had inscribed a copy of *Marco* to Agnes with one of the Great Kaan's loving tributes to his granddaughter: "You have been a golden bird singing beside a black river — the river of man's life." But now, storm-tossed and reveling in anguish, he inscribed a volume of *Lazarus Laughed* to her with one of Tiberius's bleakest speeches, starting with: "If I were sure of eternal sleep beyond there [death], deep rest and forgetfulness of all I have ever seen or heard or hated or loved on earth, I would gladly die!"

Relations between Eugene and Agnes during her fortnight in New York wavered uneasily back and forth from moments of harmony to exchanges Strindberg, or O'Neill himself, might have written. Shortly after her arrival she developed a cold and he suggested that she might benefit from his sun lamp. When he arrived at her room with the lamp, she was scantily clad, he became amorous, and they made love for what would be the last time. The intimate episode only confirmed their division, for, in Agnes's words, it was "like two ghosts sleeping together."

After considerable discussion, under the guidance of attorney Harry Weinberger, the estranged pair reached tentative agreement on the chief terms for the divorce: Agnes was to receive six to ten thousand dollars annually, depending on how much he made each year (for the past few years he had given her five hundred dollars monthly for household expenses and for her and the children's clothes), and the use of Spithead for life; if she leased the place instead of living there, she would retain the rental.

Somehow Carlotta learned of Agnes's presence at the Wentworth and, with indignation born of anxiety, demanded that Eugene force her to leave. Carlotta became so insistent and vexatious about the matter, allowing him no peace, that he flared up and declared that he was through with her. During the period of *their* estrangement he descended without prior word on the Jimmy Lights in Greenwich Village and said that after his two plays were on, he wanted to "borrow" Jimmy to accompany him on a trip to Hawaii. As the first-nighters assembled on January 9, 1928, at the Guild Theater for *Marco Millions*, the absentee author had little thought to spare for his play's prospects; he was mournfully examining the wreckage of his marriage to Agnes and of his romance with Carlotta.

Most of the reviewers were cordial to *Marco*, but with some emphasizing the serious undercurrent in the satire, others the humor of the story, it almost sounded as though the author had written two plays, in different veins, about Marco Polo. Brooks Atkinson seems, from general admiration for the playwright, to have leaned over backwards to give him a favorable notice. "There is frequently more power than magic in his artistry," the *Times* man stated, "and the simplicity of his ideas can be monotonous as well as lucid," but he concluded that the play was "an original, powerful, searching drama." Percy Hammond, usually more emphatic, said in the *Herald Tribune:* "To those who are not of the musing or Theater Guild type of playgoer [the play] may seem too long and contemplative. But to the knowing postgraduate of the Guild audience it will afford pleasure as a splendid and thoughtful burlesque."

Gilbert Gabriel of the *Sun,* among the enthusiastic, became rather lyrical: "It is full of the ease and relish of comedy. . . . It is neither deeper nor broader than Mercutio's wound; yet it is mortally meant, and the same bright scarlet of mankind's pain and grief and wasted life pours out of it, a savage and exciting dye."

Arthur Pollock of the Brooklyn *Eagle,* a dissenting voice, thought the play worth "something less" than the time required to perform it. In the *Post* Robert Littell, even more critical, found the work "surprisingly simple-minded, obvious, and at times actually foolish. . . . The eleven scenes show us, in ABCs which can be read a mile away, the contrast between Western money-grubbing and Eastern wisdom, between materialism and idealism, between the dollar and the dream."

One of the country's finest actors, Alfred Lunt was not in top form as Marco, partly because of uncertain health at the time but chiefly from dislike of both his role and the play. By default, then, the real star of the production was not Lunt but Lee Simonson's scenery and costumes — his, in Atkinson's words, "cloth of gold, rococo investiture." With ingenious economy Simonson used for most scenes an adaptable set, composed of an arch and paneled doorways, to frame different interiors evoking the ancient world from Venice to Cathay.

With one play apparently set for a moderately successful engagement, O'Neill felt further relieved when Agnes, accompanied by her twelve-year-old daughter Barbara, left for home on January 14. To practically everyone except Agnes the voyage was especially enjoyable, for it was the maiden New York–Bermuda trip of the Q.S.M.S. *Bermuda;* as the luxury cruise ship sailed down the Hudson her siren sounded continuously in reply to vessels wishing her good luck. In reporting the event Bermuda's *Royal Gazette and Colonist Daily* said on January 17, 1928, that "both crew and passengers were equally excited and enthusiastic. There was an air of fantasy about the whole proceedings; there was never such a jolly crowd ever sailed for the Isles of Rest. . . . The story of the maiden voyage would truly be [of] a fairy sail to fairyland, or a flight to

Paradise." About the time Agnes departed, Eugene and Carlotta were reconciled.

For Carlotta the future could hardly have loomed brighter; not only were she and O'Neill committed to one another but she had managed, with impunity, to ease out of her relationship with James Speyer, her protector for years. In telling Speyer that O'Neill wanted to marry her as soon as he was free, she gave a dismal picture of his life with Agnes — an ill-organized household, no peace and quiet when he worked, a wife indifferent to his career — and said that the discord was affecting his creativity. It was no romance between her and the playwright, she declared, but a situation in which he kept insisting that he "needed" her and she in turn, sorry for him, thought it her duty to help this man of genius. She asked Speyer's permission to marry the sorely tried playwright. Rising to the situation, the banker, a gentleman of the old school who came from a wealthy, cultured Jewish family in Germany, gave the proposed union his blessing and assured her that the annuity was hers for life.

On the several occasions that O'Neill and Carlotta dined at Speyer's Fifth Avenue mansion, the two men were favorably impressed with one another. From Carlotta's account, Eugene viewed the banker as simply one of her oldest friends in the city, a childless widower who had a paternal affection for her. After learning that Speyer was a prime figure in the founding of the Museum of the City of New York (besides serving as its finance chairman, he contributed nearly a half-million dollars), the playwright decided to give its theater collection some of his memorabilia, including his father's acting script of *Monte Cristo*.

Among O'Neill's friends opinion was diverse about his new love. Kenneth Macgowan, who had been close to the romance from its inception, felt sorry for Agnes and the children (he had two youngsters of his own) but at the same time thought that Carlotta "would be good for Gene — she'd get his life in shape. She had the strength of character he needed in a wife, where Agnes just wasn't strong and capable enough. And there seemed to be a strain of hostility in his feeling for her that was always ready to surface. I remember once, when they were living in Ridgefield, that he came over to my place, and he'd been drinking. 'You know,' he said, 'I don't really like Agnes,' and that seemed to me stronger somehow than if he'd said he hated her."

Carlotta's habit of holding her chin up, head tilted backward (because of her eye condition since childhood) gave her a rather haughty air. Elizabeth Sergeant was struck by her "grand manner" the first time they met, though Carlotta, knowing that Eugene was fond of the magazine writer, bent all her efforts to be gracious. Miss Sergeant, more or less sharing Macgowan's view, felt that Carlotta "would bring more order into Gene's life, would make things easier for him. He had to live in a special, very isolated way, he had to work every day, and Carlotta, I thought, would do her utmost to help him. But whether she was in love with the famous dramatist or with the man is anyone's guess."

Both Robert Rockmore and Norman Winston privately felt that the playwright was fortunate in not being able to remarry immediately, for they doubted that he and Carlotta could establish a satisfactory permanent relationship, and thought O'Neill himself would realize it before too long. Since Ben De Casseres did not care for forceful women, his opinion was predictable. He agreed with Bio that Miss Monterey was "a brilliant and scintillant being" but felt that she would be "a menace to O'Neill's creative power." Viewing both as determined characters, he expected them to clash in time.

Quietly, without introducing her to the company, O'Neill brought Carlotta to several rehearsals of *Strange Interlude*, but Lynn Fontanne already knew her; they had first met at a party given by writer Carl Van Vechten and his actress wife Fania Marinoff. Miss Fontanne remembered the occasion because she thought Carlotta "one of the most beautiful women I have ever seen . . . she had beautiful ivory skin and dark hair and mysterious big eyes, and then this rasping, husky voice came out of her, which was such a surprise — to hear the deep voice from this divine face."

Carlotta's firmest champion around the Guild was Robert Sisk, the publicity agent, who admired O'Neill and was glad that he had at last found a woman who was so protective of him, so devoted. "It seemed to me she was ideal for him," Sisk says, "and he couldn't have been the easiest person to live with." A forthright, kindly man, Sisk, who had once gone to sea, felt that this common bond helped him to establish an easy relationship with the reserved playwright. Unlike many whom O'Neill and Carlotta were to drop after a time, generally at her insistence, Sisk would remain a friend of theirs for life.

O'Neill, who hated the cold, complained so about the January weather that Carlotta, who had once delighted her former husband Ralph Barton with a fur-lined overcoat, decided that a similar gift would be even more appreciated this time. At first Eugene felt bashful at the prospect of wearing such a luxurious item — it made him feel "like a gigolo" — yet he lost no time in showing it off. The day of its delivery he called Robert

Rockmore at his office and asked him to stop by the Wentworth after work. Rockmore recalls that when he arrived, "Gene simply nodded and without a word went into the bedroom and closed the door. I didn't know what to think. In a couple of minutes he appeared wearing this long black coat with a mink collar, and then he opened it out to show that it was all fur-lined. I probably should have been more enthusiastic when he asked how I liked it. 'It's all right,' I said.

" 'Just all right?' he repeated. 'Why it comes from Revillon Frères and cost eight hundred dollars!' "

Another display of the coat was more gratifying to him. When the bell rang at the Jimmy Lights' apartment, Patti opened the door, and as she recalls, "Gene was standing there, grinning boyishly and waiting for me to comment on his splendid appearance. 'How lovely,' I said, 'it looks so right on you!' "

Despite his happiness over his new love, O'Neill was subject to "a bitter feeling of sadness" whenever he thought of his years with Agnes and "what the passage of time" had done to them. He had "the intolerable feeling" that life was against "fine beautiful things" enduring "any great length of time, that human beings are fated to destroy just that in each other which constitutes their mutual happiness." While he attributed his spells of depression to regret over the past, it seems likely that they arose also from a sense of guilt over the present. Before he could break with Agnes, he had had to persuade himself that she no longer loved him, that the fairest thing he could do was to set her free, that in the long run the children would be better off without him, for otherwise, if the marriage dragged on, they would be adversely affected by growing up in an acrimonious household. Yet all his rationalizing merely blanketed, rather than eased, his tosses and turnings of remorse.

During Agnes's visit he had tried to impress on her the importance of developing her own talent; writing meant so much to him that, indulging in wish fulfillment, he insisted it could prove her salvation too. In his first letter after her return to Bermuda he said, "I hope you will soon write me that you are really at work again on your real stuff. This isn't a mercenary wish — it's a wish for your own happiness!" And from his next letter: "Have you started to work yet? Please do, Agnes! . . . because I feel so strongly that that means peace for you and a new life all your own. . . . Don't let yourself get back in the old rut!"

But her letters left him impaled on the hook of conscience. "It hurts me," he said late in January, "to know you have such spells of loneliness — and the thought of the children carries a deep pang too. All this is not easy for me, either. . . . But one must live according to the truth inside one or life is nothing. And I do feel tremendously that, once we go through with this and readjust ourselves to the new life, it will mean happiness for both of us."

By now he and Carlotta had decided to sail for Europe after *Strange Interlude* opened, and they already were apprehensive about their private affairs becoming a matter of public interest and titillation. Several newspapers had questioned him about talk that he was having marital difficulties — he denied it — and one, the *Graphic*, said in print "it was rumored" that he and Agnes had separated. Disclosing his true plans only to his agent Richard Madden, his lawyer Harry Weinberger, and a few of his most trusted friends, he told others, including Agnes, that he was going to California, where *Lazarus Laughed* was to have its world première at the Pasadena Playhouse early in April; he intended, according to his story, to assist with the rehearsals.

A few days before *Strange Interlude* was to open, O'Neill and the Guild were furious when the February issue of *Vanity Fair* came out with a devastating review by Alexander Woollcott titled "Giving O'Neill Till It Hurts." It was generally assumed, since he was a close friend of the Lunts, that he had read Miss Fontanne's script, but no one at the Guild dared to raise the question with her. A round-faced man with a small beaklike nose who rather resembled a dyspeptic owl, Woollcott had become increasingly critical of O'Neill since *Anna Christie* and *The Hairy Ape* — he blasted both *Desire Under the Elms* and *The Great God Brown* — but none of his other attacks had been so sharp as his latest. Possibly the critic, whose appearance and manner suggested an ambiguous sex identity, was particularly offended by the character of Charles Marsden; significantly enough, he told friends that the O'Neill drama was "a play in nine scenes and an epicene." (After it had become a hit, he called it "the *Abie's Irish Rose* of the pseudo-intelligentsia.")

When the Guild complained to Herbert Bayard Swope, Woollcott's superior at the *World*, he immediately agreed that it would be unfair for the critic to cover the première for the newspaper and swore the Guild delegation to secrecy, for he intended to replace his temperamental reviewer at the last possible moment. The Guild in turn confided to O'Neill that "smart Alec" was to be superseded.

After seeing one of the last dress rehearsals, O'Neill felt that his marathon drama would hold an audience's interest to the end. When the rehearsal was over, he told Miss Fontanne: "You are so exactly right for the part that it might have been written for you." Though pleased, the actress, who had an honest, skeptical mind, wondered whether "he really meant it or simply said so because he thought it would give me more confidence and help the play." (In subsequent years O'Neill, in talking for the record about outstanding portrayals in his works, never once mentioned Miss Fontanne; perhaps he had heard that she disliked the play and that her husband used to refer to it as "a six-day bisexual race.")

The dress rehearsal was the last time the author ever saw the play. At an invitational performance before a full house on Sunday, January 29, the Guild brass first began to think that the unorthodox presentation would be a hit. Robert Sisk, his voice high with excitement, called O'Neill at Carlotta's apartment and reported that "the whole thing went over terrifically." O'Neill's only comment was: "I'm not surprised." While the actors were still removing their makeup after the preview, word began to spread around Broadway that the new drama looked like a success.

An hour or so before curtain time on the thirtieth, Theresa Helburn telephoned O'Neill in a final attempt to persuade him to attend, but he again refused. About the same time, at the *World*, Swope informed Woollcott that someone else was to cover the play, then, moving quickly to mollify the indignant critic, asked him to escort Mrs. Swope to the première. Backstage at the John Golden Theater Miss Fontanne, heading for her dressing room, groaned to Glenn Anders, "This is like giving birth — it isn't worth it!"

It was eight years almost to the day since O'Neill's arrival on Broadway with *Beyond the Horizon*. In the interval he had violated one shibboleth after another by writing plays without love interest, plays about black men, plays that made recondite use of masks, plays about such alarming matters as incest, infanticide and miscegenation, plays that were shorter and longer than standard length. At the time of *Horizon* one reviewer had declared that "however minutely he aims to analyze his characters, he must . . . not write his plays in what amounts to six acts." Another admonished him that "an audience goes to the theater to sit for an hour or two, not a day. Mr. O'Neill seems to think that time is a negligible element in the development of his ideas." Now he was awaiting the verdict on the longest American play ever given on Broadway.

When the curtain rose at five-fifteen on January 30, 1928, the reviewers were nervous, as Joseph Wood Krutch later commented: "No play of recent years has aroused as much preliminary speculation as has *Strange Interlude* . . . there was not, I fancy, a single commentator on things theatrical who did not await the fatal afternoon more tensely than a hardened observer is permitted to confess . . . each was balanced between two fears — the fear lest he be hypnotized into believing himself more impressed than he really was and the opposite fear lest he lean over backward into mere insensibility. . . . Which should he choose — the risk of going down to posterity as a soft-headed fool or the worse risk of being reminded some ten years later that he had greeted a masterpiece with wisecracks?"

When the performance broke at seven-thirty for its single intermission, Macgowan and his wife hurried to the Wentworth, where they dined with O'Neill and gave him a heartening account of their impressions and the evident audience response. Though he appeared less tense after hearing them out, the only time he smiled was when Kenneth mentioned that a drugstore near the theater was advertising "Strange Interlude" sandwiches. "I know what that is," the playwright cracked. "It's a four-decker with nothing but ham!"

The performance, which resumed at nine, ended shortly after eleven, and as the first-nighters left the theater their faces, according to one observer, "registered tiredness but not boredom, weariness but no ennui. It was the honest fatigue of people who have shared in profound emotional experiences."

As the chief model for Charles Marsden, Charles Demuth, who was among the audience, had reason to resent the play but he kept it to himself when writing to his friend Alfred Stieglitz about "Eugene's opening." The play "certainly was a surprise," he said. "You got through it, and were interested almost all of the time. Florie [Florine Stettheimer, a painter] & I decided . . . that he has used all the 'tricks' beautifully, but so far as having any real quality (or whatever you want to call it), it hasn't! — any at all. But you must see it. It's one of those things — but really not much more. . . .

"So Marsden [Hartley, another model for the *Strange Interlude* character] is again with us. What joy & sorrow — just like Life itself. Tell him not to return until I have seen him."

The press response was largely favorable, with about half of the reviewers thoroughly enthusiastic. "*Strange Interlude* stands firm and giant-sized," said Gilbert Gabriel of the *Sun*, "as a giver of new scopes, as a hewer of ways for such truths as the usual drama can scarcely imply, as a method to meet the need . . . for plays that can ably and truly cope with Freud . . . it is the most significant contribution any American has made to the stage."

To Woollcott's chagrin, Dudley Nichols, the *World* reporter who had replaced him, was among the most impressed. Nichols, who subsequently became a leading Hollywood writer (*The Informer, Stagecoach, Lost Patrol*), went on for virtually two full columns of newsprint to praise the play as "the top of O'Neill's career." The asides and soliloquies "worked," he said, enabling the playwright "to dive deep in the waters of life, as a deep-sea diver who invents for himself a new kind of armored suit, and brings up the monstrous forms which inhabit there . . . it would seem that [O'Neill] has not only written a great American play but the great American novel as well . . . a psychological novel of tremendous power and depth."

Brooks Atkinson, on the other hand, was of two minds about the asides; he felt that while some had "a dramatic quality all their own," they just as often seemed fortuitous. His chief quarrel was not, however, with the author's technical devices but with the morbid nature of his story. The playwright "has returned," Atkinson complained, "to the morbidity of his middle period, a preoccupation with dark and devious human impulses. . . . Nor does his point of view sweeten the unsavoriness of his material . . . [he] does not illumine his theme with pity or interpret its significance." He conceded, though, that the play "maintains the interest to the end." In his weekend article, after restating his objections, Atkinson was more laudatory: "Strange as it may seem, these bilious, critical comments are written by one who enjoyed Mr. O'Neill's drama. . . . Nine acts of psychopathic furies may weary but when Mr. O'Neill is the black magician they do not bore."

Like a number of others, Robert Littell of the *Post* thought that *Strange Interlude* was the finest play ever written in America. He found that it "has the space and depth, the pauses and vast convolutions of a novel, and also the surprise, the mystery, and the physical shock and reality of a play." Arthur Pollock of the Brooklyn *Eagle*, looking behind the play to the man who wrote it, made a perceptive comment: characterizing O'Neill as "something of a propagandist against life," he added, "The world must have done him an injustice at some time and he refuses to forgive."

One of the few to venture a prediction about the play's commercial prospects, Burns Mantle of the *News* said that it "will probably interest a comparatively small public. It is solid gray in tone, slow-paced and repetitious in performance, and forbidding in length."

Strange Interlude became the greatest success of O'Neill's career, the most talked-about, written-about, joked-about play of the decade (Robert Benchley called it "just an ordinary nine-act play"), and one of

[288]

the most profitable presentations in the Theater Guild's history. The O'Neill drama gave four hundred and forty-one performances on Broadway, played three seasons on the road (most of the time there were two touring companies), brought the author a third Pulitzer Prize, and eventually netted him about two hundred and seventy-five thousand dollars, a sum that included his half share of the seventy-five-thousand-dollar movie rights and his royalties from the sale of over one hundred thousand copies of the book.

Since the capacity audiences in the first weeks of *Strange Interlude* were largely composed of Guild subscribers — the John Golden was a relatively small house, only nine hundred seats — some time would pass before anyone, including O'Neill, realized that the play was going to be a spectacular hit. He felt "extremely proud" of his "great artistic success," wondered whether it would prove "commercial," and regretted that it had not opened earlier in the season, since he expected that "as soon as spring and balmy afternoons arrive, no one will want to go into a theater at 5:15 — and I don't blame them."

His predominant concern, though, was not how the play would fare but what Agnes would do, for he had been informed by a supposed friend of hers that she had no intention of setting him free. Someone had advised Agnes, according to the story he heard, to promise to do whatever O'Neill asked but to do nothing, "to hang on," thus upsetting his "new life" so that he "couldn't work and would then give up and come back" to her. Agnes liked the advice, O'Neill's informant further said, and planned to follow such a strategy.

"Naturally, I can't believe this," O'Neill wrote to her early in February. "It would be hardly an act consistent with honor or the friendship we swore to each other. And it wouldn't be practical, either — for your own sake or the children's. For it would undoubtedly make it impossible for me to work — and then there would be no new plays and no income for anyone to live on — until you decided to keep your faith with me." As for their relationship, he would justifiably hate her, he said, if she tried to wreck the happiness that now loomed before him. While he doubted the story, he repeated, he could not help being upset about it.

Several days later, after a letter from Agnes reproaching him for not sending the reviews of *Strange Interlude*, he replied that it was "a triumph. The trouble with my triumphs is that there's always so much of my own living on my mind at the time I haven't got any interest left for plays. Do you remember *The Hairy Ape* opening night, with my Mother's body in the undertaking parlor? 'So *ist das Leben,*' I guess. Or at least my '*leben.*' "

Amplifying on his previous letter, he said that he had heard so many unpleasant rumors about things she had said during her New York visit, particularly regarding her alleged scheme to hold onto him, that he was in an apprehensive state. Denying that she had any such scheme, Agnes suggested that he return to Bermuda for a week so that they could settle matters; at the same time, desperately hoping for a reconciliation, she added that she still loved him. To minimize his guilt feelings, he took the position that for him to act on her suggestion would "not be kind to you, or me, or the children. By the end of the week you and I might be hating each other again – look at your stay in N.Y.! No, Agnes, we must not see each other again for a long time – not until the 'possessive' stuff has died out in each of us. . . . It would be doing you a great wrong – re-tarding the growth of your independent personality – if I came down. I'd like to see Shane & Oona but – this is better in the long run for them too. . . .

"I'm damned sorry you are finding things so difficult – but I really can't believe you love me. . . . You could not possibly have done the things you did. You could never have touched a drink, for example. It would have choked you to death – if you really loved me. And now [that] I am really loved I see only too damned clearly by contrast all you failed to give me. I am not blaming you [this is the same pattern he would follow in *Long Day's Journey Into Night* – first the accusation, immedi-ately afterward a retraction]. It was true of me, too. It is what life does to love – unless you watch and care for it."

In his letters he always asked her to kiss the children for him and he once protested that he loved them more than she realized. "It is only that I am a bit inexpressive about what I feel toward them."

Bidding Shane farewell early in February, he wrote that he was going to California to help stage *Lazarus Laughed*. A long time would probably intervene, he said, before he saw Shane and Oona again, but "I will often think of you and I will miss you both very much. I often lie in bed before I go to sleep – or when I can't sleep – and I picture to myself all about Spithead and what you both have been doing all day . . . and then I feel very sad and life seems to me a silly, stupid thing even at best. . . . But you are not old enough to know what that feeling is – and I hope to God you never will know, but that your life will be always simple and con-tented!"

Uncertain how long he would remain abroad, O'Neill spent an evening with his older son, now a freshman at Yale, and disclosed his actual plans. The confidence meant a great deal to young Eugene, who looked up to his father, was thrilled about *Strange Interlude*, and hoped to prove his heredity by achieving literary renown of his own — a poem of his had appeared recently in *Helicon*, a Yale periodical. (While Eugene Jr. had liked Agnes, he began to view her through his father's eyes once the pair had separated and never saw her or wrote to her again. Between him and Shane relations would never be close, though in later years the half brothers often ran into one another as they drifted around Greenwich Village.)

O'Neill's affairs were in fairly good shape as the time for his departure approached. Most of his New London property had been sold piecemeal over the years; the Ridgefield place had finally been unloaded; his manuscripts were now safely stored in New York. The one major unsettled matter was his marital status, and he could only hope that Agnes would shortly give him his freedom. In the meantime Harry Weinberger, given power of attorney, was to negotiate with her and send her a monthly allowance of five hundred dollars.

Hoping to slip out of the country unnoticed, O'Neill, besides spreading the story that he was bound for California, booked passage under an assumed name on the *Berengaria*, due to sail at midnight on Friday, February 10. Too nervous to sleep Thursday night, he toured the water front with Norman Winston and pointed out some of his old hangouts, including 252 Fulton Street, the onetime site of Jimmy the Priest's, after which the two men drove around most of the night. One of the last things he did on Friday was to stop by the Guild and inscribe Moeller's script of *Strange Interlude* as follows: "To Phil: The most sympathetic and comprehending director I have ever worked with — with all my gratitude for his invaluable collaboration in making this play live in spite of the dramatist."

Long before sailing time Carlotta installed herself on the ship, and immediately began worrying about Eugene, who had his own cabin. He planned to slip aboard through third class, with Norman Winston's help, to elude the ship news reporters. It was growing late — there had been preliminary blasts of the ship's whistle — when he finally appeared.

"All he said," Carlotta has recalled, was, 'Hello, here I am,' and then Winston left. There was no thank you or I love you or anything, and here I was risking my reputation. That was bad enough but then, instead of paying any attention to me, he stood looking out the porthole, with tears rolling down his face. 'It's a terrible thing,' he said, 'to leave behind so many you love, everything that means anything to you.' 'Well, Carlotta,' I said to myself, 'you've let yourself in for it this time.' I could have strangled him!"

15

O'Neill and Carlotta

AFTER a week in London, where no one knew that "a notorious
Yank" was about, Eugene had to "confess" – and it was quite "a
confession for an O'Neill to make" – that he liked the city better than
any other he had ever known. He felt here "something so stable and solid
and self-assuredly courteous" that it was like "a soothing bath for the
nerves after the frazzle of New York."

His response to London, where he and Carlotta stayed at the Berkeley,
was partly due to his general mood. "God, I wish I could tell you how
happy I am!" he wrote to Kenneth Macgowan on February 22, 1928. "I
wander about foolish and goggle-eyed with joy in a honeymoon that is a
thousand times more poignant and sweet and ecstatic because it comes at
an age when one's past – particularly a past such as mine – gives one the
power to appreciate what happiness means and how rare it is . . . it
really seems to my mystic side as if some compassionate God, looking
back at Carlotta's unhappy life and mine, has said to himself, 'Well, they
deserve something from me in recompense for all my little jokes, they
deserve each other if they have the guts to take the gift.' . . .

"To say that Carlotta and I are in love in the sense of any love I have
ever experienced before is weak and inadequate. This is a brand new
emotion and I could beat my brains out on the threshold of any old
Temple of Aphrodite out of pure gratitude." (A strangely violent
thought for one in his mood, it suggests that some part of him rebelled
against his happiness.)

London nearly a fortnight, Paris a few days, an enchanting trip by
automobile and chauffeur along the Loire – O'Neill thought the châteaux of the Touraine "the most beautiful and dramatic places" he had
ever seen – then a brief stay in Biarritz till the couple rented a villa in

nearby Guéthary. O'Neill reveled in his "first vacation away from the burden of myself that I've ever had"; but at the same time he was eager to get to work on *Dynamo* and thought that the Villa Marguerite, which they had leased for six months, would be ideal for his purposes. Secluded among wooded grounds, with the Pyrenees for an imposing backdrop, the villa was a solid old house with stone balconies whose property included a private beach. Though the water was too cold for everyone else, O'Neill, who suspected that the local people considered him "a crazy American," began swimming regularly in the Bay of Biscay.

To conceal his whereabouts, particularly from Agnes and the press (the Paris *Herald,* which seemed anxious to locate him, ran two items about his being "somewhere in France"), he had arranged for the Guaranty Trust Company, Pall Mall, London, to serve as his chief mailing address. During his first month abroad he was completely out of touch with his affairs at home, but shortly, at Guéthary, he began receiving mail forwarded from London. *Marco Millions* and *Strange Interlude* were faring well, he learned, but personal developments were upsetting, for the New York *News* had run a story about him and Agnes "starving in the early days" and given her "all the sympathy as the pathetic deserted wife." Unreasonably, O'Neill hoped that the news story made her as "furious" as he.

He was in a peculiar emotional state that would last for months, with his joy over Carlotta (he found her "wonderfully kind and considerate" and "so deeply in love" that it filled him with "humble awe") shot through with anger toward Agnes. In corresponding with her he generally tried to be conciliatory, but almost always, directly or indirectly, his hostility is evident. "I am deeply happy now," he said in his first letter to her from abroad, "happier than I have ever dreamed I could be — and everything seems rather wonderful. I feel reborn [during this period he repeatedly declared that he felt "reborn"]. *I am sure!* At last I belong!" It was cold comfort to Agnes to read: "There is only one thing lacking in my complete happiness and that will come when you write me that you are working again, that you have readjusted your life and begin to see in your new freedom a chance for new life and happiness — and new love!"

After Agnes professed to find him "protesting too much" about his blissful state, he replied, "I am as happy as I can be, being the sort of brooding person I am . . . I have my bad hours and days, naturally, but they are due to myself alone and to my obsession with the past. . . ."

Anxious for his early freedom, he thought that they were in general agreement on the divorce terms and that she intended to leave for Reno in the near future. Agnes, however, as she told Harry Weinberger, felt "absolutely in the dark as to what final agreement it is he wants me to sign. . . . There was a more or less vague discussion when we were in New York and that is all. I do not know if I am to be allowed to stay at Spithead merely at his pleasure, or if I am to have the use of it for life, or if it is to be given to me outright. We never settled who was to pay for the children's schooling . . . the whole thing, so far as I am concerned, is up in the air. Yet both you and Gene take the attitude that everything is arranged."

When O'Neill learned of her position and that she wanted twenty-five hundred dollars as soon as possible to pay an accumulation of old bills in Bermuda, he felt "pretty hopeless" about their ever reaching a friendly settlement and charged that she was trying to "take me for all I've got." Her attitude, he said, "puts me in no right frame of mind to write any new plays. And if my work stops, my income won't be enough to keep one of us going, let alone four or five!" (By "four or five" he meant Eugene Jr. as well.)

Aside from being indignant at what he regarded as excessive financial demands (Agnes did not spell out her terms but asked for a settlement for Shane and Oona and a guarantee about Spithead, in addition to alimony), O'Neill resented the "implication" in one of her letters that she was "doing all the suffering. For Christ's sake," he exploded, "don't you think I suffer too? . . . Sometimes – and often! – when I think of Shane and Oona I suffer like hell from a sense of guilt toward them, and a deep sense of guilt because I've made you suffer. You know damn well that I'm a man who shrinks from the very notion of deliberately causing anyone sorrow. (Rages & fights and what one bitterly says then don't count.) It is in every line of my work. . . ."

Turning placatory, he said, "You will be fair, I know," but to Harold DePolo, Benjamin De Casseres and others he charged that she was trying to use "legalized blackmail" against him. It may be significant that a picture postcard he sent her from one of the châteaux showed the tomb of an "Agnes" (Agnès Sorel at Loches), especially since he told Macgowan that Agnes was "dead" to him.

Writing from Bermuda, where he had spent the past two winters, DePolo had some critical things to say about Agnes. He hoped that Eugene would not be offended at him, for he felt that he had to be honest with his old friend. (Not long after the letter DePolo borrowed some money from Agnes to help him return with his family to the States.) O'Neill replied that Harold "must have heard a lot of the gossipy dirt of

Broadway relayed through Agnes . . . but I know you know women well enough to discount that — and you know Broadway well enough. How shall one who has been a famous beauty, who comes of a fine family and has always had money of her own and fought shy of theatrical folk outside the theater, escape any variety of calumny? It has never been done. . . . I am no damn freshman in living . . . I have never made mistakes about the real true being inside people's defensive exteriors. So . . . be confident that I have found a rare and precious thing, a thing tested by time and much suffering."

Revising the past to make the present look inevitable, he painted his life with Agnes in darker colors than they had generally appeared to him at the time. He felt certain that DePolo had seen the marital split developing "long before there was a question of any third person. . . . You know, none better, what we have had to put up with in each other. . . . Speaking of my own end of it — while acknowledging that there is as much, if not more, for the other end in rebuttal! — as long as I could embark on a brain-drowning drunk once in a while, the things one can't forget didn't pile up on me to any unbearable extent. I swallowed them with old [John Barleycorn] for a chaser of memory. But when I reformed . . . it's too bad for the kids' sake. However, what can one do? There is nothing so disastrous for kids as a home poisoned by a thinly-concealed bitterness and hostility. . . . And Shane had begun to be extremely — secretively — sensitive to the undercurrents and was worried by them, I know. Without seeming to take much notice of him, I'm sure I know ten times more about what he's like inside than Agnes does — for he's very like me, God help him!"

A constant refrain in his letters to Agnes was: don't let the children forget me. To Shane he wrote, "Just now I have to stay over here on account of my plays, and I may have to go on to other countries, too, but the time won't be long passing for you and when we see each other again we'll have a grand time. . . ." Hounded by conscience, he told Agnes, "I miss him and Oona like hell at times. Don't sneer! I love them as much as you do — perhaps more — in my oblique, inexpressive fashion. At any rate, they will find out I have been a good father — (as Eugene did) — when they are old enough to understand all that has happened and when they really come to know me and about me."

It was a doubly sad period for eight-year-old Shane, because not only his father but Mrs. Clark, his devoted Gaga — one of the main pillars of his little world — had disappeared also. The previous fall Mrs. Clark, who suffered from a leg ailment that was aggravated by the moist, warm

Bermuda climate, had left the family's employ with the greatest reluctance and taken shelter with old friends in Provincetown. But, finding her separation from Shane intolerable, she became increasingly eager to return. Haunted by her own memories of the past, she walked one day, as she wrote Shane, "as far as Snail Road — you know, that's the road that went out to Peaked Hill Bars."

Although Agnes had written to her in Provincetown that she would "always have a home with us" and wanted her to rejoin them when they returned from Bermuda, the elderly woman became anxious when weeks passed without further word; she wrote O'Neill a frantic letter that "almost made [him] cry." He sent her a hundred dollars, but, as he said to Agnes, it "isn't money she needs. . . . Won't you do something about this? . . . I'll pay whatever added expense she costs you. You know I can't do anything for her. It's being near the children she loves in what for eight years has been her home." (When Agnes returned to the States, she again took in Mrs. Clark, but Shane had already suffered the fear that he would never see her again; he was learning at an early age about the instability of human relations and family life.)

Since the press was unable to locate O'Neill or to learn anything from Agnes, it could print only conjecture and rumors about the estranged pair. Vexed by certain stories, O'Neill complained to her in April that "the boys sniff so much dirt under this that they're beginning to improvise pretty impudently. One Coast paper had you going to divorce me 'it is rumored' for habitual drunkenness, because . . . another 'according to close friends of the couple' I could not 'keep my eyes off my leading ladies.' Laughable, eh — but irritating. And an Illinois one had it all scrambled — I was to divorce you — what for, not stated. A mad world!"

The two had shunned the press on Harry Weinberger's advice, but now O'Neill felt it was time for her to issue a brief statement that she was going to sue for a divorce because "we simply couldn't get along any longer" and that no "third party" was involved: "It's simply because we've been so secret," he wrote late in April, "that the story keeps hot and they keep pestering you and all my friends . . . why hide when there's nothing to hide, why keep the boys het up expecting scandal? The Sinclair Lewis case is much to the point. It was carried out with dignity and quiet in spite of the fact that it's well known he has been living with a woman [Dorothy Thompson, the journalist], in Berlin. . . . There's no news value to a simple divorce, without co-respondent, no matter how notorious the people. . . .

"Speaking of the Lewis case, I hope you read what she got — and you know damn well she bled him for every cent she could. . . . She got one-fourth of his net income up to forty-eight thousand but no more after that. She wasn't guaranteed anything per year. Quite a difference from what I'm offering you [six to ten thousand dollars annually, depending on his earnings]. . . . And his income per year for the past ten years has been at least three times mine."

Agnes returned to New York late in April, before receiving his latest letter, and denied that she planned to sue for a divorce. According to her story, published in the *World* on April 27, 1928, her husband was touring Europe with "friends" and she was shortly going to join them. As for printed reports linking him with Carlotta Monterey, Agnes said that so far as she knew, the actress was not in the traveling party. The *World* article reported at length the various rumors, touched on the marital histories of the three principals, and quoted Agnes as saying of Miss Monterey's role in *The Hairy Ape* that it was a "small one only."

Though he realized that Agnes had not heard from him in time, Eugene was irked by the interview, for he felt that "a simple divorce announcement would have . . . killed their hope for a scandal. As it is [this was written early in May] the mystery still remains to intrigue them – for they known damn well you're lying and they wonder what for.

"But don't think I'm blaming you. I realize how you've been hounded. I'm damn sorry, Agnes, to have brought you into all this! But what could I do? It was fate. But as soon as they know they're making all this fuss about just another Reno divorce . . . they'll leave us all alone. . . . It's on my mind continually and I find it hard to get any work done. So for all our sakes, let's get all this settled at the earliest possible moment."

He had previously informed her that he was temporarily in the Biarritz area but now he said that he had settled for a while near Prague, liked Czechoslovakia, and hoped "to get really down to work once this present mess of publicity clears away and you're on your way. However, if it keeps up much longer and you keep fighting for more money, there isn't much chance of any *Dynamo* for the Guild next year. . . . I can only concentrate on one thing at a time.

"And won't you be just too tickled to death to feel that you can – for the present, anyway – hurt my work! A grand revenge! But maybe I wrong you. If so, I apologize. [Here again is the *Long Day's Journey* pattern: the harsh word immediately followed by a mollifying one.] If we could talk together – our children's future, money agreements, etc. – everything would be all right and settled in half an hour, but as we can't, hence bitterness."

During their marriage finances had been a frequent subject of argument between them, for, somewhat like his father's lifelong fear of poverty, Eugene had never quite believed in his success; a side of him remained apprehensive about the future. Now, however, his circumstances were different; although still unaware that *Strange Interlude* would bring him a small fortune, he took comfort from Carlotta's financial independence. "Splitting fifty-fifty . . . as we are doing," he informed Macgowan, "our expenses, although we have done it pretty much de luxe, have been astonishingly inexpensive." Carlotta's annuity seems, indeed, to have been no small part of her attraction for him. As he became concerned that Agnes might balk at a divorce, he told Kenneth that he could "eventually starve her into it. It would, of course, entail sacrifices. I'd have to keep my plays to myself for a few years. . . . As far as finances go, I can hold out indefinitely. I've gathered a stake together over here, but quite outside of that Carlotta has enough income to keep us both in very decent comfort over here where living is cheap."

The playwright, who had started *Dynamo* during the voyage to England, resumed almost immediately once he was settled in Guéthary. Hoping to avoid "the grinding, thankless job of rewriting and cutting [he] had on *Interlude*," he proceeded more slowly this time in an effort to get the first draft "as near to final form as possible." In the first weeks he made good progress, even though his ideas and overall concept were still evolving. Although he feared that his marital "mess" might throw him off his "creative stride," by late April the drama was about half written.

From the Guild he had word that *Strange Interlude* was still playing after several months, to standees. "That," he replied to Theresa Helburn, "trends on fanaticism. . . . Myself, I wouldn't stand up for 4½ hours to see the original production of the Crucifixion!"

To whet the Guild directors' interest in his new work, he gave tantalizing glimpses of its subject matter and kept them posted on his progress. "The first part," he informed Miss Helburn, "derives from the method of simultaneous exterior and interior I used with such revealing effect (at least to me!) in *Desire Under the Elms*. The second part derives its method (use of sounds) remotely from *The Hairy Ape*. I use sounds very pronouncedly throughout the play as a definite dramatic motive. . . .

"As for the dialogue, it is Interludism. Thought will be as prominent as actual speech, probably, but there will be much less [of the] brief asides" since *Dynamo* dealt with "less cerebral people."

The play was certain, he predicted, "to stir up no end of controversy.

. . . It hits at what is the matter with us religiously speaking, with our Old Gods and our new sciences, from a psychological and symbolical angle that hasn't been touched before."

While occupied with *Dynamo* he received a script of De Casseres's latest work, for Ben wanted him to contribute a prefatory word. O'Neill found nondramatic writing so difficult that normally he said no to such requests from friends – he turned down even Macgowan and Jones when they collaborated on a book – and after his abortive attempt for Hart Crane he swore to himself that he would never make an exception. Yet he felt so strongly that De Casseres was one of the most underestimated writers in America that he promised to oblige the critic when his mind "was on an even keel once more."

"Just now," he replied on April 25, "it would be an impossible task for me mentally as I'm all shot to pieces over my gathering domestic troubles and the unceasing worry of ducking the hounding of the yellow press." Judging, however, by a letter to Macgowan two days later, he exaggerated about his mental state (probably because he wanted to continue with *Dynamo* instead of taking time for De Casseres's *Anathema!*), for he told Kenneth that he had "lots of new creative notions – the old bean is in the pink that way."

But he was not magnifying his fear that the press might track him down, something that would, in his words, "be fatal, under the circumstances, and play right into my wife's hands, to say nothing of the scandal which would injure the last person in the world I want to hurt. It's the lousiest situation," he lamented to De Casseres, "I was ever placed in – like being out in an open field with the enemy sniping at you and you can't run (for reasons connected with others). Not that I'm complaining. It's worth it and inside I'm deeply at peace and happy and confident of the future. But it's hell on the nerves and it keeps one's mind too worried and jumpy to be much good for work [he told Macgowan that *Dynamo* "has developed wonderfully . . . and is far deeper and richer than it was in scenario"]. . . . For the first few weeks here everything looked rosy but since then fresh alarms and complications . . . have been pounded at me in every mail. To use a ring expression, 'It's raining boxing gloves!' "

He warned De Casseres that the preface might be "a piece of clumsy writing. . . . I've tried several times to write Introductions to my own books . . . but although I fairly sweat blood over them, they never could be made to hang together. I wasted more labor on them than on half a play."

Influenced possibly by De Casseres's orotund style, which was at its grandiloquent worst in *Anathema!*, a kind of philosophical prose-poem that rambles on at numbing length and defies precise description, the foreword O'Neill eventually produced ranks among his emptiest pieces of writing. "An inebriate of sonorities," it says in part, De Casseres "chants disillusion and raises his panegyrics to the sky. He is swift, orgiastic and inexhaustible. He cries out his negations with a huge and resounding YES! He is that phenomenal ironist who does not want to be gentle, who, must be supremely contemptuous and fiercely assertive."

Besides using the Pall Mall bank as the address for most of his correspondence, O'Neill took other precautions to keep his whereabouts secret. He told the few to whom he confided the Guéthary address that they must not divulge it to "*anyone*" (he always underlined the word) and asked them to noise it about that they had heard from him in Prague or Vienna or "anywhere except in France." Also, exploiting the fact that Louis Kalonyme was now in Europe, he had the free-lance writer send him picture postcards from Germany, wrote messages on them, and returned them to Kalonyme to be mailed from that country. O'Neill felt that Kalonyme could be trusted since Agnes and he had never liked one another (Agnes used to think that Kalonyme fawned on her husband). Yet, for all his precautions, Eugene became so fearful that his "scent" was getting "hot," that he was about to be "smoked out," that he told De Casseres he had left Guéthary and asked both him and Macgowan to use the London address.

"A bit lonely" at times despite his deepening relationship with Carlotta (they were, he assured Macgowan, "more in love than ever"), he had Kalonyme visit him for a few days in May. The visit ended abruptly and disastrously, for O'Neill, in a nervous state about Agnes's intentions, weakened after being on the wagon for more than three years. Retiring with a bottle one night to Kalonyme's room, where they reminisced about his brother Jamie, Terry Carlin and old times, he and his guest proceeded to get drunk.

"I knew he was drinking behind that door," Carlotta recalls, "as I could hear Gene laughing out loud. I was heartsick and furious. The next morning I packed my bags, told a servant to tell Mr. O'Neill that I had left for Paris, and had myself driven to the railroad station. Then I began wondering what would happen to him — he was so helpless — and I was determined to make a go of it, so I turned around and went back."

Carlotta maintained a friendly facade toward Kalonyme, because she feared that otherwise he might talk about O'Neill's lapse and inspire rumors that the great romance was ebbing. "She used to write me,"

Kalonyme says, "about how Gene was coming along, and complain about Gene's friends — his 'false friends' she called them — writing him this and that about Agnes and keeping him steamed up instead of letting him forget her."

In his first letters to Kalonyme after the visit O'Neill repeatedly asked him to forget the drunken episode. He had grown overconfident about his self-control, he said, and now felt that he had "needed to take a good one on the chin and a long count to show me I have retired from the ring! So it may have been all for the best."

He was ill for two weeks, shortly after his fall from grace, with what he described as "a mild case of tonsillitis and flu in general exaggerated by a rundown condition due to nerves over the haggling uncertainty in my American domestic affairs. This domestic business [from a letter to Theresa Helburn on June 9] has had me in the air for over a year now and I'm beginning to develop cracks from the strain."

After his recovery, O'Neill, who had just bought a Renault, and Carlotta took a week's motor trip in mid-June along the Mediterranean, but he found the Côte d'Azur "very enervating" and "damned boring" compared to the Côte Basque. "I'm becoming quite a fan for the Basque country and its people," he told Miss Helburn, "and am getting to think . . . that it's here I may be destined to round out my days. I already have a deep feeling of home about it, even if my knowledge of French, let alone Basque! is worse than elementary [actually he could read French and when someone spoke slowly could understand it, though he could not speak it himself]. . . . But they say the Basques come from the same stock as the original Black Irish to which I obviously belong, so maybe that's it."

Finally verifying the rumors, Agnes, in an "exclusive" story published in the New York *News* on June 21, announced that she would sue for divorce in Reno or Mexico. Writing her statement in the presence of a reporter, she said in part: "We have decided to give legal form to the separation in our lives which has existed in fact for over two years. . . .

"I had attempted the experiment of giving an artist-husband the freedom he said was necessary for his dramatic success. Perhaps, from the standpoint of dramatic art and the American theater, my decision may be a success; matrimonially, it has already proved a failure. This illusion of freedom — so long maintained by the male sex, particularly by the artistic male — is very much an illusion. Now I know that the only way to give a man the freedom he wants is to open a door to captivity."

As the last words were being written, Agnes's mouth, the reporter noted, was "twisted into a sardonic smile."

The article said that "the wandering playwright" was rumored to be in Europe with Carlotta Monterey but added that Agnes, when asked if she would name another woman, replied, "No, there is no need of making Gene or anyone else uselessly unhappy."

Although the story gives the impression that the divorce was imminent, a year would elapse before Agnes filed suit. Including a photograph of O'Neill, Agnes and Shane in Bermuda, the article appeared under a two-line banner across the top of page three that read: WIFE WILL GRANT O'NEILL HIS 'ILLUSION OF FREEDOM.'

After the interview appeared, O'Neill never again wrote to Agnes, and in corresponding with their children he always referred to her as their mother, never by name.

In July he had a reunion with Saxe Commins, another whose life had changed radically. Besides getting married – to concert pianist Dorothy Berliner – Saxe, a bookish man who revered the written word, had given up his thriving dental practice to risk his future on a literary career. At college he had augmented his meager funds by "ghosting" term papers for his classmates; in Rochester, though busy with dentistry, he had managed to collaborate with a friend on *Psychology: A Simplification,* a survey of Freud, Jung et al. which was published in 1927 by Liveright; in time to come, as an editor, he would serve his religion with the total dedication of a priest. Whether he was editing the manuscripts of William Faulkner, Sinclair Lewis and O'Neill or helping the wavery flight of a fledgling, he gave everyone his best. In the hospital, dying, he meticulously went over the galleys of his final assignment; the day before his death he remembered a correction and telephoned Random House to have it inserted. "No writer who ever had him for an editor," said Murray Kempton, "would ever take another."

Saxe and Dorothy, both idealistic souls, were now in Paris for a year's stay, living off limited savings, to work at their respective careers. As soon as Eugene learned of their arrival he wrote urging his old friend to visit Guéthary and said that after much deliberation he was not inviting his wife too as her presence under "the circumstances . . . would give rise to an uncomfortable situation for all hands concerned." Agnes's lawyer, he charged, was trying "to blackmail me – legally, of course – out of so much as the price of a divorce that it would leave me in financial slavery for the rest of my life." *Dynamo,* he added, was about two-thirds written and he was "well satisfied with it." Like Macgowan,

De Casseres and others, Saxe was asked to spread the word that he had heard from O'Neill in Prague or some other place outside France.

On July 13, shortly before Saxe's visit, O'Neill wrote to Theresa Helburn that he was confident the Guild would accept *Dynamo* and that he was going to allow it to be produced without his presence because he was leaving in October for the Far East. He wondered whether she and Philip Moeller, who were vacationing separately on the Continent, could visit Guéthary or meet him in Paris at the end of August. He expected to have the play completed by then and wanted to discuss "certain very important ideas about the doing of it, and the sets."

He was concerned about getting the play typed, as he "hated to leave it out of my hands for a moment" and because of his domestic situation was unable "to let anyone come here whom I can't absolutely trust." The problem was solved by Commins, who volunteered to do the job himself and returned to Paris with the manuscript. Before long he not only was doing all the playwright's typing but spending considerable time carrying out various commissions for both O'Neill and Carlotta. The two would never have another friend so selfless and devoted, but in the end Saxe was to suffer deeply, because of Carlotta, from the relationship.

During his visit Carlotta, taking her cue from Eugene but expressing herself with characteristic vehemence, had fairly overwhelmed Saxe by treating him like one of her oldest, dearest intimates; and Saxe, eager to find her all his friend did, had been moved by her warmth toward him and impressed by her loving, solicitous care of O'Neill.

"Your more than kind letter reached me," she replied to Commins on August 9, "& I *blushed* when reading your undeserved praise. . . . I am busy now arranging all the Hong Kong business [the travel details]. Gene will have no thought of that. When we leave here in Sept. there will be no debts or strings. . . . I listen to tales of *debts, confusions,* & *indecisions* [an allusion to Agnes] & really I can't understand such half-wittedness! . . . Oh, well — someday there will be *peace* — & Gene & I will take each other by the hand & go out into the sunlight & forget the 'miasma' of the Past!"

Nothing about Carlotta endeared her more to O'Neill than her enthusiasm and anxious concern for his work. After it was arranged for a Monsieur Calmy to adapt *Strange Interlude* into French, Carlotta on August 16 wrote to Saxe: "I *do* hope he does a job of it — because I want my adored *Lazarus* translated. But the man who does *Lazarus* must not only know (in the *finer sense*) French & English — but he must be in his bones a poet! A real poet! I do now know this Calmy — perhaps he is all this!"

Gratified by Carlotta's attitude, O'Neill was also, in a way, fortunate that Agnes was balking at his alimony terms and keeping him in a kind of marital limbo; her intransigence (as he saw it) eased his burdened conscience by enabling him to feel, after he had deserted wife and children, the more injured party — a role he now began to play at every possible chance. Writing to Mike Gold, the playwright said: "I'm damned happy — in spite of . . . lying tittle-tattle in New York and much endeavor on that end to give me 'the works.' . . .

"One doesn't bust out of a rut without getting bruised a bit. . . . I'd become a writing Robot whose only living was in writing, since I'd given up life as a formula I had to be resigned to. This sort of stuff would have been as fatal to my writing as it was to living if I'd stuck in it many years longer."

When *Dynamo* was completed in mid-August, O'Neill, who generally suffered a letdown at such times, wondered (Carlotta told Saxe) "if it is *rotten* or *what not!* A perfectly healthy reaction at this stage for the Creator! I understand & soothe — ! This Lover of mine is also my child." Shortly afterward O'Neill, regaining his confidence, called the play "damn good."

Since he had been unable to arrange a meeting with Moeller and Miss Helburn, the playwright wrote out all he had wanted to say and on September 10 sent the Guild both his "dissertation" and the play. His paper dealt with various aspects of the envisioned production — casting, lighting, the sets — but dwelled largely on the sound effects. From the start of his career he had used background sounds as an important element in his plays: the oppressive silence (which has the value of a sound) and the mulatto's somber crooning in *Thirst;* the mournful foghorn as Yank lies dying in *Bound East for Cardiff;* the foghorn again in *Anna Christie,* lending ominous emphasis to old Chris's fear of the sea; the changing tenor of the street noises in *All God's Chillun;* and, most effectively, the pounding, pulse-quickening tom-toms in *The Emperor Jones.*

With his new play he was particularly concerned about a thunderstorm in the first act and the dynamo in the third. These were not, he said, "incidental noises but significant dramatic overtones that are an integral part [of] the whole play." He wanted "thunder with a menacing brooding quality as if some Electrical God were on the hills impelling all these people, affecting their thoughts and actions. The queer noise of a generator, which is unlike any other mechanical noise, its merging with, and contrast with, the peaceful soft Nature sound of the water flowing over the nearby dam also needs some doing.

"Bobby Jones once said that the difference between my plays and other contemporary work was that I always wrote primarily by ear for the ear, that most of my plays, even down to the rhythm of the dialogue, had the definite structural quality of a musical composition. This hits the nail on the head. It is not that I consciously strive after this but that, willy nilly, my stuff takes that form. (Whether this is a transgression or not is a matter of opinion. Certainly I believe it to be a great virtue, *although it is the principal reason why I have been blamed for useless repetitions* [italicized for editorial emphasis], which to me were significant recurrences of theme.)"

Once *Dynamo* was completed, the author disclosed that it was part of a projected trilogy. The other two plays, which he had "all mapped out," were to be called "Without Ending of Days" and "It Cannot Be Mad," and he thought of giving the trilogy the general title of "God Is Dead! Long Live — What?" The three were to illustrate his feeling, he told De Casseres, that any "answer" science could give to the hungry religious impulse would be "like feeding a puppy biscuit to a lion."

The envisioned trilogy was an old project of his. As early as 1922 an interviewer, after describing the playwright's more immediate projects, reported that "a trilogy analyzing and interpreting our materialistic civilization is still dimly in the back of his mind."

In a letter to George Jean Nathan that amplified on his remarks to De Casseres, O'Neill said on August 26, 1928, that *Dynamo* was "a symbolical and factual biography of what is happening in a large section of American (and not only American) soul right now . . . [the trilogy] will dig at the roots of the sickness of Today as I feel it — the death of the old God and the failure of Science and Materialism to give any satisfying new One for the surviving primitive religious instinct to find a meaning for life in, and to comfort its fears of death with. It seems to me anyone trying to do big work nowadays must have this big subject behind all the little subjects of his plays or novels, or he is simply scribbling around on the surface of things and has no more real status than a parlor entertainer."

According to O'Neill, he got his idea for the new play, which tells of a man who deifies the dynamo, from visiting a power plant near Ridgefield whose generators reminded him of the stone idols of antiquity. It appears likely, however, that the seed of the play came from *The Education of Henry Adams* ("a grand book," he once said), which he read well before he moved to Ridgefield. In his autobiography Adams, recalling his sense of awe in the Gallery of Machines at the St. Louis Exposition of 1900, said that the dynamo became to him "a symbol of infinity . . . he began to feel the forty-foot dynamos as a moral force, much as the early Christians felt the Cross . . . one began to pray to [the dynamo]; inherited instinct taught the natural expression of man before silent and infinite force. Among the thousand symbols of ultimate energy, the dynamo was not so human as some, but it was the most expressive."

Years before O'Neill ever read Adams there were indications that he found machinery strange and fascinating. In a 1912 poem about being at sea he said: "And the engines croon in a drowsy tune / And the world is mystery!" The only interesting character in "The Personal Equation," his full-length play for Professor Baker's course, was a ship's engineer, painfully shy, who was deeply attached to the machines under his care; to him they seemed almost human. After reading Adams, O'Neill's feeling in the matter became more mystical, as witness his portrait of Yank in *The Hairy Ape;* in his crude, violent fashion Yank worships power, energy, force, and imagines that he "belongs" because he is "part of de engines" that drive the great ship; his attitude, in short, is essentially religious.

For all the difference between their personalities, Reuben Light of *Dynamo* and Yank have an important common bond: both hold disastrous views of themselves in relation to the Machine. Reuben is the timid son of a bigoted minister, whom he fears, and a possessive mother, to whom he is excessively attached. Their near-oedipal relationship does not prevent him, however, from being in love, secretly, with the girl next door, an atheist's daughter. After falling into a trap set by the atheist, Reuben is outraged when his mother betrays him to his father. As the lightning flashes and the thunder rumbles — both Light males fear electrical storms (as did O'Neill) — Reuben somehow finds the spirit to defy his father, reject his mother, and forswear his religion. (James O'Neill, while deploring his sentiments, would have appreciated the theatricality of the scene.) Marching off as into battle, the boy declares: "There is no God! No God but Electricity! I'll never be scared again!"

A year or so later the boy returns a man with eyes "like lumps of ice with fire inside them," a fanatic who worships the dynamo. All life, he says, "comes down to electricity in the end." In renouncing his father's Calvinist dogma, he has merely become a zealot of another kind. Momentarily shaken on learning that during his absence his mother had died, he finds consolation in identifying her with the dynamo of a nearby power plant that is "huge and black, with something of a massive female idol about it," like "a great, dark mother! Listen to her singing . . . the hymn

[307]

of electricity . . . if you could only get back into that . . . know what it means . . . then you'd know the real God!" Kneeling, he prays before the generator: "Oh, Mother of Life, my mother is dead, she has passed back into you, tell her to forgive me, and to help me find your truth!"

As in other O'Neill plays, the new one embodied his ambivalence toward women, but this time the strain of hostility was intensified by his bitterness over Agnes. Of the three women in *Dynamo*, only one emerges alive — the atheist's wife, a dreamy, bovine kind of Earth Mother who moons sympathetically over Reuben no matter what he does. Originally he had been too shy to touch Ada, the atheist's daughter, but the transformed Reuben regards love as "just sex" and takes his pleasure of her. Shortly, however, since his mother had hated Ada and the dynamo now looms to him as a mother-figure, he renounces the flesh. Toward the end of the play, as developments crowd one another, Reuben in a moment of weakness couples with Ada before the dynamo and immediately afterward, to punish his temptress, shoots her; then, expiating his guilt — not for the slaying but for profaning the "temple" with carnal intercourse — he immolates himself by embracing the dynamo (a fate that recalls Yank's death from embracing the gorilla, another "great, dark" figure).

Clearly, *Dynamo* was, as its author said, "intensely dramatic." It also, unfortunately, was tortuous in its thought, confused in its symbolism, obviously contrived in its storytelling. It is one thing for Henry Adams to caress our imagination with a parallel between a towering dynamo and the Cross, another for O'Neill to show a half-crazed fanatic praying to a piece of machinery in language without the grace of true prayer. What Adams touched on lightly, evocatively, O'Neill dramatized with hammer blows through schematic, unconvincing characters.

Still, though among the author's poorest works, *Dynamo* could have been written only by a playwright of original talent, and, regardless of excesses and absurdities, a current of true fervor and anguish runs through practically every scene. When *Dynamo* was produced, Stark Young said that it "may be concerned at times with profound and eternal human problems and at others with what is adolescent, trite and over-familiar; but . . . the feeling behind everything is close and genuine and personal. It arises from the author's own turmoil and emotional necessity . . . we are stabbed to our depths by the importance of this feeling to him, and we are all his, not because of what he says but because saying it meant so much to him . . . as a personal document, [*Dynamo*] is significant."

This is acute commentary; without knowing the tragic facts of

O'Neill's family history, facts that would remain secret till *Long Day's Journey Into Night* became public, Stark Young sensed that the power of the play, as in so much of the author's work, was of biographical origin. Reuben's violent response to his mother's treachery reflects, in exaggerated degree, O'Neill's feeling of betrayal when he learned that his mother became a drug addict as a result of his birth. "God," he says through Edmund in *Long Day's Journey*, "it made everything in life seem rotten!" Reverend Light blames Reuben for his mother's death because she "gave up wanting to live" after his disappearance; similarly, O'Neill used to feel that the rest of his family, in the depths of their souls, blamed him for Ella's death-in-life as an addict. Finally, both in reality and in fiction the sons renounce their parents' religion after losing faith in their mother. To a limited extent, then, *Dynamo*, for all its concern with the Machine, was apprentice work for *Long Day's Journey*.

Shortly after it was completed O'Neill and Carlotta spent a week in Paris, where they saw a good deal of Saxe and Dorothy Commins. This was Dorothy's introduction to the actress, who was most charming and gracious toward her, but she and the playwright had met a few years earlier in New York at the home of Edmond T. Quinn, the sculptor. Dorothy, who lived in Westchester at the time but had a room at the Quinns' for her stays in town, was practicing one day for a Town Hall recital when Quinn, followed by O'Neill, tapped on her door and said, "Here's someone who wants to meet you."

In reply to O'Neill's question, Miss Berliner said she had been playing Bach's "Passacaglia and Fugue," and at his request performed it again. "Thank you, it's magnificent," he said, as the strong, noble chords ended. After appraising Dorothy — an ethereal-looking blond with pale blue eyes — he said wonderingly, "Where did you get the strength to play such a piece?" Momentarily stumped, she suddenly had an idea and touched her forehead. "Perhaps from up here," at which he nodded thoughtfully, "I guess you're right." Later, when he heard that Saxe had married Dorothy, one of the first things he said to him was: "Don't let her quit the piano."

During the Paris visit O'Neill hired an automobile and the two couples made a pilgrimage to Chartres on a misty day that both softened and deepened the colors in the celebrated stained glass windows. The others rhapsodized over the majestic beauty of the old cathedral but O'Neill, while appearing impressed, scarcely broke his silence. Dorothy, who was struck by the fact that all the statuary was of men, thought that one figure looked like a prophet from the Old Testament. "That reminds me," she said, "that one of the Jewish prayers for men is 'Thank God I wasn't born a woman.'" O'Neill suddenly smiled, "As far back as that!"

Earlier this year, while working on *Dynamo*, the playwright had informed Macgowan that "the grand opus of my life — the autobiographical 'Sea-Mother's Son' — has been much in my dreams of late. [Apparently he had talked about it to Kenneth before he left the States, for this is the first mention of the autobiographical project in his correspondence.] If I can write that up to what the dreams call for, it will make a work that I flatter myself will be one of those timeless Big Things."

"Sea-Mother's Son" never materialized, yet it provides evidence, together with *Strange Interlude* and the "God Is Dead" trilogy scheme, that O'Neill's ambition and drive were impelling him to literary giantism. The "grand opus," he told Nathan on August 26, would be "neither play nor novel, although there will be many plays in it and it will have greater scope than any novel I know of." Expressing himself still more extravagantly to De Casseres, he said on September 16 that it "will have scope enough to contain all of life I have the guts to grasp and make my own . . . compared to it *Interlude* ought to seem like a brief and paltry thing. It will have ten or more *Interludes* in it, each deeper and more powerful than 'S.I.,' and yet will all be a unit. Believe me, Ben, I'm going to bull's-eye a star with that job or go mad in the attempt."

Once hopeful of reaching an agreement with Agnes before he sailed for the Orient, O'Neill felt particularly aggrieved as he and Carlotta prepared for their journey. "I've been pestered to death lately," he complained on September 21 to Macgowan, "on the domestic wrangle — cables from Harry [Weinberger] every few days to answer. All sorts of decisions to make — with the only result, so far, that the miserable affair remains deadlocked. . . . It's bad on my nerves — and upsets Carlotta. But, believe me, Kenneth, once I'm free of that baby I'm going to arrange my life and affairs so I'll make her pay for this.

"Outside of the above, life is happy. That sounds like a joke but isn't. What I mean is that, while I'm worried and enraged by this, it doesn't touch me inside and I'm not hurt by it . . . she's too dead and I've too much real love inside me to protect me."

Despite his anger over his marital impasse, he occasionally felt "grateful" to it for "making it impossible for me to return to N.Y., for otherwise my author's conscience would force me to come back for rehearsals." Starting in childhood, when he used to dream over Kipling's jungle books, he had long yearned to see India and the Far East; it was "the dream of my life to live there for a while and absorb" some of the atmosphere. Feeling that such an experience would be "infinitely valuable to my future work," O'Neill expected to be away from Europe about nine months, intending to settle somewhere with Carlotta in the Orient or possibly in South Africa for a time while he worked on his next play. They were to sail early in October for Hong Kong, but the rest of their itinerary was tentative. "Enough of the old Gene O'Neill has been reborn in me," he said, "to put me in the mood — for to admire and for to see the world I've missed." . . . "I feel ten years younger — and I'm off adventuring again!"

Though he and Agnes no longer corresponded, she forwarded the children's letters and he, trying to soften the effect of his absence, replied in the most affectionate terms. But while working on *Dynamo*, he let months slip by without a word to them. In a letter Agnes wrote but never mailed, she said: "Tonight after [Oona] got to bed I said I was going to take her down to N.Y. and she immediately said, 'Can I take my trunk so I can show my toys to Daddy?' I said you weren't in N.Y. 'Where is he?' In Europe. 'Is he coming back? . . . I want him, Mummie.' (This is literal.) I said, 'he will come back, dear, & see you. Daddy loves you.' Then she said, 'Will he come back & live with us, Mummie,' and *then she began to cry.* It almost broke my heart. I think it is the most peculiar thing I have ever heard of, for a child of three to remember like that. . . . She recognizes newspaper pictures of you immediately —

". . . Why don't you write her, anyway. You don't see her. Or, perhaps, it would be kinder all around for her to be allowed to forget."

Finally breaking his silence, he asked Oona what language her letters were written in. "It looks to me a bit like Egyptian! I would love to see you again because I miss you very much."

Shane had written about Gaga taking him to the aquarium, the zoo, and the Museum of Natural History, and O'Neill, a man forever resifting the past, was reminded of his own childhood. In one of his rare references to Sarah Sandy, he said that he "used to have a nurse like Gaga when I was a boy and after I went to boarding school I used to visit her every vacation when my Mother wasn't in New York and she used to take me to every one of those places."

His letter to Shane amounted to a second farewell. "I'm sorry," he continued, "but I won't be able to come back soon, although I miss you and Oona an awful lot and think of you all the time. I've got to go on a long voyage on a ship about some plays I'd like to write." He enclosed a check for his son's ninth birthday, since he would be traveling at the time, and added, "But no matter how far off I am you'll know I'm thinking of you all that day [October 30] and maybe one of my thoughts will fly through the air and you'll hear it and think of me. Let me know if you do." This was not said lightly, for O'Neill believed in certain psychic phenomena, including mental telepathy. In *Dynamo,* for instance, he was writing from personal feeling, not merely resorting to expedient dramaturgy, when he has Reuben Light suddenly decide to return home as his mother is dying. " . . . it was about then," Reuben later reflects, "I first felt that hunch to come home and see her . . . that's damn queer."

In spite of O'Neill's early belief that the Guild was practically certain to produce *Dynamo,* he began to feel less confident once he had mailed the script, since it was "a drastic type of play and you never can predict what reactions you're going to get from a committee of six people." He had told the Guild that he hoped for its decision before he sailed, and was worried as he and Carlotta boarded the S.S. *André-Lebon* in Marseilles on October 5 that he had had no word as yet. In his cabin, though, was a cable that the play had been accepted.

"I had worried so long & was so *at end,*" Carlotta wrote to Saxe, "I wept like a fool & could have died! But it was a divine send off & Gene is resting & relaxing & is his dear *un*-worried self! — God — what a lovely soul that lover of mine has — what a fortunate woman I am! — And God knows I appreciate him & only pray . . . I'll be able to make him happy & give him Peace!"

16

Third Marriage

THE first leg of the voyage was uneventful. O'Neill, who marked his fortieth birthday (October 16, 1928) while sailing through the Red Sea, paid little attention to the other passengers, nearly all French, "a poor uninteresting crowd, petty officials off to their jobs, very depressing to look upon in the tropic heat." After days at sea, with a brief stop only at Djibouti in French Somaliland, the ship anchored for a time at Colombo, Ceylon, where Eugene "got away with swimming in the noon sun"; but at Singapore, farther south, he suffered a sunstroke from indulging in his favorite sport and became "pretty sick and whoozy." Saigon, the next stop, impressed him as the most interesting of their ports of call.

In Saigon, an old Asian hand has written, "everything happens that should happen in the quote mysterious Orient unquote. You can smoke opium, eat lichees and bears' paws (once the food of the starving, now a millionaires' delicacy), buy an exquisitely beautiful wife for $30, gamble with a fury unknown in America. You can visit the 'little flowers' whose whole life, from the day they are sold by their parents, is dedicated to the best, and more often, the worst in man." To his own surprise and Carlotta's alarm, Eugene succumbed to the endemic gambling fever when a Frenchman introduced him to a luxurious casino; he "bucked the wheel — and the game suddenly got" him. In writing about it to Harold De-Polo, he recalled his brother's passion for playing the horses: "I must have that Jim strain in me after all. I went ga-ga — without benefit of a drop of booze, either. Well, I'll slide over the horrid details. Suffice it I lost one hell of a pile. . . . Can you beat it? Me!"

Carlotta, who had remonstrated with him at Singapore for swimming under unhealthy conditions ("I begged him not to go in"), aroused his anger when she upbraided him for gambling. After a heated exchange, he returned to the casino and the roulette wheel, to let her know, he declared, that she was not going to rule his life. "He was the most stubborn man," she used to say, "I've ever known."

Before they left Saigon he came down with the flu, prevalent there at the time, and inadvertently passed it on to Carlotta. Fortunately, she had brought along on the trip a nurse named Tuwe Drew to serve as her personal maid, and Mrs. Drew, a hefty blond Swede, took care of the stricken pair aboard ship. Worn down by illness and the heat, they hoped for a more invigorating climate at Hong Kong, scheduled as the first stop in their travels, but they found it "damp and enervating" and continued on to Shanghai, where they quit the *André-Lebon* and checked into the Palace Hotel.

While the two were out walking one day O'Neill was spotted by Alfred Batson, a young Canadian he had known in Greenwich Village who was now working for the *North-China Herald*. "Do me a favor," O'Neill said as soon as he learned of the other's job, "just keep me out of the paper." After months of being sequestered with Carlotta, he was hungry for male companionship and spent some time with Batson, who had volunteered to show him sights the tourists never heard of.

"The place that interested Gene most," Batson recalls, "was the crime museum at police headquarters, a room full of murder weapons, mementoes of outstanding crimes, torture devices, and so forth. One of them, used by Chinese bandits, was part of a wall with a hole in it. The bandits used to fasten a man, with his bare stomach exposed, up against one side of the hole, and on the other side a small cage with a rat in it. Then they'd poke burning sticks at the rat, and there was only one way for him to go — toward the man's stomach. Gene was fascinated by it. The wall had the dry crusted blood of what must've been hundreds of people. Another device was called 'Death of a Thousand Cuts.' The bandits would double-track wire all over a person's body, bunching the flesh, and then slice off the skin — the one thousand cuts."

Shanghai found O'Neill in a restless, uneasy state. His relations with Carlotta had been strained since Saigon; the Orient of reality was not living up to his romantic expectations; and, underneath all, no amount of rationalizing could prevent his conscience from troubling him about Agnes and the children. For all his recent rejoicing that he was "reborn" and at last "belonged," he now felt alone again, thrown back to his old self. On a slip of gold paper used as a bookmark, he copied a passage from *Thus Spake Zarathustra* that begins:

"I am a wanderer and mountain-climber, said he to his heart. I love not the plains, and it seemeth I cannot long sit still.

"And whatever may still overtake me as fate and experience — a wandering will be therein, and a mountain-climbing: in the end one experienceth only oneself."

Had he been writing, he might have worked himself into an equable mood; as it was, the tension and dark stresses in his nature were building up to an explosive degree. He struggled with himself for a while but finally, resorting to his old anodyne, began drinking again, before he had fully recovered from his siege of the flu.

The first time he returned drunk from a night on the town with Batson, Carlotta, who had separate quarters at the Palace, was waiting in his room. "What're you doing," he demanded, "spying on me?" She protested that she had turned "sick with worry" when the hour grew late, but their exchanges escalated in bitterness when he brushed aside her attempt to mollify him. Suddenly, swinging with his whole body, as his eyes flashed, he slapped her so hard she almost fell over. "I'm not going to have an old whore," he declared, "telling me what to do!" With an effort at dignity, he stalked from the room. Carlotta returned to her suite, packed her belongings, told the hotel people not to let Mr. O'Neill know where she had gone, and moved with Mrs. Drew to the Astor House.

O'Neill was hitting the bottle again when Batson, after a telephone call from him, dropped by the Palace the next morning. In a meandering account of the quarrel, O'Neill said, "I took a poke at Carlotta, and she's gone. She's going home, I guess, but I don't gave a damn." The reporter, who had to leave for work, agreed to meet him again that evening.

After pausing en route at several bars the two, since O'Neill wanted to see some Chinese girls, ended at the St. George Dance Hall, one of the town's few late-hour spots — like most cities in the British colonies, practically all Shanghai was asleep by nine o'clock ("The dear Britons," Eugene said, "certainly put a curse of dullness on everything they touch"). The St. George, run by an American named Jimmy St. James, attracted tourists off cruise ships, commercial travelers, and sailors. Though half drunk when he arrived, O'Neill was sufficiently interested in his surroundings to size up the place, a large hall with tables surrounding the dance floor and along the walls Chinese hostesses sitting patiently. As he and Batson sipped champagne, O'Neill dwelled on the shy charm and beauty of the taxi dancers, praising them over their counterparts back in the States. It was a dull night and O'Neill, feeling sorry for the girls marooned against the walls, ordered a bottle of champagne for each, despite Batson's warning that he would be "tagged 'Mr. Moneybags' and taken in Shanghai."

His sympathy was aroused again in the men's toilet at the sight of the attendant, a sturdy peasant with a gold ring in one ear. "Why do you do this kind of work?" O'Neill asked, but the other, unable to understand English, merely grunted. "Good for you!" O'Neill cried. "To hell with the capitalists!" He pulled out a wad of money — to Batson it looked like a thousand or so in American and British bills — and handed it all to the attendant. Batson grabbed it back, tipped the man a dollar, and urged his companion to "take it easy."

Hours later the playwright and the reporter, both well liquored, made their way out of the dance hall, but at the curb O'Neill crumpled down and, starting to weep, said, "Did I ever tell you what a son of a bitch I've been to Agnes? No, well it's true and I'll tell y'all about it." Reveling in guilt, rather like the times his brother used to face a mirror and call himself the worst names he could think of, Eugene rambled through a catalogue of mea culpas, in describing his treatment of Agnes, the children and Carlotta. The two on the curb soon drew an audience — Sikh officers, dignified bearded figures in turbans from the Bubbling Well police station opposite the dance hall, who nudged one another and roared with laughter at the sight of these members of the Master Race making drunken fools of themselves.

O'Neill's recitation ended abruptly with his turning sick and starting to vomit; by the time his companion got him back to the Palace, he was trembling all over. Dr. Alexander Renner, the house physician, soon appeared, followed closely by his wife, who asked Batson, "Is this Eugene O'Neill the playwright? It is, well, I've written a play and want to read it to him. I'll be right back." While Dr. Renner attended to the patient on one side of the bed, his wife sat on the other and began reading, ever so often interrupting herself to ask, "Are you following me?" "But Gene," Batson recalls, "was trying to ignore a needle the doctor was giving him, trying to ignore her, and all this time his eyes were rolling desperately at heaven."

At the doctor's insistence, O'Neill, who initially demurred, was removed to the English-run Country Hospital on Great Western Road. According to Batson it was in a fairly quiet neighborhood, but Eugene later said he would "never forget my experience in the hospital . . . teetering on the verge of a nervous breakdown and lying awake nights listening to the night-target practice of a Welsh regiment whose garrison was two blocks away, and to the beating of Chinese gongs keeping the devils away from a birth or a bride or a corpse or something devils like. It nearly had me climbing the walls of my room and gibbering a bit."

While remaining out of sight, Carlotta kept O'Neill under surveillance the entire time, at first through informants at the Palace Hotel, now through others at the hospital, all of whom she tipped generously. In a world she distrusted and, for all her imperious air, feared, Carlotta constantly sought not merely friends but allies as part of her line of defense. Some she recruited, particularly among her social inferiors, with money, others, such as Saxe Commins, by overwhelming them with maternal solicitude and the most ardent friendliness. O'Neill had scarcely begun his stay at the hospital – he was there about ten days – when Carlotta made allies of the Renners, both of them emotional, warmhearted Austrians whose sympathies were easily engaged by the beautiful, maltreated actress.

Therez Renner, a lovely blond with aristocratic features, was particularly affected. "Carlotta turned to me," she remembers, "like a heaven-sent friend. She showered me with compliments, gratitude, little attentions [the "attentions" included fine gifts], she couldn't make enough of me. In almost no time we were like sisters, devoted sisters. We went shopping every day – I showed her the best places to get things – and she used to pour out her complaints about O'Neill. I was greatly impressed by her. The only thing I didn't like was that she treated the nurse, Mrs. Drew, like an inferior, a servant. My parents, back in Austria, had servants and we knew how to treat them."

Once O'Neill landed in the hospital, his surge of hostility toward Carlotta subsided, and on learning that she and Dr. Renner were in touch, he began pleading through the doctor for a reconciliation. After she had left him dangling in suspense for several days, the two had an ardent reunion at the hospital. In a note dispatched to her immediately afterward he said: "And God bless you! . . . I love you – always and forever! Forgive me! I'll be a good 'un in future – do my damndest best to! A million kisses, Blessed!"

Alfred Batson respected O'Neill's desire for anonymity as long as he safely could, but the playwright's hospitalization and his move subsequently to the Astor House, Carlotta's hotel, meant that more and more people knew of his presence in Shanghai. To avoid being scooped by the competition, Batson wrote a short piece for his newspaper which told of O'Neill's arrival and said that he was recovering from a recent illness. "While in Shanghai," it added, "he is anxious to live quietly and to regain his health."

Had the seclusive playwright been less worried about the press, he would have been merely minor news for a day or two, but his very efforts to forestall publicity were about to inspire page-one stories around the globe. On December 9, 1928, following the Batson account, the Associated Press correspondent in Shanghai reported, in a brief item that was widely printed in the States, that O'Neill "is confined to his bed here, but his recovery is expected within a week. His physician, Alexander Renner, said today that the playwright was suffering from a slight nervous breakdown and bronchitis as a result of overwork and the strain of travel."

After an exchange of cables with Eugene, Harry Weinberger, who had been alarmed by the report, minimized his client's illness in a statement to the press. By this time the matter was finished so far as the papers were concerned, but several days later O'Neill became front-page news when he dropped out of sight after writing Dr. Renner a rather dramatic letter. As one American paper headlined the December 13 AP dispatch from Shanghai, which quoted at length from the letter: EUGENE O'NEILL DISAPPEARS TO SEEK PEACE AND SOLITUDE AT SOUTH POLE IF NECESSARY.

O'Neill had told Dr. Renner that because of the many persons inquiring into his private affairs and trying to interview him, he felt that he could not work in Shanghai "even if well physically." He added that he had come "to China seeking peace and quiet and hoping that here . . . people would mind their own business and allow me to mind mine. But I have found more snoops and gossips per square inch than there is in any New England town of 1,000 inhabitants. This does not apply to American newspaper correspondents, who have been most decent, carrying out their duties in a most gentlemanly manner.

"I am going to Honolulu and then, perhaps, to Tahiti, if Honolulu adopts the same attitude as Shanghai, that I am a politician whose life must be public. At any rate, I will find peace and solitude to work in if I have to go to the South Pole.

"My bronchitis cough is gone, my nerves are returning to normal, and I expect to be in the pink of condition in the shortest time."

"The letter indicated," the AP dispatch continues, "that the playwright was leaving Shanghai the same day that it had been written [December 11], although no steamers had been scheduled to sail for Honolulu on that date. It is possible, however, that he might have boarded an obscure Japanese steamer for Japan, where he could catch a trans-Pacific liner." But there was also speculation, the story said, that the playwright had simply shifted from the Astor House to a hideout in Shanghai, since all the steamship lines "operating toward either Japan or Honolulu stated that no person answering his description had either sailed recently or made arrangements for transportation."

The mystery of his disappearance was cleared up when the German liner *Coblenz* arrived in Manila on December 18 with a "Reverend William O'Brien" listed among its passengers, actually O'Neill, who admitted his identity when confronted by a reporter bearing a photograph of the playwright. But still trying to mislead the press, he said he was en route to Italy, where he would finish a movie scenario at Rapallo. Carlotta, who had locked herself in her stateroom, said later that she could hear the newsmen "scurrying about and telling one another, 'She must be somewhere around here.' "

After a night aboard ship rendered sleepless by the heat and the rattle of winches unloading cargo, O'Neill looked haggard in the morning. Alarmed by his appearance, foreign correspondent Walter Robb thought that he "had been hit harder by the Orient" than he realized and that "it may yet prove to have been fatal for O'Neill to have gone on to Shanghai so soon" after his flu attack in Saigon. "But I hope," Robb wrote to H. L. Mencken on December 20, "this letter will be antiquated when it reaches you. When I saw O'Neill, his vision was dull and wandering, his attention sluggish, his mind worked only by the most obvious effort of his will. He was gracious to everyone, but he was physically *shot*."

Unlike the hare-and-hound situation in Shanghai, O'Neill cooperated with the Philippine reporters, chiefly so that they would not question him about rumors of a woman traveling with him. After a brief sight-seeing tour he told the Manila *Tribune* that the city offered "a good background for a drama. The Walled City, with its ancient churches, its towers, its narrow streets, all of it seems steeped in history and tradition. . . . But I dare not touch such a wealth of material. I cannot hope to understand it, no, not for a long time. I must tarry here for months, perhaps years. I must live it before I can write it."

When the *Coblenz* touched at Singapore on December 24, O'Neill, who had earlier had an anxious cable from Lawrence Langner, cabled back: "Feel well now. Much idiotic publicity Shanghai, Manila. My discovery, disappearance, kidnapped, bandits, death, etc. Merry Christmas to all."

In reality he was not well, and there was discord again between him and Carlotta, for he had resumed drinking. On the *Coblenz* he became friendly with F. Theo Rogers, an American newspaper executive in Manila, whose cabin, in Rogers's words, "provided a refuge where

Eugene was safe from Carlotta's nagging. He was one of the gentlest persons I've ever met, while she was the domineering sort, possessive, and wanted him all to herself. The strange thing about him, since he was so quiet and retiring, was his association with the underworld. He told me many stories about bootleggers and racketeers he'd known. Yes, he drank quite a bit, he was a brandy drinker, though I warned him that brandy was poison in the tropics."

Although Carlotta, as an acquaintance of hers said, "would hold on to the death to whatever she wanted," relations between her and Eugene became so acrimonious that she lost all heart. Without a word to him of her intention, she left the *Coblenz* at Colombo, Ceylon, on January 1, 1929, the bleakest New Year's Day she had ever known; but she took the precaution of having Mrs. Drew continue on the voyage. "I went to a hotel overlooking the bay," Carlotta has recalled, "and sat on the balcony watching the boat moving further and further away, until it was out of sight. I felt awful. 'My God,' I said to myself, 'what am I doing here?' I felt as though I'd let go of something I should've clung to. I asked the desk clerk about the American Embassy, and he said that if you want anything done quickly, go to the British Embassy (that's true throughout the East — or used to be). Well, I went to the British Embassy, and because of the holiday the head man was gone, but there was his assistant, a lamb of God, God bless him! I showed him my traveler's checks and said, 'I have jewels.' I told him I wanted to get on the next boat out. He said there's one tomorrow, and he got me on it."

It was the *President Monroe* of the American President Lines on a westering voyage around the world that had begun in San Francisco. "Away and afar," says the cruise brochure, "o'er the sparkling, sunlit seas to the lands of Romance and Adventure . . . and then that personal contact with civilizations and people throughout the world which gives you a keener, finer, more vivid understanding of life and happiness. . . ."

As soon as Carlotta was settled on the liner she wired Mrs. Drew of her whereabouts, directing her to keep it secret from O'Neill, and asked about his condition. After exchanging radiograms with the nurse for a few days and learning that O'Neill, in despair over her disappearance, threatened to drink himself to death, she began communicating with him. He was beside himself with relief and joy at hearing from her, as his replies made clear, and before long they were in constant, loving communication.

Carlotta shortly became curious about the person handling the ardent messages and, according to George H. Wiley, chief radio operator of the ship, called at the radio cabin to introduce herself. Finding him a good listener, she dropped by often. In his diary of the voyage Wiley wrote that she was "nicknamed 'Queen Mary' by the crew . . . because of her aloof manner and her criticisms. While sitting in the radio room, she told me of her former marriages, of Mr. O'Neill's charm and his great genius, and inquired if I had ever been in love. At first I was a bit surprised and, taking it as a joke, I told her that I had often been in love. Miss Monterey became somewhat indignant and explained that she meant REALLY IN LOVE. Of course I said 'no.' It is very interesting," the radio man drily concludes, "to converse with persons of wide and varied experience."

Amplifying on his diary entries, Wiley wrote later: "Carlotta's criticisms were quite general in scope; an openly expressed, arbitrary and unfavorable comparison of persons, things and ways where she presently found herself, as compared with her past, more satisfactory surroundings. In regard to Mr. O'Neill, she seemed to blame his troubles [his drinking] upon the company with which he was surrounded, and was particularly bitter in her attitude toward his friends of the press. There is no doubt in my mind that she loved and admired him deeply.

"She talked about her daughter, who was at a boarding school in California, and said she had tried to implant in the girl's mind the importance of being real. She went on about having told her daughter that she could forgive any mistakes or situations just as long as they resulted from deliberate and considered action, but that she would have no mercy if the situation were the result of stupidity, indolence or carelessness. In telling me this, Carlotta used somewhat stronger language."

As the *Coblenz* and the *President Monroe*, separated by no great distance, steamed across the Arabian Sea and approached the Red Sea, Eugene and Carlotta became excited at the possibility of their ships arriving at Port Said about the same time, thus allowing him to transfer to her vessel. They communicated so often that, Wiley estimates, her bill for radiograms (at sixteen cents a word) came to about one hundred and fifty dollars and O'Neill's nearly as high.

"It was ludicrous," Carlotta has said. "The wireless operators knew all about us, the people on the boat heard about it, and the suspense began to develop — could the two ships meet? And this went on for days. Well, we got to Port Said first, and finally we heard the police launch, putt, putt, putt, and he stumbled up the gangplank, 'Oh, darling, I love you, I need you,' and so forth. He could be so shy and afraid of public attention, yet here he was weeping and making a whole show of himself in public. Anyway, I had a room all ready for him, and helped him get to bed. I took the right shoe off the right foot and the left shoe off the left foot — 'Now just lift your foot a little.' . . . After he'd done something bad, he'd be like a little four-year-old boy, he'd put on that angel smile of his. He could have been a great actor."

Her account is incomplete, however, for she too, reportedly, made "a whole show" of herself. "Their reunion on the *Monroe*," says Second Officer George W. Stedman, Jr., "was a combination of name-calling, insults, jumping up and down, screeching, hair-pulling, stamping feet, wrestling and finally winding up in a passionate embrace smothering each other with kisses and hugs. From then on they were like a couple of lovebirds."

Booked to Marseilles, they debarked instead at Genoa on January 21, 1929, as O'Neill, who thought the whole ship was talking about them, could hardly wait to get ashore. They proceeded to the French Riviera, where Carlotta managed things so expeditiously — scouting for a residence, hiring servants, and so on — that before January ended they were installed in the Villa Les Mimosas on Boulevard de la Mer in Cap-d'Ail, just outside Monte Carlo. "The sea for my darling Gene," she wrote to Saxe Commins on January 26, "& a garden for me! — *I have found peace!* . . . Gene is lovelier than ever & an angel to me!" From another note to Saxe, on the thirtieth: "Gene is blooming — ! He has gained so much. I sit back & admire & adore! What happier lot for a woman?!"

The playwright's first word to the States was a cable to the Theater Guild: 'How is *Dynamo* moving? What opening date? . . . Wish I could be with you but domestic deadlock unchanged and will never return States until Carlotta and I are married."

To counter the impression given by the newspaper stories, he wrote to everyone that his travels in the East, despite his illness and the publicity, were "a marvelous experience." Confiding in no one about his drinking, he reported that he had suffered from both a sunstroke and influenza. "To make matters worse," he told Harold DePolo, "my friend had caught the flu from me and was sicker than I was. A pleasant time was had by all! The respectable Swedish married dame who was acting as a combination maid-secretary, although horribly shocked by events, was nevertheless romantically thrilled by the adventure of it. . . . Taking all the brunt of the notoriety barrage, she stood between us and the papers. In return they openly insinuated she was my mistress — a serious thing for her because she was happily married and had a husband and child in England. My mistress! You can't appreciate the joke of that but you would if you saw her!"

To Shane and Oona he wrote that he "wouldn't have missed [the trip] for a million dollars. I saw all kinds of strange places and met so many different kinds of people . . . that I feel as if I'd added a whole new world to my experience." From Harry Weinberger he had heard that Agnes had been ill. "Tell Mother," he went on, "I am damned sincerely sorry. Tell her when I was very sick in the hospital in Shanghai all the bitterness got burned out of me and the future years will prove this."

If he viewed Agnes more equably by this time it partly was because he had arrived at a less exalted view of Carlotta. Prior to their rows in the East, confrontations which had disclosed dark lineaments in them both, he had loved a romantic illusion named Carlotta Monterey; now he was in love with an actual woman of that name whose faults he recognized. Her image, consequently, no longer made Agnes look so flawed by comparison; but he deluded himself in thinking that "all the bitterness got burned out" of him. Before long he referred to Agnes as "the perfidious frau," and in time his resentment toward her would steadily intensify as he paid out alimony year after year.

Before sailing for the East, O'Neill had arranged through Richard Madden for a few of his friends — Nathan, Macgowan, De Casseres, Jimmy Light — to read his new play prior to production. "Not having heard from you about *Dynamo*," he wrote Nathan on February 14, "I opine it didn't hit you right in the reading. Perhaps when you saw it on the stage, you got a new light on it. I hope so. In rereading it lately it seemed so essentially a thing that must be seen and heard in a theater to appreciate its true values."

His first supposition was correct, for Nathan detested the play. In a wickedly clever article he condemned it briefly in his own words, then went on to damn it at length in its own language by quoting all the stage directions of the first act:

> Arguing tormentedly within himself
> With angry self-contempt
> Furiously clenching his fist
> His eyes lighting up with savage relish
> Suddenly horrified
> Protesting petulantly
> With indignant anger
> With evangelical fervor
> With life-long resentful frustration
> With bitter self-contempt
> With a grim resentful side-glance
> With a gloomy glance

And so forth, seriatim, for more than three full pages in the March 1929 *American Mercury*. But the use of O'Neill's own words against him was more than a clever trick; it bared in a most effective manner the ill-tempered character of the play. Nathan in conclusion called the work "amateurish, strident and juvenile," and said: "When O'Neill feels, he often produces something that is very beautiful, very moving and very fine. But when he gives himself over to science and philosophy, as in *Dynamo*, he would seem to be lost."

Nearly all the other critics felt likewise about the play, which opened at the Martin Beck on February 11, 1929. Under Philip Moeller's direction, a cast headed by Glenn Anders, Dudley Digges, Claudette Colbert and Helen Westley struggled gamely with their assignments, but to little avail. "'I remember it chiefly,'" Theresa Helburn said years later, "for the wonderful stage set, and for Claudette Colbert in a tight-fitting red dress running up and down stairs."

Usually one of O'Neill's champions, Gilbert Gabriel, who had moved from the *Sun* to the *American*, was unimpressed this time. Richard Lockridge, his successor on the *Sun*, deplored the author's "unfortunate inability to ignore the obvious. Cropping up here and there is that old, rather childish argument which the village atheist and the village clergyman have been carrying on so long to the edification – perhaps – of those . . . who are still acutely worried by the thought that we may have come from monkeys."

Another newcomer in the Broadway reviewing stand was still more severe, namely playwright-critic St. John Ervine, whom the *World* had imported to replace Alexander Woollcott. "The play opens dully," Ervine said. "The drama slowly drips out of it as we listen to infinitely dreary dialogue, and we suffer the fatigue that is felt when we are obliged to listen to some intolerable bore who will talk and talk and talk. . . ."

None of the playwright's other failures ever bothered him more than *Dynamo* (it lasted only fifty performances), and for months he wavered back and forth, now excoriating the critics, now blaming himself. After seeing the reviews he wrote to Richard Madden on February 28 that they "did not seem so disappointing to me, considering the nature of the play, and I am surprised the Guild folk thought them so antagonistic. As you know – there has always been this division of opinion about my plays – and always will be, I hope, for it is a sign of real life and guts."

But shortly, as the reviews began to rankle, he counterattacked. "The critic boys and the carping columnists seem to be real provoked with me," he replied to one correspondent. "Well, it's not the first time – nor yet the last time, please God, for when those gangrened failures get to accepting you it's a sure sign you're good and dead." To Miss Helburn he maintained that *Dynamo* would "have scored a failure" in the critics' view even "if the play had been *Hamlet!* They were out to take it out of my hide for the success of *Interlude*."

What most dismayed him, he said repeatedly, was that "no criticism, either favorable or not, got what I thought my play was about." The reviewers, he complained to a friend, were "all hot after my general abstract theme for three plays — I was a boob to let that out — and nobody saw my play, *Dynamo*, about the psychological mess a boy got into because he suddenly felt that the whole world had turned against him and betrayed him into cowardice. Most of all his mother, whose betrayal really smashes him. Psychologically, the interest in the play — for me — was how he works it out so that he electrocutes his bullying father's God, finds his dead mother again in the dynamo — a mother deified into God by the aid of pseudo-science — and is even compelled to sacrifice the girl he loves, whom his mother was jealous of and hated, to achieve that final return to his mother. His last words as he embraces the Dynamo are — in my script — 'Never let me go from you again! Please, Mother!' What could be plainer than that? . . . How anybody could think, in the light of previous work, that I would waste time writing a play on the piffling struggle between pseudo-religion and pseudo-science is more than I can make out."

He felt that "this play has been misunderstood as no other of mine except *God's Chillun*." His coupling of the two is significant, for he alone was conscious of their being rooted in his family history. Where everyone else saw in *All God's Chillun Got Wings* a story of miscegenation, he saw aspects of his parents' marriage; and in *Dynamo*, which others found a confused to-do about new gods and the old-time religion, he had sought above all to dramatize his traumatic relationship with Ella O'Neill. No wonder, then, that he thought the two plays "misunderstood."

Eventually, though, he conceded that the criticism of *Dynamo* was largely justified; he realized that the mother-son relationship "got completely lost in the obvious religious struggle in the latter portion of the play and left it dehumanized and unconvincing." To De Casseres he lamented: "I let it out of my hands much too soon — before I had a chance to get the right perspective on it. [Agnes, who had neither read nor seen the play, told a friend, "Gene has always rewritten his plays a lot, and I imagine his mistake was in letting this go on too soon."] Also, when I went over it the last time I was in a pretty hectic mental state from worry and really in no fit condition for the job."

Baring himself more frankly to Fitzi, who was still struggling to keep the Provincetown Playhouse in operation, he said the play "was written at a time when I shouldn't have written anything. The whole perfidious Agnes mess was hounding me by every mail. I had to drive it out of my head each day before I could write. I was in a continual inward state of bitter fury and resentment. . . . My brains were woolly with hatred."

After making extensive changes and writing three new scenes, he assured Horace Liveright that he had revised *Dynamo* into "a damn good play," but actually, as he told Joseph Wood Krutch, he was still dissatisfied with it: "I like it better now, but not enough. I wish I'd never written it — really — and yet I feel it has its justified place in my work development. A puzzle. What disappoints me is that it marks a standing still, if not a backward move. It wasn't worth my writing and so it never called forth my best. But a good lesson for me. Henceforth unless I've got a theme that demands I step a rung higher to do it, I'm going to mark time and play the country gent until such a theme comes."

Saxe and Dorothy Commins, who had been alarmed by the news stories from the East, spent a few days at Villa Les Mimosas in February and were relieved to find the playwright in good health. By now he looked back with some amusement at the vexations of the trip and his efforts to elude the press ("It was really the most ridiculous farce I've ever run into"), but Carlotta remained indignant on the subject of "riff-raff reporters. *I* could have murdered them!" Dorothy, a gentle, unworldly soul, was about equally impressed by her hostess's distinct personality (which also made her a shade uneasy) and her luxurious wardrobe. "Carlotta had," she says, "some of the most beautiful things I've ever seen. Showing me around one day, she opened drawer after drawer of exquisite handmade lingerie, some of it from Shanghai; then a large closet full of stunning gowns and other outfits, and finally a closet with more than thirty pairs of shoes. Her jewels, her clothes, everything was out of the ordinary. When I complimented her on the fit of her clothes, she said she didn't have to go to Paris until the final fittings, as Poiret and Mainbocher had made mannequins of her exact figure."

O'Neill was in good spirits during the Comminses' visit, for Agnes had at last accepted the terms of a separation pact and agreed to go to Reno for a divorce. Once she had done so, he wrote to George Jean Nathan on February 14, "we'll be able to have a little peace. We've sure earned it. 'God only knows the trouble we've seen' — quite enough! — through A's willful waiting. Her motives are not mercenary either. That end of it was settled long ago. The delay has been caused by her refusal to accept a clause specifying that she would write no articles about me or our married life or thinly disguised autobiographical fiction exploiting me.

"An ugly business, the whole affair! This living on the brink of a scandal, with families and children on both sides to be protected, is a wearing business which lets one in for a lot of humiliating experiences. If C and I didn't have such considerations to watch, it would be so easy to come out in the open and tell everyone to learn to like it or go to hell!"

Under the separation agreement, which permitted each "to live as though unmarried," Agnes was to get between six and ten thousand dollars annually, depending on how much he made each year, and a lifetime interest in Spithead that allowed her to live there or rent it — the same terms they had tentatively agreed upon at their last meeting in New York. The arrangement was reported in the press in mid-February, and the New York *American,* which carried the most complete story, said on the seventeenth that Agnes "covenants not to exploit her marital relations with O'Neill either in interviews, memoirs or autobiography. So important did O'Neill consider this provision that a clause in the contract makes arbitration compulsory if he feels that Mrs. O'Neill has broken the agreement. If a board of three arbitrators decides she has used her marital relations with him to earn money, he may reduce by half his payments."

The *American* account erred, however, in including "word from the Orient, where O'Neill was last reported, that the friendship of the playwright and Carlotta Monterey, the actress, was near an end. The brunette beauty is planning to return to this country soon, according to a friend of Mrs. O'Neill." To offset the false report, Eugene wrote a letter to Harry Weinberger, with instructions to "leak" it to the press, in which he said, "Carlotta and I are going to be married as soon as my wife divorces me." He had cut the eastern trip short, he added, because he had had "a strong hunch I'd never write a line east of the Suez and I felt a longing to get back on the job."

The *Herald Tribune* in a story quoting from the letter reported that Agnes still had not begun divorce proceedings, and as days passed without word of such a move, Eugene became increasingly anxious. "Ask Bio," he wrote to De Casseres on March 12, "to try concentrating on my hand. I will hold it out and imagine her looking at it at 11:30 P.M. on April 1st (I pick this date because it's easy to remember). That will be 6:30 P.M. in New York. Are you set? I want to know when that peace is coming she promised me!"

Actually, Mrs. De Casseres by this time needed no psychic powers to foretell his marital future, since the newspapers had just reported Agnes's arrival in Nevada to establish legal residence there. However, Bio, after concentrating on his hand on April 1, wrote to him that he would be free to marry in July. "Your letter with its benign prophecy," he replied on May 10, "was most welcome. . . . You will remember you said that last night [in New York] that not until I was 41 would the new era begin — and I think it will be at least then before all my affairs are smoothed out 'for keeps' and my inner self freed from the dead, consciously alive in the new, liberated and reborn."

To Harold DePolo the following day he wrote that he had "never felt half so happy and calm and conscious of the joy of being alive as I do now." His remarriage, the letter continues, would put "the final seal on my new peace. From then on I'll have a wife and friend in one, who is back of me with everything in her every minute!"

Yet all was not peaceful between them at the time, chiefly because she resented old friends of his who were fond of Agnes also, while he defended them. Since their return to Europe word had reached them of rumors around New York of conflict between them, of slanderous tales circulating about her past, of gossip that she was leading him into extravagance — talk that Carlotta blamed not only on Agnes but on his "so-called friends" in the Village. They also heard that many of his former associates sympathized with the wife who had been abandoned with two small children. Carlotta, being of a vehemently partisan nature, felt that those sorry for Agnes only proved themselves "disloyal" to Eugene, and hammered so at the question of his friends that a row exploded between them. Heartsick immediately afterward, O'Neill wrote her that he was "drowned in despair that dissension should have again sprung up between us. I am so bewildered by this ugly and mad thing, so appalled by its utter insanity, that I feel lost, defeated and done for. Why? Why? Why, in God's name! I love you! With all my soul and body I love you — with all the strength of my spirit! . . .

"And now when we are on the brink of achieving [happiness], when the goal we have paid for so bitterly is in sight, when peace is measurably within our grasp, are we going to take the side of the world against each other and ourselves work the ruin?

"Oh Dearest Heart of Mine, look at your Port Said ring and feel with me! [At their shipboard reunion they had exchanged rings as a symbol of "a new understanding" between them.] That is the truth of you and me! . . . All else is the product of nerves and the small frets and worries

[328]

of daily living. Friends? What have friends to do with Us? What has anyone to do [with] Us. . . .

"I love you! I love you! You are my life and everything! And you love me! And everything else is a lie! And we are such God damned fools to torture each other so over other things that have no meaning!"

Their quarrel was smoothed over but Carlotta was unalterably bent on relegating to the past certain of his friends. At his request she began to "edit" the news items sent by his clipping bureau, screening out stories that might distress him. The result was, she informed Saxe Commins, that "he sees about five out of a hundred! I can't edit his letters tho' – & 'some' seem determined to *not* believe he is content & happy – & equally determined to keep his entire past alive before his eyes! They'll tire of all this bye and bye, please God!?!"

Actually, though, without Eugene's knowledge, she was editing his personal correspondence as well and trying to intercept all mail from those she disliked. "You can let the PP bunch know," O'Neill wrote on April 6 to Saxe, who was about to return to the States, "that I feel fairly sore at them because not a damn one has written to me. Jimmy [Light], for example, has owed me a letter for ages." Occasionally, however, an undesirable letter escaped Carlotta's vigilance. "I was damn tickled," Eugene replied to Fitzi, "to get your letter! I had begun to think you had all forgotten my existence," and he ended: "As always, much love to you, Fitzi! You are deep in my affection ever!"

He and Carlotta remained on the Riviera only a few months. When they first moved into the villa, they had contemplated returning to America once they were married; but after he began to favor California, Carlotta cooled to the idea of their early return, chiefly because – unknown to him – she wanted to avoid living within easy reach of her mother and her twelve-year-old daughter Cynthia. Nellie Tharsing, it seems, was finding the girl difficult to handle. "My Mother writes me," Carlotta told Dorothy Commins, "she is coming to Europe this summer with my child unless I come to them! More complications! But summer is a long way off!"

The place in Cap-d'Ail was not secluded enough for O'Neill – Sacha Guitry, for instance, had a villa only a stone's throw away along the shore – and at Carlotta's suggestion, since he had been so enthralled by the Touraine, they went house-hunting in that region in April. By late May they were getting settled at Le Plessis, a gray, rather austere château of thirty-five rooms and twin round towers that was part of a seven hundred-acre estate in Saint Antoine-du-Rocher, about ten kilometers from Tours. When Carlotta first proposed living there, he thought it would be "chi-chi, putting on airs," but he soon, as he wrote Stark Young, became enthusiastic about the place: "All sorts of grand old woods and farmland, a fine old château with wonderful old carved wood furniture, including choir stalls originally from Langeais, ancient tapestries in the room downstairs — in short, it is quite perfect, and most important for me (inside) a great peace and calm broods over it all and time ceases to be a riveter's staccato of dots and dashes and becomes a flowing curved line. There is no life around but the life of a big farm. . . . The proprietors run this . . . while we have all the benefit of feeling close to animals and the soil without the disillusionment of milking and praying for rain. I will not stun your ears with the incredibly small yearly rental we pay for all this grandeur. It is a bargain even for non-tourist France."

The rent was only thirty thousand francs a year (around twelve hundred dollars in American currency at the time), but there was a reason for it. Le Plessis, for all its marble floors and other "grandeur," lacked basic comforts of modern living, such as electricity (lamps and candles were used instead), and a bathroom (Carlotta had one made from a bedroom). Moreover, the château, having been vacant and neglected for years, was grimy with cobwebs, dust and the ravages of moths. Indeed, when the American couple moved in, the place seemed a fit setting for Gothic melodrama, particularly after dark in the flickering candlelight.

"I tear (it's easily miles a day in this big house) from one end of the place to the other," Carlotta reported on June 9 to Commins, "trying to advise plumbers, painters & cleaners. But it will be nice when finished." Practically the first thing she did was fix up a work study for "Genie" in one of the twin towers, where he had a sweeping view of the fertile, well-forested countryside. Another of her early projects was, in her words, "a wee" concrete swimming pool for him behind the château, actually a good-sized one, fed by a natural stream, that cost some seventy thousand francs. In all the couple spent over one hundred and fifty thousand francs (about six thousand dollars) on improvements for the place, which they had rented for three years.

Le Plessis belonged to three sisters of the provincial nobility (the Marquise de Verdun, the Vicomtesse de Banville and Madame de la Boissière), who seemed to O'Neill "quite pleased to have a writer for a tenant." They probably, he told a friend, found it "a bit disreputably thrilling — although I hauled out my ribbon of the National Institute of Arts and Letters (what ho!) to convince the eye of my sobriety and sound doctrine!" The three sisters immediately bought and read *Strange Interlude* and, according to its author, "survived it without turning a hair, although confessing they had their own opinion of a woman like Nina."

As his new life absorbed him, he wrote less often to Shane and Oona, though he still urged them not to forget him, possibly because he, unconsciously, wished they would — so that they might weigh less on his conscience. Soon after his return from the East he had written that "sometimes I want to see you so much that I feel like taking the first boat to America — but I have such important business to attend to over here that I have to stay for a while longer." By now, though, with Agnes in Reno, the pretense was over that he would ever return to the family. In an irony that perhaps escaped him, the playwright son, who harbored a lifelong sense of grievance against his parents, a feeling he vented again and again in his plays, had egregiously failed his own children.

Though four-year-old Oona missed him more, apparently, than he imagined, his defection was far harder on Shane, nearly ten, who was approaching the age when a boy most needs a father to pattern himself on. Always inclined to be self-absorbed, he had become still more withdrawn, except with Gaga; unfortunately, she was in failing health and before long would vanish from his life forever. Shane had gone to a boarding school in New England, but he became so homesick that after a few months Agnes brought him back to the Old House in West Point Pleasant, New Jersey. For a time, regardless of what she said to him, his only reply was, "I wanna go back to Bermuda" — the last place where the family had been intact.

During Agnes's stay in Reno the two children were in the care of her sister Cecil and Mrs. Clark. "Shane was so wild," Cecil recalls, "that you couldn't manage him. His mother was away, his father was away — he hadn't seen him for a long time — and I guess he felt everybody was going to abandon him. The result was that he took it out on poor little Oona, who looked like such a frightened little waif. [Normally, Oona, according to another relative, was "a quiet, self-sufficient child who didn't make any demands on anybody."] But anything Shane wanted to do was all right with Gaga. She always defended him and made excuses."

Agnes's divorce hearing, held behind closed doors in Reno on July 1, lasted only about fifteen minutes and consisted chiefly of testimony about the separation agreement between her and O'Neill. Two days later a decree was granted in her suit, which was based on a charge of desertion. Limiting the publicity to a minimum, she "refused to see any newspaper correspondents," the *Herald Tribune* reported on the second, "and even insisted that her divorce complaint and copy of the agreement be sealed." The Associated Press on the fourth called it "one of the most secret divorces ever granted in Reno."

The separation agreement, which was incorporated with the divorce papers, contained various provisions regarding Shane and Oona. "The husband and wife shall have equal control of said children," the document stated, "and equal rights of visitation and right to sole custody at various times, to be arranged; but said arrangement shall not interfere with the health, welfare, or schooling of said children." One clause that O'Neill insisted on was that the children, at age thirteen, "shall enter a first-class American preparatory boarding school, these schools to be chosen by mutual agreement." Under the pact Agnes was to pay all "school or college fees" for the children if her alimony were at least eight thousand dollars; otherwise, O'Neill paid.

On July 6, shortly before Agnes's return from Nevada, Mrs. Clark died — she was sixty-six — and her body was shipped to Provincetown, where she had first joined the family to look after the newly born Shane. To a child the death of a parent — or surrogate parent — seems like desertion. Whether from resentment or grief, possibly from a mixture of both, Shane long would not enter the room at the Old House where Gaga had died.

The divorce stirred little feeling in the couple at the château because, in Carlotta's words, they had "waited too long & been thro' too much" to be excited about it; besides, the two already felt "married." They expected that the legal formalities would "only mean a 'ceremony'" to them, yet both were impressed by the actual event on July 22, 1929, in Paris. O'Neill "felt it meant something — not like our buy-a-dog-license variety in U.S.," while to Carlotta it seemed "the first time I'd ever really been married. The others were just legalized affairs."

In the ceremony they gave one another rings inscribed with a quotation from *Lazarus Laughed:* "I am your laughter" (in O'Neill's ring to her), "And you are mine" (in her ring to him). But the rest of their day was less romantic. Carlotta wanted to celebrate by dining at the Café de Madrid, while he as usual shied at eating in public; he yielded, however, under protest, after she announced herself ready to go alone if necessary. "When we got back to the hotel," Carlotta recalls, "he said, 'I'm exhausted, I'm going to bed,' and I told him, 'So am I.' So off he went to his bedroom and I went to mine — we always had separate bedrooms — and that was my wedding night."

The following day O'Neill cabled Saxe and Dorothy ("Grand news.

Carlotta and I married yesterday. Love from us") and, among others, Harry Weinberger. The word to the lawyer included instructions to inform the press that he and Carlotta were honeymooning in the Tyrol, but actually they returned to Le Plessis.

Eugene felt hurt that while he received congratulations from some persons he knew only casually, there was none from his old friends in Provincetown and the Village, and concluded that they must have sided with Agnes. But when word of his grievance filtered back, Frank Shay, Mary Heaton Vorse, Eben Given and others were surprised, since all had written to wish him well. "I wrote again in fact," said Mary Vorse, "when I heard about his being bitter, but he never replied. It isn't true we were on Agnes's side — we wanted both of them to be happy — but they couldn't any more, not together. He had drained her dry. I remember Agnes saying, 'I'm so sick of the theater, I don't want to hear another word about the theater.'"

Covering her tracks, Carlotta, who had "edited out" many of the wedding messages, gave Commins a different picture. "Never mention this," she wrote to Saxe on August 24, "but I was interested (tho' not surprised) when none of the Provincetowners sent Gene any word of good wishes. . . . They can't use him any more —!!!! Gene was more embarrassed on *my* account than on his own — *why* — God knows. Because I have heard all along of their disloyalties . . . I am delighted they were stupid enough to show their real colors! *Please mention this to no one — not even your sister!*" (Saxe's sister Stella and her husband E. J. Ballantine were part of the Provincetown-Village circuit.)

Harry Weinberger was a chief obstacle to Carlotta's efforts to wall off her husband from the Villagers; but since he was O'Neill's attorney, there was nothing she could do about him. After a letter from Weinberger in which he mentioned Jimmy Light and Fitzi, she exploded on August 30 to Saxe: "If I but had the words to tell you how *very, very* fed up we are with news of these two individuals! And now people are running to Miss F. & telling her Gene is 'hurt' because she sent him no letter or cable when he was married! That is a *lie* — he was not *'hurt'!* He was surprised at their lack of even *tact* — considering their endless asking of favors in the present & their having accepted so many in the past! . . .

"As Gene expressed to me the other evening — he is going thro' a *new development* — new pleasures — new riches — new objects of study — are coming into his life — the old skin is being shed! And with it the old parasites — I hope! . . .

"Gene & I want to make a *clean cut* & *go on!* You are one of the few old

ones we *want* to see! . . . we are praying for *freedom* — to *be left
alone* — for *work!* For *peace!* — One either goes forward or backward in
life — there is no standing still! . . . Gene wouldn't write anyone like
this — but he'd suffer thro' wanting to!"

She directed Saxe to "destroy this letter & forget it!"

Kenneth Macgowan fell out of her favor for a time when, thinking to
correct inflated accounts about O'Neill's life abroad, he gave a sober
picture to the *New Yorker*, which in turn reported: "Flamboyant descriptions of the château in France have exaggerated its grandeur. It is not
a show place, simply an old residence on an estate owned by three noble
ladies who rented it to the O'Neills furnished, for about half of what a
four-room apartment rents in New York. It is without electricity and has
but one bath."

Carlotta was at first *"furious,"* then flabbergasted when she discovered
that the unsigned "apologia" had originated with Macgowan as "a
friendly, kind thing." She promptly and frankly wrote him how she felt,
and afterward fumed to Saxe: "Gene's friends are free to write what they
wish about Gene personally or his *work* — (that is *his* & *their* affair), but
I happen to be *one half part of the home of the O'Neills'* — *in a cold
blooded* business *proposition.*"

It was costing her, she continued, "thousands a year" and "no publicity
can be given thro' friendly channels without consulting *me!* . . . I need
no apology to the public or Gene's old friends . . . whether I am living
in *30 rooms* or *3.* I pay as I go — & it's nobody's damned business! Gene is
not married to Agnes Boulton now but to Carlotta Monterey — &, as far
as his *personal* & *home* life is concerned it makes a *great difference!* I have
sat quietly in the background now for nearly two years — listening to
insult & unfair criticism re myself, my family — my financial position —
my morals & every other imaginable thing. Meanwhile I have gone on
paying out money — giving out energy & care — while these Provincetown people — & other of Gene's parasites — have nearly driven him &
me crazy — My patience is *exhausted.*"

Eugene owed her at least "protection from these gossiping idiots," she
declared, and if he could not provide it, she would take her own
measures!

To many Carlotta would come to seem a dragon at the gate barring
them from O'Neill, a possessive woman who wanted him all to herself;
but the situation was not as clear-cut as it appeared. Granted, she *was* of a
possessive, jealous nature; granted, she *did* seek to run his life. Yet the
essential fact remains that he wanted someone like her, capable, deter-

mined, strong, to guard and preserve his privacy, to keep the world at a distance, to devote all her attention and care to him while he devoted his life to his work. He was, in short, equally possessive and demanding. He asked much of a woman, and Carlotta gave of herself to her limits; there was a price for him to pay, and on the whole, he paid it willingly.

Part of the price was the loss of certain friends. Yet here too the picture is complicated, for in some instances it appears that he was more or less indifferent about losing them; they had meant less to him than they imagined. In other cases, though, Carlotta, indulging her dislikes and prejudices, froze out old friends he would like to have retained; but, for the sake of peace, he deferred to her in most, though not all, instances. As a result, it was generally believed that Carlotta dominated him, an impression that their appearance and manner seemed to confirm — he soft-spoken and retiring, she rather imperious-looking and with an emphatic voice. She prevailed, however, only when he allowed her to; he was far from a pliable character.

Summarizing their marriage, after his death, she said it was "a privilege to live with him because it was mentally stimulating. My God, how many women have husbands who are very stimulating?" But it was not, she added, an easy life. "I worked like a dog. I was his secretary. I was his nurse. I built and ran his houses. He wrote the plays. I did everything else." In the end her feeling was that "Gene loved me as much as he could love anyone, but the only real love he had was for writing plays. He lived completely within himself."

17

※

At the Château

For several years O'Neill had thought of writing a drama based on one of the Greek tragedies but set in America and embodying present-day concepts and insights. "Is it possible," he had wondered back in 1926, "to get [a] modern psychological approximation of [the] Greek sense of fate into such a play, which an intelligent audience of today, possessed of no belief in gods or supernatural retribution, could accept and be moved by?" His interest in the subject was sharpened later that year when he read about a fresh translation of Euripides's the *Alcestis* by Dudley Fitts and Robert Fitzgerald that made the "ancient drama moving and impressive to an audience separated from the original by barriers of time, language and a different culture." The new version, according to the review, had "something of the quality of H. D.'s [Hilda Doolittle's] fragmentary translations from the Greek." While O'Neill read the new *Alcestis*, Agnes checked on a Doolittle work and reported to him: "There's a re-creation of Greek & Roman life and characters in it — treating them like moderns — that will interest you."

After surveying the classical field, O'Neill decided to base his narrative on the *Oresteia* trilogy of Aeschylus, which he felt "has greater possibilities of revealing all the deep hidden relationships in the family than any other" of the Attic tragedies. Considering that the trilogy tells of an adulterous wife (Clytemnestra) who murders her husband (Agamemnon) and in turn is slain by her son (Orestes) at the goading of her daughter (Electra), one can only conclude from O'Neill's remark about "the deep hidden relationships" that he viewed family life as, basically, a deadly struggle. It is particularly significant too that he considered Electra the matricide "the most interesting of all women in drama."

O'Neill, who practically always had several plays germinating in his mind at the same time, never tried to "force" an idea but instead relied on the secret workings of his unconscious to develop it; he would wait until an idea surfaced and so possessed him that he knew it was time to start working on it consciously. On the voyage to the Far East he had found himself thinking about his neoclassic idea and noted in his work diary in November 1928 that he must "give modern Electra figure tragic ending worthy of character. In Greek story she peters out into undramatic married banality. Such a character contained too much tragic fate within her soul to permit this — why should Furies have let Electra escape unpunished? Why did the chain of fated crime and retribution ignore her mother's murderess? — a weakness in what remains to us of Greek tragedy is that there is no play about Electra's life after the murder of Clytemnestra. Surely it possesses as imaginative tragic possibilities as any of their plots!"

By the time he and Carlotta moved into the villa in Cap-d'Ail, his Greek project had "taken a great grip" on him and "demanded to be written." Between periods of revising *Dynamo* for publication, he began outlining the new work, which he visioned as a "modern psychological drama" in a historic setting. Examining the past for a suitable parallel to the Trojan War period of the original, he found the American Revolution "too far off and too clogged in people's minds with romantic grammar-school-history associations," the world war "too near and recognizable" for a story that required costumes and the perspective of time. The Civil War era, he concluded, was most fitting for his "drama of murderous family love and hate."

For his setting he decided on a small seaport town in New England, not primarily because he was most familiar with that milieu from his summers in New London, but because Calvinist New England, life-fearing, life-denying, was the "best possible dramatically for Greek plot of crime and retribution, chain of fate." Here, ready-made, were a place and a climate of morality where frozen silences masked violent passions, where old families decayed behind patrician facades and flagellated themselves with, in the playwright's words, "a Puritan conviction of man born to sin and punishment." Had historic conscience-plagued New England never existed, O'Neill, for his new drama, would have had to invent it. Even the period architecture of the region suited his purpose, for neo-Grecian mansions, inspired by the ancient temples, were the vogue in mid-nineteenth century New England. O'Neill's fictional family would dwell in a cold, forbidding example of the style, "a grotesque perversion of everything" the Greek temple symbolized about the meaning of life.

In the early months of 1929 O'Neill made voluminous notes as he worked on the scenario. Unlike the classical treatment, which has the gods intervening at crucial points, his narrative was to develop solely from the passions and destructive impulses of its principals. His Clytemnestra, for example, hates her husband from sexual frustration and onetime affection poisoned into gall because his "puritan sense of guilt" equates love with lust. The new Electra, moreover, is fated to be her mother's rival in love, and destined each time for defeat.

"Electra," the playwright summarized in his diary in April, "adores father, [is] devoted to brother (who resembles father), hates mother — Orestes adores mother, [is] devoted to sister (whose face resembles mother's) so hates his father — Agamemnon, frustrated in love for Clytemnestra, adores daughter, Electra, who resembles her, hates and is jealous of his son — work out this symbol of family resemblances and identifications (as visible sign of the family fate) still further." Clearly, though O'Neill always denied being a Freudian, he was using a major tenet of Freudian psychology — the oedipal complex — more schematically than ever to light the hellfire under his characters.

Once again displaying a flair for evocative titles, he called the new work *Mourning Becomes Electra,* a title with, as he said, a dual meaning: "it befits — it becomes Electra to mourn," and secondly, in an ironic sense, "mourning (black) is becoming to her — it is the only color that becomes her destiny." At first he thought the drama would be in two parts, but as it continued to expand in his mind, he decided that to realize the "full value" of his material he, like Aeschylus, would have to make it a trilogy: first part, the homecoming and murder of the husband; second part, the revenge of the daughter and the son on the mother and her lover; finally, the fate of the sister and brother. Giving the three parts individual titles, the author called them *Homecoming, The Hunted,* and *The Haunted.*

O'Neill gave his principal characters the surname of Mannon because of its resemblance both to Agamemnon and, since the family is the richest in town, to Mammon. The father, a brigadier general in Grant's army, is named Ezra Mannon, while Clytemnestra appears as Christine, Orestes as Orin, and Electra as Lavinia.

After his unhappy experience with *Dynamo* ("I blundered horribly in shooting off my mouth about a trilogy and the meaning of it"), O'Neill was wary of divulging anything about his work in progress, yet at the same time was too excited to remain silent for long. Without giving its title or any other hint of its nature, he told Saxe Commins on August 4 that he was "tremendously enthusiastic" about his present project. "It has the possibilities of being the biggest thing in modern drama – not barring anyone's plays. Whether I'll have enough stuff to realize said possibilities is another story . . . at any rate, I'd rather fail at the Big Stuff and remain a success in my own spiritual eyes than go on repeating, or simply equaling, work I've done before."

To Joseph Wood Krutch, again voicing self-doubt, he said the new project has such "possibilities" that one would "have to go back to the Greeks and Elizabethans to tie it." "Oh," he exclaimed, "for a language to write drama in! For a speech that is dramatic and not just conversation. I'm so strait-jacketed by writing in terms of talk. I'm so fed up with the dodge-question of dialect. But where to find that language?"

After the failure of *Dynamo*, which he blamed chiefly on its premature release, he had resolved to take all the time necessary to get his plays into the best possible shape. Looking back, he regretted that in eleven years he had written no less than eighteen long plays. "Too much!" he said. "At least seven of them shouldn't have been written – at least, not as they were written!"

Despite the recognition and success he had achieved, he had become, if anything, even more unhappy about the contrast between the performances he could visualize and those he saw in the theater. Thinking, presumably, of the production difficulties he would face with *Mourning Becomes Electra*, he wrote to De Casseres that acting is "quite separate from and frequently incongruous with the play as created." Of all writers, he went on, only dramatists ("I mean dramatists who aim high") had to contend with this problem. "A play may be damn well acted," he said, "and still be far from the creator's intention. I've had many plays in which the acting was excellent. I've never had one I recognized on the stage as being deeply my play." That was why, he explained, he never saw his plays after the rehearsal period.

Sounding the same refrain to Fitzi, he declared that he might wind up composing plays "to be published with 'No Productions Allowed' in red letters on the front page." He was weary not only of the "ordeal of disillusionment and compromise called rehearsals" but of "the cheap fame and notoriety *Interlude* has brought down on me – and the equally cheap defame that *Dynamo* was an excuse for." By now *Strange Interlude*, in its second year on Broadway, had become the most widely known play of the decade – "a ballyhooed freak," its author called it. Besides winning him a third Pulitzer Prize, it had run afoul of the Broadway censors, had broken house records almost everywhere its two touring companies had performed, and had scored the largest sale of any American play ever published.

Since its opening the drama had rarely been out of the news for long, and O'Neill, who was "deadly ill with being a public personage," consoled himself it had begun to fade in publicity value. "I am planning my life ahead," he told Fitzi, "so that I'll damn well go back to my old private life of unpested artist — if I have to hold back plays from production and publicity until I'm forgotten." But he was not in control of the situation. On May 27, 1929, two weeks after his letter to Fitzi, the playwright who yearned to be "forgotten" was swept up on a new wave of notoriety; or, as one newspaper put it, "The world of literature and drama was given a shock today."

On that day a woman filed suit in a New York court charging that O'Neill had stolen *Strange Interlude* from her novel *The Temple of Pallas-Athenae*, privately printed in 1924. Alleging that she had sent copies of her novel to the Theater Guild and Horace Liveright several years before the play was produced, Georges Lewys (a nom de plume) named them as codefendants with O'Neill, sought an injunction to halt performance of the play and sale of the book, and asked for damages of one million two hundred and fifty thousand dollars. As business surged at the box office from the new publicity, the Guild, which had advertised *Strange Interlude* as in its final weeks, announced that it would continue indefinitely. Less fortunately, Paramount Pictures, which was about to buy the play for seventy-five thousand dollars, withdrew its offer because of the suit.

In a statement to the press Miss Lewys listed various parallels between her novel and the play:

Both stories are built about the subject of selective paternity.

Both stories are built about young heroines, who are the leading characters. In both stories the heroines marry young men.

In both stories the young men come from insane families. In both stories the insanity is hereditary.

In both stories the heroines deliberately ask another man to become the father of a child. In both stories a boy is born. In both stories the heroines fall in love with the fathers of their boys.

In both stories the boys grow up, tall, athletic and well. In both stories the boys fall in love with beautiful young women. In both stories the mothers show jealousy of their prospective daughters-in-law.

In both stories the scientific attitude of selecting a healthy father is particularly stressed, etc., etc.

Miss Lewys, who described herself to reporters as primarily a poet, said she had written "one hundred love sonnets to one man recently, and I turned out seventy-two of them in one month — all in the Elizabethan style.

"Picture my shock and amazement when I went to see *Strange Interlude* for the first time three months ago. Eugene O'Neill had used my material but used it all wrong. He took a beautiful ideal and brought it so low that I was shocked and scandalized." (One newspaper reported that *The Temple of Pallas-Athenae* had undergone "Federal prosecution in California on an obscenity charge.")

Stunned by word of the suit, O'Neill's immediate response was that he had "never even heard" of Miss Lewys's book and that she "must be crazy." What rankled him even more than the fresh notoriety was that he would have to endure considerable trouble and expense to defend himself. The comparisons between her book and his play, as listed in the press, struck him as "farcical," and he "boiled with rage to think this neurotic blackmailer gets a million dollars worth of publicity for herself and her privately printed rubbish by deliberately slandering me!" After Harry Weinberger had sent him her book, he found it "the damndest piece of writing I've ever come across — a mixture of Laura J. Libbey, Elinor Glynn, and the Young Visitors!"

To John Francis of Provincetown he wrote that if he went in for "literary burglary I'd hold up Shakespeare — or try to — and not pick on a beggar-writer! . . . Such blackmailing fools never have a cent — you can't get anything back no matter how silly the suit is."

Replying on June 20 to a sympathetic letter from Stark Young, he agreed that he had had "as much of a certain kind of success in *Interlude* as could be hoped for. You might add, as much as my stomach could stand!" While grateful for his earnings from the play ("It has, in a way, set me free"), he felt that the plagiarism suit was "the fitting final note of cheapness to wind up the whole affair!"

But further publicity, from a new source, was in the offing. Boston, arousing a nationwide protest from people of the theater and civil libertarians, banned *Strange Interlude* on the grounds that it was, according to the mayor of that city, "a plea for the murder of unborn children, a breeding ground for atheism and domestic infidelity, and a disgusting spectacle of immorality." Under questioning by newsmen, he admitted that he had never seen or read the play. As a result of the ban, Boston became the butt of innumerable cartoons, editorials and news stories; the play was booked in the nearby city of Quincy, and what would otherwise have been just another out-of-town engagement of the O'Neill drama became a subject of national interest.

It seemed to O'Neill that, despite all his efforts, he was fated to live out his days under public scrutiny. In the midst of the publicity over the plagiarism suit, he learned, according to the newspapers, that he was in precarious health. From London the Associated Press sent out a dispatch on June 6 stating that the playwright was unable to attend the local première of his play *Welded* because he was "seriously ill with tuberculosis in Switzerland." Recalling that the papers had also reported him stricken with the disease during his Far Eastern trip, O'Neill told a friend that he had not "even bothered to deny" the latest story. "I'm getting too bored with such nonsense. And the idea that only TB could keep me away from an opening night must be a long laugh to all who know me." Boasting that he had stronger lungs than most people, he added, "My nerves are lousy, it is true, but otherwise I have my old man's constitution."

(When the National Tuberculosis Association asked him in 1933 to be on its Christmas Seal Committee, he consented on condition that his name be listed "without comment or reference to past history. My TB experience has been belabored and exaggerated to the nth degree in biographies, newspaper and magazine articles – and, candidly, I'm a bit fed up with references to it, especially when, as has happened, the profound psychological commentators try to read TB after-effects into the meaning of my plays, etc!")

While the tuberculosis reports and the Boston episode were only temporary annoyances, the court suit was a continuing concern, because it would not come to trial for a long time. "This business of the law irritates me," he told Nathan on August 3, "to the exploding point! Here is a case manifestly absurd and cooked-up on the face of it and yet our legal lights of the Guild, Liveright, & O'Neill can't seem to do anything to get it dismissed." He feared that the suit might eventually cost him as much as fifty thousand dollars in lawyer and court fees, and, as he complained to Commins, "there is always a danger that one will be up against a judge that doesn't know a book from a rabbit. . . . I am sure she stole her own book bodily from some source, probably French erotica."

What with "moving, settling down, plagiarism suits and getting married," as well as a succession of houseguests, the playwright was often interrupted in summer 1929 as he worked on *Mourning Becomes Electra;* yet he managed to finish a detailed scenario for *Homecoming* in June, for *The Hunted* in July, for *The Haunted* in August. On completing the last one he congratulated himself that he had given his "Yankee Electra [a] tragic end worthy of her — and Orestes, too."

Among the first to visit Le Plessis, George Jean Nathan and Lillian Gish were impressed not only by their hosts' baronial style of living but by Carlotta's management of the château and her concern for Eugene's welfare. She had the domestic help wear bedroom slippers so that in moving around they would not make any sounds that might interfere with his concentration. Also, at Carlotta's suggestion, they had a special chair made in England, rather resembling a padded dentist's chair, which had movable arm and leg supports to give him maximum comfort as he worked.

"All her thoughts," says Miss Gish, "were of him; she looked after him like a mother. I've been around many couples in my time but I've never known any others so close, so devoted, as Carlotta and Gene. They didn't really seem to need anyone else."

Carlotta had been somewhat apprehensive about the visit, despite Eugene's attempts at reassurance, for she had always pictured Nathan — particularly after his devastating review of *Dynamo* — as a sarcastic, overbearing individual. The visit went off smoothly, however, for Nathan, though he had private reservations about his friend's taste in wives, was on his most genial behavior, with the result that Carlotta, to her surprise, found him "a *charming* & *lovable* guest."

Nathan felt, as he has written, that the playwright had "a boyish quality, an innocent artlessness in a number of directions. . . . In it lies much of [his] charm . . . for all his solemn exterior, [he] gets an unparalleled pleasure from splashing around in a swimming pool and making funny gurgling noises, from putting on the fancily colored dressing gowns he bought in China, from watches with bells in them, and from drinking enormous glasses of Coca-Cola and making everyone believe it is straight whiskey. When his very lovely wife, Carlotta, comes down to dinner in some particularly striking gown, his face lights up like a county fair. . . . 'Do you like it?' she will delicately ask on each occasion. And, though his infinite satisfaction is clearly to be perceived, like a little boy who doesn't want to give in and admit anything too quickly, he will invariably mumble, 'Well, it's pretty, but I like blue better.' "

The critic considered him also "the hardest worker that I have ever known, and, in the roster of my writing acquaintances, I have known a number of pretty hard workers. There isn't a minute of his waking day that his thoughts are not in some way or another on his work. Even when sound asleep, Carlotta informs me, he will once in a while grunt and be heard to mumble something about Greek masks, Freudian psychology or Philip Moeller."

After swearing Nathan to secrecy, the playwright outlined *Mourning Becomes Electra;* nearly a year would pass before he confided in anyone else, but he could not refrain from arousing widespread curiosity about his current project, which he always referred to as "the biggest thing" or "the most ambitious thing" he had "ever tackled."

Carl Van Vechten and his actress wife Fania Marinoff, old friends of Carlotta's, were also guests this summer. A pink-faced, soft-looking man who wrote brittle, sophisticated novels, was fond of jewelry, and adored knowing celebrities, Van Vechten seemed the last sort of person O'Neill would have found compatible, yet the two had interests in common that formed the basis of their friendship. Both were avid readers of murder fiction, both had championed Negroes in the arts, both loved jazz and the blues, music that had been wrung from the soul of black America. Thanking Van Vechten for a gift of records, Eugene said in a note, " 'The St. James Infirmary' is right in my alley. I am now memorizing the words. Do you know Mr. [Louis] Armstrong? If so give him my fraternal benediction. He is a darb . . . 'Empty Beds' is grand and [so are] my old favorites 'Soft Pedal' and 'Sing, Sing' that Paul Robeson introduced me to."

Shortly before their arrival at Le Plessis, Carl and Fania had run into Ralph Barton in Paris, and, though he too had remarried, he was eager to know whether they had heard anything about how O'Neill and Carlotta were getting along. "He asked us," Van Vechten says, "to give her his love, but I think he actually was upset and angry at her for marrying someone more famous than himself. It was a great blow to his ego."

Like Nathan and Miss Gish, the Van Vechtens were impressed by Carlotta's care of her husband and the close relationship between them. "He was terribly dependent on her," Van Vechten says, "and she did everything possible to please him. Even when there were no guests, Carlotta told me, she always dressed for dinner; she had exquisite things from Paris that no one but him ever saw." In words reminiscent of Carlotta's, he added: "She was more than a wife to him. She fussed over him like a mother, she answered his mail, she typed up his scripts, she took care of business matters that the husband ordinarily does. She made it possible for him to concentrate all his thoughts on his work."

Late in August Eugene Jr., who had been touring Germany at his father's expense, had a reunion with him at Le Plessis that seemed to bring them closer together. Tall and good-looking — he now was two inches taller than his six-foot father — the youth was making a brilliant record at Yale in classical studies. "I am proud of him," O'Neill informed Nathan, "and our relationship is naturally brotherish with none of the forced 'pal-father-son' bunk to it. When I survey his merits and think of the rotten mess of a life I was at his age [nineteen], I have no fatherly superior assumptions, believe me! He fits in very well with us. Carlotta likes him and he likes her. And I'm sure he feels more at home with us than he ever did with me in the past." In a snapshot of the two before the château, young Eugene, lounging in a chair, looks so content that one can almost hear him sigh with pleasure, while O'Neill appears on the verge of grinning. (He later gave Eugene Jr. the Peaked Hill station, but within a year or so, after storms had lashed the coast, it slid down the shifting dunes and was broken up in the sea.)

Carlotta, who resented any talk of Agnes and her husband's friends in Greenwich Village, was grateful to her new stepson for avoiding any such subject. "A nice youngster," she wrote to Saxe on August 30, "& my God — such *tact!* He has mentioned *no one's* name since he arrived! We discuss books, music, architecture & abstract things — which makes his visit doubly enjoyable. The two Eugenes swim once or twice a day. — Life goes on — calmly & surely — with Beauty always trembling in the air — and the desire to reach up — into the completeness and fulfillment of Life & Art!"

For all O'Neill's contentment with his present, well-ordered life, he was not immune to attacks of nostalgia, according to Madeleine Boyd, another guest this year. One evening when Carlotta vanished upstairs on some chores, the other two were holding a desultory conversation by the fireplace when Mrs. Boyd happened to mention Mary Blair, a friend of hers. "Gene suddenly came to life," she recalls. "His face glowed as he began talking about the Provincetown Players, Jig Cook, Fitzi and others but mostly about Mary. He praised her talent, her courage — he said he'd always be grateful for her appearing with Robeson when no other actress would — and wound up calling her 'one of God's Chillun.' He really poured out his heart, he was so happy remembering. It sounded as though he longed for the Village and the old days. Finally, Carlotta called down, 'Gene, it's time to go to bed,' and his face instantly fell. He looked as though he'd been spanked."

An old acquaintance of both her hosts, Mrs. Boyd, a French-born literary agent, had met the playwright in the Village, and she had origi-

O'Neill and Carlotta
shortly before they sailed to Europe

George Jean Nathan

Father and elder son at Le Plessis

Carlotta
before the château

O'Neill
with his Dalmatian dog,
Blemie

nally known Carlotta during her marriage to Barton. The agent was supposed to stay a week, but Carlotta, who apparently had overheard some of the conversation about Mary Blair and the Village, indicated to her the following day that she should cut her visit short. "I always thought," says Madeleine Boyd, "that her marriage to Barton collapsed because she tried to dominate him, and it seemed to me she was falling into the same error with O'Neill."

Elizabeth Shepley Sergeant, after visiting Le Plessis the following year, had reservations of a different kind. Though she thought Carlotta was better for O'Neill than Agnes in certain important respects, Miss Sergeant regretted that Carlotta "had taken him away from the sea. She gave him a feeling of security he never had from Agnes, she saw to it everything was perfectly arranged so that he could work in quiet and comfort. But I'm not sure that handmade shoes and a château, with menus written out and placed in silver holders, were the best sort of environment for the artist in Gene."

"I taught him how to live," Carlotta has said. "This was the only time he ever made money, real money – I mean *Strange Interlude* – so I encouraged him to have everything on earth he could have that he'd never had. I thought it was good for him, that it would give him a sense of feeling just as well dressed as the next man. And it did help him, but I had to shove and push and battle all the way. Once when we were out walking he began to hobble, and I had him take his shoes off. His toes were curled up, and I said, 'For God's sake, can't you get shoes to fit?' The salesman had told him, it seems, they were long enough. He argued against it, he said I was making him a gigolo or something, but I took him to a place where shoes are made to order (he had beautiful feet, lean, strong, like his fingers) and he loved them so much he got a dozen pair. He ended up by having seventy-five pairs of shoes. Then I introduced him to tailors. When we returned to America, he never bought a suit, a pair of shoes or anything. Maybe a pair of sport pants or a jacket, but he had a complete wardrobe. It was a lucky thing he did, because the Depression was on when we returned."

Life at Le Plessis was organized around his work. As a rule he wrote four to five hours every morning, seven days a week, and his instructions were that he was never to be disturbed, not even, according to Carlotta, "if the house were on fire." For a while he used to join her at lunch but, she recalls, "I would sit here and he would sit there and actually his whole mind was on his play – acts, lines, ideas. He would not talk and I'd have to sit perfectly dumb, trying not to make even a sound with a chair or anything. It made me nervous and it made him nervous to see me sitting there, so we decided the best thing was for him to have his lunch on a tray in his study."

His afternoons were largely spent out of doors; he swam, sunbathed, bicycled on the country lanes, and, if in the mood for excitement, went riding in his Bugatti racing roadster. There were no speed limits except in the towns and he enjoyed tearing along at top speed on near-deserted roads. ("O'Neill never does things by halves," Elizabeth Sergeant had written in 1927. "When he drives a car, it must be a high-power machine which devours the miles like air. When he writes, he tries to reduce the mileage of experience by an equally intense velocity of movement.") The Bugatti, as he became more and more discriminating, was the third automobile he had bought since his arrival in Europe. The new one, he informed Saxe Commins, was said to be "the fastest roadster in the world, guaranteed to make one hundred seventy kilometers — one hundred six miles — an hour. It's a bear! It has good suspension and double shock-absorbers and good upholstery so Carlotta can ride with me in comfort. I think I shall have a lot of fun out of it."

"He had a marvelous time with that car," Carlotta says. "When he was very nervous and tired, he would go out in this racer and drive about ninety-five miles an hour, then come back looking like nineteen years old, not a wrinkle, perfectly relaxed. He took me out one day and they almost had to lift me out of the car. I was gone, I was so terrified."

Shortly after the couple had moved into the château they bought a fox terrier, an excitable creature that enjoyed swimming with O'Neill, but he faded into the background when they acquired Silverdene Emblem from England, an uncommonly bright Dalmatian who won the wholehearted love of both his masters. Indeed, Carlotta's feeling for her daughter and O'Neill's for his three children seem to have been markedly less than what they felt for their "Blemie." Until his death twelve years later, he was, in O'Neill's words, "a comfort to [us] in time of sorrow, and a reason for added joy in [our] happiness," while Carlotta said, "He's the only one of our children who never disappointed us." His collar, leash, overcoat and raincoat were made to order at Hermès of Paris, and he slept on quality linens in a miniature four-poster with a canopy. "When Gene and I read by the fireplace," Carlotta recalled, "Blemie would lie first by one of us, then go over and lie by the other, so as not to show any partiality. He didn't want to hurt anyone's feelings. A diplomatic little gentleman, our Blemie."

Lillian Gish, concurring that the Dalmatian was exceptionally winning, says that he was "a person, a full-fledged member of the family, a regular host at the château. When breakfast was brought to you, he'd trot along with an air that suggested he wanted to make sure everything was all right. Carlotta wrote me that after I left, Blemie threw himself on the ground, stretched, and gave a deep sigh, as though to say, 'Thank heaven, that's over.' He was now free of responsibility."

Starting in mid-October 1929 the O'Neills spent three weeks in Paris, where the playwright underwent extensive dental treatment. In their first theatergoing since their arrival in Europe, they saw Lenormand's *Mixture*, because he had become a friend of theirs, but Eugene declined to attend Georges Pitoëff's French-language version of *The Hairy Ape*, though he was friendly with Pitoëff also. Shortly after the play's opening O'Neill had written to Stark Young that he was unconcerned about its reception. "I am fed to the teeth," he said on September 23, "with the show-shop, American, French, Bulgarian and what not, of which I opine the French is probably the most inane. . . . So I have a strong hunch the thrill of seeing *Ape* with French actors in Russian sets is an ecstasy I am permanently going to deny myself! I don't want to become too pleasure-loving."

It appears, however, that his primary reason for shunning the Pitoëff production was his feeling that *The Hairy Ape* "can't ever really be translated. It is bound to lose in translation," he maintained on October 12 to George Jean Nathan, "just the quality . . . that is most worthwhile — its rhythm of colorful dialogue, its dynamic drive of language. And its emotional significance and meaning is nothing the French rational mind could ever get in a million years. The French theater is dead from the neck down — and that means all dead where a theater is concerned, no?"

In general he took a keen interest in his European productions. Earlier this year he had complained to Richard Madden that the Royal Theater in Stockholm had ignored his request for information about its production of *Strange Interlude*. "Isn't there some way," he asked his agent, "when you give permission for these productions that you can stick in a proviso that they must write me in full (in English, French or German) after the opening and send me notices (which I can get translated) and a set of photographs?" Ordinarily he was powerless to affect the foreign presentations but when negotiations were under way for a London staging of *Strange Interlude*, he instructed Theresa Helburn that "there must be a clause in the contract that the Guild acting script *must* be followed verbatim. I've suffered enough from European directors' antics, which I couldn't help, but let it not be said of an O'Neill that he let the English massacre him."

His nine-act marathon had been staged by now in four European countries. In Stockholm it was both a critical and a popular success; in

Budapest it was more praised than damned; in Copenhagen its preoccupation with Nina Leeds's sex life so disturbed the leader of the Conservative Party that he arose in the Danish parliament and made "a public speech of his alarm and disgust"; but the most severe response was in Berlin. "The critics yowled and hooted," O'Neill informed Manuel Komroff, "as though an American army was on the frontier! They accused me of imitating every German playwright they could think of, including Schiller, and then tacked on Ibsen, Strindberg, Chekhov, and Shakespeare for good measure. Fact! I am not exaggerating. Which is quite an accomplishment in one play! Despite their howls, the director writes me that the play is a success. Elisabeth Bergner made a great hit in the part — as everyone does who has played it anywhere."

O'Neill thought that many Europeans were "so mad at our material superiority that they will be damned if they will admit that we can produce artists!" Chauvinistic bias was again evident, though not as bad as in Berlin, when *The Hairy Ape* opened in Paris. Their anti-Americanism, he told Commins, indicated "a deep anxiety complex working underneath."

Months prior to his Paris visit O'Neill had been offered one hundred thousand dollars to write the dialogue for *Hell's Angels,* an aviation film being made by young industrialist Howard Hughes. O'Neill rejected the offer with a three-word cable — "No, No, No" — but when he saw *The Broadway Melody* in Paris, his first talking picture, he became, as once before, excited about the screen's potentialities. Back in 1921 *The Cabinet of Dr. Caligari,* which opened his eyes to "wonderful possibilities I had never dreamed of before," had led him to hope for the development of an art-film movement that would parallel the rise of the little theaters.

Now that the screen had found its voice, he was, he informed Nathan on November 12, "most enthusiastic," not about *Broadway Melody* itself but from "a vision I had of what the 'Talky' could be in time when it is perfected." Always chafing at the physical limitations of the stage, he imagined that the new film technique "could set me free in so many ways . . . free to realize a real Elizabethan treatment and get the whole meat out of a theme. Not that the 'Talky' folks are ever liable to let me realize any of these dreams but I think the day may come when there will develop a sort of Theater Guild 'Talky' organization that will be able to rely only on the big cities for its audiences."

Anticipating the multimedia movement of later decades, the visionary dramatist had one story idea that he thought should be done as "a stage play combined with a screen talky background to make alive visually and vocally the memories, etc., in the minds of the characters." He asked Nathan to "keep this notion of mine a secret" and, suddenly wondering whether he might have gone overboard, inquired, "Does my 'Talky' enthusiasm strike you as idiotic?"

At various times over the years he had attempted, unsuccessfully, to write for the screen, starting in 1913 and 1914, when he had ground out scenarios, chiefly comedies and adventure tales, in hopes of earning a quick one hundred dollars. Early in the 1920s he had worked on a novel scheme for filming *The Emperor Jones*, which he wanted to make with Robert Edmond Jones, but they failed to obtain financial backing. A few years later, trying to arouse Hollywood's interest in *The Hairy Ape* and *Desire Under the Elms*, he prepared detailed synopses, in which the original stories were changed extensively, and publicized them with the aid of Richard Watts, Jr., movie critic of the *Herald Tribune*. Watts, who discussed the two scenarios without passing judgment on them, said of the revised *Ape* that O'Neill, "with a magnanimity hitherto unknown among playwrights slumming in the films, rewrote the play by the simple means of casting aside the stage version and regarding the work as a film."

In the film treatment of *The Hairy Ape* steel heiress Mildred Douglas is both repelled by and sexually attracted to Yank, and there are several confrontations between them, including a melodramatic mob scene where he attempts to dynamite one of her father's plants. The first and last parts of the script were, however, similar to the play. Revising the *Desire Under the Elms* story even more radically, the film adaptation transforms Abbie Putnam into a Hungarian peasant girl named Stephanie who cold-bloodedly arouses the passion of all four Cabot men, father and three sons, and sets them in murderous conflict with one another; but at the end, after Eben has accidentally slain his father, the girl surrenders to the law as his accomplice.

The one similarity between the two screen treatments is that both Stephanie and the new Mildred Douglas, stronger characters than their stage counterparts, are more culpable in the hero's downfall. As O'Neill said of his *Ape* scenario, his idea was "to build up the attraction-repulsion, hate-lust thing between Yank and Mildred, to make her even more of a bitch."

In time, as one after another of his plays reached the screen almost invariably in mediocre if not in mangled form, O'Neill became disenchanted with the movies. Apparently forgetting that he had once envisioned "Elizabethan" possibilities from *The Broadway Melody*, he told

Theresa Helburn in 1944 that "the picture medium has never interested me."

Considering that hit plays and best-selling novels are snapped up today by film-makers for sums in the hundreds of thousands, O'Neill earned relatively little from Hollywood. In all, seven of his long plays (including the *S.S. Glencairn* playlets as a unit) were sold to the movies during his lifetime, and the highest ever paid, for two of them, was seventy-five thousand dollars, with the playwright obliged in most instances to split the money equally with his stage producer. Only one film from his plays ever earned big money, the second version of *Anna Christie*, which marked the talking debut of Greta Garbo, but its success was largely due to her popularity. O'Neill, whose share was twelve thousand five hundred dollars when the play was sold for a silent film, received an additional seventy-five hundred dollars early in 1929 for the dialogue rights. Arousing memories of Harvard, someone in Cambridge wrote him that the marquee of the University Theater "blazed the following announcement right into the windows of [Professor Baker's] old 'Work Shop' – O'NEILL'S 'ANNA CHRISTIE' WITH GRETA GARBO." Everywhere else, though, the film was promoted with the words: GARBO TALKS!

The O'Neills' final days in Paris in fall 1929 were shadowed by news from America of the stock market crash and letters from friends worried about the future. The Provincetown Playhouse, which had been struggling along for years, was one of the early casualties. Only weeks before the Wall Street debacle the Village group, in a desperate attempt to strengthen its position by attracting a larger audience, had moved uptown to the Garrick Theater; now the Provincetown had dissolved into history and legend.

To an anxious query from Commins, Carlotta replied on November 18: "As I *never* speculate & have advised Gene never to – neither of us was hurt in the Wall Street drop. – All that trouble was caused by the *wise ones* using Wall Street as a roulette wheel to gamble on. . . . If one uses the Market as an investment it is safe – & makes the country's financial position so much more solid."

It seems, however, that she revised fact, possibly because she wanted Eugene and herself to appear smarter than the innumerable others burned on Wall Street. Years later O'Neill told Hamilton Basso that he invested a large part of his *Strange Interlude* royalties in the stock market and lost half of the sum in the 1929 crash. Wincing at the memory, he said another time that he "didn't have [shares] on margin, but I *had* them and went right down with them."

18

❖

Mourning Becomes Electra

As O'Neill began writing *Mourning Becomes Electra* in September 1929, he felt that it "would be so easy to do *well*. The story would see to that — and that's the danger I want to avoid [from a letter on August 31 to George Jean Nathan]. It has got to have an exceptional quality to lift it above its easy possibilities and make it worthy in some respect of its classic antecedents — or it will be a rank flop in my eyes no matter what others may think of it."

Weeks later, after false starts during which he had become "terribly messed up searching for new ways and means and styles," he decided to scrap all "elaborate schemes" and strive for "the utmost simplicity and naturalness." As he resumed work in November, following the visit to Paris, he was confident that he had at last hit on the "right line" and set himself the goal of turning out an act a week "at all costs" till he had finished the first draft.

Working daily in his tower study, including Christmas and New Year's, he made such good progress that Carlotta reported to Theresa Helburn that "the new play" (the Guild had no idea that he was composing a trilogy) was "just rolling out of him! . . . he can't write fast enough!!!" O'Neill hoped, he wrote Commins, to finish the first draft by mid-February, but, remembering his unhappy experience with *Dynamo*, he added: "No, I'm not going to tell even you anything about it — not because I know you wouldn't keep it confidential but simply because I have a personal reaction against saying a word about it until I have it completed and it can speak for itself. It is the most ambitious thing I have tackled, I'll say that much, and it doesn't involve any further experiments in technique. It is so strong in itself that the less technique is apparent, the better."

The developing plays sometimes seemed "grand" to him, other times "rotten," but whatever his mood, his drive never slackened. Many days Carlotta saw him only at dinner, and often he sat there so preoccupied that he seemed scarcely aware of her presence. In November he had thought "a modified, simplified *Interlude* technique" was appropriate for the trilogy; by January "involved inhibited cerebrations" appeared out of place. He "monkeyed around with schemes for dialogue and ideas for production until [his] head ached."

Exhausted from his labors but cheered by the feeling that the first draft was good, he finished it on February 21, 1930. "I've never had anything ride me so hard," he told Nathan. "Each play is pretty intense from beginning to end and it takes the guts out of one." He intended to write three complete drafts – the second one following a motor trip in March, the final one after a hiatus of some months. He wanted to space out the drafts not only to avoid going stale, he explained, but to allow time for perspective. "When you consider that there are twelve full-sized acts in this opus, you can see I am a glutton for punishment. But I think the results will justify the pains taken."

Praising Carlotta's contribution to his work, he said she had "collaborated by keeping the old château running with uncanny efficiency so that nary an outside worry has touched me or bogged my stride even for a moment. A most marvelous wife and friend. I am steeped to the ears in gratitude – and more than gratitude. And though it has been lonely for us . . . at times, nevertheless we've been happy and made quite a pleasant life of it alone together here."

After a short stay in Paris ("Carlotta's eyes are glittering," he had told Nathan, "with that new clothes look"), the couple toured France for about a fortnight. But in their travels they were almost as isolated as at the château. "Gene didn't care anything," says Carlotta, "for being with people – they made him nervous. On ships we never dined with the others, and when we motored we always had our meals up in our rooms – always, because he would get nervous in the public dining rooms. His hands would begin to shake, his face would sort of sink . . . and he would begin to sweat." That was also why, she added, that they practically never went to the theater after they returned to America. "If we did, somebody would spy him and say, 'OH, MR. O'NEILL, IT'S SO WONDERFUL TO SEE YOU,' and people would gather around. And I could just see him sort of disintegrate. It was terrible, so we just stopped at home."

Back at Le Plessis from the trip, O'Neill, who initially had been pleased with his draft, now thought that it was "scrawny stuff," that the "bare melodrama of plot runs away with my intent." The trilogy needed above all, he said in his work diary on March 27, a stronger "sense of fate hovering over characters, fate of family." In the diary, which contains a detailed, fascinating record of his mind at work on *Electra*, he further noted on the twenty-seventh that "more of my idea was left out of the play than there is in it! — In next version I must correct this at all costs — run the risk of going to other cluttered extreme — use every means to gain added depth and scope — can always cut what is unnecessary afterward . . . must get more distance and perspective . . . more sense of the unreal behind what we call reality which is the real reality! . . . Stick to modern tempo of the dialogue without attempt at pretense of Civil War lingo. That part of 1st draft is right. Obtain more fixed formal structure for first play which succeeding plays will reiterate — pattern of exterior and interior scenes, beginning and ending with exterior in each play — with the one ship scene at the center of the second play (this, center of whole work) emphasizing sea background of family and symbolic motive of sea as means of escape and release — use townsfolk at the beginning of each play, outside house, as fixed chorus pattern — representing prying, commenting, curious town as an ever present background for the drama of the Mannon family."

All the Mannons, including their cousin Adam Brant, are haunted by images of the South Sea islands and yearn to find refuge there. O'Neill told himself, "Develop South Sea Island motive — its appeal for them all (in various aspects) — release, peace, security, beauty, freedom of conscience, sinlessness, etc. — longing for the primitive — and mother symbol — yearning for pre-natal non-competitive freedom from fear."

The first draft of *Mourning Becomes Electra* was more or less naturalistic; for the next one, which O'Neill began writing on March 31, 1930, he decided on an eclectic style that would use the half-masks of *Lazarus Laughed* and, though he had already tried and abandoned the device once, the asides of *Strange Interlude*. Through use of the masks he planned to emphasize the all-important resemblances between Christine and her daughter Lavinia, and among Ezra Mannon, his son Orin, and Adam Brant (the new Aegisthus), who is Christine's lover. In limning his principals the author aimed to "exclude as far as possible and consistent with living people, the easy superficial characteristics of individual mannerisms — unless these mannerisims are inevitable fingerprints of inner nature — essential revelations." His basic problem, he concluded, was that "the unavoidable entire melodramatic action must be felt as working out of psychic fate from past — thereby attaining tragic significance — or else! — a hell of a problem, a modern tragic interpretation of classic fate without benefit of gods — for it must, before everything, remain modern psychological play — fate springing out of the family."

His constant allusions in the diary to the family or the past as "fate" indicate that his mind was working along the same lines that eventually would produce *Long Day's Journey Into Night*, the story of his own family and of how the individual O'Neills were shaped and twisted in the crucible of their interrelations. Indeed, the guilt-wracked wife in *Electra* sounds like Mary Tyrone of *Long Day's Journey* as she laments to a neighbor's daughter: "I was like you once — long ago. . . . If I could only have stayed as I was then! Why can't all of us remain innocent and loving and trusting? But God won't leave us alone. [Devout, convent-bred Mary Tyrone would have said "Life" or "Fate" instead of "God."] He twists and wrings and tortures our lives with others' lives until — we poison each other to death!"

At the end of May the playwright interrupted his work to visit Paris with Carlotta to see *All God's Chillun* and *Desire Under the Elms* given by the Kamerny, the theater founded by Alexander Taïrov in revolt against the naturalism of Stanislavski's Moscow Art Theater. Taïrov, who trained his players for several years before he allowed them to appear before the public, aimed for a fusion of drama, music, dance and decor in highly stylized productions. After the anti-American tenor of the Berlin attacks on *Strange Interlude* and the Paris reviews of *The Hairy Ape*, O'Neill was delighted that "one of the world's most famous modern theaters" was touring Europe with a repertory that included two works by "an uncultured Yank!"

He found the Kamerny staging of his two plays "damned interesting and imaginative!" and, in a backstage visit, felt an immediate rapport with Taïrov and his actors. "God," he said afterward, "if only we had their group spirit and love of the theater — imaginative love — somewhere in our theater!"

In his enthusiasm he thought of visiting Moscow someday, as Taïrov urged, but while his visit never materialized he delighted the Russian regisseur with a letter of the highest praise. His response to the two productions, he said on June 2, was "one of amazement — and most profound gratitude! Let me humbly confess I came to the theater with secret misgivings. Not that I doubted that your presentation would be a splendid thing in itself . . . I knew the reputation of the Kamerny . . . too well for that. But I did have an author's fear that in the difficult process of translation and transformation into another language and milieu the inner

[357]

spirit — that indefinable essential quality so dear to the creator as . . . the soul of his work — might be excusably, considering the obstacles, distorted or lost." Hence his "amazement and gratitude" on finding that the productions "rang so true to the spirit of my work!" "A theater of creative imagination," his letter continues, "has always been my ideal! To see my plays given by such a theater has always been my dream! The Kamerny Theater realized that dream for me!"

Judging, however, by John Martin, the dance critic of the New York *Times,* who reviewed the two productions in Paris, O'Neill greatly over-praised them. While Martin admired Alice Koonen, Taïrov's wife and one of Russia's leading actresses, who appeared as both Ella in *All God's Chillun* and Abbie in *Desire,* he said on June 15: "The scenery and costumes are shabby from much travel, and there is a general down-at-the-heel air about the whole business that would not be tolerated for an instant in New York and is not being received too cordially in Paris. . . . Certainly it is not the perfect 'theatrical' theater of one's dreams."

Still, in spite of its negative tone, his review suggests why O'Neill, who hungered for a "theater of creative imagination," was so impressed. According to Martin, the Kamerny repertory contained two outstanding scenes — Ella's solo mad scene in *All God's Chillun* and the christening party in *Desire.* In the first one, the critic said, Mme. Koonen used stylized movement to raise the play "into the realms of transcendant tragedy." In the party scene in *Desire,* "the neighbors, dressed and made up eccentrically, stamp through a slow and heavy square dance like so many gargoyles carved from stone. At the side . . . sits Mme. Koonen with the statuesque grandeur and aloofness of another Medea. The danc-ing is broken with short dialogues and cacklings from this ominous chorus, and as it is resumed each time it increases in tempo and dynamism until the Gargantuan solo dance of old Cabot himself. Taken as a whole, it is a ballet in itself."

The O'Neills had a number of guests this spring and summer, starting, to Carlotta's displeasure, with Jimmy Light, who was in Europe on a Guggenheim fellowship. Since Light and his wife Patti were friendly with Agnes, Carlotta regarded them as hostile to herself, but she particu-larly resented Mrs. Light, for she had heard that Patti, together with Fitzi of the Provincetown and Mary Blair, had been foremost among those who had gossiped against her. Light's weekend at the château (Carlotta had flatly refused to receive Mrs. Light) was an uncomfortable one for him. At dinner the first evening he mentioned that Helena Rubenstein of cosmetic fame thought of subsidizing a theater in Paris similar to the

Provincetown Playhouse, only to hear Carlotta ridicule the idea. And the first time that he addressed her by her first name, she retorted, "I'd like you to call me Mrs. O'Neill!"

Recalling his brief stay, Jimmy says, "She hardly ever left me alone with Gene, and I think I know why — she was afraid he would complain about her." O'Neill, trying to help his old friend now that the Provincetown had folded, authorized him to negotiate for the sale of *Jones, Ape* and *Desire* to English or Continental film producers; but, out of deference to Carlotta, this was one of the last times he ever saw Light.

By mid-summer Carlotta felt like a "manageress and entertainer for a small hotel!" Following Light's visit she and O'Neill played host in succession to Theresa Helburn and her husband; Philip Moeller and Helen Westley (the two, who found Carlotta unwittingly amusing, later told friends that she paraded around with a shepherdess's crook "like Marie Antoinette in the country"); Dr. Alvan L. Barach, who had treated O'Neill in New York, and Dr. George Draper, a friend of his; Elizabeth Sergeant; George Jean Nathan and Lillian Gish; and, as Carlotta wrote to Commins on July 27, "now & then a N.Y. newspaperman thrown in to prove we are normal, healthy, human people."

Unable to keep his producers in the dark any longer, the playwright, after swearing his Guild visitors to secrecy, summarized *Electra* for them; at the same time he advised them that he probably would not have the manuscript ready for the 1930–1931 season.

When the two doctors arrived at Le Plessis, Carlotta, in a gold Grecian-style dress, had "draped herself," Dr. Barach recalls, "against a post of the driveway." At lunch the first day Dr. Draper, a brother of monologuist Ruth Draper and a gifted raconteur in his own right, charmed his hosts with a stream of stories about literary personalities. "Carlotta," Barach says, "laughed a good deal and obviously enjoyed herself." That night after dinner the conversation turned serious, to such subjects as the quest for meaning in life and the effect of the mind on the body — Draper was a pioneer in practicing psychosomatic medicine — and after a while Carlotta excused herself and went upstairs for the night. The next day the same sort of thing happened. Draper told amusing stories at lunch and Carlotta had a good time, but, in Barach's words, she "didn't stay very long when we again became philosophical at night. It seemed clear that she didn't share O'Neill's interest in the big questions. She was gay and light-hearted, and I thought O'Neill loved in her the gaiety he lacked or had repressed in himself."

The first of the journalists to visit Le Plessis, Ward Morehouse wrote a detailed account of the couple's mode of living – "thirty-five rooms . . . two eighteenth-century towers . . . swimming pool . . . Bugatti racer . . . Carlotta's magnificent French car . . . a corps of servants" – and, summing up, said: "The theater has finally made Eugene O'Neill a rich man. And, after a two-day visit with him, I have the feeling that he's also a happy man." (Shortly after his report appeared on May 14, 1930, Agnes wrote to Harold DePolo, "Did you see the article in the *Sun* re Gene?")

The other visitors from the press, all at one time, were Richard Watts, Jr., the movie critic of the *Herald Tribune;* Don Skene, a sportswriter on the same paper; and John Byram of the New York *Times.* An admirer of the playwright, Watts, who had become friendly with him in New York, thought that his "gentleness" would be a surprise to those who knew him only through his work. "No one," writes the newsman, "could be more shy, more quiet, more genuinely kindly in an embarrassed sort of way." In the trio's overnight stay at the château "the hero of the occasion," according to the film critic, was Don Skene, for O'Neill took an immediate liking to him. "After our first meeting," Watts writes, "I never found O'Neill difficult to talk to, but, with Skene, he positively blossomed. He loved sports and old popular songs and stories about colorful characters, and these were Don's special fields. The result was an evening of gay conviviality, with songs, that was sheer delight, with O'Neill the most enchanting of hosts.

"It may be merely final proof that I didn't ever get to know O'Neill really well, but my strongest recollection of him . . . is of the zest and capacity for enjoyment he revealed that night. It took a kindred spirit, such as Don Skene's, to thrust his tortured vision into the background temporarily and bring out for the moment his sense of fun, even gaiety. He was clearly a sad man . . . but far from a forbidding one."

After weeks of working from morning till night with time out only for meals ("never worked so intensively over such a long period as I have on this damn trilogy"), O'Neill finished the second draft on July 11. Feeling "drained out" and uncertain whether he was wrestling with something too big for him, he regretted that he had ever "attempted the damn thing," as it all seemed a "blur of words." Mocking himself, he noted in his diary on the eleventh that he was leaving for Paris the next day – "nice little vacation in dentist's chair scheduled! Best anodyne for pernicious brooding over one's inadequacies. . . . Anything else seems like the best of all possible when your nerves are prancing to the sweet and low down of the dentist's drill!"

On returning home a week later he thought the script "much better" than he had feared, though in need of considerable work. Once before he had tried asides and then deleted them; now he found his second attempt a mistake, for they did not "reveal anything about the characters I can't bring out quite naturally in their talk or their soliloquies when alone — [the asides] simply get in the way of the play's drive." The *Strange Interlude* technique, he concluded, was suitable for a "modern Neurotic, disintegrated soul," but when "dealing with simple direct folk or characters of strong will and passion, it is superfluous show-shop 'business.' "

Starting in mid-July he spent two months revising his second draft; besides eliminating all the asides, he rewrote the soliloquies in a stylized manner, repetitious, monotonous, rhythmic, that he hoped would be a verbal equivalent of, and have the same kind of effect as, the pounding tom-toms in *The Emperor Jones*. The new soliloquies were designed to express the "driving insistent compulsion of passions engendered in [the Mannon] family past, which constitute [the] family fate."

While occupied with the revisions he learned from Saxe Commins that Horace Liveright had been ousted from his own firm. High living, together with ventures as a Broadway producer, had taken some of his money, but a larger part had vanished on Wall Street. A publisher with flair but a poor businessman, Liveright, chronically short of cash, had from time to time sold shares in his concern to Arthur H. Pell, his head bookkeeper, a cautious, frugal man, until Pell owned a majority of the stock and took over control of the firm. Saxe, who was working for another publishing house, could tell O'Neill only the general facts, but a letter from Manuel Komroff, a veteran at Liveright's, gave O'Neill the inside story. Since Komroff felt that Pell and his associates would run Liveright's (the name was retained) on a sounder economic basis, Eugene asked him to relay word that "they will have all my cooperation."

The playwright, who had confided in only the Guild directors and several of his most trusted intimates about his work in progress, was dismayed to hear from Robert Sisk that word of *Mourning Becomes Electra* was starting to leak out and that it was being praised as his "magnum opus." "How anyone," he wrote back on August 28, "can say the play is a 'magnum opus' and 'reveals undreamt powers' when no one has read a line of it is beyond me. . . . I'll bet some at least of the present gab traces back to people who hardly know me. I've heard tales of people going back and saying they were my guests here — like one of the family — who couldn't get in except over my dead body." He told the Guild's press agent that aside from the few to whom he had outlined *Electra*, he had informed some others that it was "the most difficult job

I've ever tackled and that explained why it was taking me so long. . . . I wanted that to get around to counteract the bunk that I was over here living the life of Reilly in a château and racing cars, whirling my wealth about regardless, and forgetting to work, etc., etc. Quite a bit of such drivel got back to me."

It would be impossible, he added, to prevent advance rumors about his work, since he had had "too much notoriety for too many years and *Interlude* topped all that and put me on a par with Peggy Hopkins [Joyce, a much-married show girl]! If I stopped producing for a number of years that would do it, of course, but it's hardly worth that abstinence . . . let's hope they will discover another 'best American dramatist' this season!"

After describing *Electra* to Sisk, he said that he had written it twice in nine months — the equivalent of "six plays in long hand! Christ how I've worked . . . and still must work!" He was trying, his letter continues, "to do a big thing and I don't care who knows it. . . . I am always trying to do the big thing. It's only the joy of that attempt that keeps me writing plays. . . . I really have little interest or enthusiasm for the modern theater, and to write for success or notoriety, or even to write merely good plays, wouldn't keep me on the job a minute. Shooting at a star may be hopeless in my case, time will tell, but it gives one a rich zest in being alive."

While he was still upset over the *Electra* rumors, gossip columnist Walter Winchell launched another on September 8 by printing that "The Eugene O'Neills (Carlotta Monterey) are so thrilled!" — one of his coy ways of reporting that a couple was going to have a baby. The substance behind the erroneous item was that Dorothy and Saxe were about to become parents — if a boy, the child was to be named Eugene after his playwright godfather — but apparently the facts were twisted by the time they reached the columnist. "The news of the baby," O'Neill fumed to Theresa Helburn, "is a W. Winchell fantasy! The devil take him! [In the States Agnes too was disturbed by the column note.] He had even AP wiring us to make inquiries! No thank you! I have three already and Carlotta one, and four is certainly enough in these days of bankroll depression."

He finished revising the second draft in mid-September and was only half satisfied with it. Elimination of the asides had helped substantially, he thought, but he now found that the stylized soliloquies "held up [the] plays, break rhythm, clog flow of dramatic development" and revealed nothing about the characters that could not "be shown directly or clearly suggested in their pantomime or talk."

The half-masks of the Mannons, he further decided, should also be eliminated, since they obtruded "too much into the foreground" and introduced "an obvious duality-of-character symbolism quite outside my intent." He intended, however, to retain a suggestion of masks as a "visual symbol of the separateness, the fated isolation of this family, the mark of their fate which makes them dramatically distinct from the rest of the world." He wanted the Mannon faces "*in repose*" to simulate lifelike death masks and thought that such an image could be obtained by careful makeup. "I can visualize," he said in his diary, "the death-mask-like expression of characters' faces in repose suddenly being torn open by passion as extraordinarily effective."

Even though the stylized soliloquies had proven a mistake, they gave him new insight into his characters and fresh ideas about his recurrent themes. He now aimed to "get all this in naturally in straight dialogue — as simple and direct and dynamic as possible." Looking back on his efforts to date, he admonished himself to "stop doing things to these characters — let them reveal themselves — in spite of (or perhaps because of!) their long locked-up passions, I feel them burning to do just this!"

Once the new revisions were completed early in October, he and Carlotta, hungry for the sun and some outdoor life after a summer of constant rain, began a month's vacation in Spain and Spanish Morocco. From Tangiers he reported to Robert Sisk that the swimming "in this neck of Africa is most excellent," while Carlotta on November 5 wrote to Madeleine Boyd: "The East begins again. We went on muleback yesterday thro' the narrow streets. The Moorish children [are] like dolls!" The couple had made trips across the Spanish border while living at Guéthary but this was their first extensive tour, and O'Neill as "an old Catholic" found Spain a "wonderful experience, the most interesting country in Europe." They visited the Prado, the cathedrals in Seville and Burgos, the mosque at Córdoba, the monastery at Guadalupe, but nothing stirred O'Neill's imagination more than that somber conglomerate of structures, royal and ecclesiastical, built by Philip II near Madrid: the Escorial. For years afterward he thought of writing a drama about the ruler who had presided over the highest bonfires of the Inquisition and the gloomiest court in all Christendom.

As the couple was touring Spain they heard that Sinclair Lewis had become the first American writer to win a Nobel Prize, and the playwright sent him a congratulatory wire. "I don't envy him," O'Neill wrote to George Jean Nathan. "On careful consideration – and no sour grapes about it because I had no hopes! – I think the Nobel Prize, until you become very old . . . costs more than it's worth. Lewis will find, I think, that it's an anchor around his neck he'll never be able to shake off." (The previous year, shortly before Thomas Mann was named Nobel laureate, the Paris *Herald* had reported that Lewis, Dreiser and O'Neill were being considered, in that order, for the honor.)

"How did friend Dreiser take the blow?" O'Neill asked Nathan. "Too bad! He deserved it [the Nobel award] more than any American."

Sinclair Lewis, on sailing for Stockholm, told reporters in New York that he would have been "just as glad" had O'Neill been selected. Later, in his formal acceptance speech before the Swedish Academy, he said that O'Neill "has done nothing much in the American drama save to transform it in ten or twelve years from a false world of neat and competent trickery into a world of splendor, fear and greatness." The dramatist, he added, had seen life as "terrifying, magnificent and quite often horrible, a thing akin to a tornado, an earthquake or a devastating fire."

Before O'Neill left for Spain, he had considered his script in good shape. On his return, though, he was depressed to find the first two acts of *Homecoming* faulty and began revising them. "Would to God this damned trilogy were off of my neck!" he lamented to Nathan on December 1. "I'm beginning to hate it and curse the day I ever conceived such an idea." Nathan had offered to write an advance article, but O'Neill cautioned him to wait till he had read *Mourning Becomes Electra*. "I don't know whether it will be worth an essay or anything else.

"This isn't an author's immodest hokum! I really feel most low about it."

Expressing himself more guardedly a few days later to De Casseres, he said, "Don't ask me how good or bad it is! I have about as much perspective on the whole thing as a fly on the paper to which he's stuck. My only idea now is to get unstuck as soon as possible and get on to something else. This has been a draining, exhausting job."

He was weary by this time not only of revising *Electra* but of living abroad, and doubted that expatriation was "any answer to anything." During his early months in Europe he had "felt a deep sense of peace here, a real enjoyment in just living from day to day, that I've never known before." Anyone "doing creative work," he declared, was foolish "to waste the amount of energy required to beat life in the U.S.A. when over here one can have just that more strength to put into one's job." But now he was plagued by "a feeling of not really belonging, of having no affinity with land or people – of being rootless and growthless."

Carlotta was, if anything, even more disenchanted. Already bored from having little to do, it had come as a shock to her, since she had been generous with everyone, to discover that the manager of the estate and the tradespeople had been fleecing her with overcharges and nonexistent expenses. "The French," she complained, "think more of the *centime* than we do of the dollar."

For all his preoccupation with the trilogy, O'Neill was not unaware of what Carlotta was enduring in their isolation. Dedicating *Electra* to her the following year, he said it was in "memory of the interminable days of rain in which you bravely suffered in silence that this trilogy might be born — days when I had my work but you had nothing but household frets and a blank vista through salon windows of the gray land of Le Plessis, with the wet black trees still and dripping, and the mist wraiths mourning over drowned fields . . . days which for you were bitterly lonely, when I seemed far away and lost to you in a grim, savage gloomy country of my own. . . .

"In short, days in which you collaborated, as only deep love can, in the writing of this trilogy of the damned! . . . Let us hope what the trilogy may have in it will repay the travail we've gone through for its sake!"

Hailing her as "mother, and wife and mistress and friend!" he added, "And collaborator! Collaborator, I love you!"

As 1930 ended, they both were ill with the flu; while wrapping gifts for their servants on Christmas Eve, Carlotta fainted, and a day or so later Eugene was confined to bed. They still felt shaky as they arrived in Paris two weeks later to have his script typed, but while he managed to remain on his feet, Carlotta suffered a relapse and was in the American Hospital for over a fortnight. Writing to Manuel Komroff on January 20, 1931, O'Neill complained that "the fair land of Touraine resembles a dismal swamp. You may gather from this that I am a bit fed up with the smiling country of *la belle* France in the winter time. . . . I would not spend another winter here for anything." Congratulating Komroff on his completion of another novel, he added, "I wish to Christ my play were off my hands. In my present condition it is a hell of a labor to put on the finishing touches."

For years Manuel had done little services and favors for O'Neill at Liveright's, but now the playwright could rely on Saxe Commins, who had recently landed there as an editor through the combined influence of O'Neill and Komroff. From Paris Eugene asked Saxe to relay word to his superiors that he was against having Alexander King, who had illustrated deluxe editions of several O'Neill plays, do the same for *Lazarus Laughed*. King had written him, he said on January 24, "a very hectic sort of note in which he tells me he is dying of cancer, but he hopes to live long enough to finish the illustrations for *Lazarus* . . . something in the tone of the letter makes me believe that Alex has heard how down I am on his last illustrations . . . and that he is giving me a little sob story to work on my sympathies." (His intuition was correct: King, who became a best-selling author and a television personality in the 1950s, outlived O'Neill by more than ten years.)

A true son of James O'Neill, the playwright rarely missed an opportunity to deride the English. Informing Nathan on January 27 that *Strange Interlude* was about to open in London, he doubted that it would "last very long," for he was sure that the "dear old 'Limies' will never stand for being yanked from their afternoon tea to the theater — especially by an Irish-Yankee." Later, when *Desire Under the Elms* was finally staged in the West End for the first time, he prized a particular sentence in one review: "Yet need everyone have been quite so — brutish?" O'Neill thought it "a very, very beautiful gem of perfect British snobbery."

After he returned from Paris, his work on *Electra* in February 1931 consisted largely of eliminating things he had introduced in his previous revision, for he realized that his latest attempt to add values had simply blurred those he already had. On the twentieth, with the trilogy restored more or less to its former state, he and Carlotta left the gray, dripping Touraine for sunshine and swimming in Las Palmas, the Canary Islands; but it was not much of a vacation for him since he could not keep his hands off his script. Though it now looked "damned good" to him, he also found it "much too long" and spent many hours cutting and condensing it.

While the couple was in Las Palmas, Georges Lewys's plagiarism suit against *Strange Interlude* went on trial in New York on March 11 before Federal Judge John W. Woolsey in his chambers in the Woolworth Building. O'Neill, who had sent a deposition, told Theresa Helburn, "Five minutes on the witness stand and my goat and temper would have been lost for keeps. I was a witness once and the judge threatened me with contempt and my side wished to God they'd never thought of me. You know how some people can't stand cats. Well, a courtroom affects me the same way. I hate laws and everything to do with them."

As the trial began, the defense sought unsuccessfully to have the suit summarily dismissed on the grounds that even if the main ideas in Miss Lewys's *The Temple of Pallas-Athenae* and O'Neill's drama were similar (a view the defense disputed), ideas were not subject to copyright. Turning aphorist, Arthur Garfield Hays, Liveright's attorney, held that the first person who uses an idea is "an originator," the second "a plagiarist," the third "takes the idea from the common stock, and the fourth to use the idea does research work."

The plaintiff, a tall woman with rampant red hair and an emphatic manner, proved so evasive ₅and voluble as the first witness that both the judge and her own attorney had to caution her to limit her replies. The proceedings developed into a quick survey of world literature as the defense cited authors ranging from Plutarch and Shakespeare to Ibsen, Shaw and Amy Lowell who had used themes and situations resembling those in the plaintiff's book. Under questioning the plaintiff disclosed that she thought little of American writers, past and present. Tossing her head scornfully when asked by Harry Weinberger, O'Neill's attorney, whether she had ever read Amy Lowell's poetry, Miss Lewys declared, "She never wrote any poetry." In response to a similar question about American literature, the witness said, "I haven't found much."

During the hearings, which lasted nearly a week and were extensively reported in the press, there was considerable testimony, pro and con, about whether O'Neill might have had access to and read the Lewys novel before he wrote his drama. In her complaint the novelist stated that she had sent her book, shortly after it was copyrighted in 1924, to both the Theater Guild, for possible dramatization, and Boni and Liveright.

Like O'Neill's play, her novel dealt with a woman who goes outside her marriage, on an older woman's advice, to have a child because of hereditary insanity in her husband's family; but otherwise the two stories could hardly have been less similar. Written in purple verbiage with a kind of maidenly leer, *The Temple*, a tale of two generations, centered on a male house of assignation in Paris staffed by men bursting with virility. To quote from a resumé Miss Lewys sent to the Guild with her book: "Handsome American and European women who are married to senile, awkward or debauched husbands (*'marriages de conveniences'*) visit the house without the knowledge of their husbands in order to obtain beautiful children and to improve the human race." In time the son of one client and the daughter of another fall in love, but, unhappily, it turns out that they are cognate — their mothers had enjoyed the services of the same stud, a nonpareil named Adonis — and so the enamored young couple must part forever. (When Miss Lewys first filed her suit, she complained to the press that O'Neill's play "pandered to the licentious. He made a travesty of my work and turned pure English into the argot of the day.")

Categorically denying that his drama had been inspired by the plaintiff's novel, O'Neill stated in his deposition that he had never even heard of it, much less read it, till she filed her suit in 1929. His play was largely based, he said, on a real-life situation he had heard about in Provincetown in the summer of 1923; a few months later, according to his affidavit, he wrote the germ of the play in a notebook under the tentative title "Godfather." To document O'Neill's testimony, Weinberger offered in evidence the notebook, which contained the synopsis of "Godfather" along with ideas for over thirty plays yet unwritten.

Under cross-examination by Weinberger, Miss Lewys said she could not recall whether, after instituting her suit against *Strange Interlude*, she had offered her privately printed book to publishers Covici, Friede. The following day the attorney produced evidence establishing that she had submitted the book, without success. In an exchange between her and the attorney, she vehemently denied making the statement to someone that "whatever else I get out of this suit, I will get a million dollars worth of publicity." The defense revealed also that Miss Lewys had sued Universal Pictures in 1926 for a million dollars, charging that the studio had plagiarized another of her privately printed books. The suit was settled out of court, Weinberger said, for about five hundred dollars, but the plaintiff, when asked about it, replied only that the sum had been "satisfactory."

In her various turns in the witness stand Miss Lewys made such a poor impression that what had originally seemed merely a weak case came to look farcical; however, the judge made no attempt to shorten the trial. He apparently wanted the trial to get maximum publicity in hopes that it would discourage other plagiarism suits of little substance. A man of intellectual tastes and progressive views, Judge Woolsey later became celebrated for a landmark decision clearing Joyce's *Ulysses* of obscenity charges.

The final session, on March 16, turned into a sparring match between Daniel F. Cohalan, the plaintiff's chief counsel, and George Jean Nathan, the star witness of the day, as the lawyer constantly tried with sarcasm and blunt disparagement to anger the critic and throw him off-balance. But Nathan, although more disposed to give than to receive, generally endured the barbs without perceptible flinching. After he said that O'Neill was "not so well known" when the two of them first became acquainted, Cohalan cracked, "Oh, I see, after he met you he began to write better." "Without accepting your implication," Nathan replied, "I would say that I sold his first long play for him and published some of his one-act plays."

As he listed other instances of his aid to O'Neill in finding a producer, Cohalan interjected, "In other words you were acting as a salesman rather than a dramatic critic?" Nathan, squirming a bit but managing to grin: "As an admirer I tried to help him."

On direct examination he testified that the playwright first talked to him about *Strange Interlude* one night in 1923 as they were walking down lower Sixth Avenue. "He told me," Nathan recalled, "that it was his ambition to write a play dealing in great detail with the life of a woman from her youth until the age of forty-five. The woman, he said, would be one who had lost her ideals and vision, and the play would deal with her attempt to recapture them in some other form."

Nathan praised O'Neill as undoubtedly the foremost American playwright, but he also, to maintain his franchise as a critic, said that his friend was "a very stubborn fellow, very vain" in that he "seldom takes any suggestion concerning his plays."

In the summations Cohalan called O'Neill "too cowardly" to return for the trial and submit to cross-examination, while Weinberger countered, "One of the rackets in America is the plagiarism racket, and any successful author is likely to be its victim." Going beyond Weinberger's position, Arthur Garfield Hays asked the court not only to find for their clients but to discourage trumped-up suits by requiring the plaintiff to pay for the defendants' expenses.

Over a month later Judge Woolsey, ruling for the defense in a decision that ran forty-two pages, called Miss Lewys's suit "wholly preposterous." He ordered her to pay O'Neill seventy-five hundred dollars for his expenses, the Guild five thousand dollars, and Liveright five thousand dollars; but none of the defendants ever received a cent, for the lady, as O'Neill had suspected all along, had no funds to speak of. The following year, when pressed to pay, she said she would "get to work and write a best-seller, something nice and nasty"; a year later she entered bankruptcy and thereafter dropped from public view — no more plagiarism suits.

In Las Palmas the playwright worked so hard on *Electra* that he felt more tired than ever when he and Carlotta left the island late in March. He added some last-minute touches in Paris, had the script retyped at the hotel under his eyes — he would not allow it out of his sight — and on April 7, relieved at finally getting "the damn thing off my chest," mailed it to the Theater Guild with a covering letter in which he said: "As you will see, no departures in technique are involved. *Interlude* soliloquies and asides only got in the way of these plays of intense passions and little cerebrations. . . . The dialogue is colloquial of today. The house, the period costumes, the Civil War surface stuff, these are the masks for what is really a modern psychological drama with no true connections with that period at all. I think I have caught enough Greek sense of fate — a modern approximation to it, I mean — out of the Mannons themselves to do without any Greek theatrical effects."

He sent a script to Nathan also and wrote him: "It has been one hell of a job! To get enough of Clytemnestra in Christine, of Electra in Lavinia, of Orestes in Orin, etc., and yet keep them American primarily; to conjure a Greek fate out of the Mannons themselves (without calling in the aid of even a Puritan Old Testament God) that would convince a modern audience without religion or moral ethics; to prevent the surface melodrama of the plot from overwhelming the real drama; to contrive murders that escape cops and courtroom scenes; and finally to keep myself out of it and shun the many opportunities for effusions of personal writing anent life and fate — all this has made the going tough and the way long!"

He was uncertain of how close he had come to his objectives. "All I *do* know," his letter continues, "is that after reading it all through, in spite of my familiarity with every page, it leaves me moved and disturbed spiritually, and I have a feeling of there being real size in it, quite apart from its length; a sense of having had a valid dramatic experience with intense tortured passions beyond the ambition or scope of other modern plays."

O'Neill's finest dramas were still in the future, yet, purely as narrative, as an expression of his acute sense of theater, *Mourning Becomes Electra* remains one of his outstanding achievements. Set almost entirely in and before a neo-Grecian mansion — Christine Mannon thinks of it as a "tomb," a "sepulchre," a "pagan temple front stuck like a mask on Puritan gray ugliness!" — *Electra* wastes little time in establishing its power. From the first showdown between Lavinia and Christine, as Lavinia reviles her adulterous mother and threatens to expose her to the father, the narrative starts to coil and tighten like a huge python that will devour all members of the doomed house of Mannon, and it rarely eases its grip during most of its thirteen acts of murder, suicide, near-madness and haunting.

In at least one objective the author fell short at times, for he was not always able to "prevent the surface melodrama of the plot from overwhelming the real drama." Yet the story he tells is so lurid that only the highest art, as he himself realized, could have ennobled its violence. "Oh," he had cried earlier to Joseph Wood Krutch, "for a language to write drama in!" At the end, even though *Electra* was enthusiastically received on Broadway, he had no illusions that he had solved his central problem. In 1932 he told Arthur Hobson Quinn, who considered the trilogy "a landmark in the history of American drama," that he hoped it was "as worthy as you think it. I am very satisfied with it — (taken all around it *is* my best, I think) — but at the same time, deeply dissatisfied. It needed great language to lift it beyond itself. I haven't got that. And, by the way of self-consolation, I don't think, from the evidence of all that is written today, that great language is possible for anyone living in the discordant, broken, faithless rhythm of our time. The best one can do is to be pathetically eloquent by one's moving, dramatic inarticulations!"

Mourning Becomes Electra is the creation of a man familiar with Attic tragedy, with major aspects of Freudian theory, and, certainly not least, with the rousing head-on clashes of James O'Neill's old-time theater. In the main the trilogy, for all its base in classical tragedy, is a superstructure of austere melodrama heated by the fires of oedipal passions and frustrations. Son loves mother and hates father, daughter adores father and hates mother, each parent reciprocates in kind — *Electra* could hardly follow more closely, more obviously, Freud's view of the basic pattern of relations between children and parents. Yet its weakness as literature is a prime source of the play's strength as theater, for the schematic Freudian pattern constantly sets the stage for confrontations. A lesser man might have hit upon such a scheme for retelling the *Oresteia* trilogy, and provided an exciting show, but O'Neill endowed his version with some dignity and stature, a feeling of inevitability, by creating characters whose sheer intensity of emotion makes them larger than life; the violence of the story seems, in short, to develop relentlessly from their natures. Actually, the Mannons are not so much persons (it is difficult to think of them eating, drinking and sleeping) as walking passions, for they are totally defined by their loves, hungers and hostilities.

If the playwright misused psychoanalytic thought, his chief offense was not so much in wrapping the interfamily relationships in one neat oedipal package as in making his principals too knowing about themselves and one another. It is as though these Civil War–era figures had spent time on the analytic couch and could identify the impulses behind their unruly feelings. Christine, trying to justify her illicit romance with Adam Brant, says to Lavinia: "Well, I hope you realize I would never have fallen in love with Adam if I'd had Orin with me [her son Orin had gone off to the war]." Another time, trying to crush her daughter, she charges: "I know you, Vinnie! . . . You've tried to become the wife of your father and the mother of Orin! You've always schemed to steal my place!"

Since the Mannons' incestuous inclinations are evident early, it comes as an anticlimax in *The Haunted*, rather than as a new peak of horror, when Orin proposes to his sister that they live together like man and wife. Immediately afterward, half-crazed with grief and guilt from driving his mother to suicide, he retires and, adding another corpse to the pile, shoots himself.

Beneath its Grand Guignol aspects *Mourning Becomes Electra* bears some resemblance to *Desire Under the Elms*. Here again is a son (Adam Brant) bent on avenging a mother who had been driven into an untimely grave; an adulterous affair between that son and the wife of his adversary; and a husband whose wife shrinks from his touch. When Brigadier General Mannon returns from the war eager for reconciliation with his wife, their abortive reunion recalls the bedroom scene in which old Cabot bares himself, through his life story, to the unreceptive Abbie. In both cases the husband is unfavorably depicted at first, but finally appears in a rather sympathetic light.

After the two elder Mannons are dead and the story focuses on the relations between Lavinia and Orin, *Electra* diminishes in power; yet nothing that had transpired earlier — neither Christine's murder of her husband nor Lavinia's discovery of the deed — is quite as overwhelming as the trilogy's quiet final moments. Indeed, as Lavinia turns to enter the house while the old family retainer tries to dissuade her, *Electra* suddenly soars to a level of genuine tragedy.

"Don't be afraid," she tells old Seth. "I'm not going the way Mother and Orin went. That's escaping punishment. And there's no one left to punish me. I'm the last Mannon. I've got to punish myself! Living alone here with the dead is a worse act of justice than death or prison! I'll never go out or see anyone! I'll have the shutters nailed close so no sunlight can ever get in. I'll live alone with the dead, and keep their secrets, and let them hound me, until the curse is paid out and the last Mannon is dead! (*With a strange cruel smile of gloating over the years of self-torture*) I know they will see to it I live for a long time! It takes the Mannons to punish themselves for being born!"

She was speaking not only for herself but for her author. He, too, flagellated himself with the past; and, though he went about in the world and had some contact with his fellowman, a crucial part of him, as his writings repeatedly suggest, was forever closeted with his dead. While *Electra* is one of his less subjective works, it still expresses his somber view of what Freud called "the family romance." Or, as the playwright himself had said, he chose to retell the *Oresteia* trilogy "because it has greater possibilities of revealing all the deep hidden relationships in the family than any other" of the classic tragedies.

19

Homecoming

THE O'Neills landed back in New York on May 17, 1931, after an unpleasant crossing, due to storms and fog, that shortly would prove a fit prelude to their homecoming. Anxious as usual to avoid publicity, they managed, under a purser's guidance, to debark without running a gauntlet of ship news reporters and sequestered themselves in a suite at the Hotel Madison on East Fifty-eighth Street. They had been so secretive beforehand about their return, confiding in only several intimates, that the Theater Guild brass did not learn of their arrival until the following day, a Monday. With the playwright's reluctant consent, the Guild immediately scheduled a mass press conference for Thursday to accommodate in one sweep all the newspapers and periodicals eager to interview him; advance word on the trilogy had already aroused considerable speculation and publicity. Before the interview took place, however, both O'Neill and Carlotta – linked with Ralph Barton – were page-one news from coast to coast.

Around midnight on Tuesday the nineteenth Barton, in his penthouse apartment on East Fifty-seventh Street, only a few blocks from the Madison, carefully set the stage to exit from life with panache. He typed a farewell to the world which he headed "OBIT" in red ink; wrote a brief note to his maid and enclosed thirty-five dollars, all his cash; placed a copy of Gray's *Anatomy* on his bed, opened at pages showing illustrations of the human heart; and, attired in silk pajamas, withdrew to bed. After smoking briefly, he shot himself through the right temple. When the maid arrived on Wednesday morning, she found him propped up against the pillows, a cigarette still in one hand, the pistol in the other.

In his "OBIT" he said that everyone who knew him would have "a different hypothesis to offer to explain why I did it. Practically all of

[373]

these hypotheses will be dramatic and completely wrong. Any sane doctor knows that the reasons for suicide are invariably psychopathological and the true suicide type manufactures his own difficulties. I have had few real difficulties. I have had, on the contrary, an exceptionally glamorous life, as life goes; and I have had more than my share of affection and appreciation.

"The most charming, intelligent and important people I have known have liked me, and the list of my enemies is very flattering to me. I have always had excellent health, but since my early childhood I have suffered from a melancholia, which in the last five years has begun to show definite symptoms of manic-depressive insanity. It has prevented my getting anything like the full value out of my talent, and the past three years has made work a torture to do at all. . . . I have run from wife to wife, from house to house and from country to country in a ridiculous effort to escape from myself. In doing so, I am very much afraid that I have brought a great deal of unhappiness to those who loved me.

"In particular, my remorse is bitter over my failure to appreciate my beautiful lost angel, Carlotta, the only woman I ever loved and whom I respect and admire above all the rest of the human race. She is the one person who could have saved me had I been savable. She did her best. No one ever had a more devoted or more understanding wife. . . .

"No one thing is responsible for this and no one person – except myself. If the gossips insist on something more definite and thrilling as a reason, let them choose my pending appointment with the dentist or the fact that I happen to be painfully short of cash at the moment. . . . I present the remains, with my compliments, to any medical school that fancies them, or let soap be made of them . . . I kiss my dear children – and Carlotta."

Before word spread around town, the O'Neills, in a telephone call from Harold Ross, the editor of the *New Yorker*, were among the first to learn of the suicide and the farewell message. Carl Van Vechten and Fania Marinoff, who lunched with the couple that Wednesday in their hotel suite, found the playwright more than normally taciturn, but Carlotta was voluble on the subject of Barton.

"She couldn't understand," Van Vechten says, "why he'd dragged her into it. Barton, she insisted, hadn't loved her in years. Personally, I thought it a clear case of ego, of his wanting all possible attention at his death. He resented her marrying someone more famous than himself and wanted to upset them. I knew Ralph intimately, I'd seen him only a short time before. He was heavily in debt, he'd lived beyond his means for years, he'd seen and done everything, and saw no point in going on.

"Don't forget, too, that the Great Depression was on — people weren't in the mood for his sophisticated art. The market for his stuff had shrunk, and he could see only lean times ahead, so he decided to go out in a splash of publicity."

In the news accounts Barton's brother Homer, an actor, said that Ralph "was still in love with [Carlotta] and the realization that he had lost her broke his heart. It was a matter of impulse, I'm sure, for Ralph was very impulsive. When Mr. and Mrs. O'Neill came to New York, he paid them a friendly visit." Unable to remain publicly silent after the brother's statement, the O'Neills declared through Harry Weinberger that they had not seen Barton since their return and that Mrs. O'Neill had never heard from or seen her ex-husband "since her divorce more than five years ago."

More apprehensive now than ever about facing bombardment from the press, O'Neill thought of canceling the mass interview, but he finally had the Guild inform the newspapers that he would discuss only *Mourning Becomes Electra* and other theatrical matters. When the reporters appeared that Thursday at Guild headquarters (today the ANTA Theater), Joe Heidt, a Guild publicity man, reminded them of the playwright's stipulation. O'Neill also, to forestall a fusillade of queries, had specified that only one newsman, serving as spokesman for the group, was to question him. The choice fell on John Chapman, a drama reporter for the *Daily News* (later its theater critic). "He was pallid and shaking and sweating when he faced his lone inquisitor," Chapman says, "and so was I."

The interview, which lasted an hour and a half, proceeded harmoniously till its final moments. O'Neill sat behind a desk, "gradually but constantly," according to one account, "shifting his position, smiling shyly, recurrently lowering his deep-set eyes, his low, sad voice hesitating over his simple answers." It was apparent from a momentary brightening of his face whenever he welcomed a particular question. His major benefit from living in Europe, he said, was that it enabled him "to see America more clearly, and also to appreciate it more. . . . Most people who travel abroad get the sort of snobbish idea that they are coming in contact with something superior. I don't feel that way." Contrary to what he had expected, he found that the European stage in general was "tired out" and now thought that "the rebirth of the theater" was more likely to happen over here.

"My personal interest in the theater," he went on, "is to see just how much can be done with it — not only for my sake but for everybody's sake. The more it is pushed out, the more can be done with it. That's why I'm interested in seeing how [*Mourning Becomes Electra*] is received." Raising his voice for the first time when someone asked, "Do you care?" he replied, "Of course I care. I've been working like a Trappist monk for a year and a half."

He said of *Electra* that each play would take an evening to perform and that he favored a preliminary week for the critics' convenience during which *Homecoming* would be given two evenings in succession, then *The Hunted*, and finally *The Haunted*, after which each work would be given a week at a time.

Looking ahead, he reported that he had work "planned for at least five years," and added: "One of my principal obsessions is the reintroduction of masks. . . . My idea is that they can be made acceptable to the modern audience — as they were in ancient times — but in a new sense. People do recognize from their knowledge of the new psychology that everyone wears a mask — I don't mean only one but thousands of them. I believe people will come to accept them in the theater. I don't think *The Great God Brown* had a long run merely because it was a novelty."

Toward the end of the session several reporters became importunate about Barton and his brother's statement. "As far as I know," O'Neill replied, "I never met Ralph Barton. He did not call on us. I do not question his brother's sincerity, for Mr. Barton might have told him he called. He was in a very peculiar mental state. I know that he made no effort to see Mrs. O'Neill." Under persistent querying as to Carlotta's whereabouts, he replied only that she was "in the country."

During these exchanges he looked, the *News* reported, like a "a man repressing himself with a mighty effort. He flushed intermittently and his earnest eyes flashed. Once he seemed on the point of breaking into a rage. That was when reporters pressed him for news of his wife's whereabouts." O'Neill had just protested, "This isn't fair!" when a Guild official called him from the room, presumably to break the rising tension; on his return he closed the interview by thanking the newsmen and bidding them good-bye.

His sense of relief as the ordeal ended was cut short when Joe Heidt, at the window, observed some reporters install themselves in taxis parked before the Guild Theater; they intended, apparently, to trail O'Neill to his hideout in an effort to quiz Carlotta. Somewhat embarrassedly, Heidt, thinking that the playwright might be offended, said that the best way to escape unnoticed would be to ascend to the roof and cross over to an adjoining building with an exit on another street. O'Neill welcomed the suggestion and soon, after following the press agent up and down fire escapes and across roofs, was on his way, undetected, back to the Madison. According to Carlotta, he told her that "the men were all right but the women reporters had asked the damndest personal questions."

The couple one day made a fleeting visit to New London. After the stories she had heard of his mother drifting around the house "like a ghost" and of the countless drunken scenes between the two brothers and their father, Carlotta was surprised that her husband would ever want to see the cottage again. "Don't do it, darling," she said, attempting to dissuade him, "don't ever try to go back."

"No," she recalls, "he must go. So we took the car and we went up. But in the time that Gene had been away the town had cut a street through and built little houses along here to the water and [at first] he couldn't find it. Well, I was thunderstruck when I saw this quaint little birdcage of a house sitting there. And he said, 'I shouldn't have come.' And I said, 'Well, never mind, you have come now. Let's get out of here.' And he said, 'Yes, let's get away.'"

By mid-June the O'Neills had settled for the summer in Northport, Long Island, in a house with a private beach on Long Island Sound; once again the "Sea-Mother's Son," who had felt landlocked at Le Plessis, was living within view of the water. Originally he and Carlotta had intended to spend part of the summer in California, where Nellie Tharsing, who had reared her granddaughter since infancy, was clamoring to be relieved of the responsibility. Carlotta had promised to attend to the problem, but once her husband became involved in the preliminaries of the *Electra* production, she used him as an excuse to defer the California trip.

Although more scrupulous than Carlotta about parental obligations, it appears that O'Neill, basically, was no more of a father than she was a mother; he was too much a "son," too bound emotionally to his own parents, to be a parent himself. At the same time, however, as a man of conscience with an abiding sense of guilt, he wanted to do right by the three who bore his name. So long as they did not infringe on his special way of life and, above all, his work, he was willing to act the role of father; he wanted them to like him and to believe that they meant a great deal to him. By contrast, Carlotta's history suggests that she was more or less unconcerned as to how her daughter Cynthia felt about her.

Loath to deal directly with Agnes, O'Neill arranged through Harry Weinberger for Shane to visit him this summer on Long Island; Oona, now aged six, he intended to see later in the city. A quiet, withdrawn youngster, slightly built, Shane, at his father's suggestion, was to enter the Lawrenceville (New Jersey) School in the fall. At first the Lawrenceville authorities were going to reject him as too young — he was going on twelve — and inadequately educated, but finally the scales were tipped in his favor by his father's renown.

"Immensely pleased" at the decision, O'Neill wrote to W. A. Jameson, Jr., the assistant to the headmaster: "I think I am objective about it, and not just another parent, when I state a conviction that Shane has real stuff in him which Lawrenceville will help to bring out. His schooling in the past few years, during my residence abroad, has been so broken up and irregular that he has never really had a fair chance to get started on the right track."

Where Shane was to continue having trouble with his schooling, Eugene Jr. went from triumph to triumph at Yale. Earlier this year he had won the first Winthrop prize for his knowledge of Greek and Latin poetry; in the fall he would be among the select few named "a scholar of the first rank." "I don't know how to talk to him," O'Neill proudly complained to friends. "He's too erudite for me." In another respect, though, he was less pleased with his twenty-one-year-old son. After getting permission from the Yale faculty, as was required of undergraduates, young Eugene on June 15 had married a girl from Forest Hills, Queens, named Elizabeth Green. Although the ceremony in Long Island City was within easy driving distance of Northport, the playwright did not attend, probably to avoid an awkward meeting with his first wife.

Once O'Neill returned to this country, he never again drove, for he was too nervous to contend with the traffic, but he bought a car and hired a chauffeur. "Yes," he told Brooks Atkinson, "it's a Cadillac! But lest this sound too opulent for a serious-minded Dramatist, let me hasten to explain I secured it second-hand. Only 2,000 miles, ironclad guarantee attached, looking brand-new, over $1,000 off, who could resist this splendid gift of world depression? Not I, who have always been an A-one snob where it came to cars and boats. . . . This snootiness dates back to my early boyhood days." Although he used to deride his father as miserly, he now said, "My father, the Count of Monte Cristo, always got me the classiest rowboats to be had, and we sported the first Packard car in our section of Conn. way back in the duster-goggle era."

His summer in Northport, compared to his life at Le Plessis, was a whirl of social and professional activity. Among the guests were Shane for a fortnight, young Eugene and his bride after their honeymoon, Saxe Commins, George Jean Nathan with Lillian Gish, the Carl Van Vechtens,

arlotta in the early thirties

*O'Neill on Long Island making final revisions
in* Mourning Becomes Electra

Agnes with Oona and Shane in Bermuda in 1930

Eugene Jr. at Yale

and several from the Theater Guild. The playwright conferred not only with the Guild about *Electra* but, through Saxe, with the new heads of Liveright's. Hoping to equal the success of *Strange Interlude*, which had sold nearly one hundred and ten thousand copies, Arthur Pell and his associates were eager to publish the trilogy as soon as possible after its Broadway opening. As a promotional feature, they planned to issue a brochure of short articles on O'Neill by theatrical and literary notables, both here and abroad. Commins, who was assigned to gather the material, said in his letter soliciting comment that Liveright's wanted "to make this venture a publication worthy of the figure it honors."

Replying for Bernard Shaw, his secretary Blanche Patch wrote that he "has asked me to say that nothing is more revoltingly unreadable than logrolling and that he implores you to abandon the project before it bankrupts you. Otherwise O'Neill will probably sue you for damages."

Thomas Mann regretted that he was too busy to write an article but did say that he found in O'Neill's plays "a certain dramatic comparison to the epic writing of Ernest Hemingway" and that *Jones* and *Ape* in particular had "exercised a profound impression" on him. He was unfamiliar, he added, with the later plays and hoped that they would soon be translated and staged in Germany.

The warmest responses came from Sinclair Lewis, Alexander Taïrov of the Kamerny, and Sean O'Casey, a writer O'Neill greatly admired. Lewis, who had been so laudatory in his Nobel Prize speech, wrote that the playwright "has taken the rather stupid and tawdry drama of America, as it existed before his time, and completely revolutionized it." O'Neill, he summed up, was "a very great man."

Taïrov, returning the compliment O'Neill had paid his theater, called him "the most significant, the most interesting, and the most exciting dramatist of our time." But in the midst of praising the American, the Russian used him as a stick to beat the capitalist nations. O'Neill, he said, strips "the gilt and gaudy trappings from the contemporaneous Western-European and American cultures; and with an unparalleled profundity and truthfulness he reveals the irreconcilable conflicts and cataclysms concealed within these civilizations."

O'Casey, a man with a gift for making words sing, thought that it "might be a little impertinent for me to say why and how O'Neill is a great dramatist when, always in his published books, and often on the stage, his work is always bearing witness to the things great and the things beautiful which have saved the Theater from the shame of a house of ill-fame and a den of thieves, and have kept the ground in and around the Theater as holy as the ground around the burning bush. . . .

"Eugene O'Neill, like all men born with original sin in their souls, has, I suppose, what we, in a pensively critical mood, would call his weak moments. I remember several little playwrights, whose eyes are ever closed, whose ears are ever stopped, pointing out to me what they called weak moments in O'Neill's plays. Well, a weak moment in an hour of strength and power isn't quite so dangerous as a strong moment in an hour of weakness, so we'll leave O'Neill to himself, and the little playwrights to God.

"A playwright reviewing in a Dublin literary journal a book written about the work of O'Neill, said, 'O'Neill at any time may write a great play.' There you are, a vaudeville playwright, dancing his little dance of drama, shaking his castanets of dialogue. . . .

"Another, not a playwright, in the same journal, criticizing a performance of *The Fountain,* and complaining about the literary quality of the play, said, 'We prefer O'Neill in his rougher manner, when he uses, shall we say, "sailor talk." ' But the same man, if he heard seven syllables of sailor talk bellowed into his ear would be knocked unconscious for a week, and, even then, it would take a very, very holy saint to be able to say effectively, 'Sir, I say unto thee, get up out of thy faint and walk.'

"But never mind; Eugene O'Neill's alright, and, please God, will be given a long life to go on giving a fuller nobility and a greater power to the Drama and to the Theater."

Seeking advance opinions of *Mourning Becomes Electra,* and possibly helpful criticism, O'Neill sent scripts to, among several others, Brooks Atkinson and Barrett H. Clark. "After prolonged work on a play," he told Atkinson, "I get so damned thoroughly identified with it that it's impossible to see or feel anything but the work as a whole, its total effect. Defects in the parts, which have become simply blobs of familiar words, quite escape me. And criticism which might open one's eyes . . . never comes until after the opening when, for better or worse, it's all over. That's *one* of the *many* reasons why I'm always glad to have any critic (whose opinions I respect) read my script before the opening. Unfortunately, producers violently object to this. They want a surprise value at all costs. Also, between us, they know their acting and directing usually are judged better if the critics know nothing of the plays these are supposed (in most cases so mistakenly!) to interpret! . . . Damn it, I think in future I'll publish before production, no matter who it hurts."

After receiving an analysis from the *Times* man, who, while impressed on the whole, had reservations about parts of the trilogy, O'Neill replied on June 27 that he was "boiling over with 'I objects' but I won't let them boil over in this letter. It's too darned hot. . . . They will have to wait until you visit us and I can become vocal about it. (Not that I'm much vocally, though! This is really all to your advantage!)" Softening his position, he conceded that certain of Atkinson's criticisms were probably justified and said that he would turn "a suspicious eye" on the script when he reread it and "a suspicious ear during rehearsals."

Barrett Clark, although enthusiastic in general, thought that *Electra* had been overly influenced by Freud. In reply O'Neill countered that present-day critics "read too damn much Freud into stuff that could very well have been written exactly as it is before psychoanalysis was ever heard of. Imagine the Freudian errors that would be read into Stendhal, Balzac, Strindberg, Dostoevski, etc., if they were writing today! . . . every human complication of love and hate in my trilogy is as old as literature and the interpretations I suggest are such as might have occurred to any author in any time with a deep curiosity about the underlying motives that actuate human interrelationships in the family."

Jung, he said, interested him more than Freud, adding that he found some of Jung's suggestions "extraordinarily illuminating in the light of my own experience with hidden human motives. But as far as influence on my work goes, he has had none compared to what psychological writers of the past like Dostoevski, etc., have had."

In August the playwright, who had not looked at *Electra* for months, was moved on reading it in galley proof. It seemed to him to have "power and drive and the strange quality of unreal reality I wanted . . . there is a feeling of fate in it, or I am a fool — a psychological modern approximation of the fate in the Greek tragedies on this theme." Although pleased in general, he found a number of verbose passages and "blurry spots," chiefly in *Homecoming* and *The Haunted,* and worked late many nights on further revisions. "It is particularly important," he told Miss Helburn on August 3, "that the first play, on which so much depends, should run sharply, with no sags of extraneous ideas, sentences or phrases. There is so much *necessary* exposition of things past in it that it can't afford to carry an ounce of extra weight."

Philip Moeller, who had coped so well with *Strange Interlude,* was to serve as mahout in guiding the new O'Neill mammoth to the stage; but for the scenic artist, the Guild went outside its ranks. At the instance of O'Neill, who had been dissatisfied with Lee Simonson's contribution to *Dynamo,* Robert Edmond Jones was to design the sets and costumes. The part of Orin went to Earle Larimore, who had played Nina's husband in *Strange Interlude*, and that of Christine was given to Alla Nazimova, the Russian actress, whose career had ranged from outstanding Ibsen interpretations to years of foolish Hollywood vehicles that almost ruined her talent.

When Terry Helburn had informed O'Neill that the Guild was considering Nazimova, he replied that he too had thought of her. "She would be grand," he said, "if she can be directed to act as she did [in her] first Ibsen productions and cut out [the] ham mannerisms acquired later." The prospect of her appearing in his play had a nostalgic appeal for him, for he, while a Princeton undergraduate, had been so fascinated by her Hedda Gabler that he had seen the performance nearly a dozen times.

At the playwright's recommendation, Thomas Chalmers, who had played the seagoing brother in the 1926 revival of *Beyond the Horizon*, was cast as Adam Brant, Christine's lover, but only after prolonged wrangling about the salary. "I won't step on stage for less than two hundred dollars," Chalmers told the Guild, which was notorious for paying actors as little as possible under the plea that it was more of an art than a commercial theater.

The chief casting problem was Lavinia, the most taxing role of all. Lillian Gish was so eager to play it that she learned the entire role and during a weekend at Northport convinced O'Neill, through the intensity of her desire, that she would be ideal; after auditioning her, however, the Guild decided that her voice was too weak for a ramrod character such as Lavinia. The playwright's next choice was Ann Harding, whose radiant blond beauty and youthful fire had lighted up the Provincetown's little stage before she became a movie star, though he suspected that she was "sure to be tied up or [to] want a million a week." Miss Harding, instead, was eager for the part, but she was unable to win a release from her film contract; years later she called this "the major tragedy" of her career. The assignment finally went to Alice Brady, whose own major tragedy was that she had rejected the chance to create the part of Nina Leeds.

Before the O'Neills quit Northport they leased an eight-room duplex apartment at 1095 Park Avenue, and for weeks Carlotta was running back and forth between Long Island and Manhattan to prepare their new place. The apartment represented a drastic step for O'Neill, since he had always felt out of his element in city life, but Carlotta had persuaded him that New York would be not only stimulating but, under the proper setup, comfortable as well. After three years of seclusive living abroad, a period that had been especially boring and lonesome for her at Le Plessis, she desired some recognition and a better opportunity to enjoy being Mrs. Eugene O'Neill; but while she hoped for a degree of social life, she remained as determined as ever to stand guard over her husband's privacy.

Scheduled for seven weeks of rehearsal instead of the customary four, because of its exceptional length, *Electra* began practicing on September 7, 1931, with the playwright and his wife regularly present. Carlotta reveled in her changed status; formerly an actress who had gotten by largely on her beauty, she now was in a position to pass judgment on and criticize her superiors in talent. "I used to sit by Gene," she recalls, "and take notes and things. We sat seven weeks and I was never bored a minute. And Gene was so fascinated by the characterizations of Nazimova and Alice Brady. But as [rehearsals] went on, they were less what he wrote." O'Neill himself said in 1946: "Few people realize the shock a playwright gets when he sees his work acted. Alice Brady and Alla Nazimova gave wonderful performances . . . but they, did not carry out my conception at all. I saw a different work from the one I thought I had written."

Adding an undercurrent to the rehearsals, the two actresses clashed not only in their roles as mother and daughter but in their own characters. "They hated one another," says Carlotta, "but that was good — it added real feeling to their parts." The antagonism was largely on Nazimova's side. Passionate, intense, self-dramatizing ("My heart was born in a deep shadow," she once said, "and I can never stay out in the sun very long"), Nazimova was a hard worker and a worrier; she dug into her role like a gold miner anxious for the last speck of ore. Several years earlier, after a discouraging period, she had begun her comeback in Chekhov at Eva Le Gallienne's Civic Repertory Theater; viewing the O'Neill trilogy as her great chance to consolidate her position, she was now determined to tower over everyone else, particularly Alice Brady.

An outgoing woman who liked dogs, people, liquor and jangly jewelry — roughly in that order — Miss Brady seemed only half serious about her work. She always turned up at rehearsals with a dog or two and a copy of *Black Mask*, a detective magazine. If a scene did not require her services, she would, much to Philip Moeller's annoyance, curl up with the magazine, apparently oblivious to the play taking shape only a few feet away. Moeller would not have minded so much had she appeared to be growing into her part; she was, instead, wildly uneven. O'Neill, who kept his apprehensions to himself, considered her "a good scout but rather a roughneck, a real daughter of her father" — William A. Brady, a hard-drinking Broadway producer.

In reality Miss Brady was concerned about her part and trying harder than she appeared. Though a versatile actress who did more than exploit her own personality, she had difficulty getting under the skin of a repressed, rigid person such as Lavinia. Recalling her efforts to find the right voice for her part, she said, "For the first couple of weeks I clenched my hands so tight that I developed a sort of occupational neuritis in my forearms." Seeking guidance from O'Neill, she asked, "I don't feel that Lavinia could ever sit down and smack her lips over a good slice of roast beef. Could she?" "No," he replied, and that told her a good deal about Lavinia.

One day the O'Neills brought their Dalmatian to rehearsals, and he got into a scrap outside the theater with Miss Brady's wirehaired terrier Sammy. After parting them the playwright appeared at the actress's dressing room with her pet and reported: "Sammy met my dog outside. Sammy sniffed and said, 'My mother's appearing in your father's rotten play,' and my dog naturally leaped on him. Sammy should know better."

Initially the players, particularly those in the minor roles, were in awe of the playwright, intimidated by both his eminence and his reserved air, but he went out of his way to reassure them. An elderly actress, cast as a villager, timidly approached him once with a question. As he began to explain, Langner, conferring with Moeller on the other side of the stage, called to O'Neill to join them. "Just a minute," he said in a reproving tone, "I'm talking with this lady," and went on to discuss her part with her at some length. Another time, after he had made some cuts in the bit parts, he went to each of the actors in question and assured them that the deletions were no reflection on their playing.

Although he had pruned and polished *Electra* extensively in August and early September, once rehearsals began he found many more revisions to make, chiefly a matter of cuts, and continued tightening the work until practically opening day. After the first run-through in October, when the trilogy proved shorter than had been expected, the Guild announced that the three plays, instead of being given on separate evenings, would be performed together. The première was set for October 26 and the top price for seats at six dollars and sixty cents — the highest scale in town; Earl Carroll's *Vanities*, for example, had a three-dollar top, while the best seats for the Ziegfeld Follies were four dollars and forty cents. The O'Neill drama, the press said, would be "the major event" of the fall theatrical season.

Not long before the opening the forty-three-year-old playwright was interviewed by S. J. Woolf of the New York *Times*, who found in his eyes "a furtive sadness" that seemed "puzzlingly familiar" until he realized that "the same sadness" was to be seen in old daguerreotypes of Poe. O'Neill, Woolf stated, "is very different from what one expects him to be, more fragile, more tenuous, more apart. Behind his quiet manner is a tenseness of nerves, which his long fingers emphasized as they beat a tattoo on his thigh or dug themselves into the palms of his hands."

Recalling his father in *Monte Cristo*, the playwright, whose mind was strongly visual, said: "I can still see [him] dripping with salt and sawdust, climbing a stool behind the swinging profile of dashing waves . . . the calcium lights in the gallery played on his long beard and tattered clothes, as with arms outstretched he declared that the world was his.

"This was a signal for the house to burst into a deafening applause. . . . It was an artificial age, an age ashamed of its own feelings, and the theater reflected its thoughts. Virtue always triumphed and vice always got its just deserts. . . . The very fact that I was brought up in the theater made me hate this artificiality and this slavish acceptance of these traditions."

In the decade or so since the cautious opening of *Beyond the Horizon* on Broadway with special matinees, the New York theater had matured considerably through the work of playwrights such as Sidney Howard and George Kelly, Maxwell Anderson and Elmer Rice, Philip Barry, S. N. Behrman and Robert E. Sherwood, not to mention O'Neill himself. Plays that once would have found shelter only in Greenwich Village now were welcomed in the uptown playhouses.

Yet O'Neill, ever the visionary, found Broadway far too commercial still and, as he told Woolf, regretted "the passing of the experimental group theater where innovations are tried out" by people "inspired with real ideals." While he remained scornful of the producers as a group ("They are invariably ten years behind the times and never credit their public with as much sense and taste as it has"), living abroad had given him a new respect for American talent. "I believe," he said, "that we have the best directors, the best writers, the best actors and the best scenic artists in the world right in this country, but all of them are going along each in his own way. If all this talent could be . . . made to work together, I am certain that productions could be given here that would be unequaled."

Mourning Becomes Electra, which runs nearly an hour longer than *Strange Interlude*, was scheduled to be given regularly at five P.M., but for the critics' convenience the première on October 26, 1931, began at four. As an audience composed largely of reviewers and other theater-wise figures assembled at the Guild Theater that Monday afternoon, the question uppermost in their minds was whether they would see another *Strange Interlude* or, like *Dynamo*, a fiasco. In a wire to the cast O'Neill had said: "Like Ezra Mannon I am a bit dumb when it comes to express-ing things I would like most to say but I do want you to know how profoundly grateful I am for the splendid spirit of collaboration you have shown. . . . Good luck to you one and all tonight. And remember the Mannon dead, cheer for them as they may not like what we have done."

Alice Brady, for all her seeming self-possession during rehearsals, was painfully nervous as the performance began. "I was nearly crying from fright," she said later, "and was absolutely sure that I'd forget my lines. You see, Mr. O'Neill kept changing and changing the lines at every rehearsal. . . . So that every time I'd think of a line, I'd wonder with horror whether that was the line which had been cut or changed." In addition she had a bad knee, from an accident years earlier, that at times would suddenly slip out of place. "The most frightening part of the play is my first entrance, when I come out of the Mannon house and down the steps. No one told me about those steps!"

Fortunately, her knee behaved, she remembered the proper lines, and *Homecoming* unfolded to a tensely silent house. After a dinner break from six to seven-fifteen, *The Hunted* and *The Haunted*, with a fifteen-minute intermission between them, were given. From first to last, thanks to O'Neill's graphic sense of theater and Robert Edmond Jones's starkly noble sets, the performance offered memorable stage pictures; but the final one was the most haunting. As critic John Hutchens wrote, "In the moment when Lavinia, in black, stands framed between the white pillars of the house of Mannon, the sunset dying at her feet, the course of passion run — in that moment playwright, performer and artist come together in a superb conclusion that belongs as completely and solely to the theater as Mr. O'Neill himself."

When the curtain descended at ten thirty-five, there were cries of "Author! Author!" and many curtain calls for the players. Friends rushed over to congratulate William Brady, whose daughter had the longest, most difficult part. Grinning but trying to appear nonchalant, he said, "Alice is all right, if she just had more lines."

The reviews were the most enthusiastic the author would receive in his lifetime (only *Long Day's Journey Into Night*, produced after his death, won higher praise). Though normally restrained in his appraisals of

O'Neill, Percy Hammond became excited this time. Calling the trilogy "a morbidly fascinating series of experiences," he said in the *Herald Tribune* that "even if you prefer your plays short, as I do, you will arise from your chair, as I did, and join the others in earnest salvos of appreciation." Lauding both the author and his leading actresses, he thought that the scene in which Christine poisons her husband and is discovered by her daughter was "as shocking and as well played as anything of the kind . . . since pagan actors performed similar incidents in the theater of Dionysius, while pagan audiences ate peanuts from tigers' skulls."

John Mason Brown, a relative newcomer who was to become one of the country's best-known critics, told his *Evening Post* readers that *Electra* was "an achievement which restores the theater to its high estate . . . an experiment in sheer, shuddering, straightforward story-telling which widens the theater's limited horizons at the same time that it is exalting and horrifying its patrons."

After pronouncing the new work "artistically important and physically wearing," Burns Mantle of the *News*, who had predicted only a short run for the saga of Nina Leeds's love life, said that *Electra* "cannot hope for anything like as wide a popularity as *Strange Interlude*, being without that drama's novelty and basic human appeal." More ardent tributes were paid by Gilbert Gabriel of the *American* ("a grand scheme grandly fulfilled . . . among the dramatic masterpieces of the world today"), Richard Lockridge of the *Sun* ("O'Neill's first play of lasting importance . . . tragedy implacable and unrelenting"), and John Anderson of the *Journal* ("bears the mark of true and enduring greatness").

Brooks Atkinson, who found the revised script a substantial improvement over the one he had read, called it "an occasion for great rejoicing. Mr. O'Neill has set his hand to a tremendous story, and told it with coolness and clarity. In sustained thought and workmanship, it is his finest tragedy." In his Sunday follow-up article the *Times* critic said that *Electra* "brings the cold splendors of Greek tragedy off the sky-blue limbo of Olympus down to the gusty forum of contemporary life." As to whether *Electra* was "a great play," he said: "It falls short of true greatness, I believe. To be great a tragedy needs some traces of nobility in the characters . . . and when the house of Atreus becomes the house of Mannon you recognize the true ignobility of their personal characters." In summing up, however, he called the work "one of the supreme achievements of the modern theater."

Although many reviewers gave the trilogy the lofty rating of a tragedy, others considered it an outstanding example of a lesser genre;

Arthur Pollock of the Brooklyn *Eagle,* for one, called it "melodrama, the purest kind of melodrama, without trickery." Another of similar opinion, Robert Benchley, wondered in the *New Yorker* whether "we are not forgetting one very important source of [O'Neill's] inspiration, without which he might perhaps have been just a builder of word-mountains? Was there not standing in the wings of the Guild Theater . . . the ghost of an old actor in a white wig, with drawn sword, who looked on proudly as the titanic drama unfolded itself . . . and who murmured, with perhaps just the suggestion of a chuckle, 'That's good, son! Give 'em the old Theater'? The actor I refer to needs no introduction to the older boys and girls here tonight – Mr. James O'Neill, 'The Count of Monte Cristo' and the father of our present hero.

"Let us stop all this scowling talk about 'the inevitability of the Greek tragedy' . . . and let us admit that the reason why we sat for six hours straining to hear each line . . . was because *Mourning Becomes Electra* is filled with good, old-fashioned, spine-curling melodrama. It is his precious inheritance from his trouper-father. . . . In this tremendous play he gives us not one thing that is new, and he gives us nothing to think about . . . but he does thrill the bejeezus out of us."

Joseph Wood Krutch, among the most impressed, said in the *Nation* that *Electra* "may turn out to be the only permanent contribution yet made by the twentieth century to dramatic literature. . . . Once more, we have a great play which does not 'mean' anything in the sense that the plays of Ibsen or Shaw or Galsworthy usually mean something; but one which does, on the contrary, mean the same thing that *Oedipus* and *Hamlet* and *Macbeth* mean – namely, that human beings are great and terrible creatures when they are in the grip of great passions, and that the spectacle of them is not only absorbing but also at once horrible and cleansing. . . .

"Here is a scenario to which the most soaring eloquence and the most profound poetry are appropriate, and if it were granted us we should be swept aloft as no Anglo-Saxon audience since Shakespeare's time. . . . But no modern is capable of language really worthy of O'Neill's play, and the lack of that one thing is the penalty we must pay for living in an age which is not equal to more than prose. Nor is it to be supposed that I make this reservation merely for the purpose of saying that Mr. O'Neill's play is not so good as the best of Shakespeare; I make it, on the contrary, in order to indicate where one must go in order to find a worthy comparison."

Posterity's verdict was probably given by Kenneth Tynan, who said, after seeing a 1955 revival of *Electra* in London, that "despite the grandeur of its architecture, it remains no more than the greatest unwritten play of its century, by which I mean that O'Neill could not find words commensurate in dignity with his theme. Even so, he manages to create a stuffy, sepulchral world in which the fearful events he describes might conceivably happen; and that in itself is a mark of genius."

The playwright was still to win the Nobel Prize, but his apotheosis was virtually complete once *Electra* had opened. Recognizing him as a peer of politicians, movie stars and champion athletes, *Time* magazine displayed him on its front cover on November 2, 1931, above a line from the trilogy: "The damned don't cry." Like *Strange Interlude*, the new work became a favorite target of Broadway wits, who called it "Evening Becomes Interminable," "Mourning Becomes O'Neill" and, in a burst of inspiration, "Orestes' Development" (said quickly to make it sound like "Arrested Development").

Before the cheers had subsided, a second company, headed by Judith Anderson and Florence Reed, was sent on tour. In Boston and other northeastern cities the touring production was greeted not only by reviews, usually enthusiastic, but by editorial comment, usually condemnatory, with the latter attacking the author for depicting New England so unfavorably, first in *Desire Under the Elms*, now in *Mourning Becomes Electra*. The Boston *Herald,* for example, plaintively inquired: "Why does Mr. O'Neill find pleasure in representing New England's people as degenerates? Did he find them in Massachusetts when he sojourned here? Did he not meet any even half-respectable persons? A Bostonian in the lobby of the Colonial Theater last Monday, one well acquainted with country life, exclaimed that he would like to kill the characters on the stage and above all to murder the dramatist who put them there."

Mourning Becomes Electra gave one hundred and fifty performances on Broadway, a substantial run considering the trilogy's somber character and, especially since the Depression was deepening, its high ticket prices. However, even though few if any other American plays had ever been hailed so rapturously, *Electra* was passed over for the Pulitzer Prize; the award went instead to *Of Thee I Sing,* with a book by George S. Kaufman and Morrie Ryskind, music by George Gershwin and lyrics by his brother Ira, the first musical show ever so honored.

Following his usual practice, O'Neill waited days before he read the reviews of *Electra* (he could be almost as upset by what he considered misplaced praise as by, in his view, unjustified criticism); but in a call to the Guild the morning after the première he learned that the press notices were overwhelmingly favorable. After living with the trilogy for two years, with many weeks of rehearsal as the climax, he felt "pretty ragged." "The old booze bust," he wrote to Arthur McGinley on November 2, "was a good antidote – in its way! – but I haven't used that way out in so many years it makes me feel old to think of them."

Now that *Electra* was off his hands and he had time for personal matters, he arranged for Oona, whom he had not seen since Bermuda, and Shane to spend an afternoon with him and Carlotta. Nervous and shy about meeting a father she could not recall, Oona was relieved that the two grown-ups directed nearly all their conversation at Shane, but at the same time she felt pleased to be related to this gentle and handsome man. Luncheon was an ordeal for her, as Carlotta, unaccustomed to feeding children, served what was to six-year-old Oona an unfamiliar, distasteful-looking dish – beef kidneys. She ate her portion apprehensively, but when asked whether she would like more, politely said yes.

After the meal the four set off in the Cadillac for a drive through Central Park, with Shane next to the chauffeur and Oona between the two adults, a fur-lined car robe over their laps. While O'Neill and Shane talked of the car and Carlotta teased her husband about his "new toy," Oona, thinking of the beef kidneys, began to feel sick. When the car turned into a cobbled road and started to bounce along, she could no longer control herself and vomited on the robe, her father and her step-mother. The chauffeur immediately pulled over to the curb and, as a small crowd gathered to stare, rushed about trying to clean up things. "GOOD GOD, CHILD!" Carlotta cried, "why didn't you SAY SOME-THING?! We could have stopped the car. You must have KNOWN you felt sick! The new car! Poor Shane! It's not her fault, she felt sick, but why didn't she SAY SOMETHING!"

In mid-November the O'Neills, desiring sun and quiet, began a month's vacation at Sea Island, an exclusive resort just off the Georgia coast that had been recommended to them by actress Ilka Chase. The small island had become a resort in the late 1920s with the construction of the Cloister, a large, rambling Spanish-style hotel, only to have its development slowed by the onslaught of the Depression, so the area's natural beauty was still relatively untouched by housing and other so-called improvements. Within days of their arrival, the O'Neills decided to settle there permanently.

Eager to have the celebrated dramatist as a resident, the Sea Island Company, which owned almost all the land, sold the couple a seventeen-thousand-dollar ocean-front parcel for twelve thousand six hundred dollars. As the stock market fell again, a few weeks later, the two were able to buy an adjoining lot of equal size for five thousand dollars from private owners in need of cash. "We really can't afford it," Carlotta told George Boll of the development company, "but we *must* have *privacy*." Disabusing him of any notion that she and her husband would mingle in the community, she said that theirs would not be a home for "social life or sport" but "a workshop."

Eugene, taking a more poetic view as he inscribed a copy of *Electra* for Boll, called him "the Demon Realtor who tempted us to fall for Paradise Island." The inscription in Miss Chase's copy read: "To Ilka, who found our Blessed Isles for us, with profoundest gratitude" — a reference to the South Sea islands which loom invitingly in the minds of the tormented Mannons as "a Garden of Paradise before sin was discovered."

20

At Sea Island

IMPATIENT to be settled on "Paradise Island," O'Neill found New York less attractive than ever when he and Carlotta returned from the south. Carlotta had at least the excitement of shopping for their new home ("Bought Spanish *objets d'art* today," she wrote to George Boll, "& won't be able to even ride to Georgia if such madness continues"); but Eugene, regretting that he had ever had "the idiotic notion that there might be something in N.Y. good for work . . . nearly yawned [himself] to death with boredom."

One of his few pleasures during his final months in the city was the six-day bicycle races at Madison Square Garden, with Carlotta his constant, if unenthusiastic companion. For all his aversion to crowds, it never bothered him to be jammed in with thousand of sports fans, since he felt safely anonymous; but on the rare occasions when Carlotta managed to get him to the theater, he was apprehensive and tense lest strangers recognize and accost him. He liked to tell of once attending a play when he sat behind a man who talked familiarly and disparagingly of O'Neill as an old friend of his in Greenwich Village. Stating that the playwright had indulged in drugs, the man said that he often got calls that "Gene was lying in the gutter" and that he should come and take care of him. As O'Neill used to tell it, he leaned forward, just before quitting the theater, and told the stranger: "I don't remember you ever propping me up in the gutter. In fact, I've never seen you before, but I want you to know it was liquor — I never took dope in my life!"

At the start of 1932 Carlotta had a reunion, after five years, with her mother and her daughter, a generous-hearted girl of fourteen at once starved for affection and wary of being rejected; she masked her vulnerability behind a tomboyish manner. "I felt," says Cynthia Jane Chapman, "that I didn't belong to anybody." According to relatives, her father, who went through several marriages, had no more relish for a parent's role than had Carlotta or, for that matter, Nellie Tharsing. Nellie used to tell her granddaughter that she was taking care of her so that Cynthia in turn would eventually look after her, but once the girl began to show some spirit, Nellie became anxious to unload her on Carlotta. O'Neill, who as a child had felt rejected by his parents, took an immediate liking to Cynthia, praising her as "a game sport."

The reunion of daughter, mother and grandmother was short, emotional, less than harmonious. Cynthia, whom Carlotta had enrolled in a school in Connecticut, did not want to remain in the East, far from her friends and familiar surroundings; Carlotta, flourishing one of Cynthia's baby shoes, was upset and tearful that her daughter did not appreciate "all that was being done for her"; and Nellie, as her stay ended, was indignant at being shipped back to California before she had a chance to inspect her granddaughter's new school. During the drive to Connecticut, Carlotta and Cynthia exchanged scarcely a word, but O'Neill, normally so taciturn, kept up a running line of talk as he pointed out the sights to his stepdaughter. At the school he and Carlotta were received deferentially by the authorities; as soon as they had left, the schoolgirls came pouring out like a stampeding herd as each sought to be the first to sit in the chair the famous playwright had just graced. "Entering in mid-term is tough," Cynthia says, "because all the cliques and friendships have been formed by then, but I'd been in boarding school since I was five, so I was ringwise and knew how to take care of myself."

During the Sea Island vacation and now in New York the playwright, endlessly fertile, worked on preliminary outlines for five new plays. After deciding that two of the projects "were not yet ripe enough" for further development, he prepared detailed summaries of the others. All three were set in this country, one at the time of the Revolution, another during the 1840s, and the third in the 1920s. Presumably these outlines were his initial work on the multiplay cycle, ranging from the eighteenth century to present times, that he would start writing in several more years.

Not long after his return from Georgia he was interviewed at length for a series in the New York *News* (the articles appeared from January 24 through January 30, 1932). Thinking of what he had heard about "O'Neill, the sphinx, O'Neill, the morose," Fred Pasley, the *News* writer, approached his assignment with trepidation, but the playwright, increasingly prone to look back on his life, made him feel welcome. For several afternoons O'Neill, sitting in his book-lined study, riffled the pages of memory: the early years of touring with his parents ("Usually a child has a regular, fixed home but . . . I knew only actors and the stage. My mother nursed me in the wings and in dressing rooms"); his various schools; the gold-prospecting trip to Honduras and the voyage to Buenos Aires; his derelict days on the New York water front ("I learned at Jimmy the Priest's not to sit in judgment on people"); his brief news-paper career ("I was a bum reporter, but I gained a wonderful insight into small-town life"); his decision at the tubercular sanatorium to turn playwright; the mentally retarded boy in Provincetown who asked, "What's beyond the horizon?"

With unconscious irony the author of the nine-act *Strange Interlude* and the thirteen-act *Mourning Becomes Electra* told Pasley that Baker's playwriting course at Harvard taught him "not to take ten lines to say something that could be said in one." Recalling his early efforts for the theater, he said that his father "just thought I was crazy . . . didn't see why I should write the kind of plays I did . . . no market for them . . . [yet he] believed that I might some day amount to something — if I lived."

Talk of the old days again flowed when George Tyler, whom O'Neill had not seen in years, came to dinner. "I want to hear," Carlotta had said in her invitation, "all about a certain Irish babe." The evening proved a mixed pleasure to Eugene, for while he enjoyed reminiscing about his father and Jamie with his father's old friend, he was depressed to find Tyler full of bitterness about the decline, as he saw it, of the Broadway theater. More than nostalgia was behind Tyler's strictures; once a leading producer, he had not had a success since the mid-1920s.

Had O'Neill been inclined to forget the past, the day's mail would have prevented him, for he was continually hearing from old friends and asso-ciates: if not Tyler, then Art McGinley inquiring about tickets to *Electra;* if not McGinley, then Dr. Lyman of the tubercular sanatorium, who wanted a copy of the play inscribed to his daughter at Vassar; if not Ly-man, then Jasper Deeter, who had founded a theater outside Philadelphia where O'Neill's plays were featured — he hoped Eugene would attend a production; if not Deeter, then Harold McGee, another of the Province-town Players, with word that the old Coast Guard station at Peaked Hill had finally, after long being in peril, slid down into the sea; if not McGee, then an elderly woman in San Francisco who had rare photographs of James O'Neill and baby pictures of both Eugene and Jamie which she offered to give Eugene (her parents had been good friends of James and

Ella). "Have you one of my mother, by any lucky chance?" Eugene wrote back. "She had so few taken in her life and I have only one."

In March O'Neill met Gerhart Hauptmann, one of the few living playwrights he admired, at a small dinner party given by the Theater Guild in honor of the noted German. Shortly before, on arriving in this country to participate in academic events celebrating a Goethe anniversary, Hauptmann had told the press that the two writers he most wanted to meet were Sinclair Lewis and O'Neill. The affair on March 15 took place during the dinner intermission of *Mourning Becomes Electra*, which Hauptmann and his entourage were seeing that night. In an exchange of tributes O'Neill recalled in a low, halting voice that during his apprenticeship he had seen a production of *The Weavers* a half-dozen times and said that Hauptmann, along with Strindberg and Ibsen, had greatly influenced his work. After his remarks were translated, Hauptmann said that he had easily followed the first part of *Electra*, despite the language barrier, and had found it beautiful.

During his visit Hauptmann gave an oration at Columbia University which was broadcast in this country and, by shortwave, to Germany; was awarded academic honors; was received at City Hall by New York Mayor Jimmy Walker and at the White House by President Hoover. Sailing for home on the sixteenth, he told reporters that *Mourning Becomes Electra*, the only play he had seen here, and his meeting with its author were "the two outstanding things" of his trip. O'Neill, he said, was "a fascinating man. Every inch of him is stamped with genius."

The O'Neills' final weeks in New York were clouded not only by illness — Eugene had the flu, while Blemie was in a veterinary hospital for over a fortnight — but by the realization that they had strained their finances for a home that would cost, land and all, about one hundred thousand dollars. (To build the same house today on Sea Island would take over four hundred thousand dollars.) O'Neill had figured that his royalties from *Electra* would comfortably cover his share of the expenses, but the play, less successful than he had expected, closed in mid-April; and though Liveright's had sold over sixty thousand copies of *Electra*, a remarkable total for a play, the firm had hoped for a larger sale. Carlotta, corresponding with George Boll about domestic help, told him on April 18 that this was "'the first time in my life I have been without a personal maid — but my income has been slashed so (& expect more to follow!) I simply can't afford one. (I *loathe* being poor)." Before quitting New York at the end of April, the O'Neills took out a bank loan of fifteen thousand dollars.

In Georgia Carlotta, who had worked closely with the architect, and O'Neill were delighted with the house they found rising by the sea: a rambling brick structure painted an off-white faintly green, as though filmed with seawater. Modeled chiefly on old Spanish farmhouses, it also had, as Carlotta had specified, "a religious feeling." The guest rooms, resembling monks' cells, had massive doors with judas-holes, while the tall living room bulged at one end like an apse. Along with such decorations as Japanese noh masks, primitive African masks, Chinese statuary and Spanish artifacts, there were madonnas in niches, a crucifix behind Carlotta's bed, and spread-eagled on the living room wall a blue monk's cape with semiprecious stones.

Unlike the other twenty rooms, O'Neill's study had a nautical flavor, recalling a captain's cabin on an old sailing vessel. Sturdy-looking with oaken ribs and a beamed ceiling, its outstanding features were a mainmast encircled with marlinespikes, a bay banked with windows that suggested the high upswept stern of a galleon, and a curving iron staircase, like those in lighthouses, that led to a lookout on the roof and a panoramic view of beach, sea and sky. (Eventually Eugene grew to dislike his den, regarding it as "too much like a stage designer's idea of a writer's study.")

The oceanward side of the house, which led to a patio, was of an open, friendly personality, but the front, dominated by a massive double door that suggested a monastery or convent, looked forbidding. (The door, for all its monastic appearance, came from a New Orleans bordello.) Not many were to see the house close up during the O'Neills' four years of residence, for they erected an eight-foot wall all around the site and, to augment their privacy, planted bamboo and fast-growing shrubbery in strategic spots.

As a symbol of their oneness, their inseparability, the couple called their new home "Casa Genotta" — a neologism derived from their first names. Shortly before their arrival in Georgia, O'Neill, inscribing a book of his plays to Carlotta, quoted a line from *Marco Millions:* "In her eyes' mirror I watched myself live protected from life by her love." It was a particularly apt quotation, not only because it expressed a basic element in his affection for Carlotta — the feeling that she shielded him from the world — but because he had begun writing a play, tentatively entitled "Without Ending of Days," about a married couple who strive to make their relationship a sanctuary from the cares and uncertainties of existence.

Till their new home was ready the O'Neills stayed at a seaside cottage of the Cloister, and every day, while he worked, sunned and swam,

Carlotta supervised with "a wary eye" the construction of Casa Genotta. "I attended to all the building," she later said, "business of building, getting ideas into concrete form, and quarreling! God was good in that I worked with an architect who knew his job, and loved the unusual, and was intelligent enough to think that the one who was building the house *might* have an idea worth listening to!" She had more than "an idea" or so; she seemed to know, before the first brick was in place, precisely how she wanted everything, down to the last closet and drawer. Francis Louis Abreu, the architect, recalls that at her specification some drawers in a wall cabinet were made exactly five and seven-eighths inches deep. Satisfied that construction was progressing well, Carlotta returned to New York in May to close up the Park Avenue apartment and ship everything south.

"She's working herself to death," O'Neill wrote to Saxe Commins on the twenty-second, "to get it over and get back here, I'm afraid. Longest time we've ever been separated. I miss her like hell!" In his loneliness he wrote her a prose poem in which, after apostrophizing her as "Mistress" and "Wife," he said: "Mother, you are my lost way refound, my end and my beginning, the hand I reach out for in my lonely night, from my ghost-haunted inner dark."

Early in July, shortly after moving into their new home, the O'Neills had as their first houseguests for a fortnight Eugene Jr., his wife, and Shane. Young Eugene, freshly graduated from Yale, came wreathed with academic honors; he had won the prestigious Berkeley Scholarship, one of the oldest college awards in the country, and another fellowship, both of them for excellence in classical studies, and at the commencement exercises had been Ivy Laureate of his class. In the fall, preparing for his Ph.D. and a teaching career, he was to begin his postgraduate studies at the University of Freiburg in Germany. "He is a dyed-in-the-wool student," O'Neill boasted to a friend, "but a big 6-foot-2½ husky out-of-door manly type in the bargain. A fine guy! I am damned proud of all he has accomplished. He really seems to know what he wants from life — where he is going and how to get there. Miraculous, that!"

However, Carlotta, who had been delighted with him at Le Plessis, disapproved of his being married before he could support a wife. She now found him a shade patronizing, referred to him, privately, as "the Professor," and became impatient when he, emulating his father, began to preen himself on being a descendant of Irish royalty. As O'Neill was expatiating one day to his sons about their ancestry, Shane was too shy to say much but his half brother was all questions. "I had done some reading

O'Neill and George Boll surf-casting

Casa Genotta as seen from the beach

on the quiet about Irish history," Carlotta later recalled. "I knew there'd never been any kings of Ireland, just heads of clans and tribes, and I told them so. One of them, Gene, I think, said, 'Should we listen to her?' — as though I were an outsider or servant or something. Finally I said, 'This is getting to be too much. I'll leave you kings of Ireland to settle royal affairs. I've got more important things to do.' "

Carlotta's relations with her own child remained unsatisfactory. She freely admitted to friends that the girl disliked her, as well as the East; at the end of the school term she had sent Cynthia back to California and Nellie Tharsing. O'Neill, trying to hearten Cynthia, wrote that he had "learned to respect and admire you for yourself. . . . I want you to feel my home is always yours to come to, whenever you wish, by right of the love I bear you! . . . You are a brave girl and a true one! I am proud to be your stepfather!" No doubt he was sincerely moved by the girl's plight, but most likely he would have resented having her around for long, as she would have complicated his snug relationship with and great dependence on Carlotta.

Adding to his paternal role, he became a godfather this summer when the Comminses had a second child, a boy this time, and named him Eugene David. "Tell him," O'Neill suggested to Dorothy and Saxe, "all he has to do to have a grand youth is not to have one like mine!"

Since the Sea Island Company, which ran the island, had done its utmost to be helpful, the O'Neills entertained all the executives, with their wives, one at a time. At the succession of dinners some made the mistake of talking, or rather trying to talk, Literature and the Theater with the playwright. The only one of the company with whom he and Carlotta became friends was George Boll, a lower-echelon employee, who had sold them their land and, bombarded by daily communiqués from Carlotta, gone to infinite pains on their behalf from the start of negotiations. An easygoing young bachelor, Boll loved sports and was totally indifferent to the arts, all of which was fine with O'Neill. The two regularly went fishing together — Eugene developed a zest for the sport — and Boll was a frequent dinner guest at Casa Genotta. "Gene had a great sense of humor and did his share of talking," Boll says. "I found him a very human and normal person, which is contrary, I know, to what many thought."

The Sea Island brass had hoped that the world-famous playwright would be a social lion of the community but instead he reminded them, according to Abreu the architect, of "a gun-shy dog." Carlotta they found harder to categorize, for she was variable, now seeming a grande dame, now very much the actress. On her first visit to the company's headquarters, the sight of a large sofa in the board chairman's office set her to laughing. "My God, a theatrical office! There's the old casting couch!"

Above all, she was considered a hard worker and a perfectionist. One day while she was still getting the house in shape, an associate of Abreu's dropped by and found Carlotta on her knees scrubbing the floor. She was determined that the household operations should "go on oiled wheels." Ilka Chase, who visited the O'Neills for a few days, relates that the house "was quiet [the servants were supplied with rubber-soled shoes] and exquisitely clean, with special boxes and bags to keep the mildew out of things and with little colored maids polishing like Dutchmen." O'Neill himself marveled at Carlotta's flair for running an immaculate place. "Your Mamma," he wrote to Cynthia on July 30, "is sure a demon housekeeper! I expect any day that she's going to grab me absent-mindedly and have me varnished, vacuum-cleaned, and polished with floor wax before I have a chance to resist! Every time Blemie sees an ad for Sapolio or Dutch Cleanser he shudders with dread!"

Living conditions at Sea Island, the couple learned before long, were less than paradisical. Aside from harboring what seemed like millions of mosquitoes, the area was so damp that it was a constant struggle to keep things from turning moldy, and the window hardware had to be specially made of bronze since any metal less durable would rust away. During Lawrence Langner's first visit, with his wife and Fania Marinoff, he wondered why the lower part of the patio's bushes had been clipped bare of foliage. "That's so we can see if there are any snakes under them," explained Carlotta, and she went on to say that rattlesnakes were prevalent on the island. As the visitors looked aghast, O'Neill smilingly added, according to Langner, that the rattlers were "relatively harmless compared to the pretty little pink coral snakes" of the area. Writes Langner, "Fania, who hated snakes even more than I did, trod very gingerly around the countryside after this, and I was never quite at ease either."

"Without Ending of Days," which O'Neill had begun writing immediately after settling in Sea Island, was the second panel in the projected trilogy of "God plays" that had started with *Dynamo*. Where the first play had deified Science through a mystical view of electricity, the new one examines human love as a substitute for Divine Love.

O'Neill had written a scenario for "Days" in Bermuda in 1927, when he first conceived the idea. Two years later, shortly after *Dynamo* had opened and while he was still waiting for Agnes to divorce him, he informed Dr. J. O. Lief, his dentist in New York, that he would not proceed with the second play of the trilogy "until my personal affairs are cleared up and forgotten. It's a funny coincidence. I had the idea all mapped out before I left Bermuda and before there was any suggestion of a smash in my domestic life. It was quite objective. And yet now it would appear as most subjective and autobiographical because of the turn events have taken. A strange business! Maybe something inside me was doing a brilliant clairvoyant job."

Either he was consciously deceiving Dr. Lief or, with extreme naïveté, deluding himself in denying that "Days" was autobiographical. The play tells of a crisis in what had seemed a perfect marriage when the husband commits a single act of adultery; even before his wife begins to suspect his infidelity, he suffers the torments of the damned, for the marriage has been on such an exalted plane that he feels fallen from grace. Considering that O'Neill conceived the story idea not long after his brief romantic entanglement with Carlotta, a period when he thought their romance was over, it seems clear that the play was born of his guilt feelings toward Agnes. Thus the crowning irony behind "Days" is that by the time he came to write it, Carlotta, originally the model for the woman who seduces the hero, had become the model for his devoted wife.

As a title, "Without Ending of Days" was unwittingly inspired, it seems, by Robert Edmond Jones. Jones, who had loved Eugene and Agnes, the two of them as one, once wrote her a note which she proudly showed to her husband. The note in full: "I was so happy to see you and Gene again. There is something so living and burning about you both that I just feel everything is all right, world without end, amen, amen." While O'Neill was writing the play, the note from Bobby Jones long since forgotten, he attempted unsuccessfully to track down the source of his title; he thought he might have read the phrase or something similar in the Bible. Eventually, changing the title closer to Jones's wording, he called the play *Days Without End*.

His work, he informed Barrett Clark in summer 1932, was going well. "It has the right feel to me as I write, and flows instead of having to be torn out — which, at least, proves it's ripe for birth. Also, there is in it a fresh vision, a new understanding, an inner yea-saying, that is vastly intriguing and stimulating to me. I shall have a grand time writing this one." As things turned out, he was a poor prophet; he was to labor nearly as long and hard on it as over *Mourning Becomes Electra* — to little avail. Written out of his own spiritual hunger, confusion and conflict, the end product would be among his poorest dramas; but to those interested in the man behind the plays, it is highly significant. Properly interpreted, it helps illumine a secret source of the anxiety and the darkness in his nature.

Doggedly putting in long hours despite the hot Georgia summer, he had finished three acts by early August — there were to be four — when he hit on a fresh approach and decided to scrap the first draft. Before starting anew he took time, at the request of George Jean Nathan, to write something for *American Spectator*, a literary monthly paper due to be launched that fall. Though Nathan was listed as only one of the editors — the others were Ernest Boyd, James Branch Cabell, Theodore Dreiser and O'Neill — the periodical was largely a one-man operation by Nathan. After Eugene had made several abortive stabs at an article ("I am too enthusiastic about the scheme of the paper to send in any misbegotten amateur effort"), he wrote a piece on masks ("the only subject I can get up any interest in") which appeared by sections in the first three issues of the magazine.

Back in 1913 and 1914, when he was turning out his first plays, Eugene used to tell friends in New London that "everyone wears a mask," implying that he intended in his writings to tear off the disguises. Now older, wiser, less sure of which was the mask, which the face, he felt that everyone wears "thousands of them." He found in masks — or, rather, in the idea of the mask — a protean symbol of the human condition. "One's outer life," he says in the *American Spectator* article, "passes in a solitude haunted by the masks of others; one's inner life passes in a solitude hounded by the masks of oneself."

Advocating a greater use of the device, he held that masks were the best possible solution of the modern playwright's "problem as to how — with the greatest possible dramatic clarity and economy of means — he can express those profound hidden conflicts of the mind which the probings of psychology continue to disclose. . . . For what, at bottom, is the new psychological insight into human cause and effect but a study in masks, an exercise in unmasking? . . .

"Why not give all future Classical revivals entirely in masks? *Hamlet*, for example. Masks would liberate this play from its present confining status as exclusively a 'star vehicle.' We would be able to see the great drama we are now privileged only to read, to identify ourselves with the figure of Hamlet as a symbolic projection of a fate that is in each of us, instead of merely watching a star giving us his version of a great acting role."

The religious impulse driving him to write *Days Without End* is evident in the article. After calling for a "nonrealistic imaginative theater," he said that he meant "the one true theater, the age-old theater, the theater of the Greeks and the Elizabethans, a theater that could dare to boast – without committing a farcical sacrilege – that it is a legitimate descendant of the first theater that sprang . . . out of [man's] worship of Dionysius. I mean a theater returned to its highest and sole significant function as a Temple where the religion of a poetical interpretation and symbolical celebration of life is communicated to human beings, starved in spirit by their soul-stifling daily struggle to exist as masks among the masks of the living!"

Early in September O'Neill, who had begun a third draft of *Days Without End,* was pleasantly surprised to awaken one morning with a new play "fully in mind," one that he had never thought of before, not consciously, that is. He even had the title – *Ah, Wilderness!* a variant on a phrase in the *Rubáiyát.* Once previously, with *Desire Under the Elms,* the playwright had dreamed a complete play, but on that occasion his imagination had been set in motion, apparently, by Sidney Howard's *They Knew What They Wanted.* This time the genesis of his story idea was obscure. Setting aside *Days,* O'Neill dashed off a scenario and immediately began writing *Ah, Wilderness!,* which "simply gushed" out of him; before the month was over he had finished this affectionate, humorous picture of small-town life in yesteryear New England.

Perhaps the most striking aspect of *Wilderness* is not that the author of such somber works as *Electra, Desire* and *Ape* had written a comedy (his first and last one) but that he had extracted comedy from the same kind of characters and story material that had served him for purposes of tragedy. Here again is a sensitive youth at odds with his parents, a regretful spinster, an alcoholic ne'er-do-well and, curiously enough, considering that this is a genial play, the author's most realistic prostitute to date. But aside from her and several other minor characters, the familiar O'Neill figures are now limned with fond humor.

Denying that *Wilderness* was autobiographical, the playwright said that it was "a sort of wishing out loud. That's the way I would have *liked* my boyhood to have been." Still, though essentially true, his statement does not alter the fact, as he himself knew, that the play was rooted in his history. To find the chief model for seventeen-year-old Richard Miller, forever spouting Swinburne, Wilde and, in his more revolutionary moments, Bernard Shaw, one need look no further than the author himself. In the shadows behind Uncle Sid, a bibulous, clowning bachelor, stands the darker, more complex figure of Jamie O'Neill, who purposely drank himself to death. Lily, the old maid aunt, was chiefly based on Bessie Sheridan, a spinster schoolteacher and one of the author's favorite New London cousins.

For the fictional parents, though, the playwright went outside his family circle. Essie Miller, the mother, was modeled primarily on Evelyn Essex ("Essie") McGinley of New London, whose sons Arthur, Tom, Wint and Lawrence (their names, though not their personalities, figure in the play) were good friends of Eugene's. Finally, in tribute to a man with whom he had enjoyed a father-son kind of relationship, the playwright patterned Nat Miller, a newspaper publisher, chiefly on Fred Latimer, the New London editor who had perceived in cub reporter Eugene Gladstone O'Neill the makings of "a very high order of genius." Except that the editor was rather short, he resembled the play's description of the father: "a tall, dark, spare man . . . irregular, undistinguished features, but he has fine, shrewd, humorous eyes." Latimer, Nat Miller — the author took care to make even their names similar.

Since O'Neill attempted neither to storm the heavens nor to plumb the depths this time, it is easy to misjudge, if not to underestimate *Ah, Wilderness!;* yet the play is a significant part of his canon both in itself and for what it foreshadows. Rather than an anomaly among his works, the comedy is based on his obsession with family life and his own past, the twin foundation stones of his finest writings. The new play, despite its lighthearted tenor, contains moments that prefigure *Long Day's Journey Into Night.* Returning drunk from a Fourth of July picnic, Uncle Sid invokes the excuse that liquor is "a good man's failing" — the same defense James Tyrone would employ in *Long Day's Journey.* Lily, in words that Mary Tyrone might have used about Jamie, says of Uncle Sid that he is "irresponsible, never meaning to harm but harming in spite of himself."

Except for a rather mawkish moonlight-and-roses scene between young Miller and his palpitant fifteen-year-old sweetheart (their puppy love mildly spoofs O'Neill's romance in New London with Maibelle Scott when he was twenty-four and she eighteen), the play is one of durable charm and convincing, though idealized, characters. "The kindliness and decency of the Millers ring true enough," said Louis Kronenberger in 1941, "but they have limitations as well as virtues. Genteel, conservative, unaspiring, these people — in any age — are the guardians of the status quo, the enemies of all great emotions and discoveries. Hence, in order to obscure that fact, O'Neill made of *Ah, Wilderness!* a kind of reverie, a kind of sentimental journey – which is why the play seems minor, which is also why it does not seem false."

To prevent the sentiment from becoming excessive and cloying, the author constantly laced it with humor, with touches of realism and accurate observation. On entering the parlor, for example, Aunt Lily, who is allowed to pay only a pittance for her room and board, "goes diffidently to the straight-backed chair . . . leaving the comfortable chairs to the others." When Nat Miller discovers that Richard had been drinking the night before with a trollop, he fears that the boy might have slept with her. "I hope you're wrong," Uncle Sid says. "That kind of baby is dangerous for a kid like Dick." At that moment, as the two worry that the boy might have contracted a venereal disease, it is evident that while the play may soften reality with a haze of nostalgia, it does relate to the actual world.

Relaxed this time, not straining for poetry, not trying to express the ineffable or to find thundering words for tumultuous emotions, the playwright achieved fresh, homey language. In one of the play's highlights, it is at once amusing and genuinely touching as Miller, stiff with embarrassment, tries in a man-to-man approach to discuss with his son "certain desires of the flesh." *Wilderness*, as the author said, represented what he "would have *liked* my boyhood to have been." By the time he had reached young Richard's age, he was, under his brother's tutelage, familiar with prostitutes and whorehouses.

For months only Carlotta knew about *Ah, Wilderness!*, until O'Neill had her send the manuscript to Saxe Commins to be typed. "This is a kind of play," she wrote to Saxe, "Gene has never before done . . . and must be the *deadest* of *dead secrets* – it may be done someday" under a nom de plume.

Amplifying on Carlotta's note, Eugene told his friend that he "got immense satisfaction out of writing this play – and I feel a great affection for it – so great that I don't know whether I'll ever subject it to the humiliation of production or publication. For me it has the sweet charm of a dream of lost youth, a wistfulness of regret, a poignantly melancholy memory of dead things and people – but a smiling memory as of those who live still. . . .

"Secrecy in this case, Saxe, above all others! Don't let a soul know a damned thing – even that you have it!"

After an enthusiastic letter from Commins, O'Neill replied that he had been "doubtful if anyone would feel in it what I felt . . . it's such a simple little play . . . and its whole importance and reality depend on its conveying a mood of memory in exactly the right illuminating blend of wistful grin and lump in the throat. . . .

"But did you laugh? . . . And do you like Pa & Ma and all the rest? Fine people, all of them, to me. Lovable! I hope they will seem so to others, and it's the truth. There were innumerable such people in these U.S. There still are, except life has carried us out of their orbit, we no longer see or know them. . . . But if America ever pulls out of its present mess and back to something approaching its old integrity and uniqueness, I think it will be owing to the fundamental simple homely decency of such folk. . . . I mean I believe it's still there as a basis to build a new American faith upon."

Since he was loath to release *Wilderness* and was having difficulty with *Days Without End*, there would be no new O'Neill play on Broadway in the 1932–1933 season to relieve his financial situation. He complained to Saxe in October that Liveright's was behind schedule in paying him six months of royalties, and shortly before that he had informed Richard Madden he was against a London production of *Mourning Becomes Electra* unless he received "a substantial advance." He had "sworn off giving plays to the English for nothing," he said, adding that if "James O'Neill of Monte Cristo fame heard that I ever gave the cursed Sassenach the slightest break, he'd come back from the grave and bean me with a blackthorn! My, but didn't he love them!"

As the Depression worsened, he heard from a number of old friends in need. To Art McGinley he replied on December 10, 1932: "The enclosed is the best I can do. I am in a tough spot myself what with the beating I have taken in investments, along with everyone else — just about cash broke. All I got from *Electra* last year is sunk in the home we've built down here. . . . And I have large alimony and four children being educated, and no new play ready for a long whole year. I'm not crying poverty on you. Just a frank explanation. There is no one I would rather be of service to than you. . . . Yes, for Pete's sake, hang on to the old job! A man with one means just about he's a millionaire these days. A hell of a time this, what?"

Apologetically turning down a request from George Tyler, he said that he might be able to help later if the film of *Strange Interlude*, which had just been released, proved so successful that it encouraged Hollywood to buy other of his plays. He was pessimistic, however, for thus far he had sold to the movies only *Strange Interlude* (shortly after the plagiarism suit in 1931, with the playwright receiving thirty-seven thousand five hundred dollars, half of the purchase price, as his share), *Anna Christie*, and "a forgotten one-act play for which I got nothing. . . . They are all scared to touch my stuff."

Produced at MGM by Irving Thalberg, "the boy genius" of Hollywood, the celluloid *Strange Interlude* was only a moderate success, in spite of a stellar cast headed by Norma Shearer (Mrs. Thalberg) and the ascendant Clark Gable. O'Neill, who never saw it, had a notion that Thalberg had erred in casting his wife as Nina Leeds, but he didn't "really give a damn what they've done to it." As he said, "outside of money the films simply don't exist for me, and nothing they do or don't do seems of the slightest importance to my work as a playwright."

The "forgotten" playlet he mentioned was *Recklessness* from the *Thirst* volume ("the worst play in the book, as I remember, and that sure is low ebb"), which a minor studio bought in 1932 for five thousand dollars. The studio then scrapped the play, title and all, and turned out a film called *The Constant Woman*, with a wildly different story, that was promoted as based on a play by Eugene O'Neill. "The most amusing thing," one correspondent wrote to him, "is the way the reviewers strained their pedantic guts in an effort to associate you with the abortion . . . they saw."

Liveright's, which was having its own financial troubles, was glad to negotiate a deal, despite a low royalty rate, whereby the Book-of-the-Month Club would distribute to its members as a bonus a new collection of O'Neill's plays. It was the club's intention to have George Jean Nathan select nine plays and write an introduction, but at O'Neill's insistence he himself chose the plays and Joseph Wood Krutch supplied the prefatory word. Explaining his position to Saxe Commins, the playwright said that the volume would "stand in everyone's mind as representing the whole significant trend of my work and, between us, I don't like leaving such a choice to Nathan. . . . I by no means believe, or have ever believed, that he is any infallible critic of my work or has a comprehensive understanding of its inner spiritual trends. He has too many (frankly confessed by him) blind spots. He is antipathetic to all plays with a religious feeling (he liked *Brown* for its other aspects), all plays involving any tinge of social revolution. He liked *The Fountain, Gold!* – he despised *Lazarus*, totally misunderstood what I was driving at in *Dynamo*, thought *Hairy Ape* had radical propaganda . . . considered *Desire* [O'Neill probably meant *Welded*] imitation Strindberg. I will say nothing about the many Nathan conceptions of life he has read into my plays and praised to my irritated amusement.

"Don't misunderstand this as any panning of Nathan or any lack of gratitude for all the fights he has made for me. I'm only saying things about his criticism that I've often said in my arguments with him."

The Book-of-the-Month Club had wanted *Anna Christie* in the volume, but O'Neill was adamantly against it, for he still resented the general view that he had given the play a happy ending. *Nine Plays*, as the book was called, contained *The Emperor Jones, All God's Chillun Got Wings, Desire Under the Elms, Marco Millions, The Great God Brown, Lazarus Laughed, Strange Interlude*, and *Mourning Becomes Electra*.

Throughout fall 1932 he worked steadily, and much of the time unhappily, on *Days Without End*. "I'm batting my brains out," he lamented to Barrett Clark on November 15, and without divulging the nature of his new play, said that it was a "very difficult theme to work out clearly. Oh, for the good old days," he sighed, "when I was content to be either simple-minded or foggily mystical — now I aim to be clearly psychological and mystically clear, etc. A tough ambition!"

The final weeks of the year found him overtaxing himself; after finishing his fourth draft (the first complete one) at the end of November, he grew dissatisfied as he reread it and intensified his efforts to whip the play into shape. "I'm making Gene rest," Carlotta wrote to Commins during the Christmas holidays. "He is thoroughly exhausted. . . . It's a job looking after this child."

Utterly discouraged and suffering for the first time in his life from "nervous indigestion," O'Neill shelved *Days* at the start of 1933, thinking that he might tackle it again in a year or two, and began another play; within a few weeks he was back at *Days*. "I've tried to thrust it aside, forget it for a while, even abandon it entirely," he informed Robert Sisk on March 6, "but it won't let go its hold on me."

Although he considered *Days* to be related to *Dynamo*, it more closely resembles a blend of *Welded* and *The Great God Brown*. Here again, as in *Welded*, is a pair of possessive, romantic extremists completely engrossed in one another; and once more, like Dion Anthony of *Brown*, the protagonist is a divided man spiritually at war with himself. "Man is born broken," says Dion in what would be a perfect epigraph for *Days*. "He lives by mending. The grace of God is glue!"

It appears in fact that O'Neill's decision to write *Days Without End* was spurred by a book he had read, shortly after his return to America, which praised *Brown* as his finest work and held that if he could recapture its vision, he would secure "his ultimate liberation as a true poet of tragedy." The book was *Our Changing Theater* by Richard Dana Skinner, the critic for the Catholic periodical *Commonweal*. Skinner declared that in *Brown,* a play with "high moments of spiritual insight, of abiding faith, and of understanding of the mystic vale of tears," the author at last "began to fathom the meaning of earthly suffering. Probably no poet of the theater in recent times has always been more intensely aware of suffering than O'Neill. It has been his veritable obsession. . . . But until he wrote *Brown,* he had never seen beyond catastrophe to a possible resurrection. . . . He tells us in this play that from the tears of earth is born the eternal laughter of Heaven . . . that man should keep himself forever as a pilgrim in this earth . . . that God is!"

Even though the Catholic critic overstressed the note of Christian thought and yea-saying in *Brown,* his words were of a kind that would impress O'Neill. O'Neill himself thought highly of *Brown,* his dearest ambition was to become "a true poet of tragedy," and, above all, he hungered for redemption, for a sense of meaning in life. Yet, however strongly he may have been tempted to return to Catholicism, he was inclined still more strongly to remain outside and flagellate himself with the sound of distant prayer and the vision of a peace he would never know. Perhaps he, unconsciously, allowed himself to be tempted only so that he might put himself on the rack; as a man with deep guilt feelings and a consequent strain of self-hatred, he was inexorably bent on punishing himself, primarily, it seems (as Lavinia said of the Mannons), for the sin of "being born."

The record of O'Neill's struggle to overcome his dark impulses and, for a change, to speak out affirmatively, can be read in the various drafts of *Days,* particularly in their denouements. In the first draft the hero killed himself; in the next one, without accepting Christ as the Son of God, he saw Him as a symbol of suffering humanity; in yet another, when the hero's wife died, he ended cursing God. For his fifth draft (the second complete one), O'Neill, taking a cue from his *American Spectator* article on masks, split his protagonist in two. The article stated: "Consider Gothe's *Faust,* which, psychologically speaking, should be the closest to us of all the Classics. In producing this play, I would have Mephistopheles wearing the Mephistophelian mask of Faust. For is not the whole of Goethe's truth *for our time* just that Mephistopheles and Faust are one and the same — *are* Faust?"

Representing the opposed sides of the Faustian protagonist in *Days Without End,* "John," a Catholic apostate, longs to believe, longs for salvation, while the ironically named "Loving," a cynical nihilist, schemes for the other's ruin. The lone masked character in the play (he wears "the death mask of a John who has died with a sneer of scornful mockery on his lips"), Loving is visible only to John and of course the audience; when he speaks, the other characters take his voice to be John's. From one view he seems a malevolent incarnation of the audible-thought technique in *Strange Interlude*, as he voices the side of "John Loving" that John fears and is ashamed to 'express. He also can be seen, from a biographical angle, as a sinister version of the author's brother Jamie (in *Long Day's Journey* Jamie's face is described as having "a Mephistophelian cast"). Since the central issue is whether John will find his way back to Catholicism or succumb to Loving's diabolism, the play is largely a running argument between the opposed selves of the dual protagonist.

There is also a third voice in the debate, that of John's uncle and onetime guardian, a priest named Father Baird who strives to bring him back into the fold. Baird is to some extent an idealized image of James O'Neill (but it was the playwright's pious mother who personified to him Catholicism, just as he used to equate the Irish with his chauvinistic father). While working on *Days*, the playwright heard from an old New London friend who recalled Eugene's feuding with his father. Touched to the quick, he wrote back: "The Old Man and I got to be good friends and understood each other the winter before he died. But in the days you speak of, I was full of secret bitterness about him – not stopping to consider all he took from me and kept on smiling." In *Days* he has John say to his uncle: "You certainly didn't [take] unfair advantage of [me] in the old days. . . . When I look back, I'm amazed you could have been so fair."

Patently biographical in many respects, the new play reveals that John, a son of devout Catholics, turned renegade at the age of fifteen when his parents died in quick order, first his father, then his mother, despite all his prayers and vows to devote his life to "piety and good works." In O'Neill's case, it should be recalled, he was nearly fifteen when he learned of his mother's drug addiction and, immediately afterward, turned apostate. The play suggests, then, that both God and, in a sense, his mother died to Eugene at the same time, for he had lost his faith in them both.

Paralleling O'Neill's intellectual odyssey after he had become spiritually homeless, John successively embraces, among other secular gospels, atheism, Socialism, the teachings of Nietzsche; but he never finds an adequate substitute until he falls in love with Elsa, another rigid idealist, who joins her husband in worshiping at a private altar of complete fidelity and total union. In their religion, Marital Love is God. Thus, where O'Neill dramatized his relations with Agnes in *Welded*, *Days* affords a partial view of the feeling between him and Carlotta. In the play Elsa recalls that John once said that even "if every other marriage on earth were rotten and a lie, our love could make ours into a true sacrament." In 1934 O'Neill quoted these words in inscribing a copy of *Days* to Carlotta, then added: "And ours has, hasn't it, Darling One!"

Not only are *Days* and *Welded* marital studies based on their author's history, the new drama constitutes an ironic epilogue to the other one. It exemplifies, up to a point, the old proverb that the only thing worse than not attaining what you want is attaining it. Michael Cape of *Welded* feuded with his wife and bemoaned his lot because she resisted their becoming as one; John on the other hand is tortured after he has attained the supposedly blissful state of total union, for something in John ("Perhaps, in my soul," he says through Loving, "I hate love!") drives him to place his marriage in jeopardy by committing adultery. If John were ever unfaithful to her, Elsa tells a friend, it "would kill forever all my faith in life, all truth, all beauty, all love! I wouldn't want to live!",

True to her word, Elsa, after John indirectly confesses his guilt, invites death by pneumonia (the same illness, interestingly enough, that killed John's mother); but just in time Elsa forgives her husband, regains the will to live, and starts to recover. Behind her sudden change of heart is a mystical intuition. While she is undergoing her physical crisis, John, at the peak of his spiritual crisis, is on his knees before the Cross in a nearby church, wavering between doubt and faith. John recovers his faith in Christ just about the time Elsa relents. Loving, mortally stricken, slumps to the floor in the shape of a cross; the rising sun casts a radiant multi-colored light through the stained-glass windows; Father Baird rushes in with the happy news about Elsa; and John Loving, now a unified, harmonious soul, exults: "Life laughs with God's love again! Life laughs with love!"

Has any other major playwright ever written a play so awkwardly contrived or with such a feeble epiphany? To write it, O'Neill had to violate some of his strongest feelings and deepest convictions. As it was, he long fought against giving the play a happy ending (in his initial Faustian version, Elsa perishes), but he capitulated after more drafts and revisions, which occupied him during most of 1933. Eventually, after the play had been produced, he regretted the ending as false to himself and told friends that he intended to revise the final scene or two; but he had no heart for the job. He was weary of the play and allowed it to remain with its Handel-like coda from the "Hallelujah" chorus.

Essentially, *Days Without End* was an attempt at exorcism, hence its importance to O'Neill and his inability to abandon it when he became so discouraged. In it he sought not only to resolve his long-standing quarrel with his parents' religion but, it appears, to come to terms with a darkness in his depths, a buried strain of ambivalence concerning Carlotta. Despite his great need of her, despite his sense of security as the be-all and end-all of her existence (in a birthday tribute he called her love for him "this Stranger's only home on this earth!"), there are indications that, along with his returning her devotion, a secret part of him resented her and chafed at his dependency. If *Days* is accepted as substantially biographical and its heroine as a counterpart of Carlotta, a clue to O'Neill's feelings about her may be found in one of his earliest notes for the play. Envisioning a version of *Days* in which Elsa dies and her husband kills himself before an icon of the Virgin Mary, the note says: "Mother worship, repressed and turned morbid, ends by becoming Death-love and longing — thus it is statue of Virgin and child, identification of [the protagonist's] mother and Elsa with Her, himself with child, longing for reunion with them through Mother Goddess that really drives him to suicide . . . while at the same time it is his old resentment against mother, against Elsa as mother substitute (infidelity) that keeps him from giving in to Catholicism."

Clearly, then, even though images of the author's father and brother figure more prominently in the finished version of *Days* than an image of his mother, it was Ella O'Neill who loomed largest in her son's mind when he was conceiving the play.

To an extent, *Days Without End*, with John constantly apologizing for and trying to neutralize Loving's bitter words, foreshadows *Long Day's Journey Into Night*, in which the Tyrones oscillate between attack and apology, attack and retraction. At the beginning of *Days* Loving taunts his double with, "Afraid to face your ghosts?" to which John replies: "It is dangerous — to call things." In writing *Long Day's Journey* O'Neill would finally muster the courage "to call things," to bring into the open and face the family ghosts that lurk, in part, under various guises in *Days Without End*. For all his enthusiasm for masks, *Days*, with Loving a masked figure, would be the last time he used the device; a decisive impulse in the playwright son was driving him to write more plainly, more nakedly.

21

Controversial Drama

A FTER being financially worried for months, the O'Neills had a windfall in spring 1933 when John Krimsky and Clifford Cochran, a pair of new film-makers, bought *The Emperor Jones* for thirty thousand dollars; since the Provincetown Players, which had produced the drama, was no longer in existence, the playwright received the entire sum. At first he was hopeful about the movie, for it had Paul Robeson in his former role, Dudley Digges, one of Broadway's finest actors, as Smithers, and a screenplay by Du Bose Heyward, the author of *Porgy*, who flew down to Sea Island for a story conference and favorably impressed O'Neill. But the end product, after others had tinkered with Heyward's script to make it flashier, more exciting, proved a compromise that was neither artistic nor commercial. "However, I wail not," said O'Neill. "I got my money."

He received greater praise, though smaller remuneration (eighty dollars a performance), when an operatic version of *Jones* by Louis Gruenberg was given early this year at the Metropolitan. In the consensus of opinion the opera owed far more of its effectiveness to the playwright than to the composer. Lawrence Tibbett as the eponymous hero was well lauded, but the German tenor who played Smithers the Cockney was not exactly in character; at one point, O'Neill heard, he pronounced a line as, "I vas forgettin' dot silver bullet."

Early in April, as the playwright continued to struggle with *Days Without End*, he learned from Saxe Commins that his publisher was close to bankruptcy. For nearly three years, ever since Horace Liveright's forced departure from his own firm, Arthur Pell had staved off the day of reckoning through salary-slashing and other bone-cutting economies; but now the ills inherited from Liveright's impulsive leadership, compounded by the Depression, were taking effect.

Horace himself, at loose ends and broke (though still talking of grandiose plans), often hung around his former publishing house, till one day Pell objected to his presence. "Horace," he said, in a voice that filled the room, "I don't think you'd better come in any more. It doesn't look well for business." Horace, who almost single-handedly had fought the censors and prudish state legislators when the other bookmen feared to protest, left without a word. A few months later Liveright, showman, poseur, gambler, playboy, but one who did more than any other publisher in the 1920s to promote the new voices — Freud, Eliot, Pound, O'Neill, Faulkner, Hemingway — was dead of pneumonia at the age of forty-six. Within one period of a half-dozen years he had published seven men who subsequently won the Nobel Prize; one month six of the best sellers were Liveright books. He left an estate, it was said, of five hundred dollars.

Saxe Commins, diffident, altruistic, was too prone to let others impose on and use him, but he could be bold when the interests of his best friend were at stake. Worried that Liveright's might collapse before O'Neill received his latest royalties, he gave Pell and the other chief stockholders an ultimatum: unless he had within twenty-four hours a certified check for all the money owed to the playwright, he would inform the press that O'Neill was going to change publishers. Pell capitulated. A few days later Saxe was on his way south with the check for Eugene, who had been urging him to visit Sea Island.

This was not the first time Commins had protected his friend's financial interests. A year before, after being informed by Saxe that the publishing house was in weak condition, O'Neill had had Pell sign an agreement that if Liveright's went bankrupt, its contracts for his plays were void and all the rights would revert back to the author. During Saxe's visit in Georgia he and O'Neill drew up terms for the latter's next publisher that called for, among other provisions, a flat royalty of twenty percent (at Liveright's he had received seventeen and one-half percent, already an exceptionally high rate) and a ten thousand dollar advance when the contract was signed.

As soon as the news of Liveright's bankruptcy broke early in May 1933, a number of publishers approached O'Neill, either directly or through his agent, Richard Madden. After an exchange of correspondence, O'Neill had Thomas R. Coward of Coward-McCann fly down for an overnight visit. An affable, gentlemanly product of Groton, Yale and the squash courts, he charmed both the O'Neills, but his book list, which they received only after they had invited him, was disappointing.

O'Neill meanwhile had had a fine offer, through his agent, from

Bennett Cerf of Random House and, though he was nervously starting to envision a parade of publishers through his home, he played host briefly to Cerf also. Cerf, who thought the playwright had "the greatest natural dignity of anyone I've ever met," said, "I'm very impatient and never let a person finish what he's saying, but I never cut in on O'Neill, even though he talked slowly, very slowly – there'd be long pauses between his words."

A former vice-president of Liveright's (Horace, constantly short of cash, used to replenish his funds by selling vice-presidencies to wealthy young men eager to be in publishing), Bennett Cerf had left the firm in 1925 with its most valuable asset, the Modern Library, which he bought for two hundred and thirty-five thousand dollars. This was Liveright's fatal mistake. Despite his lavish scale of living, his unprofitable theatrical ventures, his heavy losses in Wall Street, he probably could have weathered all this and the Depression too had he retained the Modern Library, a modestly priced list of classics and near-classics that sold well from the start (in recent times it grossed over three million a year). Shortly after Cerf took over the Modern Library, in partnership with Donald S. Klopfer, the two also founded Random House to publish costly, limited editions of standard titles. For some time now the pair had planned to branch out with new books and they wanted O'Neill not only as a lure for other top authors but because his plays, even his failures on the stage, always turned a profit between book covers. For example, *Dynamo*, which all the critics had panned, sold about seventeen thousand copies – "three times," in O'Neill's words, "what the average novel sells!"

O'Neill informed Saxe on June 5 that while he felt his association with either Coward or Cerf "could not fail to be pleasant," he considered the Random House man "more able . . . [he has] a love of beautiful books, an appreciation for good literature, an ambition to . . . expand only along lines of distinction." Giving Saxe her own impression, Carlotta said on May 30 that Cerf "is a *very clever businessman*. And can get away with a lot on account of an exterior of boyish enthusiasm & a carefree manner. . . . Don't think I don't like Cerf – because I do – But he is a bit like all those N.Y. friends of his – (Dorothy Parker, Woollcott, Ross of the *New Yorker*)."

A chief stipulation of O'Neill's was that his new publisher would have to give a job, under contract, to Commins, whose life had been a financial struggle ever since his return from Europe in 1929; and now that he had two children, his situation was still more precarious. Eugene was determined that "the Liveright mess was not going to throw Saxe out on a cold, unemployed world." In choosing Random House, which met all his terms, he felt that the firm would be advantageous for both himself and his friend. "With Cerf," he told Saxe, "you will undoubtedly be called upon to contribute real imagination and judgment of real writing, once you've fitted in there." Saxe fitted in so well that in time he became not only the head editor at Random House but one of the two or three finest in the field; Auden, Faulkner, Sinclair Lewis and John O'Hara, as well as O'Neill, were only a few of the noted authors who benefited from his editorial services. Decades later Cerf said that Commins was "almost more important to us than O'Neill," while his partner Klopfer, going further, called Saxe "our prize acquisition of the two."

On rereading *Ah, Wilderness!* in June 1933, for the first time in months, O'Neill thought it a "lousy Owen Davis opus" and, still wrestling with *Days Without End*, felt dissatisfied with all his work. The Theater Guild, which had had a middling season, was eager to announce a new O'Neill play for the fall, but he was uncertain whether he would have anything ready in time. Suspending work on *Days*, he spent a fortnight cutting *Wilderness* (its first draft was so good that virtually no rewriting was necessary) and sent it to Commins to be retyped as soon as possible; he wanted a copy given to Nathan, who was shortly to visit Sea Island. On his arrival Nathan declared that the comedy was "one of the best things" O'Neill had written, but he considered *Days*, which he read in Georgia, among the author's poorest efforts.

While O'Neill was relatively undisturbed by Nathan's low opinion of *Days*, since the critic always disliked plays of a religious nature, both he and Carlotta were upset when Saxe, who had been sent the latest draft to type, failed to share their view of its new denouement. "Gene & I nearly had a fit," Carlotta wrote back, "when we saw you had taken the end of the play quite from the wrong angle. It has nothing to do with *Christianity* or *prayer* that brings Elsa back — it is her great & all-consuming *love* ["love" was underscored seven times] for her husband!

"Thro' her love she senses that her husband is in danger & that *love* [underscored four times] gives her the strength to come back & live for him — We suppose *no one* will understand that tho' — that you didn't!"

O'Neill was even more concerned that the play would be regarded as heralding his return to the Mother Church. "What a howl of discussion and misunderstanding and side-taking and reading-the-author-into-his-character's-end," he predicted to Robert Sisk, "there is going to be on this one! I grow dead with fatigue even to think of it!"

[417]

Following the Theater Guild's acceptance of both *Wilderness* and *Days* — the latter none too enthusiastically — the main question was the order in which they should be produced. Since O'Neill expected *Days* to be "controversial" and to arouse "much bitter argument," he was inclined to favor the comedy as the lead-off play, but he worried so over the problem, balancing one factor against another, that he became confused. A major reason for his indecision was the fear that both his new plays, the first since *Mourning Becomes Electra*, would be compared with that outsize achievement and suffer accordingly. He particularly wondered whether *Ah, Wilderness!* possessed something "finer" than "its obvious surface value."

The Guild decided to open its 1933–1934 season with the comedy, and at Eugene's suggestion, to present *Days* right after Christmas. He felt that "then, if ever, people remember the religious background of their past — or present — if any." (It seems significant that for years he used to sink into a depression during the Christmas holidays.)

To escape the humid heat of a Sea Island summer, when O'Neill found the water too warm for pleasurable swimming, he and Carlotta headed for a vacation in the Adirondacks. After a brief stopover in New York, where he conferred with the Guild directorate, Bennett Cerf and others, the couple spent most of August at an isolated lodge on Wolf Lake near Faust, New York; between hours of swimming, rowing and fishing, O'Neill continued revising his new drama (he privately referred to it now as "Pangs Without End"). On returning to the city the couple, with Carlotta always at her husband's side, was immediately absorbed in the casting, rehearsals and other production activities of *Ah, Wilderness!*

O'Neill was enthusiastic, the Guild dubious at first, when someone suggested George M. Cohan for the part of the father. The Guild heads considered Cohan, despite his exceptional versatility, chiefly a song-and-dance man; but at O'Neill's urging they sent him a script and, to their amazement, he accepted. For all his many years on the stage, his role as Nat Miller would be his first appearance in a play he himself had not written.

The *Wilderness* casting took everyone, not merely Helburn, Langner & Co., by surprise, for Cohan, jaunty, brash, with a disarming leer, as though mocking himself, seemed the last person to be associated with the author of *Strange Interlude* and *Mourning Becomes Electra*. The "Yankee Doodle Dandy" in an O'Neill play? Impossible! Obviously enjoying the sensation his acceptance had created, Cohan, when asked how it felt to be in a "literary play," cocked his hat over one eye and

[418]

drawled, "What t'ell, it's the same thing all over. A show's a show. There's a manuscript and a curtain and footlights and an audience out front waiting to be entertained."

Though Cohan's father and James O'Neill had been friends — they helped to found the Catholic Actors' Guild — their sons only now became acquainted. Cohan had half expected the playwright "might try to pull some of that highbrow stuff," but instead found him "just regular. Why he is as interested in the ball scores as I am. . . . He knows the show business. He wasn't born on the corner of Forty-third Street and Broadway for nothing."

Philip Moeller, nervous about directing a man accustomed to being the ringmaster and virtually the whole show in his own productions, said to Cohan as rehearsals began: "Look here, G.M., you're a director, an actor and a playwright all in one. If what I'm doing seems crazy to you, I wish you'd tell me." Cohan, who could be all graciousness when approached deferentially, replied, "I'm learning something every day." Then, placing a hand on Moeller's shoulder, "And what's more, I mean it." But he turned implacably hostile to the rest of the Guild directorate when they sent him a memorandum of suggestions and criticisms. "Tell that holy board of geniuses," he exploded to the stage manager, "never to contact me again!"

In general things went smoothly with the staging, due in large part to the easy working relationship among O'Neill, Moeller, and Robert Edmond Jones, whose sets and costumes seemed to Eugene "a marvelous job." The playwright, who usually had reservations about the shape his script assumed in performance, found rehearsals more or less of an ordeal; but this time he enjoyed himself, for he considered the cast, as a whole, "the best" ever of his productions and felt that they "really make [the play] live close to what I imagined."

Although O'Neill had previously met Russel Crouse, Robert Sisk's successor as head publicity man for the Guild, *Wilderness* marked the start of their close association and what would prove a lifelong friendship. An exception in the seismic little world of Broadway, a place subject to tremors of ego, temperament and vanity, Crouse was level-headed and kind, a man with a sense of humor, a sense of proportion. In a view he was never to change, he doubted that he or anyone else would ever really know O'Neill, would ever understand the man behind the "mask." "Gene reminded me," Crouse has said, "of the stories you read in newspapers about someone who'd been chained up for years and fed in a closet or a tiny room, until freed eventually. For a long while, every time we'd meet,

Gene would hold back like a wary animal; then he would warm up and start to wag his tail."

Most of the players in *Wilderness*, particularly the young ones, were rather timid at first around O'Neill. "He really looked," one says, "like our First Playwright — lean and gray-haired, immaculate in custom-tailored tweeds." On his side O'Neill, doing his best to encourage them, became friendly with several of the cast, but in general Carlotta served as an intermediary between him and the others. Running errands for her husband, taking notes, relaying his messages to Moeller, slipping out of the Guild Theater and back to bring him lunch, conferring with him in whispers — Carlotta was much in evidence at rehearsals. Every day in a different outfit, sometimes bearing a cane, she cut as striking a figure as O'Neill. To Ruth Holden, who played the streetwalker in the bar scene, she suggested "an unfashionable duchess [nearly all of Carlotta's wardrobe, several years old, was from the European stay]. She was a very handsome woman," Miss Holden says, "but she wore strange clothes — I remember a capelike thing — and no makeup."

O'Neill wanted the production as realistic as possible, to make the period charm of his story seem authentic, rather than so much marshmallow icing. At his request, Bobby Jones made the sets solid and habitable-looking; to Ruth Holden the playwright suggested that she add some pimples in making up ("All the tarts I knew in New London had bad complexions"). A gratuitous note of realism was added by George M. Cohan: like his fictional counterpart, he was having trouble with his son, and in certain of his scenes with Elisha Cook, Jr. (cast as young Miller), tears would start in his eyes. "If I can't play this one," Cohan told the playwright, "I might as well quit."

Both Cohan and the Guild wanted *Wilderness* shortened, though for different reasons. Cohan was more inhibited, more puritanical than his Broadway-type personality suggested; not one of his plays or musicals had ever contained a "dirty" line or a really off-color situation — any talk of sex made him uncomfortable — and now, for the first time in his career, he was in a play that contained a prostitute. He maintained that the barroom scene was unnecessary, out of key with the rest of the story, and should be dropped, a suggestion O'Neill rejected.

The Guild found *Wilderness* too long in general and hoped that O'Neill would cut it when the play tried out in Pittsburgh for a week. Unlike most playwrights, O'Neill took a dim view of pre-Broadway engagements ("I can't see or react with an audience around"). However, since an actor's timing is most important in comedy, more so than in drama, the Guild had scheduled the Pittsburgh date to give the players a chance to pace their performance and, with an audience's help, to locate the laughs in the script.

The Pittsburgh reviewers, while generally favorable, thought the play sagged at times and overall was rather mild. O'Neill, who had tentatively decided while still in New York how the script should be tightened, sliced even further after he caught the midweek matinee in Pittsburgh, yet he later insisted to Langner that he learned virtually nothing from the tryout, that all his cuts were ready prior to Pittsburgh. Carlotta, who feared that the public might "resent Gene's writing this type of play," wrote to Commins immediately after the matinee that he was "still busy cutting – (but *not* for the published book) – to get the time down." In all, he reduced the running time about half an hour.

Cordially received on the whole by the New York press, *Ah, Wilderness!*, which opened on October 2, 1933, at the Guild Theater, became the author's second biggest success (exceeded only by *Strange Interlude*) in his lifetime. The public, contrary to Carlotta's apprehension, was delighted that O'Neill could write something conventionally entertaining and flocked to it for two hundred eighty-nine performances. The reviewers, predictably, were amazed to find the author in such an affable mood (one joked that his "lightest word used to harrow up our souls and cause our knotted and combined locks to stand on end"), with some likening him to the Booth Tarkington of *Seventeen* and *Penrod*. Gilbert Gabriel of the *American,* who thought the comparison unfair to O'Neill, called his play "an evening of slyly superfine delight." Richard Lockridge hailed it in the *Sun* as "a story of much charm and truth." Brooks Atkinson, among its leading admirers, found it the author's "most attractive" work; looking beneath its humorous surface, the *Times* man thought that the final scene between father and son "caught all the love and anguish that such relationships conceal."

Not all the critics viewed the play so favorably; Percy Hammond for one considered it "more of a loaf of bread than a jug of wine, being one of the tamer items of [O'Neill's] repertory." But all were enthusiastic, indeed, virtually ecstatic about Cohan's portrayal of the father; they felt that regardless of his many past triumphs, he was now giving the performance of his career.

O'Neill dedicated the published play to George Jean Nathan – "Who also, once upon a time, in peg-top trousers went the pace that kills on the road to ruin." After the opening the playwright presented each of the cast with an autographed copy. In Cohan's he wrote: "With deep gratitude and appreciation for all your grand portrayal of Nat Miller has meant to this play — and with the real friendship of one (I hope) regular guy for another! Cheers, and then again cheers, to you and for you always!" His warm feeling for Cohan soon faded, though.

As an actor, Cohan had been delighted with his notices ("a grand and glorious piece of work" . . . "[his] ripest, finest performance" . . . "a superb interpretation," etc.). But as a playwright, he found a cutting edge to the praise. Brooks Atkinson, expressing the general view, said the new play "dipped deeper into Mr. Cohan's gifts and personal character than any of the antics he has written for himself. Ironic as it may sound, it has taken Eugene O'Neill to show us how fine an actor George M. Cohan is."

Cohan became so resentful of this aspect of the reviews that it affected his performance. Under his breath but audible enough to the other actors grouped around the Miller dinner table, he made disparaging cracks about O'Neill and his comedy. More damagingly, he slowed down an already leisurely play with new pieces of business, with longer and longer pauses in his delivery. It became a rueful joke in the company that "O'Neill took out thirty minutes and Cohan put them back." The Guild sent memorandums and emissaries requesting him to step up his performance; O'Neill berated him one night in his dressing room (Cohan had to prevent his bodyguard, an ex-policeman, from punching the playwright), but no one could sway him; he continued to perform at a deliberate pace. In later years O'Neill, who never forgot and rarely forgave, told interviewers that Cohan had been wrong for the play because he "overshadowed it" and gave it the wrong emphasis; the Miller boy, not his father, the playwright said, was supposed to be "the main figure." Talking more freely in private, he called Cohan "a vaudevillian who tried to turn the play into a one-man show."

For her husband's forty-fifth birthday, shortly after the *Wilderness* première, Carlotta gave him an old-time player piano, something he had wanted for years, similar to the one in the barroom scene of his comedy. When the couple first asked for such an instrument at Wurlitzer's on Forty-second Street, the salesman, who recognized O'Neill, felt that they were making a mistake and tried to sell them an organ, as befitting an eminent playwright; but he finally realized that their minds were set and located what they wanted.

"It was a great moment in my life," O'Neill has recalled, "when she first burst on my sight in Wurlitzer's remotest storeroom in all her gangrenous-green, festooned-with-rosebuds beauty. There sure must have been an artist soul lost to the world in the New Orleans honky-tonk – or bordello – she came from." O'Neill, who promptly named the machine "Rosie," was to spend some of his happiest hours at the old instrument as it tinkled and thumped through the strains of "Alexander's Ragtime Band" and "Mysterious Rag," "All Alone" and "Waiting for the *Robert E. Lee.*" He used to keep time with his feet and often, when carried away, would break into song.

"I'm not sure," he joked, "that listening to all those old songs I played on Rosie was a good idea. I try to remember a beautiful verse of Verlaine and come up with a line of 'Everybody's Doing It' or 'Oh, You Great Big Beautiful Doll.' "

From Hollywood Kenneth Macgowan, who had become a producer at RKO Pictures, congratulated his old friend on his latest hit and hoped that his studio would outbid the others trying to buy it. (*Wilderness* was acquired by MGM for seventy-five thousand dollars, a sum split equally between the playwright and his producers, and filmed with Lionel Barrymore as the father, Wallace Beery as the rumpot uncle.) Replying on October 16 to Kenneth, O'Neill said he felt that the play's success proved that "emotionally we still deeply hanker after the old solidarity of the family unit."

As to *Days Without End,* he expected that its ending would "astonish" Macgowan. "It was an end," he said, "I resisted (on personal grounds) but which finally forced itself on me as the one inevitable one." His latest two plays, he thought, would have Kenneth "wondering what sea change has come over me. The truth is that, after *Electra,* I felt I had gone as far as it was in me to go along my old line – for the time being, at least. I felt that to try to top myself in various other phases of the old emotional attitude would be only to crucify my work on what had become for the time an exhausted formula. . . . I felt a need to liberate myself from myself, so to speak. . . . And now, whatever the fate of *Days Without End,* I'm damned glad I did, for I feel immensely freer inside myself."

Back in Sea Island by mid-October, the playwright resumed work on *Days.* From its inception he had fought against making it a Catholic play. In his initial draft the hero's uncle was a kindly, old-fashioned country doctor; in another early version, a Protestant minister of unspecified denomination. Even after O'Neill had capitulated, in the fifth draft, and drawn him as a Catholic priest, he again changed his mind and had the uncle revert to being a country doctor, but "with a deep religiousness added." Thus, O'Neill said, he would avoid "all the Christian or Catholic priest confusion and still preserve all values." But ultimately the story, rooted in the author's own history, demanded a context of Catholicism; he subtitled the drama "A Modern Miracle Play."

On the surface his last three plays seem to have nothing in common, yet, in some degree, they are variations on a single theme: *Mourning Becomes Electra* sounds a recurrent note of Paradise Lost as, at one time or another, each of the Mannons, including Adam Brant, yearns for the innocent nudity, innocent happiness of the South Sea islanders; *Ah, Wilderness!* is a homey, middle-class version of Paradise Regained; and *Days Without End*, with its religious torment and climactic epiphany, is both Paradise Lost and Paradise Regained. Written during a period of five years, the three plays, but especially *Days*, attest to a persistent hunger in their author; while it could inspire images of secular wish fulfillment, it was essentially a spiritual hunger.

Years earlier, in the Hell Hole in Greenwich Village, Eugene used to reel off from memory "The Hound of Heaven" in its entirety; he gave the impression of communing with himself. In *Days Without End* the priest, quoting from the Francis Thompson poem, maintains to his renegade nephew that "the Hound" still pursues him. Exactly how close He came to catching up with O'Neill himself, as he worked on the play, is uncertain; the evidence is mixed. Unlike her husband, Carlotta was not, basically, of a spiritual nature, but, fascinated by the drama and color of Catholic ritual, she felt that he should return to his ancestral faith; she believed it would bring him peace.

When the couple returned to New York late in November for rehearsals of *Days Without End*, the playwright, anxious to avoid any errors in his treatment of Catholicism, had Richard Dana Skinner read the script. From both the play and several talks he had with O'Neill, the Catholic critic thought the apostate was finding his way back. "I can assure you," he wrote to a cleric friend, "that the play was written not only with the utmost sincerity but only as a result of a terrific interior and personal struggle on O'Neill's part . . . his wife is working very hard to bring about his definite return to the Catholic Church." Skinner added that since O'Neill's first two marriages were "outside of the Church," they were invalid in the Catholic view and left him "free to remain with his present wife if he returned to the Church."

At the Skinners' one evening O'Neill outlined the play to the Reverend George B. Ford, a leading intellectual of the New York diocese, who was surprised to find the playwright "so communicative," so different from his public image as a semirecluse. "I think it was characteristic of him," the priest says, "to speak freely when a subject interested him — in this case, his work — but to have nothing to say when it was just small talk. After he'd summarized his story, with the man ending on his knees before a large crucifix, I told him that a crucifix is of relatively minor significance in church architecture, that the man should prostrate himself at the altar. But Eugene said that that was not good dramatically, not as effective in the theater."

Father Ford, unlike Skinner, did not get the impression that O'Neill was wavering back to his former faith. "We never discussed religion per se that night. He simply narrated the story for my general reaction. Two or three times after that, Carlotta called and said Eugene wanted to talk with me, asked me to hold on, then came back to the phone and said he wouldn't. She always added, 'I hope you understand.' I don't know whether she wanted him to talk with me and he balked at the last minute, or whether it was his idea and he changed his mind."

With O'Neill's consent, Robert Sisk, now a movie executive, sent a copy of *Days* to Martin Quigley, a publisher of film magazines and a power in Catholic circles. "I am delighted," Eugene replied after word from Quigley, "that your reaction was so favorable — particularly so since the script you read is much too long and wordy and lacks the compact finish I hope to get . . . by the time the play is produced."

Months earlier he and the Guild had agreed to cast Earle Larimore (Nina's husband in *Strange Interlude*, Orin in *Mourning Becomes Electra*) as the tortured hero of *Days*, and Stanley Ridges as the fiendish Loving. Ilka Chase, though usually seen in comedies, was engaged to portray the family friend who tempts the hero into adultery. But the role of the wife proved difficult to fill; Carlotta was particularly anxious, since the wife was chiefly modeled on herself, that the role be well played. Before the O'Neills' return to town, Carlotta had written on November 14 to Langner: "Gene and I have been doing a lot of thinking as to Nazimova playing Elsa!! There's lots *against* and lots *for* (So few actresses feel anything under their skins — and are so artificial. [Jane] Cowl I have always loathed.) Nazimova knows what to love and to suffer means — even if her hair did become disarranged in the process!" Finally Selena Royle, a refined-looking blond who was Larimore's wife, was cast as Elsa.

From her husband, who "worshiped" O'Neill, Miss Royle had a preconceived image of the playwright that changed radically during their acquaintanceship. Instead of finding him, as Larimore did, a superior human being, she thought him "a hollowed-out, burned-out man without any tender emotion. I was impudent enough to feel sorry for him." (To

[425]

Ruth Holden of *Ah, Wilderness!* he seemed "one of the most compassionate men I've ever met, very shy, but more concerned [about you] if you were unsure of yourself than about himself.") At Miss Royle's first meeting with O'Neill, an afternoon tea in his hotel suite, Carlotta dominated the occasion with talk of "massages, hair dressings, all the luxurious things beautiful women adore." It seemed evident to the actress that Carlotta regarded *Days* as "Gene's hymn of love for her."

Unlike O'Neill's response to the staging of *Wilderness*, which he had enjoyed, he found rehearsals of *Days* a frustrating ordeal, for the production was not developing as he had hoped. He was, he complained on December 15 to Art McGinley, "busier than ever before on this one – a damned difficult play to produce and so little time to do it in – all day every day, no time out for lunch, take a sandwich to the theater – that sort of stuff." Working closely with Moeller, who was directing his fifth (and final) O'Neill script, the playwright continued revising, cutting, polishing.

Since he had had to overcome strong inner misgivings in writing a play that conformed to Catholic orthodoxy, he became incensed at the slightest criticism of it from Catholic quarters. A priest of the Catholic Writers' Guild, who knew that O'Neill was fond of Russel Crouse, invited the press agent to lunch one day and toward the end disclosed the motive behind his invitation. The Catholic Guild would endorse the play, he said, if the playwright made it clear that Elsa, who had been previously married, was not a divorcée but a widow. As Crouse had anticipated, O'Neill's reply was an unqualified No. "If *they* want to think that her first husband died," he scowled, "that's all right with me. But I won't change a word to please them!"

Explaining his position more fully when Bennett Cerf proposed seeking "advance endorsements" from "high dignitaries of the church," O'Neill declared that such a move was "the very last thing I would want done! It would throw my whole intention in writing the play into a misleading, false emphasis. It is a play about a Catholic. It is an attempt to express what I feel are the life-preserving depths in Catholic mysticism – to be fair to a side of life I have dismissed with scorn in other plays. *But* [underscored three times] it is also a psychological study whose psychological truth would be the same, essentially, if a Buddhist or a Greek Orthodox hero were involved. *It is not Catholic propaganda!* If, after it comes out, the Church wants to set the seal of its approval on it, well, that's up to them. But I don't give a damn whether they do or not – and

I certainly will not make the slightest move to win that approval in advance."

To launch *Days Without End* under favorable circumstances, the Guild scheduled a pre-Broadway engagement of one week in Boston, where the city's large Irish Catholic population was expected to assure the play a sympathetic hearing. More readily than he had gone to Pittsburgh for his comedy, O'Neill agreed to attend his drama in Boston, where it was to open two days after Christmas.

Shortly before the tryout he heard from Terry Carlin, whom he had not seen in years but whom he had continued to help support. By now Terry, who had floated through most of his life on a stream of alcohol, had been grounded by age (he was seventy-nine), ill health, and the sober realities. Presently living in Boston, in a boardinghouse at 9 Eaton Street, the old anarchist reported to his friend and benefactor that he was pressed for funds. Eugene replied that he was directing his attorney to increase the monthly check, so that Terry "needn't have any more worries on that score," and urged him not to overtax himself. "I know you! You'll be out looking for mushrooms [to use in making something alcoholic] and catch a toadstool!"

According to Jeanne Gerson, an aspiring young actress whose mother owned the Eaton Street place, Carlin became excited when the local press announced that the new O'Neill drama would be tested in Boston. "I can see him now," Miss Gerson says, "a long scrawny face, long white hair, propped up in his wheelchair. He always had a smile but he was unhappy and used to say, 'I don't want to live any more, I'm just a burden to everyone.' The thought of seeing Gene again gave him a great lift, he took on new life. He loved talking about the times he and Gene got drunk together and how they got along on practically nothing and the various characters they had known. After some correspondence it was arranged for O'Neill to visit him, but there was a heavy snowstorm that day, it went on for hours, and Terry said, 'Maybe he won't come out in all this snow — but I guess he'll let me know.' " O'Neill never did appear or telephone; he probably was deterred less by the weather than by reluctance to see his old crony in a decrepit state.

A week or so after the abortive reunion, Carlin was removed to Boston City Hospital, where he succumbed in two days from pneumonia. Following his cremation at Mt. Auburn, his ashes, Eugene was touched to hear, were taken to Provincetown by a friend and scattered over the water. O'Neill paid his medical and other final expenses; in a few years

Terry would, in a sense, repay the debt by serving as the model for Larry Slade in *The Iceman Cometh*.

Several Boston reviews of *Days Without End*, especially those in the *Transcript* and the *Traveler*, were encouraging, but the playwright remained doubtful of the outcome. A Harvard instructor named Frederic I. Carpenter, who saw the play with his wife, writes: "At its end we were walking slowly up the aisle, discussing our perplexity and dissatisfaction with the play's ending, when we became conscious of a man in the aisle seat of the back row observing the audience as it passed. For a moment the dark eyes rested on us — yet not really on us — rather on our feeling of perplexity, which his eyes seemed to share. Then he rose and hurried out into the wings. Turning to each other in startled surprise, we said: 'That was O'Neill.' "

The O'Neills celebrated New Year's Eve by having Philip Moeller to dinner in their suite at the Ritz-Carlton. Socially, in spite of the close professional relationship of playwright and director, the O'Neills saw less of Moeller than of Lawrence Langner; where Langner was eager to cultivate his friendship with the playwright, Moeller, a cultured bachelor who delighted in a one-sided intimacy with Mozart and Shakespeare, was more reserved with the living. On New Year's Day the director, who felt that *Days Without End* marked a turning point in the playwright's life, wrote down his predominant impressions of both O'Neills:

"A few notes of conversation with Gene & Carlotta after dinner last night which may be of interest to someone writing G's definitive biography fifty years hence.

"The evening was less difficult than I had anticipated. During dinner I switched the talk in the direction of the musical structure in G's plays and then to [Hitler's] persecution of the Jews. [The latter subject was of personal interest to the O'Neills because of Eugene Jr.; though he had intended to complete his postgraduate studies at the University of Freiburg, he "loathed Germany under the Hitler banner" and, after one year abroad, had returned to Yale.]

"After dinner inevitably the talk took on the direction of religion. It was obvious from what was said that [*Days*] in theme is more her play than his. They both definitely acknowledge this.

"She says Gene was and is still a Catholic and she hopes he will return definitely to the faith and that she would gladly go with him, whenever he is ready, but he must not be forced.

"There were long discussions on the mystic beauty of the Catholic faith. He said the end of the play was undoubtedly a wish fulfillment on his part. He told me about the simple trusting happiness of some of his Catholic relatives [the Sheridans and the Brennans of New London]. He wants to go that way and find a happiness which apparently he hasn't got and which obviously this perfect (?) marriage doesn't seem to bring him.

"He acknowledges the beginning of the study scene was the autobiographical projection of a life theory. This I had sensed from the beginning and had told him it was difficult to do it because of [its] closeness to himself and his personal sentiments. . . .

"Much of the strange religious hatred of the alter ego, G. said, came from his acquaintance with a lunatic boy who came to see him in Bermuda, a boy obsessed with a religious complex and persecution mania. [The playwright told someone else that the boy, who had been expelled from Fordham, had sought him out in hopes of spiritual guidance. "Can you imagine anyone," the playwright smiled wryly, "coming to me for help!"]

"All the evening G. was very direct and appealing, now that the resentment due to the way things were going has lifted. When he's in this mood he is deeply likable.

"Madam was again rich in banalities, but her striving to hold all together is somehow appealing and somehow irritating at the same time.

"The five weeks have been a difficult experience, particularly controlling myself in the face of G's hurt vanity. For an important person and surely a theater genius he has some very human crevices in his makeup. But this making spiritual peace may be his end as an important creator. . . .

"And the tragic humor of the situation is that he doesn't have what [Carlotta] wants to bring him. Psychologically, the relationship is tremendously fraught with possibilities. Will superficial ease and superficial comfort win out with his writing? Will the important element survive?"

(Where Moeller detachedly pondered the question, Robert Edmond Jones a few years later became genuinely worried. After being a houseguest of the O'Neills', he returned to New York and exploded to a friend, "She's going to kill him, she's going to kill him!" A mystic, one who thought that O'Neill's life by the sea at Peaked Hill had been ideal for him, Bobby went on to explain that under Carlotta's immaculate management "all of Gene's suits are hanging up just so in the closet, everything's neatly in place. I could've burned that closet! That's not the kind of life for Gene and his work!")

[429]

Moeller's notes conclude: "Years ago I said that G. would end on his knees before the cross, and apparently he has got there now. What will it do to the future work of America's foremost dramatist?"

The New York engagement of *Days* at the Henry Miller was to follow hard on the Boston tryout. Carlotta on January 7, 1934, wrote to Vera Massey, the cook at Casa Genotta, that she and O'Neill were "sitting on pins and needles waiting for tomorrow's opening!" The question uppermost in O'Neill's mind, he told Martin Quigley on the seventh, was whether "there is enough strength and conviction in the play to overcome the pseudo-intellectual pose of New York critics and subscriber-audiences that religious faith is an outmoded subject."

As usual he gave his first-night tickets to Saxe and Dorothy Commins. After the première Saxe, while his wife hurried home to their children, called on the O'Neills at the Hotel Madison and reported that the audience had been exceedingly attentive. Carlotta, he noted with secret amusement, was appropriately dressed for the crucial evening in a long white cashmere gown with a cowl and a ropelike gold belt – a glamorous version, in short, of a monk's habit.

The reviews, by and large, were as unfavorable as the playwright in his darkest moments had feared. John Mason Brown said in the *Post* that *Days* "must take its place along with *Dynamo* and *Welded* among the feeblest of [the author's] works . . . almost everything that was simple, straight-forward and disarmingly poignant in the miracle plays of old becomes tedious . . . turgid and artificial in this fakey preachment of our times." John Anderson thought that O'Neill's "fundamental error, dramatically, lies in the notion that Faith is an intellectual process to be touched through words. Its very point, I take it, is that it lies beyond reason." Summing up, he said in the *Journal* that the play was "all dramatically phony; that O Neill has substituted some florid emotion, and some muddy thinking, for the dignity and simplicity of religious conviction." To Brooks Atkinson it seemed that the playwright at times told his story "as though he had never [before] written a play. In view of his acknowledged mastery of the theater it is astonishing that his career can be so uneven." Another day the *Times* critic made the acute observation that "some of [the dialogue] . . . sounds as though Mr. O'Neill were trying to convince himself."

Virtually all the reviewers praised Moeller's direction, Lee Simonson's sets, and particularly Earle Larimore's performance in a difficult part; but only Richard Lockridge of the *Sun* and Burns Mantle of the *News*, among the major critics, had a kind word for the script. Lockridge, after terming it "a strange and moving play," said, "The very unsophistication of the closing scenes . . . gives to them a thrilling quality." Mantle found that it was not "an entertainment for those who frankly have little or no use for the drama of souls. But a fascinating study for students and the secretly mystified of all faiths."

As its author had predicted, *Days* aroused controversy; secular reviewers attacked it on artistic grounds and were in turn attacked by the Catholic press on religious grounds. The Brooklyn *Tablet* castigated them as "the minions of Anti-Christ," and then, in language similar to O'Neill's letter to Quigley, added: "Most of these critics are pseudo-intellectuals who hide their ignorance under the misapprehension that faith is outmoded. For this reason the grotesque reviews appearing in many papers are particularly asinine." No less vehement, the Catholic weekly *America* said the daily reviewers disliked the play because it stood "for everything they have fought against for years. . . . They called it insulting names . . . words that shallow unbelievers reserve for eternal truth."

Trying to cool the controversy, R. Dana Skinner said on January 26 in *Commonweal:* "Faith cannot be made objective in material terms. The inherent dramatic values in *Days Without End* are therefore lost to those who either have no faith or who have never experienced it.

"In fairness, then, both to Mr. O'Neill's extraordinary play and to the critics who do not see its inner beauty and dramatic strength, we can only accept the fact that when two groups of people do not speak the same language of the soul, it is very hard for them to discover a plane of mutual understanding."

One after another the Catholic reviewers lavished superlatives on the new drama ("the great Catholic play of the age." . . . "O'Neill's greatness has begun. May they be *Days Without End*"), but to the author all their high praise was more or less nullified when a Monsignor Lavelle, in charge of the matter, rejected the play for the White List, presumably because of the uncertainty over Elsa's first husband. "That makes it impossible," Skinner lamented to a friend, "to have various Catholic groups take the play for benefit performances. What strange complexities there are in the Catholic world!"

O'Neill tried to hearten his players with a telegram: "You know I told you to discount [the critics] in advance. The play was not written for that type of mind but I know you will find here as in Boston a steadily growing audience of the intelligent and unprejudiced who will know what the play is about and appreciate your grand work in making it live. . . . So carry on with confidence in the final result. . . . Are we downhearted? No!"

In reality the general verdict disturbed him deeply, more deeply than ever before — excepting possibly the response to *Dynamo*, another defective play born of his old quarrel with his parents and his parents' religion. Trying to warm himself against the cold critical winds with every possible scrap of comfort, he hugged the fact that there were, as he wrote to Macgowan on February 14, 1934, "six to ten curtain calls nightly at the end — Guild audiences three-quarters Jèwish! And yet the critical jackasses have the nerve to say the technique doesn't come off!"

To Nathan he crowed, a few weeks after the première, that the published work "has already sold close to as many copies as *Ah, Wilderness!*" It was his contention that Nathan, who had been derisive about the new play, would learn to admire it "when you at last grow that soul." (While the playwright never returned to the Church, Nathan, to the amazement of practically all who knew him, was converted to Catholicism near the end of his life.)

O'Neill's chief consolation was a cable from William Butler Yeats asking permission to stage *Days Without End* at the Abbey Theater as soon as possible. "Evidently Yeats sees what the play is all about," the author exulted on February 27 to Russel Crouse, "and likes it — and Yeats is Yeats. Also, he isn't a Catholic. Whatever bias he might have in that line would, I think, be contra rather than pro."

The O'Neill drama appeared at a strategic time for the government-subsidized Abbey, which was under attack from a powerful Jesuit for presenting allegedly irreligious plays. There were fears at the playhouse that the government, which always kept at least one ear attuned to the Church, might withdraw its support. Fortunately, Patrick McCartan, a friend of Yeats and a battler in America for Irish causes, saw *Days* and liked it. "You did us a great service," Yeats wrote to McCartan on February 16, "by recommending Eugene O'Neill's new play and by sending us a copy. . . . We have had a friendly reply [from him] and will produce it shortly after Easter. . . . It is a most powerful play, and, as you say, Catholic in atmosphere."

Under Lennox Robinson's direction, the Abbey staged *Days* with some of its finest talent, namely F. J. McCormick, Arthur Shields, Barry Fitzgerald (later of Hollywood renown), Eileen Crowe and May Craig. Yeats, in a nursing home when the play opened, had a wire from his wife: "Great success, magnificent acting, good production." The reviewers, the poet later informed McCartan, were "as favorable as they know how to be, but praise is one of the things they know little about. To praise without gushing is one of the gifts of a fine journalist. . . . The success of this perfectly orthodox play has come at the right moment for us, as we are having some trouble with the government."

Still, the play's cordial reception in Ireland could not alter the fact that on Broadway the public was, in O'Neill's words, "staying away in barbarian hordes." After the play had closed — it lasted fifty-seven performances, thanks to the Guild's subscribers — he told Russel Crouse he felt relieved, "for hoping against hope is a wearying game. . . . As you know, from the time it started rehearsing, I foresaw what we would be up against with the reviewing lads. And all the time I was sweating blood getting this opus out of my system I was never beguiled by the fancy that it would ever click as a financial success in our modern theater."

Delighted that Harold McGee, once of the Provincetown Players, had liked his new drama, he predicted that it would "come into its own" in other countries. Chafing under the widespread opinion that he was about to return to the flock, he vented his irritation in ridicule. After noting that McGee, a fellow apostate, had not been "moved by [*Days*] to the point of reembracing the Faith," he added that neither had he, "although to judge from the chatter that reached me, you'd think I was on the verge of joining the Trappist monks."

While a few critics had been annoyed to the point of derision (John Mason Brown called the hero and his alter ego "the Soul-Dust Twins"), only one person became venomous about *Days*: Benjamin De Casseres, a man of extremes. Where he had once lauded O'Neill in terms usually reserved for the titans of world literature, he now excoriated him for betraying his talent, for taking a road to artistic suicide. In a heavy-handed parody entitled "Drivel Without End" he set some O'Neill characters to mocking their creator. Here, for example, is Chris Christopherson: "So that Ol' Davil See — the Holy See — got you." And Anna Christie: "Father, I would rather see you dead drunk under a table at Jimmy the Priest's than see you one of the pope's clean little choir boys."

The lampoon almost appeared in the magazine *Panorama*, but after it was already in type Isaac Goldberg, an editor of the literary periodical who knew O'Neill, changed his mind; the article, he decided, was not worth risking O'Neill's dislike. Determined to be heard, De Casseres had the piece published in pamphlet form at his own expense and sent where it would have some impact. George Jean Nathan praised it, according to Bio De Casseres, and regretted that his friendship with O'Neill kept him from writing something similarly devastating. O'Neill's own response to the parody — De Casseres had sent him a copy — was silence; he never again wrote to or saw his onetime friend and most fervent champion.

After the long strain of trying to get *Days* into viable shape, the playwright was exhausted. A few months previously, on his forty-fifth birthday, he had boasted to Macgowan that he felt "a lot younger, body and spirit, than I did at thirty-five or twenty-five" — something he credited entirely to Carlotta's effect on him. Apparently, however, his sense of rejuvenation was largely euphoria from the successful launching of *Ah, Wilderness!;* when he returned to Sea Island after *Days*, he was in low spirits and felt years older. Informing Macgowan that he was "loafing determinedly," he said, "For twenty-two months with practically no let up — I was either writing or rehearsing — thinking nothing but plays — and I feel as stale as mousetrap cheese on the theater. I won't start anything new for a long while. I'm fed up."

He was to loaf determinedly most of 1934, for Dr. George Draper had warned him before he left the city that he was "teetering on the verge of a nervous crack-up." Unless he rested indefinitely till he "came back," he would, as Eugene summed up the diagnosis, "go on to a complete bust and be laid out for years."

Although the doctor, like O'Neill, attributed his condition to his long, unrelieved stretch of work, one suspects that the chief cause was not the *extent* but the *nature* of that work. He had labored still longer and, if anything, more arduously on *Mourning Becomes Electra* without paying for it with his health; but in *Days Without End* he had worked against his grain, he had outraged his central being, hence his present malaise. In a few years he would create *The Iceman Cometh*, another drama that deals with, among other things, a man's secret hostility to his wife; but this time the play grew easily, it "flowed right along, page after page," since O'Neill was writing true to his feelings, not violating them. The result was one of his masterpieces.

22

※

Nobel Laureate

THE O'Neills visited New York on several occasions in 1934, the first time in April because of a lawsuit; two years earlier their chauffeur-driven car had collided with one operated by a Bronx man named Louis Gans, and now his suit against the playwright for twenty-eight thousand dollars for himself and his daughter was being tried in Bronx Supreme Court. O'Neill, who hated courts, the law and everything concerned with them, in addition to dreading public appearances, would have moved heaven and hell to avoid testifying, but his state of health served to excuse him. Appearing in his stead, Carlotta told the court that he was under medical care, unable to work, and saw no one except herself and the doctor.

Carlotta, who found the trial a "horrible experience," contended on the witness stand that the plaintiff and his daughter could not have been seriously injured since they had come over and argued with her chauffeur. Questioned about the speed of the O'Neill car when the accident occurred, she said she was "terribly nervous" and did "not permit fast driving." "You don't look nervous now," the plaintiff's attorney remarked, as reported in the *Herald Tribune* on April 13, 1934, to which she replied that she was "scared to death." On quitting the stand she became faint and had to be helped into an adjoining room, where she rested a while. Several days later the jurors returned a judgment against O'Neill of three thousand and two hundred dollars.

During the couple's second visit to the city, while en route in July to another sojourn in the Adirondacks, they attended an exhibit, "James and Eugene O'Neill in the Theater," at the Museum of the City of New York. Carlotta had sent material for the show, but the institution already

[435]

had an important collection of O'Neill manuscripts and other memorabilia contributed by Carlotta and, at her instance, Eugene.

In the exhibit were costumes, masks, photographs and manuscripts, including *Beyond the Horizon,* the entire play written in the author's microscopic script on both sides of only eighteen pages of typewriter paper. Certain of the pictures must have touched off a welter of memories in the playwright: *Bound East for Cardiff* in the scrape-penny, now-historic production in Provincetown; *Thirst,* with himself and Louise Bryant, whom he had loved so desperately; *Horizon,* which his father had seen with tears in his eyes; *The Hairy Ape,* with Louis Wolheim and an actress named Carlotta Monterey who had thought O'Neill ill-mannered and whom he had considered of little talent. The photos of James O'Neill displayed him in his most noted roles — Edmund Dantès, Virginius, the Savior in Salmi Morse's *The Passion* — and one highlight of the display was the old actor's script of *Monte Cristo* with notations in his own hand.

"The O'Neills spent over a half hour looking at the exhibit," recalls May Davenport Seymour, curator of the museum's theater collection. "Carlotta put her arm around me and we didn't say a word while he slowly circled the room. I was petrified, waiting for his comment. I was most worried, I suppose, because of one particular item — a mask of Mr. O'Neill. He didn't pause longer at any one thing but gave them all close and equal attention. Finally he returned to us and put out his hand, 'Mrs. Davenport, you've made us wonderful.' "

At Wolf Lake, deep in the Adirondack wilds, where the couple spent August and September, O'Neill swam, loafed and, indulging in his favorite escapist literature, read detective stories and murder mysteries. "I'm one of the greatest fiends around," he said, "on that score." In response to queries from the press, he reported that he would not have a new play for the 1934–1935 season; actually, due to a combination of factors — recurrent illness, years of work on a gigantic project, conditions incidental to a war that convulsed the world — more than a decade would pass before a new O'Neill work was produced on Broadway.

On returning to New York, O'Neill, in the midst of his annual ordeal at the dentist's, had the pleasure of meeting Sean O'Casey. The two felt that they met as old friends, for George Jean Nathan had spoken warmly of them to one another (the critic now championed O'Casey as forcefully as he had once served O'Neill), and in addition the playwrights had exchanged cordial letters. *Within the Gates,* the Irish-American had written to the Irishman earlier, "is a splendid piece of work. My enthusiastic congratulations to you! I was especially moved — and greenly envious, I confess! — by its rare and sensitive poetical beauty. I wish to God I could write like that!

"All who admire your work here — and there are a lot of us! — are hoping the play may be placed with the right management to give it the New York production it deserves."

In *Juno and the Paycock* and *The Plough and the Stars* O'Casey had written two of the century's finest English-language plays, yet material success had eluded him. Now he was in America for the first time (also the last) for a Broadway presentation of *Within the Gates* that he hoped would improve his straitened circumstances. Wearing nearly his entire wardrobe on his back, O'Casey, who had a lean, ruddy face and a nose with character, spoke amiably to ship news reporters on his arrival, but he snorted when asked why he had abandoned Celtic themes — *Within the Gates* is set in London. "Celtic this and Celtic that!" he exclaimed. "Who ever heard of anything being Celtic? It's a generic term equally applicable to the Welsh or the Scotch. I've never in all my life — and I lived in Ireland more than forty years — seen a Celtic twilight or a Celtic dawn, or any other such nonsense."

(*Within the Gates*, which received mixed notices, gave one hundred and one performances in New York and was taken to Boston for the start of an extended tour; but after being banned there by the city officials, under pressure from Catholic quarters, it was reopened on Broadway, where it expired after a few weeks. "It was a beautiful production in every way," says O'Casey, "and any fault shown on the stage was in the play itself.")

Years later O'Casey, sharing his memories of O'Neill with the present biographer, wrote that while he saw Eugene only several times, he could "honestly say I was a friend of his. The first visit was with Mr. Nathan . . . [he] bought a few little toys for his friend — it was Eugene's birthday, I think — and this, meant as a joke, was none, for Eugene was a child as well as a great man to the end. Eugene wore a new pair of Daks — a present from Carlotta, and was very proud of them in a childlike way. The moment we met, we got close together, and were at once Eugene, Sean and George. Carlotta was there, of course, and presented herself as a very beautiful woman, devoted to Eugene.

"We spoke of many things from Daks to the Drama. When I told Eugene what I thought of him, he was pleased, but took the praise like a shy child. He wasn't really conscious of his greatness; he took this in his stride, and was concerned only with the work he had done and that which he thought of doing. The last time when I was going, we embraced, and realized that our feelings for one another came close to love."

When Brooks Atkinson, a good friend of O'Casey's, was shown this letter, his eyes twinkled: "I can guess who did the embracing."

While on their way once to lunch with the O'Neills in their suite at the Madison, Nathan and O'Casey decided to have some fun with their friend. As the critic recounts, they coached one another "to take him to task, with a great show of indignation on our part, for his burial of himself from all contact with the world and his fellowmen. Slowly and, we thought, with a pretty histrionic skill, we edged against his self-defense with lush arguments as to the necessity of an artist's — and particularly a dramatist's — mingling with the stream of life if he is to comprehend it and interpret its depths and mutations. As the hours passed, O'Neill began to indicate, first a mild restlessness, then a growing mood of irritation, and finally an open hot rebellion. Jumping out of his chair, he confronted both of us and, his face flushed, made what is the longest speech that he has made in all the seventeen years I have known him.

" 'What you fellows have been saying,' he exploded, 'is damned rot! That mingling with people and life that you talk about, far from giving anything to an artist, simply takes things away from him, damned valuable things. If he hasn't everything inside himself, he is no good. The life outside him can steal from him but it can't contribute a thing to him unless he is a rank second-rater. You talk of the thrill of cities, as against the so-called loneliness and stagnation of the country. What is the thrill? A lot of meaningless noise, a lot of crowding bores, a lot of awful smells, a swirl of excited nothingness! You talk of the thrill of a city's beauty. Well [pointing out of the window], look at those skyscrapers! What are they, what they do stand for? Nothing but a lot of children's blocks! Do you mean to say that they've got anything to do with the great soul of humanity, with humanity's deep underlying essence, and hopes, and fate? You're both bughouse!' "

O'Casey redeemed himself, though, when he told his host that he wrote "like an Irishman" rather than "like an American." "Gene was so pleased," Carlotta later said, "he didn't know what to do."

As O'Casey sailed for home and recalled the many persons he had met, prominent in his thoughts was "the long, lean figure of Eugene O'Neill . . . with a warm, welcoming smile softening his somber face, the deep-set eyes of the great dramatist burning with a light like what would glow in the eyes of a battle-scarred crusader staring from a rocky, sun-browned hill at the distant city of Jerusalem."

During O'Neill's visit in the city he saw his elder son, who was pursuing his postgraduate studies at Yale with the intention of becomng a teacher; but there was no reunion between the father and his other son, for Shane, after three years at Lawrenceville, was now at the Florida Military Academy. It was Agnes's hope that the discipline of a military academy would do him "some good," for he had made an unimpressive showing at the New Jersey school.

"He did very poorly in his work, took little interest in the various house and school activities," says William A. Jameson, Jr., the headmaster of Shane's house at Lawrenceville: "Both his teachers and the other boys felt that he was lazy, but I was never quite convinced that the answer was that simple. . . . He appeared in a constant daze. [From what Shane years later told his sweetheart Margaret Stark about his childhood — living in isolated places, piecemeal schooling — she got the impression he had been "almost another Kaspar Hauser" when he entered Lawrenceville. "He was expected to do algebra," she says, "and he didn't even know simple mathematics."] Shane was not, I think, in any sense behind the other boys in IQ or in ability; but he was behind them in maturity of thought and general mental maturity . . . my recollection is that [his IQ] was adequate to passing work and probably much better. I had innumerable sessions with him after [his teachers'] reports came out. . . . It was like talking to a blank wall. . . . He listened politely, or appeared to, said yes and no at the right spots, promised to try, and went along his usual way.

"I finally wrote his father, explaining the situation, and expressing the opinion that a visit from him . . . would make a tremendous difference in Shane's attitude and development; whether he ever saw the letter is dubious, for I had an answer from his wife to the effect that it would be impossible.

"Shane was never 'fresh' or rude, in fact at times I wished he would be. . . . In personality he had a distinct appeal. Perhaps it was the feeling [he gave one] that he needed worse than most boys interest and friendship."

Thus far O'Neill had seen his daughter only once — the 1931 meeting that ended with Oona turning sick — since his return from Europe; their contact, otherwise, had been limited to a few letters, usually around her birthday and at Christmastime. Early this year nine-year-old Oona had written that she would like to visit him in Georgia, but Carlotta, who now answered a large part of his correspondence, both personal and professional, had put the girl off.

For a while Oona had attended a Catholic school in Manhattan, but, according to a relative, it "didn't agree with her. She became very pale and quiet and serious under its influence — too much so." Oona herself recalls that she had "a fainting complex at the time which began conveniently enough when I fainted one morning at Mass & from then on associated fainting with incense — so that one whiff of the stuff & things would grow black & I would have to leave the Church — so that shortly I gave up going to Mass at all, which was what, I suppose, it was all about in the first place." After she had transferred to a secular school, she became more animated and was in better spirits.

In a letter to her father this fall Oona mentioned that she thought of becoming an actress when she grew up. Answering for him, Carlotta reproved her for such an ambition. "There are," she said on October 17, "in New York and Hollywood poor waifs, exploited by their parents, that make one's heart ache with their waved hair & talk of the theater and Movies. But you, thank God, are not one of these. Your father gives extravagantly & generously for your education and upbringing. Forget this cheap talk of Movies, dress designing & tap dancing." At her age she should be "simple, sweet and charming," and her mind occupied with school. She might consider the theater, Carlotta's letter continues, if she grew up endowed with "great beauty or great talent."

"But, if you have neither of the above qualities, train yourself to be a good wife . . . and try to marry some decent man of good family & give yourself some standing *on your own feet!*"

Occasionally Carlotta had twinges of guilt about her own daughter, but in self-defense she said, "One can serve but one god & do *anybody* any good. Otherwise one just pops about all over the place." Cynthia, now aged sixteen, had begun a new life for herself earlier this year, with the blessing of both her mother and grandmother, by marrying Augustus Barnett, a recent University of California graduate. "I really am very glad for Cynthia," one of her relatives wrote to another. "She has so longed for *her own* niche in love & in home. [She] long ago realized that she is endured, not enjoyed [by her grandmother]."

Full of energy and drive, as well as twenty pounds heavier, when he returned to Sea Island late in October, O'Neill could hardly wait to resume writing. "Loafing when you have to do it," he said, "is a damned bore!" He spent the final months of 1934 working on "The Life of Bessie Bowen," actually "It Cannot Be Mad" under a new title; but after the sour reception of both *Dynamo* and *Days Without End,* their author, understandably, was loath to let anyone know that his new project was the third panel of his "God Is Dead" trilogy. Where Science and Marital Love had been tested in the first two plays and found inadequate, in "Bessie Bowen," a drama with the automobile industry as background, "Gold was to be the God."

O'Neill had long been undecided whether to write the auto-industry story as a separate work loosely related to the other "God plays" or as part of a larger series about a family with an acquisitive strain. A year or so previously, when he had tentatively outlined the series, the press had somehow got wind of his conception and prematurely announced that the "marathon drama" would make him the "Wagner of playwrights."

At last deciding to accept the challenge ("Life is growth," he held, "or a joke one plays on oneself. One has to choose"), O'Neill set the un-finished "Bessie Bowen" aside and in the first days of 1935 began a project that would give him all the scope to grow he could possibly want, a multiplay Cycle that would span a large part of the American past as it dramatized highlights in the history of a "far from model" family. Not only was its overall theme the same as that of "Bessie Bowen" – the debasing effect on human nature of greedy materialism – but the play-wright intended to incorporate "Bessie Bowen" itself in the final panel of his panoramic work. Eventually entitled "A Tale of Possessors Self-Dispossessed," the Cycle was designed to be the ultimate statement of some of the author's central thinking, views that he had promulgated for years.

In 1922, taking issue with a critic who contended that tragedy was alien to the American character, he had said: "Suppose some day we should suddenly see with the clear eye of a soul the true valuation of all our triumphant brass band materialism; should see the cost – and the result in terms of eternal verities! What a colossal, one hundred percent American tragedy that would be. . . .

"Tragedy not native to our soil? Why, we are tragedy, the most appall-ing yet written or unwritten!"

In *The Fountain* (the face may be Ponce de León's but the voice is O'Neill's), he said of the voyagers with Columbus: "Looters of the land, one and all! There is not one who will see it as an end to build upon! . . . God pity this land until all looters perish from the earth!"

Queried in 1925 about the theme of *Desire Under the Elms,* he called it "a tragedy of the possessive – the pitiful longing of man to build his own heaven here on earth by glutting his sense of power with ownership of land, people, money."

Regarding the Cycle, he explained that he was "going on the theory that the United States, instead of being the most successful country in the world, is the greatest failure. It's the greatest failure because it was given everything, more than any other country. . . . Its main idea is that everlasting game of trying to possess your own soul by the possession of something outside of it. . . . This was really said in the Bible much better. We are the clearest example of 'For what shall it profit a man if he gain the whole world and lose his own soul?' "

Clearly, though O'Neill never became a priest, as his mother had once hoped, there was in him more than a touch of a moralizing religious.

Originally, he had envisioned "A Tale of Possessors Self-Dispossessed" as five plays, but as he outlined it in 1935 the saga soon grew to seven. Under his general plan the narrative, starting in 1828, was to deal initially with two sharply contrasted families, some Irish immigrants named Melody and an aristocratic New England clan named Harford; but after the first play the Cycle was to focus on the union of Sara Melody and Simon Harford and trace the changing fortunes of their descendants down to the early 1930s. Though Sara came out of a Catholic culture and Simon a Protestant one, religious matters were not to figure in the plays "except very incidentally as minor realistic detail."

As far as possible the dramatist wanted each play to be both a self-contained entity and a unit of the series, with each dwelling on "the final fate" of one member of the family and yet advancing, at the same time, the general family history. A major motif of the plays would be "the recurrence of family traits [with a lust for wealth and power as a predominant trait] under different conditions." Thus the Cycle would not simply visit "the iniquity of the fathers upon the children unto the third and fourth generation" but would show the familial "iniquity" reappearing in each generation. O'Neill intended also to show "the development of psychological characterization in relation to the changing times — what the railroads, what the panics did to change people's lives." In the process a large part of the American Story would get itself told — that is to say, O'Neill's view of main currents and decisive events in our national past that helped to shape our national character.

Though he realized that "A Tale of Possessors" would entail "years of the devil's own work," he was "wildly enthusiastic" about his project and its "possibilities of greatness in modern drama." After making outlines and jotting down innumerable notes, he began writing detailed scenarios, each about twenty-five thousand words, for all seven plays. His conception would later expand to eight, then to nine and finally to eleven plays, but following is his general plan for the seven as he did the spadework in 1935 (the titles, with one or two exceptions, were dreamed up subsequently):

A Touch of the Poet, set in New England in 1828.

More Stately Mansions, New England, 1837–1842.

"The Calms of Capricorn," almost entirely on a clipper ship in 1857 in Boston Harbor, the south Atlantic and the Golden Gate in San Francisco.

"The Earth's the Limit," the West Coast 1858–1860.

"Nothing Is Lost Save Honor," "around Washington [D.C.] principally," 1862–1870.

"The Man on Iron Horseback," New York City, 1876–1893.

"The Hair of the Dog" (containing "The Life of Bessie Bowen"), the Middle West (Detroit?), 1900–1932.

Russel Crouse, among the first to learn of the projected Cycle when he spent a weekend at Casa Genotta early in March, returned to New York with an account that had the Theater Guild directorate eager to learn more. Shortly afterward the Lawrence Langners vacationed briefly in Nassau and on their way home stopped off at Sea Island. Langner found the playwright completely absorbed in his work and "stripped for action like a pugilist." As O'Neill summarized the Cycle one afternoon while they sunbathed on the beach, it seemed to Langner that Galsworthy's *The Forsyte Saga* was trivial by comparison, but he wondered whether the playwright had the stamina to achieve such a titanic project in Sea Island's languorous climate. Afterward, the two men went swimming and "Gene swam out far into the sea, his head and powerful arms pushing through the green-brown water like a lonely amphibian, belonging neither to the sea nor to the land."

Theresa Helburn, reminded of Balzac rather than of Galsworthy when the project was later outlined to her, thought of it as a "dramatic comédie humaine." Flabbergasted by her husband's new venture, Carlotta told Miss Helburn, "The main thing worrying me is – now that Gene has started on plays that give him some scope for his ideas – his next will be a history of the human race!"

O'Neill, who regarded "A Tale of Possessors" as a "broadening of the *Electra* idea," informed Robert Sisk that it would be "less realistic than *Electra* in method, probably — more poetical in general, I hope — more of *Great God Brown* over and under tones, more symbolical and complicated . . . deeper probing." Dismayed that the press had run erroneous stories about his new project, he had the Guild issue a statement, he told Sisk, that corrected "a damn fool rumor in the papers that I was writing a nine-play autobiography! That would be enough to set everyone ag'in me — and I'd be the last to blame them!"

That "A Tale of Possessors" was a broadening of his Civil War trilogy seems obvious (here again the family and the past are "fate"), yet it is more illuminating to view the Cycle as the culmination of a trend in his writings that antedates *Mourning Becomes Electra*. The trend took more than one form, but at its root was a striving for apocalyptic vision and definitive statement. To trace its development, one has to survey a large part of the O'Neill canon. Excepting *Marco Millions* and *The Fountain*, moralizing costume pieces cluttered with pageantry, all the plays he wrote in the first half of the 1920s were, regardless of their respective merits, *lean* plays. *The Emperor Jones* and *Diff'rent*, *Gold*, *Anna Christie* and *The Hairy Ape*, *Welded*, *All God's Chillun Got Wings* and *Desire Under the Elms* — they all remained more or less within the frames of their stories, they had little if any excess fat, and in general none strained too hard or too obviously after universal truths. But starting with *The Great God Brown* an ambitious trend appears, an effort to pack in more story, more significance than the play can comfortably contain — hence the extensive symbolism, the complicated use of masks, the abstruse conclusion.

"It is Mystery," the author said of *Brown*, "the mystery any one man or woman can feel but not understand as the meaning of any event — or accident in any life on earth. And it is this mystery I want to realize in the theater."

As his ambition grew, it was a fairly straight line and no great distance from *Brown* to *Lazarus Laughed*, *Dynamo* and *Days Without End*, plays that grappled with the greatest of all mysteries — God and Death. If the trend led him into false profundity and turgid mysticism, it also had him striving to plumb the deepest truths of human nature, to pronounce a final word on the human condition; he was driven by a need to exhaust his subject matter. Thus, in *Strange Interlude* he aimed to tell not merely the life story of a woman but of Woman, weak and strong, benevolent and destructive, in her various roles as daughter, wife, platonic friend, mistress, mother. Thus again, for his neoclassic drama, he chose the *Oresteia* trilogy because it offered the "greatest possibilities of revealing *all* the deep hidden relationships in the family." And now he was working on, as Carlotta put it, the "political, financial, spiritual and cultural history of these grand and glorious states for a hundred years." "The amount of reading he has to do for this opus," she told Russel Crouse, "is maddening."

The O'Neills had a succession of houseguests in the spring and early summer of 1935, starting in April with Fania Marinoff and Carl Van Vechten. Several years previously Van Vechten, who had a private income and could indulge his fancy, had switched from fiction to photography; his specialty was portraits of the famous and near-famous in the arts, many of whom were friends of his. At Casa Genotta he spent a good part of his time photographing his hosts, as well as their household help. In return Eugene gave the Van Vechtens an early picture of himself, seated on a hillside in New London and hunched over a drawing pad. On Carl's print he wrote: "I drew ships in those good old days!" On Fania's, "Once an artist and now just a playwright – a study in dreams gone flooey!" The inscription on Carlotta's read: "As you see, ever your distrait artist!"

In May Carlotta had a reunion with her daughter, whom she had not seen in three years, and met for the first time her son-in-law; seventeen-year-old Cynthia, to her mother's pleasure, had gained in the interval some "poise and dignity," but Cynthia's husband was so self-conscious around his famous in-laws that he made them uncomfortable. In June Carlotta was busy "trying to be bright and gay" for Eugene Jr. and his wife ("One has to be so much more *careful*," she confided to a friend, "where stepchildren are concerned"). After the family visits, Nathan was welcomed. "He is darling with me," Carlotta said later, "and God, *how* we argue! When he leaves we are all exhausted – and still friends!!"

Regardless of houseguests, O'Neill worked seven days a week, never appearing till lunchtime. Unlike the previous two years, he remained in Sea Island all summer ("How Gene can work in this heat," Carlotta said, "I don't understand"), because he wanted to keep going till all the scenarios were completed. In the course of his preliminary work he sketched a family tree of the Harfords and their kin, outlined a map of the country on which he traced the wanderings of the clan for generations, and drew a diagram of the clipper ship in "The Calms of Capricorn," the third play, that showed where each of the principals was to be quartered. "My mind is so harassed right now by the thousand and one

Shane edited the school paper at Florida Military Academy

Carlotta's daughter Cynthia
at Sea Island in 1935

Cynthia and her second husband,
Roy Stram, about 1937

technical and psychological problems involved in rounding out the detailed outline of the interrelationships between the seven plays of this Cycle," he wrote to Clayton Hamilton on September 17, 1935, "that by the time I finish the daily stint I loathe the very mention of the word play!" Playwriting, he said, is "a torturing trade."

Even without a production on Broadway, he had a fairly sizable income from his published works and the stock productions of his plays, plus the dividends from his stocks and bonds. However, his scale of living and his obligations, particularly Agnes's alimony and young Eugene's education, took all the money he could scrape together; and since he did not expect to have anything ready for Broadway for at least several years, his financial future was a constant concern. It appeared for a time this year that Hollywood would buy *The Hairy Ape*, but the deal failed to materialize. His chief consolation was the success of a special, autographed edition of all his works priced at one hundred twenty dollars; the entire issue of seven hundred fifty sets was sold shortly after it appeared. "There's a young miracle for you!" he boasted on October 4, 1935, to Robert Sisk. "I had been afraid the Depression had ended the days when one-hundred-twenty-dollar deluxe sets could be unloaded — especially of plays."

Except for a fortnight he and Carlotta spent in New York in October, chiefly for his annual dental treatment, the playwright "slaved" steadily throughout 1935 on the Cycle. The seven scenarios were completed before the trip, and after his return home he finally began writing *A Touch of the Poet*, the initial play. Carlotta's life by now at Casa Genotta was, to a great extent, Le Plessis all over again: days and weeks on end with little to keep her occupied and only limited contact with her husband as he burrowed into his work. On her forty-seventh birthday in December he presented her with the script of *Electra*, containing his final revisions, that he had used at rehearsals. It was given, he said, "with again, as ever, my amazed wonder at [your] forbearance with my blunders and weaknesses, my wondering amazement at [your] patience with my lost preoccupations and forgetfulness."

By now he had few if any illusions about Carlotta, for he had seen her in all her moods; he knew the vehemence of her nature, with its passionate likes, fierce dislikes and sharp suspicions; but he knew also that she was totally devoted to his welfare. "All her talents and efforts," Lawrence Langner says, "went into making an attractive home and surroundings in which Gene could have privacy for his work, and to this she dedicated herself with almost fanatic fervor."

Since both were of intense, demanding natures, their relationship was not always harmonious. A servant at Casa Genotta chanced on them in the midst of a bitter argument as O'Neill was saying " . . . and there'll be a murder!" "For a couple of days after that," the domestic recalls, "she sat at the table but wouldn't eat, with the tears rolling down her face."

To the black women who worked for her, Carlotta was generous, exacting, and, in an authoritarian way, maternal. She paid above the local scale, gave them substantial gifts at Christmas, as well as at other times, and when they left for their day off, would usually stuff a five-dollar bill in their bosom as she said, "Buy yourself some peanuts." In general she seemed to regard them as not overly bright children who had to be guided firmly. When they walked on the beach, she would watch them through a spyglass, for they were under instruction not to talk with maids of other households. "She was fine," says Vera Massey, who was the cook for three years, "so long as you did exactly what she wanted." From boredom and loneliness, Carlotta made a confidante of Vera, an alert, attractive young woman, and once boasted to her of having taken O'Neill away from his former wife; but Vera, after marrying against "the Madam's" advice, found her hypercritical and finally quit.

Mattie Powell, another servant, recalls that "the house was so quiet, I felt under a strain the whole time I worked there." There were, nevertheless, currents and eddies beneath the generally placid surface of the household. During the O'Neills' first year at Casa Genotta they had, in addition to Negro help, a white couple — Herbert Freeman, a husky small-town Georgian who served as chauffeur and utility man, and his wife Lisa, a large blond German who was the leading housemaid. The pair's marriage broke up after Carlotta fired Lisa, who resented being closely supervised, but Freeman, loath to quit generous employers, remained with the O'Neills for years and became, as Carlotta used to say, "practically one of the family." Eugene enjoyed tossing around a football with Freeman, who had played the game in high school, and, like Carlotta, developed a genuine affection for their employee. But the O'Neills' feeling, contrary to what they thought, was not reciprocated. Freeman, who blamed Carlotta for his short-lived marriage, secretly harbored a grudge against her, and he seems to have had small regard, behind his respectful mask, for the playwright. Eventually he fell out of favor with both his employers.

After some five months' work, O'Neill completed the first draft of *A Touch of the Poet* in early spring 1936 and was pleased to feel that only minor revisions were needed to polish it into final shape. At his present rate of progress he would be able, he thought, to turn out an average of two Cycle plays a year. Unfortunately, although he was to work at the Cycle on and off for years, *Poet* was the only unit he would ever finish to his satisfaction. Periods of illness, turbulent world conditions that left him too disheartened to work, individual non-Cycle plays that demanded to be written — a combination of things prevented him from ever realizing the Cycle.

True to the author's general plan, *A Touch of the Poet* was at once complete in itself, encompassing "the final fate" of its protagonist, and a bridge to the projected later plays. Impressive as both character portraiture and story, it contains one of the most vivid figures in all O'Neill: a swaggering Irishman who had known days of drums and glory in the Napoleonic wars and now — the year is 1828 — runs a shabby tavern near Boston. A man with "the face of an embittered Byronic hero," he is as quick to take offense as he is to announce himself on every possible occasion, "Major Cornelius Melody, one time of His Majesty's Seventh Dragoons." His most cherished memory is that after the battle of Talavera the Duke of Wellington commended his bravery "before all the army." When alone, Con Melody likes to admire himself in the mirror as he quotes from *Childe Harold's Pilgrimage:*

> *I have not loved the World, nor the World me;*
> *I have not flattered its rank breath, nor bowed*
> *To its idolatries a patient knee . . .*

(While at Princeton, thirty years before, Eugene was fond of declaiming the same passage to his schoolmates.)

The son of a self-made man, Melody, though reared in a castle in Ireland, had never been accepted at home by the gentry, yet he "cons" himself that he belongs to the elite, even now, when his fortunes have faded. Although his tavern fares so poorly that his wife Nora is reduced to kitchen slavey, his daughter Sara to chambermaid, he keeps a blooded mare, rides about with a haughty face, and scorns the Irish laborers who patronize his taproom. If not for occasional indications of his vulnerability, Con Melody would be totally unsympathetic, especially for his contemptuous attitude toward Nora, who loves him no matter what; but under his lordly posturing he is a sorely beset man. Basically, he is a recurrent O'Neill figure: like Emma Crosby, who fancied herself "diff'rent" from all others, like Yank, who thought he "belonged," like Ella of *All God's Chillun,* who considered herself superior to her black husband, Con Melody lives a lie, or what the author was to call in *The*

Iceman Cometh, his definitive statement on the subject, a "pipe dream." O'Neill increasingly believed that man can endure life only through self-delusion, that when the dream dies, so does the dreamer, either spiritually or in reality.

Poet anticipates not only *The Iceman Cometh* but, in the ambivalent relationship of Melody and his daughter Sara, *Long Day's Journey Into Night*, in which the Tyrones (actually, the O'Neills) waver between love and hostility toward one another. Just as Edmund and Jamie are to attack Tyrone as miserly, Sara ridicules her `father's vainglory. (However, though the two fathers share a fondness for rhetoric, a weakness for drink, and a tendency to dwell on past renown, they are more dissimilar than alike; where Melody is all pose, Tyrone, at bottom, is "a simple, unpretentious man.") In the end, after a humiliating encounter with the Yankees, Melody shoots his thoroughbred, the symbol of his self-deception, and joins the Irish commoners in his bar as his own kind. Yet Sara, instead of rejoicing, is miserable and urges him to resume his aristocratic pose. Of such inconsistencies are living characters created; Sara, after Melody, is the most vital, persuasive person in the story.

As for Nora Melody, prematurely aged from worry and overwork, the author has idealized her into a household saint in broken-down brogans. Perhaps the most interesting thing about her is that she incarnates, evidently, O'Neill's feeling that a woman should devote herself to her man to the point of utter selflessness; once before, in *Servitude*, his second full-length work, he depicted a quietly noble, self-abnegating wife. (Later, about 1946, he was impressed by *Odd Man Out*, an English movie about the Black and Tan troubles in Ireland which has the heroine dying to save her lover. "That's how it should be," O'Neill said at the time. "When a woman loves a man, she should be prepared even to give her life for him.")

The "poet" in the play's title is Simon Harford, the visionary scion of a wealthy New England clan who, repudiating his materialistic forebears, intends to write a book advocating a utopian society. Now ill in an upstairs room of the tavern, young Harford remains an unseen presence, but his developing romance with Sara precipitates the drama of the story. While Sara genuinely loves him, she also is practical and, without admitting it to herself, looks on him as her great chance to rise in the world. "We'll see the day," Nora predicts to her husband, "when she'll live in a grand mansion, dressed in silks and satins, and riding in a carriage with coachman and footman." Not only is Sara to have silks and carriages but through her marriage to Simon she is destined, according to O'Neill's general scheme for the Cycle, to intensify an acquisitive strain in the Harford blood that will recur generation after generation.

Simon's mother, the only Harford who appears in *Poet*, was modeled chiefly on reclusive Ella O'Neill and the odd, idealistic mother of George Cram Cook. Fastidious, self-centered, of aristocratic tastes, Deborah Harford immures herself in her garden and listens indifferently "while the footsteps of life pass and recede . . . beyond the high wall." Acting amused, though she herself is against the match, she appears on the scene to warn Simon that his father will disown him if he marries the tavern-keeper's daughter.

Mrs. Harford has cautionary words for Sara, too. Though Simon takes after her, she says, with his noble visions, most of her husband's family have also been "great dreamers . . . in their way." The trouble is, she adds, "the Harfords never part with their dreams even when they deny them. . . . That is the family curse." Simon, she is certain, will never produce his book for reforming society, but in all likelihood, she warns Sara, "it is already written on his conscience," and thus will forever be a reproach to him, a permanent shadow on his life.

Although below the author's highest works, *Poet* remains a handsome achievement, an evocative character study and a family portrait that suggests more than its immediate concerns. In Melody's stance as a cavalier and his daughter's sniping at him we have not merely a clash of personalities, an interfamily feud, but a showdown between Old World romanticism and the ambitious, pragmatic spirit of young America; historic forces are at work here. As the self-appointed flag-bearer of a way of life increasingly anachronistic, Con Melody was bound to be defeated, yet his end is also a rejuvenation of sorts. It is some indication of the play's rich texture and ambiguity that *A Touch of the Poet* might fittingly be subtitled either "Death of a Poseur" or "Birth of an American."

While still working on *Poet*, O'Neill decided to expand the Cycle to eight plays, as it seemed advisable to introduce the Harfords at an earlier, more telling period in their history. Under his new plan, the series was to begin about 1806 with a play entitled "And Give Me Death," with *Poet* second in the sequence. When Theresa Helburn visited Casa Genotta in March 1936, she was "amazed at the amount of work involved: the preliminary research, the endless notes, the detailed scenarios." The playwright gave her a sketchy summary of the entire project and told her the Guild should not expect any scripts till he had at least several in final shape. But Miss Helburn, after conferring with her associates, wrote to him that the sooner they could read a draft, the earlier they could begin to search for the most suitable actors. The Guild intended, as O'Neill had urged, to recruit a company of players exclusively for the Cycle.

"Don't expect first drafts," he replied on April 7. "Mine are intolerably long and wordy — intentionally so, because I put everything in them . . . and rely on subsequent revision, after a lapse of time with a better perspective on them, to concentrate on the essentials and eliminate the overweight. But to a person reading a first draft, that draft is the first impact of the play on them, and it is apt to be a very misleading impact indeed. My first drafts always bore me for long stretches, so I can hardly expect them to do less for other people."

He was uncertain when the initial batch of plays would be ready, since the writing depended, his letter continues, on "so many things which cannot be foretold. For example, the old subconscious might get on the job in great shape, and I might find myself in a surge of creative energy when I could keep going on in first draft, from one to another until five or six or even all eight were written. In which case, as you will appreciate, I would be insane to pause for any interruption — especially such an exhausting interruption as production is for me, followed always by a long period of blank uncreativeness."

His hoped-for "surge of creative energy" was already, as time would disclose, behind him. The year before he had been aflame with enthusiasm as he made thousands of notes and raced ahead with outlines and scenarios; but this spring, as he completed the first draft of *Poet* and started writing "And Give Me Death," he could not help having second thoughts, and regrets. "An eight-play Cycle," he lamented to Jasper Deeter, "is something I shall never choose to attempt again though I suffer one thousand reincarnations as a playwright!" To Lawrence Langner he wrote: "Try a Cycle sometime, I advise you — that is, I would advise you to, if I hated you! A lady bearing quintuplets is having a debonair, carefree time of it by comparison."

Except for occasional press items (usually erroneous) about his progress with the Cycle, O'Neill had virtually faded out of the news; but in April the papers ran excerpts from a letter he wrote to the New York Drama Critics' Circle. Displeased with some of the Pulitzer Prize choices (the 1935 Pulitzer gave the nod to Zoe Atkins's sentimental *The Old Maid* over such superior works as Clifford Odets's *Awake and Sing!* Lillian Hellman's *The Children's Hour*, and Robert E. Sherwood's *The Petrified Forest*), the critics had recently formed the Circle to make their own yearly award — their first going to Maxwell Anderson's *Winterset*. As chairman of the group, Brooks Atkinson had asked O'Neill to speak at the awards dinner or, failing that, to send a letter.

After praising Anderson's work as a "splendid contribution . . . to what is finest in the American theater," O'Neill wrote that the critics' award deserved the best wishes of all "who have the future of our drama at heart. I confess I admit this with considerable reluctance. It is a terrible, harrowing experience for a playwright . . . to praise critics for anything. It isn't done. . . . There is something morbid and abnormal about it."

Turning serious, he hoped the awards would alert the public that "our theater is now adult and fully capable of standing comparison with that of any country in the world today; that it is no longer purely a show-shop and an amusement racket, but has grown to be a place where art may exist." (Privately, he felt the opposite; months later, wistfully recalling his association with Macgowan and Bobby Jones, he wrote to Kenneth that he often dreamed of "what a grand break it would be" if the three of them could start anew with "a resurge of the old spirit." The present New York theater was totally lacking, he thought, in any "spirit," and it seemed to him "nothing [was] left – outside of the Radical propaganda on 14th Street – which has any definite ambitions toward any goal.")

This year the couple again remained at Casa Genotta all summer, for O'Neill was reluctant to interrupt his work on "And Give Me Death." Earlier, before the full blast of hot weather, they had some familiar houseguests – Russel Crouse, the Langners, the Van Vechtens – and, for the first time, Somerset Maugham, whom they knew through Elizabeth Marbury. The several times the two writers had met in New York, O'Neill had been tense and withdrawn, but at Sea Island, within his home, he appeared to Maugham "very easy to get on with and absolutely devoid of self-consciousness." Maugham found the residence "extremely solitary," yet O'Neill, the Englishman recalls, "complained bitterly that he was surrounded by people who wouldn't leave him alone." Carlotta, airing similar feelings, wrote later to a friend: "Too many people [on Sea Island] – no quiet – no privacy!"

In reality Sea Island had changed little in the four years the O'Neills had been living there; it was still a quiet resort with, aside from the Cloister and its bungalows, only a scattering of houses. Occasionally newsmen hoping for a story or someone eager for a glimpse of the seclusive playwright tried to slip over the wall into Casa Genotta, but in general the O'Neills' resentment centered on the Jordan Lambert family next door, a young socialite couple with several children, from Pennsylvania. Yet the Lamberts, rather than latecomers in the neighborhood, had been living there prior to the O'Neills.

An energetic pair who loved sports and were enthusiastic about flying, Lambert and his wife Teresa belonged to the Pylon Club of Philadelphia. Often their fellow club members, when flying south, would stop off at Sea Island, first buzzing the Lambert house to announce their arrival and then landing at the local makeshift airport, where their hosts' limousine would shortly pick them up. O'Neill, who liked to sunbathe nude on the lookout on his roof, at first thought the planes were spying on him and had Carlotta complain to the Sea Island Company; but the noisy intrusions from the sky continued. One day Carlotta, standing on her balcony, reviled a plane hovering overhead and voiced the hope it would fall and kill all the passengers. Probably her animus was sharpened, in the isolation and loneliness of her days, by envy of the Lamberts' social life — a constant coming and going of guests, house parties, and picnics on the beach, with plenty to drink and a washboard band for music, that usually lasted till late at night.

The O'Neills' growing dissatisfaction with "Paradise Island" was intensified by an exceptionally hot summer. "Carlotta and I," Eugene complained to a friend, "are neck and neck toward the Olympic and World's sweating record! We just continually drop and drip." Stripped to the waist as he worked, the playwright, trying to keep dry, had bookkeeper's sleeves on his arms, blotters under his hands, and a bath towel to sit on. By pushing himself he managed to complete a first draft of "And Give Me Death" by mid-August of 1936, but the effort left him depressed about the "long road" still ahead. "I think after I finish this toughest of all my jobs," he wrote Harold McGee on August 18, "I shall feel I've said all I ever want to say, and turn in all the old tin medals and newspaper wreaths and . . . relax for the rest of my life."

Despite his discouragement at times, he was not through expanding the Cycle. The following year, deciding to display the Harfords at a still earlier period, he would increase the series to nine plays by writing "The Greed of the Meek," which ranges from the 1770s into the 1790s. Unfortunately, the exact contents of both "Greed" and "Give Me Death" are unknown, since the playwright destroyed the manuscripts in the 1940s; neither ever got beyond a first draft. Each was as long as *Strange Interlude* and needed extensive rewriting, O'Neill felt, and he further noted in his work diary that both were "too complicated — [I] tried to get too much into them, too many interwoven themes & motives, psychological & spiritual."

Even though the two plays no longer exist, some idea of their nature and narratives can be deduced, presumably, from *A Touch of the Poet*, for Deborah Harford, in her meeting with Sara Melody, reminisces at length about her son's paternal forebears, certain of whom, at once libertarian zealots and self-centered aristocrats, exemplified the ironic workings of the Harfords' "family curse." Jonathan Harford, Simon's great-grandfather, was slain at Bunker Hill, but Deborah suspects that he, taking an egocentric view, saw the War of Independence as merely symbolic of his personal struggle for "pure freedom." His son Evan, a fanatic of the same church, scorned the Revolution as making "too many compromises with the ideal to free him." Migrating to France, he became a follower of Robespierre and was willing to die at the guillotine with his "incorruptible Redeemer, but he was too unimportant. They simply forgot to kill him." Back home this "dry, gentle, cruel, indomitable, futile old idealist" built and lived in "a little temple of Liberty" in what eventually became Deborah's garden and refuge.

"But the point is," Deborah tells Sara, "you can have no idea what revengeful hate the Harford pursuit of freedom imposed upon the women who shared their lives."

In Deborah's summary of family history there are three spinsters who are mistakenly identified (through an error on O'Neill's part) as daughters-in-law of Jonathan; their actual relationship to the family is uncertain. In any case, "the Sisters," as they were known, seem to have been the most avaricious of the clan. Deborah, briefly flashing the claws behind her purring, says to her future daughter-in-law: "I am sorry they are dead and cannot know you. They would approve of you, I think. They would see that you are strong and ambitious and determined to take what you want. They would have smiled like senile, hungry serpents and welcomed you into their coils."

The scheme for the Cycle followed — on a grander scale and, of course, with far greater artistry — the pattern of *Monte Cristo*, James O'Neill's perennial vehicle; that is, the Cycle interwove fiction with historical fact. The pattern is particularly noticeable because the giant figure of Napoleon, who looms in the background of the Dumas fable, lurks also in the early Cycle plays: Evan Harford took part in the French Revolution, which brought Bonaparte to the fore; Con Melody fought against him in Spain; and Deborah Harford and her husband went to Paris for

[455]

their honeymoon, accompanied by "the Sisters" and others of the family, "to witness" his coronation.

The playwright, familiar with *Monte Cristo* from childhood, seems to have inherited not only his theatricality but some of his subject matter from his father. His father's professional influence on him was greater, probably, than he ever realized.

In late summer 1936 Sophus K. Winther, a professor at the University of Washington in Seattle, and his wife Eline spent a week at Casa Genotta. The playwright, who had met the professor once before, had been impressed by his book, *Eugene O'Neill: A Critical Study* ("a splendid job . . . a searching critical analysis, finely conceived and soundly carried out"), while Carlotta had developed a warm feeling for the Winthers through extensive correspondence; the two couples met, in short, virtually as old friends. By the time of the ' Winthers' visit the O'Neills, worn down by the oppressive summers of Sea Island, had decided to "give Dixie back to Tin Pan Alley" and settle in a less enervating region. After listening to their guests talk enthusiastically of the scenic splendors and bracing climate of the Northwest, they decided on an exploratory stay in Seattle in the near future. At the least, Eugene thought, he would absorb some local color and get the "feel" of the West for the part of the Cycle that occurs on the Coast.

From Carlotta's account years later, it appears that O'Neill was chiefly if not solely responsible for their departure from Sea Island. "He wanted a place by the sea," she said, "where the water wouldn't be warm in the summer or cold in the winter, and it would be sunny the year around. He was looking for Paradise, that's what he wanted. I was continually picking homes because Mr. O'Neill, not being well — I am told that many ill people are the same — feel the weather, the climate [is to blame]: it is too damp or too dry, or it's too this or too that . . . so we would sell and go to the next place and make a home."

At the time, however, she was as eager as her husband to quit Georgia. "I HATE the South (always have!)," she wrote to Dorothy Commins earlier this summer. "Some day I hope to sell this place and build a strong but simple shack in the far north."

"Carlotta," says Carl Van Vechten, "loved to build homes. But after she had everything exactly as she wanted and running smoothly, she lost interest, she became bored, she didn't have enough to do. It wasn't only Gene who used to get restless."

Once the O'Neills had decided to settle elsewhere, they felt like prisoners whose sentence was almost over and became wildly impatient for their deliverance. The seventeen-year cicadas had appeared, and Carlotta, already tense, was so unnerved by their continuous shrill buzzing that she had to fight down an impulse to scream at them. For Gene's sake, she told the Winthers, she had tried to persuade herself that she enjoyed living at Sea Island; as it was, she added, he "has never known the depth of my loneliness or apartness here."

Toward the end of September the playwright felt so poorly from "terrible night sweats, pains, a feeling of debility" that he feared a recurrence of tuberculosis. Although he and Carlotta had intended to remain at Sea Island until their house was sold, the start of October found them in New York for medical attention. While the examinations proved, fortunately, that he was organically sound, his doctors urged him to take a long rest. Carlotta too was badly run down; her physician wanted her hospitalized for a week or two, but, determined to look after her husband, she was sure the Northwest would do more to revivify her than any hospital. The couple, who stayed at the Lowell on East Sixty-third Street, spent nearly a month getting medical and dental treatments, conferring with the Guild, Random House, agents, and lawyers. They entrained for the West on the thirtieth.

In Seattle the refugees from Sea Island took shelter in a secluded house on Magnolia Bluff, which they had rented for three months, whose view took in Puget Sound, tall evergreens and the snow-capped Olympic Mountains. Watching ships glide by, listening to foghorns and the rusty cry of sea gulls, Eugene immediately, if only temporarily, felt at home.

His hope of escaping public notice proved futile at the outset, for the Seattle *Times,* tipped off by the railroad, had a reporter greet the O'Neills at the depot when they arrived on November 3. They were grateful to the paper, however, for not disclosing their hideout. To preserve their privacy they had an unlisted telephone number and Carlotta warned the telegraph office against giving their address to a single soul; within a period of days, though, as the playwright won new renown, a throng from the press, the radio and the newsreels was clamoring at his door.

On November 10 he received a wire from Russel Crouse that he was rumored to be the 1936 Nobel Prize winner in literature; instead of becoming excited, he doubted that the award would go to an American only six years after Sinclair Lewis had been honored; he thought, rather, that "a Frenchman was due — Gide or Valery." The following day the newspapers reported briefly that the American playwright, according to "well-informed Swedish sources," was the leading candidate. On the morning of the twelfth the Associated Press, unable to reach O'Neill, awoke Sophus Winther to inform him that the rumor had been confirmed by Stockholm, and he in turn telephoned Eugene. The prize carried a cash award of forty thousand dollars.

Casually attired in flannels and a gray sweater, with Carlotta and Winther flanking him, the new Nobel laureate was amiable but patently tense that afternoon in his living room as he faced reporters and photographers. He had expected, he said, that if the Nobel committee did select an American, the award "would go to Dreiser — he deserves it." Though the prize is given for overall accomplishment rather than for a particular work, O'Neill thought that *Mourning Becomes Electra* was the chief factor in his being named; but his greatest satisfaction, he volunteered, came from writing *The Great God Brown* and, next, *The Hairy Ape*. The interview was punctuated from time to time by the hoarse whistles of ferryboats on fog-shrouded Puget Sound. "I like them," Eugene remarked during a pause in the questioning. "They keep some people awake but they put me to sleep."

Grinning fleetingly when asked how he felt, he said, "Naturally I'm very happy. I feel like a horse that has just been given a blue ribbon." (Later amplifying on the image, he told a friend he was "like an ancient cab horse that has had a blue ribbon pinned on his tail — too physically weary to turn around and find out if it's good to eat, or what.") Queried about the Cycle, he thought that probably two of the plays would be given each season. "People will be seeing it for years, it will go on and on. And I hope, after all eight plays are produced once, somebody will take a chance and run them on successive nights. That will knock the audience cold and they'll never want to see another play."

Predictably, not even a Nobel Prize could induce him to participate in a public ceremony. Using the excuse that he could not arrange his personal affairs in time to appear in Stockholm on December 10, when King Gustav V was to make the presentations, he said he intended to visit Sweden at a later date.

What with a constantly ringing telephone (the number was no longer secret), a flood of congratulatory telegrams and letters, invitations to speak or simply be a guest of honor at social, cultural and literary affairs, persons eyeing the house and hoping for a glimpse of the Great Man himself, the couple on Magnolia Bluff felt besieged. "A little more excitement like this," O'Neill wrote on November 15 to Theresa Helburn, "and the remains can be condensed into an obituary." While he cooperated willingly enough with the press, he refused to oblige the radio people or a newsreel crew that had flown up from Hollywood. The film group, incredulous that he would reject a chance to appear on the screen all over the world, persisted.

"They kept after me for days," Sophus Winther recalls, "hoping I would persuade Gene to change his mind. They wanted him to pose for a faked scene of his getting the news. A telegraph boy was to be shown approaching their door, O'Neill answers the bell, with Carlotta at his side, and then a big grin as he shows her the telegram. When I told Gene about it, his only comment was, 'To hell with them!' "

Such European figures as Pirandello, the 1934 winner, Hauptmann and Lenormand sent cables, but only a few American playwrights, namely Sidney Howard, Edward Sheldon, S. N. Behrman, and Russel Crouse (Crouse had begun to collaborate with Howard Lindsay in what would be a notable partnership) bothered to congratulate O'Neill. He was particularly incensed at not hearing from Maxwell Anderson, whom he had praised generously to the New York Drama Critics' Circle. Acknowledging word from Sinclair Lewis, O'Neill agreed with him that it was "a damned shame Gorki never got the prize. When he died [this year] I wrote a tribute for the Soviet magazine in New York which exactly expressed my opinion that he had been the top of all living writers." (Partly under the influence of Gorki's *The Lower Depths*, he would in a few years write *The Iceman Cometh*, another masterpiece about a group of social outcasts.)

One photograph widely printed in the press showed the playwright seated at his writing desk, with Carlotta looking over his shoulder. At her home in Point Pleasant, Agnes preserved from the Philadelphia *Inquirer* a full-page story on December 6, headlined THROUGH THE DREGS OF LIFE TO THE NOBEL PRIZE, whose illustrations included the picture of Carlotta with her husband. (Shane sent a congratulatory wire, but his father, he learned later, never received it; the boy suspected that Carlotta intercepted it.)

Comment on the Nobel choice both here and abroad was predominantly cordial. "No one in postwar years," said the Manchester *Guardian*, "has done more to stir interest in drama throughout the world than Mr. O'Neill." The Ceylon (Colombo) *Daily News*, in an article the new laureate cherished, called him "our most modern dramatist in that he alone has succeeded in breasting back across that ocean of 2,000 years and more which rolls between our time and the ancient Greek."

In England Bernard Shaw, who was "very pleased," said he had thought "this year's prize should go either to Upton Sinclair or O'Neill, so America would have received it in any case." Other Irish writers who approved were Lennox Robinson ("O'Neill's contribution to the drama is very valuable indeed") and Yeats ("I have the greatest admiration for his work"). But what particularly pleased O'Neill, he told Crouse on November 25, was that the Irish ambassador in Washington praised him on behalf of the Irish Free State "as adding, along with Shaw and Yeats, to the credit of old Ireland. So what," O'Neill ended, "could be more perfect?" (Years later, reminiscing to Hamilton Basso, he again singled out the official tribute from Ireland.)

There were, however, a few sour notes in the symphony of praise. An AP dispatch on November 12 noted that "non-admirers" of O'Neill and of the Nobel selections in general had "pointed out that since the Prize began in 1901, some of those never tapped" were Tolstoi, Proust, Hardy, D. H. Lawrence, Conrad, Henry James, Benedetto Croce, Mark Twain and Joyce. In a sharper tone the New York *Daily Worker* declared on the thirteenth, seemingly after reading the collective mind of the Nobel committee, that O'Neill was not given the award "for being a revolutionary writer, the chronicler of workers, dreamers and rebels, of hairy apes and underdogs." He has become, the Communist paper lamented, "increasingly safe and conservative. . . . O'Neill, who started out as a dramatist of the working class, has completed his middle period as the dramatist of a sick middle class."

But the sharpest blast came in the *Saturday Review of Literature* on November 21 from Bernard De Voto, who found that at best O'Neill was "only the author of some extremely effective pieces for the theater. At worst he has written some of the most pretentiously bad plays of our time." Not content with flailing at the playwright and the movement that had nurtured him ("the little theater of cheesecloth and mandolutes"), De Voto attacked the Theater Guild, charging that its resources and prestige, its "power to compel the admiration of multitudes," were chiefly responsible for elevating O'Neill to "a grandeur" he did not deserve. (Rather than compelling "the admiration of multitudes," the organization, which had been in a decline of late, was presently under attack from various quarters. The Guild, said Richard Watts, Jr., in the *Herald Tribune*, "has had a miserable year, with three ineffectual plays in a row and with pessimism reigning among its somewhat hot-and-cold supporters . . . something has gone wrong with its creative ability and steps should be taken.")

"De Voto's article (whoever De Voto is) makes no never mind with me," O'Neill on November 30 assured Theresa Helburn, who had been worried about his reaction. "A too unanimous chorus of approval would make me feel a tombstone was planted over my head! The only writers that all writers agree are good writers are dead!"

His intention of resting and regaining his energy in the Northwest was nullified by the repercussions of his new honor. Though he managed to get in some fishing on Puget Sound and a few rides over the choppy waters of the bay, his days were largely spent staving off efforts to lionize him and acknowledging the flood of congratulations. In some of his replies a nostalgic note is evident. "You are one of the very, very few of my old friends I have heard from," he replied on December 3 to Mary A. Clark, the nurse at Gaylord Farm whom he had depicted in *The Straw*. "Most of them are dead, the rest estranged for one reason or another, the principal reason being just the wear and tear of time."

Reminded of the more recent past by word from Macgowan, he wrote back that he often thought of the time "when you worked so hard and unselfishly to help put my work across. . . . You are one of the finest guys and one of the best friends I have ever known, Kenneth, and I rate it a damn shame and loss . . . that we never get a chance even to say howdy to each other, let alone work together any more." At Eugene's urging, Macgowan flew up to Seattle for a weekend, a reunion during which one ran down Broadway, the other, Hollywood, and the two agreed that the 1920s in the New York theater had far surpassed the record of the present decade.

Speaking optimistically for the record when interviewed by Richard L. Neuberger of the *Oregonian*, the playwright found reason for hope in the Federal Theater Project, part of the government's Works Progress Administration program to ease the impact of the Depression. The WPA theater units, O'Neill said, "can present important plays before audiences that never before have seen an actual stage production. The possibilities are thrilling." Smiling wryly, he recalled that in some parts of the country where he had lived the people were so unfamiliar with the stage that the promoters of a play would "herald it as being with actual living actors."

Welcoming the federal program as recognition long overdue that the art theater needed to be subsidized, he said, "Heretofore the American idea of the theater has been dictated by business considerations. Millionaires gave money for art museums, grand opera and archaeological expeditions, but the theater budget had to balance."

Where he had once derided his father's theater to his father's face, he now looked back admiringly at the heyday of James O'Neill and Edwin Booth, when every city of any size had a stock company, and hoped that

[461]

the WPA projects would help revive "some of the culture and the color" of that period. "By reviving the best of the old playwrights, and by bringing forth the best of the new ones," he said, the WPA units "can become invaluable to our national life." (Privately, though, he was skeptical; writing on December 7 to his old friend Edward Goodman, who headed the WPA's Popular Price Theater in New York, O'Neill said he had never seen one of the WPA productions. "And I must confess, between you and me, barring the shining example of your unit, what I've heard of the productions has been . . . a sorry tale of general incompetence and bureaucratic red tape. It is the idea behind the thing I am all for.")

Neuberger, a staunch Democrat (he later was elected to the United States Senate from Oregon) led the conversation around to politics and was able to report that O'Neill "is enthusiastic over President Roosevelt's overwhelming reelection. He thinks the nation has gone ahead under the New Deal, and regards the President as a great democratic leader."

On his side O'Neill brought up the subject of John Reed, born and reared in Portland, who now lay buried in the wall of the Kremlin. Reed, the playwright recalled with affection in his voice, had been a founding member of the Provincetown Players and a man everyone had liked. Though O'Neill never mentioned her name, he doubtlessly was thinking, too, of Louise Bryant, whose life had dwindled miserably before it ended early this year. For a time after Reed's death in 1920, Louise had fared well – a glamorous career as a foreign correspondent; marriage to socialite William C. Bullitt, the diplomat; the birth of a child; a fine home in Paris. But then she had taken to drink, drugs, questionable companions, and Bullitt, charging "personal indignities," had divorced her. According to one story that filtered back to Greenwich Village, Louise was naked and holding a bottle of vodka when she tumbled down the steps of her grubby hotel on the Left Bank, not long before her death at the age of forty-one.

O'Neill spent part of November working on a speech to be read for him in Stockholm, and, doubtful that he was any better at composing speeches than at delivering them, sent a copy to Russel Crouse for his opinion. The speech was only partly sincere. Writing against his feelings, he said that "it is not only my work which is being honored but the work of all my colleagues in America – . . . the Nobel Prize is a symbol of the coming of age of the American theater. For my plays are merely, through luck of time and circumstance, the most widely known examples of the work done by American playwrights . . . since the World War."

In reality he felt aggrieved at the other playwrights as a whole. To Crouse he described the above passage as "replete with more than a little amiable phonus bolonus about my American colleagues — though why the hell I should be so amiable, I don't know, for few, if any, of them have ever had the decency to admit that my work had ever meant a thing to American drama or to them, or that my pioneering had busted the old dogmas wide open and left them free to do anything they wanted in any way they wanted. (Not that many of them have had the guts to try anything out of the ordinary — but they could have.)"

The rest of the speech, though, he assured Crouse, was totally sincere. In it he declared that it gave him "the greatest happiness" to acknowledge "the debt my work owes to that greatest genius of all modern dramatists, your August Strindberg. It was reading his plays when I first started to write . . . that, above all else, first gave me the vision of what modern drama could be, and first inspired me with the urge to write for the theater myself. If there is anything of lasting worth in my work, it is due to that original impulse from him, which has continued as my inspiration down all the years since then.

"Of course, it will be no news to you in Sweden that my work owes much to the influence of Strindberg. That influence runs clearly through more than a few of my plays. . . . For me, he remains, as Nietzsche remains, in his sphere, the master, still to this day more modern than any of us, still our leader.

"And it is my pride to imagine that perhaps his spirit, musing over this year's Nobel award for literature, may smile with a little satisfaction, and find the follower not too unworthy of his master."

Showing the speech to Sophus Winther, he said he wished there was an afterlife, for then he would have a chance to meet Strindberg. When the other remarked that that would "scarcely be enough to justify immortality," O'Neill flashed back, "It would be enough for me!"

His ardent feeling toward Strindberg sprang, apparently, from more than admiration for his literary gifts. As Agnes Boulton has written: "Gene was very impressed by Strindberg's anguished personal life as it was shown in his novels (*The Son of a Servant* and others, all autobiographical); particularly . . . his tortured relationship with the women who always seemed to be taking advantage of him. . . . These novels Gene kept by him for many years, reading them even more frequently than the plays. I don't know — but I imagine he had the same feeling of identification with the great tortured Swede up to the time of his own death."

23

Cycle Shelved

THE O'Neills had come to Seattle with the thought of possibly settling in the area, but they decided against it after weeks of almost continuous rain and fog. During a two-day automobile trip O'Neill and Winther took around the Olympic Peninsula, they had virtually no chance to enjoy the scenery; Eugene kept quoting, only half in jest, from *Anna Christie:* "Fog, fog, fog, all bloody time. You can't see vhere you vas going."

On December 15, 1936, the Seattle *Times* reported that the O'Neills had left the previous day by train "on a roundabout return tour" to Sea Island; the account was inaccurate, though. To escape public attention, a greater problem to them since "the Nobel bomb burst," they had Carlotta's daughter Cynthia come up in her car and drive them to San Francisco, for they had decided to establish a home in northern California. Cynthia had been nervous about the trip beforehand, for she was in the process of getting a divorce and had brought along Roy Stram, whom she was going to marry. To her relief, Carlotta and especially O'Neill took an immediate liking to Roy, a cheery, open-faced Californian who had worked on the big ships as a purser and been around the world a few times. While questioning Roy about his seagoing experiences, Eugene chuckled as he recalled eating hardtack with worms in it during his return voyage from Buenos Aires.

Although Carlotta had often said that she "despised" California, she now felt happy to be in "my beloved" San Francisco, where she and O'Neill took a suite in the Fairmont Hotel that overlooked the Golden Gate Bridge and the bay. O'Neill, who had always liked the town, one that rambles uphill and down and embraces the sea, had last seen it in 1909, when, fleeing from his first marriage, he had been en route to gold-prospecting in Spanish Honduras. After resting several days, he had Roy Stram drive him around in Napa, Marin and Sonoma counties in hopes of finding a sturdy old mansion that he and Carlotta might convert into their new home. One country place that particularly interested him contained a small theater on its third floor, a feature that had the playwright trying to imagine what sort of people had once lived there and put on their own plays. He revisited the place with Carlotta, but she, voicing a dislike of old houses, said she preferred "to build just what the Master wanted."

"The Master" (pronounced "Mahster") was a term she now used seriously and unselfconsciously in referring to her husband. Both Cynthia and Roy found him more natural, more relaxed when he alone was with them; around Carlotta, he appeared to them somewhat constrained, "as though he always had to be Eugene O'Neill, the world-famous dramatist."

During his final weeks in Seattle and first days in San Francisco he seemed well enough, but he was functioning on nervous energy. His health had been undermined by his working so long without surcease, especially throughout the past two summers at Sea Island, and the excitement over the Nobel award had prevented him from getting a much-needed rest. Suffering from abdominal pains, he entered the Samuel Merritt Hospital in Oakland on December 26 and three days later, after his appendix flared up, underwent an appendectomy. "I can hear horns tooting for New Year's Eve," Carlotta lamented to Russel Crouse, "& my poor Genie in pain."

She herself had entered the hospital a day after O'Neill's admittance, taking a room adjoining his, not because she was ill but the better to stand guard over his privacy and also, it appears, to prevent any possibility of his becoming romantically involved with a nurse or anyone else. In the view of Cynthia and Roy, of the Sophus Winthers, of, among others, George Boll in Sea Island, Carlotta, now forty-eight, lived under a fixed apprehension that a younger woman might try to supplant her. "You keep your chorus girls away from my husband!" she had admonished Crouse from Seattle after he relayed greetings from an actress who knew the playwright. "I've reached," Carlotta said, "the touchy age!"

Dr. Charles A. Dukes, who performed the surgery on Eugene, was an old friend of Carlotta's and her mother. When word finally leaked out about the ailing playwright — the news first appeared on January 3, 1937 — Dr. Dukes told the press that Mrs. O'Neill was ill too and had narrowly escaped pneumonia.

O'Neill made a good recovery from the operation, and, yielding to the importunities of the press, granted a group interview on January 11 from his hospital bed, next to a table piled high with detective stories and murder mysteries. In good spirits over his returning strength, though his hands trembled badly, he told the newsmen, regarding the Cycle, that the Guild "will do two a year, on as near a noncommercial basis as possible . . . a play will not continue to run even if a hit, but will be removed to make way for the next in the Cycle." He intended to withhold the plays from production, he added, till four or five were completed.

Of playwriting abroad, he said, "The Continent seems pretty dead, and I don't know of any Scandinavians. The only Englishmen who amount to anything are two Irishmen, Shaw and O'Casey."

Shortly after the interview he suffered a relapse and for several days, while his temperature mounted and he became delirious, it appeared touch-and-go as to whether he would survive. Carlotta was frantic and, though he had nurses around the clock, on the verge of collapse from watching over him day and night. The trouble was, O'Neill said later, that an "interior abscess burst and flooded my frame with poison." As he began to recover in the latter part of January, the doctors warned that after he left the hospital he should continue to rest and refrain from all work for nearly a year.

He was hospitalized for over two months. Excited to learn of his presence, another patient, a stagestruck girl named Jane Malmgren, wrote a poem in which she mentioned a recent University of California production of *Mourning Becomes Electra*, compared the Merritt Hospital, which had a neo-Grecian facade, to the Mannons' residence, and enclosed the verse with some trivial presents — balloons, candy, chewing gum. With the help of a nurse she managed to elude Carlotta's vigilance and smuggle the package to O'Neill. In a note thanking her for the gifts and "so beauteous poem," he said on January 26: "But don't insinuate this institution resembles the Mannon mansion. . . . That is too depressing a thought — for, as I remember, the male inmates didn't have much luck there, but lost considerably more than their appendices."

To the O'Neills' great relief, Casa Genotta was sold finally, and shortly afterward, in February, Carlotta spent nearly a fortnight on Sea Island packing their personal belongings and shipping other things — chiefly books and the player piano Rosie — to storage. She was assisted by Cynthia and Roy Stram, and by Freeman, whom the O'Neills retained in their employ in California. Years later the Strams thought that Casa Genotta had been sold for sixty-five thousand dollars, while George Boll recalled the price as eighty-three thousand dollars; in either case the O'Neills took a substantial loss, since the transaction covered not only the

Sophus Keith Winther and O'Neill in Seattle

O'Neill hospitalized and attended by nurse Kathryne Radovan

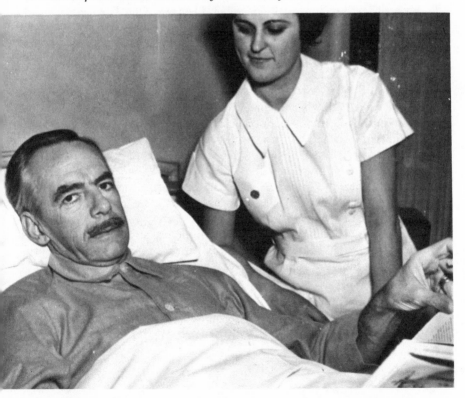

house, which had cost about one hundred thousand dollars, but virtually all the furniture and furnishings.

With Dr. Dukes and a nurse as the only spectators — Carlotta was in Georgia at the time — O'Neill on February 17 received the Nobel gold medallion and embossed diploma of award from Carl E. Wallerstedt, the Swedish consul general in San Francisco. The diploma stated that O'Neill had been selected "for his creative drama, for characters marked by virility, honesty and strong emotions, as well as for depth of interpretation." As the playwright rose to greet his visitor, his knees trembled and his hands shook; the diplomat gently placed both hands under O'Neill's shoulder and assisted him back into his chair.

"It is customary," Wallerstedt said, "for Nobel Prize winners to go to Sweden to receive their awards, and only on rare occasions is the order reversed. This is one time the custom must give way to an emergency as my nation no longer seeks to defer honor to a man who has won the highest award which can be made in his chosen field of endeavor." Smiling wanly, the playwright thanked him, signed a receipt for the medal and the diploma, and in less than five minutes the ceremony was over.

During Carlotta's visit to Georgia, O'Neill had his nurse Kathryne Radovan drive him for a call on Nellie Tharsing, who lived in Oakland. Though he and his mother-in-law had met a number of times by now, they had never had much chance to talk and get well acquainted, for Carlotta practically never left them alone together. Though she did her best to conceal it, Carlotta generally seemed uneasy whenever her mother was around. Eugene, as a consequence, had become somewhat suspicious, especially since Nellie had dropped remarks about her family that did not quite fit into the picture Carlotta had given him. And, for that matter, Nellie herself was scarcely the well-bred, cultivated lady he had once been led to expect: she had an earthy sense of humor, a hearty appetite, and at the age of seventy still played poker till one and two in the morning. (When the game was at her house, she always urged drinks on her guests, though she herself never had more than one while playing cards; as a rule, she won at poker.)

While Nellie Tharsing seemed equal to almost any situation, she was "terribly nervous" when her son-in-law turned up suddenly and proceeded to question her about his wife's background and earlier years. It is safe to assume that Nellie told him as little as possible, but another day she almost blundered as Eugene spoke warmly about the childless aunt who, according to Carlotta's story, had left her financially secure for life. Nellie's mouth was half open to correct him (*that* aunt had died near-penniless in a San Rafael nursing home), when she caught herself and clamped her mouth shut.

After his discharge from the hospital on March 4 and return to the Fairmont, he was so unhappy about being in a hotel that Carlotta intensified her efforts to find more desirable accommodations; but at first she had little success. "We are so at loose ends," she lamented to the Winthers on March 20, 1937. "No roots. No home. We have tried to rent a furnished house in the country but . . . the minute the 'name' is learned they ask ridiculous rents." The couple finally ended up in Contra Costa County; besides renting to the end of the year an estate near Lafayette, they purchased, as the site of their next home, nearly one hundred and sixty acres on a ridge of the Las Trampas Hills above Danville, an area isolated enough to satisfy even their passion for privacy.

While his wife became occupied this summer with the construction of their new home, O'Neill, careful not to overtire himself, made notes of fresh ideas for "A Tale of Possessors Self-Dispossessed." Thinking he might have one character dream up an ideal society along radical lines, he asked Saxe Commins to send him any writings by Bakunin and Kropotkin that envisioned an "anarchist Utopia." While awaiting the books he hoped that they both would not "get pinched for conspiring to pollute the mails with seditious literature!"

His new ideas dealt chiefly with expanding the series to nine plays, with one entitled "Greed of the Meek" beginning the narrative in 1775. "The Cycle," he informed Barrett Clark, "goes back to my old vein of ironic tragedy — with, I hope, added psychological depth and insight. The whole work will be a unique something, all right, if I can ever finish it . . . the technical problem alone is overwhelming. . . . I have to think in terms of nine plays, and a continuity of family lives over a space of 150 years, while I am writing each play. But given time and health I can do it."

O'Neill, whose fondest dream was to forget Broadway forever and allow his plays to be published only, told Clark he would like to withhold the Cycle from the Theater Guild till all nine plays were completed. Productions, his letter continues, are "only nerve-wracking interruptions . . . 'show business.' . . . The play, as written, is the thing, and not the way actors garble it with their almost-always-alien personalities (even when the acting is fine work in itself). But whether circumstances will permit my abstention from production for such a long time remains to be seen.

"The present status of the Cycle is one play [*A Touch of the Poet*] in good shape, needing only revising; another play ["And Give Me Death"] in a first draft as long as *Interlude,* needing complete rewriting. All the rest well thought out and scenarioed with much detail. And eight hundred million notes — more or less!"

Once when the Strams and Nellie visited the Lafayette place, O'Neill took Roy into his study to show off the family tree he had devised for the Cycle principals. "It was a huge thing," Roy recalls, "made up of many large sheets of paper, with squares and circles giving names, dates of birth, death, marriage and so forth. He had it on a big drafting board and said it was the same kind of table he had used while working as 'a bum draftsman' in South America. He created the characters, Gene said, then they *worked* for him, and he often didn't know in advance what they were going to do."

Though Stram was well read in California history, he found the playwright still better informed. "Gene knew all about the old families — the Stanfords, Huntingtons, Floods, Fairs and the rest. Once when he and Carlotta were staying at the Huntington Hotel, where their suite overlooked the old James Flood mansion [now the Pacific Union Club], he was reminded of the way some of today's fine rich families got started. He knew which [of the founding fathers] had made their money in the original gold lodes, which in silver, which of them had married whores. He got a great kick out of the fact that some of today's socialites are the descendants of rough old miners and dance-hall floozies."

When O'Neill first embarked on a literary career, he told a girl in New London that he intended to write a history of a leading American family that would expose its lowly origin. "I can't remember whether it was the Rockefellers or Vanderbilts or some others," Olive Evans says, "but he told me one of these families had an ancestor who used to peddle fish from door to door. Eugene disliked the rich and socially prominent — 'stuffed shirts' he always called them."

Basically, "A Tale of Possessors Self-Dispossessed" was the muckraking social history he had earlier contemplated writing. Projecting his own feelings onto man at large and divulging more about himself than he probably realized, he once said: "Revenge is the subconscious motive for the individual's behavior with the rest of society." Proudly Irish (though disdainful of the professional Irish in politics and of the sort who parade along Fifth Avenue on St. Patrick's Day), the playwright son never forgave the first families of New London who had looked down on James O'Neill and his family. His historical project had been motivated by a desire to get even with their kind. And now, in calling the "far from model" family of his series Harford, the playwright, who took great care in naming his characters, was gibing at the aristocratic old school to which New Englanders of any pretension sent their sons. Like some of his male forebears, Simon Harford, who figures prominently in *A Touch of the Poet* and a subsequent Cycle play, is a Harvard graduate.

During the second half of 1937, as O'Neill began to work on "Greed of the Meek," Carlotta busied herself with riding herd on contractors, carpenters, plumbers, painters and electricians. In her husband's words, she was in "a frenzy of creative activity," and he expected their new home to be "her masterpiece." Its construction took longer and was more difficult than Casa Genotta, since the task involved building not only a residence but a swimming pool, improving and paving nearly a mile of road up to the house, and creating a water system from springs on the property — all this in what the architect called "a wilderness."

The cost of labor and materials was considerably higher now than in the depth of the Depression, when the Sea Island place was built; also, the crews of organized whites were far more independent than their non-union Negro counterparts in the South. Chronically indignant at having to deal with organized labor and apprehensive that strikes might delay the construction (the plasterers "demanded" thirteen dollars for a six-hour day!), Carlotta was forever fulminating against President Roosevelt, whom she considered the chief villain behind the rise of unionism. Theresa Helburn, Saxe Commins, Robert Sisk, Eline and Sophus Winther, Robert Edmond Jones and everyone else who visited the O'Neills as their home was under construction heard the full catalogue of Carlotta's grievances and her firm judgment that the growing strength of workmen marked the decline of America.

On the whole, though, for all her complaining, both she and O'Neill enjoyed this period; establishing a new home provided an outlet for her creative impulses and driving energy, while her husband, improved in health, was glad to be writing again. Although he told friends that he was only "flirting" with work, by early fall he was pressing ahead with "Greed of the Meek." On Saturdays he usually broke his routine to attend the football games at Berkeley with Carlotta and the Strams, for he had become an ardent fan of the University of California team. "It amused and pleased him," Roy says, "to be among fifty thousand people without anyone recognizing him." On October 18, two days after his forty-ninth birthday, he wrote to Nathan that the day passed "without undue repining about Time's relentless chiseling. I can say candidly that I felt younger in health on this birthday than I have for two or three years." He ended with one of his brother's favorite expressions: "So what ho!"

Carlotta, who loved oriental things, had told Lloyd C. Simpson, her general contractor, that she wanted "something primitive on the outside but with a Chinese interior." Another of her specifications, according to architect Frederick L. R. Confer, was "space for eight thousand books and three hundred pairs of shoes." Built of concrete masonry blocks that simulated adobe, its walls painted white both inside and out, the new residence suggested an early California-Spanish ranch house; but its roof was of black oriental-type tile, all the interior doors were painted a bright Chinese orange or red, and behind the house a brick walk twisted and wound — in observance of the Chinese proverb that evil moves only in a straight line.

The dining room was Chinese Chippendale, in the living room stood a Coromandel screen that cost about eight thousand dollars, as well as a pair of old teakwood dragons — most of the furnishings came from Gump's in San Francisco — and everywhere, even along the stairway to the second floor, there were bookshelves. The most unusual item in the twenty-two-room house was O'Neill's bed, an ornate ebony couch that had once graced a deluxe opium den. Among the other furnishings were colored mirrors, including a green one in the entrance hall that startled visitors by giving back, one recalls, "a ghastly image," and a black one in the playwright's bedroom that, in Russel Crouse's words, "made you look dead. No wonder," he adds, "so many of Gene's plays ended in suicide." A more cheerful note was supplied by "Rosie's room," which contained the ancient player piano, lighting fixtures from an old-time saloon, and on its walls many photographs, chiefly portraits of James O'Neill in costume and mufti and scene shots from *Monte Cristo.*

The new residence, in spite of its bright walls and boldly colored doors, had an inward, brooding kind of atmosphere. To Cynthia and Roy the place seemed "like a fortress," and others too found it somewhat dispiriting, for Carlotta, whose eyes could not endure sunshine, had venetian blinds on all the windows and, excepting those in her husband's suite, usually kept them shut. Already isolated by their location well up the mountainside, the couple achieved still greater privacy by extending the wings of their U-shaped house with a high concrete wall, so that their immediate grounds were entirely enclosed.

The O'Neills called their new home after the Chinese word *tao*, which means "the right way of life," and on the heavy black doorway to their courtyard placed four wrought-iron symbols from Chinese calligraphy that spelled "Tao House." Contractor Lloyd Simpson estimates that the total cost of Tao House, including land, house, swimming pool and road-building, came to about one hundred thousand dollars. Carlotta herself once gave one hundred and fifty thousand dollars as the figure, but she probably, if not exaggerating, included the cost of the furnishings. When the couple moved in at the end of December, only a few rooms were ready; they expected the place to be completed in about two months, but it would be spring before the last carpenter had left. While the house was under construction, Carlotta complained that it was like "producing one of Gene's longest plays"; as the job ended, she said, "What a price to pay for privacy & a view!"

The view was magnificent, "the most beautiful," O'Neill said with proprietary hyperbole, he had ever seen. In his second-floor study he worked by a window that took in a great sweep of San Ramon Valley, with its walnut, peach and other fruit groves, and, looming in the background, Mount Diablo. The idyllic panorama before his eyes as he wrote was in striking contrast to the scenes of torment and self-torture he was to evoke in *The Iceman Cometh* and *Long Day's Journey Into Night*.

Shortly before the O'Neills moved in, Carlotta had told her mother and her daughter that they were never to visit unless invited and never, under any circumstances, to bring friends with them. "I didn't care," Cynthia says, "but Nellie, who was sociable and liked to have people in, was hurt at Carlotta's attitude. As far back as I can remember, she used to throw up her hands and say, 'I can't understand her!' In talking to me she practically never referred to Carlotta as 'my daughter' — it was always 'your mother.' I think Nellie feared her, was proud of her, was often greatly annoyed and angry at her, but never loved her. I don't think she hated her, except in her [Nellie's] final years, when she hated everybody."

Carlotta's instructions to her mother and her daughter were part of a general strategy to guard not only her husband's privacy but her own. To LaVeda Edgar, a cousin in Sacramento with whom she had once been close, Carlotta wrote with great affection, but she was evasive about a possible reunion; the reunion would never materialize in the nine years the O'Neills lived in California. Mabel E. Kuss, the couple's nearest neighbor, who lived a half-mile away on the private road that linked Tao House with the outside world, had met Carlotta at an early age when they both spent a summer with an aunt of Carlotta's. "As a child," Miss Kuss recalls, "Carlotta was quiet and reserved — a slim, pale girl — but somehow she stood out, she seemed older than her age. Shortly after the

Carlotta and O'Neill in 1938

Tao House, their new retreat

E

At the
player piano "Rosie"

Shane with his father

O'Neills settled here, her attorney notified mine that if I ever had contact with any of her servants, Mrs. O'Neill did not want me to discuss having known her or any of her family. I ran across her several times, but we talked only about current matters, never the past. I was never up to their place and never spoke with Mr. O'Neill. The only times I ever saw him were when he was driven by."

The aunt with whom Carlotta and Miss Kuss had summered in childhood was Mrs. Sophie Dahl, whom O'Neill thought had left Carlotta the annuity.

The playwright, making good progress, had completed the first draft of "Greed of the Meek" just before he and Carlotta left the estate near Lafayette; but in the early weeks of 1938, like a portent of the general ill-health that would increasingly shadow his residence at Tao House, he suffered so from neuritis, a new ailment in his life, that for a time he was unable to work. "It breaks my heart," Carlotta told Shane, "to see him as he is. So thin & nervous."

In one of the few letters O'Neill wrote during this period he declined to contribute to a volume of "Living Philosophies" by noted figures. "I would not attempt such an essay," he replied on January 8, 1938, to Clifton Fadiman, the editor of the projected book, "unless I had something positive to offer — and there is nothing. Beyond what intuitions or glimmerings of insight may be, or will be, in my plays, I don't know a single final answer as a result of my own questioning, and I cannot believe in any of the answers that are faiths to others."

Always prone to take an apprehensive view of life, he had become increasingly pessimistic during the 1930s because of the Depression — which he blamed on inept, if not corrupt, figures in public office and greedy vested interests — and the ominous developments abroad, particularly the rise of Hitler and the Spanish Civil War. "A second Flood," he often said, was needed to cleanse the world. Several months before the request from Clifton Fadiman, O'Neill, voicing what might be considered a chief tenet of his "philosophy," wrote to Barrett Clark that "we apes always climb trees — and fall out of them — with a boringly identical behavior pattern!" In a postscript he said: "The last of the above sounds pessimistic — whereas I feel full of hope these days. For, noting the way the world wags, I am sure that Man has definitely decided to destroy himself, and this seems to me the only truly wise decision he has ever made!"

The Theater Guild, still in a decline, kept pressing O'Neill for one or two of his Cycle plays. "No, absolutely no hope for any play next season," he replied to Terry Helburn on February 13, 1938. Sounding like James O'Neill, who used to talk poor-mouth to his family, the playwright said that if he could avoid "winding up in the Poorhouse or the House for the Aged and Infirm," he preferred to withhold the series from production till all nine were ready. As to when a minimum of four or five would be ready, it chiefly depended, he said, on his health. Writing a unit of the Cycle, he added, "is a much more complicated business than doing a single play, or half of *Strange Interlude* or one of the *Electra* trilogy. Often I start a work-day writing dialogue for the play I'm on and wind up writing suggested notes on a scene in the eighth or ninth play! Of course, this will all be very valuable in the later stages but it does eat up time and energy and slow up progress on the immediate job."

In a reunion with his father after two years, Shane, who had transferred from the Florida Military Academy to a prep school in Colorado, spent his spring vacation at Tao House. Each made an effort to reach the other, and they felt, for a time, that "a new understanding had sprung up" between them. Tall, thin, handsome, with a marked resemblance to his father, Shane, now eighteen, had partly emerged from his shell in Florida, where he had edited the school paper, talked of becoming a writer, and impressed the other youths with his capacity for liquor. Despite his efforts at hell-raising, though, the predominant impression he made was one of shyness and uncertainty. A chief factor in his self-doubt was that he always felt he suffered, particularly in his father's eyes, by comparison with his half brother.

Eugene Jr., besides establishing himself by this time as a brilliant young classicist on the Yale faculty, gained new distinction this year with the appearance of *The Complete Greek Drama*, a two-volume work he coedited with Professor Whitney J. Oates of Princeton. The collection, produced at the suggestion of Saxe Commins, was published by Random House. "I am tremendously pleased," O'Neill told Saxe, "at Eugene's part in it." His elder son's personal life, however, was less reassuring. The year before, his first wife had divorced him, and he remarried almost immediately; now this union was ending, and he had already chosen his third wife. "I was very worried," Carlotta wrote to Eline Winther on April 30, 1938, "that this second divorce (& from a Prof's daughter at Yale) would jeopardize his job at Yale. . . . But Gene says if he has no better sense — well, that's *his* worry!"

Cynthia Stram, on the other hand, was happy in her second marriage and expecting a baby this summer (named in part after the playwright, the Strams' only child would be called Gerald Eugene). Rather than

[477]

rejoicing at the prospect of a grandchild, Carlotta said to Mrs. Winther, "Imagine deliberately bringing a baby into this mad world. She has more courage (or less sense?!) than I would have under similar conditions."

The love she and O'Neill were temperamentally unable to give their respective children was lavished on Blemie. For a few days this spring the dog was so ill that he seemed on the verge of death. As the playwright wrote Nathan, there was "much sadness in the Hacienda O'Neill," while Carlotta, informing Sophus Winther about the pet's illness, said that he "has always been honest, amusing and charming. As well as grateful for our care and affection. Our other children have never given us that much!"

The Dalmatian could not have been more pampered; his four-poster had a place of honor in Rosie's room and, at no small expense, a full-sized bathtub with plumbing was installed in the basement for his exclusive use. Duncan MacRae, the gardener at Tao House, recalls with disapproval in his voice that "the dog had steak every day of the year." He was not the only one in the household critical of the animal's privileged existence. Although the O'Neills were under the impression that Herbert Freeman shared their feeling about Blemie, he in reality disliked the dog, chiefly because he was constantly vacuuming to keep the rugs clean of Blemie's hair.

What with O'Neill's siege of neuritis, aggravated by constant rain for over two months, and the unfinished condition of the house, with workmen still clattering around, the playwright's first winter at Tao House found him in a "vale of gloom." But by mid-April 1938, improved in health and spirits, he had resumed work on the Cycle by starting a fourth play, *More Stately Mansions*, whose title was taken in an ironic sense from Oliver Wendell Holmes's "The Chambered Nautilus": "Build thee more stately mansions, O my soul . . ."

The O'Neills' only visitors this spring, outside of Shane, were Russel Crouse, whose playwriting collaboration with Howard Lindsay was flourishing, and Bennett Cerf. To both men the playwright spoke disparagingly of the Theater Guild's course in late years, particularly its new practice of casting Hollywood "names," and said that under the circumstances he was glad none of his scripts was ready for production.

On May 7 the New York *World-Telegram* reported that O'Neill, according to a recent visitor at Tao House, "already has outlined his own plans for the production of [the Cycle] which may possibly result in his breaking away from the Theater Guild." The gist of the story was that he would hire a theater, sign a group of actors to long-term contracts, and start presenting the nine plays in 1940 under his own management. Distressed by the item, O'Neill sent a wire on the tenth to Joe Heidt of the Guild for release to the press. Calling the report "nonsense," he said that the first two Cycle plays were under contract to the Guild, that the organization had always been "fine" to him, and that his feelings toward it were those of "grateful loyalty" and "absolute confidence."

The playwright suspected that "the basis for the rumor [from a letter on May 29, 1938, to Nathan] may have been something Cerf said casually at some party or other." What most bothered him was not the falsity of the story but its timing. "Even if I hated the Guild, instead of feeling nothing but friendship for them," he explained, "I would not be such a louse as to break with them just when everyone is jumping on them and they've had a disastrous season."

Despite his publicized wire, reports persisted that he was quitting the Guild, and one story had him leasing the Broadhurst Theater for the Cycle. "Two preliminary steps would be necessary before that could happen," he assured Langner on August 2. "No. 1, I would have to be adjudged insane and committed to an asylum. No. 2, I would have to escape."

He felt, his letter continues, that while some of the attacks on the Guild may have been "arbitrarily unjust — even vindictive," that the criticism in general was justified. In his view, the Guild, by trafficking in movie stars, was betraying everything that had made it "a distinguished leader" in the American theater. "You should have stuck to your old ideal, win, lose or draw. . . . You wouldn't have lost . . . [not] inside yourselves. . . . After all, an ideal is something. Or we ought to lie to ourselves that it is, anyway, for life's sake, because if it isn't, what the hell is anything?"

Of all the places where he and Carlotta lived, O'Neill seems on the whole to have liked Tao House best. "We really have an ideal home," he told a friend, "pure country with no taint of suburbia, and yet we are only fifty minutes' drive from the heart of San Francisco." Somewhat like his father, who took proprietary pleasure in clipping the hedge before the Monte Cristo cottage in New London, Eugene liked to trim the trees around his home. However, his swimming pool, which was at the end of the serpentine path behind the house, was more of a convenience and a necessity to him than a delight — he missed the sea. On learning that the Winthers were to make an automobile trip from Seattle to southern California, Carlotta asked them to drop by and take Eugene along for a week of ocean swimming; but when the time came, he was too engrossed with *More Stately Mansions* to interrupt his work.

Without allowing anyone or anything to interfere with his stint of writing seven days a week, he and Carlotta played host late this summer not only to the Winthers but to Eugene Jr., the Robert Sisks, and some old friends of Carlotta's — Miguel Covarrubias, the Mexican artist, who was executing some murals at the forthcoming Golden Gate Exposition, and his wife Rosa. A camera fan, Mrs. Covarrubias took pictures of the O'Neills that later were widely published, including several that show the playwright, grinning boyishly, seated before his old player piano.

The first draft of *More Stately Mansions* was completed, after five months' work, early in September, at which time the author noted in his diary that it "needs lots of revision & rewriting — is as long as *Strange Interlude!* — but don't think will be able to cut length much." He devoted the rest of the year to the revisions, finishing a second longhand draft on January 1, 1939. Three weeks later Carlotta, who by now not only answered most of his mail but typed his plays — with the aid of a magnifier, since his script was so tiny — completed the first typescript. After making further revisions, in 1940 and 1941, O'Neill thought well enough of the play to preserve the typescript several years later when he burned the two longhand drafts, together with the only drafts of "Greed of the Meek" and "And Give Me Death." But at the same time he took the precaution of adding a page to the typescript that said: "Unfinished Work. This script to be destroyed in case of my death! Eugene O'Neill."

By chance the typescript, which has a running time of about nine hours, survived his death. In 1964, with Carlotta's permission, an abridged version was published by the Yale University Press with the following prefatory note: "Shortened from the author's partly revised script by Karl Ragnar Gierow [managing director of Sweden's Royal Dramatic Theater, where the condensed play had its world première] and edited by Donald Gallup [curator of American Literature at Yale's Beinecke Library]." Under the circumstances, especially since the published version is less than half the full text, a just appraisal of the play, as O'Neill's play, is impossible; what might seem flaws on his part could be the inevitable result of condensation. No doubt if he could speak from the grave, he would denounce this violation of his literary privacy. Yet anyone interested in his writings should be grateful; regardless of its defects, *Mansions*, as Gallup has said, "provides, even in its incompletely revised state, a better indication than does *A Touch of the Poet* of what [O'Neill] had intended in the Cycle." For this reason alone — although there are

[480]

others — *More Stately Mansions* occupies an important niche in the O'Neill canon.

Where *Poet* takes place on a single pivotal day in 1828 in the life of Con Melody, *Mansions* ranges from 1832 to 1841 in dealing with crises and decisive events in the entwined lives of its three principals: Simon Harford, who was only an unseen presence in the earlier play; Sara Melody, now married to Simon; and Deborah Harford, his strange, elusive mother. Like so many O'Neill protagonists, Simon is at war with himself; a true son of both his imaginative mother and his father, a hard, acquisitive businessman, he has "a touch of the poet," as expressed in his dream of a better world, but at the same time cannot deny his thirst for success and power. Under O'Neill's general plan for the Cycle, Simon's split personality symbolized a rending duality in American life, a basic condition in which the forces of greedy materialism were ascendant and threatening to destroy all that was ennobling in our national heritage.

Simon Harford intends to retire and write his book advocating "a perfect society" as soon as he has made "enough" money to assure the financial future of himself and his family; but as he grows increasingly successful, his appetite sharpens, his maw expands. And yet, though he becomes "a Napoleon" of commerce, to use a recurrent phrase in the play, the "poet" in him repeatedly spoils his victories; after each new coup, he feels "empty . . . restless and aimless."

The conflict between Simon's idealistic and materialistic sides is only one, and by no means the chief, source of his self-torment. Among O'Neill's most Strindbergian protagonists, he is reduced to a desperate state by his ambivalent feelings toward both his wife and his mother. Moreover, both Sara and Deborah also harbor warring passions within themselves, so that the play is largely a kaleidoscopic struggle in which the alliances, as well as the battle lines, are forever changing. Now Simon and Sara are leagued against Deborah, now the two women against the man, now mother and son against wife, in addition to times when each stands alone, besieged on two fronts.

While O'Neill was working on *Mansions* in 1938, he informed Macgowan that it was taking longer than he had expected, then added, "It is, I think — and hope! — the most difficult of the lot. Psychologically extremely involved and hard to keep from running wild and boiling over the play mould." The major reason why it was "psychologically extremely involved" is that in Simon's love-hate relations with Sara and Deborah the playwright was, to a considerable extent, plumbing the

[481]

depths of and dramatizing his secret feelings toward his own wife and his own mother.

The parallels between the Harford women and the predominant two in O'Neill's history begin with their very appearances and personalities. Both Ella O'Neill, as her son was to depict her under the name of Mary Tyrone in *Long Day's Journey Into Night,* and Deborah Harford have white hair, along with a girlish quality, a high forehead and, as their most striking feature, eyes uncommonly large and dark. Each is disdainful of her husband's drive for success, and each hides from reality — one in a fog of morphine, the other in fantastic daydreams. Eventually Deborah retreats forever into self-willed madness, an end that recalls the child Eugene's fear that his drug-disoriented mother was mentally unbalanced.

Although Carlotta and Sara do not resemble one another closely, both were a blend, as the playwright said about Sara, "of what are commonly considered . . . aristocratic and peasant characteristics." Carlotta, whose father was reportedly the illegitimate son of a Danish nobleman and a servant girl, looked patrician from the waist up, but she had strong hands, short, sturdy legs, and a peasantlike capacity for hard work. O'Neill used to tell her that she was everything to him, that in their relationship she filled all feminine roles. Similarly, in the play Sara says of Simon: "He has nothing left but me and my love. I'm mother, wife, and mistress in one."

Sara's remark touches on one of the strangest, and most significant, developments in the narrative, for Simon takes her into his business as his partner on condition that she will be to him like a "mistress." In return he pledges to pay her with "all my worldly goods. You can get the whole Company from me . . . piece by piece, as you earn it!" Though embarrassed at first, she soon agrees: "I'll play any game with you you like, and it will be fun playing I'm a wicked, lustful, wanton creature and making you a slave to my beauty." It was, however, no harmless "game" he was arranging; in the end, on the verge of mental collapse, he is wholly at his wife's mercy.

Time and again *More Stately Mansions* anticipates *Long Day's Journey;* indeed, certain passages in the two plays are interchangeable. Where, for instance, Simon Harford says that "the past is never dead as long as we live because all we are is the past," Mary Tyrone will sum up: "The past is the present, isn't it? It's the future, too."

If one accepts Simon as the author's persona (which, essentially, is the case), *Mansions,* despite its fictional elements, is most noteworthy for what it discloses about the author's attitude toward his mother; since he

[482]

could speak more freely from another's face, his attitude is expressed more bluntly, more violently here than in *Long Day's Journey*. Simon's feelings about Deborah run to extremes, ranging from incestuous longings and a childlike desire for complete dependence upon her to the impulses of a mortal enemy. When Sara asks why he harbors a grudge against his mother, he replies evasively: "Almost any fool of a woman can have a son, and every fool of a man has a mother! . . . all the hypocritical values we set on the relationship are mere stupidity."

Simon's grievance against her dates back to his childhood when she made up a certain fairy tale — one that ostensibly dealt with "a young King of a happy land" and "a beautiful enchantress" who dispossessed him from his realm. Actually, through the fable, Deborah disclosed to her alert, sensitive child that she found his claims on her too burdensome, that she wanted to feel free of him and belong to herself. Recalling the episode, Simon upbraids his mother: "I have never forgotten the anguished sense of being suddenly betrayed, of being wounded and . . . left alone in a life in which there was no security or faith or love. . . . By God, I hated you then! I wished you dead! I wished I had never been born!"

Clearly, O'Neill sought to make the traumatic fairy tale the equivalent of his discovery in early youth that his mother was a drug addict, a "curse" that had begun with his birth. Referring to his fall from innocence, O'Neill says in *Long Day's Journey* through Edmund Tyrone: "God, it made everything in life seem rotten!" But unlike Simon, who often turns on his mother with open hostility, Edmund practically never does.

Though *Mansions* foreshadows *Long Day's Journey* chiefly in its mother-son relationship, the two plays have other aspects in common. With regard to quality, however, there is no comparison. Where the later work is a masterpiece, the Cycle play, so far as one can judge, is wildly uneven and leaps about, covering too much territory. Perhaps in the full text the three principals are credible, but in the drastically cut version they shuttle with bewildering rapidity between love and hostility toward one another; they appear to be acting not from their own impulses and feelings but from the author's arbitrary scheme. Ultimately confused, suggesting that the author was too eager to unburden himself, *More Stately Mansions* anticipates not only *Long Day's Journey* but, at one point, *The Iceman Cometh*, a play in which the "Iceman" symbolizes death. Simon Harford, voicing his total disenchantment with life, says that "we wait day after day, hoping against hope, and when finally the bride or the bridegroom cometh, we discover we are kissing Death."

(The playwright apparently got his idea for Simon's remark, as well as his title for the "Iceman" play, from *The Bridegroom Cometh,* a novel of the time by Waldo Frank, a writer O'Neill had once known.)

While the playwright was working on the second draft of *Mansions* in fall 1938 he had a query from the San Francisco *Examiner* about how he would observe his fiftieth birthday on October 16. After a reply from Carlotta, the paper reported on the fourteenth that the day would pass "like any other" at his "great, white-walled estate. . . . The tall, graying man who keeps a hermit's seclusion within the vast estate will spend it writing, writing, writing." Terming his privacy "inviolate," the account said, "When first he began to build a year ago the school children of nearby Danville and Walnut Creek read his plays, excited that a renowned writer was making his home among them. But they never trespass beyond the series of three 'Keep Out' signs that guard the winding road to Mr. O'Neill's hilltop. And he has never been seen by any of them."

Rather than celebrating the anniversary, Eugene, as he informed Carl Van Vechten on the eighteenth, "was laid up that day with rheumatism. Blemie," he added, "remarked to the cat, 'The Old Man doesn't look a day over 183.' And he was right. I didn't feel a bit older than that, either."

The final months of the year found him increasingly apprehensive about the European situation. Critical of the concessions to Hitler at Munich, which England's Neville Chamberlain thought had guaranteed "peace in our time," O'Neill was more convinced than ever that Europe was drifting and stumbling into war. "How do you like our best of all possible worlds these days?" he wrote Macgowan on December 28. "Me, I'd as soon be a native son of a sty. . . . It's time God got plumb disgusted and unleashed a new improved Black Death. . . . I'm getting sore exasperated with the latest stupid repetition in the history of man's stupid greed."

Starting to feel stale about his "elephantine opus," he had intended to rest for a while after the second draft of *Mansions* and then begin "The Calms of Capricorn," the fifth play of the series. Instead, he spent the early months of 1939 revising *A Touch of the Poet* to link it more closely to *Mansions.* "That's the devil of this job, the amount of time spent on such revision," he complained to Nathan on May 13. "No one who confined himself to writing single plays could ever imagine how much extra thought and labor are involved. Sometimes, I feel sick about it – the constant driving on while seeming, in the light of final completion, to be making no progress."

To Stark Young he confessed that had he "foreseen the time and labor involved [in the Cycle], he would have tried to forget the idea in favor of something less soul-grinding."

Nathan had informed him that Sean O'Casey's latest work suffered from doctrinaire leftist views and O'Neill replied in May: "I suppose these lousy times make it inevitable that many authors get caught in the sociological propaganda mill. With most of them it doesn't matter. They have nothing much to lose . . . but O'Casey is an artist and the soap box is no place for his great talent. The hell of it seems to be, when an artist starts saving the world, he starts losing himself. I know, having been bitten by the salvationist bug myself at times. But only momentarily . . . my true conviction being that the one reform worth cheering for is the Second Flood [in *Mansions* Deborah Harford hopes that "the Second Flood may come and rid the world of this stupid race of men and wash the earth clean!"], and that the interesting thing about people is . . . that they don't really want to be saved."

For years, intermittently, O'Neill had been turning over in his mind bits and pieces of a "lower depths" play, a drama set in a scruffy saloon and peopled with the sort of drifters he had known in the days when he was drowning himself in booze in an effort to escape himself. Unable to conceive a unifying theme and narrative, he made no effort to force the play but, as usual, relied on the "back of my mind" to develop it. As he was revising *A Touch of the Poet* in 1939, around the time he heard from Nathan, he became aware that the barroom play had suddenly begun to crystallize in his thoughts, the bits and pieces to fall into place. Whether or not the word about O'Casey had given him the idea, his protagonist in *The Iceman Cometh* would be a self-appointed messiah, a man fatally afflicted with "the salvationist bug."

Thoroughly weary by now of "A Tale of Possessors," which he estimated would take about five years to complete, he set the Cycle aside, once he was through revising *Poet*, and early in June began the new play. Although one of his outsize dramas and among his most complex, *The Iceman* was so well formed in his mind, after years of incubation, that it developed smoothly on paper.

For all his inadequacy as a parent, O'Neill was also a man with a hyperactive conscience; in the midst of his preoccupation with *The Iceman Cometh*, he could not help being worried about Shane. The previous fall the youth, without informing his father, had once again changed schools, and now he had been dropped from his latest for "academic deficiencies." Word of O'Neill's concern was relayed to Shane by

Carlotta, who urged him on July 6 to inform his father about his plans for the future – not about "silly nonsense you'd *like* to do." Shane, presently going on twenty, dutifully reported that he was working this summer on a fishing boat at the New Jersey shore and thought of raising horses (he had spent a few months at a ranch prep school in Colorado). In a second letter shortly afterward he said that he had considered either short-story writing or a veterinarian's course but had abandoned both ideas; now undecided between horse-breeding and commercial art, he enclosed samples of his drawing.

Replying at length on July 18, O'Neill welcomed the news about his job on the fishing boat, calling it "a start in the right direction of independence," but discouraged him about horses, since he lacked experience yet apparently wanted to start at the top. Shane had no chance to succeed at raising the animals, according to O'Neill, unless he adopted an "entirely different attitude from the one you have had toward getting an education." He was "still too dependent on others," he demanded "too little of himself," his father felt. "The best I can do," O'Neill added, "is to try to encourage you to work hard at something you really want to do and have the ability to do . . . to work hard at something you want to accomplish is the only way to be happy. . . . In the really important decisions of life, others cannot help you. No matter how much they might like to. You must rely only on yourself. That is the fate of each one of us."

He rarely mentioned Agnes in his letters to Shane and Oona. His resentment of her remained acute because of her alimony, an obligation that had grown more burdensome as his income declined; he was particularly incensed that he had to pay income tax on the money Agnes received.

While he had had Shane visit him nearly every year, eight years had passed since he had seen Oona; the last time was the unfortunate ride in Central Park when the child, suddenly ill, had vomited on him and Carlotta. Earlier this year he had written her that it was time they became acquainted, and now, as he said on July 14, he was "looking forward to the great happiness of seeing you!" He confided to Macgowan, however, that he was "very apprehensive," for he had no idea of "what she might be like." Their reunion, as it turned out, proved the one "bright spot" for him in August. Before her arrival he and Carlotta had been host to Eugene Jr. and his new wife, whom O'Neill found disappointing, and even more dispiritingly, Roy Stram came down with rheumatic fever and for a time appeared close to death.

Thoroughly delighted with Oona — as was Carlotta — O'Neill praised her to Macgowan as "really a charming girl, both in looks and manner. And she has intelligence, too." Carlotta on September 8 wrote to attorney Harry Weinberger: "In this day of Progressive Schools and so-called modern education, it is a joy to find a child of fourteen with good manners, a sensitive nature, and a thought of others. . . . I hope to God she will always retain her manners and her charm." As Carlotta expected, Weinberger, who had remained on good terms with Agnes, forwarded a copy of the letter to her; apparently Carlotta wanted to seal her newly established friendship with her stepdaughter.

Dark-eyed, black-haired, exceptionally pretty, Oona, like Shane, resembled her father, but she also, in a blend of her parents' best features, had inherited Agnes's high cheekbones and shapely small nose. Unlike her brother, she had a will of her own, not stubborn but steadfast, and a capacity for inner growth. Essentially a private person, more introverted than outgoing, she managed to cover her shyness with a poise beyond her years, and found boys older than herself more interesting than her coevals. Without being outstanding at school, she did well in her studies, and she loved sports, particularly, her father was pleased to hear, swimming.

As Oona arrived for ten days at Tao House, she was exceedingly nervous; not only was she meeting in her father a virtual stranger but in his wife, from all that she had heard, a formidable figure. At dinner the first evening the girl became faint (possibly from subliminal memories of the other reunion), but fortunately Carlotta noticed her condition and rushed her to bed. Thereafter the visit went off smoothly on all sides, with Carlotta putting Oona completely at ease through a woman-to-woman approach that the youngster found most flattering; she had never been made to feel so adult. Frankly confessing that she "loathed" children, that they made her nervous, Carlotta had feared that Oona might be "a child covered in lipstick and red nail polish," hence her joy, she said, that Oona was quite grown-up. Carlotta took her to the Golden Gate Exposition, bought her presents when they went shopping in San Francisco, gave her one of the fine silk blouses she had brought back from China, and never stopped talking, always expressing herself with a forthright vigor that struck the girl as very amusing.

Oona was shortly at ease with her father too. They first met each day at lunch about one-thirty, when he stopped writing, and had an hour alone together at the pool in the late afternoon. The bathhouse by the pool interested the girl, for its interior walls were covered with posters of her paternal grandfather in *Monte Cristo* and other of his vehicles. While conversation did not exactly flow between father and daughter, neither were they uncomfortably silent, for they had sensed in one another an instant liking and respect. (O'Neill later wrote to Oona that he was "exceedingly proud" of her.) Like Carlotta, though in a different vein, he never talked down to the girl. He spoke of his difficulties with the Cycle (but never mentioned his work in progress, *The Iceman Cometh*), questioned her about Shane, and reminisced about his life in Europe and the trip to the Far East. In the evenings Oona read or talked with Carlotta, while her father played solitaire or listened to some of his records — he had a large collection of jazz and the blues. The last days of Oona's visit were darkened by events of the outside world that left the O'Neills utterly depressed, for she was still at Tao House when the Germans, invading Poland on September 1, set Europe aflame with World War II.

The girl returned home enthusiastic about both her father and stepmother. After listening patiently for several days to her daughter's rhapsodical praise of Carlotta, Agnes finally had enough and pointed out that many of Carlotta's remarks were barbs aimed at her. "Why, for example," said Agnes, "had Carlotta been dreading 'a child covered with red nail polish'?"

At Tao House O'Neill, who now spent most of his time listening to the war news on the radio, was so demoralized that for a time he quit working on *The Iceman;* the theater appeared too trivial and futile by the fiery light of the tragedy unfolding in Europe. "Jesus," he exploded to Macgowan on September 10, "the incredible, suicidal capacity of men for stupid greed! That's about the only comment I can find to make, remembering all that has been done from 1918 to date."

24

O'Neill "The Iceman"

W HAT O'Neill had to say in *The Iceman Cometh* was so important to him that his despair over the outbreak of war deterred him from working only a short time. The writing again went well, and the play, begun on June 8, 1939, was completed on November 26 in a fever of enthusiasm and excitement. He considered it among his finest plays — a view he had likewise held for a while about such flawed efforts as *Welded* and *Dynamo* — but this time he was more than justified, for his latest was his top achievement thus far. Philip Moeller, a gifted amateur musician, used to say that O'Neill's plays had a musical structure — an observation that appears particularly true of *The Iceman*, a complex, resonant work with contrapuntal effects, recurrent motifs and a symphoniclike amplitude. The play has also a sort of oceanic quality, born of slow-moving passages that recall the lazy swells of the sea, then a gradual mounting of tension which finally boils over that is like the hunching-up of the waves and their crashing on shore.

Not only his supreme work to date, *The Iceman Cometh* was also his bleakest — philosophically, that is. His view of the human condition and mankind's prospects had long been darkening; he had abandoned virtually all hope of Progress, Civilization, the Future, a perspective that the war in Europe seemed to confirm. Life appeared to him by now, as his new drama suggests, essentially a fraud. Set entirely in a squalid barroom in lower Manhattan and concerned with a raftload of social outcasts, desperate souls who are saved from the reefs by a tide of whiskey and self-delusion, *The Iceman* maintains that man cannot face the truth, especially about himself, but must take refuge in "pipe dreams." In a key speech, Larry Slade, one of the author's two spokesmen, says: "To hell with the truth! As the history of the world proves, the truth has no bearing on anything. It's irrelevant and immaterial, as the lawyers say. The lie of a pipe dream is what gives life to the whole misbegotten mad lot of us, drunk or sober."

While writing *The Iceman,* which is set in 1912, O'Neill felt that he had "locked myself in with my memories," for it contains considerable autobiography. Its bar is modeled on three in New York that he had once frequented: Jimmy the Priest's, actually James J. Condon's saloon at 252 Fulton Street, opposite the old Washington Market ("This place has a fine trade," it is said in the play, "from the Market people across the street"); the Hell Hole, actually the Golden Swan on Sixth Avenue in Greenwich Village; and the taproom of the Garden Hotel on Madison Avenue, near the old Madison Square Garden. Of the fictional dive in the play, Larry Slade says: "It's the No Chance Saloon . . . Bedrock Bar, the End of the Line Café, the Bottom of the Sea Rathskeller! Don't you notice the beautiful calm in the atmosphere? That's because it's the last harbor. No one here has to worry about where they're going next, because there is no farther they can go."

With the exception of several prostitutes and bartender-pimps, the denizens of Harry Hope's joint — onetime journalists, army officers, policemen, circus workers, law students, anarchists — have seen better days. Without exception each clings to a sustaining "pipe dream" (the term recurs constantly in the play), and most, like drunks leaning against one another in order to remain on their feet, profess belief in the others' self-delusions. The basic element in nearly all the pipe dreams is "tomorrow": tomorrow they will quit drinking, take a grip on themselves, and become respectable members of society.

The various characters, O'Neill says, were "based on people I once knew or knew of, although none . . . is an exact portrait of anyone." At least four, however, closely resemble their models. Saloonkeeper Harry Hope, who has not set foot outside his place since his wife died twenty years earlier ("Once she'd gone, I didn't give a damn for anything. I lost all my ambition"), recalls Tom Wallace, a semirecluse for years in his quarters above his place, the Hell Hole. In appearance, character and, as given in the play, personal history, Hugo Kalmar, a former anarchist, is faithful to Hippolyte Havel, one of O'Neill's radical friends in the Village and a Hell Hole habitué.

The remaining two of the fictional quartet — James ("Jimmy Tomorrow") Cameron, the leader of "the Tomorrow Movement" in the play, and Larry Slade, "the old Foolosopher" — were modeled on persons especially dear to the playwright. In life Cameron was James Findlater

Byth, the onetime press agent of James O'Neill who drank himself down to Jimmy the Priest's, at the time Eugene lived there, and who was chiefly instrumental in saving Eugene's life when he attempted suicide. Twice before, in the short story "Tomorrow" and the one-acter "Exorcism," O'Neill had tried to give Jimmy Byth literary immortality; this time he succeeded, for Cameron is among the most sensitive portraits in an O'Neill masterpiece. Apparently the playwright believed Byth's fraudulent claim that he had been a news correspondent in the Boer War, since his fictional counterpart is given such a background. And Larry Slade is really Terry Carlin — the inner Carlin O'Neill had known, the former anarchist who had ended in total disenchantment, not merely the eloquent barfly who had charmed many. In an affectionate description, the dramatist says Slade has "a gaunt Irish face with a big nose, high cheekbones . . . an expression of tired tolerance giving his face the quality of a pitying but weary old priest's."

Nearly all the characters live in Hope's shabby hotel above the saloon, and as the story begins they are eagerly awaiting "Hickey" — Theodore Hickman, a traveling salesman who turns up periodically with an epic thirst and treats the whole gang to a stream of drinks while he too wallows in booze. Cherished by the gang not alone for his generosity, he is "a great one to make a joke of everything and cheer you up." His favorite joke is to display a photo of his ultraproper wife, then remark that he left her at home in bed with "the iceman."

Like barnacles attached to an old hull, Hope's regulars appear to be in their natural habitat, but Don Parritt, a newcomer, clearly does not belong. Vaguely repugnant, he is the son of Rosa Parritt, a leading anarchist who, with several male associates, has just been jailed for life for a bombing on the West Coast; they were betrayed, apparently, by an informer within their ranks. (This background history is based on the notorious MacNamara bombing case in Los Angeles, during the 1910s, in which, as Terry Carlin told O'Neill at the time, the authorities finally captured the last of the terrorists when Donald Vose, the venal son of a woman anarchist, informed on them.) Obviously under tension, Don Parritt has come to Hope's place seeking counsel and sympathy from Larry Slade, an ex-anarchist and a onetime lover of Rosa Parritt (Rosa is modeled on Emma Goldman, an old friend of Vose's mother); but Slade, sensing something unwholesome in the youth, repeatedly tries to avoid him.

Throughout the long first act, as Slade and Parritt fence nervously, the expectant barflies bicker good-naturedly among themselves, reminisce, talk of starting a new life "tomorrow," and affectionately recall Hickey, who is due shortly for a celebration of Hope's birthday. When he appears finally, he proves different from the man they had always known: though he still wisecracks, beams at everyone, and starts treating them to drinks, he is now obsessed with saving them. Convinced that he has found the only way to personal salvation, Hickey, a preacher's son, insists that pipe dreams are what "really poison and ruin a guy's life." He maintains that he found "real peace" — a phrase he uses repeatedly — when he finally faced himself without "the old false whiskers"; now he wants the crew at Hope's, "the best friends" he ever had, to follow suit and thereby free themselves of guilt feelings over their failure to reform. It is some time before we learn the nature of Hickey's own self-delusion, but his wife Evelyn's pet dream, one she has stubbornly cherished for years, was that someday he would give up his periodic bouts of desperate drinking, his consorting with whores and other low company.

On first meeting Parritt, Hickey, detecting something familiar about him, decides that they are "members of the same lodge — in some way." "I've had hell inside me," he says another time. "I can spot it in others. Maybe that's what gives me the feeling there's . . . something between us." On his side Parritt, frightened of Hickey, feels there is "something not human behind his damned grinning and kidding."

Under continuous pressure from Hickey, Hope's derelicts reluctantly try to implement their "tomorrow" dreams, but instead of gaining peace in the attempt, as he had promised them, they fall into despair, they start hating themselves and of course one another. In desperation, Hickey, who had earlier informed them that his wife Evelyn is dead, discloses that he had shot her as she slept — but, he insists, he did it from love, for her own sake, hence his feeling of "real peace." Thus, the title of the play has both a ribald and a sinister meaning: first, it alludes to the old joke about the man who calls up to his wife, "Has the iceman come yet?" to which she replies, "No, but he's breathing fast"; in the second and dark sense the title means that Death the Iceman has come to Evelyn Hickman.

As the others shrink back in horror, Hickey, in the longest and one of the most impassioned speeches in all O'Neill, explains with diabolic logic why he had to kill his wife. He could not give her "peace" by committing suicide, as he had long wanted to, for she would "have died of a broken heart to think I could do that to her. She'd have blamed herself for it, too. Or I couldn't just run away. . . . She'd have died of grief and humiliation. . . . She'd have thought I'd stopped loving her. You see, Evelyn loved me. And I loved her. That was the trouble."

No matter what he did, even when he infected her with a venereal disease, Evelyn, "the sweetest woman in the world," always forgave him; nothing could alter her love or "kill" her pipe dream that one day he would reform. "God," Hickey cries out, "can you picture all I made her suffer, and all the guilt she made me feel, and how I hated myself! . . . I began to be afraid I was going bughouse, because sometimes I couldn't forgive her for forgiving me. I even caught myself hating her for making me hate myself so much. There's a limit to the guilt you can feel and the forgiveness and the pity you can take!"

Right after Hickey shot his wife, shortly before setting out for Hope's birthday party, he suddenly realized that he had always known that death "was the only possible way to give her peace and free her from the misery of loving me. I saw it meant peace for me, too, knowing she was at peace. I felt as though a ton of guilt was lifted off my mind. I remember I stood by the bed and suddenly I had to laugh. . . . I remember I heard myself speaking to her, as if it was something I'd always wanted to say: 'Well, you know what you can do with your pipe dream now, you damned bitch!' "

Aghast at the memory, he immediately adds: "No! That's a lie! I never said —! Good God, I couldn't have said that! If I did, I'd gone insane! Why, I loved Evelyn better than anything in life!"

As Parritt's name suggests, his situation echoes Hickey's: while he did not slay his mother, he is a matricide of sorts, for he condemned her to a kind of death in life. Initially he confides to Larry Slade that he turned informer from patriotic motives; next, that he needed funds for some fast living; finally, as Hickey bares himself more than he realizes, the youth whispers to Larry, "I didn't give a damn about the money. It was because I hated her." With Slade's anguished approval, Parritt, who can no longer endure himself, jumps from a top-floor fire escape at Harry Hope's (an end reminiscent of the death leap of James Findlater Byth in 1913 at Jimmy the Priest's). Hickey, who notifies the authorities about his deed, departs in the hands of the law.

For *The Iceman Cometh* O'Neill drew from fiction (Gorki's *The Lower Depths*, a play he greatly admired, and Ibsen's *The Wild Duck*), from his own life, and from the personal histories of others. Besides selecting and adapting things from this varied material as he saw fit, he also, of course, exercised his imagination. While his "main plot" may be, as he has said, "imaginary," large chunks of it, such as Parritt's informing on the anarchist bombers, were patently inspired by actual happenings. Another major borrowing from life was Hickey's fatal relationship with

Evelyn; in most important respects it parallels the famous murder case of Charles E. Chapin, a prominent newspaper executive, which O'Neill had followed at the time, 1918, with great interest. The city editor of the New York *Evening World*, Chapin too, like his fictional counterpart, shot his wife in the head as she slept and insisted afterward that he had been motivated by love, by concern for her welfare.

At first, in a confession left at the death scene, Chapin said that he, fearing insanity and permanent confinement, intended to commit suicide and had slain his wife because she "has no relatives and is so dependent upon me that it would be impossible for her to live on when I am gone." Uncertain why he did not kill himself, he said, after being taken into custody, that financial difficulties had reduced him to a desperate frame of mind. Though his series of explanations varied and conflicted, he steadfastly maintained that he and his wife had been "good pals," that he had "idolized" her. On the day he surrendered himself, he said that he felt "happy" for the first time in years (like Hickey enjoying "real peace" once he has killed Evelyn). "You know," Chapin told the authorities, "there was really nothing else to do. I'm quite satisfied I took the only course for an honorable man to take." Insisting on his sanity, he originally declared that he wanted the electric chair (Hickey does, too), but he later entered a plea of not guilty on the grounds of temporary insanity. After a panel of experts disputed his defense, he pleaded guilty to a second-degree murder charge and was sentenced to Sing Sing for life. In his autobiography, published in 1920, his final words are: "Almost two years have passed. In the solitude of my cell I have subjected myself to a more searching examination than the most analytical prosecutor could put me through, and the verdict that is firmly fixed in my mind is that I did the only thing that was left me to do. There was no other way of saving my wife."

The climactic period of Chapin's life foreshadows Hickey's at so many points that O'Neill, while writing *The Iceman*, must have reread accounts of the strange murder case instead of relying on memory. The important thing, however, is not that the playwright followed fact quite closely but that he exploited it masterfully.

A rich, multilayered drama that bears study on various levels, *The Iceman Cometh*, starting with its title, is full of symbolic touches and double or hidden meanings. The author, who always sought to give his characters significant names, was particularly careful this time. Aside from Parritt, and of course Harry Hope, who presides benignly over a saloonful of drifters clinging to impossible hopes, there is Hugo Kalmar, who resembles the bomb-carrying foreign radical of newspaper cartoons; his surname is an abbreviation of Karl Marx. McGloin, a larcenous ex-cop, recalls the old "Tenderloin" section of Manhattan, where the police used to fatten themselves on graft from the gambling joints and whorehouses. A bartender with a greedy streak is called Pioggi. The two detectives who take Hickey into custody are Lieb (German for "love") and Moran, which calls to mind such words as mourn and morgue, hence the two represent Love and Death; furthermore, Moran does all the talking for the two, a subtle touch that suggests Hickey's imminent fate.

Since *The Iceman* is loaded with hidden clues and meanings, it has been the subject of many interpretations; none of the author's other works has been studied so minutely. In one of the most discerning analyses, Professor Cyrus Day draws parallels between Hickey's situation and the biblical account of Christ's final days on earth. Hickey, the professor notes, "has twelve disciples. They drink wine at Hope's supper party, and their grouping on the stage, according to O'Neill's directions, is reminiscent of Leonardo da Vinci's painting of the Last Supper. Hickey leaves the party, as Christ does, aware that he is about to be executed. The three whores correspond in number to the three Marys, and sympathize with Hickey as the three Marys sympathize with Christ. . . .

"One of the derelicts, Parritt, resembles Judas Iscariot in several ways. He is twelfth in the list of dramatis personae; Judas is twelfth in the New Testament lists of the Disciples. He has betrayed his anarchist mother for a paltry $200; Judas has betrayed Christ for thirty pieces of silver. He is from the far-away Pacific Coast; Judas was from far-away Judaea. Hickey reads his mind and motives; Christ reads Judas's. Parritt compares himself to Iscariot when he says that his mother would regard anyone who quit the 'Movement' as a Judas who ought to be boiled in oil."

Thus the title *The Iceman Cometh* has not only ribald and sinister meanings but a biblical one as well. While Waldo Frank's novel *The Bridegroom Cometh* may have been the immediate inspiration for the play's title, it served primarily to remind the playwright, who was well read in the Scriptures, of the passage (25:506) in Matthew: "While the bridegroom tarried, they all slumbered and slept. And at midnight there was a cry made, Behold, the bridegroom cometh." As Professor Day notes, "In the symbolism of theology, the bridegroom is always Christ. . . . Waiting for the bridegroom symbolizes man's hope of redemption."

Surprisingly, one important aspect that the professor neglected to point out is the rich symbolism of the messianic salesman's name: Theodore,

O'Neill in 1939, when he was writing The Iceman Cometh

Real-life models for characters in
The Iceman Cometh: *Charles E.*
Chapin, right (Hickey); Hippolyte
Havel, directly below (Hugo Kalmar);
and Terry Carlin (Larry Slade)

from the Greek word *theo*, meaning god, and Hickman — hick man, man as a "hick," a credulous, deluded soul. Of all the pipe dreamers in Harry Hope's saloon, Hickey, who imagined that he loved his wife, was self-deluded most disastrously. He crucified himself for years by living a lie, till his agony became too acute to be endured. He also was a false god, a fraudulent savior, for he wanted to bring peace to his friends but instead brought them despair and the smell of death. In a fundamental sense he resembles another O'Neill salvationist, for Lazarus too sought to free his disciples of guilt and fear but succeeded only in plunging them into darker depths.

Kenneth Macgowan, among the first to read *The Iceman Cometh*, wondered whether Hickey was drawn from life. O'Neill, who never told anyone, apparently, of his debt to the Chapin case, wrote back: "No, I never knew him. He's the most imaginary character in the play. Of course, I knew many salesmen in my time who were periodical drunks, but Hickey is not any of them. He is all of them, you might say, and none of them."

However, he told George Jean Nathan, another who read the play early, "There was a periodical drunk salesman [I knew] who was a damned amusing likable guy. And he did make that typical drummer crack about the iceman, and wept maudlinly over his wife's photograph, and in other moods, boozily harped on the slogan that honesty is the best policy."

Hickey appears to have been patterned also, to some extent, on a certain other drummer, one whom O'Neill probably knew at Jimmy the Priest's. The reason for thinking so is that *Chris*, the forerunner of *Anna Christie*, contained a traveling salesman named Adams who, in the words of saloonkeeper Johnny the Priest, has "been talking me deaf, dumb and blind all day. I'm sick o' listening to him." (In *The Iceman* the others complain similarly about Hickey.) At another point in *Chris* the saloonkeeper says of Adams: "Smart fellow, too — when he's sober. . . . Never stays long on one job, though. Booze got a strangle hold on him. . . . He's one of the kind ought to leave red eye alone. Always ends up his drunk here. Knows no one'll know him here 'cept me and he ain't shamed to go the limit. Well, he's a good spender as long as he's got it."

Since O'Neill drew in Hickey a similar character twenty years later, it seems that he had in mind an actual person. Apparently, then, Hickey was largely based on two particular salesmen and Charles E. Chapin; yet even if these three models are excluded from consideration, O'Neill was less than truthful when he told Macgowan that Hickey was "the most imaginary character" and that he "never knew him."

The tragic truth is that he knew him all too well, for the Hickey who long harbored a hatred he could not acknowledge, particularly to himself, the Hickey tortured by guilt feelings and self-loathing, was O'Neill himself, just as he also was the Parritt who writhed under the knowledge that he had condemned his mother to a living death. Time and again in his works O'Neill, one of the most biographical playwrights who ever lived (probably only Strindberg equaled him in this respect), had presented images of his mother and dramatized aspects of his attitude toward her. In the interlocked stories of Hickey and Parritt he at last gave full vent to his fury against Ella Quinlan O'Neill, drug addict, the chief source of the bad conscience and the feelings of self-hatred that would fester in the playwright son till the end of his days.

In *The Iceman* Larry Slade quotes from Heine's poem about morphine: "Lo, sleep is good; better is death; in sooth, The best of all were never to be born."

The Heine lines were not lightly chosen by Slade's creator. While writing *The Iceman*, he already was conceiving his next play, *Long Day's Journey Into Night*, a fiercely honest portrait of his family in which he would reveal his mother as a morphine addict whose damnation began with his birth.

O'Neill's feelings about his parents were exceedingly complex, containing conflicting impulses toward each, but the bulk of evidence indicates that, basically, he loved his father and was hostile toward his mother. Though he knew that she fell innocently and unwittingly into addiction, he could never, on an emotional level, absolve her. As he declares through Hickey, "There's a limit to the guilt you can feel. . . . You have to begin blaming someone else, too." In another self-revelatory statement, he has Hickey say that Parritt "has to be punished, so he can forgive himself." Here, no doubt, is the chief explanation for O'Neill's bouts of desperate drinking for years, when he used to continue till he was violently sick, and the beating he gave himself in the lower depths of Buenos Aires and the New York water front, a period climaxed by his suicide attempt at Jimmy the Priest's.

But, wavering in his ambivalence toward Ella O'Neill and viewing her at times as a victim of her husband, the playwright also drew tender images of her on occasion, chiefly in Eben Cabot's recollections of his mother in *Desire Under the Elms* and, most memorably, in Dion Anthony's elegiac lament in *The Great God Brown*. Still, behind these loving sketches is the sinister fact that the two women are part of a legion of dead wives and mothers in O'Neill's writings, a clan larger than one may realize, since many of its ghostly members died before the plays begin and are referred to only fleetingly. Most likely O'Neill was unaware of the grim pattern that gradually developed in his works beneath other, more visible patterns, but this in no way alters the evidence that he had a strong matricidal impulse and through his plays took symbolic revenge again and again on Ella O'Neill, drug addict.

While it might be objected that his men likewise have a high mortality rate or suffer other unhappy fates, their downfalls are in many cases precipitated, either unintentionally or culpably, by a woman, hence they often constitute additional evidence of a misogynistic strain in O'Neill. In "Bread and Butter," his first full-length work, as well as in the one-acter *Before Breakfast,* the hero is driven to suicide by his vixenish wife. In *Beyond the Horizon* Robert Mayo, a born dreamer and wanderer, is doomed once Ruth Atkins chooses him over his brother; he remains on the farm and molders away. Yank, so swaggeringly sure of himself in *The Hairy Ape,* is set fatally adrift in a hostile universe once the society girl is horrified at the sight of him. The farmwife's seduction of her stepson launches the sequence of dire events in *Desire Under the Elms.*

But none of these plays is so revealing of O'Neill's bitterness toward his mother as *Dynamo,* in which the preacher's wife dies after she betrays her son, and the boy, half crazed at losing faith in her, turns to Science for salvation. No wonder, then, that for months after the failure of *Dynamo* the author vehemently protested to friends that the play had been misunderstood, that he had been interested primarily in the mother's treachery to her son and its disastrous effect on him, not in Science as a new gospel.

In the final analysis even the playwright's idealized women — the devoted wife in *Servitude,* an early full-length work; the Chinese princess in *Marco Millions;* Cybel in *The Great God Brown;* Nora Melody in *A Touch of the Poet;* the giant farm girl in *A Moon for the Misbegotten* — even these testify to his bias. Under the dynamics of human nature, as in physics, one extreme, like a swinging pendulum at a high point, contains within itself an impulse toward its opposite. Paralleling his mentor Strindberg, O'Neill created in the majority of his leading female characters either bitches and other agents of misfortune or impossibly noble souls. He could praise Woman only in exaggerated, unrealistic terms. One compounded of virtues and failings, the usual stuff of human nature, is rare in his writings. Generally speaking, men who romanticize women are impelled by fear or dislike or a combination of both. Unable to give women their just due, they disguise their prejudice, especially from themselves, in a flattering attitude; but the end result is that they leave their idolized ones small margin for error, scant latitude in which to be fallibly human. These romanticists set the stage, in other words, for their own disillusionment.

A complicating factor in O'Neill's feelings toward the other sex was his desire and need for a "mother," a woman strong enough to shelter him from the world. As a child, feeling rebuffed when his mother retreated into the depths of morphine, he had gratefully taken refuge under the firm wing of Sarah Jane Bucknell Sandy, his nursemaid — in effect his second mother — till he was shipped off to boarding school. While growing up, then, he had two opposite kinds of mothers rooted in his imagination: one who recurrently failed him; another who was always there when he wanted her.

Although Eugene's early attachment to Sarah Sandy and his eventual ambivalence toward Ella O'Neill account in large part, apparently, for the various O'Neill heroes obsessed with their mothers, a third person in the author's history should be considered here: his brother, the Jamie who used to paddle his hands in the scented water where his mother had just bathed, the Jamie who gave up drinking, at his mother's request, when his father died and he had his mother to himself, the Jamie who lost all interest in life once his mother was dead and proceeded to drink himself into an early grave.

There appears to be more of Jamie than of Eugene in the oedipal aspect of Orin Mannon's character, just as Simon Harford, in his turbulent love-hate feelings toward his elusive mother, suggests a blend of the O'Neill brothers. That the playwright's works contain a number of oedipally inclined protagonists is no evidence, regardless of what many O'Neill commentators have maintained, that he was ardently committed to his mother. Quite the contrary. One recalls that when O'Neill discussed Stekel's *The Disguises of Love* with Malcolm Cowley years earlier, he said that its case histories could "furnish plots to all the playwrights who ever lived." The one case he cited, significantly enough, was of a boy who went insane after his mother had seduced him.

It seems likely that O'Neill began to realize the true state of his feelings toward his mother in 1926 while undergoing exhaustive questioning by Dr. G. V. Hamilton about his parents. Toward the end of his sessions with the psychoanalyst, it should be remembered, O'Neill, who started drinking at the age of fifteen (shortly after learning about Ella's addiction), was able, rather mysteriously, to turn abstinent; except for his dissipation on the Far Eastern trip and several other isolated occasions, he would abstain the rest of his life. Similarly, after Hickey slays his wife and finally has a true glimpse of himself (though he immediately seizes on another pipe dream), he discovers that he no longer "needs" liquor and becomes a teetotaler.

Starting with the Poet in *Fog*, one of his earliest works, O'Neill drew a number of obvious self-portraits — the doomed hero of "Bread and Butter," the newspaperman in *The Straw*, the playwright in *Welded*, Dion Anthony in *The Great God Brown*, the husband in *Days Without End* — and in nearly each instance the image is more or less faithful to O'Neill in looks and personality. He was careful, however, to give his chief persona in *The Iceman* a radically different manner and appearance from himself; short and stout, Hickey "exudes a friendly, generous personality that makes everyone like him on sight." In other words, O'Neill, burning to voice through Hickey some of his darkest impulses, took pains to mislead anyone trying to follow his biographical tracks in his writings.

Aside from the analogy between O'Neill's attitude toward his mother and Hickey's toward his wife, the two have other aspects in common. Just as the playwright owed his theatrical sense to the Count of Monte Cristo, Hickey inherited his gift of gab and evangelical fervor from his clergyman father. No doubt, too, the playwright was being biographical when he has Hickey say that at the end of his periodic binges he used to look like "something lying in the gutter that no alley cat would lower itself to drag in — something they threw out of the D.T. ward at Bellevue along with the garbage, something that ought to be dead and isn't!"

Rather paradoxically, *The Iceman Cometh*, despite its bleak message about man's need for pipe dreams and its harrowing story about Hickey, is a drama of considerable warmth and humor. Among the drifters in Hope's saloon there exists a spirit of camaraderie that is immensely engaging. In the exact words that Hickey uses about them, O'Neill said in 1946, regarding their true-life models, that they were "the best friends I ever had." On the face of it this seems a curious remark, since he had, to name only a few, such devoted friends as Kenneth Macgowan, Russel Crouse, George Jean Nathan, Robert Sisk, Sophus and Eline Winther, and, above all, Saxe Commins, who was ready to go to almost any lengths for him. Behind his remark was probably the feeling that Saxe and the others were oriented in life, they "belonged," unlike himself, so that at heart he felt closest to the social pariahs he had once boozed with, drinking himself numb, in the lowest dives of the water front; it appears, indeed, that he considered himself some kind of pariah.

O'Neill and Carlotta, already distressed about the war in Europe, were further upset in the late months of 1939 by a series of mishaps in her family. Not long after Roy Stram's near-fatal attack of rheumatic fever, which left him crippled for life, Cynthia was in a collision that totally wrecked her automobile — she escaped, almost miraculously, with only a broken leg — and in the same period Nellie Tharsing came close to dying of pneumonia. Carlotta herself had the flu this fall, but O'Neill remained in relatively good health. He had never quite recovered, however, his full vigor since his siege in the Oakland hospital — he was subject to what he called "sinking spells" — and the tremor of the hands that had afflicted him on and off since childhood was becoming more troublesome.

Usually on finishing a play he would wait some months, to gain a fresh perspective, before revising it, but with *The Iceman Cometh* he knew so clearly what he wanted to say that he resumed working on it as soon as Carlotta had typed his manuscript. Written in less than six months, the four-act drama, which has a running time of about four hours, was created more easily than *Strange Interlude* or *Mourning Becomes Electra* or, for that matter, certain of his standard-length dramas; by contrast, *Days Without End*, written in large part against his grain, cost him nearly two years' work.

He spent the last weeks of 1939 and first ones of 1940 on the second and final draft. Late in January Saxe Commins, during a stay at Tao House, typed the revised script and returned to New York with a copy for safekeeping at Random House that only Bennett Cerf and George Jean Nathan were permitted to read. O'Neill swore the two to secrecy since he, to forestall any pressure for an early production, did not want the Guild or even his agent Richard Madden to know of the play's existence. Aside from his feeling that the times were wrong for the play, that audiences in wartime would be unreceptive to a drama as nihilistic as *The Iceman*, Eugene feared that he might "crack up" again, as in 1937, under the "nerve strain" of New York and rehearsals. Unwilling to risk such a possibility even if "guaranteed a great success," his sole desire was to remain well enough to continue writing — "the only thing that still interests me about my profession."

Delighted by Nathan's response to *The Iceman* (he thought it "even finer and profounder" than Gorki's *The Lower Depths*), O'Neill replied on February 28, 1940: "I was sure you would like it, but still — Well, you know how it is, you write a thing with growing confidence and elation, and you finish it in an exultant mood of accomplishment. Then suddenly the reaction comes and you become tired and empty, and what you have done grows blurred in your mind, and all you remember is a lot of dialogue and some characters that seem to have gone dead. . . . So your letter is a grand boost and I feel gratefully revived."

After word of the play leaked out months later, he permitted Langner and Miss Helburn to read it, both of whom were highly impressed. "Personally I love it!" the playwright wrote to Langner. "And I'm sure my affection is not wholly inspired by nostalgia for the dear dead days 'on the bottom of the sea,' either! I have a confident hunch that this play . . . is one of the best things I've ever done, perhaps *the* best . . . there are moments in it that suddenly strip the secret soul of a man stark naked, not in cruelty or moral superiority, but with an understanding compassion which sees him as a victim of the ironies of life and of himself. These moments are to me the depth of tragedy, with nothing more that can possibly be said."

Shortly after he had finished pruning and revising *The Iceman* early in 1940, Eugene, feeling exhausted, took to bed with what proved a recurrent case of the flu. "I am not the same as I was before my long illness [in 1937], and never will be again," he told Nathan on February 8, at the start of weeks of general poor health. The one pleasant development during the period was that Robert Sisk, a champion of O'Neill's works in Hollywood, inspired director John Ford and writer Dudley Nichols with a desire to adapt the *S.S. Glencairn* series to the screen. A superior Hollywood team whose record included such fine movies as *The Informer*, *The Grapes of Wrath* and *Stagecoach*, the two had financial backing to make the *S.S. Glencairn* film independently for release through United Artists. O'Neill initially asked for twenty thousand dollars plus a percentage of the profit if it exceeded a certain amount, but he settled finally for the flat sum.

Despite his usual reserve, he warmed quickly to the film-making pair, especially to Ford, a big hearty Irishman with a fund of irreverent stories about Hollywood, when they visited Tao House to discuss their projected movie. One anecdote of Ford's that particularly amused O'Neill concerned the filming of *Stagecoach*, today a classic Western. It seems that the studio brass, fearful of the censors, wanted the film's scarlet woman changed to a dance-hall girl or someone else less flagrant. "Finally, I hit on a solution," Ford recounted. "There's this scene where the girl walks the length of the main street followed by the stern eyes of the respectable womenfolk and admiring glances from the men. I suggested that as she approaches the stagecoach to leave town, she turns, just before entering the coach, and announces, 'Ladies and gentlemen, I am a whore no more.' "

The Ford-Nichols collaboration, entitled *The Long Voyage Home* after one of the four *S.S. Glencairn* playlets, was the finest movie ever made from O'Neill's writings (he himself praised it as "an exceptional picture, with no obvious Hollywood hokum or sentimental love bilge in it"). But in spite of cordial reviews, it was too unconventional and somber for commercial success.

Now that O'Neill had definitively expressed in *The Iceman Cometh* his hostility toward his mother, he was ready to draw a portrait of his entire family at once unsparingly frank yet compassionate. The new work was of course *Long Day's Journey Into Night*. It was already taking shape in his mind as he worked on *The Iceman*. Carlotta had first learned of the project one night in June 1939. "Whenever Gene was very upset about something or nervous," she has recalled, "he would come to my bedroom or call me to his and talk himself out. This night he told me he was going to write a play about his family. It was a thing that haunted him. He was *bedeviled* into writing it. . . . He had to get it out of his system, he had to forgive whatever it was that caused this tragedy between himself and his mother and father.

"He talked all night — it was like talking to himself. I shut up and didn't say a word. He said, 'I've *got* to write this. I'm afraid someone might find out about us one day and write something vulgar and melo-dramatic about it, even make a play out of it. But it was never vulgar! Even if my father was miserly, even if my mother used to take drugs whenever things got too much for her, even if my brother spent so much of his time in whorehouses.'

"In the evenings we used to sit before the fireplace, and I remember one night when Gene, staring into the fire, said, 'I'm just thinking of the hell every member of the family went through — separately.'

"When he started *Long Day's Journey* it was a most strange experience to watch that man being tortured every day by his own writing. He would come out of his study at the end of a day gaunt and sometimes weeping. His eyes would be all red and he looked ten years older than when he went in in the morning."

The Bible, with Freudian insight many centuries before Freud, said: "A man shall leave his father and his mother, and shall cleave unto his wife." O'Neill, clearly, never really "left" his parents. An eternal son, forever haunted by the past, he was obsessed with the subject of familial relations, particularly those between child and parent. For all his wanderings and varied experiences as a young man, he found his predominant, most fruitful theme at home. It can properly be said that *Long Day's Journey* had the longest gestation of any of his works; it was *the* play he, unconsciously, was aching to write when he first turned playwright. Indeed, he wrote bits and pieces of his family story, crudely, in "Bread and Butter," his first full-length work, and subsequently with different degrees of skill and under assorted guises in *All God's Chillun Got Wings* and *Desire Under the Elms*, in *The Great God Brown* and, among other dramas, *Dynamo*. (Professor John Henry Raleigh includes *Lazarus Laughed*, for he considers the unholy royal trio of Tiberius, Pompeia and Caligula nightmarish projections of the playwright's parents and brother.)

As O'Neill was conceiving *Long Day's Journey*, his memories of his father were sharpened when the Writers' Program of the WPA in northern California sent him the manuscript of a monograph on James O'Neill, part of a projected multivolume history of the San Francisco theater. The playwright, who was surrounded in Rosie's room by photos of his father and in the bathhouse at the pool by posters of *Monte Cristo*, carefully checked the script for error and replied at length to a list of questions. His letter, dated January 15, 1940, was included in the monograph as a kind of epilogue.

Giving advance glimpses of his family play, he reported that his paternal grandparents had been "extremely poor" and that his father, when only ten, had gone to work for fifty cents a week. He was unable, he said, to contribute a few stories that would characterize his father. "If I started on anecdotes about him I would have to write a book, because he had many extraordinary contradictory sides to his character."

His parents' wedding certificate, his letter continues, was among the few records he possessed of their early years. (The mother's wedding gown, a recurrent topic in *Long Day's Journey* as a symbol of her lost innocence and past happiness, is an agonizing sight to her husband and sons when she brings it out at the end, yellowed and bedraggled after years in the attic.) Voicing regret that he could not be more informative about his father, O'Neill, in noncommittal words that concealed a great deal, ended that once he was "old enough to take notice," he was "off at school, or wandering about, or living away from my family a lot of the time."

Pleased that the monograph, which he considered "a fine job," had been written by an O'Neill — first name, Patrick — the playwright established a correspondence with the young biographer, who was eager for the great man's advice and help. On learning that Washington was terminating the WPA Writers' Program, O'Neill sent the young man fifty dollars for a copy of an unpublished short story of his, which he was free to try and sell to the magazines, and for months took time to write to him encouraging letters. After a publishing house turned down a novel of Patrick O'Neill's, the playwright declared that "such discouraging incidents have happened to every writer who ever amounted to a damn. . . . They're a test you have to pass through to prove yourself to yourself. . . . Call the publishers all the names in the book — and then go on with your work! Because you have to . . . no matter what it costs you. . . . Publication is important, but it can wait because it is outside you. What's inside you can't wait."

He began composing *Long Day's Journey* in the early spring of 1940, but initially made slow progress. After finishing the first act, he felt exhausted, too weary to write, and then during May and much of June, as the Germans outflanked the Maginot Line, the French forces crumbled, and the British made their heroic evacuation at Dunkirk, he spent most of his time hovering over the radio. Totally demoralized by the global debacle, two months passed without his setting down a word. "With so much tragic drama happening in the world," he found it "hard to take the theater seriously." By late June, though, he had resumed work. "You can't," he said, "keep a hophead off his dope for long!" (In *Long Day's Journey* Eugene's counterpart strikes his brother when he refers to their mother as a "hophead.")

Shane, who had not seen his father for nearly two years, spent a fortnight at Tao House early this summer. Still floundering, he had taken courses at the Art Students' League in New York for the past year and, with some of his schoolmates, had begun frequenting the bars of Greenwich Village. Handsome without being vain, exceptionally shy yet pleasant, he was universally liked, arousing in his friends a protective feeling. Loath to trade on his name, he was glad that people "didn't talk about my father or ask me questions about him," but a good many pressed drinks on him when they learned his identity from other sources. At the Old Colony on Eighth Street, his favorite hangout, he once said, "I've got an idea for a play. A man in a bar announces to his friends, 'I believe I can go up in smoke.' Shortly afterward he says, 'I think I will,' and the next

thing they know, he's done it — gone up in smoke and disappeared."
Shane did not elaborate on the idea.

To friends O'Neill maintained that his younger son would be "all
right" once he had settled on his proper course in life, but privately he
was worried. Doubtful of the youth's artistic ability, O'Neill talked to
him, Carlotta informed Saxe Commins on June 18, "frankly, firmly . . .
& told him that he must get a job in a shipyard — or some such — &
prove he has the guts to work, & the desire to help himself." If he does,
she added, "Gene will help him — if not — !" She herself considered him
"a sweet kid" but was scornful of his aimlessness, his lack of drive, all of
which she blamed on his upbringing by Agnes.

Oona, after two years at a school in Virginia, where she had done well,
was to enter Brearley, a fashionable girls' school in Manhattan, this fall.
Shortly before leaving in July with Agnes for a brief stay in Bermuda,
Oona wrote to her father that she would like to visit him afterward.
While professing pleasure over the prospect, he replied that her visit
would have to be in September, for he and Carlotta would be elsewhere
during most of August (this was untrue, however). Since Oona was to
have some tutoring to assure herself a good start at Brearly, he thought
that "the important thing, for [her] own sake," was to concentrate on
her studies. But he left the decision to her and ended his letter of July 3,
"I think of you a lot and love you a lot and am very proud of you."

Perhaps he discouraged her visit, subtly, because he was so engrossed in
probing his relations with his parents as he wrote *Long Day's Journey*
that he feared her presence would be a distraction; while reliving his life
as a son, he would have to assume, for a time, the role of a father. In any
case, Oona, who had sensitive antennae, took the hint and never visited
him this year.

According to Carlotta, Eugene almost never told her to her face that he
loved her but instead used to leave ardent notes on her bed or at some
other conspicuous spot. For his customary tribute on their anniversary in
July, he wrote on the twenty-second: "Here's congratulating myself for
the blessing of you these eleven years! Time falters, civilization disinte-
grates, values perish, the old beauty becomes a gutter slut, the world
explodes, the income tax rises, the years grow heavy on us and Blemie —
But still! There is love that does not die . . . so what the hell!"

In August Terry Helburn, en route to Hollywood on a casting mission,
briefly visited Tao House, full of praise for *The Iceman* and arguments
why O'Neill should release it for production this fall. But he was

adamant, and he also told her to forget the Cycle, because he had decided to shelve it indefinitely.

In his letter to Oona he had said that it was "discouraging to feel that the Cycle . . . will have little meaning for the sort of world we will probably be living in by the time I finish it. A period of universal unrest and change is a bad period for serious creative work which is not propaganda of some sort. Not to add that conditions in the theater will be so bad that it is doubtful if anyone will dare to produce it as it should be produced — and it *must* be done my way, or I won't let it be done at all."

By the end of August, after six months, including time lost from illness and from being too demoralized by the war to write, O'Neill had finished three acts — there is a fourth — of *Long Day's Journey*. Intensifying his efforts and working longer and longer hours, like one possessed, he completed the play late in September, then immediately began revising it. Carlotta, recalling this period, says, "It nearly killed him to write this play." . . . "After his day's stint he would [be] physically and mentally exhausted. Night after night I had to hold him tight in my arms so he could relax and sleep. . . . Thus the play was written."

It was, like *The Iceman Cometh*, a masterly achievement; in the process of creating the two, O'Neill finally attained his full artistic maturity. Seymour Peck of the New York *Times*, interviewing Carlotta after O'Neill's death, asked the essential question about *Long Day's Journey*: "Do you think that there was this great burst of creative force because he had gone back so personally into his own life for the play?"

"That I couldn't tell you, I wouldn't presume, I wouldn't know," she replied, then continued with words that apply equally to *The Iceman*: "The thing is he was writing about something that came from his very guts . . . he *had* to write this play."

From the start of its composition, O'Neill had the general plan for *Long Day's Journey* clear in his mind. Without disclosing that it was autobiographical, he had told Nathan, after finishing the first act, that the play would cover one day in a family's life, "a day in which things occur which evoke the whole past of the family and reveal every aspect of its interrelationships. A deeply tragic play, but without any violent dramatic action. At the final curtain, there they still are, trapped within each other by the past, each guilty and at the same time innocent, scorning, loving, pitying each other, understanding and yet not understanding at all, forgiving but still doomed never to be able to forget."

Much of the raw material drawn upon by *Long Day's Journey* is condensed in the two papers – but particularly the full-page summary – that O'Neill produced strictly for his own eyes and self-enlightenment while undergoing intensive questioning by Dr. Hamilton back in 1926. Fascinating in itself, the summary of early family history contains several surprises, the chief one being that devout, convent-bred Ella O'Neill had, after her second child's death, a "series of brought-on abortions." (It is interesting to recall that Carlotta's mother also induced a series of miscarriages before she gave birth, unwillingly, to her first and only child.) The paper is still more fascinating, however, when juxtaposed with *Long Day's Journey*, for a comparison of the two – the literal account and the selective, dramatized family portrait – yields revealing glimpses of the way O'Neill's creative mind functioned.

The summary refers to Ella as "M," for Mother, and to Eugene as "E." Some idea of his minuscule script in the secret document (he tried to write so tiny that no one else could read it) may be gained from the fact that the entire text, which follows, is contained on one side of a single page of typewriter paper:

"M – Lonely life – spoiled before marriage (husband friend of [her] father's – father his great admirer – drinking companions) – fashionable convent girl – religious & naïve – talent for music – physical beauty – ostracism after marriage due to husband's profession – lonely life after marriage – no contact with husband's friends – husband man's man – heavy drinker – out with men until small hours every night – slept late – little time with her – stingy about money due to his childhood experience with grinding poverty after his father deserted large family to return to Ireland to spend last days (He died of poison taken by mistake although there is suspicion of suicide here in fit of insane depression – guilty conscience for desertion(?)) (In later days of his life husband periodically talks when depressed of doing as his father did, deserting family, going back to Ireland to die). Birth of first son 1 year after marriage. Father's life in profession more stable then – in stock – for long periods in one city – more sense of home than in later years when constantly touring – M physically healthy then – son is strictly brought up – is punished physically by whipping. M's mother still alive – M has still her affection for comfort when husband fails. M's father dies early in this period – her idol – spoiled her with generous gifts – she always remembers him as contrast to husband's stinginess – also as 'gentleman,' educated, in contrast to husband who is self-educated peasant. M always a bit of snob in reaction to world which finally becomes altogether her husband's world since she has little contact with reality except through him.

"Birth of second child five years after first. While still infant, M is forced to leave him to travel with husband who is morbidly jealous of her, even her affection for children. Baby is left with mother, catches measles, through carelessness of mother in allowing older brother who has measles to see baby. Baby dies. M gets back too late — dead — she is prostrated by grief — blames herself — husband for keeping her away, bitterly [sic] at mother for lack of care — elder boy as direct cause, unconsciously (?).

"Soon after elder is sent to school at husband's command, despite M's protests as to his youth (seven). But she does not feel this separation as keenly as afterward with E because she leaves him [the elder boy] with same nuns who had known her as girl — feeling of home. Her mother dies somewhere in this period. She is now absolutely alone except for husband & a brother, no good & shiftless, whom she despises and never sees, feels no affection for. Husband now 'on his own' touring nine months place to place, one-nights mostly, no chances to form contacts except for brief summers in N.L. which M hates. Her feeling [of] superiority to people there. Her poor relatives who live there make this hard. She feels they are obstacles to her socially, make that town impossible. Her husband prefers barroom companions to whom he is rich hero.

"M evidently shuns idea of another child — guilty about second — husband talks of large family but she knows his stinginess would make this difficult for her — series of brought-on abortions — (defiance of husband? — how did she justify this with religion (?) did this mark beginning of break with religion which was to leave her eventually entirely without solace?) Finally pregnant — this child, E, not wanted at first (?) then desire on both parents' parts it should be girl.

"E born with difficulty — M sick but nurses child — starts treatment with Doc, which eventually winds up in start of nervousness, drinking & drug-addiction. No signs of these before.

"E spoiled from birth — concentration of all M's love on him in her loneliness — she shares him reluctantly with nurse but makes friend and confidant out of nurse to further compensate for loneliness. Husband very proud of his birth (confirmed by stories to me) — 44 years old at time. She pleads for home in [New York] but he refuses. This was always one of her bitterest resentments against him all her life, that she never had home. M gets rid of one nurse at end of year or so (Irish woman) and gets English woman [Sarah Sandy]. (Husband hates English intensely. Always hostile to nurse secretly and she to him. Was M actuated by revenge motives on husband in this choice – to get reliable ally in war with husband (?))

"Absolute loneliness of M at this time except for nurse & few loyal friends scattered over country – (most of whom husband resented as social superiors) – logically points to what must have been her fierce concentration of affection on the child, E. This must have been further intensified by the fact that at age of 2 he nearly dies from typhoid.

"(This nurse later becomes companion in beer & stout drinking – later still (after E is in school) in whisky drinking and probably messenger for obtaining drugs (?))"

During the interval between the 1926 paper and the 1940 family portrait, O'Neill's feelings about his parents underwent, apparently, some subtle modifications. Unlike the summary, which never qualifies Ella's "fierce concentration of affection" on Eugene, *Long Day's Journey* suggests that once she stumbled into drug addiction, she began to develop a grievance against him as the primal cause, though unwittingly, of her fall. In another major difference, the play is more favorable, on the whole, toward James O'Neill than the summary.

Reflecting the author's pride of ancestry, the family in *Long Day's Journey* is named Tyrone after the county in Ireland where the earliest O'Neills had ruled as warrior-kings. Accordingly, James O'Neill becomes James Tyrone here, while his first born son is again familiarly called Jamie. Though most of her life Mrs. O'Neill chose to be known as Ella, her playwright son, using her original first name, called her fictional counterpart Mary, probably because he had in mind both the Virgin Mary and St. Mary's Academy in Indiana, where shy Mary Ellen Quinlan had been a favorite of the nuns and had thought of taking the veil herself; thus, the use of her original name suggests that her son wished she had chosen the cloister over marriage. As for his calling himself Edmund, after the brother who had died in infancy, while the dead child is renamed Eugene, the significance of the change is obvious: nothing was more true of O'Neill than that he had a strong death wish.

Where formerly the playwright had indulged repeatedly in restless, rather desperate experimentation, he now scrupulously abstained from all novelty and unusual devices, anything that smacked of theatricality, in order to show with absolute candor, with unmistakable integrity, the familial forces that had kneaded, shaped, and warped him. There is no story to speak of. It appears that O'Neill simply took some crucial, revelatory hours from his family's history and divided them into scenes

[512]

and acts; he seems, indeed, to present the raw, unadulterated stuff of life itself (one critic was to call it "a naked play, a play without a skin, so that nothing intervenes between itself and the spectator"). But such an impression, considering the shattering impact of the work, could be achieved only through unobtrusive, consummate artistry; neither reality nor, as Oscar Wilde said, sincerity is sufficient to produce a work of art.

For the sake of form and dramatic emphasis, O'Neill took various liberties with fact: he telescoped into a few hours what happened over a number of weeks, if not months; he has the play's Jamie on the scene at a time when the real Jamie was absent; he isolated the Tyrones somewhat more than they (meaning the O'Neills) actually were during this period; he suppressed certain circumstances; he invented others. Essentially, though, *Long Day's Journey* is true to the family's history.

Observing the classical unities, the play ranges from morning to around midnight on a single day in August 1912 in the living room of the Tyrones' summer place (actually the Monte Cristo cottage in New London). Formally it has only five characters, the Tyrones and a servant girl who occupies a peripheral spot, but there is an unseen presence looming over all and constituting in effect a sixth member of the household: the Past. As the author told Nathan, the Tyrones are "doomed never to be able to forget." The past is invoked so often it becomes almost visible. Each member of the family is haunted by what has gone before and plagued by vain regret for what might have been if . . . if only things had happened differently. When Tyrone, reproaching his wife for recalling old grievances and ancient sorrows, urges her to forget the past, she replies: "How can I? The past is the present, isn't it? It's the future, too. We all try to lie out of that but life won't let us."

In place of story or plot, *Long Day's Journey* follows the darkening impact on the family of two developments: first, Mary Tyrone, who has recently undergone another cure for drug addiction, succumbs once more just as her husband and sons have begun hoping that this time she has permanently recovered; second, Edmund learns that he has consumption and must enter a sanatorium (as Eugene did in 1912). With the Tyrones constantly resifting the past, to use it as either an accusation against the others or a defense of themselves, the play becomes so many continuing individual histories, all of them entwined, each affecting the rest. Also, as the family members seek at once exoneration and forgiveness — they are forever admitting and denying their offenses in almost the same breath — the play develops, in piecemeal fashion, into a series of confessions. For all his early apostasy, the author could not root out the effect of his Catholic upbringing; the Tyrones' living room gradually takes on the character of a confessional.

In a foreword to "this play of old sorrow, written in tears and blood," O'Neill said that he created it with "deep pity and understanding and forgiveness for all the four haunted Tyrones." His own portrait, as might be expected, is the sketchiest and least satisfactory, not only because in 1912 his character was still evolving — he offered a less distinct model than the rest of the family — but because it is difficult to gain a perspective on one's self at any age, and still more difficult to overcome one's defenses against giving a full and honest picture. As Travis Bogard finds, "Although O'Neill has been at pains to show what the past has made his parents and brother, it is unclear what the past has made Edmund." Clues to his personality are few. Jamie says of his brother, "His quietness fools people into thinking they can do what they like with him. But he's stubborn as hell inside." Later, Edmund admits to his father: "I have tried to make allowances for myself when I remember all the rotten stuff I've pulled!" We are told that he had been to sea, that he had sunk into the lower depths of Buenos Aires and New York, that he had once attempted suicide, yet he remains, in Bogard's words, "a strangely neutral figure," more sinned against, by all the rest of the family, than sinning.

Missing from the author's fictional counterpart are the inner darkness and tumult that drove him to become America's foremost playwright, the vein of egocentricity, if not ruthlessness, that led him to abandon his first wife and child (the play never mentions that he had been married); and despite the references to his seafaring past, it is difficult to picture Edmund Tyrone in the saloons and whorehouses of the water front, at one with the dregs of society. By comparison with his treatment of the other Tyrones, the author let himself off rather lightly.

Jamie on the other hand is graphically shown in both his destructive and self-destructive aspects, a living likeness that fairly explodes with passion in the harrowing fourth-act confession as he reveals that along with loving Edmund (read Eugene) he has always hated him too, since it was his birth that "started Mama on dope." Jamie, who feels that a part of himself has long been "dead," warns Edmund to be wary of him because "I'll do my damnedest to make you fail. Can't help it. I hate myself. Got to take revenge. On everyone else. Especially you. . . . The dead part of me hopes you won't get well. Maybe he's even glad the game has got Mama again! He wants company, he doesn't want to be the only corpse around the house!"

The parents' portraits are still richer, more complex, but in spite of the playwright son's objective of depicting them both with understanding and compassion, he was not equally successful. Tyrone, though shown full measure in his faults and weaknesses, finally appears sympathetic, but Mary, as Kenneth Tynan says, is "a subtler case. On the surface a pathetic victim, she is at heart an emotional vampire, as dextrous at reopening old wounds as she is at inflicting new ones." The difference between the parents' images develops from the fact that O'Neill eventually "forgave" his father but never, no matter how hard he tried or what he may have thought, his mother.

His approach to James Tyrone repeats a pattern discernible in other of his dramas — that is, a father, after appearing in an unfavorable light, is endowed with redeeming features or displayed from an angle that arouses our respect, if not our liking. As the most striking instance in O'Neill's early works, the miserly old gnome of The Rope proves, in an O. Henry kind of twist, to be lovingly disposed toward his prodigal son. (The one-acter was written in a period when Eugene, after years of attacking his father as tightfisted, began to warm toward him.) Ephraim Cabot is another example. If the old farmer is hard on his sons, he demands still more of himself, he has epic size; eventually we empathize more with him than with the young lovers who have cuckolded him. There is, finally, Ezra Mannon, the formidable head of the clan in Mourning Becomes Electra; from his wife's description of him, she sounds justified in fearing and hating him, but he returns from the war a different man, vulnerable, eager for love, only to be murdered by his adulterous wife.

During most of Long Day's Journey James Tyrone seems chiefly to blame for his family's unhappy course; yet, while no evident attempt is made by the author to scant his failings, he gradually emerges more victim than culprit. In a number of respects he appears even admirable. As one critic sums up, his portrait, though showing all his warts and wrinkles, also conveys the "enduring warmth of the lonely, disappointed, aging but still passionate man; his vital lifelong love for the beauty of the spoken word; the generosity of spirit which enables him to appreciate the novel poetry of Baudelaire whom he hates as well as the familiar greatness of Shakespeare whom he loves; the disciplined professional self-respect which has kept him from missing a performance in almost forty years of heavy drinking, and the self-disciplining human loyalty which has kept him from unfaithfulness through over thirty years of an often interrupted and frustrating marriage."

Some of the bitterest words in the play are hurled at Tyrone by Edmund, after the latter learns that his father wants to send him to a tubercular sanitorium for the poor. "This last stunt of yours," Edmund says, "is too much! It makes me want to puke! Not because of the rotten way you're treating me. To hell with that! I've treated you rottenly, in my way, more than once. But to think when it's a question of your son having consumption, you can show yourself up before the whole town as such a stinking old tightwad! . . . (*Bursting with rage*) And don't think I'll let you get away with it! I won't go to any damned state farm just to save you a few lousy dollars to buy more bum property with! You stinking old miser!"

Nevertheless, a deep affection between them becomes evident, particularly after Tyrone, who grew up in the meanest poverty and has been haunted all his life by a fear of the poorhouse, concedes his parsimoniousness. "Yes," he says, "maybe life overdid the lesson for me, and made a dollar worth too much."

Mary Tyrone, in contrast, blames everyone except herself for her drug addiction. No matter how tactful or loving their approach, her husband and sons find it impossible to hearten her to resist her "curse," for at the first cautionary word she collapses or else turns on them vengefully and says it "would serve all of you right" if she did backslide.

While her agony over her addiction is unmistakable, her harping on how happy she had been in her father's home and at convent school, her stubborn insistence that her ill son, who craves her solicitude, has only "a summer cold," her constant airing of grievances against the others, like one telling her beads, all tend to limit one's sympathy for her. There is in her a largeness of suffering but no enlarging of character from what she has endured. She is too concerned with herself to have much concern to spare for the misfortunes and sorrows of the others. From the start she talks of her bad eyes and during the play repeatedly seeks her glasses, without ever finding them. Her poor eyesight is symbolic, as becomes obvious near the end when she wanders about, fathoms deep in morphine, while Jamie recites from Swinburne's "A Leave-taking":

> *Let us go hence, go hence; she will not see.*
> *Sing all once more together; surely she,*
> *She too, remembering days and words that were,*
> *Will turn a little toward us, sighing; but we,*
> *We are hence, we are gone, as though we had not been there.*
> *Nay, and though all men seeing had pity on me,*
> *She would not see.*

In the end, then, the family's tragic history appears to have developed less from James Tyrone's strain of penuriousness and other flaws than from Mary Tyrone's abiding immaturity, her inability to face the realities of life and fulfill her obligations as wife and mother.

Initially O'Neill was reluctant to share *Long Day's Journey Into Night* with anyone except Carlotta. Recalling that she typed the first two drafts, Carlotta has said that the play "upset me so I wept most of the time." Saxe Commins, who retyped the play from her make-do copies when he visited Tao House in 1942, was among the few who had the privilege of reading it during the author's lifetime. Ordinarily Dorothy Commins scrupulously refrained from questioning her husband about confidential matters in his work, but she could not help being curious when he returned from the Coast with word of a play that was not to be made public till twenty-five years after O'Neill's death. "It's about his family," Saxe replied. "It's so personal, such a revelation of his father and mother that it's heartbreaking. I can't say anything more."

The only other persons allowed to read *Long Day's Journey* during the next several years, so far as can be learned, were Eugene Jr., Russel Crouse, Dudley Nichols, and Sophus and Eline Winther. Crouse was given the script during the final hours of a visit at Tao House in 1943 and had no chance to discuss it with O'Neill, but the Winthers, houseguests that same year, recall seeing him afterward. "When we joined the O'Neills in the living room," Sophus recalls, "I remember being so moved I could scarcely talk. Gene said he felt he had made his peace with his family, also that he had often wept over the various scenes as he wrote them. The thing I remember most vividly is a comment he made about the last scene. He kept his eyes fixed on Mount Diablo and was obviously struggling to retain control of his emotions as he quoted the closing lines:

" 'That was in the winter of senior year. Then in the spring something happened to me. Yes, I remember. I fell in love with James Tyrone and was so happy for a time.'

"After a long pause, Gene said, 'I think that is the greatest scene I have ever written.' "

25

※

O'Neill's Tremor

THE latter months of 1940 found the O'Neills increasingly worried about Blemie; already half blind and deaf, he went lame from falling downstairs and had to be carried around like a baby. "Gene and I spoil him no end," Carlotta told Dorothy Commins, "but always say he is the only one of our children who has not disillusioned us — & always seemed conscious (& grateful) of our efforts to do all we could for his welfare & happiness!"

Blemie died on December 17, after a long spell of dry weather, and as he was being buried in a grove not far from the house, the rattling of the leaves sounded to Carlotta like "sad castanets." Scarcely had the O'Neills returned indoors when a thunderstorm broke, the first rain in months, giving them the feeling that nature was mourning with them. To relieve his feelings that day, Eugene wrote "The Last Will and Testament of Silverdene Emblem O'Neill," a charming piece that contains echoes of Whitman's "Song of Myself" (O'Neill had been rereading the poet earlier this year). In his "Song" Whitman says:

> *I think I could turn and live with animals, they are so*
> *placid and self-contain'd;*
> *I stand and look at them long and long,*
> *They do not sweat and whine about their condition,*
> *They do not lie awake in the dark and weep for their sins,*
> *They do not make me sick discussing their duty to God:*
> *Not one is dissatisfied, not one is demented with the mania*
> *of owning things.*
> *Not one kneels to another, nor to his kind that lived thousands*
> *of years ago,*
> *Not one is respectable or unhappy over the whole earth.*

In the "Will" O'Neill wrote under Blemie's name: "I have little in the way of material things to leave. Dogs are wiser than men. They do not set great store upon things. They do not waste their days hoarding property. They do not ruin their sleep worrying about how to keep the objects they have, and to obtain the objects they have not. There is nothing of value I have to bequeath except my love and my faith . . . if I should list all those who have loved me it would force my Master to write a book. Perhaps it is vain of me to boast when I am so near death, which returns all beasts and vanities to dust, but I have always been an extremely lovable dog.

"I ask my Master and Mistress to remember me always, but not to grieve for me too long. . . . It is painful for me to think that even in death I should cause them pain. Let them remember that while no dog has ever had a happier life (and this I owe to their love and care for me) now that I have grown blind and deaf and lame . . . my pride has sunk to a sick, bewildered humiliation. I feel life is taunting me with having over-lingered my welcome. It is time I said good-bye, before I become too sick a burden on myself and on those who love me. It will be sorrow to leave them, but not sorrow to die. Dogs do not fear death as men do. We accept it as part of life, not as something alien and terrible which destroys life. What may come after death, who knows? I would like to believe with those of my fellow Dalmatians who are devout Mohammedans, that there is a Paradise where one is always young and full-bladdered; where all the day one dillies and dallies with an amorous multitude of houris. . . .

"I am afraid this is too much for even such a good dog as I am to expect. But peace, at least, is certain. Peace and long rest for weary old heart and head and limbs, an eternal sleep in the earth I have loved so well. Perhaps, after all, this is best."

After O'Neill gave Carlotta the "Will," he did not mention Blemie for months, but often, as they sat before the fireplace, she caught him glancing first at her feet, then at his own, where the Dalmatian used to divide his time. Often, too, Eugene walked up to the grave, which had a marble headstone inscribed, "Sleep in Peace, Faithful Friend," and would stand there a long time.

He was in poor health this winter, the worst since his hospitalization in 1936–1937. While revising *Long Day's Journey* he suffered from insomnia and "nervous exhaustion"; stricken just before Christmas with a bronchial cold, he rarely left his bed for over two weeks, and during the first months of 1941 he scarcely recovered from one ailment before he was afflicted by another, none of them severe but all debilitating. His uncertain health was almost as great a strain on Carlotta; of an anxious personality and zealously devoted to his welfare, she seemed to take his illnesses as a reflection on her care. Tireless in fending off anyone and anything she thought might affect him adversely, not always tactful in guarding his privacy, she inspired the suspicion that she overprotected him and made him feel more delicate than he was. However, O'Neill himself, as he wrote Macgowan on March 15, realized that if he were to retain some measure of well-being, he would have to follow "a careful routine" for the rest of his life. His blood pressure was often so low that he had hardly any energy, and the slightest untoward incident could bring on a crisis of nerves, but what chiefly worried him was the tremor of his hands, which was becoming more pronounced.

His improved health toward the end of the winter did little to raise his spirits, for he shared the universal apprehension that spring would see an all-out attempt by Hitler's hordes to invade England. Yet, for all his concern, he refused to support a petition to President de Valera to bring the Irish Free State into the war. "I have fought it out with myself," he told the sponsors of the plea, "and I find I cannot sign it. My final conviction is that we Irish-Americans owe it to the Irish people not to attempt to influence their decision by any means whatsoever. It is they who will be massacred by German bombers if they commit this act of war."

Lawrence Langner and his wife, passing through the San Francisco area this spring, dined at Tao House and found their host thinner than ever, adamant against releasing any script till after the war, and pessimistic about the Broadway theater, the Guild included. Increasingly nostalgic, he now took an exalted view of the Provincetown Players. Writing to Macgowan shortly before the Langners' visit, he said that the Provincetown was a theater "in which I knew I belonged. Now I feel out of the theater." He "dreaded" production because it "will be done by people who have really only one standard left, that of Broadway success." The fact that he would have "the final say on everything," the fact that he liked "these people personally" was "no consolation," for "the big fact" was that the production would be made "on a plane, and in an atmosphere, to which neither I nor my work belong in spirit." It seemed to him that the "idea of an Art Theater is more remote now than way back in the first decade of this century, before the Washington Square Players or the PP were ever dreamed of."

Despite his discouragement over the theater and depression from the war, regardless of periods of ill-health, his creative imagination during much of 1941 was at its most fertile. He wrote detailed outlines for six new projects, all of which he thought would make fine plays. One, the most ambitious, was for a series of seven short plays, virtually monologues, ranging from 1910 to 1928, with the overall title of "By Way of Obit" and separate titles for each. In each, he informed Nathan, the main character was to talk about someone recently deceased to "a person who does little but listen. Via this monologue you get a complete picture of the person who has died — his or her whole life story — but just as complete a picture of the life and character of the narrator. And you also get by another means — a use of stage directions, mostly — an insight into the whole life of the person who does little but listen."

Some of the characters, both the quick and the dead, were to be based on actual persons O'Neill had known — barflies, gamblers, chambermaids, petty racketeers, streetwalkers — and all the playlets were to be called after the name or nickname of the deceased. Unfortunately, *Hughie,* a playlet he composed this spring, was the only one of the series he would ever write.

Containing but two characters, Erie Smith and a hotel desk clerk who rarely says a word, and running slightly under an hour, *Hughie* is a microcosm that manages to suggest the entire Broadway macrocosm of cheap gamblers, dime crapshooters, two-dollar whores and sleazy hangers-on. It is a little gem. In a way, since it evokes so much from sparse materials, *Hughie* indicates even more clearly than *Long Day's Journey* and *The Iceman* that O'Neill, immersed in memories at his mountainside retreat, had by now mastered his art.

The reticent figure in *Hughie,* according to the playwright, "is an essence of all the night clerks I've known in bum hotels. . . . 'Erie' is a type of Broadway sport I and my brother used to know by the dozen in far-off days. I didn't know many at the time the play is laid, 1928, but they never change. Only their lingo does. As for 'Erie's' slang, I've tried, generally speaking, to stick to the type's enduring lingo, and not use stuff current only in 1928 but soon discarded. Being too meticulously timely is not worth the trouble and defeats its purpose, anyway."

Set in the lobby of a shabby hotel in the Times Square area, the playlet develops a subtle variation on the *Iceman* theme of pipe dreams. Erie Smith, short and stout, with an uncertain swagger, is a small-time horse-player hustling a marginal existence. Although he has few if any illusions about himself, he used to pretend to Hughie, the former night clerk, that he was a big sport — a hundred-buck bettor and a ladies' man with "dolls" from the Follies — because poor, gray-faced Hughie, hungry to be in touch with a glamorous, exciting world, believed Erie's stories. "Oh, I was wise I was kiddin' myself," Erie says. "But what the hell, Hughie loved it, and it didn't cost nobody nothin', and if every guy along Broadway who kids himself was to drop dead there wouldn't be nobody left. Ain't it the truth, Charlie?" Now Hughie is dead and the fat little man desolate, not only because he hasn't had a winner since his pal fell sick but because the other's credulity had been vital to Erie: in Hughie's eyes he had been everything he had once dreamed.

All this background history comes out easily, economically, atmospherically in Broadway argot as Erie Smith strives to reach the new night clerk, Charlie Hughes, who somewhat resembles his predecessor. Charlie, however, is sunk in apathy. After failing with various gambits to arouse the clerk's interest, Erie is about to retreat upstairs to his dreary cubbyhole when the clerk, finally displaying a spark of animation, asks whether he knows big-time gambler Arnold Rothstein. Lost in his own thoughts, Erie almost misses the opening, but just in time he snaps alert and starts feeding Charlie the kind of tales that will turn him into another "Hughie." Contact and communication have been established between the two; they have created an oasis in the desert of their days.

Offhand, it seems rather strange that O'Neill set *Hughie* as late as 1928, since he had been familiar with its demi-underworld of gamblers, con men and other night people a decade or two earlier; yet his dating of the play has a certain logic, stemming from the way he saw New York: he felt that the city had lost some of its onetime human quality and warmth. His critical view of its evolving personality is evident in the time scheme of *All God's Chillun*. At the start of that play, early in the century, the background sounds are pleasant — laughter in the streets, the lazy clip-clop of horsecars, singing in both the black and white neighborhoods; with the passing years, though, the city projects an increasingly hostile image. Similarly, the latter-day New York of *Hughie* seems hazardous and menacing; virtually a third character in the story, the City, though unseen, constantly intrudes as the wail of an ambulance, a police car, a fire engine.

While eminently actable, *Hughie*, its author said, was designed "more to be read than staged," since the dialogue does not tell the whole story; moreover, some of its most effective writing is in the stage directions and in Charlie's unvoiced thoughts. Here, for example, is the silent clerk at one point: "His mind has hopped an ambulance clanging down Sixth [Avenue], and is asking without curiousity: 'Will he die, Doctor, or isn't he lucky?'"

Another time, as Erie Smith rattles on: "But the Clerk's mind has rushed out to follow the siren wail of a fire engine. . . . [He] asks a fireman with disinterested eagerness: 'Where's the fire? Is it a real good one this time? . . . Will it be big enough . . . I mean, big enough to burn down the whole damn city?' 'Sorry, Brother, but there's no chance. Too much stone and steel. There'd always be something left.' 'Yes, I guess you're right . . . I wasn't really hoping, anyway. It really doesn't matter to me.' "

Actually, O'Neill doubted *Hughie*'s theatrical viability only if it were staged conventionally. Anticipating the mixed-media theater of later decades, the visionary playwright told Carlotta that ideally the playlet should be produced with a sound track for the interior monologues and stage directions that would accompany the live dialogue, in addition to a background film of the city.

Besides making outlines for the six projects that included "By Way of Obit," starting a full-length work entitled "The Thirteenth Apostle," and writing *Hughie*, O'Neill during the first half of 1941 jotted down fresh ideas for the Cycle, which intermittently occupied his thoughts. Concluding that neither "Greed of the Meek" nor "And Give Me Death" could be reduced to practicable length, he decided to expand the two plays into four and begin the series in the 1750s during the time of the French and Indian War. On May 21 he noted in his diary that he had not "told anyone yet of expansion of idea to 11 plays — seems too ridiculous . . . will never live to do it — but what price anything but a dream these days!" He later revised parts of the two plays in accordance with his enlarged scheme, but failing health, as well as depression over world affairs, prevented him from ever achieving his "dream." Eventually he destroyed the drafts and outlines of the projected first four plays, along with other material of the series.

The only available account of how the eleven-play narrative was supposed to begin is contained in a *New Yorker* profile of O'Neill, published in 1948, by Hamilton Basso. Summarizing what the playwright had told him, Basso wrote that the hero of the opening play was "an Irishman who has joined the British Army to escape the slavery of agricultural life in Ireland. It is his idea to desert as soon as he gets to America and to go into the wilderness, where, liberated from the economic and social bondage of the Old World, he can live as a truly free man. Once in this country, he strikes out for the wilderness. On his journey, wanting food and shelter, he stops at a frontier farm. It is only a clearing in a forest, but it is nonetheless the most fertile and promising soil he has ever seen. The farm is run by a young widow, who badly needs a man around the place, and who, as O'Neill saw it, also badly needs a man. The Irishman, caught between his dream of freedom and his hunger for land, and attracted by the woman's physical allure, finally abandons his dream and settles for the land. . . . According to O'Neill's scheme, the seed of greed that had thus been planted was to grow and flower throughout the Cycle."

Basso's account contradicts the impression given in *More Stately Mansions* that the Irish first become part of the Cycle family through Sara Melody's marriage to Simon Harford. In Basso's unpublished notes for the profile, he says: "O'Neill started to tell me the story of his Cycle . . . and what happened to it, but his talk was so broken and confused I couldn't follow . . . I have to get this in detail." Possibly he never did get the story straight, and the runaway soldier in the wilderness, the founding father of the acquisitive clan, was English or Welsh, something other than Irish.

From the start of the O'Neills' residence in California, Carlotta had firmly resisted attempts by cousins, aunts, schoolmates and other old friends to renew their ties with her, because she was concerned not only about safeguarding her husband's privacy but with preventing his meeting persons familiar with her early history. While she could not entirely shut out her mother, daughter and son-in-law, she brought them together with Eugene as little as possible. During her first years at Tao House she had seemed generally content, but gradually, as at Sea Island, the isolation, cares and monotony of her life began to weigh more and more heavily on her. When the alumnae of her convent school, St. Gertrude's Academy at Rio Vista, held a reunion in San Francisco in 1940, she declined to attend with the excuse that she was too busy running a household and serving as her husband's secretary; she was prominently present, however, among the gathering of over a hundred women at the annual luncheon in 1941. Already conspicuous by her attire, a long-outmoded though becoming Paris outfit, she excited further comment when she sank to her knees before an elderly nun, one of her former teachers, and gazed up at her adoringly.

Of all her old schoolmates the only one she welcomed back into her life was Mrs. Charles B. Caldwell, plump, cheerful, tolerant of human weaknesses, the wife of a noted San Francisco physician. Starved by now for feminine companionship, Carlotta phoned Myrtle Caldwell the day after the reunion and invited her, along with her husband and nineteen-year-old daughter Jane, to dinner. Relieved and delighted that Eugene also liked the Caldwells, particularly mother and daughter, Carlotta proceeded to shower the two with gifts, compliments and worldly advice, and to make a confidante of Myrtle. For the next few years, till the O'Neills returned East, they would see more of the Caldwell women than of anyone else.

A dark-eyed, strikingly pretty girl, Jane Caldwell was disquieted on first meeting the famous dramatist, for after the introductions, as they all sat around, he gazed at her a long time without a word. "Not rudely," she recalls, "but thoughtfully, for about ten minutes, as if he was looking into my soul. Later, after we became friends, he said he always did this the first time on meeting someone who interested him. He'd study them and think about them for a while, and then he felt he knew what they were like."

During one of Myrtle and Jane's early visits, Carlotta, holding forth about Eugene and herself, said she would be happy with him even if they "lived in a tent." Feeling bold, Jane interjected, "What woman wouldn't?" at which O'Neill blushed. His first gift to her, a volume of his plays, was inscribed: "To Janie – from one about to order a tent! June '41."

This summer both Eugene Jr. and Oona were guests, at different times, at Tao House. Writing to George Jean Nathan, O'Neill said that his elder son was "a fine guy and I am extremely fond of him. Also proud. He works hard, keeps his enthusiasm about his job, and is steadily moving ahead at Yale."

O'Neill was again favorably impressed by his daughter, calling her "a most delightful and charming young lady." Carlotta, however, was not overly pleased to find that the sixteen-year-old girl, who had matured considerably and gained in self-assurance since her last visit, had ideas and a will of her own. Throughout Oona's visit Carlotta talked to her about the grave state of the world, the uncertainty of the future, and the advisability of her preparing to be self-supporting – this last subject being one she had harped on for years in her letters to both Oona and Shane. Without asking Oona what she would like to do, she repeatedly urged her to become a hospital nurse. The girl, who had begun to dream of a movie career, never mentioned her ambition, for she had heard Carlotta too often regarding "the evils of Hollywood." Piqued one day when her stepmother again urged nursing on her, Oona, looking her in the eye, said, "You're wonderful, Carlotta – you cope with Daddy, the household, the typing, everything. I could never do all that, or become a good nurse." Then, impulsively, she added, "My mind is made up. I am going to marry a rich man, a really rich man!"

Carlotta was shocked. "*Dear child, what* are you saying???!!! You can't be serious!!!" When Oona mischievously insisted she was, Carlotta lectured her at length. One COULDN'T think like that — what rich man? — WHERE? — in the future there would be *no* rich men, taxes were becoming ruinous. And she must warn Oona from personal experience that NOTHING was more miserable than marriage without love to a rich man. She had married one and lived with him in a horrible castle in Scotland and had all the servants and money in the world, and never been more MISERABLE!!! She finally turned her back on it, she gave it all up, in order to be *free* and *independent!*

While O'Neill brushed off Carlotta's apprehensions about his daughter, feeling that she was needlessly dramatizing, his younger son had him more and more concerned. The previous winter, shortly after Shane's twenty-first birthday, he and Marc Brandel, a young writer from Greenwich Village, had chauffeured someone to Mexico, where they struck out on their own. They spent most of their time in the cantinas drinking and at the movies, then finally, at the instance of Shane, who often talked about his father's gold-prospecting in Honduras when he was twenty-one, set off on a camping trip to Panama. "I definitely had the feeling," Brandel recalls, "that Shane's wanting to go out and see the world was part of his wanting to relive his father's life. He used to say, jokingly, 'Let's take a slow boat to China.'" The two young men did not get very far on their journey to Panama; after various mishaps, which forced Shane to raise fresh funds by wire, once from his father, another time from Agnes, the two returned home.

More recently, shortly before Oona's visit, O'Neill had been upset by a letter from Shane in which he expressed a desire to try acting in the movies. "You seem to have no realization," his father replied on April 18, "of what is going on in the world. You write as if these were normal times. . . . Don't you know the country will almost certainly be in the war soon? Don't you know that those who became twenty-one since the draft law passed will soon be included in the draft? Don't you know that if this country gets into the war, it will probably go on for years, and that no one can possibly predict what conditions will be like even a year from now?" The farther he stayed from any job connected with the movies or the theater, the letter continues, the better off he would be.

Any resentment O'Neill may have harbored, unknowingly, against Shane and Oona as his children by Agnes does not seem to have colored, as yet, his conduct toward them. If they occupied only minor roles in his life, it was not primarily because of his hostility toward their mother but because he was not cut out to be a father. As regards Agnes herself, he probably would have felt benevolent about her had she remarried early (he once confided to Myrtle Caldwell that Carlotta gave an undue picture of his former wife) but, as it was, her alimony had long been a major irritant and now, under new and stiffer tax laws, it was a still heavier burden on him. He estimated, in 1941, that taxes and alimony would take about sixty-five percent of his income. "You have no idea," he told a friend, "what non-deductible alimony on top of these taxes can do to you. For example, if I earn thirty thousand dollars, I really get only a thousand more than if I'd earned eighteen thousand dollars. So what's the use? It makes me more indifferent than ever about the production of new plays." Cutting expenses in line with their reduced income, the O'Neills discharged two outdoor men and the butler, leaving them with only Freeman, a cook and a gardener. Carlotta, who had always worked indoors and out, was now busier than ever with domestic chores, in addition to her secretarial duties.

Despite their reduced funds, O'Neill gave one hundred dollars to the Norwegian Refugee Fund, saying in an accompanying note on July 11: "I wish I could send more. I am honored to serve on your Committee to help Norwegian war sufferers."

Again this summer and fall he was unwell at times. "Not long after Lawrence and Armina were here," he informed Miss Helburn on July 29, "I faded out to a state where I could hardly swim – and that's pretty bad, because swimming comes easier for me than walking."

Since none of his new scripts was available, the Guild decided to revive several of his plays in popular-priced engagements and hoped to sign Lionel Barrymore for *Ah, Wilderness!*, Walter Huston in his original role and Tallulah Bankhead for *Desire Under the Elms*, and Charles Bickford for *The Hairy Ape*. O'Neill was delighted at the prospect, not alone for financial reasons; for years he had felt aggrieved that his plays vanished, seemingly forever, from the Broadway stage after their original productions, while in Europe works of merit were kept before the public in repertory or revived from time to time.

With a cast headed by Harry Carey of the films, rather than by Barrymore, *Ah, Wilderness!* opened at the Guild Theater on October 2, 1941, to generally fine notices. Though the reviewers agreed that Carey lacked George M. Cohan's authority and finesse, he was well praised, as were the other actors. More than one critic commented that the comedy appeared a stronger, better work than originally, and all said that the production, at a two-dollar top, was the best bargain on Broadway.

Gratified by the reviews, O'Neill took for granted that the revival would run at least several months, but, sparsely attended, it closed after twenty-nine performances and at the same time ended the Guild's plan to revive other of his works. The brief engagement convinced him that revivals had no chance on Broadway unless they offered "a lady star with a big following," and he also felt that theatergoers, rather than welcoming a bargain, "suspect they are going to be swindled!"

Pleased to hear from Elizabeth Shepley Sergeant after years of silence, O'Neill on October 20 gave her a rundown on his life and writings since he started work in 1935 on "A Tale of Possessors Self-Dispossessed." He reported that he had written four Cycle plays, three of which were double-length, and said of *Long Day's Journey* and *The Iceman:* "I love both these plays. They are, I know, as fine drama as I can ever write. In '41 so far, I've written scenarios for five non-Cycle plays [though he thought *Hughie* had "its own quality," he apparently regarded it as too minor to mention here], but I can't seem to decide which I want to write first. My health has been poor, too, and my mind distracted by world tragedy. But I've started one now and hope to go through with it. . . .

"So you see, as far as labor goes, counting the three double-length plays as six . . . I've written nine plays in seven years, illness or no illness. Not such a bad record of industriousness!"

The new drama he hoped "to go through with" was *A Moon for the Misbegotten,* which deals with his brother, again called James Tyrone, Jr., near the end of his life. Apparently Eugene had come to view *Long Day's Journey* as too severe on Jamie and an incomplete family portrait because it did not adequately convey Jamie's deep feeling for his mother, the only woman he ever loved, the "Cynara" to whom he had been "faithful" in his dissipated fashion. *The Misbegotten* was designed, in other words, as a kind of fifth act to the four-act *Long Day's Journey.*

Although O'Neill began the play rather tentatively, he became enthusiastic and worked well until the Japanese struck at Pearl Harbor on December 7. For the past two years, as the Germans spread death in Europe and rained death on the English, he had struggled against the feeling that the theater and his work were unimportant; now, as this country went to war, he lost almost all desire to write. "Gene is nervous, upset & in a terrible stew," Carlotta reported to Russel Crouse. "But — life will not be too easy for any person from now on. God help us all." While she and Freeman made blackout curtains, as the West Coast braced itself for possible aerial attack from the Japanese, O'Neill practiced shooting, in case he might be needed for civil defense, and by holding the revolver with both hands, to offset his tremor, succeeded in hitting the target.

In his Christmas greeting to Carlotta he said: " 'To hell with the torpedoes!' Love marches on!" His note on her birthday, December 27, read: "In this time of chaos, when all old dreams and hopes are blown to dust, there remains for me — as ever, but now so much more than ever! — only you! I love you, Darling."

After Pearl Harbor he had to "drag [his] mind through the rest" of *A Moon for the Misbegotten*, and late in January 1942 finished what he regarded as "way below par for even a first draft." Periodically in the next several years he was to work further on the four-act drama. While its central concern is Jamie's desperate state after the death of his mother, the play approaches the heart of its subject matter slowly and warily, as though the author had to force himself to come to grips with something intensely painful to him. Considering what is to follow, the play opens deceptively on a humorous, boisterous note and in fact for much of its length seems more O'Casey than O'Neill. Set in September 1923 on a farm in Connecticut — the locale is actually New London — the story involves Jamie Tyrone, who is drinking himself to death; Phil Hogan, a wily farmer with a gift for rhetoric and invective — he is closely based on John ("Dirty") Dolan, a onetime tenant of James O'Neill — and his daughter Josie, who is almost freakish in size.

Always loath to compromise his visions for the sake of convenient staging, as evidenced by his extra-long works and his demand for super-human laughter in *Lazarus*, O'Neill, with Josie Hogan, posed a formidable casting problem. Nearly six feet and weighing around one hundred and eighty pounds, Josie "is more powerful than any but an exceptionally strong man. . . . But there is no mannish quality about her. She is all woman." And, clearly, another instance of the author's obsession with Earth Mothers.

Like Jamie, she, figuratively, wears a mask: where he, behind a facade of cynical banter, is a despairing child in search of a mother, she boasts of being shameless and pretends to have slept with nearly all the men of the community but actually is a virgin. The confrontation between the two is among the most moving scenes in all O'Neill. Perceptive enough to see and appreciate the true Josie, Jamie seeks her out. In turn Josie, who has long loved him and seen through *his* masquerade, tries to help him, hoping that her devotion and strength can make a new life for them both. After guardedly circling one another, they at last drop their pretenses, but she learns it is too late. He has come to her not for love but for confession, forgiveness, absolution for an outrage that profanes his memories of his mother. Borrowing from the life of Jamie O'Neill, the play tells how Jamie Tyrone, while on a train bearing his mother's body back East for burial, slept his way across the country with "a blonde pig who looked more like a whore than twenty-five whores. . . . It was as if I wanted revenge — because I'd been left alone — because I knew I was lost."

Sitting before the Hogans' ramshackle farmhouse, he tears the confession out of himself, then falls asleep, nestled like a child at Josie's great breast, and awakens at dawn feeling "sort of at peace with myself . . . as if all my sins had been forgiven."

The final words, directed toward his departing figure, are Josie's: "May you have your wish and die in your sleep soon, Jim, darling. May you rest forever in forgiveness and peace." But of course it was actually O'Neill speaking through the farm girl, pronouncing benediction over a ghost that had haunted him ever since his brother's death.

Although too long for the story it tells, dawdling chiefly in the first half, *A Moon for the Misbegotten* is, nevertheless, one of the author's superior achievements, original, vital, richly Irish in its mixture of lusty humor and bone-deep sadness. Toward the end, as the debauched alcoholic and the tremulous giantess struggle to make contact in the moonlight, the drama builds to an overwhelming climax of agonized compassion; like *Long Day's Journey*, it was written in the author's "tears and blood."

Carlotta practically never ventured to question her husband's writings, yet she had conceived such a violent dislike of his brother from all she had heard about him that she protested when Eugene decided to write *The Misbegotten* and include the episode on the train. "I told him," she later said, "it's too unpleasant, too sordid. How would a mother feel seeing this play and thinking of how her own son might act after her death? But, no, his mind was made up, he was stubborn; he felt he had to complete the picture of his brother."

Reliving the past, as during his composition of *Long Day's Journey*, O'Neill was again in an overwrought state while writing *The Misbegotten* and often wept over its scenes. One night, after some lovemaking with Carlotta, he suddenly leaped off her bed, his eyes blazing, and, before dashing out, yelled, "You goddam whore!"

"I sat there on the bed, my mind numb," Carlotta has said. "I wondered if he was going to come back and kill me. A few minutes later I heard a noise in his room. I went in and there he was on the floor, stretched out, face down, crying. I knelt down beside him. 'Forgive me, forgive me, I didn't mean it, I can't help myself,' he said. And then he went on to tell me that Jamie had introduced him to sex before he was ready for it, at a whorehouse, and ever since then he'd never been able to rid himself of a dirty feeling about sex, even with someone he loved, a feeling that all women were whores.

"Gene," she added reflectively, "was a peculiar mixture. He was soft-spoken, he had a smile like a child of five. You would forgive him anything. But then he would turn around and, like that . . . I don't think the word 'savage' exaggerates what he was like in those moods. . . . He was very much of a sadist at times, but when his mood changed, he suffered terribly from guilt if he had hurt anyone that he liked. And his guilt, to watch his guilt, hurt me more than when he was a sadist. I couldn't stand to see my child so miserable."

In February 1942, shortly after finishing the first draft of *The Misbegotten*, he pressed his doctor for a diagnosis of the tremor of the hands that had intermittently afflicted him ever since childhood and which was now growing worse. Just as he had dreaded, he was told that he had Parkinson's disease. "You should have seen his eyes afterward," Carlotta mourned to Myrtle Caldwell on the seventeenth. "I thought I'd die. And he'd look at me and smile that sweet old smile with his eyes looking hurt and alone!"

His tremor varied from one day to the next, and at times, partly by dint of sheer determination, he managed to accomplish a good day's writing; but too often, dropping him into despair, his hands trembled so that he could not hold a pencil. Unfortunately, medications that alleviated the condition of some Parkinson's victims had on him only an adverse effect. Since his mother's hands and shoulders had trembled slightly, he believed that he had inherited from her a predisposition for his ailment.

Not long after the diagnosis of Parkinson's, O'Neill was thrown into another depression when Oona was chosen "Debutante No. 1" of the year at a glamorous New York night spot and widely written up in the press. Actually, for all the frivolity of the event and, in view of the war, its questionable taste, Oona came out looking rather well. To a reporter's query as to whether she was "lace-curtain or shanty Irish," she said, "I'm shanty Irish and proud of it." Asked for her view on world conditions, she replied, "Wouldn't it be silly for me, sitting here in the Stork Club, to comment on that?" She felt "a bit timid," she confessed, about her father's probable reaction to her publicity.

His reaction was extreme. "I have never seen Gene," Carlotta said, "so coldly bitter about anything." Though he shortly became loath even to mention her name, he unburdened himself on April 24, in the first rush of his anger, to Robert Sisk: "I did not congratulate the young lady. . . . Somehow, it didn't strike me as quite the correct kind of success to rejoice about in the year 1942 — or any other year. I would rather have one Red Cross Nurse or airplane factory worker for a daughter than fifty million glamour girls — to put it mildly. . . . As my father often used to remark with feeling, 'God deliver me from my children!' At that I'm getting a better break than he did until his very last days. One of mine is doing a grand job of himself on his own merits, and I'm immensely proud of him."

He and Carlotta suspected that Agnes was pushing Oona into the spotlight and exploiting his name for her own and their daughter's benefit. In reality the Stork Club publicists were behind Oona's emergence as a celebrity; they began to promote her on learning of her parentage, and she went along with their campaign in hopes it would help her to a theatrical career. Despite appearances at the time, she was basically shy, essentially serious, as her father might have recognized; but since she was on his conscience, he was eager to find her unworthy and shut her out of his life. He had to establish himself as the injured party, hence his outrage over the lighthearted pursuits of a girl still not seventeen.

Unknown to O'Neill, Carlotta during this period had her own cause to be agitated. The previous winter James Speyer had died, leaving a net estate of over two millions, and now his heirs, chiefly nephews and nieces, threatened court action to eliminate the secret trust fund that gave Carlotta her lifetime annuity. In a panic that Eugene would learn the true source of her funds, she at first feared to tell a soul, outside of her attorneys in New York, about her precarious situation, but finally, desperate for comfort, she confided in Myrtle Caldwell. The prospect of an unsavory court action and newspaper notoriety loomed nightmarishly over Carlotta for months, till the heirs decided against a suit that, unavoidably, would have tarnished the old banker's name. A few more years were to pass before O'Neill learned, somehow, that Speyer had been his wife's benefactor and onetime lover.

Increasingly squeezed by taxes, alimony, and a reduced income — after a drop in the stock market the O'Neills estimated that on paper they had lost over nineteen thousand dollars in three months — the playwright thought of seeking a cut in his payments to Agnes. He abandoned the idea, though, after learning that he would have to apply for relief to the Reno courts. It would cost "a lot in both dough and bum publicity," he complained to Robert Sisk. "Reno is strictly a female racket." Probably his resentment of the alimony, which supported Oona along with her mother, served to exacerbate his feeling against the girl.

This spring he had an infection from an abscessed wisdom tooth that spread to various parts of his body and kept him ill for nearly a month with fever, chills and aches. Shortly after recovering from the infection, his back began ailing him and he was obliged to wear "a belt-corset affair" with a wide steel plate that made his movements difficult. "He nearly went crazy the first few days," Carlotta said, "getting up and down."

From a number of causes — the war, Oona's publicity, his Parkinson's and other ailments — the playwright sank, both mentally and physically, to a nadir. Trying to relieve his feelings by verbalizing them, O'Neill, who at one time had dreamed of becoming another Swinburne or Baudelaire, wrote several poems. Following is one:

So am I isolate,
Inviolate,
Untouchable,
Bitterest of all, ungivable,
Unable to bestow,
Break from my solitude
A lonely gift,
Myself.

Oh, I have tried to scream!
Give pain a voice!
Make it a street singer
Acting a pantomime of tragic song . . .

But something was born wrong.
The voice strains toward a sob.
Begins and ends in silence . . .

All this,
As I have said before,
Happens where silence is;
Where I,
A quiet man,
In love with quiet,
Live quietly
Among the visions of my drowned,
Deep in my silent sea.

Another poem, in its entirety:

> *Through indolence,*
> *Irony,*
> *Helplessness, too, perhaps,*
> *He let the legends go,*
> *The lying legends grow;*
> *Then watched the mirror darken,*
> *Indolently,*
> *Ironically,*
> *Helplessly, too, perhaps*
> *Until one final day*
> *Only a ghost remained*
> *To haunt its shallow depths —*
> *Himself,*
> *Bewildered apparition,*
> *Seeking a lost identity.*

Carlotta also was unwell this year. Taped up and forced to sleep on boards for relief, she suffered from an arthritic spine at a time when she could least afford to be indisposed, for Freeman, after ten years in the O'Neills' employ, was shortly to enter the armed forces. "You can imagine what that will do to our household," Eugene wrote on May 21 to Nathan. "We depend on him so much as a man of all work, who is more like a member of the family than a servant, who can be absolutely trusted and is able to take care of almost any job that comes up. When you live in the country this means a lot. It is practically impossible to hire anyone now to do anything. They are all in ship yards or in the service. . . . And we couldn't afford to hire more help, if we could get them."

After Freeman enlisted in the marines this summer, Carlotta's only regular help were a cook and a gardener; she now had to do all the household chores, excepting the preparation of meals, in addition to attending to her husband. The couple felt "marooned" on their mountainside, since O'Neill, because of his tremor, could no longer drive and Carlotta had never learned. Improvising as best they could, they arranged for the hardware man in Danville to drive Eugene to his semimonthly "imperative treatments" for a prostate condition by a urologist in Oakland; Carlotta made her shopping trips to Danville in the gardener's truck; and, since she had scarcely any time for her husband's typing, her daughter Cynthia was hired to take over the bulk of her secretarial work.

The Strams needed Cynthia's salary because Roy, crippled from rheumatic fever, was unable to work.

Theresa Helburn, stubbornly hoping that O'Neill might relent, wrote to him that the Broadway theater was spiritually poorer without his works and urged him to release one or more of his new scripts. Rejecting her plea, he replied that at a later time "there will again be an audience able to feel the inner meaning of plays dealing with the everlasting mystery and irony and tragedy of men's lives and dreams. . . . People are too damned preoccupied with the tragedy of war now – as they should be – to want to face such plays."

His health had so deteriorated, he reported, that he had had "to give up the physical work around the grounds – I used to take care of quite a lot – because it brings on spells of complete exhaustion when I feel like a wet anemic fly crawling up a cold windowpane."

Practically the only bright moments in the O'Neills' life were sparked by Myrtle Caldwell and her daughter Jane, who visited Tao House more often than was convenient for them, in response to importunate invitations. Outgoing, uncomplicated, Myrtle was a steadying influence, if only momentarily, on the couple, while Jane, attractive, charming, was another cheerful presence in a house the Caldwells found oppressively quiet. Like Eugene, Myrtle was fond of the old-time songs, knew many of the lyrics, and the two, in what they agreed were "cracked voices," would vocalize as Rosie thumped out a melody. While Carlotta disapproved of his vagabond period and if possible would have censored his memories, Myrtle enjoyed his ribald tales of Buenos Aires and Jimmy the Priest's. Shortly before one of her visits, Washington asked O'Neill to speak on the radio to the soldiers overseas, a request he turned down because of his tremor and general nervous state. In telling Myrtle about it, he said, "I could never talk in a room with strangers about. But if you must know what I would've said, I'd have recommended that the government open whorehouses for the GIs at five cents a lay."

Jane Caldwell, who thought him "the kindest human being I've ever known," recalls being at the swimming pool "when a large insect crawled on him. I wanted him to kill it – I have a thing about bugs – but instead he gently removed it."

Despite his tremor and periods of fading out, as well as his feeling that the war made everything else seem trivial ("The world drama you hear over the radio every day, or read in the papers, is the one important drama of the moment"), he managed to revise *A Touch of the Poet*. He also worked on "The Last Conquest" (originally entitled "The Thirteenth Apostle"), which he had begun the year before, a "symbolic fantasy of the future" envisioned in a prologue and eight scenes, but he was never to complete it. The projected play, he informed Nathan, was "not the usual obvious stuff either in theme or technique, but something which hits at what is behind all this chaos, the realistic attitude which has lost the knowledge of the opposites of Good and Evil within Man and their struggles for possession of Man's soul. I know you regard the word 'soul' with skepticism, but I don't mean it in any special orthodox religious sense. Perhaps if I said Man's spirit it would be as close, but 'spirit' is another word that has been worn thin and meaningless by stupid misuse. Anyway, I like the idea for this play, which could be subtitled 'An Outmoded Prophetic Fantasy for the Blind and the Deaf.' "

"In many ways," he said another time, "it could better be done as a picture than as a stage play, that is, if Hollywood could ever treat a subject of depth and integrity with depth and integrity — which, of course, is a fantastically impossible notion."

According to actor E. G. Marshall, to whom O'Neill told the story of "The Last Conquest" a few years later, one of the final scenes finds a young man and an old one in a whirlpool, in mortal danger, and the junior pushes the other to safety before he himself is pulled under and drowned. (The episode seems a bit reminiscent of the escape from the Château d'If in *Monte Cristo*.) "At this," Marshall says, "the devil, who has come back to earth, gives up, defeated, for the young man's sacrifice proves that there is some good in man, that he is not totally corruptible." Jane Caldwell, who read the unfinished manuscript, which the author destroyed later, says that the devil, "a particularly evil devil, was the Thirteenth Apostle. He was in control of the world, or the most power-ful figure — I'm not sure which now — and the forces of good, repre-sented by the other Apostles, are being mobilized against him. The play, as I remember, was supposed to end with the ringing of church bells all over the world to signal the devil's defeat."

Reasonably confident that this country and its allies would win the war, O'Neill was already apprehensive about its aftermath. "My own prediction is for the same kind of peace treaty which has followed all wars," he wrote to Nathan on October 24, 1942, "because the same greedy politicians and monkey diplomats will make it. These boys' trade is never to learn anything. . . . I cannot understand how anyone who has read history can waste time in sentimental wishful thinking about the next peace." He ended: "Yours, Comrade, for any old kind of post-war revolution."

Months passed before he had his first word, in November, from Oona since her Stork Club publicity. During the interval she had been accepted at Vassar (but had decided against college), had been offered screen tests and modeling jobs, and had made her stage debut, fleetingly, in a summer stock production of *Pal Joey* in New Jersey. Vivienne Segal, the star of the musical, recalls her as "a delightful, friendly child. I remember she insisted on going barefoot. She was like some wild Irish sprite. We all loved her."

Voicing a desire to see him and explain that some of the newspaper and magazine stories had been foisted on her against her will, Oona wrote to her father while en route to California by train, in company with her friend Carol Marcus. Also seventeen, Carol was bound for Sacramento to see her fiancé — writer William Saroyan, who had recently been inducted into the army. Carol's mother, loath for the girl to go alone, had consented to the trip on condition that Oona, whom she regarded as more mature, would accompany her as "chaperone." In the letter to her father Oona had given the name of the Sacramento hotel where she was to stay.

Rejecting her attempt at a reconciliation, O'Neill replied on November 19 that she should have written first and explained what her "present plans and ambitions are in these war torn days. Then I could tell you if I wanted to see you. As it is, all I know of what you have become since you blossomed into the night club racket is derived from newspaper clippings of your interviews . . . all the publicity you have had is the wrong kind, unless your ambition is to be a second-rate movie actress of the floosie variety — the sort who have their pictures in the papers for a couple of years and then sink back into the obscurity of their naturally silly, talentless lives. . . .

"The thing I cannot forgive you is that you never wrote me to tell me about anything or to take advantage of my experience and ask my opinion — while all the time you were riding on my name! I could have warned you against every stupid blunder you have made — from the standpoint of your own self-interest, I mean. . . .

"To get back to your request to see me: you don't want to see me. Your conduct proves that. So let's cut out the kidding. And I don't want to see the kind of daughter you have become in this past year. . . .

"Here's hoping you change as you grow out of the callow stage. I had hoped there was the making of a fine intelligent woman in you, who would remain fine in whatever she did. I still hope so. If I am wrong, good-bye. If I am right, you will sometime see the point in this letter and be grateful – in which case, au revoir."

Oona informed Agnes that she had had "a horrible letter" from "Daddy [that] hurt me very much." As things turned out, it was "good-bye," not "au revoir," though Oona in subsequent years was to make several more attempts at a reconciliation. Considering that she was only two years old when he left Agnes, practically her entire acquaintanceship with her father, outside of their correspondence, was limited to her two short stays at Tao House.

For a change O'Neill, in the midst of his chagrin over his daughter, could regard his younger son favorably. A few days after Pearl Harbor Shane had obtained seaman's papers ("I'm an able-bodied seaman," he told friends, "just like my father was") and early in 1942, around the time that Oona's name began to appear in the press, he had shipped out. For the next year and a half, till his health broke down, he was to make a number of voyages, through waters infested with German submarines, to England and North Africa.

Shortly before sailing in December 1942 he gave some money to Margaret Stark, his sweetheart and a gifted young painter, and asked her to send Christmas presents to his father and stepmother. When a letter arrived weeks later from Tao House, Margaret forwarded it unopened to Shane and relayed to O'Neill some messages from his son. In an immediate reply Carlotta said that the letter thanking Shane for his gifts was from her and that she had decided not to show her husband Miss Stark's letter about Shane. She felt, as Miss Stark recalls, that "it would be much better if Shane himself wrote his father of his voyages. After all, it was wartime and such news, secondhand, might upset her husband and make him unable to work."

When Shane returned, Margaret exploded about Carlotta: "Who does she think she is – St. Peter, opening and closing the gates?! Why does your father allow such a thing to happen? You are his son. Doesn't he have any feelings of responsibility to you? Does she open all his mail?"

Shane, who rarely became emotional, shrugged. "It must have been a good letter. That's why she didn't show it to my father. I wonder how many of my letters, or all of his children's letters, he's received. After he won the Nobel Prize, I sent him a wire. I really did! Then one day, during my last visit in California, he said he was hurt because I had never written to congratulate him. Carlotta must've intercepted it. I told him I did, but I don't think he believed me."

O'Neill's other son, now aged thirty-two, was being frustrated in his attempts to share in the war effort. Versed in five languages, aside from classical Greek, he applied for a commission in the Intelligence Corps but was successively turned down — why, he never learned — by the three armed services. (According to a friend of his at Yale, Professor Norman Holmes Pearson, who served in Army Intelligence, he was rejected because of a record of leftist political leanings.) Expecting to be drafted, Eugene Jr. resigned from Yale and underwent training as a mechanic in hopes of landing in some branch other than the infantry. He failed, however, to pass the army physical because of a fractured skull he had sustained in boyhood and a slight tremor of the hands; he had had the tremor for years and, in view of his father's condition, believed it to be of hereditary origin. Badly shaken by his series of rejections, he went to work for a cable factory in New Haven and began turning into a heavy drinker.

The couple at Tao House observed Christmas 1942 in an elegiac mood by laying a wreath on Blemie's grave and "hoping he would look down from the Paradise of Ten Billion Trees and Unrationable Dog Biscuits and pity us."

O'Neill's Christmas greeting to Carlotta, entitled "Song in Chaos," begins:

> *What if the world be mad?*
> *You are near.*
> *What if the mind be sad?*
> *You are here*
> *In my heart,*
> *My dear. . . .*

While the tenor of the poem is that their relationship compensates him for all that is "mad" and "sad" in life, one remembers the poem, written earlier this year, in which he saw himself as a "Bewildered apparition, / Seeking a lost identity."

26

Rejected Children

SHORTLY after this country entered the war, both Yale and Princeton, prompted by the nationwide feeling of apprehensiveness, had offered O'Neill safekeeping for his manuscripts "for the duration." In response he gave the bulk of his old plays to the two schools, with Yale getting the larger share, and the rest, at Carlotta's suggestion, to the Museum of the City of New York. Although he was financially pressed and could have sold the scripts for several hundred thousands (years earlier, it will be recalled, he had thought of selling them to a collector or autograph dealer), he was more concerned now about posterity; he wanted his holograph drafts and revised typescripts in institutions where they could be studied by future generations of scholars. He had a generally accurate idea, without conceit, of the size of his contribution to American drama, and he knew, without regret, what that contribution had cost him. "His work," Carlotta told a man at Yale, "is his life – nothing else counts."

Princeton's Firestone Library, preparing an O'Neill exhibit early in 1943, asked his permission to display not only its manuscripts but some of his correspondence with George Tyler, which it had acquired through another channel. While the playwright could be severe on the subject of actors, he also – most likely because of his father – was protective about their feelings. He replied on January 28 to Julian P. Boyd, the Princeton librarian, that the exhibit could include any of his letters that did not contain "sharp cracks about actors or actresses now alive. (As I remember the miscasting of the two plays Tyler produced, there might well be!) Such cracks are remembered, passed on, and finally appear in theatrical gossip columns and someone's feelings are hurt, even though it dates back twenty years or more. I would not want that to happen."

Boyd had commented on the difference in size between O'Neill's script in his letters and in the plays. "The more concentrated and lost in myself my mind became," the playwright explained, "the smaller the handwriting. . . . The minute style grew on me. I did not wish it on myself, God knows, because it made it so hard to get my scripts typed. . . . Of late years I can't write anything but minute, but there is a physical reason for that — the curse of Parkinson's disease — it's easier to control tremor in minute writing."

For the next several years he would recurrently revise and polish his unproduced plays, in addition to working on "The Last Conquest," but so far as substantive results were concerned, his writing career, after thirty years, had ended. *A Moon for the Misbegotten* was the last play he ever completed. He had long ago learned that he could not create on a typewriter. As his tremor grew worse, he acquired a Soundscribe and tried to dictate the ideas developed in his mind and pressing to be born, but his creative process balked at the new approach; having no alternative, he returned to a pencil held in trembly fingers.

His frame of mind was not helped any by the news that his daughter had turned up in Hollywood, a place he detested above all others. After her stay in Sacramento with Carol Marcus, Oona had proceeded to the movie colony, where she was joined by Agnes. Before long the young would-be actress had met some leading filmland figures, including Charlie Chaplin, who thought of casting her as Bridget in a movie version of *Shadow and Substance*, the fine Irish play by Paul Vincent Carroll; but Chaplin's interest in Oona soon became more personal and ardent than professional. When the girl told Agnes in spring 1943 that she was in love with Chaplin and intended to accept him, Agnes wondered "if she realized what she was letting herself in for" — not only had the famous comedian been married and divorced three times but he was fifty-four, exactly thrice her age. As Agnes recalls, Oona said: "I will never love another man in my life."

Chaplin had just become embroiled in a paternity suit brought by a onetime protégée of his named Joan Barry, and the press was already licking its chops over what promised to be a juicy, scandalous trial. Anxious to shield Oona, Charlie suggested that they postpone their marriage till his innocence had been proven, but she wanted to be by his side while he was under attack. (The case did not come to trial till the following year.) After elaborate precautions to elude reporters, climaxed by an automobile chase through Santa Barbara, the two were quietly wed on June 16 in the village of Carpinteria, with the press learning of the ceremony several hours later.

O'Neill was heartsick, yet it also seems likely that a side of him welcomed Oona's latest step, for, in his view, it vindicated his having "severed relations" with his daughter previously. After her latest wave of publicity had subsided, Oona wrote to him that she had married for love, not from material considerations, and still hoped for their reconciliation, but he remained adamantly silent. Several old friends of his tried to serve as an intermediary; their efforts were fruitless. To Carlotta, who widely publicized her view, Oona's new life was simply a cold-blooded fulfillment of her declared intention "to marry a rich man, a really rich man." But eventually, when the marriage had proven durable and happy, Carlotta confided to a visitor (after O'Neill's death) that she was "proud of Oona and hoped for a chance some day to tell her so."

(In a 1960 interview Oona said of her life with Chaplin: "He has made me more mature and I keep him young. When you are happy, you don't go in for self-analysis. He has given me a great sense of security which has nothing to do with his wealth. I could be happy [with him] in any other environment." Sounding a little like her father, she confessed that she was reluctant to socialize. "It's a protective instinct and a selfish one. Our happiness depends to a great extent on our being left alone. Charlie has to remind me when we owe an invitation. I might forget on purpose. Yet we enjoy having houseguests stay with us."

By this time the Chaplins had seven children — there would be an eighth — and were living in Switzerland. Her husband, Oona recalled, had wanted to send their elder son to a boarding school in England when he was ten, but, though she almost always acceded to his wishes, she objected: "I don't like sending them out into the world too young. A family is a unit and should remain together as long as possible."

At the end of his autobiography, published in 1964, Chaplin says: "For the last twenty years I have known what happiness means. . . . I wish I could write more about this, but it involves love, and perfect love is the most beautiful of all frustrations because it is more than one can express. As I live with Oona, the depth and beauty of her character are a continual revelation to me. Even as she walks ahead of me along the narrow sidewalks of Vevey [Switzerland] with simple dignity, her neat little figure straight, her dark hair smoothed back showing a few silver threads, a sudden wave of love and admiration comes over me for all that she is — and a lump comes into my throat.")

Oona's elopement in 1943, with the ensuing publicity, left the couple at Tao House feeling buffeted on all sides. Already contending with ill health — aside from Eugene's chronic affliction, Carlotta's arthritic back was again troubling her – they lost their cook, their last indoor help, so that Carlotta had to struggle alone with the preparation of meals and other household chores. "A remarkably capable and gallant lady, my spouse!" Eugene wrote on June 4 to Nathan. "But at the end of each day she is utterly exhausted. I feel like hell having to watch her do so much work she shouldn't do.

"I dry dishes – and this and that. Outside, help the farmer . . . but have to watch my step. A little too much of it and bang, I suddenly fade out, and my latent ills begin to act up."

Carlotta urged her husband to sell the place – it was too difficult, too costly to maintain in wartime. Her domestic situation was finally eased somewhat, after several months, by a new cook, but she was kept in an apprehensive state by O'Neill's physical condition.

In August the playwright, weighing only one hundred and thirty-eight pounds (he was five feet eleven), began undergoing an exhaustive series of tests and experiments by Dr. Fletcher B. Taylor of Oakland aimed at relieving not only his Parkinson's but his general state of nervousness and malaise. "Gene is *bad*," Carlotta lamented to Myrtle Caldwell, "so many things wrong – all the damnable medicine they gave him almost drove him mad. He 'cracked' again today – wept & shook . . . & nearly broke my heart. . . . If I didn't love him it would be so much easier!"

He complained to the doctor that even minor upsets or excitements left him with a feeling in the pit of his stomach that was, in Taylor's paraphrase, "like the visceral component of fear, as one would have in real danger." Not long after the series of tests had begun, he was ill for over a month, first from an infection that spread through his system, and next from a siege of bronchitis. Concerned about a possible recurrence of tuberculosis, he was particularly alarmed one morning when, in the midst of coughing, he spit up blood. "Of course, all this didn't improve the nerves," he told a friend, "and the old Parkinson's went wild and woolly."

From his notes to Carlotta it appears that all was serene between them; on their anniversary in July he had said: "Every day, in every way, you are more & more beautiful, & I love you more!" Regardless, however, of the state of his affection, his deteriorating health had diminished his sex drive and left Carlotta, as she confided to Mrs. Caldwell, feeling physically unsatisfied.

For a time this summer and fall she had regular treatments to ease her arthritis by a masseuse who visited Tao House and occasionally stayed the night. Carlotta became fond of the masseuse, a large and hearty woman, but the treatments and the friendship ended abruptly when O'Neill found

*Oona and Charles Chaplin in their first public appearance
after their marriage*

Oona and her mother in the early forties

Oona with the four children she had had by then, on the liner Queen Elizabeth *as she and her husband were about to sail for England in 1952*

The Chaplins at the London airport in 1961, en route to their home in Switzerland from an Irish vacation. Left to right: Geraldine, 16; Eugene, 7; Victoria, 9; Chaplin, Oona holding Annette, 18 months; Josephine, 11, and Michael, 14. Three-year-old Jane adamantly declined to pose with the family

them in circumstances that suggested to him a lesbian attachment. At Carlotta's plea, Myrtle Caldwell soon arrived to help pacify the incensed playwright and talk him out of his suspicions. Though harmony was gradually reestablished between the pair, he never forgot the equivocal episode; when the O'Neills were temporarily estranged a few years later, he confided to intimates his doubts about his wife and the masseuse, while Carlotta once asked Russel Crouse whether he had heard any rumors about her being of lesbian proclivities and was distressed at his affirmative reply.

Feeling that she herself would crack up if they remained at Tao House indefinitely, Carlotta, close to exhaustion from worry and overwork, won her husband's permission to sell the place. During their early years there she had declared, "I love the country because I love being away from people," and said that the privacy and beauty of their surroundings repaid her a hundredfold for her labors. Now, however, she confessed to her friend Myrtle, "I *loathe the country*, for more than a few days. *I always have!* I have lied to everyone, *& myself*, all these years trying to *make* myself like it! I knew Gene couldn't work in a town." She would go out of her mind, she added, if she had to spend the rest of her days "listening to sweet woodland noises!"

Sounding even more desperate in a letter to Eline Winther on October 29, 1943, she said, "I feel imprisoned — and want to scream my way out. . . . I want to go back where I belong. The East. I want to see my friends. People who are doing things. I would rather live in one room and be in the midst of activities. I can't stand this [being] stuck away from living people. . . . *Pray we'll be able to sell!*"

The couple's financial situation was eased this fall when the playwright, after several years of tentative nibbles by Hollywood, received thirty thousand dollars for *The Hairy Ape;* he sold it, however, reluctantly. "I've never liked having distorted pictures made of my plays," he told Theresa Helburn. "I thought long ago when I saw *Caligari* that there could be a genuine, original art form developed along that line. Talking pictures seem to me a bastard which has inherited the lowest traits of both parents. [He had forgotten, apparently, that he had once been enthusiastic about the possibilities of "the talkies."] It was the talkless part of *The Long Voyage Home* — the best picture ever made from my stuff — that impressed me the most." *The Hairy Ape*, his letter continues, remained one of his favorite plays: "I sold it because, with Tao House and ranch overhead on my neck, I had to sell it or sell some of my securities whose income pays the alimony! . . . I knew no one in Hollywood had the guts to film *my play*. . . . I remember that its first stage production was one of my most satisfying times in the theater . . . I don't want to have that memory spoiled. So when I tell you I am not going to see the film . . . nor even admit that it exists, I sure mean it! But all the same, I will always feel guilty."

His strictures against Hollywood were touched off by a report from Miss Helburn that she was reviving an old campaign to interest the movies in *Mourning Becomes Electra* — she had originally suggested Greta Garbo and Katharine Hepburn as the two Mannon women — and had again enlisted Hepburn's support. O'Neill thought that Hepburn would be "splendid as Lavinia," but feared that the rest of the picture would be "a dreadful hash of attempted condensation and idiotic censorship," as the *Strange Interlude* film was. "How about General Mannon's speeches about war, death, etc., and what Orin has to say when he returns? Would these be ruled out as morbid pacifism or something? Yet to me these contain an implication, at least, of deep spiritual truth. Do you remember when Orin says to Lavinia . . . : 'I had to kill another in the same way. It was like murdering the same man twice. I had a queer feeling that war meant murdering the same man over and over, and that in the end I would discover the man was myself!' "

While O'Neill was unhappy at the prospect of leaving his retreat for a hotel in San Francisco, not least because of his tremor, Carlotta was wildly impatient for the move. Making the household situation worse than ever, the cook fell ill in the final days of 1943, so that Carlotta had to nurse her in addition to bearing the full weight of the household chores and her husband's care. In his Christmas tribute to her, Eugene said: "Along with all my love, my admiration for your courage in carrying on so bravely and gallantly in this Yuletide of many trials! Well, we have love, so what the hell! I adore you, Darling One!"

Their privacy already broken by real estate agents and prospective buyers, the O'Neills in the early weeks of 1944 had to contend also with the press, which was eager to learn the playwright's response to the impending paternity trial of his famous son-in-law. After Chaplin was indicted by a federal grand jury on several charges, including an alleged violation of the Mann Act, a United Press dispatch said: "The intimate details of the love life of Charlie Chaplin and Joan Barry promised today to provide Hollywood with the most lurid criminal trial in its history" (a "promise" that the hearings would scarcely fulfill). When the press failed to reach O'Neill on the telephone, reporters and photographers tried, but unsuccessfully, to crash his retreat. In the end, after blood tests proved that Chaplin had not sired the plaintiff's child, he was acquitted on all charges.

Tao House, which had cost about one hundred thousand dollars, was sold in February for what Carlotta called "a good price," yet it appears that the couple, as with Casa Genotta, sustained a substantial loss. Dr. Clifford Feiler, one of O'Neill's several physicians, recalls that the estate was offered to him for seventy thousand dollars. More substantively, the realty tax stamps for the transaction — the purchasers were Arthur Carlson, an Oakland attorney, and his heiress wife — indicate that the price was around sixty thousand dollars. (Today, Tao House with its acreage is worth about a million dollars.) When the Carlsons opened negotiations, the playwright remained out of sight, but after the sale was arranged he materialized and impressed them as "very charming." Discussing the surrounding countryside, he thought that the hills had a "corduroy texture," which led the new owners to rename the place "Corduroy Hills Ranch." Carlotta did most of the talking, however, and more than once urged the Carlsons to keep Blemie's grave in good condition.

During his final days at Tao House the playwright screened his unproduced writings and on February 21, 1944, burned the manuscripts of "Greed of the Meek" and "And Give Me Death" ("because they no longer fitted into my revised plan"), as well as the holograph drafts of More Stately Mansion, but the typescript of Mansions was preserved. He also retained his notes and outlines of the projected plays of the Cycle, for in spite of his worsening tremor he stubbornly hoped for a change in his condition that would enable him to complete his magnum opus. Carlotta was distressed at the destruction of work that had cost him so much time and stress of mind and spirit, but she knew it was useless to try and dissuade her husband.

His stockpile of new works that were more or less in finished shape consisted of the one-act Hughie and four full-length dramas — Long Day's Journey Into Night, The Iceman Cometh, A Moon for the Misbegotten and A Touch of the Poet.

Retaining only a few choice items, the O'Neills sold most of their fine Chinese furnishings back to Gump's, shipped the player piano and "a hundred boxes of books" to storage in New York, and took an apartment at the Hotel Fairmont on Nob Hill. Right after the couple moved late in February, Carlotta, generally run-down, fell seriously ill from an infection in her kidneys and bladder, but penicillin and other new "miracle drugs" helped pull her through. At the height of her illness, O'Neill was saddened by word that Harry Weinberger, his attorney and among his oldest friends, had died. "He sat by my bed all night," Carlotta said, "like a ghost! Poor darling, my heart ached for him. He has had tough going this past year."

To George Jean Nathan, another of Weinberger's clients, Eugene wrote on March 6 that the lawyer's death "hit me hard. Twenty-eight years of friendship. It started with his doing work for me for nothing — as he did for so many. . . . I shall miss his ever loyal and generous friendship."

Once the O'Neills were at the Fairmont, Carlotta never again saw her daughter, though Cynthia lived with her husband and son not far away in Lafayette. Since mid-1942 she had worked for her stepfather, typing his scripts and some of his correspondence; but now that Carlotta felt she could dispense with her help, she once more shut her daughter, as far as possible, out of her life. (Clifford Odets, who knew Oona, has said of O'Neill that he apparently "could not forgive his children because *he* had abandoned them." The same seems equally true of Carlotta in regard to her daughter.) By this time, too, Carlotta had almost no contact with her mother, who was senile, hostile, and becoming an impossible presence in the Stram household — one day she bit her granddaughter on the hand. When Cynthia afterward "blew up" on the telephone to Carlotta, Carlotta countered by denouncing her; but finally she arranged for Nellie Tharsing to enter a nursing home.

O'Neill, whose rootless early years of touring with his parents had left him with a lifelong aversion to hotels, felt confined and edgy in a small suite at the Fairmont. Though aware that he was being unreasonable — housing accommodations were scarce because of San Francisco's swollen wartime population — he complained so that Carlotta at last managed to obtain a larger apartment at the Huntington Hotel, one consisting of two bedrooms, a living room and a combination kitchen and dinette.

For years now, whenever one of the O'Neills was ill, they had summoned Kathryne Albertoni (formerly Kathryne Radovan), who had nursed the playwright during his hospitalization in 1937. Once the couple was settled at the Huntington, they had Kaye, an attractive brunette with a serious disposition, taking care of them regularly, five days a week, and would retain her in their employ till they returned East. "Not that either of them was so ill the whole time that they needed a nurse," she says, "but I was like a buffer, a mediator, between them. Also, I gave them daily injections. He got Oreton, for the change of life — it had a calming effect, it helped his tremor — while she got Theelin. But mostly I was company for Carlotta, someone always around for her to talk to."

To spur her husband's efforts at writing and help keep him occupied, Carlotta, who was indisposed for months from a succession of ailments, suggested that Jane Caldwell be hired to type his work as he revised. He welcomed the proposal, for he had become attached to the girl, more attached than Carlotta suspected, more, perhaps, than he himself yet realized. As she began working for him in spring 1944, he warned her, "If you give me a Father's Day present, I'll bite your ear off!"

There was rarely any considerable amount of typing for her to do, but, putting in time five days a week, she, like Mrs. Albertoni, would continue a regular part of the household practically to the end of the O'Neills' stay on the West Coast. Going back to his first love, Eugene composed a number of poems. Letters came from all over seeking his professional advice and, though Carlotta complained about these strangers bothering him, he took an interest in the correspondence. To a literary aspirant in India, he replied: "Write, write, write, tear it up and try again." Most of his working hours were spent on polishing his unproduced plays. At times tears rolled down his face as he revised *A Moon for the Misbegotten*, a sight that always sent Jane slipping quietly from the room, and she used to feel on her return that he had been too lost in himself to be aware of her absence.

Grace Cathedral, an unfinished structure opposite the Huntington and overlooked by the O'Neills' tenth-floor suite, fascinated him, according to Miss Caldwell. "He said it was so depressing that he might use it in one of his plays." His feeling about the church seems to have been the chief source of a recurrent dream of his at the time; as Jane recalls, he told her that the dream always found him "in the sea, with the seventh wave, the largest wave, rolling upward, turning into a cathedral, and crashing down on him."

In a visit to the Coast this summer the Langners were cheered to find the playwright at last willing to discuss plans for postwar productions of *The Iceman Cometh* and other of his plays. Cautioning them against staging *The Iceman* too early, he said that the general euphoria as peace began would prevent the play, with its bleak view of the human condition, from getting a sympathetic hearing. But after a year or so, when disillusionment was likely to set in, he predicted that audiences would be more receptive to *The Iceman*.

Against Carlotta's private advice, O'Neill allowed the Langners to read *The Misbegotten*, *A Touch of the Poet* and *Hughie*. Since he had been away from Broadway a full ten years, a period during which the theatrical scene had changed considerably, Carlotta had urged caution on him in renewing his association with the Guild. "I begged him not to sign for more than one play," she says, "but he was the most stubborn man I've ever known. I'd make suggestions I thought would be helpful, and he'd do the opposite."

Her wariness about the Theater Guild was not unjustified, as it had lost much of its onetime vitality and luster and no longer was preeminent in the New York theater. A few years earlier, after behind-the-scenes feuding with other board members, director Philip Moeller and designer Lee Simonson, the most talented of the founders, had resigned (or been pushed out), and more than once in the past decade the organization had appeared on the verge of folding. Fortunately, at one of its lowest ebbs it had come up with Katharine Hepburn in Philip Barry's *The Philadelphia Story*, the most profitable play in its history, and more recently it had tapped a still richer gold mine by teaming Richard Rodgers and Oscar Hammerstein II for the epochal musical *Oklahoma!* But a society comedy, however successful, and even a pioneering musical provided something other than the rousing dramas and intellectual excitements of the Guild's earlier years.

O'Neill himself was well aware of a decline in the Guild's operations, yet he was grateful for its excellent productions of *Strange Interlude* and *Mourning Becomes Electra*, both uncommonly difficult plays to stage, and its sponsorship of such flawed efforts as *Dynamo* and *Days Without End*. But beyond the matter of gratitude, he knew that the Guild heads viewed his new scripts as potential steps toward regaining their former eminence and would do their utmost to give them the best possible production.

Langner and his wife Armina Marshall (with Theresa Helburn they now comprised the entire Guild directorate) were enthusiastic about the new O'Neill plays, particularly *A Moon for the Misbegotten*. However, their initial delight over the script was tempered when they thought of the difficulty of finding an actress built like an Amazon but with depths of tender femininity for the part of Josie Hogan. Despite its casting problem, O'Neill and his visitors decided that *The Misbegotten* should be produced first, shortly after the war, then *The Iceman*, and finally *Poet*. According to Langner, the playwright said that he had another one-act play, not quite finished, that would make a full evening with *Hughie;* but the promised companion piece never materialized, and *Hughie* would not be seen on Broadway till a decade after its author's death.

Where Carlotta could hardly wait to quit California ("I loathe the state, I've *always* loathed it"), Eugene, in her words, *"wants* to go East — & *hates going!* He dreads meeting people — & [is] afraid of publicity." For months they had expected to leave before 1944 ended, but on their doctors' advice they reluctantly postponed their departure to the following spring. "The doctors have said no, decidedly precarious to jump from seven years of Coast weather into a New York winter — in the present state of both our health," Eugene on October 9 informed Nathan. "I want to be East again. Ever since we sold our house — or even before that, when it became a worry and a burden — I've felt that life out here had become meaningless."

He "celebrated" his fifty-sixth birthday in October by visiting (from his account on October 19 to Carl Van Vechten) "a really swell columbarium. California, as is well known, leads the world in the swellness of its columbariums, designed apparently to keep the dead lively, cheerful and constantly amused." He had "intended to price a few snappy urns . . . but as neither the curator of the dump nor I could hear each other above the roaring of ten thousand savage canary birds and the horrible gush of innumerable fancy fountains," he left in disgust, "swearing I'd live forever to spite those damned canaries." To another friend he said that the columbariums "would be comic were it not that they reveal a passion for unreality. . . . Nothing strikes deeper in the American character than its fear of death."

Sophus Winther, in a visit to the Huntington this fall, found O'Neill in low spirits. After showing his guest around the attractive apartment, whose view took in a panoramic sweep of the city and the bay, Eugene remarked, "I'd rather be at Alcatraz. I might learn something if I were over there."

The sight of Grace Cathedral launched him on one of his favorite themes — namely, that all religions, however noble and wise in their origins, become corrupt in the workings of their establishments. "Man," he said, "has been told the truth. He has been shown the way to the good life in simple language. Jesus, Confucius, Lao-tze, a little more complex . . . Socrates, but it has been futile. Great and simple truth has been perverted into worldly power by organized institutions. The church in our world has no relationship to Christianity. The church is a fraud."

Airing another of his standard jeremiads, regarding the shoddy ethics of Hollywood, he reported that he had recently rejected an offer of one hundred thousand dollars for an original screenplay because he knew they would "simply use [my] name and prostitute [my] idea." The movie agent had next offered the same sum if he would allow two film writers to talk with him. "Two, no less. They were to consult with me, but I would not have to write a word. When I looked skeptical, the agent went further. I would not even have to consult with the writers."

Silent for a time, O'Neill suddenly laughed derisively. "If I had let them do that, and then if someone had asked me if I had a bear in the story, I would have to answer, 'I don't know. I haven't seen the picture.'"

Stimulated by the presence of an attentive listener — Carlotta had heard it all before, many times — the playwright ranged widely in unburdening himself. He had hoped for "a new and vital drama" in this country after the last war, but his hopes had been disappointed, and now, he added, "the overhead cost of production is so great that any serious play is doomed before it starts."

Implicitly dismissing the fine residences he had shared with Carlotta, not to mention the places where he and Agnes had lived, the prisoner of the past lamented, "I have never had a home, never had a chance to establish roots. I grew up in hotels. My mother never had a home. *Long Day's Journey* is her story and my autobiography. It's strange, but the time I spent at sea on a sailing ship [the voyage to Buenos Aires on the *Charles Racine*] was the *only* time I ever felt I had roots in any place."

To Winther's distress, Eugene reported that not only was his hand tremor becoming worse but that sometimes his entire body shook. A poor sleeper, he usually woke about 3 A.M. and heated a pot of coffee Carlotta had prepared for him. He liked to stand by the window while sipping the coffee and "look out over the city at that time of night. It's dead at three in the morning, and when it's dead it's really interesting."

Standing tall and slender, his arms folded in order to minimize the shaking of his hands, he told Sophus, "Remember that this is what I want on my tombstone:

EUGENE O'NEILL
THERE IS SOMETHING
TO BE SAID
FOR BEING DEAD."

Though Carlotta screened her husband's correspondence and tried also to bar newspapers with stories likely to disturb him, her efforts were not always successful. Word reached him that Mrs. Charles Chaplin had had a child, a girl, and that his former wife had published a novel. After striving on and off for years to establish herself as a writer, Agnes finally won some acclaim this fall with *The Road Is Before Us,* a story of four widely assorted persons on an automobile trip to Florida. Praising Agnes on October 14 as a "talent worth following," the *New Yorker* found that most of her principals "emerge with startling clarity in a series of pictures done not only with skill but with compassionate understanding." The New York *Times* said on the fifteenth the novel "leaves a definite hope that Miss Boulton will keep her feet on the very promising road that lies before her."

(Agnes's second and final book, *Part of a Long Story,* a memoir of her and O'Neill's earliest years together, was published after his death. Overall a fine achievement, in spite of some shortcomings, it gives a vivid, persuasive portrait of her onetime husband and recalls with considerable sensitivity a bygone bohemia of Greenwich Village and Provincetown.)

At O'Neill's desire, with Carlotta agreeing reluctantly, they decided that on quitting the West Coast they would resettle in Sea Island, rather than in New York; but this time, as Carlotta put it, they would build "a five-room house — no work — furniture out of Woolworth's. I want to eliminate all fuss and feathers. I'm getting old. I want to take it easy." She was living, she felt, "on the edge of a volcano until I can get Gene . . . out of doors again," and gloomily predicted to George Boll that "if he discovers he is unable to swim — he'll go mad! And so will I!"

Reviewing his situation, O'Neill told Elizabeth Shepley Sergeant on December 3, 1944, "We sold our old home at Sea Island because we had become too blind to its virtues and too impatient of its minor defects. We wanted a change — and the house was too large for two people. . . . So was the one we built out here. We *will not* make that mistake again!"

Regarding his Parkinson's, he said the "worst part" was the "fits of extreme melancholia that go with it. God knows I have had enough of Celtic Twilight in my makeup without needing any more of the same. And this isn't the same. It isn't sadness. It's an exhausted horrible apathy."

From one month to the next the O'Neills, reduced to an indecisive state by wartime conditions on the home front as well as by conflicting desires within themselves, changed their plans. For a while they thought of returning to Georgia the following spring, but early in 1945 they decided to remain longer at the Huntington, chiefly because of the conveniences and services, particularly good medical care, available in San Francisco. Looking ahead, Carlotta spelled out their needs, wants and specifications in a stream of correspondence with George Boll and quizzed him exhaustively about present circumstances on Sea Island. By the time the war ended in Europe, in May, the O'Neills owned several oceanfront lots in the island resort and, intending to arrive in October, had leased a house nearby, so that Carlotta could supervise construction of their new home.

One reason why O'Neill agreed to defer their departure for Georgia, in spite of his dislike of hotel living, was his reluctance to part from Jane Caldwell. He knew she was dating an army dentist (whom she later married), yet he half-courted her in a half-joking manner. Talking once about reincarnation, he hoped that they would return as sea gulls; while she rested on a piling or some other perch, he would fly about and keep her supplied with fish. He daydreamed about her accompanying him to Russia, where they would spend the pile of rubles owed to him as royalties. With a jade-handled mirror he gave her for her birthday on April 3 was a note that began: "I must warn you that this is an enchanted, haunted mirror, for whenever you gaze in it you will see in its secret depths someone staring back at you with — well, let us say, with an emotion befitting the loveliness the surface of the mirror reflects."

The O'Neills decided in July to remain on the Coast another winter and arrive at Sea Island in spring 1946. It is uncertain whether they revised their plans chiefly because of Eugene's health, as Carlotta informed George Boll, or because of wartime shortages at the Georgian resort, as she told Sophus Winther, or because O'Neill, concealing the state of his feelings about Jane Caldwell, raised objections.

Carlotta, who handled most of her husband's correspondence, used to "magnify his illness" in writing to his friends, according to Miss Caldwell: "Except for his Parkinson's," Jane recalls, "he was not really ill the entire time I worked for him. Almost every day before lunch he used to put on some records and we'd dance — the Bunny Hug, the Turkey Trot, occasionally the tango. He liked to dance fast, but he wasn't very good.

"He knew that Carlotta discouraged people from coming to see him and made him sound worse than he was. One time after she'd written a letter — I can't remember whether it was to Nathan or Langner — he said, 'Who's it for? Let me see.' Carlotta tossed the sealed letter on the sofa and told him to go ahead, but she looked worried that he might open and read it. The next day Gene told me she'd risen during the night and written another letter in its place."

With neither in good health — Carlotta too was ailing on and off this year — and the playwright scarcely able to work, they both were on edge, quick to take offense at one another. "Gene told me that his tremor was worse on days when she was angry at him," Jane Caldwell says.

"Sometimes, out of spite, she'd give him his soup in a bowl, with a spoon, instead of a coffee cup, which was easier for him to handle."

Kaye Albertoni, who had been reared strictly, felt that relations between Miss Caldwell and O'Neill were overly friendly, if not indiscreet; the two always kissed on the mouth at her arrival and departure, and the door to O'Neill's room was usually closed when Jane was with him. Considering Carlotta's jealous nature and her vigilance against other women, particularly those her junior, she was surprisingly indulgent about Jane; apparently she long thought that Eugene's feeling toward her was merely avuncular and platonic. But at last, a full year after Jane began working there, Carlotta called a halt to the overt expressions of affection.

In August 1945 Jane and her mother vacationed for ten days in Pasadena, where they saw *Mourning Becomes Electra* at the Pasadena Playhouse. Even though Carlotta's suspicions were aroused by now, she telephoned Jane several times and urged her to return early, because Gene was making her life "a hell." He wanted Jane back as soon as possible so that he could continue with his work. In a showdown between the O'Neills late this month he admitted being attracted to the girl, he said she had given "a lift" to his life, but that he did not want a divorce or separation. Storming and weeping all at once, Carlotta wrung him through one of their worst scenes ever. While she castigated him in the harshest terms ("a nasty, dirty senile old man" was one of her epithets), with a side attack on Jane, he countered with his old charge about her and the masseuse. The next morning Carlotta, still in an overwrought state, told Kaye Albertoni she had thought of committing suicide by slashing her wrists but did not want to leave "a mess" for Kaye.

The atmosphere in the apartment for the next few weeks, as Jane continued in her job, was Strindbergian. No longer able to unburden herself to Myrtle Caldwell, Carlotta poured out her heart in a telephone call to a friend in New York. On his side O'Neill, rather than feeling conscience-stricken or contrite, told Myrtle during one of her last visits that Carlotta "loves being Mrs. Eugene O'Neill, she loves the name, but if a millionaire came along who wanted her, she'd drop me in a minute." Of his feeling for Jane, he said, "I didn't want it to happen, but it did."

Near the end of September the situation boiled over. During an argument between the pair on the twenty-seventh, Carlotta directed Mrs. Albertoni to help her pack; she wanted to leave immediately for New York, while he insisted she would have to remain. They were still wrangling when Kaye walked out. Carlotta's first words to her the fol-

O'Neill
in the early forties

Jane Caldwell

lowing morning were: "Let him stay away from me. I'll kill him!" When the nurse appeared on the twenty-ninth, Carlotta tearfully reported that the previous night "he threatened to kill me with his gun and I came in with a butcher knife." In the ensuing brawl, according to her account, he began choking her and she dug her fingernails into his hands, then he, releasing her, "knocked her out cold" with a blow to the jaw. Apparently verifying the essentials of her story, her jaw was swollen slightly, and so was his right hand.

In the following day or so Carlotta talked of taking a fatal overdose of sedatives, Kaye telephoned the pair's doctors to report on the situation and express her fears ("There is a loaded gun somewhere in the apartment"), and one time O'Neill began packing to leave. In the end the warring pair patched together a truce (though he vowed to himself that "she would pay for this"). After he had bidden Jane good-bye early in October, he and Carlotta prepared to depart as soon as possible for New York; they did not want to be isolated with one another at Sea Island.

How serious was O'Neill's feeling for Jane Caldwell? Less serious, probably, than any of the principals in the imbroglio thought, even though the repercussions were quite serious. It appears that Eugene, bored, restless, depressed by his inability to work and at the same time touched by the girl's fresh beauty and charm, indulged in a middle-aged spree of emotionally recapturing his youth (he told Jane that she reminded him of Beatrice Ashe, his great love in New London some thirty years previously). Also, now that he was unable to express his feelings, fantasies and aggressions on paper, it seems that he had begun to dramatize his own life, to set up provocative situations in which he was a leading player while part of him watched from the sidelines as the little dramas developed.

Years earlier he had said that of all the modern plays, he would most like to have written *The Dance of Death*, Strindberg's mordant account of a married couple locked in coils of loving hate. O'Neill had tried and failed in several plays to equal the Swedish master; it now appeared that if he were unable to write a *Dance of Death*, part of him sought to live out such a story. As a man loaded with guilt feelings, he derived some kind of satisfaction from flagellating himself and being tormented. Other than the impression he gave Jane and her mother that he would like to start a new life with her, there is no evidence that O'Neill ever seriously considered leaving Carlotta, whom he had long known would protect him from everyone except herself. Torture and be tortured; for one of his nature, Carlotta was, more or less, an ideal mate.

As most girls would have been, Jane was flattered at inspiring the great man's ardor, but at the same time, from all available evidence, she was no coquette; already engaged to a man of her own generation, she never, it seems, gave Eugene reason for thinking that her affection for him was of a romantic nature. It was, then, a *safe* romance for O'Neill in every respect: the girl had no desire to take him away from his wife, and his wife, he knew, would hold on to him to the death.

Although the war with Japan was now over, train accommodations were still at a premium, but Carlotta managed through a friend of hers, a railroad executive, to obtain reservations for October 17, a day after the playwright's fifty-seventh birthday. Shortly before the pair's departure, Cynthia Stram had a message that her stepfather wanted her to have a farewell lunch with him.

"Carlotta was nowhere in sight when I got there," she recalls. "Gene told me she had to go out, but at one point the phone rang in the next room and someone — my mother, I guess — answered it. He was so nice to me during the visit that I was embarrassed for him. I felt he was thinking of the raw deal I was getting from Carlotta, that I'd always gotten, and he wanted me to know that he sympathized with me. His tremor was very bad that day. As I was leaving, I said, 'Please tell Mother good-bye for me.' Maybe it wasn't nice of me, but I added in a sarcastic tone, 'I'm sorry she had such an important errand that she couldn't be here to see me,' and his eyes twinkled."

The playwright's friends in New York were shocked on first seeing him again — he now appeared so frail and so much older than his age. O'Neill himself, though, felt revivified at being surrounded by persons devoted to him and, despite his old dislike of the city, enjoyed a sense of homecoming. Feeling, like Carlotta, that they had been under "a curse" in California, he called the East "God's country!" in writing to Robert Sisk in Los Angeles and said, "You will find the climate here so much more healthy, so much more sunshine, the oranges are better, the date trees in Central Park so much more fruitful, and one light on Broadway makes Wilshire Boulevard look like a dismal blind alley!" As his favorable reference to Broadway suggests, he also felt stimulated at resuming contact with the theater. In a change of plans, he and the Guild decided to give *The Iceman Cometh* priority over *A Moon for the Misbegotten* and go to work immediately on long-range plans for its production next fall.

Offsetting his pleasure over his reactivated career, relations between him and Carlotta were uneasy and tense as they settled into a two-room suite at the Barclay on East Forty-eighth Street, where, because of the tight housing situation, they had to share a bedroom for the first time in their many years together. Dining with them shortly after their return, Saxe Commins found the playwright in an obvious state of nerves and Carlotta looking forbidding. When the meal ended, O'Neill told Saxe that his Cycle papers — *Poet, Mansions,* outlines and notes for the other units of the series — had disappeared; he had checked over them a few days previously when they arrived in a trunk from the Coast, but earlier this day he had looked for them without success. During her husband's unhappy account, Carlotta interjected that his mind was deteriorating and that he must have misplaced the scripts. Under Saxe's urging, Eugene, with his friend's help, proceeded methodically to examine every inch of the suite, every shelf and drawer — all the drawers, that is, except those containing Carlotta's underclothes. At her insistence, the two men, feeling embarrassed, removed the garments, to an accompaniment of gibes from Carlotta. Still no papers.

Several days later O'Neill told Saxe to forget about the missing scripts and never to mention the incident to anyone, for they had reappeared. Carlotta, he confided, had removed them from the apartment and temporarily stored them elsewhere, to punish him for some reason unknown to him (he never told Saxe about Jane Caldwell). "Only Strindberg," he said, could appreciate how he felt and could fathom the thinking behind his wife's cruel hoax.

His frightening experience with the Cycle papers led him to make certain that *Long Day's Journey Into Night* would be safe. On November 29, 1945, he delivered a copy of the play to Bennett Cerf, who was not allowed to read it, and Saxe at Random House. At the playwright's instance, the envelope containing the script was fastened with sealing wax, after which it was stored in the publisher's top-security vault. Finally O'Neill dictated and signed a paper, which Cerf also signed, that began: "I am this day depositing with you, on condition that it not be opened by you until twenty-five years after my death, a sealed copy of an original play which I have written, entitled *Long Day's Journey Into Night.*" Shrinking from the thought of his family, including himself, being impersonated on the stage, he said that *Long Day's Journey* could be published at the future date but should never be performed.

After years of seclusive living that had declined into ill health, inactivity, and heartache, O'Neill hungered for diversion and social contacts. He welcomed old friends, made new ones, and quietly relished the attention shown him at Guild headquarters, where he was treated as visiting royalty. Accompanied usually by George Jean Nathan, Guild press agent Joe Heidt or his new attorney, Winfield ("Bill") Aronberg, who had been Harry Weinberger's associate, he attended football games, prize fights, ice hockey matches and of course the six-day bicycle races. Like the playwright, Aronberg loved jazz, and the two spent a number of evenings on The Street (Fifty-second between Fifth and Sixth avenues), as it was pronounced with affectionate emphasis by the followers of Billie Holiday and Art Tatum, Coleman Hawkins, "Hot Lips" Page and other great performers. "On Fifty-second Street," according to pianist Marian McPartland, "you could walk through the history of jazz. In several hours, nursing a few drinks, you could travel musically from New Orleans up to Harlem and bop."

"Gene," says Aronberg, "was the politest man I ever knew. In those stinky Fifty-second Street joints he would thank the waiters for every little service, and he tipped generously. A helluva good guy."

Between the lawyer and Carlotta, relations were never more than polite and cool, as was to be expected. She had always disliked Harry Weinberger (to intimates she used to refer to him as her husband's "Jew lawyer") and was prejudiced in advance against his successor, while Aronberg was antagonistic to her, sight unseen, from what Weinberger had told him. An emotional, intense man who masked his nature behind an offhand, humorous manner, Aronberg says of Carlotta: "She was always onstage, always playing the grande dame, but she also liked to cry poverty. She once said to me, 'Do you know what we're having for dinner tonight? Beef kidneys. The poor buy steak, but with our taxes and alimony we can't afford steak.' What a phoney she was! She liked kidneys, and when she was through fixing them with wine and sauces, they must've cost twelve dollars!"

By this time relations were cool also between her and Eugene Jr. Carlotta, who thought he had become "a mess," disapproved of his incipient paunch, of the Vandyke beard he had grown as the outcome of a wager, and, above all, of his leftist political views. For a short period before the Nazi-Soviet pact of 1939, he had been a member of the Communist Party, but according to his friend Frank Meyer, he was more "confused and anarchistic" than anything else. The two friends used to argue constantly, for Meyer, at one time a leading Communist functionary, had swung to the right and eventually would become an associate of William F. Buckley, Jr.

Carlotta's politics can be gauged from the fact that she regarded

Roosevelt as radical and in her moments of darkest suspicion thought him intent on becoming a dictator along Stalinist lines. The first time Eugene Jr. appeared at the Barclay, he greeted her with: "Well, how does an old Tory like you feel having a Communist to dinner?" Recalling the incident, she complained that "Gene just sat there, he didn't say a word. His children could say anything to me, and he'd never interfere."

Following years of brilliant promise as a student and of superior achievement on the Yale faculty, Eugene O'Neill, Jr., aged thirty-five, was now on a course generally downward. Thrice married and divorced, he had been too restless when the war ended to return to Yale. Endowed with a fine, resonant voice, which he considered a heritage from his paternal grandfather, and a striking presence — over six feet tall, broad-shouldered, he was distinctive-looking even without the Vandyke — he hoped for a career on radio and television, if not in the theater. After his wartime stint in a factory, he had worked briefly as a radio announcer in Hartford before gravitating to his father's old haunt, Greenwich Village, where he presently lived with a statuesque blond, an artists' agent named Ruth Lander; drank rather heavily; and constantly ran into Shane. For the next few years, till his life ended abruptly, he would manage to get by on periodic jobs of teaching and lecturing and assignments in the electronics media. During a course he gave at the New School for Social Research, he once committed a Freudianism: "When I wrote *Mourning Becomes Electra* . . ."

Charles T. Harrell, a director at the ABC network and a fan of O'Neill's plays, tried to further Eugene Jr.'s career. After auditioning him, Harrell found that he had "very little talent as an 'actor' in that he lacked the control of his voice to give nuance to the vapid lines that make up the bulk of radio writing. But he did have a fine quality for narration. On 'mike' he sounded not unlike Orson Welles, when Welles was a tower of talent rather than the oafish buffoon of today. I felt that O'Neill could, with experience and training, equal many of the regular narration performers." The novice "did a satisfactory, though undistinguished job" the first time Harrell employed him, but "there was no improvement in his technique on several other occasions."

Although some acquaintances thought him comfortable with his name and glad to exploit it as much as possible, Harrell, who drank with him a few times, received the opposite impression. "He was most reluctant to talk about his father," the network man recalls, "till one day the liquor spoke. I can't remember his exact words, but he declared that he was cursed with his father's name. He knew that it was a useful tool to gain him entrée into theatrical circles, but he felt ambivalent about it. He used to curse himself silently, he said, for his weakness in using it, in view of his father's lack of simple human feelings toward his children. But he probably was speaking from a frustrated love for his father."

Shane was unaware of O'Neill and Carlotta's return East till his half brother stopped by to say that their father wanted to see him. Now married and soon to be a father himself, the twenty-six-year-old boy (essentially, he would remain a boy most of his life) was, if anything, more unsure of himself than ever. His onetime girl friend Margaret Stark recalls that he "never sat *in* a chair; he sat *on* it. You always had the feeling he might, at any moment, run away or just disappear."

Late in 1943, after voyages during which he had seen ships torpedoed and bodies aflame in the water, he had been in such a nervous state that Margaret had persuaded him to quit the sea. Following a short period of treatment for shock at a federal hospital for seamen, he drifted from one inconsequential job to another; most of the time, though, he was unemployed. Miss Stark, a bright and very attractive girl, as well as a gifted painter, was deeply in love with Shane and did her best to help him, but he was bent on self-destruction. Often he was dead drunk when she returned from work, and on two occasions she found him unconscious, with all the gas jets open. Following the second suicide attempt, she and other friends persuaded him to undergo psychiatric care. He went faithfully for a while, then began appearing later and later for his appointments, till finally he stopped going at all.

The Greenwich Village he haunted was more frenetic than the one his father had known; there was less striving in the arts and a greater restlessness, a sense of futility and discontent, a desire to escape that no amount of alcohol could assuage. Many of the young, Shane among them, took to "sticks of tea" (marijuana cigarettes). "I started it," he recalls, "because everybody else seemed to be doing it. I didn't want to be different." His friend Marc Brandel, who likewise indulged, says, "The idea was to get yourself feeling anything but natural. The thing is, most of us outgrew it. Shane didn't."

Since Shane said little and, being without guile, was easily taken advantage of, some thought him not overly bright; but actually he had a good mind, a potentiality that, from paralyzing self-doubt, would never be realized. Miss Stark, who considered him "too good to cope," says, "He hated to mistrust or not understand anyone. In this way he was a little like Prince Myshkin, Dostoevski's 'Idiot.' He was too innocent."

Marc Brandel, in a similar view, feels that Shane "had exceptional qualities of kindness and gentleness — and a certain *virtue* — it is difficult to define but I suppose it was a sense of decency . . . that was very rare. . . . Of course in time it all got screwed up. . . . Then, too, so much of Shane's energy, which might have helped him to survive, was squandered in nostalgia — into romantic admiration for his father and his uncle, the reluctant actor and successful alcoholic. '*He* was the really great one,' Shane once told me about his uncle. He must have identified with him very strongly."

On the verge of marriage for several years, Shane and Miss Stark finally parted. Long afterward, looking back, she said, "I was dazzled by the O'Neills, but I had a sense of survival, which kept me at last from being dragged into the whirlpool of the established tragic ambiance."

In one of his recurrent attempts at rehabilitating himself, Shane went to work for a Greenwich Village studio that made ornaments for window displays and proved clever with his hands; he was particularly good at fashioning animals of straw and papier-mâché. After Margaret Stark, he took up with Catherine Givens, whom he knew from the Old Colony bar, a blond, thin and pretty, with a faintly scornful air. From a well-to-do Connecticut family, Cathy had been reared with material advantages — private schools, etc. — but there was discord between her parents, little rapport between them and their children. Rejecting her elders' way of life, Cathy settled in the Village and supported herself as a sales-girl in department stores. In common with Shane, she had little drive and was indifferent to the conventions; at the same time, though, she was too in love with Shane to be content with just sleeping with him and thought that marriage would give her a sense of security. She was twenty, he four years older, when they were married in July 1944.

Since Cathy was in her final weeks of pregnancy in fall 1945 when Shane received the message from Eugene Jr., he went alone to the Barclay for a reunion with his father after five years. In a succinct account afterward, he told Cathy that his father and in particular Carlotta had questioned him closely about her and were eager to meet her.

On November 19 she gave birth to a boy, who was named after his celebrated grandfather. Visiting the hospital several days later with gifts, Carlotta explained that O'Neill had not accompanied her for fear of running into Agnes, and stressed that Cathy was never to mention his former wife's name in his presence, because it would upset him. After Cathy returned home to 49 King Street, Carlotta again called on her, this time with a complete layette for the baby, and said that Eugene was unwell that day. According to Cathy, her visitor was "obviously uncomfortable about our cold-water flat and its meager furnishings," but during her stream of talk Carlotta said it was "important for a young couple to stand on their own feet" and expressed satisfaction that Shane was working — by this time, in a factory. She promised to have them to dinner shortly and once more warned the girl against mentioning Agnes's name to O'Neill.

O'Neill's first words on meeting her: "Why, you look just like Agnes!" While he did not kiss his daughter-in-law, he smiled warmly and soon had her at ease. She had "sort of expected the old sailor, the saloon guy I had read about," but instead found him "a very elegant man. He was extremely well dressed and had an Old World air about him. He was very gallant, had beautiful manners." The evening at the Barclay went off pleasantly. O'Neill nodded approvingly when Cathy, under questioning, said that Yeats and Edna St. Vincent Millay were among her favorite poets, and he became animated as the dinner talk got around to jazz. Carlotta momentarily dampened the conversation when she dismissed jazz as "savage" music. According to Cathy, Carlotta said that it was " 'the music of Negroes, and that they go by their instincts.' She did not believe jazz was true art."

Eugene O'Neill III, whose paternal grandfather never saw him, lived only briefly. On February 10, 1946, Cathy, finding the baby cold to the touch, rushed him to a sister of hers who lived nearby and then to St. Vincent's Hospital, where he was pronounced dead on arrival. After an autopsy the probable cause of death was listed as "postural asphyxia from bed clothes. Accidental."

(Decades later medical science began an intensive study of what is called Sudden Infant Death Syndrome [SIDS], the leading killer of children between the ages of a week and a year. According to a 1972 news account: "It happens at least 10,000 times a year in the United States: A happy, apparently healthy child — usually 2 to 3 months old — is diapered, burped and bedded. In the morning it lies dead. . . . And nobody knows why.

"Such a death strikes the parents to the core of their psyches. They feel they did something wrong. . . . As of this moment, there is only a strong suggestion that a virus is the culprit. . . . Crib deaths are more common in winter than in summer. . . . There is not even a clue to the prevention of SIDS. So effort now turns on meliorating the psychic aftermath for the surviving parents, to remove the blame, the recrimination and to have them understand it was not their fault. . . . So things are a little better than in the nineteenth century when most physicians believed that the children smothered in bed clothes improperly arranged by a careless mother.")

Cathy and Shane, feeling guilty over the infant's death, were devastated. Agnes, in Los Angeles at the time, where Oona was expecting her second child, tried on the telephone to comfort them and suggested a change of scene, namely, Spithead. Through Bill Aronberg she arranged for an advance payment on her alimony to be given to the young couple for their visit to Bermuda. The night before they sailed, O'Neill had them to dinner, but Carlotta, whose mother had died on the Coast a few days previously and who was indisposed, did not appear. Most likely she would have shunned seeing them under any circumstances, for on hearing of the baby's death she had denounced them as "bohemians," immature and shiftless, with no right to have children. O'Neill himself was greatly upset over his namesake's fate — he regarded it as symbolically significant — but he refrained, for a while, from becoming critical.

In his wife's absence O'Neill seemed more relaxed to Cathy, more outgoing. She had developed an immediate affection for her father-in-law (she thought him "shy and sweet like Shane") and sat back silent most of the time, listening to the two men reminisce about Bermuda. "Gene," she recalls, "spoke of how much he had loved Spithead, about the times he and Shane had had there." On both sides, throughout the evening, there was a warm feeling, but this would be the last time Shane and his wife ever saw O'Neill.

As the young couple ran out of funds during their months in Bermuda, they gradually sold virtually the entire contents of Spithead — furniture, linens, barrels of dishes, including some fine china that had belonged to Ella and James O'Neill — and they even disposed of the ceiling heaters in the bathrooms. It is unknown whether someone in Bermuda informed O'Neill that they were stripping Spithead or whether Carlotta's censorious attitude finally influenced him, but, whatever the cause, he cooled toward his son and daughter-in-law.

Shortly after their return to New York in 1946, Shane came down with the flu and Cathy, since they were broke, telephoned her father-in-law. Carlotta, who answered, said that her husband did not care to see them and hung up, but Cathy kept calling back till O'Neill got on the wire. On learning that his son was ill, he said he would have his attorney attend to the matter. By the time Aronberg arrived with a doctor at the couple's hotel in the Village, Shane, feeling hungry and slightly better, had gone out with Cathy for a meal; but they left behind a friend named Seymour who had been drinking and wanted a nap. Since Aronberg had never before met Shane, he and the doctor assumed they had the right patient. After being examined by the doctor and given an injection, Seymour finally grasped the situation. "He laughed like hell," the lawyer recalls, "and said, 'I'm not Shane — he went out.'"

Aronberg too thought the incident amusing but, evidently, O'Neill felt that he had been hoaxed by a hopelessly irresponsible son. From time to time he would make efforts to learn how the boy was getting along; he would quietly try once or twice to help him; but he would never again have direct contact with him. He was less forbearing than James O'Neill, who used to say, with sufficient provocation: "God deliver me from my children!"

27

❖

Return to Broadway

S t. Patrick's Day 1946 saw a reunion of the playwright and Barrett H. Clark, one of his earliest champions. When Clark asked why "a man who called himself O'Neill" was not marching at that moment on Fifth Avenue, his host merely grinned. At first the theater historian, who had not seen O'Neill for ten years, was distressed at his appearance ("Painfully thin and shrunken . . . a man who looked as though he should be in a hospital"); but as the playwright became animated, Clark found that "the O'Neill I remembered was again sitting before me. He spoke . . . with good humor and graciousness. His interest in the world about him seemed deeper and broader than ever . . . he seemed no longer to object to being a part of the practical theater. . . . I thought I could detect in him even a little pleasure and excitement in the prospect of casting his new play, being on hand at rehearsals."

In lending Clark a script of *The Iceman Cometh*, its author said, "Mere physical violence, mere bigness, is not important. You'll see that *The Iceman* is a very simple play: one set; I've certainly observed the unities all right, characterization, but no plot in the ordinary sense; I didn't need a plot; the people are enough."

With the Guild brass and Eddie Dowling, who was slated both to direct the play and to appear as Hickey, O'Neill was involved by now in casting *The Iceman*, which was to start rehearsing in September. Dowling had been recommended for the part of Hickey years earlier by George Jean Nathan, chiefly on the basis of his portrayal in William Saroyan's *The Time of Your Life*, another saloon story, and O'Neill had endorsed him after they had had a long talk at Tao House. Besides helping to cast the production and making further revisions in his script, the playwright was engaged in conferences with his old friend Robert Edmond Jones, who was designing the sets and costumes.

A perfectionist, Jones had been working on the O'Neill project since the first of the year. After steeping himself in the script, he had sought out Manhattan's ancient saloons, starting with McSorley's, and worked his way from South Ferry to Harlem. "There are so many things," he said, "bound up in designing a play by O'Neill. There's knowledge of the man, of course, and friendship and memories. It's hard to say, otherwise, why you spend twelve hours of every day trying trimmings for dresses, looking for 1912 underthings, hanging around disreputable saloons, getting the exact type of keg to look right on the bar, selecting mosquito netting to keep the flies off the mirrors, raiding a water-front hash house for dirty, checked tablecloths, exploring junk shops for straight-backed iron chairs, traveling upstate for a nickel-in-the-slot Edison talking machine, searching photograph collections for pictures of John L. Sullivan and Dick Croker [a onetime head of Tammany Hall].

"Gene knows exactly what he wants. His descriptions are definite. All a designer has to do is to follow them. I've been complimented on the colors for the sets and costumes [he was interviewed shortly after *The Iceman* had opened], but it was really all Gene's idea. He knew so well that dirty white would be the best background. . . . Without ever having painted, he's a true artist. His creativeness embraces the visual aspect.

"Gene has a tremendous sense of living. A high-voltage person. He disturbs people by just being around and therefore all kinds of theories are made up about him. His great virtue is that he writes close to the quick of life. The public regards him as a mystic, cynic, dreamer, prophet, a dark, brooding spirit. Actually, the wellspring of his influence is his astonishing instinct for the theater. In the final analysis he is first, last and foremost the son of James O'Neill, a great actor."

Of the new friends the playwright had made since his return to New York, none responded to him with greater sensitivity than Sherlee Weingarten, a production assistant at the Theater Guild. Quick in mind and spirit, a slight brunette with fine blue eyes, she was detailed by the Guild to serve as O'Neill's secretary in the afternoons. The first time Sherlee saw him, he and Carlotta were in front of Guild headquarters waiting for a taxi. "I didn't know who they were," she recalls, "but even in profile they were two extraordinary persons. There was something unmistakably special about them. They stood out."

Sherlee was "terrified" at the prospect of working for O'Neill, for he

[569]

was "like a legend" to her, he was "in the textbooks at school." The playwright had been given a small office at the Guild, and the first time Sherlee appeared, he stood up. "Please don't," the girl said, "it isn't necessary in an office." Later, she brought him a cup of tea and immediately regretted it, because his hands shook so that the liquid sloshed over. In an agony of embarrassment, Sherlee looked at the walls, the ceiling, out the window, and finally in desperation said, "Maybe it's too warm for tea [the day was cold]. How about a Coca-Cola?" At his assent, she dashed without a coat to a nearby drugstore and returned with the soft drink, which he drank easily through a straw.

Touched by her concern and tact, he praised her to Carlotta, who likewise was favorably impressed when she met the young Guild employee. Though on guard against any more Jane Caldwell episodes, Carlotta decided that Sherlee was trustworthy. At Carlotta's initiative, the two shortly were on a first-name basis, but the girl always, despite the warm feeling that developed between her and the playwright, addressed him as "Mr. O'Neill" and referred to him as such.

Before long a frequent luncheon guest of the O'Neills, Sherlee found that the close association confirmed her first quick impression of them. "They both," she says, "had the gift of making everything seem special, more interesting, more alive. Most people who have this quality are very much involved in life, are deeply involved with people and things they believe in, but O'Neill and Carlotta weren't, yet they had this thing. If Carlotta gave you a glass of sherry and a biscuit, they were special because she gave them to you. The grass seemed greener, the sky bluer, everything more interesting because you saw them and knew them, were involved to some extent in their lives."

Initially Carlotta had not looked forward to resettling in Georgia, but the prospect became more attractive the longer she and Eugene remained at the Barclay. Writing in March 1946 to an acquaintance in the Sea Island area, she said that her husband "loathes towns" and that they were "living in two rooms & miserable!" Instead of returning South, though, they chose an alternative more desirable to Carlotta; they moved into a six-room penthouse at 35 East Eighty-fourth Street that became available this spring with the death of playwright Edward Sheldon. With Carlotta urging him to be sensible and remain where good medical care was available, Eugene had finally agreed that Sea Island was no longer a suitable place for him.

Under the circumstances he felt that if he had to live in New York it was symbolically appropriate that he should inherit Sheldon's apartment, since the other man's life had also been darkened by illness. Sheldon's in fact had been a far crueler fate, yet he had transcended it. Blind, immobilized, and in almost constant pain throughout his final two decades, Sheldon after becoming bedridden had attained serenity of spirit, along with a heightened appreciation of life, that exalted his parade of visitors; many considered him a kind of secular saint. Shortly after the O'Neills' return to New York, Carlotta had accompanied friends to meet the distinguished invalid and had come away awed. Though O'Neill himself never called on him, he was moved by Carlotta's account; where he had once disparaged Sheldon's works, he now called him "very good for his day."

After Carlotta was through redecorating, the penthouse glowed with color — walls of deep purple, royal blue, Chinese red — and was tastefully furnished with things the couple had collected in their travels. Hanging in the playwright's combination bedroom-study were depictions of old sailing vessels and an oil study of Broadway at the height of the theater rush hour. "There's the whole story of the decline of America," he remarked to a visitor, indicating the artwork. "From the most beautiful thing America has ever built, the clipper ship, to the most tawdry street in the world."

During the pair's seven months at the Barclay the strain of living in close quarters had led to disagreements and rehashing of old grievances that still rankled, chiefly on Carlotta's side, as they settled into the penthouse. In his anniversary note to her this July, Eugene said: "With the same old love deep in my heart I felt for you on that day in Paris, 1929!

"In justice, as everyone but ourselves seems to know, our marriage has been the most successful and happy of any we know — until late years.

"Here's for a new beginning!"

Mourning Becomes Electra was at last sold to the movies this year, chiefly through the efforts of Dudley Nichols, who was assigned by RKO Pictures to produce and direct it from his own screenplay. Nichols conferred a few times with O'Neill and at his request brought along one evening Katina Paxinou, Greece's foremost actress, who was slated for the part of Christine Mannon. "I was trembling, so nervous about meeting him," she recalls. "O'Neill kissed my hand, and over his protests, I kissed his. In dress he looked like a French gentleman — striped trousers, black jacket, black tie — and topping everything those burning black eyes. We arrived at eight and were supposed to be there only half an hour, as he wasn't well, but he kept us till after two. He had me recite from the old tragedies, in the original Greek, and we discussed my part in the movie."

(Released the following year with Rosalind Russell, Miss Paxinou, Michael Redgrave and Raymond Massey as the Mannon family, the picture was a respectful but static and uninspired adaptation; Redgrave's was the only meritorious performance.)

Since *The Iceman Cometh* was another of the author's outsize dramas, with a running time of over four hours, there were again differences between him and the Guild over the question of length. O'Neill tried to cut three-quarters of an hour from the four-act drama but found that he could trim it no more than fifteen minutes without diminishing the play's impact. Trying to persuade him to cut further, Langner had an assistant check the script for the number of times it declares that "the lie of a pipe dream is what gives life," etc., and found that the thought was expressed eighteen times. When Langner pointed this out, the playwright replied in a quiet but emphatic voice, "I *intended* it to be repeated eighteen times!"

Summarizing his view to Kenneth Macgowan, who also, like the Guild brass, felt that the play was too long, O'Neill had said earlier that he had tried to write a drama "where at the end you feel you know the souls of the seventeen men and women who appear — and the women who don't appear — as well as if you'd read a play about each of them. I couldn't condense much without taking a lot of life from some of these people and reducing them to lay figures. You would find if I did not build up the complete picture of the group . . . in the first part — the atmosphere of the place, the humor and friendship and human warmth and *deep inner contentment* of the bottom — you would not be so interested in these people and you would find the impact of what follows a lot less profoundly disturbing. You wouldn't feel the same sympathy and understanding for them, or be so moved by what Hickey does to them.

"It's hard to explain exactly my intuitions about this play. Perhaps I can put it best by saying *The Iceman Cometh* is something I want to make life reveal about itself, fully and deeply and roundly — that it takes place for me in life, not in a theater — that the fact it is a play which can be produced with actors is secondary and incidental to me — and even quite unimportant — and so it would be a loss to me to sacrifice anything of the complete life for the sake of stage and audience."

Besides working with Saxe Commins on the text for the published version, which was to contain material cut from the performed script, O'Neill enlisted the services of his wife Dorothy. While out walking one day he and Carlotta dropped by the Comminses, who lived on East Ninety-fifth Street, and Eugene asked Dorothy to help him with the music for a number in *The Iceman* and another in *A Moon for the*

Misbegotten. "I hope you won't mind my croaking voice," he said, as she picked out the notes from his rendering of the songs.

The elevator in the O'Neills' building opened directly into their apartment, and the doorman was under strict instructions to announce anyone who wanted to see them. However, Saxe and Dorothy had been there so often that the doorman passed her in without a word when she arrived several days later to give O'Neill the sheets of music. At Dorothy's sudden appearance, Carlotta, instead of being cordial as usual, said, "How did you get up here? Who let you in?" Dorothy gave her the papers — Eugene was out at the time — and left almost immediately, giving little thought to her brusque reception; but she would later recall the cold face Carlotta turned on her.

After auditioning actors for months, O'Neill and the Guild decided that Eddie Dowling should only direct *The Iceman*, assigned the part of Hickey to James Barton, who originally was listed to portray Harry Hope, and gave the part of Hope to the fine old character actor Dudley Digges. Few plays in the Guild's history were cast with as much care; eager to regain its onetime eminence, the Guild had great expectations for the Nobel laureate's return to the theater after twelve years.

With O'Neill adamant against a pre-Broadway tryout ("Maxwell Anderson may revise and rewrite on the road, but I can't do it"), Actors' Equity granted his play a fifth week to rehearse, as well as other concessions. *The Iceman* entered production on September 3. O'Neill, who attended all the afternoon sessions, relied so by now on Sherlee Weingarten that he always had her by his side at rehearsals. Previously a moderate smoker, Sherlee became "a cigarette fiend" around O'Neill, since it was difficult for him to light his own. "Whenever he took one out, I would," she recalls, "so I could light his at the same time without being too obvious about it." The copy of *The Iceman* he later inscribed to her said: "With affection and gratitude for all she has done since the first typing job — all the kindnesses in the many small things that only the sensitive do, or the sensitive appreciate. I have a guilty feeling I have not been sufficiently appreciative at times . . . taking it for granted you should light cigarettes for playwrights!"

Though he seemed to come alive and gain in energy as the production was taking shape, he still, chiefly because of his tremor, gave an impression of fragility. In taking notes he clasped his right wrist with his left hand while he wrote; as one actor recalls, it was "painful" to see him shakily turning the pages of his script. Occasionally he sat on the stage, at one of the tables in Harry Hope's Bedrock Bar, and at times, lost in thought, appeared to be reliving a phase of his past rather than watching a rehearsal.

Despite his reserve, he inspired affection in some of the players, chiefly the younger ones, who were delighted at being in an O'Neill production and gratified that the Great Man, instead of striking a Great Man attitude, was approachable and courteous. "Unlike many if not most playwrights," says Miss Weingarten, "O'Neill was not disdainful of actors, he didn't dislike them as a group — personally, I mean. How he felt about their work in his plays was another thing, but he didn't share the usual bias of playwrights against them. One of his finest qualities was that he gave dignity to everyone he met, he treated everyone with great respect. Waiters, waitresses, cabdrivers, elevator operators, he reacted to them, he *saw* them, he was aware of them as individuals."

E. G. Marshall (cast as Willie Oban) felt at their first meeting that he "had known O'Neill a thousand years." Tom Pedi (the bartender Rocky) says that he "never went over and talked with him, as some did. I wanted to, and didn't know how, but I felt he liked me. I think he knew I was the underdog there — the Guild had wanted all 'names'. — and I hadn't done much. But O'Neill was always for the underdog. I felt he understood."

Covertly, to keep from alarming Carlotta, O'Neill had a mild crush on redheaded Marcella Markham (Cora, the eldest of the three prostitutes) — he thought she had "sensual haunches" — and enjoyed teasing her. When she asked if he had ever known a "Cora," he said, "Yes — but I won't say how well!" In general, however, the atmosphere at rehearsals was solemn and heavy, and all the actors were under a pledge not to reveal the story to anyone. James Barton, who had starred in vaudeville and musical comedy before distinguishing himself as Jeeter Lester in *Tobacco Road*, cracked that "it's as bad as being in church."

At first Eddie Dowling tried to enliven the leisurely drama with some movement and pieces of "business," but every afternoon the playwright eliminated what the director had introduced in the morning. The playwright wanted no unessential action that might distract, even momentarily, from his words. After being told by the Guild brass to follow the text scrupulously — no stage business unless specified in the script — Dowling, according to cast members, was "cowed," "like a whipped child," "afraid to suggest anything." Dowling himself confided to stage manager Karl Nielsen: "I dread their [the O'Neills'] coming in the afternoon."

On his side, O'Neill, who had become thoroughly dissatisfied with the director, felt that he had been unduly influenced by George Jean

Nathan's enthusiastic recommendation. "Nathan," he complained privately, "may know plays, but he doesn't know actors and directors."

Years later many of the cast called *The Iceman* the most trying play they had ever appeared in. "The main trouble," says John Marriott (Joe Mott, the black gambler), "was that you couldn't relax a minute, you always had to be in character, though you just sat there for long periods at a time and didn't say a word. It was a real ordeal, and the same was true of rehearsals. One of the fellows started doing a crossword puzzle once, but he immediately got a note to pay full attention to what was going on."

Some actors found that the play seeped, in disturbing ways, into their private lives. According to Joe Marr (the bartender Chuck) another of the cast confided that he was having "violent nightmares, some of a suicidal nature." Nicholas Joy, accustomed to playing well-tailored, sophisticated characters, grew so disturbed by his role as a raggedy alcoholic (Captain Smith) that he not only gave up liquor for months but became more immaculate than ever in his dress outside the theater. "There was something about this play," Jeanne Cagney recalls, "that affected you personally. A few of the older players, men who'd been in many things, said this was the first time they couldn't maintain a professional distance from their parts. One or two, in fact, told me, 'I think this is going to be my last play, Jeanne.' There was this strong feeling of death, you know, in the play." Miss Cagney herself, a devout Catholic, was so uncomfortable playing a streetwalker that she took to wearing a large crucifix.

As O'Neill and Dowling stood before the theater one day, a large bearded face suddenly bent down toward them and said, "Hello, Pop. Can I see a rehearsal?" In giving his own consent, O'Neill politely asked Dowling for his. Eugene Jr. afterward told his father that the play was "great" and disappeared. Although he attended several more rehearsals, the actors were unaware of his presence, for he always sat unobtrusively in the rear of the auditorium and was never introduced to them. He also kept his distance at the theater from Carlotta, since their relationship had so deteriorated that he rarely visited the penthouse any longer.

Now that the Nobel Prize winner had emerged from seclusion after more than a decade, the newspapers and magazines were eager to question him and bring his history up to date. In California, thinking of his tremor and general physical decline in recent years, he had dreaded the prospect of becoming involved with Broadway and meeting people, yet in the months prior to the opening of *The Iceman*, he readily submitted to a number of interviews. Perhaps he was heartened by the example of Edward Sheldon's heroic success in rising above his afflictions.

Robert Sylvester of the *News*, the first in a parade of men with pencil, paper and questions, found the playwright in a genial mood. Appearing amused at photographers who were "turning him this way and that" at Guild headquarters, O'Neill laughed silently, his whole body shaking, over one of Theresa Helburn's remarks. When a cameraman asked if the playwright should assume a "typical" pose, Miss Helburn retorted, "Yes, take him giving us a definite 'No.' " Apologizing for his hair being rather long, O'Neill said he was not trying to look "artistic" but had been too busy for a barber.

Before *Post* columnist Earl Wilson saw the playwright, the Guild's Joe Heidt warned him, "He may try to light a cigarette – but don't help him. He'll resent that." During Wilson's hour and a half at the penthouse, the matches repeatedly burned out without one ever reaching his host's cigarette. Questioned about the play that was not to be released till twenty-five years after his death, O'Neill said, "It's a real story, also [like *The Iceman*] laid in 1912. There's one person in it who is still alive." Eager to learn more of the secret play that had aroused great curiosity around Broadway, Wilson was on the verge of asking, "Do you mean it's you – it's your autobiography?" but before he could frame the question, O'Neill added, "I won't tell you a word about it." As the columnist left, his host was still trying to light a cigarette.

According to an account in the *Journal-American* by George Jean Nathan, he asked his old friend what he considered "the greatest present need of the American stage." O'Neill, who often sounds more like Nathan than himself when quoted in Nathan's writings, allegedly replied, ". . . another Lotta Faust. There, my boy, was a love apple, and who said anything about acting? . . . When Lotta sang 'Sammy,' all the great Shakespearean actresses of the day felt like going into hiding."

A Moon for the Misbegotten was to enter rehearsal shortly after *The Iceman* opened, he informed the critic, and added that he was already concerned about finding a suitable actor for Con Melody in *A Touch of the Poet*. "What that one needs," he said, "is an actor like Maurice Barrymore or James O'Neill, my old man. One of those big-chested, chiseled-mug, romantic old boys. . . . Most actors in these times lack an air. If a playwright doesn't work up entrances fifteen minutes long for them and have all the other characters describe them in advance as something pretty elegant, noble, chivalrous and handsome, the audiences wouldn't be able to accept them for much more than third assistant barkeeps, if that."

Unable to accommodate the many individual requests, O'Neill gave a mass interview to the press on September 2 at the Guild offices. At the outset he apologized for his low, indistinct voice ("Even my own family complains about it"), then said that he didn't "know Broadway any more. It's all changed. They've even torn down the Cadillac Hotel [originally the Barrett House] where I was born fifty-seven years ago. There is only empty air now where I came into this world. That was a dirty trick." To one newsman he seemed to wear "a tragic mask of concentrated sorrow," but when he said "a dirty trick," he suddenly flashed a broad grin, as though "another mask had suddenly been superimposed. Then, instantaneously, this fleeting mask of comedy disappeared, and the mask of tragedy was donned again. One was shocked by the sudden transition."

Decades ahead of his day, O'Neill said cautionary things at the press conference that would be accepted gospel among the more thoughtful in the 1960s and 1970s; but in 1946, with the national mood one of confidence and optimism over our emergence as the predominant power from the most catastrophic war in history, he stood an isolated Jeremiah. Voicing some of his central thinking when asked about the theme of his nine-play Cycle, he declared that he considered America, "instead of being the most successful country in the world, is its greatest failure . . . the greatest failure because it was given everything, more than any other country. Through moving as rapidly as it has, it has never acquired any real roots. Its main idea is that everlasting game of trying to possess your own soul and the things outside of it, too."

He kept rubbing his trembly hands, folding and unfolding them constantly; his attitude toward his tremor, he said, was one of "enraged resignation." At times his voice almost died in his throat, but now and then, in his effort to speak up, it suddenly filled the room with a booming bass. He sensed, he said, "a feeling around, or I'm mistaken, of fate. Kismet, the negative fate; not in the Greek sense. . . . It's struck me as time goes on, how something funny, even farcical, can suddenly without any apparent reason, break up into something gloomy and tragic [At this point he seems to anticipate the dark comedy and black humor so prevalent in the writings of subsequent decades]. . . . A sort of unfair *non sequitur*, as though events, as though life, were being manipulated just to confuse us; a big kind of comedy that doesn't stay funny very long. I've made some use of it in *The Iceman*. The first act is hilarious comedy, *I think*, but then some people may not even laugh. At any rate, the comedy breaks up and the tragedy comes on."

Another day, talking onstage during a rehearsal break to Croswell Bowen of the newspaper *PM*, he again pursued his thesis about this country as the "greatest failure." "Of course America is due for a retribution," he declared. "There ought to be a page in the history books of the United States of all the unprovoked, criminal, unjust crimes committed and sanctioned by our government since the beginning of our history. . . . There is hardly one thing that our government has done that isn't some treachery — against the Indians, against the people of the Northwest, against the small farmers."

As he spoke, he seemed to Bowen "in the tradition of all the great half-drunken Irishmen who sound off in bars all over the world. Their talk is always the same, extravagant, rambling, full of madness and violence, but studded with enough essential truth and insight to force you to listen with troubled fascination."

Fondling a prop bottle filled with "whiskey" (water and caramel syrup), the playwright continued: "This American Dream stuff gives me a pain. Telling the world about our American Dream! I don't know what they mean. If it exists . . . why don't we make it work in one small hamlet in the United States?"

He banged his fist on top of the bar. "The big business leaders in this country! Why do we produce such stupendous, colossal egomaniacs? They go on doing the most monstrous things, always using the same excuse that if we don't, the other person will. It's impossible to satirize them if you wanted to."

In a more relaxed mood the afternoon Kyle Crichton of *Collier's* called at the apartment, O'Neill took evident pleasure in reminiscing. It seemed to the visitor that the playwright looked back on his relations with his father with amusement. "There's no secret," he suddenly grinned, "about my father and me. Whatever he wanted, I wouldn't touch with a ten-foot pole!"

Of his brief newspaper career in New London, he said that he had written poems that imitated "Kipling and people like that. Dante Gabriel Rossetti would have a chance for a pretty good lawsuit if he could get himself out of that grave and come back." At the end Crichton expressed pleasure at finding him "a down-to-earth humorist rather than the solemn philosopher I had expected." "Oh, yes, some days," O'Neill replied with a sad smile. "Other days, other moods."

Thanks to his being recommended by Robert Edmond Jones, Tom

Prideaux of *Life* was granted several sessions and other preferential treatment. Though O'Neill maintained a "mysterious silence" about *Long Day's Journey*, he delighted Prideaux by giving him a passage from the play, with permission to publish it in his article. The extract, from the fourth act, was Edmund's lyrical recollection of his ecstatic moments at sea, ending, "It was a great mistake my being born a man."

The New York *Times* considered O'Neill's return important enough to have S. J. Woolf interview him for its weekend magazine in mid-September, and Karl Schriftgeisser for its Sunday drama pages later that month. "Almost the first words of my father I remember," O'Neill told Woolf, "are, 'The theater is dying.' . . . It was when he was starring in *The Count of Monte Cristo*. . . . I can still see him in that play . . . rising from a canvas sea shouting, 'The world is mine!' It was a time when artificiality was as prevalent on the stage as . . . in everyday life. The simplest lines had to be declaimed.

"It was a prudish age which left its impress in the form of present-day censorship. This to me is one of the biggest obstacles in the artistic development of the theater. Now, before a play can safely be produced, somebody has to say it will not corrupt the morals of six-year-olds."

At the mass interview he had called *The Hairy Ape*, of all his old works, his favorite, but to Woolf he said that he probably was fondest of *The Great God Brown*. (In both plays, it is worth noting, the protagonist is a man who doesn't "belong.") O'Neill added, however, that he had "never been completely satisfied with anything that I have done and I constantly rewrite my plays until they are produced and even then I always see things which I could improve and I regret that it is too late to make more changes. For, after all, anyone who creates must feel deeply. Like Shaw, he may cover up his sincerity with humor, he may make light of his efforts, but those efforts are nevertheless heartbreaking."

Recovering from the flu when Schriftgeisser interviewed him, the playwright appeared to recede into himself between answering questions, but as the afternoon wore on he became more animated. After outlining the subject matter of *The Iceman*, he said, "I do not think that you can write anything of value or understanding about the present. You can only write about life if it is far enough in the past. The present is too mixed up with superficial values; you can't know which thing is important and which is not."

His new drama, he summarized, was "about pipe dreams. And the philosophy is that there is always one dream left, one final dream, no matter how low you have fallen, down there at the bottom of the bottle. I

O'Neill at a rehearsal of The Iceman Cometh. *The players, left to right, are Ruth Gilbert, Dudley Digges and Marcella Markham*

Saxe Commins at work at Random House

know, because I saw it." Emerging from a long silence, he voiced a main article of his credo: "It will take man a million years to grow up and obtain a soul."

At one of the last rehearsals, when the actors were given a chance to question their author, he was asked for the meaning of the play. He smilingly countered, "What does it mean to you?" and listened intently as some gave their views. One actor, politically radical, said of the play that "it's depressing, there's no solution. What's the good of it?" Instead of being offended, O'Neill spoke at some length but without satisfying the dissenter. Asked about his own politics, he called himself "a philosophical anarchist, which means — Go to it, but leave me out of it!"

The physical act of writing had become so difficult for him by now that it took him ten to fifteen minutes merely to sign his name. Hoping to inspire his actors to give their best, he spent days writing inscriptions at once humorous and flattering in copies of the published play for every one of the large cast. On opening day the actors, especially those in dressing rooms on the third and fourth levels, were surprised to see the uncertain figure of O'Neill bearing the gift books. The inscription in John Marriott's book is representative: "Many, many thanks for your grand impersonation of 'Joe.' *The Iceman Cometh* owes a lot to it and you.

"And when your new gambling house opens, please make an exception and let me in. But don't let me near the faro layout. I was once lucky at that — welcome me to the Wheel. Boy, the money I'll lose!"

Lagging behind schedule from the time it entered production, *The Iceman Cometh* ended its final rehearsal at 3 P.M. on October 9, 1946, only an hour and a half before the première performance was to begin. The actors felt both tired and keyed up. The request for press tickets was so heavy that correspondents from all over — Australia, Italy, Greece, South Africa, the Scandinavian countries — had to content themselves with standing room. In the audience were some who had paid scalpers as high as twenty-five dollars for their seats. An hour before curtain time the lobby and the sidewalk at the Martin Beck were jammed with people clutching the prized tickets and others present to gawk at the celebrities. O'Neill, prowling nervously about backstage, waited just long enough to hear the applause and beelike buzz as the curtain went up, then Sherlee Weingarten shepherded him through the stage-door alley to Forty-fifth Street, where she hailed a taxi for him. None of the throng, craning for a glimpse of Hollywood bosoms and famous profiles, noticed the playwright.

The Comminses, who had O'Neill's tickets, were sitting next to Brooks Atkinson, and the moment the curtain rose on Robert Edmond Jones's setting, Dorothy breathed to Saxe, "Why, it's a Daumier!" Atkinson immediately leaned over and whispered, "May I quote that in my review?"

The audience as a whole gave the play strained attention from start to finish. At the close of the hour-long first act, there was a seventy-five-minute intermission for dinner, and the performance — after near-disaster in the final act — ended at ten. James Barton, instead of resting during the long dinner break and conserving his voice for Hickey's torrential confession, one of the longest speeches in modern drama, played host to a line of well-wishers in his dressing room. As a result, in a scene where Barton should have been most forceful, most impassioned, he was almost inaudible at times; moreover, he "blew up" once or twice. Since it had been apparent at rehearsals that he was having difficulty memorizing the part, the Guild had taken the precaution to station prompters in both wings and beneath the bar onstage. When Barton first limped to a silence, the prompters could be heard from the first rows. "Please, boys, please!" the rattled actor cried, but he soon managed to continue in character.

As the first-nighters streamed out, many were debating whether Hickey was supposed to be insane (Barton's interpretation failed to clarify this point), and shortly afterward, as one account has it, "Sardi's and Twenty-One, Walgreen's and El Morocco seethed with indignant argument" concerning the merits and the meaning of the play. *The Iceman Cometh* had immediately established itself as the most controversial play in town.

Considering the damage to the evening from Barton's inadequate portrayal, the reviews, though several were sharply critical and others only lukewarm, were somewhat better than might be expected. Almost without exception the critics, including those favorably impressed, found the play repetitious and decidedly too long. While Eddie Dowling's direction was widely praised, Stark Young, an astute judge of acting, was so dissatisfied that he said in the *New Republic:* "I am not even sure as to the extent to which I can judge *The Iceman Cometh* after seeing such a production of it."

John Chapman of the *News*, thoroughly responsive to the play itself, called it "a magnificent drama — magnificent in plan, in size, in scope . . . a frightening play, too — terrifying and shocking . . . a part of life itself." It seemed to him that some first-nighters were "so intent upon finding hidden meanings, so afraid they might miss the master's message that they had little time left for doing the very simple thing an audience is supposed to do — to sit in a comfortable chair and take in a play." O'Neill's latest, he concluded, was "great theater."

Equally enthusiastic, Richard Watts, Jr., said in the *Post:* "There is a wild, cascading power in O'Neill's dramas, which, if tamed, would destroy the freedom and scope of his fierce and brooding imagination, and the excessive length of an O'Neill play [is] a small price to pay for keeping his essential quality intact. Editing might make *The Iceman* seem more efficient, but it would endanger the magnitude of its spirit." The play, he added, was "a superb drama of splendid and imposing stature."

Brooks Atkinson, though critical of the play's length, declared that "the only thing that matters is that [O'Neill] has plunged again into the black quagmire of man's illusions and composed a rigadoon of death as strange and elemental as his first works. . . . The Lord knows [the characters] talk too much. . . . But it is good talk — racy, angry, comic drumbeats on the lid of doom [and the play itself is] a notable drama by a man who writes with the heart and wonder of a poet." Taking his cue from Dorothy Commins, the *Times* critic said that Jones's setting "glows with an articulate meaning, like a Daumier print, as one alert spectator observed."

While Louis Kronenberger of *PM* thought that the play "should be seen," he found that the characters "are not probed very deeply (we know almost as much about them in the first act as in the last); they do not grow, but they grow beautifully familiar and hence fairly real: the four hours of *The Iceman* have the cumulative value of a very long novel, where abundance does well enough what art would do much better. . . . For all its fine scattered scenes, [the play] left me cold."

To Ward Morehouse of the *Sun* the saloon saga, though "often too slow, too long-winded," was, if not the author's finest, "certainly one of stature and importance." Arthur Pollock of the Brooklyn *Eagle*, another who chided the playwright for being verbose, conceded, however, that he had created living people "all the way, characters we will remember for years."

Howard Barnes of the *Herald Tribune*, among the dissenters, felt that the author's "erratic genius flames uncertainly" this time, while Robert Garland, even more critical, said in the *Journal-American* that the play was "neither first-rate Broadway, first-rate Theater Guild, nor first-rate Eugene O'Neill . . . you feel as if a revival of *The Lower Depths* and a revival of an old-time vaudeville show were being staged concurrently."

In the principal yes-and-no verdict, *Time*, which displayed O'Neill on its front cover a second time, held that "this often static, enormously protracted play lacked the depth to match its length. . . . As theater, much of the play was first-rate O'Neill. But as drama, for all its honest brooding, *The Iceman* was scarcely deeper than a puddle." Using the occasion to review the playwright's career, the anonymous *Time* reviewer said: "O'Neill does not seem to be a man of great, searching or original intelligence. And however vivid his emotions and intuitions . . . he generally lacks the ability to stand aside from them and give them final hardness, clearness, earthiness, eloquence. . . . That O'Neill is a poet is evident in almost any line he has written. That he lacks the ultimate (and primary) requirement of a great poet (to arrange words in eloquent and unimprovable order and beauty) is equally evident in the same lines. Lacking deep perception of real people, O'Neill constantly scores his points and gets his effects by external tricks.

"But as a playwright, O'Neill remains the greatest master of theater the U.S. has produced. He is a marvelous craftsman, and one of the most high-minded who has ever worked. If he often undertakes too much, that is far better than undertaking too little. This habitual exorbitance goes far toward accounting for the compelling tone which resounds through all of O'Neill's work like the ringing of red iron on an anvil."

George Jean Nathan, likewise scanning the dramatist's career, concluded that "the great body of his work has a size and significance not remotely approached by any other American . . . he is plainly not the mind that Shaw is, not by a thousand leagues . . . he is not the poet O'Casey is, for in O'Casey there is the true music of great wonder and beauty. But he has plumbed depths deeper than either; he is greatly the superior of both in dramaturgy."

With characteristic generosity, O'Casey, after reading Nathan's article (*American Mercury*, November 1946), wrote to him: "I think you are right in saying [O'Neill] goes far deeper than Shaw or I do. I've often envied him this gift. I've pondered his plays and tried to discover how he came by it, and, of course, never could; for the man doesn't know himself. He's got it, and we just have to leave it with him. It is a powerful gift and Gene, thank God, uses it with power and ruthless integrity."

The Iceman Cometh was the last new O'Neill work that would be presented on Broadway in his lifetime. That most of the reviewers could not see the play for the performance became evident ten years later when *The Iceman*, given a rousing off-Broadway production at the Circle in the Square, loomed in its proper titanic size. The revival had three distinct advantages over the Theater Guild presentation: sympathetic direction by José Quintero; an unforgettable, indeed thrilling portrayal of Hickey by Jason Robards, Jr., which brought him stardom; and arena staging in a onetime nightclub that proved ideal for the saloon story. "You are apt to feel," said one reviewer, "as if you were sitting right in Harry Hope's bar, along with all the other lovely bums." Where Brooks Atkinson, like so many others, had once thought the play too long, he now felt that its length was "an essential part of its power. . . . It seems not like something written, but like something that is happening." Where originally Wolcott Gibbs, the fastidious critic of the *New Yorker*, held that *The Iceman*, "while an interesting play, was by no means comparable to its author's best efforts," it appeared to him in revival as "a great play . . . a tragedy that, for all its defects, states a terrible truth with extraordinary power and compassion."

Produced by the Guild for about fifty thousand dollars, *The Iceman* had a weekly "nut" of twenty thousand dollars. Even though its length allowed only six performances a week instead of the customary eight, at capacity it netted the playwright three thousand dollars, his highest weekly income ever from a single production. A month or so after the première, when it developed that about ten percent of the audience never returned from the dinner intermission, the Guild, which had instituted the dining period at O'Neill's insistence, won his permission to eliminate it. Under the new schedule, the performance ran from seven-thirty to eleven-twenty, with fifteen minutes cut from the original running time by quickening the pace.

Despite the number of adverse reviews and those of qualified praise, O'Neill remained confident that *The Iceman* was one of his two finest works (*Long Day's Journey* being the other), but his spirits were not helped any by the sniping that continued. During his long absence from Broadway there had emerged some young Turks, among them Mary McCarthy and Eric Bentley, eager to proclaim that the Emperors to whom their elders genuflected were actually and embarrassingly naked. O'Neill became one of their favorite butts.

Miss McCarthy declared in the *Partisan Review* of November–December 1946 that the playwright "belongs to that group of American authors, which includes Farrell and Dreiser, whose choice of vocation was a kind of triumphant catastrophe; none of these men possessed the slightest ear for the word, the sentence, the speech. . . . What they produce is hard to praise or to condemn; how is one to judge the great, logical symphony of a tone-deaf musician?" After a sarcastic summary of the *Iceman* story, Miss McCarthy, who evidently believed that she had been objective, indulged in jactitation: "The odd thing about *The Iceman Cometh* is that this rather bony synopsis does it perfect justice; in fact, it improves it by substituting, whenever possible, the word *illusion* for the word *pipe-dream.*" The playwright's intention, she cracked, "is symbolic and philosophical, but unfortunately you cannot write a Platonic dialogue in the style of 'Casey at the Bat.' "

Judging by the text before *The Iceman* opened, Eric Bentley said in the *Atlantic Monthly* (November 1946) that in performance it was "likely to be less 'terrific' " than *Strange Interlude* or *Electra*, but he found it "a more interesting play." "To everyone except O'Neill-worshipers," he continues, "the two earlier colossi seemed contrived, labored, overloaded, and at times false." However, Bentley, who looked abroad for his gods — he favored such cerebral, politically committed writers as Sartre, Camus and Brecht — was not particularly impressed by *The Iceman* either. "Since most of the characters," he says, "are rather wooden and diagrammatic — the whores are stage whores, and so on — since the raciness of the speeches is the raciness of Broadway convention rather than that of great realistic dialogue, we have the impression less of fine dramatic form . . . than of a skeleton's rigidity. Of course there is much emotion in the play. But you cannot pass off a skeleton as a man merely by enveloping it in a cloud of emotion."

The pronouncements of Bentley and Miss McCarthy were among the opening shots in an attack that would diminish O'Neill's reputation among the intelligentsia and the young. While still alive, he would come to appear more of historic than of lasting importance to the American drama. Until his resurrection in the mid-1950s through *Long Day's Journey*, he would be merely a gray eminence, a dusty name to a new generation of Broadway patrons who looked to Tennessee Williams and Arthur Miller, among others, for their stirring nights of theater.

Except for a few brief lapses O'Neill was, for him, in relatively good health during 1946, thanks in part, probably, to the stimulation of seeing *The Iceman Cometh* brought to life on the stage. On November 1 he wrote to his old friend Charles O'Brien Kennedy that he had been "laid up, not from the punches I took, hither and yon, from the critics, but from just plain fatigue and flu." By mid-November he "looked much healthier" to Barrett Clark than when the theater historian had seen him in the spring. Noticing a dozen or so books on Robespierre in his host's crowded bookshelves, Clark wondered whether he intended to write a play about the French revolutionary. "I was thinking about it for a time," O'Neill replied. "Robespierre sums it all up: the idealist at first, the righteous man; he gets power; he uses it; he misuses it; tragedy. The perfect pattern, you see."

One of the O'Neills' most frequent and welcome visitors, Russel Crouse had become by now, in partnership with Howard Lindsay, an outstanding figure on Broadway as a playwright (*Life with Father*), a producer (*Arsenic and Old Lace*), and a musical comedy librettist. Serenely happy with his second wife — his first had died — he was delighted that both O'Neill and Carlotta took to her immediately, for she had been apprehensive at the prospect of meeting them. "I was terrified," says Anna Crouse, "out of respect for his work and because of things I had heard about her. But they were warm and friendly, and it was obvious that they loved 'Buck' [Crouse's nickname]."

For years Crouse had talked of bringing O'Neill together for an evening with Irving Berlin, since he was so fond of Berlin's music, and the date finally was set for November 23, a Saturday. At Eugene's request, he and Carlotta were the Crouses' only dinner guests, for he disliked eating with a large party, and stew was served, since he could not readily manipulate knife and fork. Around nine the Berlins arrived and shortly afterward, Howard Lindsay and his actress wife Dorothy Stickney. A faulty, self-taught pianist, Berlin almost never performed at parties (he had a specially constructed piano at home that was relatively simple to play), but within ten or fifteen minutes of his arrival he was at the Crouses' piano, with the playwright seated alongside, hoarsely, joyously singing.

O'Neill, says Mrs. Crouse, had "a remarkable memory for the lyrics, and Berlin knew which singers had made them famous, which companies had published them, the years they came out, and so forth. Soon everything was so warm and jolly that I asked the O'Neills if I could phone Phyllis and Bennett Cerf, who lived around the corner, and they said yes. So there they all were at the piano, singing abominably and having the times of their lives. Berlin and O'Neill kept saying to one another, 'Do you remember such-and-such?' and almost invariably the other remembered.

"Around midnight the doorbell rang. It was the Berlins' chauffeur, who'd been told to wait in the car, as they had expected to visit only about fifteen minutes. It was a cold night, and the chauffeur wanted to thaw out. I was pregnant at the time and sitting on the sofa with Carlotta, who kept saying to me, 'You shouldn't be staying up this late.' The party didn't break up till three in the morning, and I don't think I ever saw anyone have such a good time as O'Neill did."

Summing up in his diary a "wonderful party," Crouse noted that "Gene sang some [old songs] we didn't know and Carlotta unburdens herself to me. And we all really had fun."

Irving Berlin is another who glows when he thinks of that night, though he recalls that he was nervous beforehand: "I was worried about what I was going to say to him. I'd read a few of his plays but didn't really know his work, not the way my wife does. I figured on saying something of the usual, how much I respected him, but I didn't have a chance to say anything. Soon as we got there I found he was interested in my old songs, he knew them, he knew them all, even some I'd forgotten. It all started when he asked if I remembered 'I Love a Piano.' He had to sing in one key because that's how I play, I don't play well.

"Do you get the picture? It was like some songwriter in Britain going to meet Bernard Shaw. How many are there whose plays have lived? Shakespeare, Shaw, O'Neill. . . . I don't want to sound gushy and sentimental, but I found him a wonderful human being. I've met a great many with talent and importance — should I drop some names? [said in a voice of mock snobbery] — but none of them gave me the feeling as much as O'Neill did that he respected me."

Carlotta afterward wrote to Anna Crouse that "Gene couldn't get to sleep until four he was so full of pleasure & song & delicious stew! . . . We so seldom go out that Saturday was indeed a gala! So much so that the night man here wasn't going to let us in! He couldn't believe his eyes when he saw us at that hour."

Escorted by the Crouses and the Lindsays, Eugene and Carlotta had another gala evening a fortnight later when they saw Irving Berlin's *Annie Get Your Gun*, starring Ethel Merman. The rare times O'Neill attended the theater he usually was so apprehensive that someone might recognize him that he would slip out before the lights went up; but he was so enjoying himself that he remained to the end and, at Crouse's suggestion, went backstage to congratulate Miss Merman. As word of his presence spread and chorines fluttered around him in the star's dressing room, his face lit up at the sight of a particularly beautiful show girl; at the same time, Anna Crouse recalls, Carlotta looked "more and more frozen."

O'Neill's occasional social activities found Carlotta worried that he might be overtaxing himself, but in some cases his socializing, such as the backstage visit, had her more concerned for her own sake. As part of her vigilance against possible rivals, she once asked Sherlee Weingarten to be present whenever her husband was interviewed by a woman. While

Sherlee herself was attractive, Carlotta apparently considered her too serious and idealistic, too respectful of O'Neill, to be a romantic threat. Nearly fifty-eight, Carlotta was still handsome; though her figure had thickened in time, she had a flawlessly smooth face and looked younger than her years. As early as Sea Island, however, she had lamented being middle-aged, and the Jane Caldwell episode had left her feeling increasingly insecure. Between her and Eugene there was often an undercurrent of tension; gradually their life together was developing into a pattern of disagreements and amnesties.

A few weeks after the impromptu musicale that had costarred Berlin and O'Neill, the Bennett Cerfs gave a party attended by the O'Neills, the Crouses and the Saxe Comminses at which Burl Ives entertained. Accompanying himself on a guitar, Ives sang numbers that became, in Cerf's words, "more and more dirty." Carlotta, plainly, disapproved. Further irked when her husband began to sing ribald songs he had learned as a seaman, she tried to persuade him to leave, insisting that he was not well enough to be out so late; finally, unable to budge him, she picked herself up and departed alone.

In a note to her in December, probably at Christmastime, Eugene said: "I am sorry for the unhappiness I have caused you. How unhappy it has made me, you have seen and know.

"Let us forget and forgive, Darling. . . . We have love still, Sweetheart. We [have] the chance of a new life!"

28

Misbegotten Production

U SUALLY O'Neill paid little attention to his productions once they had
opened, but *The Iceman Cometh* was a different story; knowing
that the Guild considered the play repetitious and too long, he kept an
eye on the proceedings at the Martin Beck to prevent any secret cutting
of the text. Without notifying the Guild in advance, he had Carlotta, on
a number of evenings, station herself unobtrusively backstage where she
could hear everything and check the performance against the script. On
learning that stage manager Karl Nielsen had told the two detectives to
delay their entrance till just before the climax of Hickey's confession,
O'Neill warned the Guild that he had the right to close the play unless
his stage directions were strictly adhered to; and thereafter, though he
had formerly been kindly disposed toward Nielsen, he never spoke to him
again.

In another departure from practice, the playwright, who hardly ever
saw a regular performance of his works, went one night when James
Barton was indisposed and the part of Hickey was filled by E. G.
Marshall (who regularly played Willie Oban). Pleased to find him better
than Barton, O'Neill became friendly with the young actor and had him
to lunch or tea a few times. "The audiences," he complained to Marshall,
"don't laugh at my plays, they're afraid to, they don't know whether
they're supposed to or not. Someday I'm going on a grand binge and
explode the great man myth, the impression that I'm all gloom and
tragedy."

Several months later he saw *The Iceman* again, this time accompanied
by Katina Paxinou and her actor husband Alexis Minotis, who had just
arrived from Greece. During the evening the playwright writhed in his
seat at times, he was so unhappy about the performance, and kept

muttering imprecations against Dowling's direction. The Greek couple, who likewise took the theater seriously, endeared themselves to the playwright by commiserating with him; indeed, they went further and suffered with him. O'Neill told them that he began devouring the Greek classics when he turned playwright, while the couple, returning the compliment to their heritage, said that when they appeared in *Desire Under the Elms*, a prominent Athens critic called O'Neill the first dramatist since Sophocles with the classical sense of tragedy.

Carlotta telephoned the couple one day to say that her husband wanted them as dinner guests, but she thought it inadvisable, as he was not in good health; at this point he took over the phone and urged the invitation. During the meal the Minotises recalled that while touring in this country in 1930, a young man met them at the railroad station in New Haven, assisted them with their luggage, and, reading from a paper, wished them well in Greek. As their host started to beam knowingly, they added that the young man identified himself as a Yale student and the son of Eugene O'Neill.

After dinner O'Neill told the couple that he wanted them to know the tragic inside story of his family as contained in a play he had written that was not to be released till long after his death. Minotis, tactfully objecting (in part because Carlotta had an air of disapproving of her husband's intent), said that he might later rue confiding in them. But Eugene, as Miss Paxinou recalls, was determined: "He led us into his bedroom and took the play from a small sailor's trunk which was filled with scripts, all of them perfectly aligned, not one sticking out a fraction of an inch from the others. First he described the members of his family — the pious mother, but a drug addict; the miserly father; the alcoholic brother. . . . O'Neill had closed the door, but Carlotta was in and out a few times, on household errands, I guess. After he had told us about his family, he read the last act from the time the father turns out the lights, and once as he was reading the tears rolled down his face. But the thing I particularly remember is an error he made. Instead of saying, 'The Mad Scene. Enter Ophelia!' he said, 'Enter Lady Macbeth!' Then he corrected himself."

As Miss Paxinou evoked that moment, she hunched forward in her chair, put her hands over her mouth, shrugged, her eyes wide with mock-innocence, and added, "I can't say what he had in mind, why he said 'Lady Macbeth' instead of 'Ophelia,' but she [Carlotta] was outside, moving around." Another shrug. "I can't say anything."

The next morning on the telephone Carlotta upbraided the couple for not dissuading Eugene from reading the play. He was so upset and had such a bad night, she reported, that she had summoned the doctor.

The *Iceman* production, which lasted for one hundred thirty-six performances, proved a source of vexation to its author and producers to the end. At O'Neill's insistence, E. G. Marshall was given the part of Hickey for the road tour and James Barton was asked to switch to Harry Hope's role; Barton refused, however, and since he had a run-of-the-play contract, the Guild was obliged to pay his salary, while Marshall took over his part, till the production folded.

Shortly before the tour began, the Boston authorities announced that *The Iceman* could not be given in their bailiwick unless some "objectionable" dialogue was changed. O'Neill, denouncing the verdict as a recurrence of the "stupid censorship" that had led to the banning of *Strange Interlude*, refused to change "one word" of his drama. Boston audiences, he declared, "do not want plays weakened and made silly by ignorant censorship which knows and cares nothing about dràma." Boston was dropped from the play's itinerary. (Sherlee Weingarten suspects that the Guild instigated the Boston controversy with the hope it would help the play's receipts elsewhere.)

When *The Iceman* opened at the National Theater in Washington, D.C., the playwright was again upset, because the theater was under attack for its policy of barring Negroes, and the Guild was unable to break the booking. After an appeal from Reverend Wilfred Parsons of the Catholic Inter-Racial Council in the capital, O'Neill sent him the following wire, with permission to publicize it: "I am and always have been opposed to racial discrimination of any kind and I assure you I will insist on a non-discrimination clause in all future contracts. Surely my past record as a dramatist and a producer has shown where I stand on this issue."

For all their troubles with *The Iceman Cometh*, O'Neill and the Guild were fated to be still more unfortunate with *A Moon for the Misbegotten*. Well before the play entered rehearsal in January 1947, the Guild instituted a search in Hollywood, Dublin and London, as well as in New York, for an outsized Irish actress with "a range from farce to Greek tragedy" to portray farm girl Josie Hogan. In the end Mary Welch, a relatively unknown Broadway actress, was selected, but it was uncertain for months whether she would be signed; in addition to being of limited experience, she was scarcely a giantess in build. "Are you Irish? What percent?" the playwright asked when they first met. "I want as many people as possible connected with my play to be Irish. Although the setting is New England, the dry wit, the mercurial changes of mood, and the mystic quality of the three main characters are distinctly Irish."

Encouraged by his smile when she said she was all Irish, with parents from County Cork, Miss Welch slipped into a brogue and recalled that her grandmother used to say, "I'll never eat a plate of stew — those dishes of mystery!"

From their first moment together, O'Neill's eyes probed into her face, but instead of making her self-conscious, they seemed, she reports, "to put me on my absolute honor to express myself as clearly and as simply as I could [Leona Hogarth reacted similarly, one recalls, when O'Neill interviewed her in 1925 for *The Great God Brown*] . . . he just kept staring, as though he were burning me down to a purer core. I always felt the same way with him — as though I were purified."

After talking more about the Irish than about *The Misbegotten*, the playwright gave Miss Welch a script and told her to return in two weeks. Emotionally shaken on reading the play, she noted in her diary: "Every bluff and hurt and discovery of Josie's seems to have occurred to me. . . . For once I feel moved by fate. I know I have to play this part and will."

At her first audition the Guild heads thought she looked "too normal," but the playwright was inclined to waive his own physical specifications for the part. According to the actress, he said: "She can gain some more weight, but the important thing is Miss Welch understands how Josie feels." While the search continued for someone more experienced and better qualified physically, Miss Welch was called in for further testing, and at each appearance she was pounds heavier from a "diet of potatoes, bananas and pies." Just before the final audition of the surviving candidates, O'Neill had Miss Welch to tea and assured her that she was his choice. Later that day, after a reading with James Dunn, who was to enact James Tyrone, Jr., she was given a contract with an unusual clause: "The artist agrees to gain the necessary weight required for the role."

As a rule the director is signed early and participates in the casting of a play, but, after difficulty in finding one around Broadway acceptable to O'Neill — he had to be Irish — Arthur Shields, an Abbey Theater veteran and Barry Fitzgerald's brother, was summoned from Hollywood at almost the last minute. The upshot was that Shields found himself working with players he himself did not particularly favor. In addition to James Dunn, who had been chosen on the basis of his portrayal in the film *A Tree Grows in Brooklyn*, and Miss Welch, the other principal was J. M. Kerrigan, as Josie's father.

From what Dunn said later, it appears that he was as reluctant as Mary Welch was eager to be in *A Moon for the Misbegotten.* "I didn't really like the play; I like to do comedy, I love to hear people laugh, but my wife, she told me I ought to do it — Eugene O'Neill, the Theater Guild, a big prestige thing. I let her talk me into it." Kerrigan was no admirer of the play, either; to intimates he confided that he disapproved of its strong language and the impression it gave of the Irish, but he hoped to tone down what he considered his role's more offensive aspects.

At the first rehearsal, while reading passages about Jamie's feeling toward his mother and his shameful conduct on the train, James Dunn broke down and began weeping. As he struggled to resume, Mary Welch also became tearful and, looking around the table, observed that the playwright and the three Guild directors were wet-eyed too. "Oh, here we go again," O'Neill remarked humorously. "I wept a great deal over Josie Hogan and Jim Tyrone as I wrote the play. I loved them." At last getting himself under control, Dunn, more of a prophet than he could have imagined, said: "We're *all* crying now. I guess it will be the management's time to cry later."

Where the Guild was doubtful of Miss Welch, the playwright was chiefly dissatisfied with Dunn and complained to Langner that the actor was not making Jamie Tyrone enough of a "gentleman." Langner, unaware that Tyrone was actually O'Neill's brother, felt that the playwright held an "idealized" image of the character that was not limned in the play itself. Indisposed during most of the rehearsal period, O'Neill attended only a few of the sessions; but at one he advised the principals that they "were playing the tragedy of the work too early" and should give more emphasis to the comedy in the first two acts.

Arthur Shields felt, he says, that the play "should have a minimum of action, and Mr. O'Neill agreed with me. The hardest thing in the theater is to get actors *not* to do something. Langner, the players, everybody wanted to break it up, to do something, especially during Tyrone's long speeches in the third act. And Langner wanted some cuts, drastic cuts, that would have weakened points Mr. O'Neill was trying to make. I'd been told he wouldn't allow any cutting, so I was absolutely floored when Mr. O'Neill asked me one day whether I thought the play should be shortened. My twenty years at the Abbey Theater — which was definitely a playwright's theater — had taught me not to tamper with the work of an established author. It just wasn't done. I truthfully told him that I hadn't thought of it and hoped that no drastic alterations would be made."

O'Neill became so dissatisfied as rehearsals progressed that he would have welcomed cancellation of the production, but the Guild was already having difficulty in filling the season's quota of plays for its subscribers. With O'Neill's unenthusiastic consent, the producers scheduled a few out-of-town engagements 'in hopes of substantial improvement before the Broadway opening.

Attended by a stylish audience that included the governor of Ohio and, "in a halo of roses and a black satin dress," Mrs. James Dunn, the world première of *A Moon for the Misbegotten* took place in Columbus on February 20, 1947. The playwright, who remained in New York, sent Mary Welch a dozen roses with a card that read, "Again my absolute confidence." At the second intermission, when Langner noticed a group gather their overclothes and depart, he asked the doorman whether some of the dialogue had offended them. "No," the man replied. "They just said they were Irish."

The reviews were mixed. Elliot Norton of the Boston *Post*, one of the few out-of-state critics to cover the première, called the play "profoundly beautiful" and added regretfully, "It is not likely to get to Boston." The Columbus *Citizen*, on the other hand, pronounced the new drama "unimportant."

In Pittsburgh *The Misbegotten* was roundly attacked not only by reviewers, columnists and editors but by heads of the business community. Terming the play "evidence of deterioration" in O'Neill, a columnist in the *Press* declared that "vulgarity is a bad enough dish" and that "corn added to vulgarity makes slop." The president of the chamber of commerce, while freely admitting that he had not seen the play, said that he had received "an unbiased report from reputable business leaders, and was shocked at what they reported."

Alerted by the outcries in Pittsburgh, the Detroit censor, eager to protect the morality of his domain, was ready when the Guild production opened there on March 10. The following morning Theresa Helburn and Armina Marshall, who were in Detroit for the tryout, were stunned when they saw the local *Times*. Across the top of page one in red letters was the banner: O'NEILL PLAY CLOSED FOR OBSCENITY.

"The whole theme is obscene," thundered police censor Charles Snyder in the news account. "It is a slander on American motherhood. The play will have to be thoroughly rewritten before I will let it go on."

When the two Guild women conferred with Snyder at the theater, they learned that he particularly resented the words "mother" and "prostitute" being used in the same sentence. He also demanded, among other things, that "louse" be substituted for "bastard," "tart" for "whore," and that a reference to a girl as a "pig" be eliminated.

"You've allowed *Maid in the Ozarks* [a tawdry piece about "a moonshiner and a slightly soiled waitress"] to play here in Detroit," countered Miss Marshall, "and yet you [bar] a play by Eugene O'Neill, who won the Nobel Prize?"

Snyder: "Lady, I don't care what kind of prize he's won, he can't put on a dirty show in *my* town."

The argument was shortly interrupted by the arrival of James Dunn, who had been in touch with a top Michigan official he knew; using his friend's name, Dunn proceeded to pacify the censor. But the censor, while agreeing to review the situation with the actor, insisted that the women be excluded.

The controversy ended, according to Miss Marshall, with the two men deleting "about eight words." Guild publicist Joe Heidt, also making light of the outcome, told the press that the changes involved thirteen words and one sentence, and that after they "had been agreed to, we called Mr. O'Neill in New York. The changes were so slight that Mr. O'Neill just laughed about the matter and agreed completely."

Arthur Shields, though, giving a different account, maintains that more than eight or thirteen words were cut: "I'd expected the Guild to fight that kind of censorship and was surprised when word came that the police officer would be allowed to dictate what could be said. I got the impression that when O'Neill was contacted on the phone by the Guild, he was so fed up that he told them to do what they liked. The whole episode was so distasteful to me that the following morning I left for the Coast."

But this time, unlike the reception in Pittsburgh, the press was cordial. Indeed, *The Misbegotten* would never receive a more sympathetic review than Russell McLaughlin's on March 11 in the Detroit *News*. "It is wise to bear in mind, while watching O'Neill's new play," said McLaughlin, "that he is an Irish poet, for all his unassailed position as America's first dramatist. His present characters, although they use some of the worst modern language ever heard on a stage, are actually dark, eerie, Celtic symbol-folk, probably contemporaries of Cuchulain or Ossian, who beat their breasts at the agony of living, battle titanically and drink like Nordic gods, but finally are seen to wear the garb of sainthood and die for love.

"That simple touchstone to the essential O'Neill was, perhaps, not universally comprehended by a big audience which saw [the play] last night. Both bewilderment and shock were freely expressed in the lobby. Take the word of a fellow who has some dark Celtic blood of his own, that this sort of thing, barring its profanity and raw speech, has been agitating bardic souls in Erin and the Scottish Highlands for more than 1500 years. . . . Don't forget, whatever they say, that it's all a love-lament played on ancient pipes."

Dissatisfied with both Dunn and Miss Welch, the Guild closed *The Misbegotten* after two weeks in Detroit and a week in St. Louis, intend- ing to recast it, with the author's help, and open the new production the following season. However, O'Neill, who had begun to turn against the play (in 1952 he said he had "come to loathe" it), kept stalling the Guild with one excuse or another. Also, since no latter-day Maurice Barrymore or James O'Neill was in sight for the part of Con Melody, he told the Guild to postpone all plans for *A Touch of the Poet*. Neither play would be seen on Broadway in his lifetime, but, under financial pressure, he allowed *The Misbegotten*, not long before his death, to be published.

After being successively occupied for over a year with the *Iceman* and *Misbegotten* productions, O'Neill found himself at leisure in spring 1947, a silenced playwright of uncertain health. He once mentioned to Sherlee Weingarten that he had a play, a comedy, all thought out in his mind that would have to remain there because of his tremor; Sherlee immediately volunteered to quit the Guild and work for him, so that he could dictate his plays to her, but he declined her offer. Sadly contemplating his hands, he explained that he could find the right words only with pencil and paper.

His present restlessness sometimes led him, Carlotta felt, to overexert himself. In a note to Charles O'Brien Kennedy on June 8, she said that O'Neill was in bed with an upset stomach and a temperature from "doing too much. I try to guard him against this evil — but who can keep an Irishman from stepping over a cliff?

"However, I'll be going on trying — angels can do no more."

Whenever Kennedy visited the penthouse, the two men usually talked sports, baseball especially, for Kennedy was a devout believer in "dem Bums," the Brooklyn Dodgers, while O'Neill, who followed the game on the radio, was a Giant fan. The conversation tended to be more intellec- tual when E. G. Marshall called. Curious about O'Neill's opinion of exis- tentialism, the reigning philosophy of the day, Marshall gave him a book of Sartre's, but his host was unimpressed. "Do they know what it's all about?" he asked in a skeptical tone; his own philosophy, he remarked, was best expressed by Nietzsche and Spengler.

Bill Aronberg was just leaving the apartment one day as Marshall arrived, and the playwright said with a wry smile, "There goes my alimony dispatcher." This year finally saw the end, however, of his annual payment to Agnes; after negotiating with her through Aronberg, he paid his former wife seventeen thousand dollars to settle her claim on him. (Not long afterward Agnes married one Morris Kaufman, a free-lance writer whom she had known for years.)

While Carlotta used to make Marshall and Kennedy feel welcome, she only tolerated Walter ("Ice") Casey, one of Eugene's old friends from New London, a large, genial, red-faced bachelor with a weakness for liquor. He had arrived in New York years earlier with literary ambitions, but after drifting for a time as a hack writer had ended as a desk clerk in third-rate hotels. Frequently in New London, where he had a half-dozen or so sisters, Casey used to return with news of Art McGinley, Ed Keefe, Tommy Troland (now a judge), "Doc" Ganey and others of the old gang. To Carlotta's dislike, Casey's visits sometimes set her husband to reminiscing about his two great loves in New London, Maibelle Scott (the model for the girl in *Ah, Wilderness!*) and Beatrice Ashe; perhaps he dwelled on the subject precisely because he knew that it annoyed Carlotta.

At a play being rehearsed at the Guild for the Westport (Connecticut) Country Playhouse, the Langners' summer theater, O'Neill was impressed by the acting of Patricia Neal. He had met her once before, when she had auditioned for the part of Josie Hogan in *The Misbegotten;* later, he had had an enthusiastic letter from her when she saw *The Iceman,* and he in turn had sent her a congratulatory note when she scored a personal success in Lillian Hellman's *Another Part of the Forest.* At the rehearsal, O'Neill told Miss Neal he thought she would be right as the daughter in *A Touch of the Poet* and afterward sent her a copy of the script. Charmed by the bright, spirited young actress, who obviously admired him, Eugene saw her a half-dozen or so times; while their relationship was innocent, he arranged the meetings as discreetly as possible to avoid trouble with Carlotta.

"The Guild would phone that Mr. O'Neill wanted to see me," Miss Neal remembers, "and we'd meet in one of their offices and talk about the theater, jazz, Hollywood, books we'd liked. He said he'd let me do any of his plays I wanted. I was thinking of accepting a movie offer, and he told me to go ahead; he said the theater wasn't worth sacrificing for. For years I had a clause in all my Hollywood contracts that I could take a leave of absence if I was wanted for *A Touch of the Poet.* One day after he'd mentioned an ice cream parlor in New London that had the most wonderful sodas, I said they couldn't be any better than those at Hick's, near Fifth Avenue, and persuaded him to go with me. His tremor wasn't too bad that day and he looked so pleased with himself that he could manage the soda."

When Carlotta learned somehow of his friendship with Patricia Neal, she was furious. (Her antagonism to the young actress never lessened; a few years later Miss Neal was on the verge of being signed for the part of Abbie Putnam in a Broadway revival of *Desire Under the Elms*, but as soon as Carlotta learned of the proposed casting, the negotiations were broken off.)

In the second half of 1947 a frequent visitor at the penthouse was Hamilton Basso, who was working on a profile of O'Neill for the *New Yorker* (it appeared in three installments in February and March 1948). Practically everyone Basso approached in his research, he noted, spoke of the playwright in "terms of complete affection. Even [Edmund] Wilson, who is getting more and more like a meat-chopper, hasn't anything to say against him. 'He's absolutely on the level,' Bunny says."

At first the *New Yorker* man was discouraged, for many who knew O'Neill best refused to help. Nathan and Langner said they intended to write their own pieces about the playwright; Madden wanted a list of questions beforehand that would be shown to O'Neill for his approval (a proposal Basso rejected). Others, such as Commins, declined chiefly from a protective feeling toward O'Neill, but in addition nearly all were wary from fear of Carlotta's displeasure. Finally, to Basso's surprise, in view of his subject's known diffidence, O'Neill himself proved the most cooperative and helpful source of information. For months, in two afternoon sessions a week, he reviewed his past for Basso's benefit in what would be the last time he ever was interviewed; initially he had to be prompted with questions but after the introductory session he began to reminisce at his own initiative.

"He was the most incorrigibly honest man about himself I've ever met," Basso says. "He never spoke editorially, if you know what I mean; he never stopped to think, 'How will the answer sound, how will it seem to others?' Afterward, I felt that he opened up because he could no longer work and was terribly alone, that I was the first person from the outside he'd seen in a long time, so he was ready to talk."

A tactful, gentlemanly Southerner, Basso early won the playwright's favor by recalling that they had once met many years before, in passing. It seems that Basso was descending the subway steps at Times Square and quoting aloud from Cybel's final speech in *The Great God Brown* ("Always spring comes again bearing life! . . .") when he noticed that a lean stranger, approaching, had overheard him and was grinning shyly — a stranger he suddenly recognized as O'Neill.

"O'Neill not working now," Basso wrote in his notes, after surveying his host's bedroom-study, "but his desk is kept in readiness for him to do so. Something very sad about that desk."

During one of their first afternoons, sitting out on the terrace, which surrounded the penthouse on three sides and offered a panoramic view of the city, O'Neill had been animated and cheerful as he and Basso discussed "mutual remembrances and mutual friends." But a humid day in July found him indoors suffering from "a bad case of the New York blues" and longing for his onetime mountainside home in California. As Basso remembered how O'Neill had looked the first time he saw him and thought of stories he had heard about his prowess in the water, he was reminded of "a clipper-ship on the rocks."

It seemed to him that O'Neill was the only person he knew "whose face, in repose, wears an expression of almost unbearable intensity" — chiefly from the burning expression in his large dark eyes. Dante must have had a similar expression, Basso felt, thinking of the old legend that the Florentines used to avoid the poet in the belief that his eyes "had looked into the bottom level of hell."

There were such long silences at times that Basso thought he had been forgotten, but when O'Neill resumed talking it was evident that he had been shuffling his memories for the more significant ones. Scanning his entire life, he began with the years of trouping with his parents that had left him with "a fondness for order" and "a deep, abiding hatred of hotels." Ella O'Neill figured only passingly in his conversation, but he constantly returned to the subject of his father. Ironically, considering his treatment of his own children (though the irony seems to have escaped him), he recalled that there were times, in his years of feuding with his father, when his father had "just about given me up. Not that I can blame him. If anything, he was too patient with me. What I wonder now is why he didn't kick me out. I gave him every chance to."

Reviewing his acquaintanceship with O'Neill, Basso thought that "it might be interesting, someday, to show how creative writers all end up like one of their own characters. Nothing mysterious or profound about this; the creative imagination feeds on itself and *all* a writer's best characters — best in the sense that they are most alive — are reflections, to a greater or less degree, of himself. Getting down to people I've actually known, Scott Fitzgerald was certainly a person out of one of his books; Gatsby, I would say, more than anyone else. Thomas Wolfe, of course, is an obvious example and Hemingway, who is something of a mess, seems to have decided that his whole life should be led in imitation of his fiction. Sherwood Anderson was one of those half-articulate, muggy-minded people that turn up in Winesburg and Edmund Wilson, Lord knows, is one of the old natives of Hecate County. Willie Maugham is a character out of Willie Maugham, Dreiser was Sister Carrie's big brother, and, to come to the point, O'Neill, at the present time, could be a figure waiting in the wings for his cue in a play by Eugene O'Neill — the tragic life thrice compounded."

One fall afternoon, as the light was waning, O'Neill got around to the subject of his work, especially its frustrations. "After you've finished a play and it goes into rehearsals, it begins to go from you. No matter how good the production is, or how able the actors, something is lost — your own vision of the play, the way you saw it in your imagination."

When Carlotta, who had been out shopping, returned, she reproved her husband for sitting in the dark. "Why don't you turn some of the lights on? It's so *gloomy*." His face emerged from the shadows as she went about switching on lamps. "I'm supposed to be a gloomy fellow. Haven't you heard?"

"You can be gloomy enough, sometimes," she replied. "But why do they always have to exaggerate? Nearly everything that has been said about you is all wrong." After she had left to make coffee, he remarked: "What Carlotta just said is true. Nearly everything that has been said about me *is* all wrong."

Basso never sensed anything unusual in the O'Neills' relationship. "After all, they were worldly people, with a sense of dignity," he says, "and would keep up appearances before others." But at times on his arrival at the penthouse, "the atmosphere seemed *heavy*, as though hard words had been exchanged."

With O'Neill bored from inactivity and Carlotta prone to magnify into major offenses what were at most peccadillos on his part, such as his friendship with Patricia Neal, tension was building up between them. Carlotta had delighted in New York on first returning from the Coast ("I'm home, home, home! Glory be to God!" she exulted at the time. "I haven't been so happy in years!"); but now she "loathed" the city, chiefly, it seems, because it contained too many old friends of her husband whom she disliked, too many young actresses eager to know the eminent dramatist. She did her utmost to monitor and curb his social activities, but at the same time he appears to have been equally possessive and suspicious about her. After a chance meeting one evening with Sherlee Weingarten's fiancé, a production aide at the Guild named Steve Alexander, Carlotta was apprehensive that Eugene might hear that she and Alexander had had coffee together; the next day she asked Sherlee to say, if Gene should question her, that she too had been present.

Although Miss Weingarten was unaware of it at the time, Carlotta began to cool toward her this fall, initially, it seems, over Djuna Barnes's *Nightwood*, a strange novel written with style about lesbians, transvestites and other desperate souls. When Sherlee mentioned the book to O'Neill, he said he would like to read it, since he had known Djuna, a strikingly handsome girl, at the Provincetown Players. Carlotta, who hated the little she read, was at first incredulous when O'Neill said that the book came from Sherlee. "Our Sherlee gave you this dirty book, our little Sherlee?!" she kept repeating. O'Neill pointed out that *Nightwood* carried an enthusiastic introduction by T. S. Eliot (has "a quality of horror and doom very nearly related to that of Elizabethan tragedy"), but no one could alter Carlotta's view of it as "a dirty book."

Sherlee was again an innocent source of displeasure to Carlotta through a wedding party the Langners gave for her and Steve Alexander. At the Langners' instance, Sherlee gave them a list of persons to invite and, without expecting the O'Neills to attend, included their names. Carlotta, declining the invitation, told Sherlee that she and O'Neill never attended social affairs but would have the young couple to dinner the following week.

To the surprise of the bridal pair and the Langners, O'Neill appeared alone; he seemed in such good spirits at the party that no one could have guessed that he was present against his wife's wishes and, in fact, had just come from an argument with her. His tremor was scarcely visible as he took a few sips of champagne and lit his own cigarettes, beaming all the while at some pretty girls who had grouped themselves on the floor around his chair. "My wife was firing questions and comments at him," actor Edmond Ryan recalls, "but he obviously was enjoying her somewhat intoxicated talk. When I told her not to badger him, he waved me aside."

"I was wound up about politics that night," says Ann Sergeant, Ryan's wife. "There'd been some picketing of Kirsten Flagstad at Carnegie Hall because she was said to have been pro-Nazi during the war. That was all right with the liberals, but they were angry when a rightist group demonstrated against Larry Adler the harmonica player. It seemed to me, I told

O'Neill, that if it was fair to picket Flagstad, it was equally fair to picket Adler. I also said that philosophically I was an anarchist but in practical matters a capitalist, and O'Neill called me 'the wisest woman he had met in a thousand years.' He had a good sense of humor. I felt he was the warmest, friendliest person I ever met. He liked people, I'm sure of that, but he was shy — that's all."

As Sherlee kissed him good-night before his apartment house, O'Neill murmured that he was "going to catch hell," and most likely Carlotta did not disappoint him when he appeared with lipstick on his cheek.

At their dinner party for the young couple, the O'Neills gave them a check for one hundred seventy dollars, a week's royalty from a Czechoslovakian production of *The Iceman Cometh*. Sherlee vaguely sensed that Carlotta was somehow "different" that evening — she looked heavier and ate more than usual — but she presented an agreeable front to her guests. As it turned out, this was the last time Sherlee would ever see her.

Eline and Sophus Winther, visiting New York in November, dined with the O'Neills on the twenty-first after a note of invitation from Carlotta in which she said, "Freeman is here — but not darling Blemie, alas!" In the pair's early months at the penthouse they had had a German butler, but Eugene grew to dislike him — he thought the man had a face like "a tub of lard" — and they had summoned Herbert Freeman from San Francisco, where he had been working as a longshoreman since the war's end. Though the dinner on the twenty-first went off smoothly, the O'Neills privately were again at odds. Shortly after the Winthers arrived for a second visit — they spent most of Thanksgiving at the penthouse — Carlotta closeted herself in her bedroom with Eline and for nearly two hours poured out a stream of complaints about O'Neill.

She was wearing a plain kitchen apron, had a thin gray shawl over her shoulders, and, in Eline's words, "her whole costume lacked the *color* and *style* I was accustomed to think of as inseparable from her. She spoke in a rather 'gray' voice, new to me, because if there was anything about Carlotta that I loved more than anything else, it was her vibrant, beautiful voice and her trained diction." Before Carlotta launched into her grievances, she, as Eline put it, "set the stage" by assigning Eline to a comfortable armchair, while she herself sat on a backless stool in the middle of the room.

In Carlotta's bill of particulars against her husband, Mrs. Winther recalls, she charged that he had "been drinking with his cronies" in the apartment and that he often prevented her from sleeping by lying beside her, on top of the covers, and reminiscing for hours about his past, particularly his marriage to Agnes. (Carlotta now felt, it seems, that he "had treated Agnes brutally," and she warned Eline never to mention Agnes to him.)

"She told how Gene and she," Mrs. Winther's account continues, "would get into great tempestuous arguments. Gene, she said, 'would hold me like this,' indicating an embrace, his arms locked across her back, holding her so she could not move, 'and then,' she said, 'once he threw me to the floor, hard. My head struck against the radiator.

"'You did not manage that right, Gene,' she quotes herself. 'You should have thrown me closer to the radiator and killed me!'

"'For that matter,' she quotes Gene, "I have a pair of belaying pins in the next room.'"

As Carlotta's recital went on, Mrs. Winther became increasingly skeptical, yet by the end, against her will, she was tearful. After she had bathed her eyes and Carlotta had given her a glass of sherry, they rejoined the two men in the living room. "When I came out," Eline remembers, "Gene gave me an intense, anxious look. When I smiled at him, he visibly relaxed."

The rest of Thanksgiving passed pleasantly enough, with the talk largely about literary matters. Eugene had given Winther a copy of *The Iceman Cometh* inscribed, "To my friend Sophus — *Usque ad finem!*" a reference to Conrad's *Lord Jim*, and the two men threw choice lines at one another ("How do you shoot a spectre through the heart?" etc.) from what each called his favorite novel. In the evening Sophus read aloud Browning's "Childe Roland to the Dark Tower Came," a poem that O'Neill felt was symbolically true of his own life.

Whenever the Winthers had previously visited the pair, Freeman had always appeared to say hello, but this time he remained out of sight; the Winthers knew of his presence only because Carlotta said that he was "in the kitchen slicing the turkey." Not long after the holiday, O'Neill, harboring jealous suspicions about the Southerner, fired him. (Some months later, back in California, Freeman called on the Strams and, as they recall, sounded rather amused while reminiscing about his former employers.)

At Christmas Eugene forgot to write Carlotta a holiday greeting and, in his words, "paid for that in tears." On her fifty-ninth birthday three days later he gave her "my love, and my great need of your love, which is my life." He urged her not to "sneer at this, for it is the one truth that counts, that can support us in our old age against the sneers of the world. . . . I love you, Carlotta, as I have loved you, as I always will!"

Years after her husband's death, Carlotta told this biographer: "To me he was like a wayward child, a delinquent. He didn't love me, I don't think he ever loved anybody — just his work. He needed me to look after him. He was impotent the last ten years of his life, and he hated me for it. If he'd known anything about love, this wouldn't have bothered him. . . . Things would be going along all right between us when out of the blue he would say, 'I don't know whether I hate myself more or you.' " But another time she conceded that "Gene probably loved me as much as he could love anyone."

Richard Lebherz, the poet, was at the Metropolitan Museum one day when O'Neill, whom he recognized immediately, and Carlotta preceded him into an elevator. Like Hamilton Basso, Lebherz was distressed by the playwright's eyes — "two dreadful spots of agony, the eyes of a man in hell looking out at the world about him." Lebherz was uncertain, he says, "whether this was due to the physical pain he might have been experiencing but I am rather inclined to believe that it was more the result of a man who had stripped away every illusion from his mind only to find there was nothing in the end. I also got the impression that he was a man terribly riddled with guilt. When the elevator stopped and he shuffled out, with his wife attentively behind him, I felt I had been in the presence of one who had suffered terribly spiritually and all that was left of him was a faint flicker of life just about to be blown out by time."

O'Neill was more durable, though, than he appeared; he was to live another six years.

One evening in mid-January 1948 when Saxe Commins was at the apartment, the telephone rang; after listening for a few moments, Carlotta in a cold voice summoned her husband. While he spoke ("Yes, of course, Fitzi, I'll be glad to, how much do you want? Will one hundred dollars be enough?"), Carlotta paced back and forth, fuming, "Those bohemians, those leeches, always wanting something, the dirty scum," and so on. The call was from M. Eleanor Fitzgerald, who had been a real-life Earth Mother to so many at the Provincetown Playhouse; indisposed and fearful of cancer, Fitzi was about to enter Mt. Sinai for an examination, but the hospital required an advance payment. After he hung up, O'Neill tried to calm his wife by explaining that he owed a great deal to Fitzi, but Carlotta was not to be pacified. Saxe, pained with embarrassment, whispered good-night and slipped away.

From attacking O'Neill's "bohemian" friends, Carlotta turned to abusing him; he retreated into his bedroom (according to his account later to Commins), but she followed him and at the height of her rage broke a glass covering some photos on his bureau, among them a picture of himself as a baby nestled on his mother's shoulder. Crying, "Your mother was a whore!" she tore the picture into little pieces, whereupon O'Neill, calling her names, slapped her. Hysterical by now, she threw a few clothes into a suitcase and stormed out.

The following morning Eugene, after discussing the situation with Saxe, summoned Walter Casey for an indefinite stay, but he lost no time trying to win back Carlotta. Addressing her as "Darling" in a note sent on January 19 in care of her attorney, he said: "For the love of God, forgive and come back. You are all I have in life. I am sick and I will surely die without you. You do not want to murder me, I know, and a curse will be on you for your remaining days.

"I love you and I [always] will! Please, Darling!"

Carlotta, who had taken refuge in the New Weston Hotel, ignored his plea. After Bill Aronberg located her through a private detective, she moved to another East Side hotel, but she kept in touch with the Crouses, the Van Vechtens and other friends, pouring out her grievances in long monologues on the telephone.

O'Neill's tremor was at its worst and his physician, Dr. Shirley C. Fisk, hoping to forestall any injuries ("either accidental or self-inflicted"), privately advised Saxe and Casey that the playwright should never be left alone in the apartment. Saxe, who remained there late on January 27, felt apprehensive, for his friend was in a particularly low mood. After Saxe's departure, O'Neill had some drinks with Casey before retiring to bed. Later, while heading for the bathroom during the night, he lurched and as he struck the floor felt a sharp pain in his left arm. Unable to stand again, he kept crying out to Casey, but Casey was lost in alcoholic sleep. Cupping his hands around his mouth, O'Neill tried to make himself heard in the apartment below, and eventually, after rolling himself in a rug against the cold, fainted. Full of remorse when he awoke, Casey immediately telephoned Dr. Fisk, then Commins, after which O'Neill, suffering from a fractured left shoulder, was removed in an ambulance to Doctors' Hospital.

Dr. Fisk could not determine how much O'Neill had drunk since "alcohol, even a little, would be potent on top of the bromides and other medications" he was taking for his Parkinson's. A young man with a reassuring personality whose practice included a number of literary and theatrical figures, Dr. Fisk had taken an immediate liking to O'Neill the first time they met, only a short while before the accident; at the hospital Fisk found him appreciative and stoical, in short a model patient. "I gave him special attention, more time than I usually do," the doctor says, "not because he was a famous playwright but rather because he had a very appealing personality. You wanted to do your best for him, and Dr. Patterson [Robert Lee Patterson, an orthopedist whom Fisk brought into the case] felt the same."

Echoing his colleague's sentiments, Dr. Patterson says, "Regardless of his pain, O'Neill always greeted me with a little smile. It was difficult knowing when to prescribe sedation, since he never complained."

Unaware of the O'Neills' estrangement, Sherlee Weingarten, as soon as she heard of the accident, sent a note of sympathy. A day or two later Carlotta telephoned Armina Marshall at the Guild, but since she was out, the operator gave the call to Sherlee. "Ordinarily Carlotta identified herself to the operator as 'Mrs. O'Neill,'" Sherlee recalls, "but this time she had said 'Miss Monterey.' 'Is that you, Carlotta?' I asked, and she replied, 'I want to speak to Miss Marshall. Get off the phone!' Her voice was so full of hate that I dropped the phone, and while I'm not the fainting kind, I almost blacked out. It was the last time I ever spoke with her."

Eugene Jr., who was at the hospital almost daily — he had scarcely seen his father during the past year — hoped that he was through with Carlotta. But O'Neill told him, "I can't live without her." While discussing his children once with Dr. Fisk, he expressed the belief, in the doctor's words, that "his elder son was not unlike himself in emotional makeup, and he feared that the young man would come to an unhappy end."

Although in despair over his marital crisis, O'Neill made some pretense of taking the situation lightly. On February 3 he dictated a note to Russel Crouse: "I'd love to see you any time in the evening beginning next week. By then I ought to be able to cook up a smile of welcome or sing to you faintly, 'Oh, Come and Be Sweet to Me, Kid.'" To E. G. Marshall he gave a humorous account of his accident. "He was laughing silently the whole time he told me about it," Marshall says, "not in hysteria but at the whole ridiculous picture of himself that night, the absurdity of it."

Certain of the O'Neills' friends, including the Crouses, the Langners, Theresa Helburn and the Van Vechtens, felt that in the end they would be reconciled, but others, particularly Commins and Aronberg, who regarded Carlotta as a blight on her husband's life, hopefully believed that the rupture would be permanent. At first O'Neill led Dr. Fisk to think that he had broken with Carlotta and intended to establish bachelor quarters, with Casey looking after him. To Sherlee Weingarten, who visited him regularly and took care of his correspondence under his direction, he divulged his suspicions about the masseuse in California and said he had finally learned that Carlotta's annuity came from James Speyer, her onetime lover. Yet, regardless of his suspicions and grievances, his dearest wish was for their reunion.

On February 10, 1948, the twentieth anniversary of their secret departure for Europe, he wrote to her in a tremulous hand:

> *Please, O Dear God, let this anniversary . . . not make you think of a flop! You have been life to me, and the greatest beauty and joy, and without you I am nothing!*
>
> *Please, Sweetheart, I have been through hell and you have. I could never act again as I have acted.*
>
> *I love you, Darling, Darling! I love you! I love you! I am yours. Don't leave me!*
>
> *Your*
>
> *Gene*

But Carlotta was not yet ready to end his anguish, or her opportunity for dramatics. She would telephone Dr. Fisk to inquire about her husband's condition, then, launching into a long tirade, call him a sadist, "an old lecher," and accuse him of affairs with actresses from his productions. In a conference with Aronberg, she announced that she was leaving shortly with a friend for Europe. Days later, though, after seeing Dr. Patterson about her arthritic condition, she herself entered Doctors' Hospital, where she had a room on the floor below her husband's. "I had a nine-dollar one," she remembered complainingly, "while the Master had one for thirty-five dollars, with his friends trooping in and out." In Dr. Fisk's opinion, she had herself admitted simply to spy on her husband — something she managed to do quite effectively with the help of Freeman, who stationed himself near the playwright's room and asked all his callers for their names. Carlotta remained in the hospital only a short time, however.

O'Neill, whose tenth-floor corner room overlooked the East River, spent much of his time watching the various vessels gliding up and down. During a visit from Rouben Mamoulian, now a movie director, and his wife, the playwright was his usual reticent self at first, but he became animated on learning that they had just returned from touring South America. "He began telling," Mamoulian recalls, "about the time he'd spent down there, on ships, sleeping on park benches, and he was fascinating. For the first time in my experience he talked the way he wrote. He'd never been so eloquent and graphic. It was obvious that he had a great nostalgia for those days. He talked of sleeping on benches the way Zeus would talk of sleeping on a cloud. He went on for an hour or more, his talk was really poetic. I'd been shocked by his appearance when I first saw him, but as he spoke he looked almost healthy and young."

In mid-February the playwright, suddenly worried about his manuscripts and other papers at the penthouse, had Casey bring them to Saxe at Random House, where they were stored in a safe. The nine packages of material included, according to Commins's listing, two typescripts of *Long Day's Journey* and the scenario in the author's hand; three typescripts of *A Touch of the Poet*, two with revisions in the author's hand; a package marked "Cycle"; one marked "Ideas for plays not in Cycle"; one marked "Revolt"; and another bearing the titles, "By Way of Obit," "The Last Conquest" and "Gag's End."

Carlotta formerly had so trusted Commins that for years he had had a key to her safe-deposit box in a Manhattan bank and the authority to use it whenever she required; but right after the blowup at the penthouse she retrieved the key through her attorney. On February 26 Commins had a telephone call from her which began with her demanding to know whether he had removed the manuscripts from O'Neill's desk. Immediately abusive when he said no, she declared, in the midst of defaming both him and O'Neill, that she had "enough on" Saxe to send him to prison, where he had "belonged for years," and again demanded that he divulge where the papers were hidden.

"Don't ask me about them," Saxe replied. "They are not mine."

Losing all self-control, she screamed that Hitler had not killed enough of "your kind," called him "a crook, a Jew bastard," among other epithets, and slammed down the receiver. Trembling when he returned home to his wife that night, Saxe broke down weeping.

In writing the next day to O'Neill of the telephone call, he said: "What else could I have done, Gene, but tell her that I did not take the scripts? Without authorization from you, I cannot even mention them. Under the circumstances, I want you to know and approve of whatever I say or do whenever it touches you."

To Russel Crouse it seemed that "Gene and Carlotta were both fascinated and repelled by one another. That's not," he added, "an uncommon relationship." At the beginning of March, largely through his intercession, Carlotta at last visited her husband, but their reunion broke up in recriminations. She was shaking and in tears when she called on Crouse, and after listening to her he noted in his diary on March 3 that "it's all a tragedy." From O'Neill later, however, he heard "another story." According to his version, she at one point moved his injured arm, intentionally, and caused him great pain.

After the embattled pair, Saxe Commins was the one most unhappy about the situation. On hearing that Carlotta had seen her husband, Saxe wrote to him on March 2: "I have been giving much tormented thought to the possibility that my frequent visits to the hospital and my daily phone calls . . . might have been causing you embarrassment. Nothing, as you must know, could be farther from my mind or heart. Yet if it will save you the slightest need of explanation I shall stay away until you summon me. All I want you to know is that as long as I live I'll be available, when the chips are down or at any other time, on the moment of your call."

Although both Eugene and Carlotta wanted a reconciliation by now, each held the other chiefly to blame for their discord, and more than once a patchwork truce between them fell apart. Their negotiations dragged on for weeks. On March 5 Carlotta informed the Crouses that Gene intended to join her about the first of April at the Lowell, a residential hotel on East Sixty-third Street; apparently they did not care to return to the penthouse, the scene of so many ugly incidents between them. But a month later Eugene was still in the hospital, and Carlotta, declining a dinner invitation from the Crouses, explained on April 8 that she was "terrified to go out after dark. Ever since I have returned here [at the Lowell] the Master has had two detectives (& a car) following me, or hanging about the hotel. I am terrified! What in the name of God he expects to find I don't know. After living with him 20 years he knows me so little. And the last five years with him have cured me of [desire for] any version of sex or love. . . .

"He *does* know how I *loathe* all this sordid, horrible, exhibitionistic, common sort of thing. It is done to humiliate & worry me into a mad house. He has told me so often how easy it would be for him to get in touch with the gangsters he used to know somewhere down in the Village, & have anyone 'bumped off' or 'beat up' "! — I would welcome being shot — but I would *loathe* being beat up! I go out only when I have to, & then I'm scared crazy. . . .

"You see, dear Russel, Gene hasn't been able to work for *years*. But all these sordid tales go on in his brain — This thing, between us, that is happening now, gives him a beautiful chance for drama. He will, *in his*

[610]

head, dramatize everything, until he will have *no* conception, in his present state, *what* is truth & *what* is drama! But it would be wonderful if something *strange* & *horrible* could happen to me — Then — what a fine third act there could be.

"So, my dear Russèl & Anna, pray for me."

Only several days later, however, she and Eugene were reconciled at the hospital. "He needs me, he can't live without me!" she crowed to Dr. Fisk, while her husband smiled in assent.

After talking things over they agreed to settle near Boston, one of the country's leading medical centers, and establish a home overlooking the water. "God, if you knew how I long to get back to and in the sea," O'Neill had written to a friend in 1944, while living at the hotel in San Francisco. "One thing our ranch in the San Ramon Valley taught me was that no matter how beautiful the hills and woods and meadows . . . I can admire it objectively but in any deep spiritual sense I don't belong. . . . Beach grass is the only verdure I really understand, dunes are my hills, the beach-sun is my only sun and the sea is the symbol of the mystery of life to which I belong, and has been that for me since I was a small boy."

The O'Neills' happiness over their rapprochement was dampened, during their final days in New York, by an article in the *Times Literary Supplement* of London in which the playwright was "figuratively torn to shreds." Summarizing the diatribe, which covered two and a half pages of newsprint, the New York *Times* said on April 12, "It is rare for this staid and most important of Britain's literary publications to attack with such vigor."

Touched off by the publication in England of *The Iceman Cometh*, the anonymous article (all pieces in the *Literary Supplement* were unsigned) railed at O'Neill as a "puritan" whose "fury against puritans is so fierce that it appears to be pathological." His "philosophy" was dismissed as a "mass of undisciplined emotions and jejune opinions." As for his work as a whole: "The O'Neill world is a dirty pub, frequented by drunks and disorderlies and shiftless loafers; and periodically raided by corrupt cops. . . . Wandering through his underworld, and holding our noses as we wander, we have difficulty in believing that even it could have existed without one positively good and likeable inhabitant."

O'Neill, the article sourly noted, was merely forty-eight when he won the Nobel Prize, but Shaw "had to wait for it until he was sixty-nine." The only one of the American's plays to win the unqualified approval of the anonymous critic was *Ah, Wilderness!*

Brooks Atkinson counterattacked in the New York *Times* that even "for a critic the animadversions of the *Literary Supplement* writer are excessively obtuse and prejudiced . . . the genius of O'Neill is the raw boldness and the elemental strength of his attack upon outworn concepts of destiny. Don't be misled by the crudeness of his characters and the gutter argot they speak. . . . He thinks the spiritual glories of America have been sold out for materialistic gains, which is a moral idea. He thinks that modern civilization is godless and that it has not found a substitute for God — and that, too, is a moral idea. . . . The peevish article in the *Times Literary Supplement* overlooks the one thing in O'Neill that is inescapable: the passionate depth and vitality of his convictions. Nothing said about him is worth the paper it is printed on unless it recognizes the vitality he had brought into the theater. Nobody is so impervious to vitality as a writer who has none."

When the reconciled couple left for Boston on April 19, O'Neill, though born in Manhattan, felt homeward bound. As a playwright he "felt closest to the battle of moral forces in New England," and as a person he "loved that region best." In time his settling there would prove "becoming" in an unhappy sense; traditionally a place of strong-willed individuals, of interfamily feuds that finally break with a gray fury like that of a nor'easter battering its rocky coast, New England would seem as appropriate a background for O'Neill and Carlotta as for the hapless clan in *Mourning Becomes Electra*.

29

※

By the Sea Again

B EFORE they had been in Boston a month the O'Neills purchased an old cottage, built around 1880, at the very tip of Marblehead Neck. From here one has a magnificent view that embraces all at once the harbor, the coast and the open sea. Jutting out from Marblehead proper, about twenty miles north of Boston, the Neck is the choicest part of one of the most picturesque towns in all New England, as well as a watery paradise for yachting and sailboat enthusiasts. To Carlotta their new refuge seemed, after Tao House and Casa Genotta, "a birdcage," but Eugene was pleasurably reminded of "the first home my father bought in New London" — the Monte Cristo cottage. Exulting over its site, "*right on the ocean*," he felt that "I shall be able to write again, and have some roots — of seaweed — with my feet in a New England sea."

The house on Point o' Rocks Lane was purchased in spring 1948 but fall would be near before the couple could quit their suite at the Ritz-Carlton for the Marblehead place, since it required extensive alterations for year-round living. "I was horrified when I saw it," says architect Philip Horton Smith, who designed and supervised the remodeling. "It was just a wooden summer cottage, open underneath with latticework, so all the cold ocean wind could blow under it, and no heating system, no electric wiring to speak of, no basement, no proper kitchen. I felt they had made a great mistake, but according to the real estate broker, O'Neill liked its location at the northeastern end [of the Neck], where it would get the full brunt of storms from the sea."

During the months of renovation the O'Neills became friendly with Philip Smith, a gentlemanly New Englander about their age who, like the playwright, loved the old-time songs and had vivid memories of the yesteryear theater. "As a boy growing up in Salem," he recalls, "I used to hang around the railroad station and carry the actors' bags to their board-inghouses. That's how I got to see all the shows. When I mentioned that I'd seen his father in *Monte Cristo,* O'Neill said, 'I'm not surprised — he played in that practically all his life.'"

The O'Neills were cordial also toward the architect's wife Elinor, attractive, pleasant-natured, considerably his junior; both Smiths were fond of the arts, enjoyed reading, and doted on their only child, a mannerly boy of nine. Envious of the architect's manifest closeness to his son, O'Neill repined to Smith that he and his father had not "understood" one another and now a similar situation existed between him and his own children. The Smiths, in view of the kind of plays he had written, were happily surprised to find him "gentle, quiet, shy, courteous, so unassuming in manner," and in addition were delighted that his wife was so gracious and warm. The O'Neills seemed to the other couple "very happy," with Carlotta wholeheartedly dedicated to his welfare.

Cheered by the prospect of again living by the sea, Eugene was grateful to Carlotta, for she had sold her nest egg of stocks and bonds, netting some forty-eight thousand dollars to buy their new home. The cottage cost twenty-five thousand dollars, and she expected that the rest of her money would take care of the alterations.

Calling her "my love and my life," O'Neill on July 11 wrote in a copy of *The Iceman Cometh:* "Out of great sorrow, and pain, and misunderstanding, comes a new vision of deeper love and security and above all, serenity, to bind us ever closer in our old age." Later this month, inscribing a volume of Christina Rossetti's verse to her on their nineteenth anniversary, he said: "Now, with our sixtieth birthday looming close upon us . . . I want to say to you — 'You are my love — forever my love, Sweetheart! And I want to promise you that I will do my utmost to cast out whatever remains in me of selfishness or thoughtlessness that could possibly harm you, wishing with all my heart only for that which will make you happy; for your happiness is my happiness!"

Thanks to an unaccountable lessening of his chronic affliction for a time, his handwriting in both inscriptions and in the few letters he wrote during this period was more legible than in several years. Euphoric for the moment, he thought, as he told Saxe Commins on July 26, that he might be able to resume playwriting. "The tremor is better," he said, "but I'm just crowned with it for life, I guess, and the best to hope for is to circumvent it. . . . And why complain when the world itself is one vast tremor."

At the end of July the couple, with the Smiths as their guests, attended a private screening of Laurence Olivier's *Hamlet* at a movie company's headquarters on Green Street. Afterward, as they strolled back to the Ritz-Carlton, Smith wondered about the playwright's opinion of the film. Thinking perhaps of Barrymore's great portrayal, his only comment was, "Shall I say, now that I'm outside?" But Carlotta later reported that they had "fought like hyenas," as she, unlike her husband, had loved the film.

Thus far only a small number knew of the playwright's presence in Boston, a situation that changed right after the *Hamlet* screening when someone at the movie company tipped off the press. The newspapers reported his purchase of a home in Marblehead and tried to interview him, while Carlotta complained to the Smiths that the publicity was making their life "miserable." Their apprehensions were as nothing, however, compared to their fear and anger after a telephone call in mid-August from Bill Aronberg: Shane had been arrested on a heroin charge, and Cathy, who had had another child, wanted help for both Shane and herself.

After years of alcohol and marijuana, Shane had become a heroin addict, cursed with an appetite that grows sharper from the stuff it feeds on. Gaunt, unkempt, shabbily dressed, indistinguishable from the other junkies in the developing drug subculture of Greenwich Village, he devoted all his efforts to a desperate hustling up of money to buy "horse" or "H," as heroin was called by the addicts. "Shane once told me," says Marc Brandel, "that he took to heroin because it was 'a way of life.' I think I know what he meant; it gave him a definite aim, an inescapable purpose, every day of his life: to get the damned stuff."

Arrested on August 10, 1948, on a charge of possessing three capsules of heroin, Shane, while Cathy frantically tried to raise his bail of five hundred dollars, had to remain in jail till the disposition of his case. Cathy informed Aronberg that Shane had the alternatives of pleading guilty and entering the federal hospital in Lexington, Kentucky, for treatment – a plea that would draw only a minimum of publicity – or of fighting the case, in which event the notoriety was certain to engulf O'Neill also.

Forever haunted by memories of his mother's addiction, O'Neill felt devastated about Shane, torn with guilt feelings. The arrest had not yet become public knowledge when Philip Smith, who knew only that the O'Neills had had bad news from New York, called at their hotel suite; both looked to him "wrung out and much older" than when he had seen them a few days earlier. Under insistent prodding from Carlotta ("It's better that he learns about it from us, instead of the papers"), O'Neill reluctantly began, "Much as I hate to say it, my son Shane is a complete rotter," and he went on to tell the general facts. He was uncertain, he said, whether or not it was his fault that the boy "had turned out this way, but he had spent untold sums on his education, sending him to good schools, and so forth."

Her voice rising over her husband's, Carlotta pictured Shane and Cathy as "the lowest dregs of humanity," told "an incredible and revolting story of their smothered baby," and said that the two had tried to "blackmail" Gene with threats of sordid publicity. In the present mess, she wanted her husband to make "a complete break" with his son and have nothing further to do with him, so that they could have some "peace" in their old age. Turning to her own history, she said that her daughter "had broken her heart and done just about everything possible to her, but that she had now steeled herself not to care any more what the girl did, and she wanted Gene to be the same way with his son."

While Shane was bitter that no one loved him enough to provide the five hundred dollars' bail money, he was defensive about his father when Cathy relayed word from Aronberg that O'Neill would not come to his help; his father, the boy said, was in poor health. At the hearing of the case of the United States of America versus Shane Rudraighe O'Neill on August 20, the defendant pleaded guilty and was given a two-year suspended sentence on condition that he undergo treatment in Lexington for a minimum of four months, or till his discharge as cured. (Perilously adrift for years and unable to provide for his family – he and Cathy had four children after their short-lived first one – Shane would have several other brushes with the law over narcotics charges before he eventually rehabilitated himself with the aid of methadone. The family was sustained for a period by a legacy from Cathy's mother, a windfall with blood on it, for it came to Cathy after her stepfather, like a figure in an O'Neill drama, stabbed his wife to death.)

Though Philip and Elinor Smith would always think fondly of the playwright, they began to have mixed feelings about his wife; she bewildered them. While Smith busied himself one day with workmen at the cottage, Elinor was moved as Carlotta spoke compassionately of her husband, who had remained behind at the hotel: he was so unhappy now that he could no longer write; he had nothing to look forward to, but she hoped that he would feel better after they had moved into the cottage, where he could "look at the water and dream." When Mrs. Smith reported the conversation to her husband, he was surprised, for just before Elinor's arrival, Carlotta had denounced O'Neill and spelled out a compendium of grievances. Another day Carlotta complained to the architect

[616]

that Gene was selfish, yet "everyone thinks he's so sweet and gentle, and likes him. Me — No!"

O'Neill in turn could be sharp with his wife when provoked, the Smiths said, but generally he confined his response to "dirty looks."

The Smiths had been flattered at first when Carlotta spoke frankly of private family matters — in almost no time they felt that they had known her "a long time" — but finally her confidences were of a kind that embarrassed them. O'Neill was so helpless, she said, that in order to bathe him she had to strip and get into the tub with him. Disclosing that they had been estranged for a time, shortly before their move to Boston, she stated that the trouble began with a homosexual incident, that she had returned to the penthouse and found him in bed with an old acquaintance of his. Later, after he fell and injured his shoulder, her story continued, his "fine friends" deserted him, so he had to "send for Mama." She felt that he showed "consideration to everyone" except herself, as he knew that she "would stick by him." She had turned over to him most of her money, for him she had given up her kind of life and lived in isolated, lonely places, but he did not appreciate all her sacrifices. "A genius? Bah!"

Carlotta was in an aggrieved mood from both the Shane episode and the rapidly mounting expense of renovating the cottage. During her early months in Boston she had bought antiques and other quality furnishings at Carbone's (according to a decorator at the Boylston Street place, which is no longer in existence, she spent close to ten thousand dollars); but by late summer both she and O'Neill were "crying poverty" to the Smiths. Contrary to her original expectations, the Marblehead place with alterations cost around eighty-five thousand dollars. O'Neill supplied fifteen thousand dollars and they obtained a twenty thousand dollar mortgage after she had paid out nearly fifty thousand dollars. "She couldn't get over the fact," Smith recalls, "that a small wooden cottage was costing almost as much as Tao House. But their place in Georgia and even Tao House were built when things were relatively cheap, whereas the cottage was done over during the postwar construction boom, when labor and materials were priced higher than ever before. The cottage was more costly, also, because they were in a hurry to move in. Normally, the job would have taken months longer."

The remodeling crew found the playwright's wife exacting, generous, unpredictable, inclined to be explosive. "I can't complain about her," says one contractor, a man of forbearance and calm speech. "She treated *me* all right. But I liked him, I really liked him — he was a nice, mild old fellow." Another of the group, more outspoken, said, "She could be sweet as pie one minute and cut your throat the next."

As the two settled on Point o' Rocks Lane in September, Carlotta, who now realized that she had "bought too much" at Carbone's, was almost frantic trying to find room for everything and talked of holding an auction. After two huge vans arrived with furniture and furnishings from storage in New York, she showered presents, including some costly things, on the Smiths and the head workmen, all the while talking poormouth. Upset over the contents of one carton — two shotguns and a hunting rifle that Freeman had used in Georgia and California — she declared, "I won't stay in this house a single night with those things here!" The guns were given immediately to the building contractor.

Under the renovation the cottage gained a glassed-in porch in the rear, facing the sea, an immaculate kitchen, a maid's room, and among other improvements, built-in bookshelves everywhere, downstairs and up. The four small rooms on the second floor consisted of two bedrooms, Carlotta's workroom, and Eugene's study, with a window that overlooked "nothing but ocean." The interior of the gray house gleamed with color — doors of Chinese red, pink walls, blue tile floors, multihued ceramic elephants and Sicilian donkeys, Chinese screens — with a six-foot African mask lending a touch of drama. Yet the overall effect was less vivid than its colorful parts, for Carlotta, who suffered from double vision and could not endure sunshine, kept the daylight muffled with both venetian blinds and heavy draperies on nearly every window. To other residents of the vicinity the cottage appeared to have a closed-up, rather secretive personality; they used to wonder, like the villagers speculating about the forbidding mansion in *Mourning Becomes Electra*, what went on in the house.

Several days after moving in, Carlotta remarked cryptically on the telephone to Elinor Smith: "You find when you get to the other side of the lake that it is just the same as the one you left."

To the Smiths' bewilderment and regret, their friendship with the O'Neills ended suddenly. Not long before quitting Boston, Carlotta had told Mrs. Smith, "Don't disappear when we get to Marblehead — drop by soon and help me decide where to put things." Taking her at her word, Elinor called on them without telephoning in advance. "The maid showed me right in," she says, "and pointed toward the porch. My first sight of them gave me a start. They looked like two murderers, with the body still on the premises, who were being visited by the police. He was at one end of the porch looking fearful, and she was at the other end glowering. A great smile spread over his face as soon as he saw me, but she stormed off upstairs. She later came back and made an effort to be pleasant, but I was shocked at the change in her. She'd always been so friendly before, she couldn't make enough of Philip and me."

Carlotta wrote to Mrs. Smith on October 7 that they had "never seen people without an appointment. . . . We live differently from other folk — and, added to that, now neither of us is well. Gene spends certain hours in his study & is *never* disturbed for *no one!* . . . I have all his secretarial work to do — & I must have a rest period."

In the architect's turn to be rebuffed, Carlotta took vehement exception to an aspect of the renovation; and where she had formerly welcomed his help in arranging for the mortgage, she now said that she had always managed for herself and must have been "in a coma" for the past four months to allow him "to do so much." It was a mistake, she said, "to mix business with pleasure." Before long Carlotta, who had snubbed not only the Philip Smiths but others of the area ready to be friendly, began to complain of being lonely. To Earl Finney, the building contractor for the alterations, it seemed that Carlotta did her utmost to isolate her husband, to make him feel that he could not do anything for himself, so that he would be more dependent on her. However, now that O'Neill, a kind of amphibious Antaeus, was again living by the water, he appeared to gain in strength and spirit.

On October 16, his sixtieth birthday, he received a congratulatory telegram from Dorothy Commins; actually, as both O'Neills knew, it came from Saxe, but Saxe had figured that Carlotta would intercept any communication bearing his name. Replying for Eugene on the twenty-first, Carlotta thanked Dorothy in a letter that dwelled on the high cost of the Marblehead place. "I had the beautiful idea," she said, "that if I sold all the securities I had left I would have enough to re-do some little house and, when finished, go to Master O'Neill and say, 'Here, young man, is a home for you all ready!' But, like everything I have attempted with the Master, it did not work out that way. . . . I hope things go well with you and yours." No mention of Saxe by name.

Although the trembling of O'Neill's legs had become so bad that some days he could hardly walk, the condition of his hands continued somewhat better. "I hope to return to my old occupation of playwriting before too long," he told Nathan on December 3, 1948. "God knows I have plenty of ideas, and the tremor, which had me stopped for so long — along with war, cities, hotels and apartments — seems now to affect my hands less. . . . At any rate, there is hope in what appeared hopeless — as this letter, written without aid of medicine or psychiatry, proves." To Bill Aronberg, on the same day, he wrote that he and Carlotta were "happier than in many years . . . the house is a home as only Carlotta can make," and in a letter to Dudley Nichols he reported that he was "planning to start a new play."

Addressing Carlotta as "Dearest One," he said in his Christmas greeting (the handwriting is fairly good): "May Santa Claus bring you a more understanding, more tender and gentle one — I mean, husband — I mean the same old one, but better!"

Largely a haven for summer colonists, Marblehead Neck had a forlorn air during the cold months, when most of the houses were shuttered and dark, the trees bare, and the ocean gray under bleak skies. Occasionally the quiet tenor of the O'Neills' first winter at the cottage was shattered by storms, including a nor'easter that sent water cascading down the chimney, dislodged boulders on the grounds, and tore away an iron door at nearby Marblehead Light. "Jesus, I don't know how they stood it," says Frank Orne, the couple's utility man, "with the ocean pounding and roaring at them! I know I couldn't have taken it." Carlotta herself has said that "we were tied to rocks by steel cables and when the storms came up, of course they came up over our heads. I expected to go out to sea any moment."

Late in the winter, after the playwright had had experimental medication at Boston Hospital, the press erroneously stated that he was recovering from his tremor and had begun a new drama. The timing of the report was sadly ironical, for it was during this period that his affliction worsened and he finally abandoned all hope that he would ever write again. Adding to his distress, mail poured in from Parkinson's victims in this country and abroad asking what medicine had cured him, the name of his doctor, and so on. "I can only answer," he told Nathan on March 20, 1949, "that I have tried everything too, with only bad results. Most of these letters are extremely sad and anything but a boost to my morale."

Dudley Nichols, who visited the O'Neills this spring, gave Oona a report when he returned to California and she relayed his account to Agnes in the thought that Shane "would like to know" their father's situation: "Dudley says that he sits in his study watching the waves on the rocks, listens to his records, reads; he never leaves the place to go to New York or anywhere — he doesn't write at all . . . the disease is getting steadily worse. . . . Esta Nichols [Dudley's wife] said that Carlotta wrote her that Gene's memory leaves him sometimes for several days —

and Dudley immediately pounced on her and said that Carlotta was hysterical and neurotic and not to go by anything she said!!

"He showed me two pictures of Gene taken several months ago, and I must say he looked *terrible!* His life now must be pretty awful. . . . Dudley says he is philosophical and resigned and not too pulled down. . . . Personally I think he should be a little more bitter, it would be better!!!"

Now that he no longer had his life's work to occupy his time and sustain him, O'Neill was grateful whenever old friends — the few still acceptable to Carlotta — visited him. Like Dudley Nichols, the others — Russel and Anna Crouse, the Langners, Kenneth Macgowan, Eline and Sophus Winther, Charles O'Brien Kennedy — generally found him philosophical and resigned, but occasionally the face behind the mask showed through. Kennedy remembers sitting with him one sunny afternoon as sailboats were gliding in and out of the harbor. "After a while," Kennedy writes, "he leaned forward. Anyone familiar with his life could surmise that his thoughts were back in the days when he was a young sailor . . . free to wander at will, free from bodily ills or anguish of spirit . . . the longing in his eyes was almost unbearable."

Since the cottage could not accommodate overnight guests, most visitors remained only a few hours, but late in summer 1949 the Winthers, who stayed at a hotel in Salem, saw the O'Neills for several days. "Here in the gray house on a rock washed by the Atlantic," Sophus recalls, "O'Neill felt that his life had come full circle. As we sat on the porch one night, with the full moon hanging in a faint mist, Gene suddenly said, 'Good-bye, old moon, fall out of the sky. I don't need you any more.'"

(Years earlier, one remembers, O'Neill used to say that the ideal way to commit suicide would be to swim out, under a full moon, till one eventually went under. However, various circumstances in his history suggest that his envisioned drowning, rather than expressing a death wish, represented a mystical desire to "die" in the sea and be reborn as another person in a better kind of life. Thus, his apostrophe to the moon was more than egocentricity or bathos; it seems, instead, that what he had endured and suffered in his time had finally killed all desire for reincarnation.)

In his study, under sloping eaves that reminded him of the Monte Cristo cottage in New London, the silenced playwright showed Winther his desk, all arranged with notebook, paper and pencils. "It's a hell of a thing," he said, "to want to write, to have everything except the control of your hands." Winther, recalling his words, says, "So it was. It was the saddest moment of all the years I had known Gene."

(A few months later O'Neill, in an almost illegible hand, inscribed a book of his plays to the Strams' son Gerald Eugene with his "deepest hopes that your life to come may be one of hard work at something you love better than yourself — in short, may you find happiness!")

Carlotta told Sophus and Eline that she found her husband "aging in so many ways," but the couple, without venturing to disagree with her, thought that he had not deteriorated visibly since their visit to the penthouse nearly two years earlier. "The day we left," Winther says, "Gene lent us manuscripts of *A Touch of the Poet* and *A Moon for the Misbegotten* that were to be mailed back. Carlotta obviously disapproved, but when he made up his mind . . ."

Partly for his own benefit but chiefly to please Carlotta, who complained that the stairway was hard on her arthritic condition, O'Neill had a small elevator installed this year. He wanted to make the cottage more comfortable and attractive to her, but after her original interest in furnishing it, she never liked the place; she found it too hot in summer, too cold in winter, and was annoyed the year round at her husband's musicmaking. Unlike their previous homes, where he could play his records without disturbing her, the acoustics here were so sharp, from thin walls and tile floors, that almost any sound could be heard in the rest of the place. To a workman at the place this fall, she said that they did not want to spend additional money on the house because they might sell it, but more than another year would pass before their tenancy on Point o' Rocks Lane came to an unhappy climax and abrupt end.

Excepting their domestic help — a Japanese houseman, who lived in, a Marblehead woman who cooked for them, and a part-time utility man — the only persons in regular contact with the O'Neills were a barber, who came to the house every two weeks, and their physician, Frederic B. Mayo of nearby Swampscott. A lanky, young New Englander with a pleasing personality, Dr. Mayo liked O'Neill from the start ("He was a delightful man, very charming and gracious"), but in time developed private reservations about his wife. The doctor, who saw the couple on an average of once a month, treated them in the main for colds and other minor indispositions; he sometimes felt that he was summoned "just because they were lonely and wanted to see someone else. I felt that about him especially — he was all cooped up there."

While O'Neill rarely said much, the doctor, who shared his love of boats and jazz, found him easy to talk to. Concerned about the other's inactivity and seclusive existence, Mayo, who had a good-sized schooner at his disposal, invited him to go sailing some Sunday afternoon; brightening with anticipatory pleasure, Eugene accepted immediately. But later, when Mayo tried to arrange the date, his offer was politely declined. "It's my impression," he says, "that she was against it."

Although O'Neill's tremor was bad enough to prevent him from writing, he was not, according to Mayo, a severe case of Parkinson's. "His body didn't tremble violently or all the time, his hands didn't shake violently against his body, as I've seen in some instances. He had what I would say was moderate difficulty in walking. Some days his tremor was hardly noticeable, but other times, especially when he was upset, it would be bad."

As for Carlotta's affliction — for years she had complained of arthritis of the spine and in her feet — Dr. Mayo finds it "difficult to say how bad her spine was. But I took X rays of her feet, and nothing was wrong there. She dramatized and made a great deal of her aches and pains." She told Mayo that she had been, in his words, "a fine actress and could have become one of the best in the theater, except that her marriage to O'Neill cut her career short." The doctor, unfamiliar with O'Neill's personal history, made a faux pas the first Christmas he knew the couple by asking whether Oona was to visit them for the holidays. "Please don't ever mention that name in this house again," Carlotta said. "We've disowned her."

In their isolation the couple always welcomed the fortnightly visits of Alfred DiDonato, the barber from Salem who attended to them both; an artist in his work, he had once trimmed the hair of Presidents Taft and Coolidge. A short, bespectacled man of generous feelings who loved grand opera and baseball, he had long had two idols — Giuseppe Verdi and, as a collective entity, the Boston Braves; now O'Neill was added as a third god in the barber's pantheon. "I'd seen several of his plays and read some," DiDonato says, "and then when I met him personally and found him so simple and spontaneous, so wide open. . . . He was very polite, very. Any little thing you did for him, it was, 'Thank you, thank you, Fred.' He had an expression in his eyes like a child who'd lost something or had something taken away from him. It's hard to describe the expression. It was pleading-like, but not begging, not suppliant, he didn't ask for sympathy. . . . When I admire somebody — if I'd ever met 'Papa' Verdi, I would have genuflected, and I felt the same way about O'Neill. If he had told me to jump into the sea, I would've said, 'Yes, Mr. O'Neill, yes.'

"He had a wonderful smile, it was angelic, and I would say things just to get a reaction. My brother used to send me a paper from Italy, and I once told him that *Ah, Wilderness!* was going to be done on the radio with some of the best actors in Italy. He wanted to know the value of a lira, and how much it might bring him. 'Leave it over there,' I said, 'me and your wife, we'll go over and have a good time on it.' His whole face lit up and his body shook with laughter, but he didn't make a sound."

Till nearly the end of the pair's residence on the Neck, Fred never sensed anything amiss between them or that either was under any particular stress; he felt that Carlotta "worshiped" her husband and was "very devoted" to him. "I used to love going over there," he says. "They both were so natural – nothing put on." The two men usually talked baseball but one day the subject of sleeping pills and drugs in general came up. As DiDonato recalls, O'Neill said, "I feel sorry for anyone who has to depend on those things. God help those who become real drug addicts. My boy had that trouble." Then, in a voice scarcely audible, he added that his mother too had been an addict.

Shortly before Christmas 1949 the O'Neills were driven almost frantic by a putrid smell in the kitchen area whose source defied detection for several days. It finally turned out to be a large water rat that had managed somehow to crawl under the house and, trapped there, had died from eating fiber glass in the insulation panels. Eventually the noxious incident would seem symbolic of something that sickened and festered beneath the surface of life at the cottage.

The previous Christmas the playwright had still clung to a hope that he might be able to resume his career; now, in Carlotta's words, they could only wait for "the fiery chariot to come & take us on High!" In his holiday greeting to her, Eugene said: "To 'Mama' – and still as over all the years, 'Sweetheart' and 'Darling' and 'Beloved Wife' and 'Friend' too! – in these days of sickness and toil (on your part) and despair –

"Well, there is always us, there is still love, My Own!"

In their first year at the cottage, Carlotta had contended with inadequate domestic help, but she now had, in Mataichiro Narazaki the houseman and Doris Manning the cook, two who suited her. Like all the O'Neills' previous servants, they were under strict instructions from Carlotta never to discuss their employers with anyone, and they obeyed her faithfully to the end. If a finicky, difficult mistress, she also could be most generous. "Saki," as the houseman was familiarly called, was particularly discreet, according to John Snow, the policeman who patroled Marblehead Neck during the off-season, when most of the houses were vacant. "When I first knew him," the patrolman says, "he used to talk broken English and act as if he didn't understand it very well, but later on, after we became friendly, he spoke English as well as anybody. He was a college graduate, educated over here."

Despite the curtain of silence that Carlotta sought to draw around her life with O'Neill, she herself ripped it back occasionally and disclosed that they were not in general accord. Patrolman Snow recalls that "Mrs. O'Neill wanted me to drop by once a week — she was afraid out there. But I had too much to cover. I used to go by three or four times during the fall and winter. She told me that if she had her way, they wouldn't live out there. It was too lonesome. But he liked it, the pounding on the rocks, the sea right there, with that wonderful view."

The differences between the pair took a violent turn at least once in 1950. The incident involved the door of O'Neill's bedroom, which had to be fixed and repainted this spring after it had been forced by some kind of instrument; in addition, the inside of the door was "scratched, like from a dog," according to Rodrique Berube, who did the repainting. While it seems probable that Carlotta broke the jamb, since the door had been forced from the outside, she told Berube that her husband had done it. "She was in a rage," the painter recalls, "and told me, as she tapped her head, 'He's a sick man. I can't control him any longer and am going to have to put him away.'" To old friends who visited them this year, however, they seemed more or less comfortable with one another — no perceptible change in their usual relationship.

Increasingly a tenant of the past, O'Neill found himself dwelling not so much in the years of his Broadway acclaim as in earlier periods — the New London summers, his various schools, Jimmy the Priest's, and, with the waves ceaselessly washing just outside the cottage, his voyages to Buenos Aires and across the Atlantic. Replying to a letter from Dr. David Lyman, Eugene said on April 28, 1950, that his health "has been extremely poor for the past ten years. . . . All the drugs tried on me [for Parkinson's] had made me feel worse instead of better. I wish I were back at Gaylord Farm lolling on one of the rest chairs!"

Occasionally the past intruded unpleasantly into the present. An obscure publishing house announced this spring that it was going to issue what it called *Lost Plays of Eugene O'Neill:* namely, the one-acters *Abortion, The Movie Man, The Sniper* and *Wife for a Life,* and the full-length *Servitude,* all written between 1913 and 1915. Actually, they had never been "lost"; the author had simply forgotten to renew his copyrights, so that a few of his most callow works had passed into the public domain. When Aronberg informed him about the unauthorized collection, O'Neill initially thought of taking legal action to prevent its publication, but he no longer had the will or the strength for a fight. *Lost Plays*, as Jordan Y. Miller reports in his O'Neill bibliography, "met with a varied, but generally unenthusiastic, reception, calling down the ire of most critics for the publisher's attempt to make capital on obviously inferior works at the expense of their creator."

Rarely did O'Neill venture outside his walls any more. During his first year or so at the cottage he used to consult medical specialists in Boston; he once, with Carlotta, attended a play in the city, and, under Fred DiDonato's urging, the couple twice accompanied him to the movies in Salem. By now, however, the playwright's contacts with the outside world were limited almost entirely to the visits of his barber and his physician and the fleeting appearances of a few old friends. In the midst of constantly looking back, he occasionally thought ahead and considered whether to be cremated; but on one thing his mind was fixed: he wanted his funeral, he told DiDonato, to be as simple as possible, without any "fanfare."

Unwittingly, DiDonato, like Dr. Mayo, "stepped out of line" once by asking something about Oona. After a terse reply that he had severed relations with his daughter, O'Neill, to change the subject, added that he had an elder son who "had taught at Yale" — "had taught," past tense, for the father could no longer talk proudly of the course his son's life was taking.

It now appeared that Eugene Jr. had decided, perhaps unconsciously, that if he could not become a replica of his celebrated father, he would prove himself a true O'Neill by turning into a second edition of his scapegrace uncle. Such a view is more than idle theorizing, for the playwright began to romanticize his brother once he was dead; consequently, both Eugene Jr. and Shane grew up hearing affectionate, humorous tales about Jamie O'Neill. Like his uncle, Eugene Jr. drank too much and, though averse to wallowing in whorehouses, he slept around widely in Greenwich Village, both before and while living with Ruth Lander, a blond, bosomy divorcée involved with bohemia as an artists' agent; their romance tended to be turbulent. But the most curious parallel between uncle and nephew was that Jamie had had a fixed apprehension that he would become impotent at the age of forty, and now Junior, under a similar obsession, feared that once he was forty (in 1950), he would become sexually unattractive to women.

In his professional life he seemed torn between a desire for universal acclaim (his status in academic circles as a brilliant young classicist was insufficient for him, hence his resignation from Yale) and, recalling his uncle, an impulse toward self-ruin. For a while he made steady if unspectacular progress toward establishing himself as a learned figure in radio and television, with columnist John Crosby calling him "a classical scholar of frightening erudition who likes virtually nothing written since the birth of Christ." One night, however, as a panelist on a television series that had as its guest Adolphe Menjou, the suave movie actor, young O'Neill turned up intoxicated and slovenly attired. Since Menjou was supposed to be "the best-dressed man" in the country, Eugene had told Ruth Lander that he would appear as "the worst-dressed." End of his television career, for that was the last time he was ever tapped for the series, or for any other TV program. Through the good offices of Professor Whitney J. Oates of Princeton, who had collaborated with him years previously on the two-volume collection of Greek plays, he became a guest lecturer at the university; after acquitting himself creditably during the first semester, he began coming later and later to class, with liquor on his breath, until finally someone else had to take over his duties.

Trying to straighten himself out, he settled with Ruth in 1947 in the artists and writers' colony of Woodstock, New York, where he rented a house near his good friend Frank Meyer. He also, with collateral supplied by his father, borrowed four thousand dollars to purchase twenty-odd acres on which he hoped to build a house someday. His widowed mother Kathleen Pitt-Smith supported herself by working as the editor of a small Long Island weekly; but Eugene, worried about her situation in old age should something happen to him, took out a twenty-five-thousand-dollar insurance policy, listing her as the beneficiary, and told Frank Meyer and his wife Elsie that "now he could kill" himself, for his mother would be financially secure. Occasionally he was so pressed for funds that he would have a beer at the Yale Club in New York and make a meal of the cocktail-hour snacks, but he never failed to pay his insurance premiums.

In Woodstock he indulged his love of chopping down trees, cooking, and arguing about everything under the sun, generally with Meyer — they were brothers from choice, rather than by blood. His work desk was from the Peaked Hill station, the one on which his father had written *The Emperor Jones* and *The Hairy Ape*. "Being the son of a great writer," he told an interviewer in 1948, "made me feel obligated to do well whatever I did. Naturally I haven't always succeeded, but I regard the stimulus of having a famous father as a very valuable influence in my life. . . . Anything at all that I've done in academic life has been primarily due to this urge."

While some recall that in private he tended to be critical of his father, Frank Meyer thinks that "Gene was hurt but not bitter about O'Neill's treatment of himself and Shane. When he saw his father in the hospital in 1948 and O'Neill said that he couldn't live without Carlotta, Gene took it to mean that once they were reconciled, he could never see his father again. He'd hoped that he and his father would live together."

In Meyer's opinion his friend made "his great mistake and took the wrong turn when he left Yale, but he felt he wasn't appreciated there, there were too many restrictions. For four thousand dollars a year he had to follow a narrow academic line. Yale wouldn't let him go on any radio programs except academic stuff. Gene hankered to be an actor, he had a rich deep voice which he figured he'd inherited from his famous grandfather. For a class at the New School, he once read poetry the entire hour, and they all burst into applause at the end. He loved languages and he loved words, he had a real gift for them."

After several years in Woodstock, the Yale alumnus felt further than ever from making something of his life. Professionally, it had dwindled to his giving a course at a small New Jersey college and two at the New School for Social Research in Greenwich Village. Personally, it consisted chiefly of a bickersome relationship with Ruth Lander; occasionally he struck her, but what seems to have rankled her most was the derisive postscript he inserted in her inscribed copy of *The Iceman Cometh.* Beneath his father's inscription, "To Ruth Lander with all the best of good wishes. Eugene O'Neill," he added, "My father wrote this in ignorance of the real nature of this woman. Eugene O'Neill, Jr."

"Gene ran pretty wild," Meyer said, referring to the period after Ruth left him in spring 1950; while not their first separation, the rupture seemed permanent this time. Obviously depressed at a celebration in May of his fortieth birthday, he looked as though he would have preferred to be elsewhere; but usually he sought to be the center of attention.

A tolerant colony, with a good many struggling to express themselves in the arts, Woodstock had known other unhappy souls and insecure, clamorous egos, so it was not unduly disturbed over young O'Neill this summer, but his conduct would be remembered for years. While having an affair with a wife in the community, he (sounding somewhat like his uncle Jamie) went around bragging of the number of times they had intercourse in a night. "He was sort of . . . well, Rabelaisian," says Stephen Barr, a painter. "He'd pass wind in mixed company and laugh about it. He did it on purpose to startle us, but when we ignored it, he tried other tactics." Making himself an instant cynosure at one social gathering, he stripped off all his clothes and dived into his host's swimming pool. Frank Meyer recalls another time "when the artist Kuniyoshi was present with his wife, a tiny beauty. Gene picked her up, as though she were an oriental doll, an *objet d'art*, and looked admiringly up at her." But after all his misbehavior, the end impression he made on many, as writer Robert Phelps says, was that he "wanted desperately to be loved."

With September and the approach of his classes at the two schools, he grew dispirited at the thought of returning from New York to an empty house in the long fall and winter that lay ahead. At the same time he became determined to win back Ruth Lander, who now had a new friend, a garment-maker identified here by the fictitious name of Lesser. Whenever Eugene ran into her in the local bars he would plead with her, even before Lesser (who was no physical match for the six-foot-three lecturer), for a reconciliation. At one of their chance meetings, after Eugene had vowed that he loved her and wanted to marry her, that he would hang himself unless she said yes, Ruth removed her slippers and, throwing them at Lesser, cried, "Take back your shoes!" The reunited couple then made the round of the bars, announcing their intention to be wed. A day or so later, however, Ruth decided that the two of them could never be happy together, and she again left him.

The pair's reconciliation and final breakup occurred in the week starting September 18. In a visit to New York this same week, Eugene, worried over his finances, called on Saxe Commins at Random House. He feared, he told Saxe, that he might lose his acreage on Ohayo Mountain in Woodstock, since he had been unable to reach his father about the four-thousand-dollar bank loan, which was due for reendorsement; Carlotta, her stepson figured, was intercepting his letters and telegrams. Hoping to improve his financial state, Eugene had conceived a weekly radio program on which he would review books, and he wanted Saxe's help in lining up about a half-dozen publishers as sponsors. Though doubtful of the project, Saxe made some telephone calls, without success.

On Saturday evening the twenty-third, Stephen Barr and his wife were having dinner at the White Horse Inn in Woodstock when Eugene, as the painter recalls, "came in, glowering thunder and lightning at everybody. He went by without saying hello, then returned and asked whether he could come around to the house. I told him to go ahead, that the house was open. When we got there, he was drinking – he'd been drinking before — and began talking about killing himself. He hadn't done his schedule yet for the new term, which began the following week — the notes for his lectures — and this was very much on his mind. He'd put it off too long and now he wouldn't have time."

Frank Meyer and his wife Elsie, aware of Eugene's depressed state, became worried this same evening as they checked at his home, scouted the bars, and telephoned around without locating him (he spent the night at the Barrs'). "Not that I thought he would ever kill himself over Ruth," Meyer says, "but I felt he was equal to such an act. We'd often discussed the subject and we agreed that when a man finds his lot intolerable, he has a right to end it all. Neither of us believed in the orthodox view that suicide is some kind of sin."

Meyer, who lived near the top of Ohayo Mountain, while Eugene's place was on the same road toward the bottom, found his friend at home on Sunday and invited him to dinner that evening. Pale and drawn, he accepted so reluctantly that Frank was doubtful, till his appearance, whether he would come. The Meyers, disclosing their fears of the previous evening, said that they had even searched his grounds in the apprehension that he might have hanged himself from a tree. Looking grave, he disquieted the couple by replying that he *had* considered it, while Elsie reproved him for such talk and insisted that she knew he was too sensible to throw away his life. Drinking moderately, he and Frank had several bourbon highballs at dinner and some beer afterward. Throughout the evening there was a kind of stillness about him. When he left shortly after ten, he said he would come back if he were unable to sleep.

Awaking about 3 A.M., he wanted a drink and, since he was out of liquor, returned to the Meyers. "I got up," Frank recalls, "and we sat around drinking bourbon, not heavily, and talking." The two reminisced about their lives since their meeting in Maine in 1926, the same summer that saw Eugene O'Neill and Carlotta Monterey renew their acquaintanceship. "I stayed in bed," Elsie Meyer says, "but my door was open and I could hear them. Gene seemed in a peaceful frame of mind, but at one point he said, 'If I live through this, I'm a man of iron.'"

About 5 A.M. he went to sleep on a couch, with the bottle, now down to a few drinks, close at hand. When the Meyers awoke about eleven, both their guest and the bottle were gone. Eugene was scheduled to resume his courses at the New School with a class late that Monday afternoon, September 25, and the couple assumed that he had followed his usual practice of driving his jeep to Poughkeepsie, where he would catch a train for New York.

The telephone at the Meyers' rang that afternoon about one. "It was Ruth Lander," Elsie recalls. "She wanted to pick up her clothes at Gene's place but was afraid to go alone, in case he might be there. He'd been so wild the week before, she said — I think he hit her — that she didn't want to take any chances on his being around. She asked me to pick her up at the bottom of the hill and go with her. I was surprised she'd call us — she knew we despised her — and started to tell her to go to hell, but for Gene's sake, to avoid any further mess, I agreed.

"Driving down to get her, as I went by Gene's house, I saw his jeep still out front and immediately knew something must be wrong — he should've been in the city by now. One of my boys was with me, and I told him to stay in the car. After I knocked on the door and there was no answer, I opened it and went in. He was at the bottom of the stairs, all sprawled out."

A broken line of blood led from the body to the bathroom upstairs. A classicist to the end, Eugene, taking his cue from a favorite mode of suicide among the ancient Romans and Greeks, had filled the tub, slashed his left wrist and ankle with a straight razor he normally used for shaving, and settled into the water. Some minutes later, either decisively or from instinctive panic, he got out and, though he fell several times, managed to reach the stairway; but he fell again, rolling to the bottom, where Elsie Meyer found him.

Before slashing himself, he had finished the bourbon from the Meyers and written the following note, which he left with the bottle in the bathroom: "Never let it be said of O'Neill that he failed to empty a bottle. *Ave atque vale.*"

Elsie's first sight of the body sent her flying to the telephone, but the service was off from nonpayment of bills, so she ran to the nearest neighbor, where she called a doctor, then her husband. Eugene, who had last been seen about ten that morning in the village, killed himself, the doctor said, at noontime.

Every Monday or Tuesday Eugene used to take his mother to dinner in the city; if he did not phone her the first day to arrange their date, Kathleen Pitt-Smith knew that he would call on Tuesday. Late Monday afternoon of the twenty-fifth she had a call from a New York *News* reporter who wondered whether she had heard anything about her son that day. "I was cagey," Mrs. Pitt-Smith recalls, "because I thought it was about Eugene getting married suddenly to Ruth, as he was going to, and wanted to know why he asked. He said Eugene had been in an accident in Woodstock, about one o'clock, and I said he must be mistaken, since

Eugene was supposed to be in the city by then for his classes. The reporter urged me to call Frank Meyer — and that's how I found out. . . .

"A week or two later, after I started to come out of my daze, I was very grateful to that newspaperman for the way he handled the matter. When Mr. Pitt-Smith's son died [from a fall that may have been a suicide], a reporter called up the mother and started right off by asking her about the funeral arrangements. They tell me you could have heard her scream a block away."

Although the Meyers could not steel themselves to take the initiative in informing Eugene's mother, they promptly notified Saxe Commins. He in turn telephoned Bill Aronberg, who agreed to call the Marblehead cottage and report to Commins afterward. The lawyer was furious when he spoke to Saxe again. According to his account, Carlotta answered the phone and as soon as Aronberg told her the unhappy news, she replied, "How dare you invade our privacy!" and slammed down the receiver.

Carlotta, giving a different version, maintains that when "the lawyer phoned and said, 'Eugene has killed himself,' I said, 'What?' The phone was here and my husband was sitting right over there. So you couldn't expect me to say, 'Oh, how funny,' or something, and I said, 'Are you sure,' and he said, 'Yes,' and I said, 'I don't believe it.' 'I tell you,' he answered, 'I'm sure.' . . . Well, I hung up the phone and you can imagine what I felt like, with Gene watching me with those black eyes of his.

"He said, 'Well, come out with it, what is it?' And I said, 'Eugene is ill, very ill,' and he said, 'When did he die?'"

Carlotta then told him as much as she knew.

Wracked with guilt feelings, he sealed his lips on his agony. Carlotta recalls that "as time went on and this hurt . . . and that hurt would arrive [because of his children], there was no criticism, there was no anything, he just became more ill, more unhappy, but never said anything." O'Neill paid for the funeral and sent a blanket of white chrysanthemums that, in Mrs. Pitt-Smith's words, "virtually covered the casket," while Carlotta sent a wreath, but he never found it in himself to write a word of sympathy to the mother of his first child. Probably he felt too culpable about what had happened, and all words now seemed to him hollow.

In the remaining three years of his life, he mentioned his elder son's name to Carlotta only once more, according to what she told Seymour

Aging playwright

Eugene Jr. in Woodstock in the summer of 1950

Shane in a New York subway station in 1970

Peck of the New York *Times* in 1956 as *Long Day's Journey Into Night* was about to open on Broadway. Following in essence is her story:

When Eugene Jr. read *Long Day's Journey* at Tao House, he thought it a "very wonderful play," but asked his father to withhold it for twenty-five years because he felt it would not "be good for my social position at Yale," and O'Neill assented to his request. However, Carlotta knew nothing at the time of her husband's reason for imposing the restriction. In the early 1950s, by which time the couple lived in Boston, Carlotta was moping around the apartment one day, and when Eugene asked what troubled her, she replied, "Money, money, money." Whereupon he allegedly told her that they had "a nest egg" in *Long Day's Journey* and divulged for the first time that Eugene Jr. had urged the twenty-five-year ban. " 'Now,' he said [from her recapitulation], 'if things get worse, we'll publish it.' And then he made a literary trust and paid me the greatest compliment he could have done [with] the will in which I have complete and absolute control of everything, and he said I could publish [*Long Day's Journey*] if and when I pleased." End of Carlotta's account.

In 1955, two years after O'Neill's death, Carlotta directed Random House to publish *Long Day's Journey*, but Bennett Cerf, on reading the personal testament "written in tears and blood" decided to abide by the playwright's twenty-five-year interdict. Thereupon Carlotta gave the publication rights to Yale University Press. When word of the new play reached Karl Ragnar Gierow, director of Stockholm's Royal Dramatic Theater, where O'Neill is a prime favorite, he opened negotiations with the widow through United Nations secretary general Dag Hammarskjöld, a friend of his, for permission to stage the play.

The world première of *Journey* took place in Sweden in February 1956, where it was received enthusiastically, while the text, published over here around the same time, became a best seller. Initially Carlotta said she would allow it to be released only in book form in America, because the American theater had not properly "appreciated" her husband; next, that she might allow a concert reading version limited to touring the colleges; but finally, as every leading producer in New York sought the rights, she gave the nod to the young trio at Circle in the Square because of their fine revival of *The Iceman Cometh*. With Fredric March and Florence Eldridge as the elder Tyrones, Jason Robards, Jr., as Jamie, and Bradford Dillman as Edmund, *Long Day's Journey*, under José Quintero's direction, was the dramatic sensation of the 1956–1957 Broadway season and won its author a posthumous Pulitzer Prize, his fourth in all.

While there was only mild, scattered criticism in the press about O'Neill's widow going against his wishes, Carlotta eventually became so nettled that she told the story about his imposing the ban at his elder son's request. Frank Meyer has a memory, however, that casts doubt on her account: "Gene once told me that his father had written a play about his family that was not to be done for twenty-five years, and he didn't think it was a good idea; he thought it should be released without delay. He was mysterious about the play, but he seemed to feel there was a curse on the family or something in the blood. He wasn't consistent about this, he wavered between the two views, but on one thing he was fixed — that there was something special about the family."

Not only Meyer's recollection but documentary evidence contradicts Miss Monterey's assertion that her husband reversed himself about *Long Day's Journey*. In 1951, nearly a year after his elder son's suicide, O'Neill, on receiving the scripts and other material that had been cached at Random House, wrote to Bennett Cerf: "No, I do not want *Long Day's Journey Into Night*. That, as you know, is to be published twenty-five years after my death — but never produced as a play."

Another witness against Carlotta is Carlotta herself. Shortly after she became a widow, she wrote to Anna Crouse: "I have but one reason to live & that is to carry out Gene's wishes. I have my Eugene O'Neill Collection to put in order. What I call the 'twenty-five-year box' is the most interesting part of it — all personal except *Long Day's Journey Into Night* — & not to be opened until twenty-five years after Gene's death."

When Saxe Commins heard, in the mid-1950s, that Carlotta was about to publish *Long Day's Journey* and allow it to be staged, he told his wife, "She's determined to exhume Gene's body and give him no peace — even in death." The matter can be viewed, however, from more than one angle: legally, as the playwright's executrix and sole heir, she had the authority to do as she pleased; morally, her act is something else again; yet at the same time all interested in the American drama can be grateful that she released at an early date what many consider the finest American play ever written.

30

Estranged Pair

AFTER months of pressure, Carlotta won her husband's permission in 1950 to sell their cottage; the prospect of another winter on Marblehead Neck appeared to her too bleak to be endured. Since they failed, however, to find a buyer, she had no choice but to resign herself — though resignation was alien to her nature — to remaining indefinitely in a place where she could not shut out the sound of her husband's record-playing. "That music of his," she often said, "is driving me crazy." The wash of the waves perpetually beating at the shore was also audible within the house, but while Eugene welcomed the sound, that, too, was unsettling to her.

Dr. Frederic Mayo, continuing to call about once a month, found both his patients and the atmosphere at the cottage more or less as usual. Kenneth Macgowan, who visited them in December, says that "Gene complained of some difficulty in walking. Carlotta lamented, 'Mama's got arthritis, Mama's getting a middle-aged spread,' but they seemed fairly happy with one another." Despite appearances, however, the cottage was becoming a cauldron of simmering hostilities, as Carlotta, increasingly tense, provoked disputes with her husband, who, unwell since his son's suicide, was already nervous and depressed. It was only a question of time before the cauldron boiled over. Unlike previous years, there was no loving message from Eugene to his wife at Christmas or on her birthday several days later. His handwriting, always at its worst when he was upset, is a tortuous scrawl, barely decipherable, on his Christmas card to Commins. "Dear Saxe," he wrote, "As ever, all best to all of you. Gene / '50."

Of the few callers, the only one aware of trouble looming ahead was Alfred DiDonato, who had a standing appointment with the couple for every other Monday. While O'Neill appeared to him unchanged, Fred, as he recalls reluctantly, found Carlotta "becoming queer." "I came there once," he says, "and she didn't have much on; you could see her [at this point he abashedly pantomimed breasts]. . . . I must've looked surprised, because she said, 'That's all right, come in, Fred.' Another time, while I was trimming her hair, you could see her [he again mimed breasts], and she asked me, 'How do you like them?' . . . I felt I could've had it if I wanted, but I wouldn't have taken it if she'd given it to me on a golden platter. I had too much respect for him."

During this climactic period, no one, including Carlotta herself, suspected that she was starting to suffer from bromide poisoning, a condition that temporarily affects the mind, impairing a person's judgment and state of orientation. For years she had occasionally taken a sedative without being toxically affected, but once she increased her use of the medicine to offset her growing tension she proved sensitive to bromides and began undergoing periods of cloudy and paranoid thinking. It is uncertain, though, whether bromism or the dark side of her nature, activated by mounting discontent, was chiefly responsible for the blowup between her and O'Neill in February 1951.

On the night of the fifth, Eugene, abruptly terminating a bitter quarrel, walked out of the house, thinly clad and without his cane, possibly with the intention of ending his life in the nearby icy waters. While making his way beside the house he tripped over a rock hidden in the snow and, as he struck the ground, felt a sharp pain; he had fractured his right leg at the knee. Fearful of freezing to death, he kept crying for help, till finally Carlotta opened the door. Standing at the entrance and looking down at him, she said: "How the mighty have fallen! Where's your greatness now, little man?" Shortly after she had closed the door, he blacked out.

The preceding account, pieced together from several sources, conflicts with Carlotta's version of the night's happenings. She says that O'Neill, "bundled up" warmly, went out "for some air," and that when she heard "something" outside ("It sounded like it might be a kitten caught in the bushes — I love animals") went to investigate and found her husband lying in the snow. "I asked him," she continues, "if he could get up, what was wrong, and just then a car drove up. I was surprised, as we didn't expect anyone, but it was our doctor."

Dr. Mayo, while making house visits this night, was notified by his office about nine that someone had telephoned from the O'Neills' (most likely the caller was Narazaki the houseman). Leaving the O'Neills to the last, since there had been no mention of an emergency, the doctor arrived at the scene around ten; apparently, then, O'Neill lay out in the snow at least an hour.

"As I approached the house, I heard this moaning," Mayo recalls, "and when I investigated, found him lying in the snow. He had come around to the side of the house. Planning to kill himself? It's possible. It looked as though he was headed for the water, but that's only a guess. He didn't say anything that I can remember. He must've been in too much pain to talk, and too frozen. I lifted him up and half carried him into the house."

As soon as Eugene was indoors, he covered his eyes with his hands to shut out the sight of his wife ("He'd never done that before," she said later). Dr. Mayo, too engrossed with his patient to notice Carlotta's agitated state — she fluttered around, expressing her concern in half-coherent words — summoned an ambulance, and shortly O'Neill was on his way to Salem Hospital. While Carlotta remained behind, the doctor trailed the ambulance in his car and saw the playwright safely bestowed in the hospital. Himself a man of reticent dignity, Mayo did not question O'Neill about the circumstances surrounding the accident, and O'Neill volunteered nothing, but from the look of stark misery in his eyes, the doctor had the painful impression that he was suffering in more than body.

Carlotta's version again: "We got Gene inside and stretched him out. I asked him how he felt, then Saki came in and said the ambulance is here. I hadn't called for an ambulance. There was something going on, I didn't know what was happening, something wicked. I asked, 'Where are you taking my husband?' and that doctor said, 'To the hospital.' He didn't ask me whether it was all right or anything.

"I became so worried I put on my heavy coat and walked out, figuring I'd get to the main road and catch a cab to the hospital. They used to have a policeman going around the neighborhood, he'd stop in for coffee sometimes. He came along and asked me what I was doing, and I told him I wanted to get to the hospital to see my husband. So they put me in the car and took me there. . . . After that, I don't remember anything, I must've fainted. . . . The next thing I knew, I tried to move and couldn't. I was in an ambulance and a voice said, 'You're all right, I'll loosen the straps.' . . . They'd ruined one of my shoes, the way they strapped me, and there I was with just one shoe. . . . The next thing I remember is waking up and there were bars on the window. The door was glass but there were bars there, too. God, I was terrified! I didn't know where on earth I was! I heard somebody approaching and closed my eyes. A nurse came in, felt my pulse, my forehead, and I peeped out.

'That's right,' she said, 'open your eyes. You're all right now, you're safe, don't worry.' . . . They were wonderful to me at McLean's."

From Carlotta's account it sounds as though she set out for the hospital shortly after O'Neill's departure in the ambulance on Monday, February 5. Actually it was on Tuesday night the sixth that Patrolman John Snow, making his rounds on fŏot, saw "this figure up ahead, and when I caught up with her it was Mrs. O'Neill in a fur coat. I saw right away something was wrong with her. I told her she oughtn't be out in weather like this — it was a very cold night — but she said, 'I'm not going back to that house, I'm never going back there. The air is full of people.' I walked along with her to where the Quinbys live and tried to get her to go in where she'd be warm, but she wouldn't.

"Leaving her outside, I went in and called for a police car, then waited with her till it came along, with Norman Powers and John Tucker. We finally persuaded her to get in the car and drove her home, but she wouldn't go in. I went in, waited a minute or two, then came back and said, 'The people are all gone; there aren't any more people in the air,' but she still wouldn't. One of us phoned Dr. Mayo and he had her taken to the hospital."

John Tucker recalls that when he and Powers first appeared, Carlotta sounded rational: "She said, 'I'm Mrs. O'Neill. My husband's in the hospital and I must go see him, I must see him.' We knew about his being hospitalized and thought she'd heard he was dying or something, and somewhat distraught had started out. We told her she'd never get a cab out there and offered to drive her to where she could. She seemed to think that was a good idea and got in the back of the car, but suddenly she became hysterical, screaming and crying, so we drove her back to the house."

When Dr. Mayo arrived, he obtained permission from the police station to have Carlotta transported in the patrol car, and for the second night in a row he trailed one of the O'Neills to Salem Hospital. Although he thought Carlotta should be transferred as soon as possible to a mental sanatorium, Mayo, who had the authority to commit her on a temporary basis and had done so previously with other cases, was loath to act on his own this time in view of the patient's prominence. He arranged for her to be examined early the next day by a psychiatrist on Salem's staff.

The nurse who undressed and settled her in bed found her "rigid as a board." She kept looking around nervously, as though fearing harm from some quarter. Elinor Smith, the architect's wife, who was visiting a friend at the hospital that night, happened to glance into a room that contained "an odd-looking man," then realized with a shock that the "man" was Carlotta, her hair cut short, her face heavier than when Elinor had last seen her.

O'Neill was tight-lipped the following morning when Dr. Mayo informed him that Carlotta, acting irrationally, had been admitted to the hospital. Mayo went on to say that he and the staff psychiatrist thought she should be transferred immediately to an institution for mental cases. Taking O'Neill's silence for consent, the doctor proceeded to make the necessary arrangements. Several hours later Carlotta, who afterward remembered nothing of her stay at Salem, was transferred by ambulance to McLean Hospital, a private institution with psychiatric facilities in Belmont, a suburb of Boston.

For all his despondency during his early weeks in the hospital, O'Neill never tried to impose his misery on those around him; his doctors and nurses thought him in fact an ideal patient. Dr. Paul W. Hugenberger, a Boston orthopedist who set his injured leg in a cast, says he "never complained of his disability or pain; he didn't try to make you feel sorry for him. After a couple of weeks, the cast was reduced, a painful procedure, but he took it gamely, even though he didn't have any anesthesia. I found him delightful, in spite of his low spirits at first. I used to spend some time with him on my visits.

"The circumstances of his accident *were* peculiar and we considered the possibility that he intended suicide, but we couldn't come to any definite decision. It was only conjecture."

Claire Bird, his day nurse, calls him "one of the best patients I ever had. He appreciated everything you did for him, he asked for little, he liked to do things for himself. Some people when they have a private nurse think you ought to stand on your head for them." His only fault was that he endangered himself and alarmed others by his attempts to be self-sufficient. The nurse was frightened once on returning to his room to find it empty. "When I looked in the bathroom," she recalls, "there he was — in the tub, on his back, with an inflated ring cushion around his head where it'd fallen, and his crutches in the tub with him. 'What're you doing?' I said, though I realized he must've been on his way to the john and slipped. He began laughing and so did I; I couldn't help it, he looked so funny."

A charming young blond, both tactful and freshly beautiful, Mrs. Bird won O'Neill's liking from the start. Among other things in her favor, she was not in awe of the Great Man. "My husband," she says somewhat indulgently, "is the 'intellectual' of the family. He reads all the time. He was excited when I was called to be O'Neill's nurse but I had to ask who he was." Initially she had difficulty understanding her famous patient, he spoke so low, and also if he were upset, he tended to mumble. Moody above all, he scarcely said a word some days, but other times was fairly communicative. "One day," the nurse remembers, "he talked for two hours, going on about his children, the sons mostly, very little about Oona, as far as I could make out. Once I heard him say, 'What a miserable mess, what a miserable mess . . .' "

Concerned that he scarcely ate, Mrs. Bird, after realizing that he was embarrassed at being fed and watched, changed the routine; she "cut up everything into little pieces" and went for her own meals while he fed himself. His tremor varied from one day to the next, but it always took him, according to the nurse, "five to ten minutes just to sign his checks."

Paralyzed in will, uncertain what to do about his future, he appeared disinclined even to think about it. After a month he could have been treated just as well at home — his leg was healing satisfactorily — but when Dr. Hugenberger so informed him, he shrank from the prospect. "He seemed content," the doctor says, "to remain at Salem forever; he didn't want people bothering him, he liked being cared for." Dr. Mayo, agreeing with his colleague, says that O'Neill "was in no state during his time at Salem to make any decisions."

Soon after the press reported his hospitalization, some of his friends started to visit him, including several — Commins, Aronberg, Sherlee Weingarten — whose way had been barred by Carlotta. O'Neill had to brace himself for the reunions, because he was seeing nearly all the friends for the first time since one of his sons had been arrested as a drug addict and the other had killed himself. To Saxe he confided that the night of the accident he had walked out of the house during a row with Carlotta, but to offset possible rumors of a suicide attempt, said he was returning to get his overcoat when he fell in the snow.

Although O'Neill had long taken a mixture of bromide and chloral hydrate for his tremor without ill effect, he too, like Carlotta, was suffering by now from bromide poisoning, but in his case less seriously. Instead of experiencing spells of extreme disorientation and mental confusion, he occasionally had hallucinations. While lying in bed once, when Saxe was with him, he imagined that Carlotta was climbing in at the window and, though hampered by the cast on his leg, he clambered back in terror from the apparition. Other times he thought he saw the long-dead members of his family.

Now married for a second time, to a literary agent named Robert

Lantz, Sherlee Weingarten came to Salem after Langner had relayed word that O'Neill wanted to see her. "At my first visit," Sherlee recalls, "he said sort of accusingly that I had changed. He kept looking at me suspiciously till he realized that I had my hair different, then he felt relieved to find me the same person he'd known. Apparently he didn't like the thought of his friends changing after he had a certain image of them." On her side Sherlee was troubled that he never once referred to Carlotta's sudden hostility to her, that he never explained what lay behind it, a question that was to haunt Sherlee for years.

His most frequent visitors from New York were Aronberg, who now — in place of Carlotta — was handling O'Neill's financial matters, and Langner, who flew up once or twice a week. Worried about his funds, especially now that he was under heavy medical expense, O'Neill authorized Random House to publish *A Moon for the Misbegotten* and *A Touch of the Poet* at will, but, despite Langner's pleas and arguments, refused to allow a production of either drama. It was Claire Bird's impression that her patient found the visits of his lawyer and his producer rather tiring. Langner, who had just completed his autobiography, was full of reminiscences and often could be heard laughing as he sat with the playwright.

Narazaki the houseman and Doris Manning the cook called on O'Neill only once, at the same time, to bring him pajamas and other personal effects; their first loyalty was to Carlotta, who had always treated them so generously. The playwright's most constant visitor, Fred DiDonato once said jokingly that O'Neill was "like a baby," and O'Neill sadly agreed; the comparison was apt, he thought, since he shared an infant's inability to walk. But under the barber's urging, O'Neill, with Fred and Mrs. Bird flanking him, ventured as far as the hallway. According to Dr. Hugenberger, he seemed reluctant to regain mobility, possibly in the thought that it would hasten his discharge and force him to start making decisions.

After he had been at Salem several weeks, Dr. Mayo informed him that Carlotta, whose condition had been diagnosed by McLean as temporary psychosis from bromide intoxication, wanted to visit him. Immediately breaking out in sweat, he cried, "Oh, don't let her near me, don't let her come here!"

Later, changing his mind, he consented to her visit. Accompanied by a nurse from McLean, Carlotta appeared with her hair unkempt, a fur coat thrown carelessly over one shoulder, and wearing sunglasses. When she removed them briefly, Claire Bird noticed that her eyes were glassy, probably, the nurse thought, from sedation. At the doorway she said

"Gene!" and he, pronouncing her name, extended a hand. As she took it and kissed him, the two nurses left the room; her visit lasted about an hour. "He was upset and mumbling the next day," Mrs. Bird recalls. "I heard her name a couple of times but couldn't make out what he was saying." He was intelligible enough, though, as he told Mayo that he never wanted to see her again.

Shortly after the abortive reunion, Carlotta, feeling in need of an intermediary, telephoned Kathryne Albertoni on the West Coast and asked her to fly East. Giving Kaye a wrong impression, she said, "Papa needs you." Mrs. Albertoni, who arrived in mid-March and called first at Salem Hospital, was shocked to find O'Neill "so thin and changed" since California — he weighed slightly under a hundred pounds — and from his reticence felt that he "was hiding something." When she visited McLean the following day, Dr. William H. Horwitz, a staff psychiatrist, said in briefing her, "You can help — she trusts you." As soon as Carlotta saw her, she cried, "Oh, Kaye, you don't know how much this means to me. The Master hates me!"

While Mrs. Albertoni was to have no appreciable effect on relations between the pair, their situation became aggravated through the tactics of Merrill Moore, a well-known Boston psychiatrist. Brought into the picture by Langner, who felt that O'Neill needed psychiatric guidance, Dr. Moore was scarcely a disinterested party in the case, since he was a cousin of the late Ralph Barton, had once met his ex-wife, and thought that "Carlotta loved only Carlotta." An eccentric individual who wrote poems and prescriptions with equal facility, he sometimes felt "like a lesser (poetic) Balzac" and hoped to produce "a kind of *Comédie Humaine* in sonnets for our times."

Neither Mayo nor Hugenberger questioned their patient's sanity, but Dr. Moore, discounting his bromism, stated in a diagnostic report on March 19, 1951, that O'Neill was mentally unfit to take care of himself and recommended either an asylum or a legally appointed guardian. Advising further that O'Neill be indefinitely separated from Carlotta, the psychiatrist attributed his unfortunate mental state, as Moore saw it, to anxiety over his son's suicide and his wife's commitment. O'Neill's doctors dismissed Moore's diagnosis without giving it a second thought, while O'Neill himself never knew about it.

Convinced that Carlotta was mentally unbalanced, from what O'Neill, Aronberg and Langner had told him, Moore called on her at McLean on March 22, a visit that left her apprehensive and furious. Mimicking an unctuous, insincere voice, she recalls that he kissed her hand and murmured, "The beautiful Carlotta Monterey." He went on to say, according to her, that "I must forget O'Neill, never see him again, that he was very ill and the sight of me upset him. He called me young and beautiful — I could've slapped him for treating me like a fool — and said I should start a new life for myself. When he left, he had the nerve to kiss my hand again. I'd taken the precaution to have my doctor with me and as Moore went out, my doctor threw a look at me. I knew he could've killed him!"

Frantic over O'Neill's continuing rejection of her, Carlotta took only minimal comfort from McLean's intention to release her shortly. Unburdening herself to Sophus Winther, she wrote on March 24 that she had been through "*hell*," that O'Neill had "decayed" in mind and body since the Winthers last saw him. " 'Whore' has echoed about my ears continually," she said. "He couldn't express enough hatred for me, & all the sadism of his nature came out until my body reeled with fear & heartbreak." Wildly inventing details and distorting fact, she charged that Eugene and his doctor had concocted a scheme to have her committed and said that the night she was to be removed, O'Neill had had his accident when he walked outside to avoid facing her.

In another letter to Winther she declared that O'Neill "failed his children & his wives. He *loathes* women, except when he needs them. When he no longer needs them — out they go! But, with Nietzsche & Strindberg as his gods one can understand all this. The final play is being written (in his imagination) & I should commit suicide, or he should kill me — (by having someone to do it, of course)." "I wish I believed in hell," she said another time, "it would help."

For weeks Aronberg and Langner had been urging O'Neill to transfer to a New York hospital, where his friends would be at hand to help him; but their chief thought was that such a move would increase the chances of the O'Neills' split becoming permanent. Long mired in indecision, O'Neill, under Dr. Moore's prodding, took a drastic step on March 23, the day after the psychiatrist's visit to McLean. With Moore as a signatory, he signed a petition which alleged that his wife was "an insane person . . . incapable of taking care of herself," and requested that James E. Farley "or some other suitable person" be appointed her guardian. A balding Salem attorney with a perpetual, masklike smile, Farley had been asked by Aronberg to serve as the playwright's attorney in Massachusetts. The petition, which listed O'Neill and Cynthia Stram as Carlotta's nearest of kin, was filed in the Salem probate court on March 28, with the hearing set for April 23.

Releasing Carlotta on March 29 with a prognosis of "Good," McLean advised her to consult an outside psychiatrist and recommended Dr. Harry L. Kozol, a young expert in forensic medicine. Shortly before seeing Kozol on the day of her discharge, Carlotta first learned of the guardianship petition and was so close to hysteria by the time she reached his office on Bay State Road that she feared she would have a heart attack. At his suggestion, she took rooms for herself and Mrs. Albertoni at the Hotel Shelton, opposite his office, and immediately got in touch with her lawyers. Filing suit in the Salem probate court the following day for separate support, Carlotta stated that she was dwelling apart from her husband for "justifiable" cause and charged that on or about February 1 and "at diverse other times" he had been "guilty of cruel and abusive treatment" of her. Her petition was also returnable on April 23.

Unknown to her at the time, O'Neill left for New York on Friday, March 30, the same day that she filed her petition. Accompanied by Aronberg and Claire Bird, he was taken from Salem in an ambulance to South Station, Boston, where he boarded a train shortly before noon. Both Dr. Hugenberger, who saw him on the morning of his departure, and Mrs. Bird recall that he went most reluctantly. "He felt that his friends had gone to a lot of trouble on his behalf, the arrangements were all set, so he couldn't let them down," says Hugenberger. According to the nurse, Langner had told her that O'Neill "wouldn't leave unless I went with him. Well, I couldn't go and stay the whole time but I promised to see him settled. I don't think he really wanted to go. It seemed to me he just wanted to be left alone, but they kept after him."

The day, bleak with rain, paralleled O'Neill's mood. Rarely uttering a word during the entire trip, he kept the shade down in his compartment and never bothered to peer out when the train paused briefly in New London. From Grand Central, where he was greeted by Commins and Langner, he was taken in an ambulance to a nursing home on East Sixty-first Street with the quiet, impersonal atmosphere of a hotel for the elderly. (In the mid-1960s Carlotta, turning senile, was a guest there.) After an uncomfortable night, O'Neill said, as soon as Mrs. Bird appeared the following morning, "Get me out of here immediately." A few hours later he was transferred to Doctors' Hospital for his second stay there in three years.

Russel Crouse, who saw him briefly just before he left the nursing home, was saddened to find that his "amazing personality is slowly fading." At Doctors' Hospital Dr. Shirley Fisk, though prepared for changes in his old patient, since he had had a report from Dr. Mayo, was still dismayed at his appearance — his weight remained a little under a hundred pounds — and his "marked deterioration." As one nurse recalls, he was "just skin and bones."

O'Neill tried to joke when Claire Bird bade him good-bye that weekend, but his eyes were tearful as he kissed her on the cheek.

On March 31, the day of his admission to the New York hospital, the press first carried word about O'Neill's guardianship petition and his wife's countersuit for separate support. In Boston Carlotta, who collapsed in tears when the stories appeared, began telephoning Crouse and finally reached him at eleven that night; for a full hour she poured out a rambling account of anguish and accusation. Charging that O'Neill was the one whose mind was slipping, she said that one night at the cottage she woke up and screamed for their Japanese houseman when she found O'Neill standing over her with a belaying pin. Crouse's wife says, "The only hitch in this story — I remember thinking at the time — was that Gene was so frail and shaky I didn't see how he could be much of a threat."

In another account of the alleged incident, Carlotta said that during their final weeks on Marblehead Neck O'Neill "was getting queerer and queerer. Somebody had given him a shillelagh; it was like iron; you could kill somebody with it, easily. I was afraid of what he might do. He asked me to move my bed into his room, in case he needed something during the night, but I told him my room was so close I could hear if he called. One night he came over to my bed talking to himself, 'I'm going to smash her skull in, and all the blood will run down her face — I know you hear me, you're just pretending to be asleep.' "

Shortly before Kaye Albertoni's return to California she had a private meeting with Dr. Kozol, who asked whether she considered Carlotta sane. Her answer was yes. "Next," in her words, "he wanted to know whether she had any friends, and I said, 'Some.' Then he asked, 'Is she bitchy?' and I told him, 'She drives hard.' "

As soon as Cynthia Stram in Sausalito, California, learned from the newspapers about the guardianship petition, she telephoned Salem Hospital, but someone there, keeping secret that O'Neill had left for New York, said that he refused to speak to her. "That's the only thing I hold against Gene," says Cynthia. "I wanted to find out whether my mother was actually crazy or being railroaded. If she were really mental, I had no objection to her commitment. I just wanted to make sure she wasn't being framed."

After being notified about the petition, Cynthia replied in part to the

judge of the probate court in Salem that if "there is sufficient evidence
. . . for you in your judgment to consider her incapable of caring for
herself, I have no objection to the appointment of . . . some . . . suitable person to act as her guardian. My paramount consideration is her
welfare and proper treatment.

"Living at such a great distance and working at a job that pays forty-
eight dollars per week, which goes for the support of my crippled husband, twelve-year-old son, home and myself, I am in no position to
actively participate in the care of my mother. I . . . request . . . the
selection of a considerate person of responsibility and integrity . . . and
that a periodical report be made to me concerning her affairs and
welfare."

Carlotta's bitterness over the petition was intensified when she learned
that O'Neill had changed his will to eliminate her as the executrix. By
letter and telephone she vented her feelings to Crouse, charging Langner
with scheming to get her out of the way so that he could produce *The
Misbegotten* and *Poet*. She maintained that Moore had committed a crime
by swearing in the petition that she was insane, since he had never "examined" her, and threatened to sue the psychiatrist and Langner for conspiracy; in her letters of the period the word "conspiracy" appears repeatedly.

From hindsight it is clear that Langner showed poor judgment in
introducing Merrill Moore into the pair's imbroglio, but, despite Carlotta's suspicion of Langner's motives, it also appears that the Guild man,
who had a genuine regard for O'Neill, felt he was serving the other's best
interests. Like a number close to the situation, he was apprehensive about
O'Neill being, as he saw it, at Carlotta's mercy, and thought that O'Neill
could enjoy more or less tranquil final years if he and his wife were
permanently separated. But what he and the others never realized,
apparently, was that Carlotta, in both a good and a dark sense, was virtually an ideal mate for Eugene O'Neill.

Her virtues and strong points almost everyone recognized, but few if
any seemed to realize that her sadistic impulses and unforgiving nature
also served as a welding factor between her and O'Neill. Had he, with his
deep guilt feelings, been married to someone like Hickey's Evelyn, a
stubborn good woman, endlessly forgiving, his troubled conscience
would have become intolerable. As it was, he unconsciously welcomed, in
some part of his being, the anguish he suffered at times through Carlotta:
she gave him opportunities to do penance for his sin of having been
born.

Toward the end of O'Neill's first week at Doctors' Hospital he was stricken with pneumonia and for a day or so appeared on the verge of dying — his weight fell to about ninety pounds — but with the aid of penicillin he rallied and, eating ravenously, made a good recovery. His early days there were marked also by occasional hallucinations and passing moments of mental confusion, until Dr. Fisk, eliminating bromide from his medication, prescribed straight chloral for his tremor.

Now slower and more halting in speech than ever, he gave some of his visitors the erroneous impression that he had deteriorated in mind. Probably his labored speech, his disinclination to talk, were due in part to emotional weariness, for he was torn in his feelings about Carlotta and carrying on a running debate with himself about his future course. He must have known, once McLean had discharged her, that there was little if any chance of his guardianship petition being granted unless he was ready to disclose certain incidents in their private life, all of which would lead in turn, he knew, to melodramatic testimony on Carlotta's part and sensational publicity.

Carlotta was presently in fact seeing a *Time* magazine correspondent in Boston, one Francis Wylie, and threatening to let the world know "the whole story" of her troubles with O'Neill. Besides repeating her standard charges against Langner and Moore, she told Wylie that O'Neill in the midst of their estrangement was writing her "love letters" (this was not so) and sending her red roses (the reverse was true: she had sent him roses at Salem Hospital).

Wylie reported on April 6, 1951, to his editors in New York that Carlotta "says that she loves [O'Neill] and feels that he needs her more than anything else." A friend of Dr. Kozol's, the *Time* man said that the psychiatrist was certain of Mrs. O'Neill's sanity, "though admittedly she has her temperamental quirks." Kozol, he continues, "is confident that there will be a reconciliation in three weeks." After outlining what Carlotta had told him, Wylie added that the facts are "pretty sordid and much of them would be . . . unprintable. . . . What I think we should try for is the tragic story of the last years of America's greatest dramatist, with all the undertones and emotional highlights of his literary and domestic struggle."

Ten days later Wylie informed *Time*'s home office that Carlotta was threatening to sue O'Neill, his attorney and Moore for conspiracy unless the petition was withdrawn. "Once she is cleared," he added, "there is a good chance that she will go to New York and try to get a guardianship over O'Neill." After weighing the matter, *Time* decided that the O'Neill story was "too sad" for its readership.

Dr. Robert Lee Patterson, who was again associated with Fisk in treating O'Neill, kept after him about his tremor, for he felt that O'Neill could minimize it if he tried hard enough. At Patterson's suggestion, Sally Coughlin, the playwright's day nurse, likewise tried to persuade him to cope with his affliction. "He felt," she recalls, "that life had dealt him a dirty deal. I told him, Parkinson's doesn't kill, it only impairs, but he said it kept him from writing, the thing that meant most to him." As countless others had done, she suggested that he ought to dictate his plays, but, according to her, he replied that "the ideas wouldn't come unless his hand was moving over the paper. His tremor wasn't so bad; I felt that he could train himself to write if he really tried. I got him to the desk once and gave him pencil and paper, but he pushed it away."

A frank-spoken New Englander of middle years, Miss Coughlin at first regretted having him as a patient. "He was difficult," she says, "though not unpleasant. He never got pettish or pouted or raised Cain about anything, like some patients, but it was hard to get him to do things that were good for him." Sounding very much like Olive Evans, the nurse who had taken care of Eugene in 1912, just before he left for the tuberculosis sanatorium, Miss Coughlin added, "You could never get him to do anything he really didn't want to.

"Other people," she continues, "put him up on a pedestal, but I didn't. I talked to him the way I would anyone else. Sometimes when I said something, he wouldn't answer; he'd pretend he didn't hear me. I'd repeat it and say, 'If you don't feel like talking, that's up to you, but wiggle your ears or do something so I'll know you heard me,' and he'd smile. There were days he didn't say a word."

Somehow Carlotta learned the nurse's name, and sent her notes of thanks for taking good care of her husband. Several times she enclosed photos from the Tao House period, and on the back of one wrote that it was taken "in happier days"; but the photos and notes stopped after a while, since Miss Coughlin never acknowledged them. "Dr. Patterson," the nurse says, "seemed fond of them both. In telling me about their previous separation, when he also had Carlotta in Doctors' Hospital, without O'Neill knowing it, Dr. Patterson laughed as though he was talking about the antics of two difficult children."

A woman of strong family feeling, Sally Coughlin was critical of O'Neill as a father. "A man came to see him," she recalls, "who wanted to tell him that Oona was getting along fine, that she was highly thought of in California. O'Neill didn't want to see him, but I thought he should. The man was in there just a short time. I once asked him if he didn't feel guilty about Oona, the way he'd treated her, and he said that everyone has to make their own life and do what they think is best for them."

Where Miss Coughlin was a bracing cool shower to O'Neill, Mrs. W. Earl Beatty, his evening nurse, was a soothing warm bath. "I liked him very much," she says. "I felt so sorry for him — he was so, I don't know . . . lost. I found him very cooperative, very kind and gentle." The widow of a doctor, a cultivated lady who had spent time abroad, Mrs. Beatty found a receptive audience in her patient when she spoke of her travels. She played canasta with him ("His tremor varied, but he usually had no difficulty in handling the cards") and introduced him to radio station WQXR, whose programs of classical music he came to enjoy. "I did everything I could to divert him," she says. "Left to his own thoughts, he became depressed."

By now he had lost virtually all interest in world affairs, but once, after listening to a newscast, he predicted, in Mrs. Beatty's words, that "Russia would never start a war. Its policy, he said, was to bankrupt the United States."

Many of Eugene's friends, particularly those Carlotta had antagonized, thought that the estrangement would be permanent. A few, recalling the outcome of the 1948 separation, expected a reconciliation. Still others didn't know what to think, since O'Neill, prey to conflicting emotions, spoke variously of his wife. He tried to make excuses for her — both to himself and others — but constantly returned to the fact that he would have died the night she left him out in the snow had the doctor not arrived in time. "He sounded terribly hurt," Miss Coughlin recalls, "in telling me about it."

When Macgowan, in town briefly from California, visited him, O'Neill took one of Kenneth's hands in both his own and said, "It's good to see you *alone*." Kenneth had the impression he was through with Carlotta.

Emotional, devoted, Commins was the one most anxious that O'Neill should never return to her, for he had been inconsolable at being barred by Carlotta. His friendship with O'Neill was "the most meaningful one" of his life, and he was ready to do his utmost to prevent another enforced separation. Presently building a home in Princeton, New Jersey, Saxe kept urging his friend to take permanent refuge with him and his family, but O'Neill remained evasively silent about his intentions.

Sherlee Lantz, who likewise had been distressed over her expulsion from the playwright's life, was another who spent considerable time at the hospital. No longer with the Theater Guild — she was expecting a child — Sherlee, at O'Neill's request, took care of his mail. Not only was he too indifferent to read the letters, he didn't even care to know who had written, so that Sherlee, without knowing whether the correspondents were close to O'Neill, had to rely on her own judgment in answering for him, in her name. "I was uneasy about it. I felt as though I were usurping a daughter's place," she recalls, "and asked if he wanted me to write Oona, for her to take over. All he said was, 'No.'"

During his 1948 hospital stay he had talked as though he had lost all interest in life, yet Shirlee felt that he wanted to be persuaded out of his mood, that he still clung to shreds of hope. By this time, however, it seemed to her that he really had "given up." Unlike many others, Sherlee, who was keenly responsive to O'Neill and intuited how he felt, expected him to reconcile with Carlotta; this, she felt, was now the only thing in the world of any consequence to him.

Sherlee generally visited him every other day for an hour or two, but his difficulty in talking pained her so that sometimes she phoned that she could not see him that day. "As word got around about his condition, people would come to see him in twos," she recalls, "and sit there chatting between themselves to spare him the struggle of talking. He joked to me that it was like presiding at a conference."

Thinking to relieve Sherlee's concern over the playwright, a staff man at Doctors' Hospital told her that O'Neill's mind would deteriorate but that he would not suffer mentally or be in anguish because he would become "like a vegetable." "When I heard that," Sherlee says, "I wanted to kill the doctor."

In mid-April O'Neill became so depressed that he spoke of suicide; as a precautionary measure, Miss Coughlin kept his windows locked. He slept poorly, and when he did fall off was frequently startled awake by weird dreams. In one he dreamed that he killed his night nurse (not Mrs. Beatty but someone he had for a short time); in another, as he told Crouse, "I dreamed I was in Japan two thousand years from now and the Japanese were the only surviving race. They showed me the scientific developments of the day, which were wonderful, but they would not tell me how they were done."

Only Crouse, of all the persons engulfed by the O'Neills' troubles, was in regular touch with both principals, each of whom kept asking him about the other. As soon as he appeared at the hospital on April 17, Eugene said, "I want to go back to Carlotta"; by the next day, however, he was "very nervous and shaky" and had changed his mind. Crouse, like Sherlee Lantz, felt almost certain from the outset that the two would eventually reconcile.

In Seattle the Sophus Winthers, who had heard from Carlotta by telephone and mail — she wanted them to file an affidavit in support of her suit — were worried about O'Neill. Sophus wrote to him on April 12: "My understanding of you and my loyalty to you makes it impossible for me to accept [Carlotta's] story on its face value. I feel very sorry for her. She is trapped by her own nature and from that there can be no escape."

Sally Coughlin, who handled her patient's mail on days when Sherlee was absent, replied to Sophus and Eline on April 18 that she hesitated to give O'Neill their letters because they would "add to the already heavy burden he is carrying. . . . I feel dreadfully sorry for him and the worst part . . . is that there is very little any of us can do to help him. His one desire now seems to be return to Carlotta, even though he regards her as a mental case." His friends had brought him to New York, she said, "hoping to clarify things in his mind and hoping he would make the break with her and live out the remainder of his life in a measure of contentment. His plea is loneliness. . . . As with most paranoids she writes letters and makes telephone calls which hurt his old friends."

Pressed for funds because of the guardianship petition, which barred her from touching her own bank account, Carlotta had to quit the Shelton and return to Point o' Rocks Lane. Sounding like Christine Mannon in *Mourning Becomes Electra,* she now called the cottage "a tomb." A friend who flew up from New York to comfort her and bring some money was dismayed to find her so worn-looking and tense.

Her circumstances were eased after the hearings in Salem probate court on April 23, for O'Neill, through attorney Farley, withdrew his petition. At the same time he asked that her suit for separate support be dismissed for lack of jurisdiction, on the grounds that their legal address was in New York.

Once the two suits were out of the way — Carlotta's became inactive — efforts for a permanent settlement of the O'Neills' split began to accelerate, with one faction pressing for reconciliation, another trying to consolidate the estrangement. Merrill Moore, who unaccountably was still in the picture, thought that O'Neill should remain in New York, where he could take an apartment and be attended by a manservant, while Carlotta should live in Boston. They would see one another occasionally, according to his idea, but would never again live together. Trying to make his scheme seem more attractive to both parties, Dr. Moore asked Crouse to propose it as his plan. Crouse declined, and later, after visiting the hospital, noted in his diary on April 26 that "Gene wants none of the Moore separation plan."

By the end of April, after a month in New York, O'Neill was determined on reunion but, in Crouse's view, the lawyers were "in the way" and Crouse was uncertain "what to do about it." Now that the guardianship petition had been dropped, Carlotta, rather than feeling relieved, seemed more outraged than ever at her public humiliation. Once when Russel phoned, to keep her posted on the latest developments, she was "hurt and savage," and another time she greeted him with "a blast!"

As a substitute for Richard Madden, now fatally ill, his secretary Jane Rubin (who succeeded him as O'Neill's literary agent), was a frequent visitor at the hospital. "One day," she says, "I told him, 'I'm here to help you. Do you want to go back to Carlotta?' and he broke down as he said yes. It was heartbreaking to see him cry.

"I don't know whether they ever heard about it, but Arthur Hopkins for years used to say that he cursed the day he introduced Carlotta to Gene."

Early in May Carlotta's attorney notified Aronberg that she wanted Dr. Kozol to interview her husband to determine "if Gene really wanted her back or if [it were] a trick." The lawyer assured Aronberg that Carlotta, contrary to a report by Merrill Moore, had no intention of trying "to commit" O'Neill.

Russel Crouse had been hesitant to intervene actively in the O'Neills' affairs since lawyers and legal matters were involved, but finally Aronberg, whom Crouse considered a chief stumbling block in the proceedings, gave him permission to do all possible to end the separation. After hearing from Crouse, Dr. Kozol visited New York on May 9 and during an interview with O'Neill became convinced that he was eager to rejoin his wife. Four days later Eugene, appearing "very gay," told Crouse that he and Carlotta were to live at the Hotel Shelton, opposite Kozol's office.

He was returning under Carlotta's terms, one of her chief stipulations being that he would again change his will and rename her as his executrix and sole heir. According to Jane Rubin, O'Neill thought "the joke was on her, since his plays were bringing in little by then — he seemed to be passé.

"Most people didn't realize it," Miss Rubin adds, "but he had a sense of humor. He once told me, 'If I had used all the money my wives cost me to open a string of whorehouses from New York to San Francisco, I would have a nice income today — and I'd have had a lot more fun.'"

O'Neill, whose spirits and health began to improve markedly once the months of separation were coming to an end, kept his plans secret as long as possible from those who would, he knew, be saddened by his decision.

[653]

His final days were marked by farewells. One evening Aronberg brought along Ruth Lander, who had met the playwright once before when she attended a rehearsal of *The Iceman Cometh* with Eugene Jr. "I was uncertain," Ruth says, "whether he'd remember me, but he put out his arms and dropped his head on my shoulder as he wept. I felt that he was saying good-bye to Gene, to his dead son."

During his hospital stay he had put off old friends from the Province-town Players eager to call, in part, probably, because he expected them to be appalled at the changes time and illness had wrought in him; now that his departure was near, he received a few, including Jimmy Light, whom he had not seen for over twenty years. The reunion with Light, who had always hero-worshiped O'Neill and formerly been close to him, must have stirred the depths in them both, but they kept the conversation on the surface.

"The first thing he said to me," Light recalls, "was, 'Give me a cigarette, will you?' His hands were all shaky as he took it, and I started to light it for him, but he took the book of matches and said, 'Thanks for nothing.'

"Can you top that? The guts of the man! It took him a few matches, but he finally managed to light it himself."

O'Neill was to leave for Boston on May 17. When Saxe and Dorothy Commins saw him for the last time, on the evening of the fifteenth, Saxe gave him a large envelope from Oona, which he placed under his pillow. Whether he ever looked at its contents — or discarded the envelope unopened — is unknown; the only certainty is that Oona Chaplin never heard from her father in reply. The communication from her was the result of a visit that Dudley Nichols, in town from Hollywood, made at Doctors' Hospital. Nichols, after hearing about O'Neill's final days at the cottage, had telephoned Oona, urging her to fly East; he hoped for a reconciliation of father and daughter that would forever eliminate Car-lotta from O'Neill's life. Oona told Nichols, however, that the trip was out of the question, for she was in her final month of pregnancy (the Chaplins had their fourth child on May 19, two days after the reunion in Boston). Trying to be of some comfort, Oona had written to her father, in care of Saxe at Random House, and enclosed photographs of her children and herself.

"Gene was dressed and standing when we arrived," Dorothy Commins recalls. "We again pressed him about living with us. We would love to have you, I told him, for years, as long as you like. But Gene said, 'I couldn't, I'd only be a burden, I can't even hold a cup of water.' "

Self-conscious and embarrassed about his palsy, which robbed him of dignity, he added that he could not bear the thought of anyone except Carlotta looking after him. In general she took good care of him, he went on, and there were things to be said on her side: with her beauty, she should have had a far more enjoyable life than she had known with him; she had sacrificed a great deal to devote herself to him and his work.

"We were there only about twenty minutes," Mrs. Commins says. "It was too painful to be prolonged. Gene put his arms around Saxe and said, 'Good-bye, my brother.' I was in tears as we went out."

The following morning, the sixteenth, Saxe wrote to Oona that her letter had arrived just in time, for her father was leaving the next day to rejoin "his wife" (throughout the letter he never once mentions Carlotta by name — her name was anathema to him). Reporting that Eugene was "well on the road to recovery," he said that "his leg is entirely healed; his tremor is immensely improved; his speech is clearer; his strength is returning and his will to live has been restored."

When her father arrived in New York, the letter continues, "the doctors and his friends had grave fears that he would not live. But those anxieties are, happily, past and now he is doing what he wants to do, namely, go back to what may be happiness for him or perhaps even death. In any case, it is what he wants and that is all-important.

"His friends, acting with the purest motives of devotion, did what they could and, in my opinion, saved his life. Now they must withdraw . . . and perhaps even face the prospect of being accused of acting against his interests and wishes. . . . My hope is that your father's strength will be restored completely, so that he can work again in all serenity. He has had more than anyone should be asked to bear of torture and physical hurt."

Dudley Nichols, he concludes, "has told me wonderful things about you and I was immensely pleased to learn that you are a happy and completely fulfilled woman."

(In the late 1960s Oona met Dr. Kozol and asked him "*why* my father returned to Carlotta after all he'd been through." Kozol said, according to her, that "there had been talk of making Aronberg and Langner his legal guardians — and my father immediately got frightened because he felt Langner might get control of his plays, and the only person he trusted in this respect was Carlotta!")

During her final visit at the hospital Sherlee Lantz was in agony over how to end it. "How do you say good-bye," she asked rhetorically, "to someone you love when you know you'll never see him again? Conventional words of affection and regret weren't enough, and any emotional expression would have been painfully embarrassing to us both. The whole time I was there I kept turning over in my mind, what would be the easiest way to get from his bedside to the door? It was only a few steps but it seemed a long distance."

Finally she said, "I'd like to take you to the train tomorrow" — knowing that it was already arranged for Sally Coughlin to do so. O'Neill, understanding immediately, replied, "I'd like that." Sherlee kissed him, said she would telephone the next morning, and, before tears could well up, vanished.

O'Neill's precautions to quit New York as quietly as possible were so effective that some first learned that he was going after he had gone. Bennett Cerf, who saw him on the eve of his departure, was among those left in the dark. Unaware of O'Neill's rejection of "the Moore separation plan," Cerf had arranged for a suite at the Carlyle on Madison Avenue, where a male nurse was to look after him, starting on May 17; instead, that was the day of the Boston reunion.

Now weighing one hundred and seventeen pounds, twenty more than when he had arrived in New York, the playwright still was gaunt. As he prepared to check out of the hospital, he told Miss Coughlin to leave behind everything that could not be crammed into his luggage, as he would not take along any paper bags. "He wanted to travel like a gentleman," says the nurse, who was to accompany him. "I think he wanted to put up his best front for his girl."

Bill Aronberg, who escorted the two to Grand Central, said, "This is good-bye, Gene. I'll be fired as soon as you get back. I know she hates me." O'Neill politely demurred, though he knew that Carlotta would have her way.

Tense as the journey began, O'Neill, who had a roomette on the Yankee Clipper, seemed only half reassured when Miss Coughlin told him that, at Dr. Patterson's instructions, she had sedation for him. "I was supposed to wait till after the halfway point," she recalls, "but he was so nervous I found it necessary to give him the hypodermic injection earlier." He slept most of the way and was unaware when the train paused briefly in New London, the last time he would ever pass through the locale of some of his most poignant memories.

Dr. Kozol was awaiting him with a wheelchair at Back Bay Station, and soon O'Neill was on his way in the psychiatrist's car to the Hotel Shelton on Bay State Road, which was to be his final home and the scene of his death.

31

✦

A Private Funeral

"THEY'D told me Gene had strong guilt feelings from what he'd done, but I didn't know how he would act when he returned," Carlotta said of the reunion in 1951. "The nurse came with him. Well, he walked by me and said [here she burlesqued a sad voice], 'I love you, forgive me,' and he went right on by, into the bedroom, *without even stopping!*"

Sally Coughlin gives a different picture, one more favorable to them both: "I must say, Carlotta handled the situation beautifully. As soon as we came in, she threw her arms around him, hugging and kissing him. I saw his face — he looked so relieved. I was there for a few hours, and he smiled more than in all the weeks I'd known him. He was happy to be home."

Before leaving New York he had borrowed five thousand dollars from the Guild and given an IOU. "When Gene came back," Carlotta says, "he owed seventeen thousand dollars in hospital and doctor bills. I told him, 'All right, Gene, I'll take care of it.' And he said he owed Langner five thousand dollars, and I said I'd pay that too." In their final exchange of correspondence, Carlotta sent Mrs. Langner a check and asked for the IOU, which she received without ever acknowledging. The Langners as well as Aronberg, who had been fired immediately, were now part of the growing list of people forever cut off from O'Neill.

"Carlotta lives in an 'ivory' mind," playwright Marc Connelly said. "She made herself into a necessity for Gene. Wives of writers are as predatory as anything you know. It's just a way for them — and Carlotta specifically — to justify their existence near a famous husband in this sort of stewardship. . . . For the rest, she dressed herself up in an attitude of dedication. O'Neill was always a sort of submerged fellow, and the progression of his illness did not help any against this tendency. . . .

[657]

Carlotta completed the job by practically wrapping Gene up in swaddling clothes."

The cottage on Marblehead Neck was sold, shortly after O'Neill's homecoming, to the Richard S. Robies of Boston. Mrs. Robie, who met the playwright once, recalls him as "very quiet and very gracious. Mrs. O'Neill did all the talking." According to Carlotta, she was in such a hurry to raise funds that she disposed of the place, which had a twenty-thousand-dollar mortgage, for forty thousand dollars; the word around the Neck, however, was that it brought fifty thousand dollars.

At last through with the trouble of running a home, Carlotta had minimal domestic cares at the Hotel Shelton. The couple's suite in 401, which overlooked the Charles River and Cambridge, consisted of a living room, furnished partly with the last of their fine Chinese things, and a bedroom with twin beds; all their meals were brought up from the hotel kitchen. Except for occasional visits to a doctor and several short hospital stays, O'Neill was not to leave the apartment during the rest of his life. His waking hours were largely spent in reading mysteries, listening to ball games on the radio, and, unless sunken in thought, studying with mournful eyes the scene from his chair at a living room window – sailboats, racing shells and other craft on the river; Cambridge, where he had studied playwriting under Professor Baker in another decade, another world. "I want," he had written to Baker in 1914, "to be an artist or nothing."

Initially Carlotta was, in her words, "on twenty-four-hour duty," but this was reduced to sixteen, except on weekends, when she engaged a nurse named Jean M. Welton, whom she pronounced "an angel." A quiet woman, serious and loyal, Mrs. Welton would be Carlotta's confidante and, together with Dr. Kozol, chief support during the trying times that lay ahead.

Before O'Neill had been at the Shelton a fortnight he made out a new will, designating Carlotta as his executrix and sole heir, which said: "I desire to be buried in a burial lot with my wife and I authorize my executrix to purchase such a lot and erect a simple stone thereon . . ." (Carlotta later remarked to Brooks Atkinson that Gene could not have found her "so bad" if he wanted her beside him "for eternity.") He further stated in the document of May 28: "I purposely exclude from any interest under this will my son, Shane O'Neill, and my daughter, Oona O'Neill Chaplin, and I exclude their issue now and hereafter born."

Early this June he received from Random House the galley proofs of *A Moon for the Misbegotten*. On one set he wrote, in a fairly legible hand:

"To Carlotta, my beloved wife, whose love I could not possibly live without, in a spirit of the humblest gratitude for her love which has forgiven my recent shameful conduct toward her." He signed it, "Your Gene, Sweetheart."

Days later Random House sent him, at his direction, the scripts and other papers he had deposited with the publishing house for safekeeping in 1948, when he was in the hospital and worried about Carlotta gaining possession of them. The cache included a box containing holograph drafts and typescripts of some of his produced works and about a dozen parcels containing, among other things, unfinished work and unproduced scripts. Not all the material is extant today. According to a list made by Saxe Commins, some of the parcels were identified as: "Cycle," "By Way of Obit," "The Last Conquest," "Gag's End." Unfinished work (part of Cycle, Reporter's Notebook, French Revolution data); Notes, outlines, ideas for plays; and "Revolt."

O'Neill's life at the Shelton soon fell into a pattern: the morning would be nearly half over before Mrs. Welton had him bathed, dressed and ready for breakfast; in the afternoon he napped. Often he would lie there pretending to sleep but listening to the two women, or with his eyes open just enough to see them. "One time shortly after he came back, after that dreadful business," Carlotta said, "I noticed he was watching me. This was the only time I ever said anything to him about it. I said, 'How could you have done that to me?' His face started to get dark, then suddenly he smiled, 'Well, it was a helluva fourth act.' 'Yes,' I said, 'it *was* a helluva fourth act, and I was the one who suffered.' "

The first time she had stayed at the hotel, under the name of Carlotta Monterey during the estrangement, she was so impatient and demanding that the employees, thinking her on the verge of a nervous breakdown, had avoided her as much as possible. But after they learned that she was Mrs. Eugene O'Neill and began to enjoy her largesse — she tipped most generously, unless she took a dislike to someone — they fell over themselves to be of service.

"She dressed old-fashioned," says Joan Orlando, a dining-room hostess, "mostly in black — black stockings, high-neck dresses, black hat, long black coat, and always wore sunglasses. Her cane fascinated me, a black one with a black marble head. She used it in talking, for emphasis, and whenever she approached the door would raise it imperiously. The doorman was afraid of her. When she wanted the elevator, she would tap on the little window with her cane, as if to say, 'All right, hurry up, I'm here and I want the elevator immediately!' "

Another employee, who remembers her in a fur hat and coat, with the cane, thought of her as "a Russian czarina. She had a strong voice," says Virginia McArdle, "and carried herself proudly."

Among the few from Broadway ever to breach the wall around suite 401, Maxwell Anderson, who had never before met his eminent fellow dramatist, and Jerry Stagg, a television producer, called on O'Neill this spring regarding a TV series planned by the Playwrights' Company. Anderson and his colleagues in the playwrights' group – S. N. Behrman, Elmer Rice and Robert E. Sherwood – wanted to launch the program with an O'Neill work. Stagg later chose *Ah Wilderness!* and *Anna Christie* for the series, but at the meeting in the Shelton the conversation, steered and monopolized by Anderson, scarcely touched on theatrical matters; instead Anderson, who had been married twice – his second wife committed suicide – and who had four children, dwelled on family life. Tactlessly, since he must have known something about the unhappy fates of O'Neill's two sons and his estrangement from Oona, Anderson said: "The great tragedy is to discover that you have not armed your children for life." O'Neill, without betraying any emotion, nodded thoughtfully.

Eager as he had been to rejoin Carlotta, O'Neill became restive after several months, chiefly because of his aversion to hotel living. As Carlotta was giving him a rubdown one day, Eugene, in her words, "squirmed around resentfully. 'What's the matter with you?' I said. 'How can I do this unless you lie quiet?' 'I don't like it here,' he said. 'I want to go.' 'Very well, you can leave,' I told him. 'But this time you're going like a gentleman, quietly. I'll have all your things packed, and you can go back to New York. But there's one thing: if you leave here, that's the end. You can never come back again, *never.*' He gave me a look with those eyes – God, could he give looks! And he was quiet. He never mentioned the subject again."

Perhaps not, but they found other things to wrangle about. Joan Orlando, whose room was close by, used to hear angry voices from suite 401, and James Hunter, a room-service waiter, sometimes came down from the O'Neills with a show of mopping his brow. "It's hell up there," he would say.

A major issue between the two for months was *A Moon for the Misbegotten*, which she wanted him to revise before publication. Her chief objection was to the part about Jamie sleeping with the "blonde pig" on the train carrying his mother's body. By now O'Neill himself had come to "loathe" the play, yet he resisted his wife's importunities to make it more palatable, in her view, for the public. When Crouse later this year thought of coproducing *The Misbegotten* with Howard Lindsay, Carlotta insisted that the scene in question be cut; but their production never materialized.

O'Neill's smoking was another source of contention, because he occasionally burned himself when a cigarette dropped from his trembly fingers; yet keeping cigarettes from him only made the situation worse, for he would get up during the night and rummage around trying to find a smoke. His quest ended more than once with his falling and injuring himself.

Most of his life had been shadowed by his mother's addiction, and now, in an ultimate irony, he himself became, in Carlotta's words, "a drug addict." Not that he was hooked on hard drugs — he never, as Ella O'Neill had done, isolated himself beyond reach — but he increasingly craved sedation. Carlotta, who kept Nembutal locked in a drawer and the key to it in a locket at her throat, privately complained to Anna Crouse, when the Crouses visited this summer, that O'Neill "tries desperately to get" the medicine. "He used to twist the chain," she recalled another time, "and leave marks on my neck. Once he grabbed hold of me and said he was going to choke me till I gave him more, but I told him I'd given the doctor my word. He could choke me or push me from the window, as he threatened, but I didn't care any longer."

While her words suggest that she doled out the Nembutal most cautiously, Dr. W. Richard Ohler gained an opposite impression. "He was under *sedation* [the doctor's voice emphasized the word] a great deal of the time. She told me she had to keep it under lock and key because sometimes he wanted more than he was supposed to get. She said he needed the sedation, as otherwise he might be unmanageable. An assistant of mine took over once when I was away, and it was also his feeling that O'Neill was getting more sedation than necessary."

Ohler began to attend O'Neill at the suggestion of Dr. Kozol, who felt that the playwright should also be under the regular care of an internist. The physician found him "a likable, relatively genial man, but by the time I knew O'Neill he was burned out, like a dried-up cinder. Maybe that's too severe, as I did sense a spark there. Since he was always reading detective stories, I once kidded that he ought to write one, and he went along with the joke by saying he'd give it some thought.

"It was a regimented household, medicine by the clock, that sort of thing. He did pretty much as he was told. He was never enthusiastic

[661]

about anything, he lacked spirit. I once suggested that he be taken for a ride, but nothing happened.

"While taking his history, I asked him something about Oona, and Mrs. O'Neill afterward said that she ought to have warned me against it, as he always got upset when her name was mentioned. I had the feeling he'd have liked more company. He seemed rather glad to see me, though sometimes he wouldn't say a word. He never talked much . . . she and Kozol ran the show. My general feeling was that maybe he was *over-treated*, made to feel too much of an invalid."

In the past many had been charmed by O'Neill's smile, which was best described, perhaps, by Sherlee Lantz; she felt that "every light in the world went on when he smiled. The contrast between the somber face, full of pain, and when he smiled — it was the most astounding, beautiful thing."

But now, presumably under the effect of sedation, he sometimes had what seemed to Dr. Ohler "an almost foolish smile." Though Russel Crouse was too fond of O'Neill to use a word such as "foolish" in describing him, he has a memory that seems to parallel the doctor's impression. During one visit at the Shelton, when Carlotta began attacking Saxe Commins, Crouse defended him, maintaining that he had always been "a good friend" to both her and O'Neill. What particularly remained in Crouse's mind years later was that "Gene just sat there and grinned." Probably he was too sedated to be concerned or to speak up for Saxe; if his medication did not entirely shut out reality, as in his mother's case, it apparently blunted the sharp edges.

Ever since their first rupture in 1948, Carlotta had sought to spread the impression that her husband was mentally unstable, that his mind was failing, and the estrangement this year spurred her efforts. Indeed, she maintained in a letter to Macgowan (just before O'Neill rejoined her in Boston) that periods of "mental confusion," rather than the tremor, had forced him to quit writing in the mid-forties. However, according to Dr. Ohler and others in contact with him, he remained rational to the end.

While O'Neill seemed resigned to his declining prestige around Broadway, Carlotta was chronically incensed, particularly since the theaters of Europe found him worthy of revival. But if unproduced in New York, he was not entirely forgotten. In the summer 1951 issue of the magazine *Theater Time* John Gassner declared that "the most distressing aspects of the current American theater are its . . . neglect of O'Neill's plays and the apparent indifference with which he is regarded by the young." Noting that some of the new generation thought that O'Neill's crown had descended on Tennessee Williams (*The Glass Menagerie* and *A Streetcar Named Desire*) or Arthur Miller (*Death of a Salesman*), Gassner was reminded of "the neo-classic playwrights who succeeded the 'noble brood' of Shakespeare and his fellow Jacobeans after 1660. They are free from the awkwardness of the giants," Gassner adds, "but they are not giants."

Applauding Gassner's view, Brooks Atkinson said in the *Times:* "In originality, size and passion [the O'Neill canon] is the finest dramatic literature we have. Only an improvident theater, like the one we have, would neglect work of such power and magnitude."

Late in November 1951 O'Neill, suffering from a gastrointestinal disturbance, entered Faulkner Hospital, but the newspapers did not learn about it till a week later, when they reported him in "serious condition." His wife, according to United Press, was "in constant attendance." Actually, by the time the word leaked out, Eugene had begun to recover; he returned to the two rooms and his circumscribed existence at the Shelton on December 11.

His illness, which alarmed Carlotta and turned her all solicitous, introduced a generally harmonious period of some months in their relationship. About a fortnight after his discharge from the hospital, on the sixty-third birthday of his "wife, friend, helper & lover," he gave her a typescript of *Long Day's Journey Into Night* bearing the inscription: "To Carlotta, my beloved wife, this play, written in blood and tears, is dedicated. She did the slavery on it, typing it twice, encouraging me, giving me faith and love and making it possible for me to go on with work which daily broke my heart with poignant memory! . . .

"I have loved you for twenty-three years now, Darling, and now that I am old and can work no more, I love you more than ever!"

In a more substantial expression of his devotion, several months later, he had his attorneys draw up a detailed document which "irrevocably" gave Carlotta full ownership and command of all his writings, published and unpublished. The paper is evidence not only of his attachment to her but of his fading interest in life and the things of this world; he says near the beginning: ". . . being desirous of relieving myself of the burden of dealing with, managing or otherwise handling my literary properties to enable effective utilization thereof . . ." For more than thirty years, with incorruptible integrity, he had dreamed of and fought for "effective utilization" of his works; now he was letting go.

"I make these provisions," he stated, "in recognition of the loyalty and care afforded me by my said wife as well as the expenditures by her of her own substantial funds as well as funds I provided her with which were prematurely disbursed because of compelling needs." He added that he made "no provisions for my children since I have otherwise provided for them heretofore."

In the first weeks of 1952 the New York theater, possibly as a result of the Atkinson and Gassner articles, staged two O'Neill plays: *Anna Christie* at the City Center and, as part of the American National Theater and Academy series, *Desire Under the Elms* at ANTA Playhouse. Despite shortcomings in both — Celeste Holm made a lightweight Anna, Karl Malden had but a thin vein of granite as old Cabot — the revivals were, the critics generally agreed, absorbing fare and among the superior offerings of the season. Yet *Anna Christie* lingered a mere twenty-nine performances, while *Desire* eked out a run of only forty-six. Rather than signaling a new generation's interest in O'Neill, the productions suggested that theatergoers had relegated him to the past, that they considered him at best to be of historic importance, not of permanent value and interest.

O'Neill was again in the news this year when *A Moon for the Misbegotten* was published finally — intact, without the cuts Carlotta had urged. Seeking background data for a review *Time* magazine was to run, Francis Wylie sent the playwright a list of questions. In response Carlotta telephoned the correspondent "to rant about how sick O'Neill was, how they don't want to be bothered about cheap publicity and about how she has no right to speak for him." After she had calmed down, she told Wylie that, in his words, "there was no particular reason why the play should be published at this time." Speaking for himself, in a report to *Time*, he added: "Off the record, I have it on good authority that the play was published . . . because the O'Neills are very hard up. But that's off the record, and the source [probably Kozol] tells me if we use it, Carolotta would wreak vengeance, since she would know where it came from."

Publication of the play added nothing to its author's reputation. With the chief exception of Richard Watts, Jr., of the *Post*, who thought it "a drama of unusual force and power, with a strange beauty," the important critics who reviewed it — Brooks Atkinson, Eric Bentley, Walter Kerr — rated *The Misbegotten* one of the playwright's lesser works. Neither did it relieve the O'Neills' financial situation; indeed, it sold so poorly that most of the edition was remaindered in bookstores for a dollar. Like the short-lived revivals of *Desire* and *Anna Christie* early this year, the fate of the new play suggested that the public had permanently turned from

O'Neill. He could only hope that at a distant day, after he had long been in his grave, *Long Day's Journey* would refurbish his name.

On July 22, 1952, in a surprisingly good hand, he inscribed a copy of *The Misbegotten* to

> . . . *darling Carlotta, my wife, who for twenty-three years has endured with love and understanding my rotten nerves, my lack of stability, my cussedness in general —*
> *This token of my gratitude and awareness — a poor thing — a play she dislikes, and which I have come to loathe. . . .*
> *I am old and would be sick of life, were it not that you, Sweetheart, are here, as deep and understanding in your love as ever — and I as deep in my love for you as when we stood in Paris . . . on July 22, 1929, and both said faintly "Oui!"*
>   *Your*
>   *Gene*

The above tribute to her is the final entry in a collection of birthday, wedding anniversary and Christmas messages, as well as dedications, which Carlotta published under the title *Inscriptions: Eugene O'Neill to Carlotta Monterey O'Neill*. The 1952 entry is not, however, the last thing he ever wrote to her; the final one, according to her, was "quite bitter."

From leading a sedentary existence, O'Neill, though his appetite was only fair, gained weight. He was heavier and in fact looked healthier than in years, but his lack of control over his body continued to worsen. He swayed when he stood, even while bracing himself with two canes, and, in Carlotta's words, he "would go to step forward and instead of that he would fall backward . . . it angered him, it embarrassed him." With nothing to look forward to, time yawned emptily before his despairing eyes; day after day after day, from bed to his chair by the window, then bed again.

Russel Crouse, whose theatrical activities occasionally took him to Boston, was the only one of his old friends the playwright saw any more. Otherwise, except for Carlotta, Mrs. Welton the nurse and his doctors — Kozol dropped by about twice a week — practically the only faces in O'Neill's small orbit were the hotel employees who served the suite and a barber from the outside.

"They both were very generous," says James Saia, the barber, "but especially her. The haircut was three dollars, a shave, one dollar. I used to shave him at least every other day, and he always tipped me one dollar, then she'd tip me too. She always walked me to the elevator and every time gave me two, three or five dollars. She'd keep me awhile and talk — I guess she was lonely. He didn't talk much, just a little about baseball. I once showed him a picture of my wife, my children and my grandchildren, but he never said anything about his own. She never talked of hers, either."

Although Carlotta always warned others against mentioning Oona or Chaplin to her husband, she herself could not keep off the subject this fall when Chaplin was again on page one. On September 18, 1952, the newspapers reported that he and his family had sailed for six months abroad; some of the news photos showed Oona beaming over their four children. Two days later the press broke out in headlines that Attorney General James P. McGranery hoped to prove Chaplin, who had never been naturalized, an undesirable alien and bar his return to this country. Before he could reenter, he would have to undergo a hearing based, according to one Justice Department source, on a section of the law regarding persons who advocate overthrow of the government.

For years Chaplin had been under attack from conservative and reactionary elements as a supporter of Communist and other leftist causes. In reply, when the notorious House Un-American Activities Committee asked him in 1947 to come to Washington for a quizzing, he sent a telegram: "While you are preparing your engraved subpoena, I will give you a hint on where I stand. I am not a Communist. I am a peacemonger."

Weary of the "lies and vicious propaganda" he had endured in America, the world-famous performer finally, rather than submit to the indignity of a hearing by the immigration authorities, chose to remain abroad, settling in Switzerland. The Chaplins went on to have eight children in all, with Oona naming their second son, born in 1953, Eugene.

When the cottage on Marblehead Neck was sold, Carlotta had given, with her husband's consent, a treasure of his holograph writings to Yale — plays, poems, diaries, notebooks crammed with ideas for future works. Now he was concerned about the disposition of the manuscripts and other papers that had been cached at Random House. One day in the winter of 1952–1953 he told Carlotta that he had decided to destroy the detailed scenarios and rough drafts of the Cycle. "It isn't that I don't trust you," he said, "but you might drop dead or get run over or something, and I don't want anybody else finishing up a play of mine."

When asked later whether she had tried to dissuade him, Carlotta replied, "Why, certainly not. I'd not be so presumptuous. No one would get very far trying to persuade him to do anything. . . . He wasn't that kind of a man."

The two of them tore up a few pages of the scripts at a time and when there was a heap of scraps, Carlotta set it aflame, a task that lasted for hours. "It was awful," she recalls, "it was like tearing up children."

While O'Neill intended that only *A Touch of the Poet* should survive from the Cycle, the mass of material sent to Yale from the Marblehead cottage inadvertently included a typescript of *More Stately Mansions*. It was from this draft, which would take some nine hours to perform, that Karl Ragnar Gierow of Stockholm's Royal Dramatic Theater, with the assistance of Donald Gallup of Yale, culled the version that is in print today.

In what would prove the final time they ever saw the playwright, Russel Crouse and his wife, visiting Boston in spring 1953, called at the Shelton. "He said very little," Anna Crouse remembers, "just sat there and beamed at us. Buck spoke about Gene's plays, while Carlotta complained bitterly that the theater had forgotten him. She did most of the talking. I had the curious feeling, the whole time we were there, that when you called on them you left the world outside the door."

The Crouses' visit was possibly the last pleasurable hour O'Neill ever knew; he spoke more and more longingly to Carlotta of death. One day, according to what she told Gierow, she "found him lying on the floor unable to raise himself, crying because death wouldn't take him."

"He suffered horribly from his illness — in his soul," she said another time, "and though no longer Catholic, he still feared this Hell might continue after death, and was afraid to take his life."

Due chiefly to his added weight, O'Neill had a deceptive appearance of health ("He looks years younger," Carlotta informed Kaye Albertoni on July 29, "than he did 10 yrs. ago!"), but all the while the disease that was destroying his control of his body intensified. Once in the middle of the night Carlotta found him toppled over in the bathtub and injured her spine dragging him back to bed. Except when under heavy sedation, he was in a highly nervous state, quick to take offense at Carlotta, while Carlotta, feeling exhausted, grew increasingly short-tempered from the strain of looking after him and leading such a circumscribed existence. The doctor, she has said, wanted her to go to the hospital and rest, but Gene said, " 'No, she's my wife and she promised to stay with me for better or worse. Her place is here.' And he said, 'If she dies, well let her die!' And he meant it. . . .

"He kept talking those final months of throwing himself out the window, and I was terrified. I told the doctor, and he said I shouldn't worry, that people who're going to do it don't talk about it. 'The next time he threatens to,' the doctor said, 'tell him you'll open the window for him and dust off the sill, so he won't get dirty.' Well, I followed the advice. The very next time he began, I said, 'Wait, Gene, I'll get the window open for you.' He looked at me! God, if looks could kill! After that he didn't talk much about jumping out."

Their relationship turned more peaceable early this fall when he no longer could get out of bed unaided; clearly, his progress toward death was starting to accelerate. From September on he almost never left his bed except to take a few tottering steps, once or twice a day, for exercise. He often spoke now of how he wanted the funeral and other final matters arranged. "He looked at me one day with those quiet dark eyes," Carlotta recalls, "and said, 'When I'm dying, don't let a priest or Protestant minister or Salvation Army captain near me. Let me die in dignity. Keep it as simple and brief as possible. No fuss, no man of God there. If there is a God, I'll see Him and we'll talk things over.' "

Rather like his father, who had died plagued with regrets, Eugene rued the course his life had taken in recent years. He felt, according to Carlotta, that they should have killed themselves in California, for then they would have escaped the disappointments of the *Iceman* and *Misbegotten* productions, the grief over his sons, the suffering and notoriety of their estrangements. "I put you through Hell," she quotes him as saying, "but I have killed myself!" It was Carlotta's own feeling that the "real" O'Neill died in the early 1940s when the tremor forced him to quit writing. "Writing was his life," she repeatedly used to say. "Nothing else really mattered to him."

On October 16 he marked another birthday, his sixty-fifth, with a sense of relief that it would be his last. By this time he was being attended by a night nurse in addition to his wife and Mrs. Welton. It was so difficult to move him, merely to change his pajamas or the bed linens, that he seemed to Carlotta like "a stone man."

The strain on Carlotta is evident in a letter she wrote to an acquaintance the day after the birthday. "Our patient continues to sway, lurch and fall," she said. "The doctor was here yesterday to wish him well & go over him. He said the patient must be made to walk & exercise. To which I replied, 'And *who* is to *make* the patient do anything *he doesn't wish* to?' — He has fallen once today — & the other times I have almost had to carry him. Not so simple, my friend. He pays NO attention to what anyone says. What he thinks of — I don't know. He believes in nothing — just *takes, absorbs* — with rarely a 'thank you'! He's a 'hard man.' They say a writer always writes of himself? !

"God knows what will happen!"

When she answered the telephone one day early in November, the caller was the Reverend Vincent Mackay of nearby St. Cecilia's Roman Catholic Church, who was downstairs. Having heard that the playwright was gravely ill, he thought that O'Neill might like to have the Sacrament. Carlotta cut him short by replying that the sight of a priest "would upset him, and that it was against the doctor's orders."

The priest thereupon wrote O'Neill a letter expressing his readiness to come to him any hour of the day or night. "The next morning," Father Mackay recalls, he had "an indignant, violent call from Mrs. O'Neill. 'Of all the sneaky, underhanded things to do!' she said. She called it outrageous, said I was badgering him, since she'd already told me that I couldn't see Mr. O'Neill. I let her carry on till the first opening, then I mildly pointed out that the letter came in an envelope with St. Cecilia's on it and that I took for granted that she received all the mail. I wanted to put into writing what I'd tried to say, since she hadn't given me much chance when I phoned.

"Well, she calmed down and told me she knew all about the Church, as she had been educated in a convent school. Mr. O'Neill, she said, was really not a Catholic any more; he hadn't been to church since he was a boy; he had indicated no desire to see a priest, and that was that. But if he ever changed his mind, she would let me know.

" 'Don't call us,' she ended, 'we'll call you.' "

Now that he spent practically all his time in bed, Eugene liked to have Carlotta lie beside him — he under the covers, she on top of the spread. Generally, according to her, "he was silent, and I'd think he was napping, but every so often he'd open his eyes and mention something that had happened long ago. His mind had been going all the time.

"I'd read and heard so much about people dying, but this was happening so quietly — there was nothing dramatic about it. We had two doctors who came by regularly. They were amazed; they knew he was dying, but he looked so well. They couldn't find anything wrong except that he had this temperature. He wasn't in pain, at least he didn't say so, except when he shifted in bed. Parts of him were sore, I guess."

As she was once passing his bed, he reached out and took one of her hands, "You're my Mama, now."

"No, Gene, I'm not your Mama, I'm Carlotta."

"But he was insistent," she recalls, "and repeated that yes, I was his

Mama. And, you know, I really was — his mother, wife, mistress, secretary, everything. He was always looking for a mother."

In the latter part of November, as an infection attacked his already weakened body, he began to sink rapidly. He was treated with antibiotics but, says Dr. Ohler, "He no longer had a will to live." One day he suddenly struggled up to a half-sitting position and, staring wildly around the room, cried, "I knew it I knew it! Born in a goddam hotel room and dying in a hotel room!"

Stricken with pneumonia, he lost consciousness on Thursday the twenty-sixth and lay in a coma for the next thirty-six hours. Carlotta remained at his bedside virtually the entire time, until there was, in her words, "a terrible silence." The silence fell at 4:37 P.M. on November 27, 1953.

Joseph Walker, a desk clerk, saw the playwright only twice during his two-and-half year residence at the Shelton: at his arrival for the reunion with Carlotta, and when he was removed. "It hurt me," Walker says of the second time, "to see this great man, wrapped in a dark blanket and strapped to the undertaker's stretcher, being carried out . . . like anybody else."

The following day Carlotta had an autopsy performed "because I wanted to know what in the name of God was the matter with this man I had nursed so long." It disclosed that one lung was abnormally large and the other shrunken, but his heart and, despite his heavy drinking in early years, liver were in excellent condition. Finally, refuting what his doctors had said for years, the post-mortem examination proved that Parkinson's disease was not primarily responsible for the ultimate disaster of his life.

Dr. Robert S. Schwab, an expert on Parkinson's who examined O'Neill once while he was living in Marblehead, says the autopsy revealed that he had "suffered chiefly from a familial tremor and only to a minor degree from Parkinson's. After having this familial tremor for years, he developed in later life some Parkinson's, but only to a mild degree, while his familial tremor became worse. Alcohol allays a familial tremor, so that a person suffering from it will have to drink to relieve his condition.

"The cause of a familial tremor is unknown. O'Neill's was not caused by drinking or by a venereal disease. In a familial tremor the shaking is slight when the person is at rest but *intention* movements cause it to be violently agitated. [One of O'Neill's nurses at Salem Hospital had noticed that his hand would be steady as he started to raise it with food or a cigarette, but that the closer it came to his mouth, the more his hand shook.] The exact opposite is true of Parkinson's; the tremor is greatly in evidence when the person is at rest, but under control when he is moving."

In an article based in part on the autopsy report, Karl Ragnar Gierow says that the playwright's affliction, "a degeneration of the cells of the cerebellum," was a "rare disease" about which little is known. According to him, the autopsy findings left unsettled the question of whether O'Neill had inherited the ailment but did note that "the initial symptoms are generally trembling hands and speech impairments" and that both his mother and brother had had such a tremor. O'Neill's disease, Gierow continues, is of a kind that gradually destroys only "the motor system — the coordination between the nerves and the muscles . . . from top to toe the body loses all control; a helpless wreck, a foundering ship. . . .

"Thus the horror of it is that the cerebrum remains unharmed. O'Neill's mind was completely clear the entire time, able to comprehend his misery, able, too, to create, but short-circuited, charged with electricity but with the wires leading to the apparatus broken. While the sickness wrought its havoc . . . inside him, visions of new dramas grew with the power lent by desperation, dramas doomed to perish [unwritten]. . . . His life was a tragedy, and from the moment when he first grasped his pen, the words choked in his throat and his hands trembled before the unknown fate which was to be his."

Carlotta took elaborate precautions to assure that her husband would be interred as privately as he had lived. Through Dr. Kozol she notified the Associated Press of his death but kept secret the funeral parlor — the body was at J. S. Waterman's in Kenmore Square — and all burial plans. The employees at the hotel were under strict orders not to give out the slightest scrap of information. As soon as the newspapers got word of O'Neill's death, the Shelton was besieged; according to Philip McBride, the manager, "That was the worst time we ever had at the hotel — from the press and phone calls."

Carlotta herself says: "I carried out every wish of Gene's to the letter, and it was very difficult. He wished no publicity . . . nobody to be at his funeral . . . no religious representative of any creed or kind. . . . Well, what we [Mrs. Welton and Carlotta] went through, I must say! But the people in the hotel, and particularly two men who were strong of arm and determined, good Bostonians, they were throwing people downstairs and I don't know what. And my nurse and I, we used to go around blocks and change taxis and everything to finally get to the undertaker's, which was only two blocks from where we lived. We'd ride miles to keep [the undertaker's] a secret."

In New York O'Neill's friends, many of whom wanted to attend his funeral, were dismayed at the shroud of silence thrown around the final arrangements. Some tried to telephone Carlotta, but she had isolated herself in the suite and was not accepting any calls; even Russel Crouse, who happened to be in Boston at the time, was unable to get through to her.

Saxe Commins, too pained to remain silent, wrote to Oona on December 1 about being shut out of her father's life during his terminal years and added: "But I was not alone in the general proscription. All his friends, one by one, were kept outside the wall built around him.

"Right now it is very, very important that I tell you how deeply I've felt the enforced alienation by a will not your father's. You have probably felt it yourself, as I have reason to know.

"But even all that is to be forgotten. Gene is now beyond being forbidden; he is beyond fear. I've been told that his passing was peaceful and painless. That, at least, is something gained. The torment is over. The gentlest and noblest man I ever knew is finally at rest. There is nothing any of us can do except revere his memory and be very proud and very sad, too, that so fine a spirit became a prisoner and never knew freedom until he died."

The friends were not the only ones upset. After several days the Health Department asked Waterman's how long the body was going to remain unburied (Carlotta kept deferring the funeral in hopes of foiling press coverage). Also, at the local police station Sergeant Edward J. Schofield was irked that the playwright's death was never, contrary to law, reported to the police. "Whenever someone dies in a public place, such as a hotel," he says, "we're supposed to be notified." Schofield became "suspicious and angry," in fact, when a Shelton employee informed him that the O'Neills had often been at odds and that he had once "threatened to kill her." The sergeant was ready to press an investigation, but his superiors, in view of O'Neill's prominence, instructed him "not to stir up things."

After the undertaker had obtained a burial permit from the Health Department at the last possible moment on December 1, the newspapers finally learned that O'Neill was at Waterman's and due to be interred the following day at Forest Hills Cemetery. The funeral was scheduled for 10:30 A.M., but on Wednesday the second Carlotta, to elude "the scavenger press," advanced the time a full hour.

As Bostonians bustled about their affairs that morning, a cortege too meager to be noticed, particularly at the height of the rush hour, slowly threaded its way through traffic. Formally, it consisted of only the hearse and a limousine containing Carlotta, Dr. Kozol, and Mrs. Welton, but two other vehicles were shadowing them — Alfred DiDonato, the barber from Salem, in one, and in the other David Silverstein, an English instructor at Brandeis University who loved O'Neill's plays, with a friend. At the cemetery the unofficial attendants remained in their cars and, from a distance, watched a minimal ceremony held under a pale December sun.

"Carlotta bowed her head," DiDonato recalls, "and the nurse took her arm. The whole thing couldn't have lasted more than six or seven minutes. No fanfare — that's what he wanted, that's what he always said."

The only detailed account appeared in the Boston *Post* on the third, written by Warren Carberg, whose informant had pledged him to secrecy about his source of information. His report in part: "There were no formal prayers. Even the sounds coming across the cemetery from distant traffic were muted. . . . A funeral director's assistant stepped forward and placed a single spray of white chrysanthemums on the casket [a plain black one] and then the three mourners turned and walked to the automobile.

"Not a word was spoken. No hymns were sung. Mrs. O'Neill wore simple black clothing, with no mourning veil. She was pale and appeared without makeup. There seemed to be tiny lines of grief about her eyes and mouth. No tears showed in her eyes."

Days later she was distressed to learn from a cemetery official that the coffin had inadvertently been placed six inches beyond its plot. As though O'Neill's spirit were as unquiet in death as in life, he was dug up and reburied.

His headstone, a boulder of New England granite, was installed in March 1954. Carlotta had told the monument people that she wanted something "simple, vigorous, powerful, in keeping with my husband's character." On the stone were simply his name and vital statistics, the same regarding Carlotta, with a blank space for the place and date of her death (she died in a New Jersey nursing home in 1970), and the traditional phrase: Rest in Peace.

But O'Neill's true epitaph is to be found in *Long Day's Journey Into Night*, when he says through Edmund: "It was a great mistake, my being born a man, I would have been much more successful as a sea gull or a fish. As it is, I will always be a stranger who never feels at home, who does not really want and is not really wanted, who can never belong, who must always be a little in love with death!"

[673]

Bibliography

WITH one exception, mentioned in its proper place, the page references in the Notes to O'Neill's plays are to the editions (or, in one
case, the unpublished script) listed below. In the Notes involving quotations from the plays, the number at the start of a key phrase refers to a
page of this book, while the italic number at the end refers to a page of
the play text.

The Plays

"Chris Christopherson." Unpublished. Three acts. Copyright Division,
Library of Congress, and Theater Collection, Harvard College Library.

Hughie. New Haven: Yale University Press, 1959.

Long Day's Journey Into Night. New Haven: Yale University Press,
1956.

A Moon for the Misbegotten. New York: Random House, 1952.

More Stately Mansions. New Haven: Yale University Press, 1964.

A Touch of the Poet. New Haven: Yale University Press, 1957.

The Plays of Eugene O'Neill, 3 vols. New York: Random House, 1951.
Contains all O'Neill's published plays except those listed above and certain
of his early works contained in *Ten "Lost" Plays* (New York: Random
House, 1964).

The Plays of Eugene O'Neill, 12 vols. Wilderness Edition. New York:
Scribner's, 1934–1935. Referred to in the Notes as *Wilderness,* this
limited, autographed edition is used in this book only for O'Neill's commentary regarding certain of his plays.

[675]

Other Sources

Each of the following entries is preceded by the abbreviated form used in the Notes. Many sources, particularly articles in newspapers and periodicals, are not listed below but are cited only in the Notes.

Alexander   Alexander, Doris. *The Tempering of Eugene O'Neill.* New York: Harcourt, Brace & World, 1962.

Atkinson   Atkinson, Brooks. *Broadway.* New York: Macmillan, 1970.

Basso (A)   Basso, Hamilton. "The Tragic Sense." *New Yorker,* February 28, March 6, and March 13, 1948.

Basso (B)   ———. Notes for the *New Yorker* series.

Bentley   Bentley, Eric. *In Search of Theater.* New York: Knopf, 1953.

Bogard   Bogard, Travis. *Contour in Time: The Plays of Eugene O'Neill.* New York: Oxford University Press, 1972.

Boulton   Boulton, Agnes. *Part of a Long Story.* Garden City: Doubleday, 1958.

Bowen (A)   Bowen, Croswell. "The Black Irishman." *PM,* November 3, 1946. Reprinted in *Cargill.*

Bowen (B)   ———, with the assistance of Shane O'Neill. *The Curse of the Misbegotten.* New York: McGraw-Hill, 1959.

Brown   Brown, John Mason. *The Worlds of Robert E. Sherwood.* New York: Harper & Row, 1965.

Brustein   Brustein, Robert. *The Theater in Revolt.* Atlantic–Little, Brown, 1964.

Cargill   Cargill, Oscar, *et al.,* eds. *O'Neill and His Plays.* New York: New York University Press, 1961. Contains a number of articles listed in this Bibliography, together with a wealth of other material on the subject.

Carpenter   Carpenter, Frederic I. *Eugene O'Neill.* New York: Twayne, 1964.

Chaplin   Chaplin, Charles. *My Autobiography.* New York: Simon & Schuster, 1964.

Chase   Chase, Ilka. *Past Imperfect.* Garden City: Doubleday, 1942.

Clark   Clark, Barrett H. *Eugene O'Neill: The Man and His Plays.* New York: Dover, 1947.

Cowley (A)   Cowley, Malcolm. "Eugene O'Neill: Writer of Synthetic Drama." *Brentano's Book Chat,* July–August 1926.

Cowley (B)   ———. "A Weekend with Eugene O'Neill." *Reporter,* September 5, 1957. Reprinted in *Cargill.*

Craig Craig, Gordon. *The Theater Advancing.* New York: Benjamin Blom, 1963.

Crichton (A) Crichton, Kyle. "Mr. O'Neill and The Iceman." *Collier's,* October 26, 1946.

Crichton (B) ———. *Total Recoil.* Garden City: Doubleday, 1960.

Deutsch Deutsch, Helen, and Stella Hanau. *The Provincetown: A Story of the Theater.* New York: Farrar & Rinehart, 1931.

Diary (A) Diary kept by Kathryne Albertoni.

Diary (B) One kept in 1925 by Agnes Boulton.

Diary (C) One kept by Russel Crouse.

Diary (M) One kept by O'Neill while writing *Mourning Becomes Electra.* Extracts first published in New York *Herald Tribune,* November 8, 1931. Reprinted in Barrett H. Clark's *European Theories of the Drama* (New York: Crown, 1947).

Diary (O) One kept by O'Neill in 1925.

Diary (S) One kept by Elinor C. M. Smith.

Downer Downer, Alan S. *Fifty Years of American Drama: 1900–1950.* Chicago: Regnery, 1951.

Engel Engel, Edwin A. *The Haunted Heroes of Eugene O'Neill.* Cambridge: Harvard University Press, 1953.

Falk Falk, Doris. *Eugene O'Neill and the Tragic Tension.* New Brunswick: Rutgers University Press, 1958.

Fitzi "In Memory of Fitzi." Privately printed. New York, issued by Pauline H. Turkel.

Ford Ford, Torey. "From Pullman Porter to Honor Guest of Drama League." New York *Herald Tribune,* March 13, 1921.

Frazer Frazer, Winifred D. *Love as Death in The Iceman Cometh.* Gainesville: University of Florida Press, 1967.

Gassner (A) Gassner, John, ed. *O'Neill: A Collection of Critical Essays.* Englewood Cliffs: Prentice-Hall, 1964.

Gassner (B) ———. *Eugene O'Neill.* Minneapolis: University of Minnesota Press, 1965.

Gelb Gelb, Arthur and Barbara. *O'Neill.* New York: Harper's, 1962.

Gierow Gierow, Karl Ragnar. "Eugene O'Neill's Posthumous Plays." *World Theater,* Spring 1958.

Gilmer Gilmer, Walker. *Horace Liveright: Publisher of the Twenties.* New York: David Lewis, 1970.

Glaspell Glaspell, Susan. *The Road to the Temple.* New York: Stokes, 1927.

Goldberg Goldberg, Isaac. *The Theater of George Jean Nathan.* New York: Simon & Schuster, 1926.

Bibliography

Goldman Goldman, Emma. *Living My Life*. New York: Knopf, 1931.

Hamilton (A) Hamilton, Dr. G. V. *A Research in Marriage*. New York: Albert & Charles Boni, 1929.

Hamilton, (B) ———, and Kenneth Macgowan. *What Is Wrong with Marriage*. New York: Albert & Charles Boni, 1929. A popularized version of the preceding book.

Hansford Hansford, Montiville M. "O'Neill as the Stage Never Sees Him." Boston *Transcript*, March 22, 1930.

Helburn (A) Helburn, Theresa. "O'Neill: An Impression." *Saturday Review of Literature*, November 21, 1936.

Helburn (B) ———. *A Wayward Quest*. Boston: Little, Brown, 1960.

Hopkins Hopkins, Arthur. *Reference Point*. New York: Samuel French, 1948.

Kenton Kenton, Edna. "The Provincetown Players and the Playwrights' Theater, 1915–1922." Unpublished manuscript.

Kinne Kinne, Wisner Payne. *George Pierce Baker and the American Theater*. Cambridge: Harvard University Press, 1954.

Kronenberger Kronenberger, Louis. *No Whippings, No Gold Watches*. Boston: Atlantic–Little, Brown, 1970.

Krutch (A) Krutch, Joseph Wood. Introduction to *Nine Plays by Eugene O'Neill*. New York: Liveright, 1932. Reissued by Random House and Modern Library.

Krutch (B) ———, *The American Drama Since 1918*. New York: Braziller, 1957.

Langner Langner, Lawrence. *The Magic Curtain*. New York: Dutton, 1951.

Lawrence Lawrence, D. H. *Studies in Classic American Literature*. Garden City: Doubleday, 1953.

Merrill Merrill, Flora. "Fierce Oaths and Blushing Complexes Find No Place in Eugene O'Neill's Talk." New York *World*, July 19, 1925.

Miller (A) Miller, Jordan Y. *Eugene O'Neill and the American Critic*. Hamden: Archon, 1962. The most complete O'Neill bibliography.

Miller (B) ———, ed. *Playwright's Progress: O'Neill and the Critics*. Chicago: Scott, Foresman, 1965.

Mollan Mollan, Malcolm. "Making Plays with a Tragic End." Philadelphia *Public Ledger*, January 22, 1922.

Nadel Nadel, Norman. *A Pictorial History of the Theater Guild*. New York: Crown, 1969.

Nathan Nathan, George Jean. *The Intimate Notebooks of George Jean Nathan*. New York: Knopf, 1932.

[678]

O'Casey   O'Casey, Sean. *Rose and Crown.* New York: Macmillan, 1952.
O'Neill (A)   O'Neill, Eugene. "Strindberg and Our Theater." Playbill for *The Spook Sonata* at the Provincetown Playhouse in 1924. Reprinted in *Deutsch*, 191–193, and *Cargill*, 108–109.
O'Neill (B) ———. "Are the Actors to Blame?" Playbill for *Adam Solitaire* at the Provincetown Playhouse in 1925. Reprinted in *Deutsch*, 197–198, and *Cargill*, 113–114.
O'Neill (C) ———. "Memoranda on Masks," November 1932; "Second Thoughts," December 1932; and "A Dramatist's Notebook," January 1933, all in *American Spectator.* Reprinted in *Cargill.*
O'Neill (D) ———. *The Last Will and Testament of Silverdene Emblem O'Neill.* Privately printed "for Carlotta." New Haven: Yale University Press, 1956.
O'Neill (E) ———. *Inscriptions: Eugene O'Neill to Carlotta Monterey O'Neill.* Privately printed. New Haven: Yale University Press, 1960. Copyright by Yale University Library.
O'Neill (P)   O'Neill, Patrick. *James O'Neill.* History of the San Francisco Theater, vol. 20. San Francisco: Writers' Program of the WPA in Northern California, 1942.
Pasley   Pasley, Fred. "The Odyssey of Eugene O'Neill." New York *News*, January 24–30, 1932.
Peck (A)   Peck, Seymour. Transcript of a taped interview with Carlotta Monterey O'Neill in 1956.
Peck (B) ———. "Talk with Mrs. O'Neill." New York *Times*, November 4, 1956. An article based on the preceding entry. Reprinted in *Cargill.*
Prideaux   Prideaux, Tom. "Most Celebrated U.S. Playwright Returns to Theater." *Life*, October 14, 1946.
Quinn   Quinn, Arthur Hobson. *A History of the American Drama.* New York: Crofts, 1945.
Raleigh (A)   Raleigh, John Henry. *The Plays of Eugene O'Neill.* Carbondale: Southern Illinois University Press, 1965.
Raleigh (B) ———, ed. *Twentieth Century Interpretations of The Iceman Cometh.* Englewood Cliffs: Prentice-Hall, 1968.
Sanborn   Sanborn, Ralph, and Barrett H. Clark. *A Bibliography of the Works of Eugene O'Neill.* New York: Random House, 1931. Contains all his early published poetry.
Schriftgiesser   Schriftgiesser, Karl. "The Iceman Cometh." New York *Times*, September 29, 1946.

Sergeant   Sergeant, Elizabeth Shepley. "O'Neill: The Man with a Mask." *New Republic,* March 16, 1927. Reprinted in Miss Sergeant's *Fire Under the Andes* (New York: Knopf, 1927).

Sheaffer   Sheaffer, Louis. *O'Neill: Son and Playwright.* Boston: Little, Brown, 1968.

Sifton   Sifton, Paul. "A Whale of a Play." *McCall's,* May 1932.

Simonson   Simonson, Lee. *The Stage Is Set.* New York: Harcourt, Brace, 1932.

Skinner (A)   Skinner, Richard Dana. *Our Changing Theater.* New York: Dial, 1931.

Skinner (B)   ———. *Eugene O'Neill: A Poet's Quest.* New York: Longmans, Green, 1935.

Sweeney   Sweeney, Charles P. "Back to the Sources·of Plays Written by Eugene O'Neill." New York *World,* November 9, 1924.

Tiusanen   Tiusanen, Timo. *O'Neill's Scenic Images.* Princeton: Princeton University Press, 1969.

Törnqvist   Törnqvist, Egil. *A Drama of Souls.* New Haven: Yale University Press, 1969.

Weissman   Weissman, Philip. *Creativity in the Theater.* New York: Basic Books, 1965.

Welch   Welch, Mary. "Softer Tones for Mr. O'Neill's Portrait." *Theater Arts,* May 1957. Reprinted in *Cargill.*

Winther   Winther, Sophus Keith. *Eugene O'Neill: A Critical Study.* New York: Random House, 1934.

Woolf (A)   Woolf, S. J. "O'Neill Plots a Course for the Drama." New York *Times,* October 4, 1931.

Woolf (B)   ———. "Eugene O'Neill Returns After Twelve Years." New York *Times,* September 15, 1946.

Woollcott   Woollcott, Alexander. *Shouts and Murmurs.* New York: Century, 1922.

Young (A)   Young, Stark. *Immortal Shadows.* New York: Scribner's, 1948.

Young (B)   ———. "Eugene O'Neill: Notes from a Critic's Diary." *Harper's,* June 1957.

Zolotow   Zolotow, Maurice. *Stagestruck: The Romance of Alfred Lunt and Lynn Fontanne.* New York: Harcourt, Brace & World, 1965.

For further bibliographical data, see *Cargill,* 487–517; *Miller (A)*; *Sanborn;* and *Törnqvist,* 266–274.

Notes

Quotations from O'Neill's Plays

In the play listings, (R.H. 1), (R.H. 2), and (R.H. 3) refer to the three-volume Random House set. The volumes are numbered by one, two or three diamonds on their spines.

AH, WILDERNESS! (R.H. 2)

405	"a tall, dark, spare," *188.*
405	"a good man's failing," *225.*
405	"irresponsible, never," *313.*
406	"goes diffidently," *188.*
406	"I hope you're wrong," *267.*
406	"certain desires," *295.*

ALL GOD'S CHILLUN GOT WINGS (R.H. 2)

119	"a dirty nigger," *337.*
119	"Will God forgive," *341.*
119	"You with your fool," *336.*
119	"looking at her wildly," *339–340.*
120	"street noises," *301.*
120	"The street noises are now," *305.*
120	"There is no laughter," *312.*
120	"The buildings have," *318.*

ANNA CHRISTIE (R.H. 3)

25	"There ain't nothing," *65.*
69	"I was in a house," *58.*
464	"Fog, fog, fog, all bloody," *78.*

CHRIS CHRISTOPHERSON

498	"been talking me deaf," *2.*
498	"Smart fellow," *6.*

[681]

DAYS WITHOUT END (R.H. 3)

DESIRE UNDER THE ELMS (R.H. 1)

DIFF'RENT (R.H. 2)

DYNAMO (R.H. 3)

THE EMPEROR JONES (R.H. 3)

THE FIRST MAN (R.H. 2)

THE FOUNTAIN (R.H. 1)

53	"I begin to know," *448.*
53	"Look at the men," *395.*
111	"lands beyond strange," *385.*
201	"Age — Youth," *442.*
441	"Looters of the land," *395.*

GOLD (R.H. 2)

12	"one of the smartest," *644.*
13	"Hands off, ye dog!" *630.*
13	"It wasn't me," *652.*
13	"What man that's," *665.*

THE GREAT GOD BROWN (R.H. 3)

167	"You're not weak," *285.*
167	"Why must I," *264–265.*
169	"No! That is merely," *298.*
169	"But you like him," *287.*
169	"Old Sacred Cow," *285.*
169	"Old Filth," *285.*
169	"Haven't I told," *288.*
169	"the hardened prostitute," *279.*
171	"Who are you?" *266.*
171	"Dion! Don't!" *292.*
171	"What aliens," *282.*
201	"Always spring," *322.*
409	"Man is born broken," *318.*
600	"Always spring," *322.*

THE HAIRY APE (R.H. 3)

73	"I belong," *215–216.*
73	"Aw yuh make me," *217.*
74	"Take me away!" *226.*
74	"she'd seen a great," *230.*
74	"spit in her," *235.*
74	"all de factories," *248.*
74	"I ain't on oith," *253.*
74	"Christ, where do I," *254.*
92	"Toin off dat," *225.*
175	"Jenkins — the First," *208.*
269	"Sure! *You* get me" *253.*
307	"part of de," *215.*

HUGHIE

522	"Oh, I was wise," *29.*
522	"His mind has hopped," *26.*
523	"But the Clerk's," *27–28.*

THE ICEMAN COMETH (R.H. 3)

489	"To hell with," *578.*
490	"This place has," *594.*
490	"It's the No Chance," *587.*
490	"Once she'd gone," *603.*
491	"a gaunt Irish face," *574.*
491	"a great one," *580.*
492	"really poison," *622.*
492	"real peace," *passim.*
492	"the old false," *641.*
492	"the best friends," *621.*
492	"members of the same," *624.*
492	"I've had hell," *642.*
492	"something not human," *648.*
492	"have died of a broken," *705–706.*
493	"the sweetest woman," *714.*
493	"God, can you," *713.*
493	"I began to be," *714–715.*
493	"was the only," *716.*
493	"I didn't give," *716.*
499	"There's a limit," *715.*
499	"has to be punished," *642.*
502	"exudes a friendly," *618.*
502	"something lying," *713.*

ILE (R.H. 1)

39	"old Vikings in the storybooks," *546.*

LAZARUS LAUGHED (R.H. 1)

200	"Laugh! Laugh with me!" *280.*
280	"If I were sure," *353.*

LONG DAY'S JOURNEY INTO NIGHT

xi	"good bad luck," *150.*
xii	"When you're in agony," *74.*
26	"His face has begun," *13.*
27	"None of us can help," *61.*
39	"different from all," *105.*
154	"It was a great mistake," *153.*
191	"It was right after," *118.*
200	"a little in love," *154.*
309	"God, it made," *118.*
450	"a simple, unpretentious," *13.*
482	"The past is," *87.*
483	"God, it made," *118.*
507	"hophead," *161.*
513	"How can I?" *87.*
514	"this play of old," *dedication.*
514	"His quietness fools," *35.*
514	"I have tried," *145.*

514	"started Mama on dope," *166.*
516	"This last stunt," *145.*
516	"Yes, maybe life," *149.*
516	"would serve all," *47.*
516	"a summer cold," *26.*
516	"Let us go," *174.*
517	"That was in," *176.*
673	"It was a great mistake," *153–154.*

MOURNING BECOMES ELECTRA (R.H. 2)

357	"I was like you," *73.*
370	"tomb," *17.*
371	"Well, I hope," *32.*
371	"I know you, Vinnie!" *33.*
372	"Don't be afraid," *178.*
392	"a Garden of Paradise," *24.*

STRANGE INTERLUDE (R.H. 1)

170	"The mistake began," *42.*
239	"one of those poor," *34.*
239	"our lives are merely," *199.*
241	"guinea pigs," *84.*
241	"dear old Charlie," *passim.*
241	"My three men!" *135.*
242	"how dim his face," *4.*
242	"immune to love," *33.*
242	"doesn't care for," *33.*
244	"Christ! . . . touch of," *97.*
244	"How we poor," *39–40.*
245	"dive for the gutter," *35.*
245	"needs normal love objects," *37.*
263	"we must all be," *11.*

A TOUCH OF THE POET

449	"the face of an embittered," *34.*
449	"before all the army," *38.*
449	"I have not loved," *43.*
450	"We'll see the day," *63.*
451	"while the footsteps," *86.*
451	"great dreamers," *82.*
451	"it is already written," *85.*
455	"pure freedom . . . their coils." *83.*
456	"the Sisters" and "to witness," *84.*
482	"of what are commonly," *15.*

WELDED (R.H. 2)

100	"His unusual face," *443–444.*
100	"blue-gray eyes," *443.*
100	"You can't imagine," *456–457.*
100	"Thanks for that," *457.*
100	"I've grown inward," *453.*
101	"It's so beautiful," *453.*
101	"stamp [his love]," *460.*
101	"we'll torture," *488.*
101	"You and I," *448.*
102	"Oh, it was beautiful," *447.*
102	"I want to say," *488.*
103	"speak, ostensibly to," *452.*
103	"you're such a relentless," *447.*

132   "becomes impossible," *488*.
133   "I love you!" *489*.
201   "To learn to love," *478*.

Sources Other Than the Plays

Whenever someone is quoted and no published or other written source is given, the remarks, unless otherwise specified in the text or Notes, were obtained through personal interviews. For the sake of smoother reading, elisions in quotations from published material or from correspondence are no always indicated; and occasionally the order of a quotation has been revised, but never in such a way, the biographer believes, as to modify the meaning.

Following are abbreviations used in the Notes. For a full listing of sources given in abbreviated form, see the Bibliography.

GB	George Boll	AM	Arthur McGinley
AB	Agnes Boulton	KM	Kenneth Macgowan
JC	Jane Caldwell	RM	Richard Madden
MC	Myrtle Caldwell	CM	Carlotta Monterey
OOC	Oona O'Neill Chaplin	GJN	George Jean Nathan
BHC	Barrett H. Clark	EO	Eugene O'Neill
DC	Dorothy Commins	SO	Shane O'Neill
SC	Saxe Commins	OS	Oliver Sayler
RC	Russel Crouse	ESS	Elizabeth Shepley Sergeant
BD	Benjamin De Casseres	LS	Louis Sheaffer
HD	Harold DePolo	RS	Robert Sisk
FTZ	M. Eleanor ("Fitzi") Fitz-gerald	CCS	Cynthia Chapman Stram
		RoS	Roy Stram
TH	Theresa Helburn	GCT	George C. Tyler
MK	Manuel Komroff	CVV	Carl Van Vechten
JWK	Joseph Wood Krutch	EW	Eline Winther
LL	Lawrence Langner	SKW	Sophus Keith Winther
JOL	Dr. J. O. Lief	SY	Stark Young
HL	Horace Liveright		

1. THE OLD ACTOR'S FINALE

3   "Oh, Gene": Dated only "Saturday," probably 1/3/20.
3   "I just can't": Dated "Late Saturday night," probably 2/7/20.
3   "I'll be back": 1/31. "After this": 2/6. "God, how I": 1/28, all 1920.

3	"Oh Beloved": Dated "Friday night," probably 2/6/20.
4	"If you and I": Dated "Sunday," probably 1/25/20.
4	"plague spot": 1/24/20.
4	"it would all": Dated "Sunday," probably 2/15/20.
4	"You'll see what": 2/4/20.
4	"My Own, I have": 2/5/20.
4	"*Beyond* is now": 2/6/20.
5	"trace of pneumonia": EO to AB, 2/7/20.
5	"Now you must": Dated "Wednesday," probably 2/11/20.
5	"alive at all": Dated "Monday," probably 2/16/20.
5	"I tried to drag": As James Light recalled what EO told him.
5	"curse . . . fallen for": EO to GCT, 12/9/20.
6	"Life with me": Probably 2/16/20.
6	"If that's fame": EO to AB, 2/6/20.
6	"Success has meant": EO to AB, dated "Thursday," probably 2/12/20.
6	"Exact hour": 4/12/20
6	"punk and pessimistic": Dated "Saturday," probably 2/21/20.
6	"I am proud": 2/18/20.
7	"four years' experience": EO to AB, 1/26/20.
7	"Well, never again!": Dated "Wednesday," probably 2/25/20.
7	"rough-necks . . . brother": 2/27/20.
9	"principally composed": 3/11/20.
9	"all wrong and": EO to GCT, 3/14/20.
9	"pleasant surprise": EO to GCT, 3/17/20.
10	"technical experiment": EO to GCT, 3/26/20.
10	"looseness and a certain": 2/8/20.
10	"You remember": 3/13/20.
11	"new imaginative": 2/7/20.
11	"a good deal": 3/29/20.
11	"very intelligent": 4/1/20.
11	"to produce a play": 3/30/20.
11	"the Bostonians": 1/17/21.
12	"uncommonly good": New York *Times*, 4/4/20.
12	"moments of intense": 4/1/20.
12	"most depressing": *Variety*, 4/2/20.
12	" 'Exorcism' has": EO to Frank Shay, 1/12/22.
12	*Where the Cross* symbolism: See *Sheaffer*, 430–431.
13	"hated . . . the punkest": EO to AB, 4/27/20.
13	"in the back": 6/19/20.
13	"I am familiar": 6/20/20.
14	"Fifine is lost": Dated "Sunday," probably 4/24/20.
14	"like him to show": Undated, circa February 1922.
14	EO at *Horizon*: E. J. Ballantine.
15	"We could understand": *Kenton*, p. 149.
15	"these earnest amateurs": Ibid., p. 142.
15	"Fitzi was touched": *Fitzi*.
16	"*Romeo and Juliet*": EO to GCT, 6/3/20.
16	"pretty wise crowd": 6/4/20.
16	"over-strained letters": 10/24/20.
17	"Oh, a damned medal!": AP, 11/28/53.
17	"Yes, it was": EO to Nina Moise, 8/29/20.
20	"Friday night and Saturday": Undated, circa 5/17/20.
21	"You could get": Mrs. Pearl Sanford, one of the nurses.
22	"an unhappy one": AB to EO, 7/30/20.

22 "Oh, My Own, we": 7/29/20.
23 "Helluva time": Tom Dorsey, Jr., who drove them to the hospital.
23 Ella's reaction to the death: Mrs. Pearl Sanford.
23 One relative recalls: Daniel J. O'Neill, a relative through marriage, not by blood.
23 "mourned their father": *Bowen (A)*.
24 "absolutely ignored": EO to George Middleton, 11/12/33.
24 Mrs. Platz episode: Mrs. Elliott W. Sherman, née Claire Rogers, a cousin of EO.
24 "written indelibly": EO to GCT, 12/9/20.

2. THE PROVINCETOWN'S COSTLY SUCCESS

25 "the Atlantic for": EO to GCT, 6/8/19.
25 The seal episode: AB.
25 "chanties sung": "Playwright Finds His Inspiration on Lonely Sand Dunes by the Sea," Boston *Post*, 8/29/20.
27 "When I get": *Sweeney*.
27 "his enemies would": *Wilderness*.
27 "but I couldn't": *Sweeney*.
28 "the woods were unmoved": Joseph Conrad, *Three Great Tales* (New York: Random House, Vintage Books, 1958), p. 282.
28 "The monotonous beating": Ibid., p. 290.
28 "the beat of the drum": Ibid., p. 302.
28 "Dancing, Pantomime": *Craig*, pp. 117–118.
28 "in its dramatic": *Bogard*, p. 136.
29 "the condition": Ibid., p. 137.
30 "thrilling struggle": *Glaspell*, p. 286.
30 "This marks": Ibid., p. 287.
31 "What Jig hasn't": *Kenton*, pp. 153–154.
32 "actual sense of infinity": Ibid., p. 159.
32 "Are you Charles?": Cleon Throckmorton.
32 "Away we'd start": *Ford*.
32 "A colored man": Ibid.
33 "deeply excited": *Kenton*, pp. 155–156.
33 "The last five": Ibid., p. 155.
33 Charlie Chaplin episode: James Light.
34 "Episodes of glorious": KM, New York *Globe*, 11/4/20.
34 "A persistent drum": A. B. Walkley, London *Times*, 9/11/25.
34 "deep in the hole": EO to George Middleton, 12/18/20.
35 "we were not getting": *Kenton*, p. 161.
35 Gilpin's behavior: Pauline H. Turkel.
36 "about four minutes": *Ford*.
36 "Yes, Gilpin is": Undated letter from EO to Michael Gold, circa June 1923.
37 "No, Slim, I": *Gelb*, p. 450.
37 "a timeless resignation": Moss Hart, *Act One* (New York: Random House, 1959), p. 87.
37 "effect was shattering": Ibid., p. 88.
37 "As I look back": *Woolf (B)*.
38 "Fifine has handed": Dated "Tuesday," probably 4/27/20.
39 "Old Man's business": 7/30/20.
40 "[My father's] leaving": 12/9/20.
40 "taking a real": 12/13/20.
40 "a wasted talent": Daniel J. O'Neill.

[689]

41   "Being your father's": 10/26/20.
41   "very much indeed": GCT to EO, 12/13/20.
42   "the very deplorable": 1/14/21.
42   "the real estate theater": *Sweeney.*
42   "one of the best": EO to John Peter Toohey, 12/6/20.
42   "His speech was slow": Charles O'Brien Kennedy, *Lambs Script*, of the Lambs Club, March–April 1954.
43   "so brutal and ugly": New York *Times*, 2/6/21.
43   "To see dramatic": New York *Herald*, 2/1/21.
43   "A chap walked": 1/15/21. Since the librarian was a prisoner, he is not identified here.
43   "The characters are": Louis V. De Foe, New York *World*, 2/1/21.
43   "the man who writes": KM, New York *Globe*, 12/31/20.
43   "Life is too": New York *World*, 2/1/21.
44   "*Diff'rent*, as I": "Eugene O'Neill's Credo and the Reasons for His Faith," New York *Tribune*, 2/13/21. Reprinted in *Cargill.*
44   "extracted from": *Crichton (A).*
44   Sketch of Willie Fernandez: AB, among others.
45   "Did you hear": *Cowley (A).*
45   Second Avenue restaurant episode: AB.
46   "Art may not": *Craig*, p. 47.
46   "A work of art": *Mollan.*

3. UNEVEN PLAYWRIGHT

48   "I wanted you": *Boulton*, p. 68.
48   "to be alone": Ibid., p. 172.
48   "I am one": Dated "Sunday," the letter was probably written 11/2/19. Her grandson Shane was born Thursday, 10/30/19.
49   "We considered the O'Neills": *Gelb*, p. 95.
49   The basement nursery: AB.
50   "everyone who does": Georges Simenon, *Writers at Work* (New York: Viking, 1958), pp. 146–147.
50   "most generous": EO to GCT, 1/14/21.
50   "I wonder if": 2/11/21.
50   "My principal reaction": 3/18/21.
51   "*The Spring* has": New York *Tribune*, 2/2/21.
51   "a remarkable and arresting": New York *Globe*, 2/2/21.
51   "will have a new": Alison Smith column, New York *Globe*, 5/7/21.
51   Cook's sketches and prospectus drafts are in the C. Waller Barrett Collection at the University of Virginia Library.
52   "It's too great": GCT to EO, 1/15/21.
52   "too inexperienced": 3/5/21.
52   "possesses absolute genius": 3/8/21.
52   "to smolder for a while": EO to KM, 3/18/21.
52   "the recurrence in folklore": Note by EO in playbill for *The Fountain.* Reprinted in *Wilderness.*
52   "Could you suggest": 3/18/21; "If you should happen": 3/29/21.
53   "worked harder": EO to SC, 9/5/22.
54   "frightfully dilapidated": EO to SC, 3/12/21.
54   "I warn you": Ibid.
54   "tiresome bickering": EO to AB, 4/24/21.
54   "Our finances had got": *Kenton*, p. 168.

54	Sketch of SC's parents: DC.
55	"Saxe's people are fine": Dated "Friday," probably 4/22/21.
55	"a large cash and "hawked *Gold*": EO to GJN, 3/31/21.
55	"outrageously inept": EO to AB, dated "Saturday," probably 4/23/21.
55	"doesn't sound so": EO to AB, dated "Wednesday," probably 4/27/21.
55	"For Christ's sake": Dated "Thursday," probably 4/28/21.
55	EO's early efforts as a movie scenarist: *Sheaffer*, pp. 311–312.
55	"loud, strident voice": 5/1/21.
56	"Williams is on": EO to AB, 4/30/21.
56	"got good and pickled": EO to Ralph Block, 6/10/21.
56	"an amazing mixture": New York *Tribune*, 6/2/21.
56	"his propensity to look": Louis V. De Foe, New York *World*, 6/5/21.
57	"Admirers of Eugene": 6/3/21.
57	"Every hat in Indianapolis": George Somnes to EO, 3/30/21.
57	"It's a great": 7/1/21.
58	"God, how I": Dated "Friday," probably 4/22/21; "I feel quite": Dated "Saturday," probably 4/23/21.
58	"Mrs. Clark . . . Clarkie": Josephine Johnson, a friend of Mrs. Clark.
58	Mrs. Clark "used" Shane: Silvio A. Bedini.
59	"Is he sick?": Agnes Carr.
59	"He was headed": AB.
59	AB and Jamie's relationship: AB.
60	"There are already": Agnes Carr.
60	"need vacations": EO to Dr. David R. Lyman, 8/18/24.
60	"Too weak to live": "Mabel Dodge Writes About Robert Edmond Jones," New York *Journal*, 9/14/17.
60	"He is essentially": "The Emperor Jones," *New Yorker*, 5/9/31.
60	"It is dreadful": Undated. At Beinecke Library, Yale University.
60	"It is horrible": Undated. Beinecke Library.
61	"I never felt": EO to KM, 8/9/21.
61	"as a critic": EO to KM, 3/29/21.
61	KM's background: KM.
62	Carlin's wine-making and bosun's chair: James Light.
62	"Skunk cabbage": Peggy Baird.
62	"I'll have to stop": *Cowley* (B).
63	"The ordeal of the conflagration": Dated "Sunday," probably 8/21/21.
63	Refuge in a closet: Wilbur Daniel Steele, a guest of EO the night of the storm.
64	The scene of violence: Agnes Carr.
64	"You must keep her": Dr. Daniel Hiebert.
64	"anticipate making": EO to SC, dated "Tuesday," probably 9/27/21.
64	"is to release": *Hopkins*, p. 20.
64	"should be done": Ibid., p. 32.
64	"We have heard": Ibid., p. 50.
64	"A performance that is": Ibid., p. 51.
64	"The greatest gift": Ibid., p. 55.
65	"That's all I": Ibid., p. 95.
65	"in conference": OS.
65	"hectic, nerve-wracking": EO to Edward Keefe, dated "Monday," probably 11/14/21.
66	Reluctant to meet his son: KM.
66	Eugene O'Neill, Jr.'s early years: Kathleen Pitt-Smith.
67	"peculiar. . . . They hit": *Bowen* (B), p. 136.

67   "Anna forced herself": 2/1/21. The order of the quotation has been changed.
67   "the morbid young": New York *Mail*, 11/3/21.
67   "is gradually degenerating": New York *Sun*, 11/3/21.
67   "Towers above": Burns Mantle.
67   "For sheer realism": KM, New York *Globe*, 11/3/21.
67   "not a defense": "The Mail Bag," New York *Times*, 12/18/21.
68   "to force Chris's": *Bogard*, p. 153.
68   "the very worst": 12/5/21.
68   "Sure, use your": JWK, "O'Neill's Play, Being Revived Wednesday, Was a Public Pet But He Rejected It: This May Reopen the Argument," New York *Herald Tribune*, 1/6/52.
69   "The goats are": AB.
69   O'Neill's huddle with Charles O'Brien Kennedy: Charles O'Brien Kennedy.
69   "If O'Neill writes": Charles O'Brien Kennedy.
70   Mrs. O'Neill at *The Straw* in New London: Alice Sheridan.
70   "The Brennans are": Dated "Monday," probably 11/14/21.
70   "probably write a musical": New York *American*, 11/11/21.
70   "Only that which": New York *World*, 11/20/21.

4. THE MOTHER'S END

73   "The search for": *Wilderness*.
73   "New York tough": EO to KM, 12/24/21.
73   "Steel barbwire": Carl Sandburg, *Complete Poems of Carl Sandburg*, p. 153 (New York: Harcourt Brace Jovanovich, 1970), p. 153.
74   "a symbol of man": "O'Neill Talks of His Own and the Plays of Others," New York *Herald Tribune*, 3/16/24. Reprinted in *Cargill*.
75   "write about happiness": *Mollan*.
76   "is a wonder": 2/12/22.
76   "drama of disorder": A. R. Thompson, *Anatomy of the Drama* (Berkeley: University of California Press, 1946), p. 342. Contains an excellent discussion of Expressionism in the theater.
76   "direct descendant": *Wilderness*.
76   "I personally do": "O'Neill Talks," etc., New York *Herald Tribune*, 3/16/24.
76   "unconscious autobiography": *Sergeant*, p. 97.
77   "ghastly joy": EO to KM, 1/22/22.
79   Scene at the Brevoort: Floyd Dell.
79   "It is time": *Glaspell*, p. 311.
80   "the big man": *Clark*, p. 31.
80   "That guy smeared": "Broken Nose Step to Stardom for Wolheim, Film Roughneck," Brooklyn *Eagle*, 2/22/31.
81   "That preposterous little": Alexander Woollcott, New York *Times*, 3/10/22.
81   "all the figures": "Second Thoughts," *O'Neill* (C). Reprinted in *Cargill*.
82   "No question of temperament": Date unknown, circa 2/20/22.
      "a fine type": EO to Frank W. Dart, 4/3/22.
83   Mrs. O'Neill's final days: Mrs. Drummer to a Mrs. Phillips, undated letter, circa 3/20/22.
86   Scene at Grand Central Station: Frank Wilder.
86   Central Park episode: Based on a written account by SC and an interview with DC.
87   The funeral service: AB and Frank Wilder.

88   "No, my brother": EO to Joseph A. McCarthy, 2/18/31.
88   Benchley, 3/30; Woollcott and Towse, 3/10; Pollock, 3/20; and Broun, 3/12, all 1922.
88   "of the professional": EO to RS, 10/15/33.
89   "I like to read": Alfred Batson.
89   "It seems rather": 3/10/22.
89   "O'Neill has done": *New Republic*, 11/15/22.
89   "In my opinion": *Hopkins*, p. 47.
89   "No actor we": New York *Mail*, 3/10/22.
90   "in full of your": 3/30/22.
90   "While James O'Neill": Marion Reed to Judge Arthur B. Calkins, 4/12/22.
90   "I have information": Marion Reed to Hull, McGuire & Hull, 4/15/22.
91   "They looked like": DC.
91   "Javanese or Russian": *Chase*, p. 61.
91   "always dressed rather": Ibid., pp. 61–62.
91   EO and CM's first meeting: CM.
92   "Gee, Kid, you": Eben Given.
92   "This stupidity was": New York *Herald Tribune*, 5/20/22.
93   "I seem to be": 5/25/22.

5. ECHOING STRINDBERG

96   Episode with Jones and Carlin: KM.
96   Jones's letters to Mabel Dodge: Undated, at Beinecke Library, Yale University.
97   EO's conduct the night of the ball: Eben Given and Hazel Hawthorne Werner.
97   The séance: Lucy L'Engle, who participated.
99   "violence and death": Kathleen Pitt-Smith.
99   "regular attack of August": EO to AB, 8/21/21.
99   "I can't tell": Dated "Saturday," probably 9/2/22.
99   "I've done a lot": 9/5/22.
100   "demands evolving": 9/23/22.
101   "Love is the mysterious": *Lawrence*, p. 74.
102   "I wanted you": *Boulton*, p. 68; "I want it": Ibid., p. 70.
102   "So there you are": *Lawrence*, p. 74.
102   "The central law": Ibid., p. 75.
102   "But the secondary": Ibid., p. 75.
102   "a carbon copy": Si Liberman, "She Lived with O'Neill's Genius, Tragedy," Asbury Park *Press*, 4/20/58.
103   "Who can you": 9/23/22.
103   "Here's the difference": *Young* (*B*).
104   "delightful surprise": *Merrill*.
104   "the lady was damn": EO to Grace Rippin, 4/4/30.
106   Jamie at Darien: HD and Helen DePolo and William F. Batterham.
107   "Why shouldn't my brother": William F. Batterham.
107   "most disgraceful scene": 2/17/23.
107   EO's violent behavior: AB.
107   "preliminary imperfections": EO to OS, 4/16/23.
108   "an attempt at the last": EO to Michael Gold, undated, summer 1923.
108   "too painfully bungled": "Second Thoughts," *O'Neill* (*C*).

109 "wildly demonstrative": New York *Mail*, 4/12/23.
109 "Apart from his admiration": Rudolf Kommer, "O'Neill in Europe," New York *Times*, 11/9/24. Reprinted in *Cargill*.
109 "thought they could": Ibid.
109 "The first act": Date of letter unknown, but contents printed in New York *Sun*, 11/17/24.
110 "It's wonderful": EO to FTZ, undated, spring 1923.
110 "I can't write": EO to KM, dated "Friday," apparently early summer 1923.
111 "grand pleasure": Ibid.
111 "The real Greeks": Undated.
111 "*My* Provincetown Players": Undated.
114 "*experiment in production*": Dated "Sunday," circa September 1923.
114 "the old bickering": Dated "Sunday," apparently early summer 1923.
114 "Frankly, things are": Undated.

6. LEGACY FROM JAMIE

116 "bad booze": EO to SC, 8/7/23.
116 Sheridan and Campbell's visit to the sanatorium: Both men interviewed.
117 "on the road to": Letter from Philip Sheridan to his fiancée, 10/16/23.
117 Funeral arrangements for Jamie: AB, her sister Margery, and Dorothy Day.
117 "I have lost": EO to Mary A. Clark, 5/28/24.
119 "I am a white": New London *Telegraph*, 9/13/12.
119 "God pity a poor": New London *Day*, 9/12/12.
119 "drift around the house": EO so described her to AB.
121 "roisterous time!": Hart Crane to Susan Jenkins Light, 11/13/23; John Unterecker, *Voyager: A Life of Hart Crane* (New York: Farrar, Straus & Giroux, 1969), p. 327.
121 "extraordinarily kind": *Cowley (B)*.
121 "to furnish plots": Ibid.
121 "so meagerly furnished": Ibid.
121 "the Lord's Prayer": Ibid.
121 "pipes radiating": Ibid.
121 "I can see": Ibid.
122 Crane learning of EO's suspicions: AB.
122 "I consider him": EO to Silvio A. Bedini, 12/14/41.
122 "the O'Neills rattle": *Cowley (B)*.
122 "To avoid trouble": Ibid.
123 "madly riding": EO to KM, 10/3/23.
123 "I think I've": Dated "Thursday," probably 12/7/23.
123 "full and final": Minutes of a meeting on 11/18/23 of the new Provincetown Theater group.
123 "gravestone for a pile": James Light.
124 "much ado about": New York *Sun*, 1/7/24.
124 "it is negligible": New York *Post*, 1/7/24.
124 "which Strindberg wrote": *Judge*, 2/2/24.
124 "establishing a modern": *O'Neill (A)*.
125 "Be sure and go": 1/21/24.
125 "When the word": "George Cram Cook," playbill for *The Saint* at the Provincetown Playhouse in 1924. Reprinted in *Deutsch*.
125 "one of the best": 5/26/24.
126 "steered just the right": *Deutsch*, p. 103.

Howard's play: KM told the present biographer that *They Knew What They Wanted* was never submitted to the Triumvirate for possible production, but his memory seems in error. For a different account, see *Bogard*, pp. 201–203.

126   "These people — unlike": *Clark*, p. 97.
127   "I intend to use": *Mollan.*
130   "I always have": EO to KM, 9/21/28.
131   "a house full": "Protean Artist," *Sergeant*, p. 39.
131   "The memory of": Ibid., p. 40.
131   "violent, passionate": Ibid., p. 40.
131   "The temperature": Curtis Cooksey to LS, 1/6/61.
131   "I know that Gene's": *Young (B).*
132   "The actors did": *Clark*, p. 91.

7. BESIEGED PLAYHOUSE

135   "The play requires": 2/22/24.
135   Mary Blair's joke about her obituaries: Letter to LS from Lois Jansen, Mary Blair's sister.
136   "Yesterday a persistent": 3/1/24.
137   "SECRET DRILLS": 3/17/24.
138   "base metal from": New York *World*, 4/7/24; "collaboration": New York *Sun*, 4/7/24.
138   "let the splinters": *Mollan.*
138   "Any mention of Negro": Provincetown playbill No. 4, 1923–1924.
138   "intensely harmful": *American*, 3/15/24.
138   "only harm": Ibid.
138   "an educated, high-minded": 3/11/24.
139   "Othello through his": 4/23/24.
140   "It seemed for a time": *Fifteen-Year Record of the Class of 1910 of Princeton University*. Published by the class, 1925, p. 212.
140   "a voice that": *Deutsch*, pp. 110–111.
141   The party and EO's drumming: AB, James Light, and Barney Gallant.
141   "in the face": 5/12/24.
141   "a genuine prejudice": Louis Kantor, "O'Neill Defends His Play of Negro," New York *Times*, 5/11/24.
142   "is that the woman": Carol Bird, "Eugene O'Neill — the Inner Man," *Theater*, June 1924.
142   "the tender age": New York *Times*, 5/17/24.
142   "There will be some": Hart Crane to Charlotte and Richard Rychtarik, 3/5/24.
143   "dreadful anti-climax": *Fifteen-Year Record of the Class of 1910 of Princeton University*, p. 213.
143   Reviews by Broun of the New York *World*, Mantle of the New York *News*, Hammond of the New York *Herald Tribune*, and Woollcott of the New York *Sun*, all 5/16/24.
143   "It seems the most": Gene Fowler, 5/16/24.
143   "The production, long": *Life*, 6/5/24.
144   "sensation-mongers": EO's statement to the press, 3/19/24.
144   "Ah, well, it": EO to RS, 3/11/29.
144   "heard dramatic critics": EO to RS, 3/12/29.
144   "divided into three": "A Eugene O'Neill Miscellany," New York *Sun*, 1/12/28.

144 "received more publicity": KM, New York *Times*, 8/31/24.
144 A white Jim: EO to LL, 5/8/32.
145 "It's my very": EO to OS, 7/2/24.
145 Bernard Simon at Ridgefield: Bernard Simon.
146 Felton Elkins' visit: AB.
147 Padraic and Mary Colum's visit: Padraic Colum.
147 EO's typescript of "The Reckoning" is at Houghton Library, Harvard University.
148 "No one else dares": Dated "Sunday," circa July 1924.
148 "It's the best": 8/19/24.
148 "much more adventurous": Ibid.
148 "Am working hard": Dated "Sunday," circa July 1924.
149 "Next month is": 8/19/24.
149 "Either he's there": 9/6/24.
149 "Unless I get": 9/4/24.
149 "go together in great": EO to KM, 8/19/24.
150 "cast up on our": AB to HD, 10/6/24.
150 "I've spent too": *Morning Telegraph*, 10/9/27.

8. A DRAMA OF MASKS

153 "experiment . . . repertory": A leaflet issued by the Triumvirate at the end of their 1923–1924 season.
153 "Life was a bewildering": *Deutsch*, p. 114.
154 "some of the best": EO to KM, 9/4/24.
154 "autobiographical . . . the grand opus": EO to KM, 4/27/28.
154 "It's a hell": EO to KM, 10/12/24.
155 "The individual plays": New York *Herald Tribune*, 3/16/24.
155 "as good as": 2/18/25.
156 "There have been": *Basso (A)*, 3/13/48.
156 "every detail": *Clark*, p. 117.
156 "There has never": EO to KM, dated "Monday," probably 8/23/26.
158 *Desire Under the Elms* reviews: Alan Dale, 11/14; New York *Post*, 11/12; *Time*, 11/24; Burns Mantle, New York *News*, 11/14; Heywood Broun, New York *World*, 11/12; Alexander Woollcott, New York *Sun*, 11/12; Stark Young, 11/12, all 1924.
159 "What I think": 3/26/25.
159 "has done the better": *Life*, 12/11/24.
160 Howard's letter published 12/14/24.
160 "vicious, vulgar": *Sheaffer*, p. 372.
161 "feel a true": Pierre Loving, "Eugene O'Neill," *The Bookman*, August 1921.
162 "non-smoke record": *Diary (O)*, 3/24/25.
162 "chest, 40": Ibid., 2/23/25.
162 "very interesting and applicable": Ibid., 1/22/25.
162 "This is a recurrent": Sir James Purves-Steward, "Alcohol and the Nervous System," *The Practitioner*, October 1924.
163 "one long evening": *Diary (O)*, 1/14/25.
163 Belasco "loved" the play: Ibid., 2/14/25.
163 "Weren't they swimming": *Diary (B)*, 2/8/25.
163 "very near the truth": Ibid., 5/4/25.
164 "which means that": EO to a Mr. Perlman, 2/5/25.
164 "coming out all": *Diary (O)*, 2/4/25.
164 "a wild cable": Ibid., 2/21/25.

165   "to shock the theatergoing": New York *Times*, 2/20/25.
165   "a theatrical suicide": New York *Times*, 2/14/25.
165   "irreclaimably vicious": New York *Times*, 2/17/25.
165   "worse . . . advertise": Ibid.
165   "too thoroughly bad": 2/21/25.
166   "God bless Gene!": EO, in 3/1/25 letter to KM, repeats what KM had written previously.
166   "the low-minded": EO to JOL, 3/28/25.
166   "culminating in a": Burns Mantle, ed., *The Best Plays of 1924–1925* (Boston: Small, Maynard, 1925), p. 6.
166   "comical . . . guiltless": New York *Times*, 3/14/25.
166   "range of worry": *Diary (O)*, 3/1/25.
167   "so damn complicated": Ibid., 2/19/25.
167   "in tears": Ibid., 3/22/25.
167   "For what, at bottom": "Memoranda on Masks," *O'Neill (C)*.
167   EO's "explanatory" article on *The Great God Brown* appeared in several New York papers on 2/13/26 and 2/14/26. Reprinted in *Clark*, pp. 104–106, and *Quinn*, II, pp. 192–194.
168   "In one sense": *Clark*, p. 106.
169   "I want to be": EO to Professor George Pierce Baker, 7/16/14.
170   "I feel the impulse": Letter dated "Friday night," envelope postmarked 2/5/15. EO's letters to Beatrice Ashe are in the Berg Collection of the New York Public Library.
170   "I had a frightful": 8/4/20.
171   "What moved us": *New Republic*, 2/10/26.
171   "I still consider": Whit Burnett, ed., *This is My Best* (New York: Dial, 1942), p. 738.
172   "Of all the plays": *Basso (A)*, 3/6/48.

9. DION ANTHONY'S COURSE

173   "very intriguing looking": *Diary (O)*, 2/18/25.
174   "very interesting": Ibid., 3/10/25.
174   "interesting but dully": Ibid., 1/21/25.
174   "Playwrights are either": EO to Mr. Perlman, 2/5/25.
174   "The Freudian brethren": EO to Dr. William J. Maloney, 2/18/25.
174   "wonderful stuff": *Diary (O)*, 2/4/25.
174   "most stimulating book": Ibid., 3/25/25.
174   "immersed in a book": *Hansford*.
176   "I wish we": 3/14/25.
176   "grand stuff": Undated, circa April 1925.
176   "But the man?": 3/14/25.
176   "Your Hamlet": Undated, circa December 1923.
176   "Am taking liberty": 7/6/25.
177   "old, married, child-bearing": *Diary (B)*, 2/12/25.
177   "a play with a jinx": EO to GJN, 3/26/25.
177   "three drinks": *Diary (B)*, 5/4/25.
177   "raved bitterly": Ibid., 5/9/25.
178   "How many we": 5/3/25.
179   "the only very little": *Diary (B)*, 5/16/25.
179   "liked the sound": OOC to LS, 2/18/73.
179   "It's a goil": 5/14/25.
179   "dog fleas": *Diary (B)*, 5/17/25.

179   "something 'important' ": Ibid., 5/18/25.
180   "much impressed": *Diary (O)*, 6/6/25.
180   "too primitive": AB to HD, 6/18/25.
180   "it might make": *Gelb*, p. 595.
181   "the Old Master": EO to AB, dated "Wednesday," probably 7/18/25.
181   "I'm damn lonely": Ibid.
181   "the morose, silent": *Merrill*.
182   "I must have": Undated, circa 7/27/25.
183   "not inspiring": *Diary (O)*, 7/27/25.
183   "Not for mine": Ibid.
183   "get interested": EO to KM, undated, circa late August 1925.
183   Edward Keefe episode: Edward Keefe.
184   "enormously excited": EO to KM, 9/28/25.
184   "much prefer": Ibid.
184   "faith in theaters": Undated, circa September 1925. See *O'Neill (B)*.
185   "Decay & ruin": *Diary (O)*, 10/5/25.
185   "debauch with": 4/9/27.
186   "I'd been playing": Leona Hogarth to LS, 12/23/60.
187   "disgusted": 11/24/25; "bust": 11/23/25, both *Diary (O)*.
187   "Ridgefield is no": Ibid., 12/9/25.
187   "I liked him": Cecil Boulton.
187   "how bad they": *Diary (O)*, 12/11/25.
187   "bit corned up": Ibid., 12/23/25.
187   "must get in shape": Ibid., 12/30/25.

10. O'NEILL'S REFORMATION

188   "Kenneth has made": 12/27/25.
188   "in a measure" and "almost from the day": *Hamilton (A)*, p. vi.
189   "interrelated, nearly": Stella Bloch Hanau.
189   "erotic self-love" and "emotional upset": *Hamilton (A)*, p. 18.
189   "studies [of sex]": Dust jacket of *Hamilton (A)* when reprinted at an unspecified later date by Medical Research Press, New York.
189   "drug habit": Ibid., p. 240.
190   "At early childhood": See diagram in *Sheaffer*, p. 506.
191   "feels he has": *Clark*, p. 4.
192   "when all is said": Ibid., pp. 7–8.
192   "like a ship": Anne Shoemaker.
192   "there was so": Leona Hogarth to LS, 12/23/60.
193   Vreeland and Watts reviews: 1/25/26.
193   Gabriel and Atkinson reviews: 1/25/26.
194   "cramp the actors": New York *World*, 1/25/26.
194   "Coming on and off": *New Republic*, 2/10/26.
194   "only get across": EO to KM, 8/23/26.
194   "we had neither": EO to BD, 6/22/27.
194   "There was some": "Memoranda on Masks," *O'Neill (C)*.
195   "You simply must": 3/12/26.
195   "*Lazarus* is going," 3/12/26, and "*Lazarus* is coming," 3/25/26.
197   "I'm going in": 3/22/26.
197   "no stage except": Boston *Transcript*, 4/21/26.
199   "staked all the members": EO to KM, 4/27/28.
199   "Dreiser had written": SC's affidavit at the *Strange Interlude* plagiarism trial in 1931.

201   "is the root": *Quinn*, pp. 252–253.
202   "I mean the one": "Dramatist's Notebook," *O'Neill (C)*.
202   "It would be": Undated, circa late December 1926.
202   "He's the only": 9/11/27.
202   Mumford, New York *Herald Tribune*, 11/20/27, and Aiken, New York *Post*, 12/24/27.
203   "It is as a pageant": George C. Warren, San Francisco *Chronicle*, 4/10/28.
203   Atkinson, New York *Times*, and Watts, New York *Post*, both 4/9/48.
203   "just a shell": EO to Grace and Jessica Rippin, 8/18/26.

11. ACTRESS IN MAINE

206   "Why doesn't Gene": MK.
207   Foreword to *White Buildings:* John Unterecker, *Voyager: A Life of Hart Crane* (New York: Farrar, Straus & Giroux, 1969), p. 408.
207   "wasn't qualified": 8/21/26.
208   "should recognize": *Kinne*, p. 258.
208   "Coming from Yale": Ibid., 258.
208   "it meant so": EO to SC, 2/24/43.
209   "the epitome": HD, who saw O'Neill shortly after the Yale commencement.
209   "a tremendous ovation": New Haven *Journal-Courier*, 6/24/26.
209   "To my surprise": EO to Harold McGee, 7/10/26.
209   "a torture, not": EO to SC, 2/24/43.
210   "as colorful a scene": New York *Times*, 6/26/26.
210   "a long, heartbreaking": Ibid.
210   "very slowly and reminiscently": EO to Grace and Jessica Rippin, 8/18/26.
210   "atrocities": Ibid.
211   "so dashing and handsome": Barbara Burton to LS.
211   "I found him": Frank Meyer.
212   "aren't the sea": EO to Isaac Goldberg, 7/7/26.
213   "the best thing": Dated "Sunday," probably 10/10/26.
213   "has ever walked": *Sergeant*, pp. 81–82.
213   "When O'Neill steps": Ibid., p. 104.
214   "this Actors' combine": 8/7/26.
214   "three hellish seasons": 8/12/26.
215   "What's the use": Dated "Monday," probably 8/23/26.
215   "could do with more": 8/7/26.
216   "One might trace": *Sergeant*, p. 83.
217   "to be all sufficient": OOC to LS, 3/4/70.
217   "an incredible stew," p. 59; "life together," p. 61; and "used to love," p. 62, all *Chase*.
218   CM's background: From interviewing her; CCS and ROS, her daughter and son-in-law; Frank and Ceil Shay and LaVeda Shaffer, her cousins; Melvin Chapman, her second husband; and MC, a schoolmate and subsequent intimate.
221   "Hazel always made": Mrs. Maynard W. Butler.
221   "You know, I always": *Hill Crest*, St. Gertrude's school magazine, 6/15/07.
221   "Miss California" contest: San Francisco *Call*, 5/5/07 and 6/2/07.
222   "I would rather": "Life on the Road," *Green Book*, November 1916.
223   "philanthropies were": New York *Herald Tribune*, 11/1/41.
223   "made to order": *Chase*, p. 61.
223   "he had 8,000 books": Frederick L. R. Confer.
229   Miss Marbury wanted to adopt CM: CCS.

229   "friends to talk": EO to KM, 8/7/26.
229   "absolutely the most": Florence Reed.
231   "a damn fine": 8/26/26.

The audience in Ralph Barton's between-the-acts curtain for the *Chauve-Souris:*

First row, left to right: David Belasco, Lenore Ulric, John Barrymore, Michael Strange (Mrs. Barrymore)

Lower right box: Lucrezia Bori, Madame Alda, Feodor Chaliapin

Second row: Theodore Roosevelt, Jr., Marie Jeritza, Gatti-Casazza, Geraldine Farrar, Mary Garden

Third: Conde Nast, Irene Castle, Frank Crowninshield, Mrs. H. Payne Whitney, Kenneth Macgowan, Alan Dale, Ray Long

Fourth: Alexander Woollcott, Mrs. Lydig Hoyt, Franklin P. Adams, Neysa McMein, Heywood Broun, Doris Keane, Percy Hammond

Fifth: Walter Catlett, Sophie Braslau, Dorothy Gish, D. W. Griffith, Lillian Gish, Elizabeth Marbury, Leon Errol, Zoe Akins

Sixth: Adolph Zukor, Robert G. Welsh, Fay Bainter, Lawrence Reamer, Gertrude Hoffman, Walter Damrosch, Mary Nash, Wilhelm Mengelberg, Charles Darnton, Otto H. Kahn, Frank A. Munsey, Flo Ziegfeld, Arturo Bodanzky, Adolph Ochs, John Rumsey

Seventh: Ludwig Lewisohn, George S. Kaufman, Lynn Fontanne, Marc Connelly, George M. Cohan, John MacMahon, Henry Krehbiel, Mrs. Enrico Caruso, Jacob Ben-Ami, Dorothy Dalton, David Warfield, Robert Benchley

Eighth: Karl Kitchen, Antonio Scotti, Fanny Hurst, Hugo Riesenfeld, Vera Fokina, Michel Fokine, Avery Hopwood, Constance Talmadge, Anna Fitziu, Reginald Vanderbilt, Dr. Frank Crane, Jascha Heifetz

Upper left box: Maude Adams, John McCormack, Charlie Chaplin, Marshall Joffre

Upper right box: Laurette Taylor, Frances Starr, Clare Sheridan, Hartley Manners

Ninth row: Eugene O'Neill, Professor Roerich, Joseph Urban, Arthur Hornblow, Jr., Paul Meyer, Elsie Janis, Paul Bloch, John Farrar, Sergei Rachmaninoff, Herbert Hoover, John Golden, Winchell Smith, Jay Gould

Rear, standing room only: A. D. Lasker, Samuel L. ("Roxy") Rothafel, Nicholas Murray Butler, Ralph Barton, Jesse Lasky, Edward Ziegler, William Guard, Louis Untermeyer, J. J. Shubert, Lee Shubert, F. Ray Comstock, Morris Gest, Oliver Sayler, Boris Anisfeld, Robert Edmond Jones, Ring Lardner, Stephen Rathbun, Armand Vecszy, Andreas De Segurola, Papi, Raymond Hitchcock

12. STRANGE INTERLUDE

232   "Old Doc. O'Neill": Dated "Friday," probably 10/8/26.
233   "troubles" and "rows": EO to AB, 10/15/26.
233   "only chance": AB to HD, circa 10/16/26.
233   "mighty uncertain": EO to CM, 12/1/26.
233   "He came up": CM's remarks are a mixture of *Peck* (B) and LS interview with her.
234   "wonderful days": EO to AB, 9/8/27.
235   "rolling now": From a draft of the letter, undated, probably 11/28/26.
236   "play solitaire": EO to KM, 8/7/26.
236   "The two days": From a draft of the letter, undated, probably 12/1/26.

236	"There are some": Ibid.
236	"I think of you": Undated, circa 12/20/26.
237	"I'm not what": Dated "Thursday," probably 12/2/26.
237	"shot into the sky": EO to CM, 12/1/26.
237	"playing Carlotta": Hubertine Zahorska.
238	"a wonder when": EO to KM, 12/30/26.
238	"a hell of an overcrowded": Ibid.
238	"How Gene works": AB to her mother, 2/6/27.
238	"deep . . . groaning": EO to KM, 1/12/27.
239	"wedding the theme": "A Letter from O'Neill," New York *Times*, 4/11/20.
239	"heard from an aviator": EO's affidavit in the *Strange Interlude* plagiarism suit in 1931.
240	"if women were": George Bernard Shaw, *Selected Plays of Bernard Shaw* (New York: Dodd, Mead, 1952, III, p. 497.
240	"that's the devilish": Ibid., p. 537.
242	"I like 'Marsden' ": EO to JWK, 7/15/27.
244	"the most golden": John Davies: *The Legend of Hobey Baker* (Boston: Little, Brown, 1966), p. xv.
244	"indisputably the best": Rex Lardner, New York *Times*, 9/11/66.
244	"an ideal worthy": "The Romantic Egotist" (the original draft of the novel that became *This Side of Paradise*), chap. 2, p. 20.
244	"no conscious use": EO to Martha C. Sparrow, 10/13/29.
245	"an exception among": New York *Post*, 1/30/29.
247	"It was as if": *Bowen* (*B*), p. 170.
247	"They did not recognize": Ibid., pp. 170–171.
249	"the family *en masse*": 4/1/27.
249	"to keep the theme": 4/4/27.
249	"probably the bravest": *Nadel*, p. 89.
251	"impressed — but didn't": AB to EO, undated, circa 4/20/27.
251	"bad financial": Ibid.
252	"only a first cutting": EO to TH, undated, circa 5/17/27.
252	"arrogantly critical": *Zolotow*, p. 205.
252	"a difficult ordeal" and "fought family quarrels": *Brown*, p. 270.
253	"a lone eagle": *Helburn* (*A*).
253	"The Provincetown did": Robert Rockmore.
253	"For the sake": James Light.
253	"It's just like turning": *Langner*, p. 235.
253	"wildly excited": Lawrence Langner, *G.B.S. and the Lunatic* (New York: Atheneum, 1963), p. 4.
253	"a fantee Shakespeare": St. John Ervine, "Is Eugene O'Neill's Power in Decline?" *Theater*, May 1926.
253	"He'll probably never": *G.B.S. and the Lunatic*, p. 5.
253	"to see in him": *Krutch*, p. xiv.
254	"somewhat naughty": JWK to LS, 5/2/59.

13. O'NEILL'S "VULTURES"

255	"You get so": EO to KM, 8/7/27.
256	"should certainly be": 7/15/27.
256	"almost awed me": *Popular Biography*, April 1930, pp. 31–38.
256	"Your long letter": 6/22/27.
256	"get the affirmative": 6/3/27.
256	"found something": 6/22/27.

257   "a slow mover": *Hansford.*
258   "Everything seems so": Dated "Sunday," apparently 8/28/27.
260   "very sad": Dated "Sunday," apparently 9/4/27.
261   "great fatigue": Dr. Alvan Barach.
261   "has given it": EO to AB, 9/15/27.
261   "the exact opposite": EO to AB, 9/8–9/27.
261   "beautiful" and "a face": Lillian Gish.
261   "it would wreck": EO to AB, 10/4/27.
261   "rotten about everything": 9/8–9/27.
261   "The place is": Undated, circa 9/4/27.
262   "Please do anything": Undated, circa 9/9/27.
262   "prize fisherman": Undated, circa 9/10/27.
263   "is the thing": Undated, circa 9/16/27.
265   "years, rather than": Undated, circa 9/22/27.
265   "I felt that": Undated, circa 9/28/27.
267   "do a better": Seattle *Times,* 11/12/36.
267   "a grand time": 9/23; "a fine show": 10/7; and "the lousiest musical": 10/4, all 1927, EO to AB.
268   "taken all over": EO to AB, 10/4/27.
268   "there can be": 7/15/27.
269   "there is absolutely": 7/25/27.
269   "No one thought": Dated "Thursday," probably 9/29/27.
269   "a one-woman man": Nina Moise, who discussed EO with Dr. Hamilton.
269   "Sure! *You* get me": *O'Neill (E).*

14. END OF A MARRIAGE

271   "the event of": *Zolotow,* p. 155.
271   "tango lovers": GCT to EO, 3/10/20.
271   "remarkable" and "will give": Dated "Sunday," probably 11/27/27.
272   "a long boring": EO to AB, dated "Friday," probably 12/2/27.
272   "Oh, I wouldn't": Robert Sisk.
273   "Bayreuth fashion": EO to Katharine Cornell, 7/25/27.
273   "like hell": EO to AB, dated "Tuesday," probably 12/15/27.
274   "strangely and deliberately": Theresa Helburn, "Staged by Philip Moeller," *Theater Guild,* May 1929.
274   "We used to say": *Helburn (B),* p. 185.
274   "special zone": Philip Moeller, "Silences Out Loud," New York *Times,* 2/26/28. Moeller's remarks continue in the following two paragraphs.
275   "I thought she": *Zolotow,* p. 155.
275   "I respect authors": Combination of *Zolotow,* pp. 156–157, and LS interview with Lynn Fontanne.
275   EO's visits to Ben and Bio De Casseres: Bio De Casseres.
276   "*must* go. I was": Dated "Sunday," probably 11/27/27.
277   "a loss of": Dated "Friday," probably 12/2/27.
277   "*Don't forget*": Dated "Friday," probably 12/16/27.
278   "Dearest Aggie": Dated "Tuesday," probably 12/20/27.
279   "loved someone else": Dated "Monday," probably 12/26/27.
280   "You have been": 4/29/27.
280   "If I were sure": 12/30/27.
280   EO and CM's estrangement: AB and James and Patti Light.
280   *Marco Millions* reviews: all 1/10/28.
283   "one of the most beautiful": *Zolotow,* p. 155.

284   "a bitter feeling": EO to AB, dated "Monday eve.," probably 12/26/27.
284   "I hope you": Dated "Thursday," probably 1/19/28.
284   "Have you started": Dated "Monday night," probably 1/23/28.
284   "It hurts me": Dated "Tuesday," a postscript to 1/23/28 letter.
285   "it was rumored": EO to AB, dated "Tuesday," probably 1/31/28.
285   "a play in nine": *Zolotow*, p. 157.
286   "six-day bisexual": Ibid., p. 155.
286   "This is like giving": Glenn Anders.
286   "however minutely": Louis V. De Foe, New York *World*, 2/7/20.
286   "an audience goes": Anonymous reviewer, New York *Sun*, 2/8/20.
286   "No play of recent": *Nation*, 2/15/28.
287   "registered tiredness": Dudley Nichols, New York *World*, 1/31/28.
287   "Eugene's opening": 2/5/28. For smoother reading, the punctuation has been revised. Demuth's letter is at Beinecke Library, Yale University.
287   *Strange Interlude* reviews: All appeared on January 31, 1928, except Atkinson's weekend article and Pollock's, both February 5.
289   "extremely proud": EO to AB, dated "Tuesday," probably 1/31/28.
289   "as soon as spring": EO to AB, dated "Friday," probably 2/3/28.
289   "to hang on": Ibid.
289   "Naturally, I can't": Ibid.
289   "a triumph. The trouble": Dated "Tuesday," probably 2/7/28.
290   "not be kind": Ibid.
290   "It is only": Dated "Friday," probably 2/3/28.
290   "I will often": Undated, circa 2/5/28.

15. O'NEILL AND CARLOTTA

293   "a notorious Yank": EO to KM, 2/22/28.
293   "the most beautiful": EO to KM, undated, circa March 1928.
294   "first vacation away": EO to KM, 2/27/28.
294   "a crazy American": EO to SO, circa 3/14/28.
294   "somewhere in France": EO to RS, 4/10/28.
294   "starving in": EO to AB, 3/10/28.
294   "wonderfully kind": EO to KM, undated, circa March 1928.
294   "I am deeply": Circa 2/20/28.
294   "I am as happy": Undated, circa April 1928.
295   "absolutely in the dark": Undated, circa 3/2/28.
295   "pretty hopeless": Undated, circa 3/15/28.
295   "must have heard": Undated, circa April 1928.
296   "Just now I": Undated, circa March 1928.
296   "I miss him": Undated, circa April 1928.
297   "as far as Snail": Undated, circa March 1928.
297   "always have a home": Undated, circa February 1928.
297   "almost made [him] cry": EO to AB, undated, circa April 1928.
297   "the boys sniff": Undated, probably mid-April 1928.
298   "a simple divorce": Undated.
299   "Splitting fifty-fifty": Undated, circa 3/8/28.
299   "eventually starve": 4/27/28.
299   "the grinding, thankless": EO to AB, undated, circa April 1928.
299   "as near to final": EO to TH, undated, circa 3/25/28.
299   "mess" and "creative": EO to TH, 4/8/28.
299   "That trends on": Ibid.
299   "The first part": Undated, circa 3/25/28.

| 299 | "to stir up": EO to TH, 7/13/28. |

299 "to stir up": EO to TH, 7/13/28.
301 "An inebriate": Foreword to *Anathema! Litanies of Negation* (New York: Gotham Book Mart, 1928).
301 "hot" and "smoked out": EO to BD, 4/25/28.
301 "A bit lonely": EO to HD, undated, circa April 1928.
301 "more in love": 4/27/28.
302 "very enervating": EO to TH, 7/13/28.
303 "No writer who": New York *Post*, 8/1/58.
303 "the circumstances . . . would": Undated, circa 7/2/28.
304 "hated to leave": EO to TH, 7/13/28.
305 "I'm damned happy": 8/13/28.
305 "if it is *rotten*": 9/5/28.
305 "damn good": EO to KM, 9/21/28.
306 "all mapped out": 9/16/28.
306 "a trilogy analyzing": OS, "The Real Eugene O'Neill," *Century*, January 1922.
306 "a grand book": EO to SO, 1/18/40.
307 "a symbol of infinity": Henry Adams, *The Education of Henry Adams* (New York: Modern Library, undated, p. 380.
307 "And the engines croon": *Sanborn*, p. 153.
308 "intensely dramatic": EO to TH, 4/8/28.
308 "may be concerned": *New Republic*, 2/27/29.
309 "Here's someone who": DC.
310 "the grand opus": 4/27/28.
310 "grateful" and "making it": EO to RM, 9/14/28.
311 "infinitely valuable": EO to JOL, 10/2/28.
311 "Enough of the old": EO to KM, 4/27/28.
311 "I feel ten": EO to BD, 9/16/28.
311 "It looks to me": Undated, circa September 1928.
311 "used to have": Undated, circa September 1928.
312 "a drastic type": EO to RM, 9/14/28.
312 "I had worried": 10/7/28.

16. THIRD MARRIAGE

313 "a poor uninteresting": EO to SC, undated, circa 10/28/28.
313 "everything happens": Nöel Barber, "Saigon," *Holiday*, February 1953.
313 "bucked the wheel": EO to HD, 5/11/29.
314 "damp and enervating": EO to SC, undated, circa November 1928.
314 "Do me a favor": Alfred Batson.
315 "I am a wanderer": Friedrich Nietzsche, *Thus Spake Zarathustra* (New York: Modern Library), p. 161.
315 "What're you doing?": CM.
315 "I took a poke": Alfred Batson.
315 "The dear Britons": EO to HL, 2/17/29.
316 "never forget my": EO to JWK, 7/27/29.
317 CM and the Renners: Dr. and Mrs. Renner.
317 "And God bless": *O'Neill (E)*, December 1928.
319 "a good background": 12/19/28.
319 "Feel well now": *Langner*, p. 240.
319 F. Theo Rogers interviewed in Manila in 1963 by Mrs. Virginia Capotosto for this book.
320 "would hold on": Eileen Curran Herron.

321 "nicknamed Queen Mary": George Wiley to LS, 9/27/61.
321 "Carlotta's criticisms": George Wiley to LS, 11/26/61.
322 "Their reunion": George Stedman to LS, 9/26/61.
322 "How is *Dynamo*": 1/23/29.
322 "To make matters": 5/11/29.
322 "wouldn't have missed": Undated, circa February 1929.
323 "perfidious frau": EO to HD, 5/11/29.
324 "I remember it": *Helburn (B)*, p. 261.
324 *Dynamo* reviews: Gabriel and Lockridge, 2/12/29; Ervine, 2/13/29.
324 "The critic boys": EO to JOL, 3/16/29.
325 "have scored a failure": 5/10/29.
325 "no criticism, either": EO to RS, 3/16/29.
325 "all hot after": EO to JOL, 3/16/29.
325 "this play has": EO to BD, 3/12/29.
325 "got completely lost": EO to SC, circa 3/15/29.
325 "I let it out": 3/12/29.
325 "Gene has always": AB to Frank B. Elser, 4/29/29.
326 "was written at a time": 5/13/29.
326 "damn good play": 6/14/29.
326 "I like it better": 7/27/29.
326 "It was really": EO to GJN, 2/14/29.
326 "riff-raff reporters": CM to SC, 1/30/29.
327 "Carlotta and I": New York *Herald Tribune*, 3/8/29.
328 "drowned in despair": *O'Neill (E)*, spring 1929.
329 "he sees about five": 8/24/29.
329 "I was damn": 5/13/29.
329 "My Mother writes": 3/8/29.
330 "chi-chi, putting on": *Peck (B)*.
330 "All sorts of grand": 6/20/29.
330 "quite pleased": Ibid.
331 "sometimes I want": Undated, circa February 1929.
331 "I wanna go": Cecil Boulton.
331 "a quiet, self-sufficient": Pamela Bianco.
332 "waited too long": CM to SC, 7/13/29.
332 "felt it meant": *Langner*, p. 276.
332 "the first time": CM.
334 "Flamboyant descriptions": "The Talk of the Town," *New Yorker*, 9/28/29.
334 "Gene's friends are": Undated, circa 11/14/29.
335 "a privilege to live": *Peck (A)*.
335 "Gene loved me": CM.

17. AT THE CHÂTEAU

336 "Is it possible": *Diary (M)*, spring 1926.
336 "ancient drama moving": New York *Times*, 10/11/26.
336 "There's a re-creation": Undated, circa November 1926. She probably read HD's *Palimpsest* (Boston: Houghton Mifflin, 1926).
336 "has greater possibilities": EO to RS, 8/28/30.
336 "the most interesting": Ibid.
337 "taken" and "demanded": EO to JOL, 3/16/29.
337 "modern psychological": *Diary (M)*, April 1929. This diary is the source of the other quotations in this paragraph and in the following two.
338 "it befits — it": Ibid., May 1929.

338 "I blundered horribly": *Langner*, p. 241.
339 "possibilities" and "have to": EO to JWK, 7/27/29.
339 "Too much! At least": EO to SY, 5/8/29.
339 "quite separate": Undated, circa late March 1929.
339 "to be published": 5/13/29.
339 "a ballyhooed freak": EO to SY, 6/20/29.
340 "The world of literature": Brooklyn *Eagle*.
340 The plagiarism suit was extensively reported in the press on May 27, 28 and 29, 1929.
341 "one hundred love sonnets": New York *Herald Tribune*, 5/28/29.
341 "never even heard": Cable to Harry Weinberger, reported in press, 5/28/29.
341 "farcical" and "boiled with rage": EO to BHC, 6/21/29.
341 "the damndest piece": EO to GJN, 8/31/29.
341 "literary burglary": 6/15/29.
341 "a plea for the murder": *Helburn (B)*, p. 234.
342 "even bothered": EO to JOL, 6/22/29.
342 "without comment": EO to a Mr. Emerson, 10/20/33.
342 "there is always": 4/29/30.
342 "moving, settling": *Langner*, p. 275.
343 "Yankee Electra": *Diary (M)*, August 1929.
343 "a *charming* & *lovable*": CM to SC, 8/30/29.
343 "a boyish quality": *Nathan*, pp. 30–31.
343 "the hardest worker": "O'Neill," *Vanity Fair*, October 1933.
344 "The St. James Infirmary": 9/30/29.
345 "I am proud": 8/31/29.
348 "I taught him how": A combination of *Peck (A)* and LS interview.
348 "if the house": *Peck (A)*.
349 "O'Neill never does": *Sergeant*, p. 85.
349 "the fastest roadster": 12/5/29.
349 "He had a marvelous": *Peck (A)*.
349 "a comfort to [us]": *O'Neill (D)*.
350 "Isn't there some": EO to RM, 5/10/29.
350 "there must be": Undated, circa October 1929.
351 "a public speech": *Langner*, p. 277.
351 "The critics yowled": 11/23/29.
351 "so mad at our": Ibid.
351 "a deep anxiety": 12/5/29.
351 "No, No, No": EO to RS, 5/11/29.
351 "wonderful possibilities": EO to Ralph Block, 6/10/21.
352 "with a magnanimity": 3/4/28.
352 "to build up": EO to RS, 3/21/35.
353 "the picture medium": *Helburn (B)*, pp. 276–277.
353 "blazed the following": Ralph Sanborn to EO, undated, circa May 1930.
353 "didn't have [shares]": *Crichton (B)*, p. 126.

18. MOURNING BECOMES ELECTRA

354 "terribly messed up": EO to GJN, 11/12/29.
354 "the new play": CM to TH, 12/18/29.
354 "No, I'm not": EO to SC, 12/5/29.
355 "a modified, simplified": EO to GJN, 11/12/29.
355 "involved inhibited": EO to GJN, 1/7/30.
355 "I've never had": 2/19/30.

355   "Gene didn't care": Combination of *Peck* (*A*) and LS interview.
356   "Develop South Sea": *Diary* (*M*), 3/27/30. Also the source of the quotations in the following paragraph.
357   "one of the world's": EO to Madeleine Boyd, 5/19/30.
357   "damned interesting": EO to SC, undated, circa 6/6/30.
357   "one of amazement": His letter was published in the New York *Herald Tribune* 6/2/30. Reprinted in *Cargill.*
359   "manageress and entertainer": CM to SC, 7/27/30.
360   "Did you see": 6/9/30.
360   "gentleness" and "No one": New York *Herald Tribune*, 6/8/30.
360   "the hero of the occasion": New York *Post*, 12/8/57.
360   "never worked so": *Diary* (*M*), 7/11/30.
360   "much better": Ibid., 7/18/30.
361   "driving insistent": Ibid., 7/19/30.
361   "they will have": 8/23/30.
362   "The news of the baby": 11/17/30.
362   Agnes "disturbed": As indicated in a letter to HD, 9/11/30.
362   "held up [the] plays": *Diary* (*M*), 9/20/30.
363   "visual symbol": Ibid., 9/21/30. This letter is also the source of the quotations in the following paragraph.
363   "in this neck": Undated, circa 11/5/30.
363   "an old Catholic": EO to BD, 12/5/30.
363   "I don't envy": 12/1/30. In *Nathan*, p. 36, the critic makes the letter seem part of a conversation he had with EO.
364   "just as glad": Mark Schorer, *Sinclair Lewis* (New York: McGraw-Hill, 1961), p. 550.
364   "has done nothing": New York *Times*, 12/13/30.
364   "Don't ask me": 12/5/30.
364   "any answer to anything": EO to Frank Shay, 10/3/30.
364   "felt a deep sense": EO to GJN, 8/26/28.
364   "a feeling of not": EO to GJN, 2/2/31.
365   "The French think": Ilka Chase.
365   "memory of the interminable": Dedication, written 4/23/31, in the published *Mourning Becomes Electra* (Liveright: New York, 1931). Facsimile of handwritten original in *O'Neill* (*E*).
366   "a very, very beautiful": EO to RS, 2/18/40.
366   "damned good": *Diary* (*M*), 3/8/31.
366   "Five minutes": 4/7/31.
367   "She never wrote": New York *Sun*, 3/12/31.
367   "Handsome American": The résumé is quoted in Judge Woolsey's decision, released on 4/22/31.
367   "pandered to": New York *Herald Tribune*, 5/28/29.
368   "whatever else I": the New York *Sun*, 3/13/31.
368   "not so well": New York *Herald Tribune*, 3/17/31. Also the source of the Nathan-Cohalan exchange in the following paragraph.
369   "He told me": the New York *Sun*, 3/16/31.
369   "a very stubborn": Brooklyn *Eagle*, 3/16/31.
369   "too cowardly": New York *Times*, 3/17/31.
369   Judge Woolsey's decision: Reported by the press on 4/22 and 4/23/31.
369   "get to work": New York *Times*, 9/8/32.
369   "the damn thing": EO to SC, 1/24/31.
370   "It has been": 4/7/31. Reprinted in *Nathan*, pp. 28–29.
370   "as worthy as": *Quinn*, II, p. 258.

19. HOMECOMING

373	Barton's "OBIT" was extensively printed in the press on 5/21/31.
375	"He was pallid": John Chapman, "The Seven Haunted O'Neills," New York *News*, 12/16/56.
375	"gradually but constantly": "Exile Made Him Appreciate U.S., O'Neill Admits," New York *Herald Tribune*, 5/22/31.
376	"As far as": the New York *News*, 5/22/31.
376	Heidt suggests the roof: Joe Heidt.
377	New London visit: *Peck (A)*.
378	"I think I": 8/10/31.
378	"I don't know how": Lillian Gish.
378	"Yes, it's a Cadillac!": 8/16/31.
380	*Strange Interlude*'s success as a book: *Gilmer*, p. 263, n. 21.
380	"to make this venture": Undated, circa January 1931.
380	Blanche Patch's reply: 2/5/31. Those of Mann, Lewis and Taïrov, undated.
380	Sean O'Casey's reply: 2/10/31.
381	"After prolonged work": 8/16/31.
382	"read too damn": 6/6/31.
383	"She would be": 4/28/31.
383	"I won't step": Thomas Chalmers.
383	"sure to be tied": EO to TH, undated, circa August 1931.
384	"I used to sit": *Peck (A)*.
384	"Few people realize": *Woolf (B)*.
384	"My heart was": Alexander Kirkland, "The Woman from Yalta," *Theater Arts*, December 1949.
384	"a good scout": EO to AB, 11/27/27.
385	"For the first couple": *Sifton*.
385	"Just a minute": Arthur Hughes of the cast.
386	"a furtive sadness": *Woolf (A)*.
387	"Like Ezra Mannon": Undated, probably 10/26/31.
387	"I was nearly": *Gelb*, p. 751.
387	"The most frightening": *Sifton*.
387	"In the moment": *Theater Arts*, January 1932.
387	"Alice is all": *Sifton*.
387	All the 1931 *Electra* reviews quoted here appeared on 10/27 except "brings the cold": Atkinson, 11/1; Benchley, 11/7; and Krutch, 11/18.
390	"despite the grandeur": Sunday *Observer*, 6/12/55.
390	"Why does Mr. O'Neill": 4/24/32.
391	Shane and Oona's meeting with EO: OOC to LS, 8/28/69. Also the source of the quotations in the following paragraph.
392	"We really can't": 1/2/32 and "social life": 1/23/32.
392	"To Ilka, who": *Chase*, p. 24.

20. AT SEA ISLAND

393	"Bought Spanish": Undated, circa 12/24/31.
393	"the idiotic notion": EO to BHC, 6/6/32.
393	"Gene was lying": George L. Fogle, stage manager for *Ah, Wilderness!*
393	Account of the reunion: CCS.
394	"were not yet ripe": EO to RS, 2/24/32.
394	"O'Neill, the sphinx": 1/24; Usually a child": 1/25; "I learned at": 1/24; "I

was a bum": 1/26; "What's beyond": 1/24; "not to take": 1/27; and "just thought I": 1/27, all *Pasley.*

395 "I want to hear": 11/23/31.

396 "Have you one": EO to Katherine M. Black, 6/21/31.

396 "the two outstanding": New York *Times*, 3/17/32.

397 "a religious feeling": Francis Louis Abreu, the architect for Casa Genotta.

397 "too much like": CM.

397 "In her eyes' ": *O'Neill (E)*, 4/28/32.

398 "a wary eye": CM to CVV, 9/10/42.

398 "Mistress" and "Wife": *O'Neill (E)*, 5/25/32.

398 "He is a dyed-in": EO to Frank B. Elser, 1/13/33.

400 "learned to respect": 5/16/32.

400 "Tell him all": Undated, circa July 1932.

401 "My God, a theatrical": Alfred W. Jones, chairman of the board of the Sea Island Company.

401 "go on oiled": CM to GB, 4/18/32.

401 "was quiet and exquisitely": *Chase*, pp. 62–63.

401 "That's so we": *Langner*, p. 281.

402 "until my personal": 3/16/29.

402 "I was so happy": Undated.

402 "It has the right": 6/6/32.

403 "I am too enthusiastic": EO to GJN, 8/6/32.

403 "thousands of them": New York *Herald Tribune*, 5/22/31.

403 "One's outer life": "Memoranda on Masks," *O'Neill (C).*

404 "nonrealistic imaginative": "A Dramatist's Notebook," *O'Neill (C).*

404 "fully in mind" and "simply gushed": EO to SC, 1/3/33.

404 "a sort of wishing": *Basso (A)*, 3/6/48.

405 "a very high order": *Clark*, p. 20.

405 "The kindliness and decency": *PM*, 10/21/41.

406 "This is a kind": 1/1/33.

406 "got immense satisfaction": 1/3/33.

406 "doubtful if anyone": 1/12/33.

407 "a substantial advance": 9/24/32.

408 "a forgotten one-act": EO to GCT, 9/3/32.

408 "really give a damn": EO to RS, 7/4/32.

408 "the worst play": EO to RS, 3/6/33.

408 "The most amusing": Ralph Sanborn to EO, 3/27/33.

408 "stand in everyone's": Undated, circa October 1932.

409 "I'm making Gene": Undated, circa 12/30/32.

409 "nervous indigestion": EO to SC, 1/3/33.

409 "his ultimate liberation": *Skinner (A)*, p. 43.

410 "high moments": Ibid., p. 44.

410 "began to fathom": Ibid., p. 46.

410 "Consider Goethe's *Faust*": "Memoranda on Masks," *O'Neill (C).*

411 "The Old Man": EO to AM, 12/10/32.

412 "And ours has": *O'Neill (E)*, January 1934.

413 "this Stranger's only": *O'Neill (E)*, 12/28/35.

413 "Mother worship": The note is at Beinecke Library, Yale University.

21. CONTROVERSIAL DRAMA

414 "However, I wail": EO to KM, 2/14/34.

414 Eighty dollars a performance: CM to GCT, 1/20/33.

414   "I vas forgettin' ": Ralph Sanborn to EO, 1/28/33.

415   "Horace, I don't": *Kronenberger*, p. 37.

416   "the greatest natural": Bennett Cerf.

416   "three times what": EO to GJN, 5/9/33.

417   "the Liveright mess": EO to GJN, 5/31/33.

417   "With Cerf you": 6/5/33.

417   "lousy Owen Davis": 6/10/33. Though Davis won the 1923 Pulitzer Prize for his play *Icebound*, he was only a hack writer.

417   "one of the best": EO to SC, 7/5/33.

417   "Gene & I nearly": Undated, circa 7/9/33.

417   "What a howl": 10/15/33.

418   "controversial" and "much bitter": *Langner*, p. 283.

418   "then, if ever,": EO to RS, 10/15/33.

418   "literary play": S. J. Woolf, New York *Times*, 10/1/33.

419   "might try to pull": New York *Herald Tribune*, 8/26/33.

419   "Look here, G. M.": Helen Ormsbee, "Philip Moeller, Director, Hollywood and Here," New York *Herald Tribune*, 9/9/34.

419   "Tell that holy": George L. Fogle, the stage manager.

419   "the best" and "really make": EO to KM, 10/16/33.

419   "Gene reminded me": RC.

420   "He really looked": Ruth Holden.

420   "If I can't play": George L. Fogle.

420   "I can't see": EO to LL, 11/8/33.

421   "resent Gene's writing": CM to SC, 9/28/33.

421   Except for "lightest word used" (Percy Hammond, New York *Herald Tribune*, 10/8/33), all the other quotations about *Wilderness* are from reviews on 10/3/33.

422   "a grand and glorious," John Mason Brown, New York *Post*; "ripest, finest," Atkinson; and "a superb," Lockridge.

422   "a vaudevillian who": Sherlee Weingarten Lantz.

422   "It was a great": EO to RS, 10/18/37.

423   "I'm not sure": *Basso* (B), 6/14/47.

423   "with a deep": EO to SC, undated, circa 7/5/33.

424   "I can assure": EO to the Reverend Michael Earls, 1/11/34.

424   "so communicative": Reverend George Ford.

425   "I am delighted": 12/18/33.

425   "worshiped" and "hollowed-out": Selena Royle to LS, 3/7/64.

426   "If *they* want to": RC.

426   "advance endorsements": 11/6/33.

427   "needn't have any": Dated "Friday," circa December 1933.

427   "I can see": Jeanne Gerson to LS, 6/5/57, 11/18/59, and 12/7/59. Carlin died on 1/9/34.

428   "At its end": *Carpenter*, p. 64.

428   "A few notes": Philip Moeller lent the present biographer his notes.

428   "loathed Germany": CM to SC, 5/12/33.

429   "Can you imagine": Reverend Vincent Donovan.

429   "She's going to kill": Belinda Jelliffe.

430   Review of *Days Without End:* The quotations in this paragraph and the following one are from reviews published on 1/9/34, excepting "some of the [dialogue]," Atkinson, 1/14/34.

431   "the minions of Anti-Christ": Quoted in New York *Post*, 1/22/34; "for everything they," Ibid.

431   "the great Catholic play": *The Queen's Work*, February 1934, and "O'Neill's greatness": *Christian Century*, 2/7/34.
431   "That makes it": R. Dana Skinner to Reverend Michael Earls, 1/28/34.
431   "You know I": 1/9/34.
432   "Great success, magnificent": *Yeats and Patrick McCartan: A Fenian Friendship*, Yeats Centenary Papers, vol. x (Dublin: Dolmen Press, 1968), p. 364.
432   "as favorable as they": 4/21/34.
433   "staying away in barbarian": EO to Charles O'Brien Kennedy, 2/18/34.
433   "for hoping against": 2/27/34.
433   "come into its own": 3/2/34.
433   "the Soul-Dust Twins": New York *Post*, 1/9/34.
434   "a lot younger": 10/16/33, and "loafing determinedly": 2/14/34.
434   "teetering on the verge": EO to Sherwood Anderson, 4/23/34.
434   "flowed right along": *Schriftgeisser*.

22. NOBEL LAUREATE

435   "horrible experience": CM to SKW, undated, circa 4/30/34.
436   "I'm one of the greatest": Oakland *Tribune*, 1/11/37.
436   "is a splendid piece": 12/15/33.
437   "Celtic this and": New York *Times*, 9/18/34.
437   "It was a beautiful": *O'Casey*, p. 270.
437   "honestly say I": Sean O'Casey to LS, 1/28/57.
438   "to take him": GJN, "The Recluse of Sea Island," *Redbook*, August 1935.
438   "like an Irishman": *Peck (A)*.
438   "the long, lean": *O'Casey*, p. 321.
439   "He did very": William Jameson to LS, 2/24/58 and 3/5/58.
440   "didn't agree with her": Barbara Burton, her half sister, to LS, 5/8/69.
440   "a fainting complex": OOC to LS, 10/16/69.
440   "One can serve": CM to SC, undated, circa July 1933.
440   "I really am": "Aunt Tina," Nellie Tharsing's sister, to LaVeda Shaffer, 1/28/33.
440   "Loafing when you": EO to CC(S), 12/16/34.
441   "Gold was to be": EO to F. I. Carpenter, 3/24/45.
441   "Life is growth": EO to SC, 8/4/29.
441   "far from model": AP dispatch, 1/12/37.
441   "Suppose some day": *Mollan*.
441   "a tragedy of the possessive": EO to Mrs. Dupré Hills, 3/21/25.
442   "going on the theory": Said at a mass press interview, 9/2/46.
442   "except very incidentally" and "the final fate," EO to RS, 7/3/35.
442   "the recurrence of family": New York *Times*, 11/13/36.
442   "years of the devil's": EO to RS, 3/1/35.
443   "stripped for action," *Langner*, p. 285.
443   "Gene swam out": Ibid., p. 286.
443   "dramatic comédie humaine": *Helburn (A)*.
443   "The main thing that": 9/3/35.
444   "broadening of the *Electra*": 7/3/35.
444   "It is Mystery": Statement to the press, New York *Post*, 2/13/26.
445   "political, financial": 6/10/35.
445   EO's photograph as a child reproduced in *Sheaffer*, p. 61, and *O'Neill (E)*
445   "poise and dignity": CM to RC, 6/10/35. Also the source of the other quotations in this paragraph.
445   "How Gene can": Undated, to Joe Heidt.

447   "with again, as": *O'Neill (E)*, 12/28/35.
447   "All her talents," *Langner*, p. 281.
448   "and there'll be": Mattie Powell.
449   EO declaiming the Byron passage at Princeton: *Sheaffer*, p .120.
450   EO regarding *Odd Man Out:* Sherlee Lantz.
451   "amazed at the amount": *Helburn (A)*.
452   "An eight-play Cycle": 6/25/36.
452   "Try a Cycle": *Nadel*, p. 94.
453   "splendid contribution": New York *American*, 4/6/36.
453   "what a grand break": 11/15/36.
453   "very easy to get": Somerset Maugham to LS, 7/10/58.
453   "Too many people": CM to MC, undated.
454   Account of the Lamberts: Mrs. Jordan Lambert.
454   CM voiced hope the plane would fall: Mattie Powell.
454   "Carlotta and I": *Nadel*, p. 94.
454   "too complicated": Prefatory Note to *More Stately Mansions*, p. vii.
456   "a splendid job": EO to SKW, 7/7/33.
456   "give Dixie back": EO to KM, 11/15/36.
456   "He wanted a place": A combination of *Peck (A)* and LS interview with CM.
456   "I HATE the South": Undated, circa July 1936.
457   "has never known": CM to EW and SKW, 9/8/36.
457   "terrible night sweats": CM to SKW, undated, circa September 1936.
457   "a Frenchman was": EO to GJN, 11/16/36.
458   "would go to Dreiser": The nation's press, 11/12 and 11/13/1936.
458   "like an ancient": EO to KM, 11/15/36.
459   "damned shame Gorki": 11/25/36.
459   Comment on Nobel award: Manchester *Guardian*, 11/13/36; Ceylon *News*, 11/27/36; Shaw, New York *Times*, 11/13/36; and Robinson and Yeats, New York *Times*, 11/15/36.
460   "has had a miserable": 1/24/37.
461   "when you worked": 11/15/36.
461   "can present important": "O'Neill Turns West to New Horizons," New York *Times*, 11/22/36.
462   "it is not": New York *Times*, 12/11/36.
463   "replete with more": 11/25/36.
463   "scarcely be enough": SKW, "Strindberg and O'Neill," *Scandinavian Studies*, August 1959.
463   "Gene was very": *Boulton*, pp. 76–77.

23. CYCLE SHELVED

465   "to build just": RoS to LS, 7/9/62.
465   "as though he": Unless stated otherwise, the remarks of CCS and RoS were obtained in a series of interviews.
465   "You keep your": Undated, circa 11/20/36.
466   "will do two": Newspapers of the Bay Area, 1/11 and 1/12/37.
466   "interior abscess burst": EO to TH, 2/26/37.
468   Presentation of the Nobel Prize: Oakland *Tribune*, 2/18/37, and Carl Wallerstedt to LS, 10/3/60.
468   EO's visit to Nellie Tharsing: Mrs. Ceil Shay, Mrs. Tharsing's niece.
469   "anarchist Utopia": Undated, circa June 1937, and "get pinched": 7/24/37.
469   "The Cycle goes": Undated, circa September 1937, *Clark*, p. 144.

470 "Revenge is the subconscious": *Bowen (A)*.
471 "a frenzy of creative": EO to GJN, 8/30/37.
472 "something primitive": Lloyd Simpson.
472 "space for 8,000": Frederick Confer.
473 "producing one of": CM to KM, 8/26/37, and "What a price": CM to SKW, 4/30/38.
476 "It breaks my heart": Undated, circa 2/20/38.
476 "we apes always": 9/22/37.
477 "a new understanding": EO to SO, 7/18/39.
477 "I am tremendously": 7/10/38.
478 "much sadness": 5/29/38, and "has always been": 5/30/38.
478 "vale of gloom": EO to SKW, 5/15/38.
479 "We really have": EO to SY, 2/17/39.
480 "needs lots of revision" and "Unfinished Work": Prefatory Note to *More Stately Mansions*, p. x.
480 "provides, even in": Ibid., p. xii.
481 "It is, I think!": 12/28/38.
485 "foreseen the time": 2/17/39.
486 "very apprehensive," "what she might," and "bright spot": EO to KM, 9/10/39. This letter is also the source of "really a charming," in next paragraph.
487 "a child covered": OOC to LS, 7/29/69.
488 "Why, for example": Ibid.

24. O'NEILL "THE ICEMAN"

490 "locked myself in": *Bowen (A)*.
490 "based on people": EO to RS, 10/13/40.
490 Havel's history: See *Sheaffer*, pp. 327–329; Byth's history, Ibid., pp. 129–131; Carlin's history, Ibid., pp. 335–338.
491 Vose the informer: Carlin and Vose were together, visiting Emma Goldman, when one of the MacNamara case fugitives suddenly turned up.
493 "main plot" and "imaginary": EO to KM, 12/15/40.
494 The Chapin murder case was extensively covered in the New York press, 9/17 through 9/20, 9/25 through 9/27, 10/18, 10/19, 10/25, 11/1, 11/2, 11/5, all 1918; 1/17 and 1/18, both 1919.
494 "Almost two years": Charles E. Chapin, *Charles E. Chapin's Story* (New York: Putnam, 1920), p. 334.
495 "has twelve disciples": "The Iceman and The Bridegroom," *Modern Drama*, May 1958.
498 "No, I never": 12/30/40.
498 "There was a periodical": 2/8/40.
503 "crack up": EO to RS, 8/3/40.
503 "even finer and profounder": *Liberty*, 10/12/40.
504 "Personally I love it!" *Nadel*, p. 95.
504 Ford's *Stagecoach* anecdote: As SKW recalls EO's account.
505 "an exceptional picture": EO to OO(C), 10/25/40.
505 "Whenever Gene was very": Combination of *Peck (B)* and LS interview. Also the source of the following three paragraphs.
506 Raleigh concerning *Lazarus*: Raleigh, p. 47.
506 "extremely poor": p. 118; "If I started": p. 117; "old enough": p. 121; and "a fine job": p. 115, all *O'Neill (P)*.
507 "such discouraging": 11/29/40.

507   "With so much tragic": EO to OO(C), 7/3/40.
507   "You can't keep": *Langner*, p. 398.
507   "didn't talk about": *Bowen* (*B*), p. 266.
507   "I've got an idea": Margaret Stark.
508   Helburn's visit: CM wrote RC on 8/29/40 that TH urged EO to release *Iceman*. EO wrote GJN on 8/30 that TH did not press him. However, since GJN had long been critical of the Theater Guild, it seems likely that EO did not want to supply him with new ammunition. In short, CM's account sounds more credible.
509   "It nearly killed": CM to Hallie Flanagan, 1/17/56.
509   "After his day's": John Chapman, New York *News*, 12/12/56.
509   "Do you think": *Peck* (*A*) and (*B*).
509   "a day in which": 6/15/40.
513   "a naked play": Dwight MacDonald, *Esquire*, December 1962.
514   "Although O'Neill" and "a strangely neutral": *Bogard*, p. 432.
515   "a subtler case": London *Observer*, 5/26/57.
515   "enduring warmth": Annette Rubinstein, "The Dark Journey of Eugene O'Neill," *Mainstream*, April 1957.
517   "upset me so": *Peck* (*A*).
517   "When we joined": SKW to LS, 7/27/71. (For two particularly fine discussions of *Long Day's Journey Into Night*, see *Bogard*, pp. 422–445, and "O'Neill's *Long Day's Journey Into Night* and New England Irish-Catholicism," by John Henry Raleigh, in *Gassner* (*A*), pp. 124–141.)

25. O'NEILL'S TREMOR

518   "Gene and I": 1/20/40.
519   "I have little": *O'Neill* (*D*).
519   "nervous exhaustion": EO to KM, 12/30/40.
520   "I have fought": EO to William R. Agar, 2/15/41.
520   "in which I knew": 11/29/40.
521   "a person who does": 6/19/42.
521   "is an essence": Ibid.
522   "more to be read": EO to GJN, 9/19/41.
523   "told anyone yet": Prefatory Note to *More Stately Mansions*, p. vii.
523   Destruction of drafts and outlines: For the fullest reconstruction of the Cycle narrative, see *Bogard*, pp. 371–407.
523   "an Irishman who": *Basso*, 3/13/48.
524   St. Gertrude's reunion: Mrs. Maynard W. Butler, MC, and JC.
525   "a fine guy": 9/19/41.
525   "a most delightful": EO to Charles O'Brien Kennedy, 7/17/41.
525   "You're wonderful, Carlotta": OOC to LS, 7/29/69. Also the source of CM's rejoinder in the following paragraph.
526   "I definitely had": *Bowen* (*B*), p. 272.
527   "You have no idea": EO to GJN, 9/19/41.
528   "a lady star": EO to RC, 10/16/41.
528   "Gene is nervous": Undated, probably December 1941.
529   "To hell with" and "In this time": *O'Neill* (*E*).
529   "drag [his] mind": EO to RS, 4/24/42.
530   "I sat there": Combination of *Peck* (*A*) and LS interview.
531   Oona's Stork Club publicity: AP dispatch, 4/12/42 and New York press, 4/13/42.
531   "I have never": CM to EW, 5/21/42.

532 "a lot in both": 4/24/42.
533 "a belt-corset affair": CM to TH, 8/31/42.
533 "So am I": Written on 8/17/42.
534 "Through indolence": Written on 9/10/42.
534 "marooned" and "imperative treatments": EO to RC, 12/18/42.
535 "there will again": *Helburn* (B), p. 275.
535 "I could never": MC.
535 "The world drama": EO to GJN, 10/24/42.
536 "symbolic fantasy": *Clark*, p. 147.
536 "not the usual": 5/2/42.
536 "In many ways": EO to Sean O'Casey, 8/5/43.
537 "a delightful, friendly": *Bowen* (B), p. 288.
538 "a horrible letter": Undated.
538 "I'm an able-bodied": Marc Brandel.
538 CM's rebuff to Margaret Stark: Margaret Stark.
538 "Who does she": *Bowen* (B), pp. 284–285.
539 "hoping he would": EO to SKW, 12/26/42.
539 "What if the world": *O'Neill* (E).

26. REJECTED CHILDREN

540 "His work is": CM to Gilbert McC. Troxell, 5/5/42.
541 "if she realized": Asbury Park *Press*, 4/20/58.
542 "severed relations": EO to SC, 6/30/43.
542 "proud of Oona": Said to LS.
542 "He has made": Frederick Sands, "Oona: In Her First Interview, Charlie Chaplin's Wife (35) Describes Her Life With a Legend (71)," *Journal-American*, 6/19/60.
542 "For the last": *Chaplin*, p. 497.
543 "Gene is *bad*": Undated, summer 1943.
543 "like the visceral": From Dr. Fletcher Taylor's records.
543 "Of course, all this": EO to GJN, 9/25/43.
543 "Every day, in every": *O'Neill* (E), 7/22/43.
546 "I love the country": CM to OO(C), 3/25/38.
546 "I *loathe the country*": 8/25/43.
546 "I've never liked": *Helburn* (B), pp. 276–277.
547 "How about General": Ibid., 277–278.
547 "Along with all": *O'Neill* (E).
548 "a good price": CM to RC, 3/21/44.
548 "very charming" and "corduroy texture": The Carlsons.
548 "because they no": As SKW recalls EO's explanation.
549 "He sat by": CM to SKW, undated, circa 3/10/44.
549 "could not forgive": *Bowen* (B), p. 299.
550 "If you give": JC.
550 "Write, write, write": JC.
552 "I loathe the state": CM to GB, 9/15/45.
552 "*wants* to go": CM to GB, 7/25/44.
552 "would be comic": As recorded by SKW. Right after visiting EO at the Huntington on 10/22/44, Professor Winther wrote down his recollection of EO's more interesting remarks. The quotations starting with "would be comic" and running through the next eight paragraphs are from the professor's account.
554 "a five-room house": CM to GB, undated, circa June 1943.

554 "on the edge": CM to GB, 12/15/44.
556 The conflict between EO and CM over JC. The account here is based on *Diary (A)* and interviews with JC, MC, and Kaye Albertoni.
559 "a curse": EO to RS, 1/1/46.
560 Missing Cycle papers: Based on a written account by SC and an interview with DC.
561 "On 52d Street": Arnold Shaw, "Swinging Again Down Swing Street," New York *Times*, 10/10/71.
562 "When I wrote": Edward Jablonski.
562 "very little talent": Charles Harrell to LS, 3/13/71 and 4/17/71.
563 "never sat *in*": *Bowen (B)*, p. 274.
563 "I started it": Ibid., p. 296.
563 "had exceptional qualities": Marc Brandel to Margaret Stark, 1/8/72.
564 "obviously uncomfortable": *Bowen (B)*, p. 302.
565 "Why, you look": Ibid., p. 303.
565 "It happens at least": Earl Ubell, "10,000 Victims a Year, Cause Unknown," New York *Times*, 1/30/72.
566 Shane and Cathy's visit with EO: From interviewing the couple.
566 The wrong patient episode: Winfield Aronberg.

27. RETURN TO BROADWAY

568 "a man who": *Clark*, p. 152.
568 "Painfully thin": Ibid., pp. 150–151.
568 "Mere physical": Ibid., p. 151.
569 "There are so many": Russell Rhodes, "Robert Edmond Jones Says It Was O'Neill Who Really Did Designing for *The Iceman*," New York *Herald Tribune*, 12/29/46.
569 "I didn't know": Sherlee Lantz.
570 "loathes towns": CM to James D. Gould, 3/9/46.
571 "There's the whole": *Basso (A)*, 2/28/48.
571 "With the same": *O'Neill (E)*, 7/22/46.
572 "I *intended* it": *Langner*, p. 405.
572 "where at the end": 12/30/40.
573 "I hope you": DC.
573 "Maxwell Anderson may": SKW's notes on 10/22/44.
574 "had known O'Neill," Marshall, and "never went over," Pedi: From interviewing the two actors.
574 "sensual haunches": E. G. Marshall.
574 "it's as bad": As recalled by Jeanne Cagney.
574 "I dread their coming": Karl Nielsen.
575 "Nathan may know": Sherlee Lantz.
575 "Hello, Pop.": Eddie Dowling.
576 "turning him this": "O'Neill Sets Aside Drama for Staging 25 Years After Death," New York *News*, 6/20/46.
576 "He may try": 11/30/53, and "It's a real story": 8/2/46.
576 "the greatest present": "Eugene O'Neill Discourses on Dramatic Art," 8/26/46.
577 The mass interview was extensively reported in the press and national periodicals.
577 "a tragic mask": Herbert J. Stoeckel, "Memories of Eugene O'Neill," Hartford *Courant*, 12/6/53.

577 "enraged resignation": *Time*, 10/21/46. The article is also the source of his other remarks in this paragraph.
578 "Of course America": *Bowen (A)*.
578 "There's no secret": p. 115; "Kipling and people": p. 119; and "a down-to-earth": p. 131, all *Crichton (B)*.
579 "mysterious silence": *Prideaux*.
579 "Almost the first": *Woolf (B)*.
579 "I do not think": *Schriftgeisser*.
581 "What does it": Sherlee Lantz.
581 "a philosophical anarchist": *Bowen (A)*.
582 "Why, it's a Daumier!" DC.
582 "Please, boys, please!": From interviewing a number of the cast of *The Iceman Cometh*.
582 "Sardi's and Twenty-One": Rosamund Gilder, *Theater Arts*, December 1946.
582 *The Iceman*'s 1946 reviews: Stark Young, 10/21; John Chapman, Richard Watts, Jr., Brooks Atkinson, Ward Morehouse, Arthur Pollock, Howard Barnes, and Robert Garland, all 10/10; Louis Kronenberger, 10/11; *Time*, 10/21.
584 "I think you": 10/31/47.
585 "You are apt": Wolcott Gibbs, *New Yorker*, 5/26/56.
585 "an essential part": New York *Times*, 5/20/56.
585 "while an interesting": 10/19/46, and "a great play": 5/26/56.
586 "looked much healthier": *Clark*, p. 161.
588 "Gene couldn't get": Undated, circa 11/25/46.
589 The Bennett Cerfs' party: Bennett Cerf.
589 "I am sorry": *O'Neill (E)*.

28. MISBEGOTTEN PRODUCTION

590 CM backstage at *The Iceman Cometh*: Karl Nielsen.
590 "The audiences don't": E. G. Marshall.
590 The Paxinou-Minotis episodes: From interviewing the couple.
592 "stupid censorship": International News Service, 2/19/47.
592 "I am and always": 3/23/47.
592 "a range from farce": *Welch*. Also the source of the quoted remarks in the following four paragraphs.
594 "Oh, here we": Ibid.
594 "We're *all* crying": *Langner*, p. 407.
594 "were playing the tragedy": *Welch*.
595 "in a halo of roses": *Time*, 3/3/47.
595 "Again my absolute": *Welch*.
595 "No. They just": *Langner*, p. 408.
595 "evidence of deterioration": *Variety*, 3/12/47.
596 "louse" and "bastard": *Variety*, 3/19/47.
596 "You've allowed": *Nadel*, p. 98.
596 "a moonshiner and a slightly": Burns Mantle, ed., *Best Plays of 1946–1947* (New York: Dodd, Mead, 1947), p. 416.
596 "had been agreed": New York *Times*, 3/12/47.
596 "I'd expected the Guild": Arthur Shields.
597 "come to loathe": *O'Neill (E)*, 7/22/52.
597 "Do they know": E. G. Marshall.
599 "terms of complete": *Basso (B)*.

600 "O'Neill not working": *Basso* (*B*). Also the source of the quotations in the following paragraph.
600 "a fondness for order": *Basso* (*A*), 2/28/48.
600 "it might be": *Basso* (*B*).
601 "After you've finished": *Basso* (*A*), 3/13/48.
601 "I'm home, home": CM to GB, dated "Sunday," probably 10/21/45.
602 "Our Sherlee gave": Sherlee Lantz.
602 "a quality of horror": T. S. Eliot, Introduction to *Nightwood* (New York: Harcourt, Brace), 1937.
603 "going to catch": Sherlee Lantz.
603 "a tub of lard": As SKW recalls.
603 "her whole costume": The quoted remarks in this paragraph and the following eight, EW to LS, 7/27/71 and 10/18/71.
604 "*Usque ad finem!*": Joseph Conrad, *Lord Jim* (New York, Modern Library, undated), p. 215. Just before the Latin phrase, in Conrad's novel, Stein says: "To follow the dream, and again to follow the dream" — words that sum up so much of O'Neill's life.
604 "paid for that" and "my love": *O'Neill* (*E*), 12/28/47.
605 "two dreadful spots": Richard Lebherz to LS, 3/8/60.
605 The row between EO and CM: Based on a written account by SC and an interview with DC.
606 "For the love": *O'Neill* (*E*), 1/19/48.
606 "either accidental": Dr. Shirley Fisk.
607 "I can't live": As Frank Meyer recalls what Eugene Jr. told him.
608 "Please, O Dear": *O'Neill* (*E*).
609 CM's telephone call: Based on a written account by SC.
610 "another story": *Diary* (*C*), 3/15/48.
611 "He needs me": Dr. Shirley Fisk.
611 "God, if you": EO to ESS, 12/3/44.
611 "puritan" and "fury against": "Counsels of Despair," 4/10/48.
611 Atkinson's counterattack: 4/25/48.
612 "felt closest to": Herbert J. Stoeckel, "Memories of Eugene O'Neill," Hartford *Courant*, 12/6/53.

29. BY THE SEA AGAIN

613 "a birdcage": CM to Elinor C. M. Smith, 9/5/48.
613 "the first home": EO to SC, 7/26/48.
614 "my love and my": *O'Neill* (*E*).
614 "Now, with our sixtieth": Ibid., 7/22/48.
615 "Shall I say" and "fought like hyenas": *Diary* (*S*), 7/29/48. Elinor Smith recorded in her diary not only what she saw or heard but her husband's accounts of his contacts with the O'Neills.
615 "Shane once told": Marc Brandel to Margaret Stark, 1/8/72.
615 "wrung out and much": *Diary* (*S*), 8/17/48.
617 "fine friends" and "send for Mama": *Diary* (*S*), 9/15/48.
617 "I can't complain": Earl P. Finney.
618 "She could be": Rodrique E. Berube.
618 "bought too much": *Diary* (*S*), 9/15/48.
618 "nothing but ocean": EO to GJN, 12/3/48.
618 "Don't disappear": *Diary* (*S*), 9/1/48.
619 "in a coma": Ibid., 10/1/48.
620 "planning to start": As OOC reported to AB in an undated letter.

620   "Dearest One": *O'Neill (E)*.
620   Erroneous press reports: 2/18/49.
620   "would like to know": Undated letter.
621   "After a while": Charles O'Brien Kennedy, "Eugene O'Neill," *Lambs Script,* of the Lambs Club, March–April 1954.
621   "Here in the gray": SKW to LS, 11/4/69.
622   "deepest hopes that": February 1950.
622   "aging in so many": EW and SKW.
623   "He was a delightful": Dr. Frederic Mayo.
624   "the fiery chariot": CM to SKW, 4/20/49.
624   "To 'Mama' — and still": *O'Neill (E)*, Christmas 1949.
626   "met with a varied": *Miller (A)*, p. 127.
626   "stepped out of line": Fred DiDonato. Also the source of the other quoted remarks in the paragraph.
627   "a classical scholar": New York *Herald Tribune*, 1/23/48.
627   "the best-dressed man": Ruth Lander.
627   "now he could kill": Frank and Elsie Meyer.
627   "Being the son": Mary Bragiotti, "Bearded Giant, Mighty Arguer," New York *Post*, 11/3/48.
629   "Take back your!": Elsie Meyer.
629   Eugene Jr.'s radio project: From a written account by SC.
631   The suicide: From press accounts, 9/26/50.
632   "How dare you": Winfield Aronberg.
632   "Eugene has killed" and "as time went": *Peck (A)*.
634   "a very wonderful": Ibid.

30. ESTRANGED PAIR

636   "That music of his": Frank Orne, the couple's part-time utility man.
637   EO's accident: The account here is based on one written by SC, summarizing what EO had told him, and interviews with Dr. Frederic Mayo and Sally Coughlin, one of EO's nurses.
637   "bundled up": CM.
639   "this figure up": Patrolman John Snow.
641   EO's hallucinations: DC.
643   "Papa needs you": Kaye Albertoni. Much of her quoted recollections in this paragraph and following ones are based on *Diary (A)*.
643   "Carlotta loved only": Dr. Merrill Moore.
643   "like a lesser": "Greetings and Salutations from Merrill Moore," a pamphlet (Boston, 1957).
644   "failed his children": 4/17/51.
644   "I wish I": CM to SKW, 4/9/51.
645   "amazing personality": *Diary (C)*, 3/31/51.
646   "The only hitch": Anna Crouse to LS, 4/14/71.
646   "was getting queerer": Told to LS.
646   Dr. Kozol quizzed Kaye Albertoni: *Diary (A)*, 4/6/51.
647   "there is sufficient": CCS to Judge V. Phelan, 4/8/51.
648   "the whole story" and "love letters": Wylie to *Time* headquarters, 4/6/51.
650   "the most meaningful": SC to OOC, 5/16/51.
651   "I dreamed I": *Diary (C)*, 4/7/51.
651   "I want to go": Ibid., 4/17/51.
653   "in the way": 4/29/51, and "hurt and savage": 5/2/51, Ibid.
653   "if Gene really": Winfield Aronberg's diary, 5/4/51.

653   "very gay": *Diary* (C), 5/13/51.
655   "*why* my father": OOC to LS, 10/28/70.

31. A PRIVATE FUNERAL

657   "Carlotta lives in": Tom Wenning, "Dead Man Triumphant," *Newsweek*, 6/17/57.
658   "I want to be": 7/16/14.
658   "so bad" and "for eternity": 4/25/54.
659   "To Carlotta, my beloved": *O'Neill* (E), 6/3/51.
660   "The great tragedy": Jerry Stagg.
660   "squirmed around resentfully": CM.
661   "tries desperately": *Diary* (C), 7/31/51.
661   "He used to twist": Told to LS.
663   "In originality, size": 8/19/51.
663   "serious condition": 12/6/51.
663   "To Carlotta, my": *O'Neill* (E), 12/27/51.
663   "being desirous of": 3/3/52.
664   "to rant about": Wylie to *Time* headquarters, 7/16/52.
664   "a drama of unusual": 8/31/52.
665   "would go to step": *Peck* (A).
666   "While you are": New York *Times*, 9/20/52.
666   "lies and vicious": AP, London, 4/17/53.
666   "It isn't that": *Peck* (B).
666   "Why, certainly not": *Peck* (A).
667   "It was awful": *Peck* (B).
667   "found him lying": A written account by Karl Ragnar Gierow, parts of which appear in his article, *Gierow*.
667   "He suffered horribly": Ruth Link, "The Royal Dramatic, Where O'Neill's Genius Found a Home," *American Swedish Monthly*, May 1962.
667   "to go to the hospital": Ibid.
667   "He kept talking": Told to LS.
668   "I put you": CM to Brooks Atkinson, 12/12/53.
668   "a stone man": Ibid.
668   "Our patient continues": CM to Dale Edward Fern, 10/17/53.
669   "would upset him": Reverend Vincent Mackay.
670   "I knew it": CM.
670   "a terrible silence": CM to Anna Crouse, 1/4/54.
670   "because I wanted": *Peck* (A).
671   "a degeneration": *Gierow*.
671   "I carried out": *Peck* (A).
672   "the scavenger press": CM to Anna Crouse, 1/4/54.
673   Coffin beyond its plot: RoS to LS, 5/14/70.
673   "simple, vigorous": Mrs. Henry Decatur, head of the monument firm.

Acknowledgments

CERTAIN of the persons, publications, publishing houses, libraries and other institutions to be mentioned here have already been named, with gratitude, in *O'Neill: Son and Playwright*, the first half of this biography, published in 1968. It is fitting and just, however, that I should thank them again, some more fully this time, since their contributions to my work figure largely in the present volume.

The major boon of being allowed to quote from letters, poems and other writings of O'Neill, much of this material hitherto unpublished, was granted by Yale University (under the provisions of Carlotta Monterey O'Neill's will) through the courtesy of Rutherford D. Rogers, the university librarian, and Donald C. Gallup, curator of the American Literature Collection in Beinecke Library. I am likewise grateful to attorneys Richard N. Crockett and Jacquelin A. Swords of Cadwalader, Wickersham and Taft for their support in this matter.

For the privilege to quote from the letters and other writings of the late Agnes Boulton, I am indebted to her children, namely Barbara Burton, Mrs. Oona O'Neill Chaplin, and Shane O'Neill. For the same privilege in regard to the private papers of Carlotta Monterey, I am indebted to her grandson, Gerald Eugene Stram.

All three of O'Neill's wives, by granting me numerous interviews and helping in other ways, contributed greatly to this biography. Though his first wife, Kathleen Pitt-Smith (née Jenkins), had ample cause to regret that she ever met O'Neill, she never once spoke against him to me or even gave the slightest indication of harboring any hostility toward him. Her forbearance was impressive. While my copies of the extensive correspondence between O'Neill and Agnes Boulton were obtained from Houghton Library of Harvard University, Miss Boulton made available for my use a copious amount of other important material, including O'Neill's diary of 1925, her own for that same year, and his letters to their children, Oona and Shane.

In Carlotta Monterey, a woman of sharp contradictions, there was a strong impulse to cover up, to revise and edit her history, and an opposed, equally strong desire to bare all, or nearly all. And she loved to talk. In the course of many four- and five-hour sessions with O'Neill's widow I heard a vast amount of autobiography, parts of which seemed adulterated

[721]

with fiction, particularly when concerned with her years prior to O'Neill. By measuring her accounts against the memories of persons who knew her at different periods of her life, starting with childhood acquaintances, I hope that I have approached the neighborhood of truth. However, I learned early in my research that the quest for certitude about a person and his life has aspects of a Pirandellian undertaking.

Biographical works, especially those based almost entirely on original investigations and research, are among the most costly of literary endeavors. This two-volume life, which has taken me over fifteen years and had me doing field research nearly every place O'Neill lived any length of time — New London, Cape Cod, Ridgefield, Bermuda, Sea Island, California, Marblehead, Boston, every place except Buenos Aires and France — could not have been realized without subsidies. Hence my deep gratitude to the John Simon Guggenheim Foundation — particularly Henry Allen Moe, long its director; Gordon N. Ray, now the president; and James F. Mathias, the secretary — for awarding me fellowships in 1959, 1962 and 1969. I am likewise grateful to the American Council of Learned Societies for grants-in-aid in 1961 and 1962, and to the National Endowment for the Humanities for a grant in 1971. Needless to say, the findings, conclusions, etc., in this biography do not necessarily represent the views of the National Endowment, the Council of Learned Societies, or the Guggenheim Foundation.

For acting as sponsors for one or more of my many applications for scholarships, I am indebted to Brooks Atkinson, my earliest and longest supporter; Professor Travis Bogard; the late John Mason Brown; Malcolm Cowley; the late Professor Alan S. Downer; Professor Howard E. Hugo; Granville Hicks; Louis Kronenberger; the late Kenneth Macgowan; Professor Jordan Y. Miller; Dr. Whitney J. Oates; Professor John Henry Raleigh; Philip Van Doren Stern; and Richard Watts, Jr.

There is no one to whom I am more grateful than to Dorothy Berliner Commins, whose late husband, Saxe Commins, was not only O'Neill's editor but his most devoted and trusted friend. With characteristic generosity Mrs. Commins has allowed me to use the voluminous collection of letters from O'Neill and Miss Monterey to Saxe and her, even though Mrs. Commins herself is using these papers, with others, for a book on her husband, one of the outstanding literary editors of our time. Faulkner, Auden and Adlai Stevenson, as well as O'Neill, were among the many who benefited from Mr. Commins's editorial talent. In addition to the letters, Mrs. Commins's memories of the O'Neills and of her husband's relations with them were also very helpful.

The late Cynthia and Roy Stram, Carlotta Monterey's daughter and

Acknowledgments

son-in-law, who gave me their trust the first time I called on them in California, gladly and untiringly did their utmost for this book. It is largely due to them that I gained detailed knowledge of Miss Monterey's early years, and they contributed importantly to my picture of O'Neill and Carlotta in California. They gave me exclusive access to their O'Neill letters, dredged their memories for every scrap of remembrance that might be helpful, and for years Roy, replying for them both, wrote me long, frank letters in response to my frequent queries. For similar reasons I feel particularly grateful to Professor Sophus Keith Winther and his wife Eline, who became good friends of the O'Neills in the mid-thirties and saw them often. Professor and Mrs. Winther have shared with me their many letters from the O'Neills, their recollections of them, and from their home in Seattle have written me at length to answer my questions. I was glad to have a chance to meet and interview them twice, once in California, again in New York.

In Switzerland Mrs. Oona O'Neill Chaplin has kindly taken time more than once from her busy days to write me what she recalled of her father and to answer my numerous queries. On her own generous initiative, she sent me some important material, hitherto untapped by O'Neill biography, and many photographs. Miss Boulton's other daughter, Barbara Burton, and her sisters, Cecil and Margery Boulton, have likewise gone to considerable trouble to be of all possible assistance; they added materially to my fund of information.

Supplementing the help Russel Crouse, her late husband, had given me, Mrs. Anna Crouse made available their letters from O'Neill and Carlotta, transcribed extracts from Mr. Crouse's diary, and by mail and interview, shared all she could recall of my subject. Others from whom I also gained copies of O'Neill letters and, through interviews, glimpses of the man were Robert Sisk; Madeleine Boyd; Mrs. Rebecca Grubb, whose first husband, Frank D. Elser, was a friend of O'Neill's; Bio De Casseres; Jasper Deeter; Winfield Aronberg; Edward Keefe; Charles O'Brien Kennedy; Joseph Wood Krutch; Manuel Komroff; Arthur McGinley; Oliver Sayler; and Stark Young (with the exception of Mr. Komroff and Mr. McGinley, all now deceased).

For their remembrances of O'Neill and/or other principals in his life I am particularly obliged to Philip Moeller, Dr. Alvan L. Barach, William F. Batterham, Silvio A. Bedini, Irving Berlin, Sally Coughlin, Mrs. W. Earl Beatty, Helen DePolo, Reverend George B. Ford, Jeanne Gerson, Sherlee Lantz, Ilka Chase, Richard Lebherz, Katina Paxinou and her husband Alexis Minotis, Jane Rubin, Susan Jenkins Brown, Dr. Shirley C. Fiske, Lillian Gish, Patti Light, Rouben Mamoulian, Patricia Neal,

[723]

Frank W. Wilder, and the following, now deceased: E. J. Ballantine, Hamilton Basso, Bennett Cerf, Harold DePolo, James Light, Somerset Maugham, Sean O'Casey, Elizabeth Shepley Sergeant, and Cleon Throckmorton. Others to whom I am similarly obliged are Floyd Dell, Joseph Heidt, Florence Reed, May Davenport Seymour, Padraic Colum, Louis Kalonyme, Dr. Merrill Moore, Gilbert Miller, Robert Rockmore, Sam Schwartz, Philip Sheridan, and Carl Van Vechten, all deceased, and Jed Harris, Reverend Vincent Donovan, Jerry Stagg, Daniel J. O'Neill, Tom Dorsey, Jr., Alice Sheridan, Mrs. Claire R. Sherman, Belinda Jelliffe, Kyra Markham, Howard Lindsay, Allen Delano, Aline MacMahon, Lucian Cary, Jr., John H. G. Pell, Isidor Schneider, Keith Baker, Pearl Sanford, and Mrs. Frank Wilson.

For providing me with O'Neill letters or other material I am beholden to Dr. Frederick Ives Carpenter, Professor Travis Bogard, Mrs. Bogard (formerly Jane Malmgren), Dale Edward Fern, Celia C. Francis, Grace Dupré Hills, Professor David Krause, Dr. J. O. Lief, Mrs. Harold McGee, Arvid Paulson, and Seymour Peck.

My accounts of certain O'Neill productions owe considerably to the remembrances of the following, who appeared in the plays or had some other share in the proceedings:

Welded, Jacob Ben Ami, Curtis Cooksey and director Stark Young; *The Great God Brown,* William Harrigan, Leona Hogarth, Anne Shoemaker, and William Stahl; *Marco Millions,* Morris Carnovsky and Alfred Lunt; *Strange Interlude,* Glenn Anders, Lynn Fontanne, and Ethel Westley Hjul; *Mourning Becomes Electra,* Thomas Chalmers, Grant Gordon, and Arthur Hughes; *Ah, Wilderness!,* Elisha Cook, Jr., Eda Heineman, Ruth Holden, William Post, Jr., and stage manager George L. Fogle; *Days Without End,* Richard Barbee, Ilka Chase, and director Philip Moeller; *The Iceman Cometh,* Jeanne Cagney, Russell Collins, Paul Crabtree, Nicholas Joy, Joe Marr, John Marriott, E. G. Marshall, Al McGranary, Tom Pedi, Carl Benton Reid, Frank Tweddell, director Eddie Dowling, and stage manager Karl Nielsen; *A Moon for the Misbegotten,* James Dunn and director Arthur Shields.

For my reconstruction of O'Neill and Agnes's later years in Provincetown, I am indebted to Eben Given and his wife Phyllis Duganne, Thelma Given Verdi, Mrs. William Perry (the former Agnes Carr), Louise Enos, Josephine Johnson, Mrs. Lucy L'Engle, Dr. and Mrs. Daniel H. Hiebert, Wilbur Daniel Steele, and Hazel Hawthorne Werner.

For the O'Neills in Bermuda: Chester M. Goldman, the present owner of Spithead, who allowed me to inspect the place; Mrs. Rutledge Robinson (the former Hubertine Zahorska); Mrs. Frieda Wardman; Mrs.

Acknowledgments

Gladys C. Hutchings; Ronald John Williams, editor of *The Bermudian;*
Philip Hurn; Mrs. William Dickey (the former Mrs. Hurn); Mr. and
Mrs. Clyde Leseur, Earl and Lucy Anderson; E. C. Barnes; Robert D.
Aitken; Dr. Henry C. Wilkinson; Walter Usher; George Powell; Mrs.
John Johnston; George A. H. Lightbourne; and William A. Henderson.

Carlotta's background and life prior to O'Neill: I am most indebted for
my account, after Cynthia and Roy Stram, to Mr. and Mrs. Frank Shay,
her cousins; Melvin Chapman, her second husband; LaVeda Shaffer, a
cousin; Mrs. Myrtle Caldwell; Mrs. Maynard W. Butler; Mabel E. Kuss;
Mrs. Alexander Paladini; Mrs. Thomas Schartzer; and Mrs. A. W. Lasher.

O'Neill and Carlotta in France: On my behalf Michelle Weiller, an
American scholar in Paris, visited Le Plessis, where she interviewed
Jacques Vassor, present owner of the château, and Mme. Albert Real,
widow of the farm manager during the O'Neills' tenancy. Also, Miss
Weiller located and interviewed Mme. Josephine Rulfo, Miss Monterey's
personal maid in Cap-d'Ail and at Le Plessis.

The Far East trip: Alfred Batson, Dr. and Mrs. Alexander Renner,
George H. Wiley, G. W. Stedman, Jr., Eugene F. Hoffman and Paul B.
Clover of the American President Lines, Ltd., San Francisco, and Mrs.
Virginia Capotosto of the Philippines, who interviewed F. Theo Rogers
for me.

The O'Neills in Sea Island: My greatest debt for this period is to
George Boll of the Sea Island Company, the O'Neills' only close friend in
the resort. Mr. Boll made available his extensive O'Neill correspondence
and shared his memories of the couple. Others who helped were Alfred
W. Jones, James D. Compton, Francis Louis Abreu, J. L. McDonald,
James L. Robeson, T. M. Baumgardner, S. C. Kaufmann, Vera Massey,
Penny Ora Davis, Hazel Floyd, Mattie Powell, Edna Senior, Ira L. Estes,
Walter E. Estes, Richard A. Everett, Jr., Carrie Miller, Mrs. Arthur H.
Ballard, Mrs. J. Foster Bowers, Boyd Donaldson, C. O. Svendsen, Ray
Coddington, Mrs. Robert W. Chambers, Senator James D. Gould, Jr.,
Mrs. Theresa M. Lambert, Mrs. Edwin McCarty, Margaret McGarvey,
Mr. and Mrs. Norman Pancoast, Doles Edward Wilshar, and Mrs. John
Grondahl.

The O'Neills in Seattle: Professor and Mrs. Sophus K. Winther, Mrs.
Paul J. Paschke and Mrs. Kathleen P. Johnston.

In California: After Cynthia and Roy Stram, my chief informants
regarding this period were Mrs. Myrtle Caldwell and her daughter Jane,
and Mrs. Kathryne Albertoni (née Radovan). Other contributors were
Ralph Coffey; Frederick L. R. Confer; John L. Duke; Dr. Clifford Feiler;
Mrs. Thalia Brewer; Donald MacRae; James Schevill; Lloyd C. Simpson;

Dr. Fletcher B. Taylor; the Hon. Carl E. Wallerstedt, formerly the Swedish consul general in San Francisco; Philip Harris; Curtis R. Haskell; and Mrs. Lillian M. Kearney.

In Marblehead: My most important sources of information were Alfred DiDonato, Dr. Frederic B. Mayo, Philip Horton Smith and his wife Elinor, who kept a diary during this period. Other contributors were J. T. Barry, Louise Barrett, Thomas H. Barry, Rodrique E. Berube, Mrs. L. C. Copeland, Mrs. Mildred Crowley, Mrs. Rufus Cushman, Earl P. Finney, Mrs. Emerson E. Glass, Fred Goddard of the Lynn *Item*, Charles Lee, Doris Manning, Dr. Frank R. Ober, Frank W. Orne, Francis Tuckerman Parker, Mrs. Lucille W. Paul, Norman Powers, Mr. and Mrs. Richard S. Robie, Andrew Sarno, Dr. Robert S. Schwab, Dr. and Mrs. Bernard L. Willett, John Snow, and John Tucker. At the Salem Hospital: Mrs. Claire Bird, Dr. Paul W. Hugenberger, and Miss D. P. Petelle.

In Boston: Rudolph Bergeron, Mrs. Henry Decatur, Mrs. Katherine Gould, Mrs. Marie Hannon, James Hunter, Mrs. Ellen Kirby, Reverend Vincent Mackay, Virginia McArdle, Philip V. McBride, Elliot Norton, Dr. W. Richard Ohler, Kay O'Malley, Joan Orlando, James Saia, Police Lieutenant Edward J. Schofield, Loretta Senior, Horace W. Smith, Gaetano Pantano, and Joseph Walker.

For close-up views of Eugene O'Neill, Jr., I am indebted to Frank and Elsie Meyer, Ruth Lander, George T. Harrell, and Robert Phelps. For the same concerning Shane O'Neill, I am obliged to Margaret Stark, Marc Brandel, William A. Jameson, Jr., Dorothy Dort, John Dunn, Thomas Martin, and William A. Raidy.

The libraries have been of immeasurable help to me. At Yale's Beinecke Library, which has by far the largest, most important collection of O'Neill papers anywhere, I am beholden to Donald C. Gallup for many kindnesses. Comparatively recent acquisitions at Beinecke include the letters to Kenneth Macgowan, Robert Sisk, Elizabeth Shepley Sergeant, and part of O'Neill's letters to his children, Oona and Shane. At Princeton University's Firestone Library, the repository of the O'Neill–George C. Tyler correspondence, some scripts and other O'Neilliana, I am particularly grateful to Alexander P. Clark, and the Harvard College Library, where the O'Neill–Agnes Boulton correspondence is a prized feature, I am indebted to Helen D. Willard, who retired recently as curator of the Theater Collection.

Cornell University promptly furnished me with copies of its second and final batch of letters from the playwright to George Jean Nathan, one of its famous alumni. I am indebted also to Dartmouth College for material, including papers from the Ralph Sanborn Collection; to the

Humanities Research Center of the University of Texas for various O'Neill letters; to Columbia University libraries for O'Neill letters to Bennett Cerf and others by Hart Crane and Edna Kenton; to the Berg Collection of the New York Public Library, which has O'Neill's letters to Beatrice Ashe, one of his major New London romances; to the Theater Collection of the Museum of the City of New York; and to New York University's Fales Collection. My work has been substantially facilitated by the invaluable Theater Collection, headed by Paul Myers, at the Lincoln Center branch of the New York Public Library; a recent acquisition at Lincoln Center is Brooks Atkinson's letters from O'Neill and other notables. Aid for my work has also been readily forthcoming from Louis A. Rackow of the Walter Hampden Library at The Players. Among the private collectors, C. Waller Barrett kindly made his material available before he gave it to the University of Virginia.

A number of illustrations in this book were supplied by Margery Boulton, Barbara Burton, Oona O'Neill Chaplin, Jere Hageman and Daniel W. Jones, while most of the Nicholas Muray photographs came from his widow, Margaret Muray, who has been generously helpful. To Samuel B. Melner, president of Liveright Publishing Corporation, I am indebted for data on O'Neill's earnings from his published works by that house.

I am obliged to Eileen O'Casey for permission to quote from several of her husband's letters, to Sally Coughlin for the use of her letter to Sophus and Eline Winther, to Sirius Cook and Mrs. Harl Cook for quotations from the writings and letters of George Cram Cook and Susan Glaspell, to John G. Evans for his assent to the use of letters from Robert Edmond Jones to the former's mother, Mabel Dodge.

In regard to published works, I am indebted to Random House, Inc., for permission to quote from the following O'Neill plays: *A Moon for the Misbegotten*, 1945; *Ah, Wilderness!*, 1933; *All God's Chillun Got Wings*, 1924; *Anna Christie*, 1920; *Days Without End*, 1933; *Desire Under the Elms*, 1924; *Diff'rent*, 1921; *Dynamo*, 1928; *Gold*, 1920; *Lazarus Laughed*, 1926; *Ile*, 1918; *Marco Millions*, 1925; *Mourning Becomes Electra*, 1931; *Strange Interlude*, 1927; *The Emperor Jones*, 1921; *The First Man*, 1921; *The Fountain*, 1921; *The Great God Brown*, 1925; *The Hairy Ape*, 1922; *The Iceman Cometh*, 1940; and *Welded*, 1923. (All of the above copyrighted by Eugene O'Neill.) The Random House permission covers distribution of my biography in the United States and Canada. For its distribution in the British Commonwealth and Empire, excluding Canada, I am obliged to Jonathan Cape Ltd.

It is by permission of Yale University Press that I quote from *Hughie*

(Copyright © 1959 by Carlotta Monterey O'Neill), *More Stately Mansions* (Copyright © 1964 by Carlotta Monterey O'Neill), *Long Day's Journey Into Night* (Copyright © 1955 by Carlotta Monterey O'Neill), and *A Touch of the Poet* (Copyright © 1957 by Carlotta Monterey O'Neill).

I am grateful to the *New Yorker* for permission to quote from the following articles: "The Tragic Sense," Hamilton Basso's three-part profile of O'Neill; "The Emperor Jones," a profile of Robert Edmond Jones by Gilbert Seldes; Robert Benchley's review of *Mourning Becomes Electra;* and Wolcott Gibbs's review of *The Iceman Cometh.* My quotations from Seymour Peck's "Talk with Mrs. O'Neill," © 1956, are reprinted by permission of the New York Times Company, and I am grateful for extracts from other articles in the *Times,* which are credited in my text or Notes.

For permission to quote other published material, I am indebted to Dover Publications (*Eugene O'Neill, the Man and His Plays,* by Barrett H. Clark), to the *Nation* (reviews by Joseph Wood Krutch), to Mrs. Margaret Kocher (*A Wayward Quest,* by Theresa Helburn), to Mrs. Elizabeth Bowen Elton (*The Curse of the Misbegotten,* by Croswell Bowen with the aid of Shane O'Neill), to Harcourt Brace Jovanovich ("Smoke and Steel" from *Complete Poems of Carl Sandburg*), to Julie Haydon Nathan (O'Neill's "Memoranda on Masks," "Second Thoughts," and "A Dramatist's Notebook," *American Spectator*), to Floyd Barger, the executive editor, and the New York *News* ("Odyssey of Eugene O'Neill," by Fred Pasley, and reviews by Burns Mantle and John Chapman), to the New York *Post* (reviews by J. Ranken Towse, Conrad Aiken, Robert Littell, John Mason Brown, and Richard Watts, Jr.; articles by Mary Braggiotti and Murray Kempton, all copyright by the New York Post Corporation), and to *Time* magazine (several reviews and articles copyright Time, Inc.). Quotations from other newspapers, periodicals and books are fully credited in the text or the Notes.

The present volume, like my previous one, benefited greatly from the seasoned editorial judgment of the late Stella Bloch Hanau, who read most of this biography in manuscript. I am indebted also to William D. Phillips, my editor, for sound, helpful criticism. Roberts Jackson of Culver Pictures and Daniel W. Jones provided expert advice regarding the illustrations, while Jack Hamilton, Sam Hindel and Calvin Hoffman aided my research. For providing a quiet refuge in summertime from cacophonous New York City, I gladly acknowledge my thanks to the MacDowell Colony in New Hampshire and Yaddo in upstate New York, where much of this book was written.

Index

Index

Index

Index

Index

Index

Index

Index

Goldwyn, Sam, 61
Good Bad Woman, A, 165, 166
Good News, 267
Goodman, Edward, 462
Goodman Theater, 232
Gorki, Maxim, 459, 493, 503
Grace Cathedral, 550, 552
Grapes of Wrath, The, 504
Great God Brown, The, 103, 147, 164, 173, 179, 180, 198, 269, 408, 409, 444, 502, 506, 593, 600; discussed, 166–172; masks in, 167; O'Neill on, 167–168, 172, 176, 376, 458, 579; production, 182, 184, 186, 187, 191, 192–194, 197; reviews, 193–194, 285; life theme, 201; Skinner on, 409–410; women in, 499, 500
Great Pacific War, The, 211–212
Greatness and Decline of Rome, The, 197
"Greed of the Meek, The," 454, 469, 471, 476, 480, 523; burned, 548
Green, Elizabeth. *See* O'Neill, Mrs. Eugene, Jr.
Green, Paul, 253
Greenwich Village, xiii, 29, 44, 92, 117, 242, 280, 291, 345, 386, 393, 424, 554; Shane in, 507, 562, 563, 564, 615; Eugene Jr. in, 562, 626. *See also* Provincetown Players
Greenwich Village Follies, 160
Greenwich Village Theater, 70, 126, 136, 144, 148, 153, 158, 175, 180, 181, 184, 186, 187, 192, 194, 197, 249, 269; merger with Actors' Theater, 206, 214, 215
Gregory, Lady, 147
Groton, 415
Group Psychology and the Analysis of the Ego, 174, 245
Gruenberg, Louis, 414
Guéthary, France, 294, 299, 301, 303, 304, 363
Guild Theater, 280, 376, 387, 389, 420, 421, 528
Guilty One, The, 147–148, 166
Guitry, Sacha, 329
Gustav V, King of Sweden, 458

"Hair of the Dog, The," 443
Hairy Ape, The, 69, 94, 104, 119, 132, 154, 157, 159, 163, 167, 175, 197, 214, 216, 217, 269, 285, 289, 299, 307, 359, 380, 404, 408, 444, 447, 500, 527, 627; discussed, 72–77; productions, 77–81; 85, 86, 91, 92, 139, 350, 351, 357; O'Neill on, 81, 350, 458, 546, 579; reviews, 88–89; Carlotta in, 91–92, 139, 272, 298, 436; film, 352, 546
Hamilton, Clayton, 447

Hamilton, Dr. Gilbert V., 188–190, 233, 269, 501, 510
Hamlet, 57, 103, 208, 389, 615
Hammarskjöld, Dag, 634
Hammerstein, Oscar, II, 551
Hammond, Edward Crowninshield, 209
Hammond, Percy, reviews: *All God's Chillun,* 143; *Marco,* 281; *Electra,* 388; *Wilderness,* 421
Hanau, Stella Bloch, 126, 153, 188
Hand of the Potter, The, 78
Hansford, Montiville M., 257–258
Harding, Ann, 383
Hardwicke, Cedric, 221
Hardy, Thomas, 460
Harkness, Edward S., 208–209, 215
Harkness Theater, 232
Harlem, 29, 32, 182
Harrell, Charles T., 562–563
Harrigan, William, 187
Hart, Moss, 37
Hartley, Marsden, 242, 287
Harvard Dramatic Club, 61
Harvard University, xiii, 146, 208, 353
Hasenclever, Walter, 175
Haunted, The: as early title for *Strange Interlude,* 240; third part of *Electra,* 338, 343, 371, 376, 382, 387
Hauptmann, Gerhart, 148, 396, 459
Havel, Hippolyte, 490
Hawkins, Coleman, 561
Hawthorne, Hazel, 25
Hayes, Helen, 4, 7, 11, 41, 181
Hays, Arthur Garfield, 366, 369
Hays, Blanche, 81
Heart of Darkness, 28
Heidt, Joe, 375, 376, 479, 561, 576, 596
Heine, Heinrich, 54, 499
Helburn, Theresa, 275, 305, 354, 418, 471, 551; and O'Neill, 252–253, 256, 258, 286, 299, 302, 304, 350, 353, 359, 362, 366, 458, 460–461, 477, 527, 535, 576, 607; on Moeller, 274; and *Dynamo,* 324, 325; and *Electra,* 382, 383; and Cycle, 443, 451–452, 509; and *Iceman,* 504, 508–509; and films of plays, 546–547; and *The Misbegotten,* 595
Helicon, 291
Hell Hole, xiii, 7, 44, 122, 150, 424, 490
Hellman, Lillian, 452, 598
Hell's Angels, 351
Hemingway, Ernest, 207, 380, 415, 601
Henry Miller Theater, 430
Hepburn, Katharine, 547, 551
Heyward, Du Bose, 272, 414
Hick's, 599
Hiebert, Dr. Daniel, 64
Hippolytus, 127
Hitler, Adolf, 428, 476, 484, 520

Index

Index

Index

Index

Index

Index

Index

Pulitzer Prize: for *Beyond the Horizon*, 16–17; for *Anna Christie*, 93; for *They Knew What They Wanted*, 160; for *In Abraham's Bosom*, 253; for *Strange Interlude*, 289, 339; for *Of Thee I Sing*, 390; for *The Old Maid*, 452; for *Long Day's Journey*, 634
Punch and Judy Theater, 163
Purves-Steward, Sir James, 162
Pylon Club, Philadelphia, 454

Q.S.M.S. *Bermuda*, 281
Quigley, Martin, 425, 430, 431
Quincy, Mass., 342
Quinlan, Mary Ellen. *See* O'Neill, Ella
Quinn, Arthur Hobson, 201, 370
Quinn, Edmond T., 146, 147, 179, 309
Quinn, Mrs. Edmond T., 146, 147
Quintero, José, 585, 634
Quintessence of Ibsenism, The, 253

Radovan, Kathryne. *See* Albertoni, Kathryne Radovan
Raleigh, John Henry, 128, 506
"Rand, Eleanor." *See* Boulton, Agnes
Random House, 416, 417, 457, 477, 503, 629, 642, 654; mss. at, 560, 609, 659, 666; and *Long Day's Journey*, 634, 635; and *The Misbegotten*, 658
Rathbun, Stephen, review of *Anna Christie*, 67
Rauh, Ida, 15, 32, 54
Reamer, Lawrence, review of *Diff'rent*, 43
Recklessness, 408
"Reckoning, The," 147–148
Red Falcon, The, 217
Redemption, 60, 65
Redgrave, Michael, 572
Reed, Florence, 229–230, 390
Reed, John, 242, 462
Reed, Marion, 83–85, 90–91
Reinhardt, Max, 60, 108, 160, 232
Renner, Dr. Alexander, 316, 317, 318
Renner, Therez, 316, 317
Research in Marriage, A, 189
"Revolt," 609, 659
Rice, Elmer, 252, 386, 660
Richard III, 65
Richmond, Va., 32
Ridgefield, Conn. *See* Brook Farm
Ridges, Stanley, 425
Rippin family, 210, 216
Riverlawn Sanitarium, Paterson, N.J., 116
RKO Pictures, 423, 571
Road Is Before Us, The, 554
Robards, Jason, Jr., 585, 634
Robb, Walter, 319

Robeson, Paul, 140–141, 182, 202, 344; in *Jones*, 37, 140, 414; in *All God's Chillun*, 135, 139, 140, 143, 345
Robespierre, 586–587
Robie, Richard S., 658
Robinson, Lennox, 147, 432, 460
Rochester, N.Y., 54–55, 303
Rockefeller, John D., Jr., 214
Rockmore, Robert, 262, 264, 266–267, 273, 283–284
Rodgers, Richard, 551
Rogers, 70
Rogers, F. Theo, 319–320
Romance, 131
Roosevelt, Franklin D., 462, 471, 562
Rope, The, 515
Roseanne, 135
Rosenbach, A. S. W., 277
Ross, Harold, 374, 416
Rossetti, Christina, 614
Rossetti, Dante Gabriel, 578
Rostand, Edmond, 197
Royal Gazette and Colonist Daily, 161, 281
Royal Theater, Stockholm, 350, 480, 667; première of *Long Day's Journey*, 634
Royle, Selena (Mrs. Earle Larimore), 425–426
Rubenstein, Helena, 358
Rubin, Jane, 653
Russell, Rosalind, 572
Ryan, Edmond, 602
Ryskind, Morrie, 390

S.S. *André-Lebon* (ship), 312, 314
S.S. *Glencairn* (collected sea plays), 149–150, 163, 175; reviews, 155; film, 353, 504–505
S.S. *Themistocles* (ship), 79
Saia, James, 665–666
Saigon, 313, 314
Saint, The, 153
St. Aloysius Academy. *See* Mount St. Vincent, Academy of
St. Cecilia's Roman Catholic Church, 669
Saint-Gaudens, Augustus, 56
St. George Dance Hall (Shanghai), 315
St. Gertrude's Academy, 220, 524
St. James, Jimmy, 315
St. Joseph's Roman Catholic Church (New London), 24
St. Leo's Church (New York), 87
St. Louis, Mo., 597
St. Mary's Academy (Indiana), 512
St. Mary's Cemetery (New London), 24, 87, 117
St. Stephen's Church (New York), 117
St. Vincent's Hospital (New York), 20, 565
Salem Hospital, 638–643 *passim*, 646, 670
Saltus, Edgar, 197

[746]

Index

Index

Index